Matthew

VOLUME 1

This thoughtful and thorough commentary on the First Gospel comes from a scholar who has obviously spent many years at the feet of Matthew the teacher, and even more importantly, at the feet of the One to whom Matthew bears witness.

Jonathan T. Pennington
Assistant Professor of NT Interpretation,
Southern Baptist Theological Seminary, Louisville, Kentucky

My head hurts when I think of how Knox Chamblin weighed and worried over every Greek word or phrase in every sentence of Matthew's Gospel and then has pulled it all together into a lucid and connected whole. And my heart is grateful for a commentary like this--that is thorough (he simply 'milks' the text), clear (both in its organization and in his positions), and 'pushy' (in driving us to worship). Chamblin clearly wants me to understand Matthew and to stand amazed in the presence of Jesus the Nazarene. Knox Chamblin is in vintage form here: relentlessly nailing us to the text and always wobbling on the edge of doxology.

Dale Ralph Davis,
Pastor, Woodlands Presbyterian Church,
Hattiesburg, Mississippi

Matthew

VOLUME 1

A Mentor Commentary

J. Knox Chamblin

MENTOR

To the Memory of my Parents

Jones Miller Chamblin (1893–1970)
&
Olivia Knox Chamblin (1906–2001)

both of whom acquainted me
with the sacred writings
from my childhood

(2 Tim. 3:15)

Scripture quotations, unless otherwise indicated, are the author's own translation.

Scripture quotations marked NIV are from *The Holy Bible, New International Version*. Copyright 1973, 1978, 1985 by International Bible Society. Used by permission of Zondervan. All rights reserved.

Scripture quotations marked ESV are from *The Holy Bible, English Standard Version*, copyright © 2001 by Crossway Bibles, a division of Good News Publishers. Used by permission. All rights reserved.

Scripture quotations marked NASB are taken from the *New American Standard Bible*®, Copyright © 1960, 1962, 1963, 1968, 1971, 1972, 1973, 1975, 1977, 1995 by The Lockman Foundation Used by permission. www.lockman.org

J. Knox Chamblin was ordained to the gospel ministry in 1971. He did graduate work at Cambridge University, and received his Th.D. from Union Theological Seminary in Virginia in 1977. He taught for thirty-four years in Jackson, Mississippi, first at Belhaven College, then at Reformed Theological Seminary until retirement in 2001. He is author of *Paul & the Self: Apostolic Teaching for Personal Wholeness* (1993). He and his wife Ginger have two daughters, two sons-in-law and five grandchildren.

This is the First Volume of Matthew.
The Second Volume is 978-1-84550-379-6.

Copyright © J. Knox Chamblin 2010

ISBN 978-1-84550-364-2

10 9 8 7 6 5 4 3 2 1

Published in 2010
in the
Mentor Imprint
by
Christian Focus Publications,
Geanies House, Fearn, Tain,
Ross-shire, IV20 1TW, Great Britain
www.christianfocus.com

Cover Design by Daniel van Straaten
Printed and bound by MPG Books, UK

Contents

Abbreviations

ACC   *Ancient Christian Commentary on Scripture: New Testament.* Thomas C. Oden, general editor. Downers Grove: InterVarsity Press, 1998–2002.

apud   'with,' 'in agreement with.'

BAGD   W. F. Arndt and F. W. Gingrich, with F. Danker. *A Greek-English Lexicon of the New Testament and Other Early Christian Literature.* 2nd ed. Based on the 5th ed. of the German lexicon of Walter Bauer, 1958. Chicago: University of Chicago Press, 1979.

BBR   *Bulletin for Biblical Research,* a publication of the Institute for Biblical Research.

BDB   Francis Brown, S. R. Driver and Charles A. Briggs. *A Hebrew and English Lexicon of the Old Testament.* Oxford: Clarendon Press, 1957.

BDF   F. Blass and A. Debrunner. *A Greek Grammar of the New Testament and Other Early Christian Literature.* A translation and revision by Robert W. Funk. Chicago: University of Chicago Press, 1961.

BJRL   *Bulletin of the John Rylands Library* (Manchester, England).

CMM   D. A. Carson, Douglas J. Moo, and Leon Morris. *An Introduction to the New Testament.* Grand Rapids: Zondervan, 1992.

DBA   *Dictionary of Biblical Archaeology.* E. M. Blaiklock and R. K. Harrison, editors. Grand Rapids: Zondervan, 1983.

DCC   *The New International Dictionary of the Christian Church.* J. D. Douglas, general editor. Grand Rapids: Zondervan, 1974.

DJG   *Dictionary of Jesus and the Gospels.* Joel B. Green and Scot McKnight, editors. Downers Grove: InterVarsity Press, 1992.

DNTB   *Dictionary of New Testament Background.* Craig A. Evans and Stanley E. Porter, editors. Downers Grove: InterVarsity Press, 2000.

DNTT   *The New International Dictionary of New Testament Theology.* Colin Brown, editor. 3 vols. Grand Rapids: Zondervan, 1975-78.

DPL   *Dictionary of Paul and his Letters.* Gerald F. Hawthorne, Ralph P. Martin and Daniel G. Reid, editors. Downers Grove: InterVarsity Press, 1993.

DSCHT   *Dictionary of Scottish Church History & Theology.* Nigel Cameron, organizing editor. Downers Grove: InterVarsity Press, 1993.

EBC   *The Expositor's Bible Commentary.* Frank E. Gaebelein, general editor. 12 vols. Grand Rapids: Zondervan, 1976-1992.

EDT   *Evangelical Dictionary of Theology.* Walter A. Elwell, editor. Grand Rapids: Baker Book House, 1984.

Eng. tr.   English translation.

ESV   *English Standard Version.* Wheaton: Good News Publishers, 2001.

GGBB   Daniel B. Wallace. *Greek Grammar Beyond the Basics.* Grand Rapids: Zondervan, 1996.

GGNT   A. T. Robertson. *A Grammar of the Greek New Testament in the Light of Historical Research.* Nashville: Broadman, 1934.

GHG   *Gesenius' Hebrew Grammar.* Edited and enlarged by E. Kautzsch. 2nd English edition revised by A. E. Cowley. Oxford: Clarendon Press, 1910.

GNT   *Greek New Testament.* 4th revised ed. Kurt Aland *et al.*, editors. United Bible Societies, 1993.

GNTG   James Hope Moulton and Nigel Turner. *A Grammar of New Testament Greek.* 4 vols. Edinburgh: T. &T. Clark, 1957–76.

GT   Joseph Henry Thayer. *A Greek-English Lexicon of the New Testament.* Based on the German lexicon of C. L. W. Grimm, 1868. New York: Harper, 1897.

HE	*Historia Ecclesiastica (The History of the Church)* by Eusebius (ca. A.D. 265 to 339), according to the Greek text in the Loeb Classical Library (London: Heinemann, 1925), and largely according to the Eng. tr. of G. A. Williamson, *The History of the Church from Christ to Constantine* (Baltimore: Penguin Books, 1965).
IB	C. F. D. Moule. *An Idiom Book of New Testament Greek,* 2nd ed. Cambridge: University Press, 1959.
IBD	*The Illustrated Bible Dictionary.* 3 vols. J. D. Douglas and N. Hillyer, editors. Wheaton: Tyndale House, 1980.
ibid.	'in the same place' (i.e., cited just before).
idem	'the same' author
in loc.	*in loco,* i.e., in the place indicated.
ISBE	*International Standard Bible Encyclopedia,* revised ed. G. W. Bromiley, general editor. 4 vols. Grand Rapids: Eerdmans, 1979–88.
JETS	*Journal of the Evangelical Theological Society.*
JSNT	*Journal for the Study of the New Testament.*
LSJ	George Liddell and Robert Scott. *A Greek-English Lexicon.* Revised and augmented by Henry Stuart Jones. 9th ed. Oxford: Clarendon Press, 1996.
LXX	Septuagint, the standardized Greek translation of the OT (in *Septuaginta,* edited by Alfred Rahlfs, no date).
mg.	margin.
MS. or MSS.	Manuscript or manuscripts.
MT	Massoretic Text, the standardized Hebrew text of the OT (in *Biblia Hebraica Stuttgartensia,* edited by Karl Elliger and Wilhelm Rudolph, 1967 and 1977).
NASB	*New American Standard Bible*: Updated Edition. Anaheim, CA: Foundation Publications, 1997.
NB	*Nota Bene,* 'note well.'
NBC:R	*New Bible Commentary: Revised.* Donald Guthrie, J. A. Motyer *et al.,* editors. Grand Rapids: Eerdmans, 1970.
NEB	*The New English Bible.* New York: Oxford University Press, 1976.

NIV	*New International Version.* Colorado Springs: International Bible Society, 1984.
NJB	*New Jerusalem Bible.* London: Darton, Longman & Todd, 1985.
NKJV	*New King James Version.* Nashville: Thomas Nelson, 1982.
NLT	*New Living Translation.* Wheaton: Tyndale House, 1996.
NRSV	*New Revised Standard Version.* Nashville: Thomas Nelson, 1989.
NTS	*New Testament Studies,* a scholarly journal.
OTP	*Old Testament Pseudepigrapha.* 2 vols. James H. Charlesworth, editor. Garden City: Doubleday & Co., 1983-85.
pace	'against,' 'in disagreement with.'
passim	'everywhere.'
PGL	G. W. H. Lampe, editor. *A Patristic Greek Lexicon.* Oxford: Clarendon Press, 1961.
REB	*The Revised English Bible.* Oxford University Press, 1989.
s.v.	*sub voce,* 'under a (given) word,' denoting an entry in a dictionary.
TB	*Tyndale Bulletin* (of Tyndale House, Cambridge).
TC	*A Textual Commentary on the Greek New Testament,* by Bruce Metzger. 2nd ed. United Bible Societies, 1994.
TDNT	*Theological Dictionary of the New Testament,* 2nd ed. G. Kittel and G. Friedrich, editors. Translated by G. W. Bromiley. 9 vols. Grand Rapids: Eerdmans, 1964–74.
TNIV	*Today's New International Version.* Colorado Springs: International Bible Society, 2001.
WCF	*Westminster Confession of Faith.*
Whiston	William Whiston, translator. *The Works of Flavius Josephus.* London: Routledge & Sons, 1899.
WSC	*Westminster Shorter Catechism.*
WTJ	*Westminster Theological Journal.*

Preface

Earlier – and much shorter! – versions of this work appeared in the *Evangelical Commentary on the Bible*, edited by Walter Elwell and published by Baker Book House in 1989; and in a syllabus prepared for my students at Reformed Theological Seminary during the 1990s. As the present work comes to publication, I want to express special thanks

• to my colleagues in Biblical Studies at RTS from 1980 to 2001, both in Old Testament (John Currid, Ralph Davis, Ken Howell, Julie Möller, Richard Pratt and Willem VanGemeren) and in New Testament (Jim DeYoung, Paul Fowler, Dennis Ireland and Sam Kistemaker), for whose joint labors I am newly appreciative since learning how Matthew joins 'things new and old' (Matt. 13:52);

• to the members of my immediate and my extended family for their support over many years, and especially to Ginger (who has been my loving and faithful wife for forty-five years), our younger daughter, Claire Holley (who read most of the commentary and offered valuable suggestions), our older daughter, Beverly Harmon (who was caring for our triplet granddaughters while Claire read the commentary!) and my parents Jones and Olivia Chamblin (who financed my earliest serious study of Matthew in graduate school during the 1960s, and to whose memory this volume is dedicated);

• to the many people both within and beyond my family who remained steadfast in prayer for me even as the commentary progressed at an almost unbearably slow pace (and as I recalled the words of my friend Palmer Robertson: 'nine months to bear a baby, nine years to produce a book');

• to Christian Focus Publications, for their invitation to write this commentary for their Mentor series; to my editor

13

Malcolm MacLean, who encouraged me throughout the project, and who was remarkably forbearing in face of my several 'false prophecies' about the date of completion; and to my friend Boyd Luter, who helped edit the commentary's final draft;

• to the many whose writings have helped me better to understand the Gospel according to Matthew, and to whom my indebtedness will be evident everywhere, especially in the footnotes and the bibliography (it has been said that if you borrow from one person, they call it 'plagiarism'; but that if you borrow from a thousand, they call it 'research'!);

• to the writers of hymns whose words have captured the glory and the grace, the joy and the wonder, of Jesus the Messiah, and have supplied headings for the whole of the commentary;

• to the evangelist Matthew himself, for his fidelity to his Master's commission (28:20a); his artistry in the use of the Greek language (which the commentary employs); and the literary and theological masterpiece he has produced under the Spirit's direction;

• to the Triune God supremely (28:19): to God the Father for the gift of his beloved Son and the promise of his kingdom; to God the Son, for the unsearchable riches of his glory and grace so splendidly displayed in the Gospel according to Matthew; and to God the Holy Spirit for his inspiration of this gospel, and for his enlivening, enlightening and empowering presence throughout this study. *Soli Deo Gloria!*

* * * * *

Notes. 1. This commentary is largely devoted to exegesis. Most application is left to the readers! Attention may be drawn to the volume on Matthew by Michael J. Wilkins in *The NIV Application Commentary: From biblical text...to contemporary life* (Grand Rapids: Zondervan, 2004).

2. A survey of the bibliography will show that there is far more reliance on books than on articles in scholarly journals. For extensive interaction with the latter, see the commentaries

by Donald A. Hagner (1993 and 1995), W. D. Davies and Dale C. Allison, Jr. (1988, 1991 and 1997), and Craig S. Keener (1999).

3. Translations of Matthew and other biblical writings are my own, unless otherwise indicated. In renderings of Old Testament texts, where most English versions use 'the LORD' for the personal name of Israel's God, I have usually chosen 'Yahweh' instead (cf. J. Alec Motyer 1999: 12).

4. *The Gospel of Matthew*, by John Nolland (Grand Rapids: Eerdmans, 2005), *The Gospel of Matthew*, by R. T. France (Grand Rapids: Eerdmans, 2007), and *Matthew*, by David L. Turner (Grand Rapids: Baker, 2008), appeared too late for me to consult.

Section 1
Approaching the Gospel according to Matthew

I.
THE STORY

Before us is a book of twenty-eight chapters which covers forty-five pages in my edition of the New International Version (hereafter *NIV*). It is the first document in the NT canon, which matches its pre-eminence throughout the church's history.[1] In that regard, the NT scholar Theodor Zahn found himself at a loss to find its equal in the literature of antiquity; and Ernest Renan, the historian of religion, called Matthew the most important book ever written.[2]

Beyond its monumental significance, the key background questions must be addressed. What sort of book – what kind of literature – is Matthew? Who is its author? On what basis – with what qualifications and for what purposes – does he write? Within what historical, literary and theological contexts does he stand? To whom and to what are he and his work indebted? For whom did he write? Are we among his intended readers? What effect can an ancient document from a foreign culture be expected to have upon us? Why, even given its long and distinguished history, should we take the time to read and study Matthew? Such are the major questions before us.

The Gospel according to Matthew takes the form of a story. The book contains much of Jesus' preaching and teaching, but it is all set within the framework, or drawn into the flow, of an underlying *narrative*.[3]

---

[1]On the prominence of Matthew in the church's life from post-apostolic times onward, see France 1989: 13-20. Cf. Howard Clarke, *The Gospel of Matthew and its Readers: A Historical Introduction to the First Gospel* (Bloomington: Indiana Univ. Press, 2003).

[2]These statements are cited in Morris 1992: 1.

[3]Bauer 1988: 142; Ryken 1987: 31; Combrink 1983: 61-90. The basic shape of Matthew is discernible in the other three gospels. All four offer, in the language of Luke 1:3 (*kathexēs*), an 'orderly account' of Jesus' life and work, whether order is conceived in temporal, spatial or logical terms (cf. BAGD

What story is being told? Answering this question calls for attention to *characters* and to *plot*. 'Characters are necessary for the actions which move the story along, but actions help define characters, so there is a dialectical relationship between plot and character in the Gospels.'[4] Plot denotes the arrangement of episodes within a story, and the progress from one event to another down to a climax and a conclusion. 'Central to most plots is *conflict*, which provides movement and heightens the tension, leading to a climax of success or failure.'[5] To what characters, then, are we here introduced? How do they help shape the story, and how are they affected by unfolding events and by other persons participating in them? How does the action progress from beginning to end? What conflicts are described, and what is their outcome? How are we affected as we move through the story to its climax and conclusion?

It should be observed that, as readers, we may be deeply moved, even radically changed, by a story without knowing who wrote it. But being affected that way, as innumerable readers of this story have been, heightens our interest in the *storyteller*, to whom we will turn our attention at the close of this section.

A. The Characters

The figure introduced in the opening verse ('Jesus Christ the son of David, the son of Abraham') remains central throughout the story. We learn about certain events of his life, including his birth in Bethlehem, his family's flight to Egypt and return to Galilee, his baptism in the Jordan River, his testing in the wilderness, his preaching and teaching and miracle-working in Galilee and Judea, his encounters with various individuals, his table fellowship with 'tax collectors and sinners', his conflicts with adversaries both human and demonic,

---

s.v. *kathexēs*). Each document, moreover, takes the form of a 'narrative' – Luke's language again (1:1, *diēgēsis*).

[4]E. V. McKnight, 'Literary Criticism,' *DJG*, 479.

[5]Burridge 1994: 19. Pratt 1990: 179 recalls Aristotle's definition of plot as 'the arrangement of incidents,' and Pratt himself speaks of 'plot, or dramatic flow, as the heightening or lessening of tension through the arrangement of scenes.'

his calling and training and commissioning of disciples, his transfiguration, his final journey to Jerusalem, his triumphal entry, his cleansing of the temple, his debates with the religious authorities, his last meal with the disciples, his agony in Gethsemane, his betrayal and arrest, his trial before Jewish and Roman courts, his crucifixion, his resurrection from the dead and his concluding commission to his followers.

All other characters are presented in relation to Jesus. We are early introduced to his distinguished ancestors and to Mary and Joseph, to King Herod and to magi from the east, to John the Baptist and to certain Pharisees and Sadducees. As the story unfolds we find three groups around Jesus: the crowd; the authorities, both religious and secular; and the disciples. There are also memorable representatives from each group, such as (respectively) a Jewish leper, a Roman centurion and a Canaanite woman; Herod the tetrarch, Caiaphas the high priest and Pilate the Roman governor; and Simon Peter, Mary Magdalene and Judas Iscariot. There are also frequent references to Old Testament figures, such as Abraham, Noah, Moses, Elijah, David, Solomon, Isaiah, Jeremiah, Jonah, Daniel and the Son of Man. Also featured in the story are non-human characters – angels, Satan and the demonic powers, God the Father and the Holy Spirit.

B. The Plot
The opening verse causes us to ask: Who is Jesus, and why is his story being told at such length? Why is he called 'Christ' and 'Son of David' and 'Son of Abraham?' The genealogy readies us for the arrival of a regal figure. Anticipation is heightened into wonder when we learn of the angel's appearance to Joseph, and of the magi's journey to Bethlehem. But both the magi and Jesus' family must flee from Herod, and our joy over Jesus' birth and deliverance is nearly eclipsed by the slaughter of the innocents. Even after Herod's death, Judea remains a dangerous place, and Joseph takes his family to Galilee.

John the Baptist appears on the scene, announcing the dawn of God's rule. We wonder how this event will affect Israel and her leaders, here addressed as 'a brood of vipers'.

And we wonder, in view of John's prophecy, what Jesus is about to do, and why he receives John's baptism. The Son and Servant, now anointed by the Spirit and appointed by the Father, is led into battle with the devil; and we suspect, even as we celebrate Jesus' victory, that the war is not over.

Jesus' return to Galilee following John's imprisonment (4:12) recalls earlier dangers in Judea (2:16), and makes us wonder what is in store for Jesus, especially as his message is the same as John's (3:2; 4:17). Throughout the ministry on which he now embarks, Jesus does battle with demonic powers and says and does things that provoke opposition from the Pharisees and teachers of the law. On the surface of the ensuing chapters, there is an ebb and flow of tension both within and between episodes. But as the larger story progresses, the tension steadily builds. Jesus teaches his followers that adherence to him and to God's rule assures fierce opposition and puts their lives at risk (5:11-12; 10:16-23). Yet the fiercest hostility and the most blasphemous charges are directed at him, calling forth his sternest words of judgment (12:22-45). Toward the end of this period, following Peter's declaration that Jesus is 'the Messiah, the Son of the living God', Jesus expressly tells his disciples that he, like John, will suffer and die at the hands of the authorities.[6]

Soon thereafter, Jesus 'departed from Galilee and came into the region of Judea beyond the Jordan' (19:1). One reads the ensuing narrative with a mounting sense of impending disaster. Enlarging on his earlier prophecies, Jesus foretells his betrayal, mockery, flogging and death by crucifixion, (20:17-19). By the self-understanding implicit in his entry into Jerusalem and his cleansing of the temple, Jesus confirms his enemies' worst suspicions about him. Knowing that his parables of judgment, notably the one in which a vineyard's tenants slay the owner's son, are directed at them, the chief priests and the Pharisees look for a way to arrest him (21:33-46). In a series of debates, Jesus rebuts or deflects his antagonists' questions (about his and John's authority, paying taxes to Caesar, and life in the resurrection), then raises a

---

[6]See Matthew 16:13-21; 17:11-13, 22-23, with 14:1-12.

question of his own about Messiah's sonship. That paves the way for his devastating exposé of Pharisaic and scribal sins, and for his discourse on the future (in which he traces developments from present turmoil, foretells persecution but ultimate vindication for God's people, and depicts the horrors of Jerusalem's coming destruction (chapters 23–25).

Hereafter, the narrative swiftly moves to its climax. Jesus' enemies, now determined on a course of action, find a willing ally in Judas. Jesus interprets his anointing at Bethany as preparation for his burial. During his last meal with the disciples, he verbally and visibly portrays his approaching death. Following his anguished prayer in the garden, he is arrested, tried before Jewish and Roman authorities, sentenced to die and crucified (26:17-27:56). His enemies' triumph is complete. On his way to death, Jesus has been betrayed by one of his followers, denied by another and forsaken by them all (26:56). At the end, he is even abandoned by the One who had declared him to be his 'beloved Son' at the baptism and the transfiguration.[7] We now better understand the baptism at the Jordan and the agony in Gethsemane. Yet even amid our sorrow over the crucifixion, we sense, especially if we have read Matthew carefully to this point, that it is God and Jesus, not their enemies, who have determined this outcome, that it was to this very end that Jesus embarked on his ministry, that this event is essential, if the promise of 1:21 is to be fulfilled, and thus that, in a real sense, Jesus' mission has succeeded in the very place it appears to have failed. In the very hour of his death, Jesus is the Father's obedient Son, as the centurion testifies (27:54).

But the story was not designed to end on Golgotha, as close attention to the foregoing narrative would have assured us. Each time Jesus foretold his suffering and death, he also promised that he would rise from the dead (16:21; 17:22; 20:19). His restoring a girl to life (9:23-26) foreshadows such an event, as do his promise of 'the sign of Jonah the prophet' (12:39-40; 16:4), his transfiguration (17:9) and his response to the Sadducees' question about the resurrection (22:29-32). And

---

[7]See Matthew 27:46, with 3:17 and 17:5.

so it happens. 'He is not here, for he has been raised, just as he said,' declares the angel, (28:6). The Father has vindicated his beloved Son, the suffering Servant, by raising him from the dead, and by this action has ratified and assured the saving effects of Jesus' death.

The risen Jesus attends to his followers. As at the first, he summons them by his sovereign command, and he gathers them to a place of former instruction (28:7, 16; see 5:1). As before, they worship him (28:17; see 14:33). Again he commissions them. Only now, in keeping with the authority granted him, they are to go to 'all the nations' (28:18-20a; see 10:5-6). In accord with the name given him at the beginning, Jesus promises to be with them always, even to the close of the age (28:20b; see 1:23, 'Immanuel'). With the sounding of the three major chords of victory, fulfillment and resolution, the story comes to a close.

C. The Storyteller

The teller of the story does not advertise himself, but keeps us focused on the plot and on the characters, especially on the story's central figure. He does not reflect upon his psyche or feelings or troubled past. It is not his temperament or his personality that defines him, but the Christian community from which he wrote this book.[8] What C. S. Lewis says about poets applies (*mutatis mutandis*) to him: 'The poet is not a man who asks me to look at *him*; he is a man who says "look at that" and points; the more I follow the pointing of his finger the less I can possibly see of *him*.'[9]

From acquaintance with modern literature, we are accustomed to knowing who wrote the stories we read. Sometimes the story itself identifies the author, as in an

---

[8]'In the ancient world, individuals were defined by the groups to which they belonged. Psychological factors were insignificant as explanations of human behavior. Ancients approved of the "individual" who represented group norms and values; modern westerners value those who stand out from the crowd.' (Aune 1987: 28).

[9]Lewis and Tillyard 1939: 11. Lewis contends that a poet 'does not express his own personality .... [His is] a voyage beyond the limits of his personal point of view, an annihilation of the brute fact of his own particular psychology rather than its assertion' (ibid., 26-27).

autobiography, or a biography penned by an acquaintance of the subject. But often we must rely entirely on external sources for this information. In Stephen Ambrose's *Undaunted Courage*, an account of the nineteenth-century explorations of Meriwether Lewis and William Clark, the author's name appears on the title page, but never in the story. We are likewise dependent on outside information for the identity of most novelists, for only rarely does such a writer assign himself a part, and identify himself by name within the story. Yet in other instances, from knowing about the author in advance, we can detect his personal traits and experiences in his characters.[10]

The book we are studying is both like and unlike such works. It is unlike them in that it comes from the ancient past; but like many of them in that it does not expressly identify its author. It is like them in that its authorship is attested from outside sources; it is unlike most of them in that this external evidence is strongly contested. In certain respects, it is like modern biography and historiography; but given its age, its claims and its motivation, it is distinguishable from both. It is emphatically not an ancient counterpart to a modern novel; but here, as with some novels, study of its text offers clues about the author's identity, experiences and purpose. Such are the matters to be addressed in the following sections.

---

[10]W. Somerset Maugham appears as himself in his novel *The Razor's Edge*. His name does not appear in *Of Human Bondage*; but he says in the Foreword that it is 'an autobiographical novel,' and its main figure, Philip Carey, is in many ways a self-portrait. One suspects that traits of Jane Austen's own character are often subtly present in her novels' heroines (e.g., in Elizabeth Bennett of *Pride and Prejudice*, and in Elinor Dashwood of *Sense and Sensibility*).

II.
THE APOSTLE

I believe that this gospel was written by Matthew, a Jewish tax collector also named Levi, who became a disciple of Jesus, a member of the twelve and a commissioned apostle; and that we here possess splendid evidence of his fidelity to that commission. Considerable support for this view comes from both the early church and from the book itself.

A. The Testimony of the Early Church

This witness, insofar as it is available to us and speaks to the matter, is unanimous in its judgment that the author was Matthew, the very Matthew whose call and commissioning the book records.[1]

The Superscription
This gospel, like the other three, is anonymous in the sense that the writer does not identify himself by name. The same is true for many another documents from ancient times, both within and beyond the Bible. Yet such a work is often ascribed to a given author by means of an attached heading or closing inscription (a colophon).[2]

The gospels are a case in point. The earliest existing texts bear the superscriptions 'The Gospel according to Matthew' (*EUANGELION KATA MATTHAION*), 'The Gospel according to Mark' (*EUANGELION KATA MARKON*), etc. Joined to the nominative absolute *euangelion* are the preposition *kata*

---

[1]See Matthew 9:9; 10:3; France 1985: 30; Davies and Allison 1988: 129, n. 93.

[2]France 1989: 50. John 21:24 serves as a kind of colophon; yet it identifies the author not by name but as 'the disciple whom Jesus loved' (v. 20, and it stands within the document [the author is granted the last word]; v. 25).

and the proper name in the accusative case.[3] There is only one *euangelion*, the gospel of Jesus Christ; only later do we find references to the four 'gospels' (*euangelia*).[4] One purpose of the prepositional phrase is to ascribe authorship to the person whose name is given.[5] Another is to distinguish *this* presentation of Christ from the others.[6] The above heading is therefore not equivalent to 'the Gospel *of* Matthew' (with the genitive *tou Matthaiou*). The latter phrase is doubly misleading: it suggests that there is a plurality of gospels (i.e., one belonging to Matthew, another to Mark, and so on), when in fact there is only one; and it obscures the gospel's fundamental identity as 'the gospel of Christ' (*euangelion tou Christou*) or 'the gospel of God' (*euangelion tou Theou*).[7] Other forms of the heading are to

---

[3]The nominative absolute is common in headings and titles; for other examples, see the opening words of Matthew 1:1 (*Biblos*), and Mark 1:1 (*Archē*). Cf. *GGBB*, 49-51.

[4]For plural forms of *euangelion* in this sense, see *PGL* s.v., B.

[5]According to Plummer 1911: vii, the *kata* 'neither affirms nor denies authorship; it implies *conformity to a type*, and need not mean more than "drawn up according to the teaching of."' *Kata* with the accusative may indeed be so used, as e.g. in Romans 2:16, where *kata to euangelion mou* means 'in accordance with my gospel' (BAGD s.v. *kata*, II. 5. a.) and in the title 'Gospel according to the Hebrews' (*HE* 3.39.17). 'But [Plummer adds] it is certain that the Christians of the first four centuries who gave these titles to the Gospels meant more than this: they believed, and meant to express, that each Gospel was written by the person whose name it bears.' Hengel 1985: 65-66, (i) acknowledges that *kata* with the accusative need not denote authorship, and that the expression is so used only rarely in Greek literature of the period, but (ii) also observes that the closest parallel to the gospel-headings are references to Greek versions of the OT 'according to the seventy [*kata tous hebdomēkonta*],' 'according to Aquila [*kata ton Akylon*],' and 'according to Symmachus [*kata ton Symmachon*]' – i.e., to parties responsible for producing them. BDF, par. 124 (p. 120), judges that the *kata* of the superscription designates 'the author of this form of the Gospel.'

[6]Thus Plummer 1911: vii, who cites Irenaeus' expression *euangelion tetramorphēn*, 'the gospel in four shapes.'

[7]Against the view that the *kata* of the headings is 'a simple periphrasis for the *genitivus auctoris* [a genitive denoting the author],' as represented e.g. in BAGD s.v. *kata*, II. 7. c., Hengel rightly notes that 'the concern was in fact to avoid the genitive' (1985: 65). BDF also notes the choice of *kata Matthaion*, 'according to the presentation of Matthew,' rather than *tou Matthaiou*, 'the [special] Gospel of Matthew' (par. 163, p. 90). For 'the gospel of Jesus Christ,'

be found in the textual tradition. But *euangelion*, where present, is always singular. Moreover, 'according to Matthew' is always present; never does a heading attribute this book to someone else.[8]

When were these earliest headings first joined to the gospels? One judgment is that they 'originated no later than A.D. 140 and in all probability were handed down with the Gospel texts as early as A.D. 125.'[9] Yet by then, according to the same judgment, the gospels were already associated with an earlier generation, and old enough for it to be claimed 'that actual apostles and their associates had written them'; and it is highly improbable that they circulated anonymously for sixty years or even for thirty.[10] On the contrary, it is highly probable – for reasons both practical and theological – that authors' names were attached to the gospels from the earliest days of their circulation.[11] In any case, we possess no evidence that a gospel ever existed without such a heading. Even on the view that the gospels were written relatively late, and over a thirty-year period (i.e., from Mark in the mid-60s to John in

---

see Mark 1:1; for 'the gospel of God' (1:14) usage to which the headings' choice of *euangelion* may be traced (cf. Hengel 1985: 84).

[8]The same is true for the other gospels. Other forms of the superscription for Matthew: *KATA MATTHAION* ('According to Matthew'); *ARCHĒSYN THEŌ TOU KATA MATTHAION EUANGELIOU* ('The beginning, with God, of the Gospel according to Matthew'), *HAGION EUANGELION KATA MATTHAION* ('The Holy Gospel according to Matthew'), *EK TOU [EUANGELIOU] KATA MATTHAION* ('From the [Gospel] according to Matthew'). See France 1989: 50; Davies and Allison 1988: 129.

[9]Stonehouse 1964: 16. Cf. Davies and Allison (1988: 129): 'a date as early as A.D. 125, although not absolutely demanded by the evidence, is quite reasonable.' As both sources note, the suggestion of 125 goes back to J. H. Ropes (1934) and G. D. Kilpatrick (1946).

[10]The quotation is from Stonehouse, ibid. (recounting the view of J. H. Ropes). To speak of the gospels' circulating from thirty to sixty years (i.e., from ca. A.D. 65 to 95) reflects varying views about the dates of their composition (cf. the later discussion of this area).

[11]See Hengel 1985: 64-84, on 'the titles of the Gospels.' A theological reason was to assure that no unauthorized person was credited with the writing (see ibid., 69, for Tertullian's criticism of Marcion). A practical reason, as already noted, was to distinguish one Christian's writing from another (see ibid., 74-81, on 'the practical necessity of the titles').

the mid-90s), the superscriptions may be reasonably dated no
later than about A.D. 100.[12]

Evidence from Papias

Papias lived from ca. A.D. 60 to 130, and became bishop of
Hierapolis.[13] We learn of his work from two later bishops, Irenaeus
of Lyons (who flourished from ca. A.D. 175 to 195) and Eusebius
of Caesarea (who lived from ca. A.D. 265 to 339).[14]

1. Papias' work

In Book 3 of *HE*, Eusebius refers to a five-volume work by
Papias entitled 'Exposition [*Exēgēsis*] of the Oracles [*Logia*] of
the Lord'. He then quotes Irenaeus: 'To these things [Jesus'
oracles] Papias, who had listened to John and was later
a companion of Polycarp, and who lived at a very early
date, bears written testimony in the fourth of his books; he
composed five' (3.39.1).[15]

'That is what Irenaeus says [continues Eusebius]; but Papias
himself, in the preface to his work [the 'Exposition'], makes
it clear that he was never a hearer or eyewitness of the holy
apostles [*apostolōn*], and tells us that he learnt the essentials
of the faith from their former pupils [Eusebius now quotes

---

[12]Hengel affirms that 'in the present state of our knowledge the titles
of the Gospels are by no means late products from the second century but
must be very old. With a considerable degree of probability they can be
traced back to the time of the origin of the four Gospels between 69 and 100
A.D. and are connected with their circulation in the communities' (1985:
84). Cf. Hengel 2000: 48-56. France, who finds Hengel's proposals attractive,
calls the proposal of A.D. 125. (noted earlier) 'a scholarly guess' (1989: 51).
The use of superscriptions need not have awaited the collection of all four
gospels. Would they not have been needed when *two* such documents (e.g.,
Mark and Matthew) began circulating among the churches? Some of the
points raised here anticipate later discussion.

[13]See D. F. Wright, 'Papias,' *DCC*, 746. Hierapolis was about twelve miles
northwest of Colossae and six miles north of Laodicea. In all probability,
a church was first established there through the ministry of Epaphras,
a colleague of Paul (see Col. 4:13, with Acts 19:10).

[14]On Irenaeus, see D. F. Wright, *DCC*, 516-17; on Eusebius, J. G. G. Norman,
ibid., 356-57.

[15]Here, and again in verses 15 and 16, I have translated *logia* 'oracles'
instead of 'sayings' (Williamson's choice). See the later discussion.

from Papias]: "I shall not hesitate to furnish you, along with the interpretations [*hermēneiais*], with all that in days gone by I carefully learnt from the presbyters [*presbyterōn*] and have carefully recalled, for I can guarantee its truth. Unlike most people, I felt at home not with those who had a great deal to say, but with those who taught the truth; not with those who appeal to commandments from other sources but with those who appeal to the commandments given by the Lord to faith and coming to us from truth itself [cf. John 14:6]. And whenever anyone came who had been a follower of the presbyters, I inquired into the words [*logous*] of the presbyters, what Andrew or Peter had said [*eipen*], or Philip or Thomas or James or John or Matthew [*Matthaios*], or any other disciple of the Lord; and what Aristion and the presbyter John, disciples of the Lord, were still saying [*legousin*]. For I did not imagine that things out of books would help me as much as the utterances of a living and abiding voice."' Eusebius appends his opinion that Papias is speaking of two Johns, one 'the apostle' and author of the gospel, the other 'the elder' and probably the author of Revelation (3.39.2-7).

Eusebius next refers to Papias' record of some miracles (including, from his own time, the raising of a dead person) and of 'some otherwise unknown parables and teachings of the Saviour'; and to Papias' belief 'that after the resurrection of the dead there will be a period of a thousand years, when Christ's kingdom will be set up on this earth in material form'. Eusebius then comments: 'I suppose he got these [millennial] notions by misinterpreting the apostolic accounts and failing to grasp what they had said in mystic and symbolic language. For he seems to have been a man of very small intelligence, to judge from his books. But it is partly due to him that the great majority of churchmen after him took the same view, relying on his early date; e.g. Irenaeus and several others, who clearly held the same opinion' (3.39.8-13).

Having noted that Papias in the same work 'gives us accounts [*diēgēseis*] of the Lord's sayings [*logōn*] obtained from Aristion or learnt direct from the presbyter John,' Eusebius quotes what Papias has to say 'regarding Mark, the writer of the gospel: "This, too, the presbyter used to say: 'Mark, who had been Peter's interpreter [hermēneutēs], wrote down carefully, but not in order [taxei], all that he remembered of the Lord's sayings and doings. For he had not heard the Lord or been one of His followers, but later, as I said, one of Peter's. Peter used to adapt his teaching to the occasion, without making a systematic arrangement [syntaxin] of the Lord's oracles [logiōn], so that Mark was quite justified in writing down some things just as he remembered them. For he had one purpose only – to leave out nothing that he had heard, and to make no misstatement about it.'" These things, then [oun], are related by [or to] Papias concerning Mark. "Concerning Matthew [continues Papias] these things were said [by the same presbyter]:[16] 'Matthew [Matthaios] therefore [oun] compiled [synetaxato] the oracles [ta logia] in the Hebrew dialect [Hebraïdi dialektō], and everyone interpreted [hērmēneusen] them as well as he could'"' (3.39.14-16).[17]

This passage has been quoted at length in order to relate the statement about Matthew to the other quotations from Papias, and also to Eusebius' remarks about Papias. We shall have occasion to refer to the passage more than once; for now, we limit ourselves to the following observations.

---

[16]Williamson's translation of 16a – 'Such is Papias' account of Mark. Of Matthew he has this to say' – gives the impression that 16b comes from Papias. But heretofore in chapter 39, when quoting Papias himself, Eusebius uses phēsin, 'he says' (2, 7, 12), whereas here the verb is eirētai (a form of eipon used for legō in the perfect tense), 'these things were [or have been] said' – which matches the imperfect elegen of 15a, 'the presbyter used to say.' On my translation, Papias is indicating that the words about Matthew, like those about Mark, come from the presbyter John. This sense is yet stronger if 16a means 'these things are related to Papias [tō Papia, a dative of indirect object],' rather than 'by Papias [an instrumental dative of agency].' Cf. Gundry 1994: 613.

[17]Williamson leaves this oun, like the earlier one in 16a, untranslated. He has 'translated' rather than 'interpreted' for hērmēneusen, even though he renders the hermēneiais of 2 'interpretations,' and the hermēneutēs of 15 'interpreter.' In place of his 'Aramaic language,' I have chosen the more literal 'Hebrew dialect.' On these matters, see the later discussion.

2. Papias' sources

Papias testifies that he learned what 'the presbyters,' that is, the disciples of Jesus, 'had said' by inquiring of their followers. Among the seven presbyters whom he names—all of them members of the twelve—are the brothers James and John, and Matthew.[18] Papias also inquired (he tells us) into 'what Aristion and the presbyter John, disciples of the Lord, were still saying.' Eusebius' distinction between John the apostle and John the presbyter is to be rejected.[19] Papias refers to one John only: the son of Zebedee and member of the twelve, whom he twice identifies both as 'presbyter' and as 'disciple of the Lord'; it is Eusebius, not Papias, who speaks of 'apostles.' What this John 'had said,' Papias learned from his followers. But 'the utterances of a living and abiding voice' were not confined to intermediaries. John was still alive, and Papias had access to what he was 'still saying.' Some of Jesus' words Papias 'learnt direct from the presbyter John.'[20] The testimony that Papias 'had listened to John,' 'was later a companion of Polycarp,' and 'lived at a very early date,' comes from Irenaeus, who himself had been taught by Polycarp. In a later quotation preserved by Eusebius, Irenaeus recalls how Polycarp 'spoke of his intercourse with John and with the others who had seen the Lord' (5.20.6), evidence which, when joined to that of 3.39.1, suggests that Polycarp may have been one of the main 'followers' on whom Papias relied. If Papias lived from A.D. 60 to 130, and Polycarp from A.D. 70 to 155/160, and if John died around A.D. 100. (all reasonable, though approximate, datings), then we may place the writing of

---

[18]The list of the twelve in Matthew 10:2-4 includes 'James the son of Zebedee, and John his brother,' and also 'James the son of Alphaeus.' Papias almost certainly has the first James in view, for he joins the names of James and John (39.4) and is more likely to mention the better known James.

[19]See the arguments in Gundry 1994: 611-15. Cf. France 1989: 55.

[20]Papias receives present testimony from both John and Aristion (3.39.4, 14). But only the former is identified as 'the presbyter'; for Aristion, though an original disciple, did not become an apostle (so Gundry 1994: 612).

Papias' 'Exposition of the Oracles of the Lord' sometime between A.D. 95 and 110.[21]

3. Papias' reliability

On the above reading of the evidence, Papias (i) received testimony from followers of Jesus' first and closest disciples, including Matthew, and from at least one of those very disciples, the apostle John, and (ii) recorded and interpreted that tradition toward the close of the first century or the beginning of the second. Thus we would expect him to be more trustworthy than someone further removed from the events concerned.[22] Moreover, to judge from his own words, Papias considered the witness of his predecessors to be thoroughly reliable, and was determined to faithfully and accurately impart what he received from them: 'I shall not hesitate to furnish you... with all that in days gone by I carefully learnt from the presbyters and have carefully recalled, for I can guarantee its truth' (3.39.3).

To be sure, Eusebius observes that Papias 'seems to have been a man of very small intelligence'; but this is a judgment about Papias' millennial views, whose materialism Eusebius rejects and whose influence he regrets (3.39.12-13).[23] Eusebius

---

[21]The dates for Papias and Polycarp come from *DCC*, s.v. Polycarp became bishop of Smyrna (Eusebius 3.36.1); it was probably here that Irenaeus came under his teaching (*DCC*, 516, 791). According to Irenaeus, John died during Trajan's reign (A.D. 98-117; see Eusebius 3.23.1-4). After a careful study, Yarbrough concludes (1983: 190) that the 'generally accepted date of 130 or later' for Papias' writings 'has little to commend it,' and that 'Papias wrote his five treatises ca. 95-110.' For strong arguments in favor of 'a date before Trajan's persecution (i.e., before ca. 110) for Papias' report concerning Mark and Matthew,' see Gundry 1994: 610-11.

[22]Gundry 1994: 611. Let modern students of Matthew remember that, in one sense, we are the furthest removed from the events concerned. 'It is not prudent for scholarship 1,900 years later to dismiss too facilely as complete fiction or ignorance the affirmation of Papias, an ancient spokesman living within four decades of the composition of canonical Matt' (Brown 1997: 211).

[23]In this regard, cf. Gundry 1994: 612: 'Eusebius does not like the Book of Revelation—the millenarianism that Papias, Irenaeus, and others have drawn from it seems crassly materialistic to him...—so he wants to belittle the book by making it unapostolic, i.e., written by an elder named John as opposed to the apostle named John [3.39.5-6].'

has earlier presented Papias, together with Polycarp and Ignatius, as a distinguished bishop (3.36.1-2).[24] And while he thinks that Papias 'was never a hearer or eyewitness of the holy apostles' (3.39.2), he proceeds to quote directly from him; and when doing so, he casts no doubt on the accuracy of Papias' reports.[25] Indeed, given his explicit disapproval of Papias' millennial views—which are summarized, not directly quoted—the absence of such remarks about the quoted material amounts to tacit approval. In short, Eusebius offers us no reason to doubt that Papias accurately represents his sources, only reason to doubt Eusebius' own ability to characterize them correctly (39.5-7)![26]

4. Papias' testimony about Matthew

'Of Matthew [says Papias] these things were said [by the presbyter John]: "Matthew [*Matthaios*] therefore [*oun*] compiled [*synetaxato*] the oracles [*ta logia*] in the Hebrew dialect [*Hebraïdi dialektō*], and everyone interpreted [*hērmēneusen*] them as well as he could"' (39.16).

Papias learns about Matthew both from followers of the first disciples (39.4, where Matthew is named, as again in 39.5) and from Matthew's fellow apostle, 'the presbyter John' (39.4, 14), to whom the testimony of 39.16 is ascribed.[27] Having just read the presbyter's witness about 'Mark, the writer of the gospel,' 15, we are disposed to think that 16 likewise refers to

---

[24]There is some textual support for the comment (i.e., in 36.2) that Papias was 'highly proficient in all kinds of learning and expert in Scripture.' Is this a spurious addition to defend Papias against Eusebius' charge in 39.13? Or was it deleted to show respect for Eusebius' judgment, or to remove an inconsistency? See Petrie 1967: 24, n. 1.

[25]The words of 39.13 ('a man of very small intelligence, to judge from his books') first applied to Papias' exegesis of Revelation, might also be applied to *interpretations* which he attached to received tradition (cf. 39.3), but which lie beyond the material Eusebius quotes.

[26]Writes Wenham (1991: 127): 'Eusebius is generally recognized as an honest transcriber of valuable sources, but also as a person of unreliable critical judgment.' Petrie comments that 'Eusebius is disposed to quarrel with Papias in matters of opinion, not of facts; although... he may turn the latter to his own account' (1967: 24, n. 1).

[27]See note 16 above.

a completed gospel. This expectation is strengthened by the direct juxtaposing of the phrases 'concerning Mark' (*peri tou Markou*) and 'concerning Matthew' (*peri de tou Matthaiou*) in 16a. Let us see how this judgment is affected by the language of the quotation in 16.

The verb chosen for Matthew's activity is *synataxato*, from *syntassō*, 'to put together in order,' 'to arrange, organize.'[28] This word recalls two terms in 15: 'Mark... wrote down carefully, but not in order [*taxei*], all that he remembered... Peter used to adapt his teaching to the occasion, without making a systematic arrangement [*syntaxin*] of the Lord's oracles.'[29]

This evidence strongly suggests that Matthew writes with Mark's gospel in view, and with the intention (expressed in the *oun*, 'therefore,' of 16a) of presenting 'the oracles' (*logia*, 15 and 16) in a more orderly fashion than Mark had done, without sacrificing Markan accuracy (see the end of 15).[30]

What did Matthew 'arrange,' according to Papias and the presbyter John? What do they mean by 'the oracles' (*ta logia*, 16), that is, 'the oracles of the Lord' (1, 15)? In what language were they written, and to what effect? A common view is represented by Williamson's rendering of 16: 'Matthew compiled the *Sayings* in the Aramaic language, and everyone translated them as well as he could.' Thus interpreted, *logia* denotes a major component of the gospel rather than the gospel itself.

One version of this view is voiced by T. W. Manson: 'Matthew made a collection of oracles, i.e. sayings analogous to those of the old prophets, uttered by divine inspiration and

---

[28]LSJ s.v. The form in 39.16, an aorist middle, may have a reflexive force, 'to arrange, organize, for oneself.' All three NT instances of *syntassō* are in Matthew (21:6; 26:19; 27:10); all are aorist active, with the meaning 'order, direct, prescribe' (BAGD s.v.).

[29]*Taxis* here denotes 'fixed succession' or 'order' (BAGD s.v., 1); *syntaxis* (cognate of *syntassō*), 'order, arrangement' or 'organization, system' (LSJ s.v., 1).

[30]Thus too Gundry 1994: 614. The later patristic judgment – voiced, e.g. by Irenaeus (*HE* 5.8.2-3), by Clement of Alexandria, ca. A.D. 155 to 220. (*HE* 6.14.5), and by Origen, ca. A.D. 185 to 254. (*HE* 6.25.4) – that Matthew was written before Mark, may be traced in part to the emerging canonical order (Origen is said to be 'defending the canon of the Church,' 6.25.3), which depended in turn on Matthew's greater suitability than Mark for liturgical reading, and (to judge from that reference to Clement) on Matthew's opening

containing the commandments and promises of God for the new Israel, the Church of Christ.' He further argues that Matthew's collection is the very document identified as 'Q' in modern scholarship; that Matthew 'composed it in the vernacular of Palestine [i.e., in Aramaic]; that it consisted for the most part of sayings and speeches of Jesus; that various renderings of it (into Greek) were made; and that one of these renderings furnished material for the First Evangelist.'[31]

I wish to defend a different reading of 39.16, however, one reflected in the translation at the opening of section 4. We begin with *ta logia*. According to the immediately preceding testimony, Mark's practice of writing down carefully, 'but not in order [*taxei*], all that he remembered of the Lord's sayings and doings [*kyriou...lechthenta... prachthenta*],' 15a, matches Peter's habit of adapting his teaching to the occasion 'without making a systematic arrangement [*syntaxin*] of the Lord's oracles [*tōn kyriakōn... logiōn*],' 15b, which indicates that the *logia* of 15b embraces the words and the deeds of 15a, and thus denotes Mark's completed gospel.[32] That strongly suggests that the *logia* of 16 correspondingly denotes Matthew's entire gospel, which concurs with testimony from the early church (see the next paragraph). My chosen translation for *logia* ('oracles') indeed suggests speech ('oracle' comes from the Latin verb *orare*, 'to speak'), but it is speech of a particular kind. All

---

genealogy, forming as it did a link with the OT (thus Gundry 1994: 614). On Matthew's use of Mark, see III. below.

[31]Manson 1946: 75, 86. 'Q' is taken up later in our discussion. A less likely version of this view is that *ta logia* denotes a collection of OT texts fulfilled in Jesus; note the link between 'the sayings' (39.16) and 'the sayings of the Lord,' i.e., Jesus (39.1, 15).

[32]Thus too, e.g., Hendriksen 1973: 89; Gerhard Kittel, *TDNT* 4: 141 (s.v. *logion*). The participles *lechthenta* and *prachthenta* come, respectively, from *legō* ('to speak') and *prassō* ('to do'). In 39.4, which speaks of what the presbyters 'had said [*eipen*]' or what John and Aristion 'were still saying [*legousin*],' Papias reports that he 'inquired into the words [*logous*, not *logia*] of the presbyters.' *Logos* is a cognate of *legō*, for which forms of *eipon* serve in the aorist; so Williamson rightly translates *tōn tou kyriou logōn* [a genitive plural of *logos*], 14a, 'the Lord's sayings.'

four NT instances of the term denote *the utterances of God*; and in the patristic period the word is used 'especially of oracular or inspired utterances.'[33]

It should be observed that the entire ministry of Jesus is revelatory in character. His deeds, no less than his words, disclose that the rule of God has drawn near for salvation and judgment. In light of Jesus' sayings about the event, the crucifixion becomes an 'oracle,' a visible word.[34] Indeed 'the Lord' (*ho Kyrios*) whose 'oracles' Papias expounds is himself a revelation; and nowhere is this plainer than in the gospel according to Matthew, with its declaration that Jesus is 'God with us' (1:23).

Moreover, recognizing that this gospel is written under the authority of the risen Lord and with the tutelage of the enlightening Spirit, there is yet more reason to conclude that *logia*, or 'oracles' of the kind just indicated, is a fitting term for the book as a whole.[35] Having said that, we may note that perhaps one reason for Papias' choice of *ta logia* for this gospel is the presence of the five great discourses. It is not that *ta logia* consist exclusively of 'sayings of the Lord,' but that the

---

[33]*PGL* s.v., 3. The four NT instances are Acts 7:38 (on Sinai Moses 'received living oracles'); Romans 3:2 (Jews 'were entrusted with the oracles of God'); Hebrews 5:12 ('the basic elements of the oracles of God'); and 1 Peter 4:11 (by the gift of the Spirit and the grace of God, 10, one may speak the very 'words of God'). Warfield 1948: 408 finds in the first three passages 'convincing evidence' that the NT writers esteemed the OT 'as an oracular book, which in itself not merely contains, but is the "utterance," the very Word of God.' For corroborative evidence from the patristic period, see ibid., 391-403.

[34]Jesus' proclamation of the kingdom (Matt. 4:17) is unfolded both in the sermon of Matthew 5–7 and in the miracles of Matthew 8–9. Jesus declares the saving significance of his death in, e.g., 20:28; 26:26-28. Romans 3:2, according to Kittel, speaks of Jews' being given 'the whole event of salvation history'; and Hebrews 5:12, of Christians' being instructed 'in the event of revelation which has taken place in Jesus' (*TDNT* 4: 139).

[35]Cf. Matthew 28:18-20 and III. below. Warfield concludes that the obvious meaning of *HE* 3.39.1 is that 'Papias wrote an "Exposition of the Gospels," and that he speaks of Matthew's and Mark's books as themselves sections of those "Scriptures" which he was expounding' (1948: 397).

collection of these sayings into the five discourses is a striking and dominant feature of this gospel.[36]

If *ta logia* denotes the gospel as a whole, how are the accompanying words 'in the Hebrew dialect [*Hebraïdi dialektō*]' to be understood? The prevalent view, in accord with (i) the principal uses of *dialektos* in ancient times, (ii) all occurrences of the term in the NT, and (iii) the testimony of the early church, is that Papias and the presbyter are referring to the Hebrew or Aramaic *language*.[37] In this case *Hebrew* is the better alternative, since the text speaks of a written rather than an oral compilation.[38] Some who

---

[36]But the fashioning of these discourses (on which see III.) is integral to the writing of the gospel itself, unlike the constructing of 'Q,' which would have occurred (as Manson noted) before the writing of Matthew.

[37]The first three usages in LSJ, s.v., are (1) 'discourse, conversation'; (2) 'common language, talk'; (3) 'speech, language.' *Dialektos* means 'language' in all six NT instances, Acts 1:19; 2:6, 8; 21:40; 22:2; and 26:14 (cf. BAGD s.v.). Early testimony comes from Irenaeus ('Matthew published a written gospel for the Hebrews [*Hebraiois*] in their own tongue [*dialektō*],' *HE* 5.8.2; cf. Irenaeus' words about Papias in 3.39.1); from Pantaenus, who died ca. 190 A.D. (who claims to have found 'the Gospel according to Matthew [*to kata Matthaion euangelion*]' among Christians in India, the apostle Bartholomew having 'left behind Matthew's account in Hebrew letters [*Hebraiōn grammasi*: Williamson, 'in the actual Aramaic characters'],' *HE* 5.10.3); from Origen (Matthew's gospel 'was published for believers of Jewish origin, and was composed in Hebrew [*grammasin Hebraïkois syntetagmenon*: Williamson, 'in Aramaic'],' *HE* 6.25.4; cf. 3.39.16, with its *synetaxato*, a form of the same verb); and from Eusebius himself ('Matthew had begun by preaching to Hebrews [*Hebraiois*]; and when he made up his mind to go to others too, he committed his own gospel [*to kat' auton euangelion*] to writing in his native tongue [*patriō glōttē graphē*],' *HE* 3.24.6). For similar testimonies from Epiphanius, Cyril of Jerusalem, and Jerome, see Wenham 1991: 118-19. France thinks it 'most unlikely' that a Greek reader would understand the combination of *Hebraïdi dialektō* and *hermēneuō* to mean 'anything other than translation from one language to another' (1989: 57).

[38]Writing on 'the languages of Palestine,' M. O. Wise concludes that 'most religious writings were not inscribed in Aramaic at all. The chosen linguistic vehicle for such works in first-century Palestine was ordinarily LBH [Late Biblical Hebrew]' (*DJG*, 444). Acts 21:40; 22:2; and 26:14 all contain the very phrase of *HE* 3.39.16, *Hebraïdi dialektō*. As the words in all three instances are *spoken*, NIV's 'Aramaic' is probably a better choice than NASB's 'Hebrew.' BAGD says of these instances, '*the Hebr. language*...i.e., the Aramaic spoken at that time in Palestine' (s.v. *Hebraïs*). Wenham thinks Matthew could have been published in Aramaic or in Hebrew (or in Greek), but he considers Hebrew 'the most suitable language in which to record the fulfilling of the Old Testament scriptures' (1991: 201).

thus interpret the phrase think that in this matter Papias was mistaken.[39] Yet we have thus far found good reason to consider Papias a trustworthy witness. So if this is his meaning (and it may well be), I think it likely (i) that Matthew indeed 'compiled the oracles' (i.e., wrote a gospel) in the Hebrew language; (ii) that others translated and otherwise interpreted the document as well as they could, both by word of mouth and in writing; (iii) that our gospel according to Matthew came into being as a Greek document, not as a *translation* of that Semitic original but as a *thorough revision* made in light of Mark's gospel;[40] (iv) that the apostle Matthew, the very one who 'compiled the oracles in the Hebrew language,' wrote the Greek gospel as well;[41] and (v) that the loss of the Semitic original is to be explained (at least in

---

[39]Stonehouse, having concluded 'that Matthew was originally written in Greek,' thinks that 'the statement of Papias [about the Hebrew language of the original] is obviously mistaken' (1964: 90, 91). Reasons for the mistake, as suggested by Stonehouse, 91-92, and France 1989: 64-66: (i) the thoroughly Semitic character of the gospel, and the author's constant use of the OT in portraying Jesus and interpreting his mission; (ii) evidence that the gospel is addressed to Jewish-Christians, together with non-Christian Jews; and (iii) confusion between this gospel and another work, such as the apocryphal 'Gospel according to the Hebrews,' or between the original Greek Matthew and a Hebrew text based upon it.

[40]The scholarly consensus that our Matthew was originally written in Greek is based on such judgments as the following: (i) Matthew's quotations from the OT depend on Greek versions as well as the Hebrew; (ii) Matthew's Greek is heavily indebted to that of Mark (as noted, *HE* 3.39.15- 16 suggests that Matthew wrote in light of Mark); and (iii) Matthew as a whole does not show signs of being a translation from a Semitic original. Writes Wikenhauser (1958: 195): 'It may be taken as certain that an Aramaic original of the Gospel of St. Matthew can be defended only if we regard Greek Mt. not as a literal translation of the Aramaic, but as a thorough revision made with frequent use of the Gospel of St. Mark.' So too Tasker 1961: 12-13. Butler (1951) argues that the Greek Matthew is a translation of a Palestinian Aramaic Matthew and a source for both Mark and Luke. Wenham's views are similar, though he thinks the original is more likely to have been Hebrew (1991: 198-213).

[41]To state the obvious: the superscriptions, which uniformly ascribe this gospel to Matthew, are attached to the *Greek* document. If Matthew previously wrote a Hebrew (or Aramaic) gospel, and if he was also fluent in Greek (as I believe), then who better qualified than he to revise that document for conveying its message to Greek-speaking readers? According to Gundry 1994: 618, 'those who believe in an Aramaic Gospel of Matthew usually say that because people had difficulty translating it, Matthew wrote another gospel as well, viz., the

part) by the existence of the author's own revision in a language suited to a wider audience.

But also attractive is the view that 'Hebrew dialect [*Hebraïdi dialektō*]' is *literary* rather than *linguistic* in intent, and that the phrase refers to our Greek Matthew, namely to its 'Hebrew way of presenting Jesus' messiahship.' It is argued (i) that the substance and the style of Matthew agree with such a description;[42] (ii) that the contrast between Matthean order and Markan disorder (39.15-16) is better served by a literary than a linguistic term; (iii) that the adjoining verb *hermēneusen*, to judge from its cognate forms in 39.3, 15, denotes expository rather than linguistic skills; (iv) that the comprehensive reference ('everyone interpreted') better applies to the commonly used Greek than to the lesser known Hebrew and Aramaic; (v) that the absence of the definite article favors this sense; and (vi) that *dialektos* 'commonly carried a stylistic meaning, especially when referring to debate.'[43]

While it is hard to choose between those two readings of *Hebraïdi dialektō*, the arguments for the latter are in my judgment slightly more persuasive. In any case, the Greek Matthew is all we

---

Greek gospel we now have, not translated from the earlier Aramaic gospel but probably incorporating materials from it.'

[42]The *substance* of Matthew is thoroughly Hebraic: cf. e.g., the frequent references to OT persons, events, institutions and teachings; and the portrait of Jesus as Messiah, Son of Abraham, Son of David, Son of Man, and New Moses (see further below). So is the *style*: the Greek of Matthew often employs Semitic idiom and shows signs of indebtedness to a Hebrew or Aramaic original – as, of course, do the other gospels. For evidence of Aramaic and Hebraic influences on the style of Matthew, see *GNTG* 4: 31-37. Yet Matthew remains a *Greek* document (see n. 40). Black (1967: 274, 275) stresses that the 'Evangelists... are for the most part writing Greek Gospels, even where they are dependent upon [Aramaic] sources'; and that their records of Jesus' sayings 'are not all literal translations of Aramaic, but translations which have passed through the minds of the Greek Evangelists and emerged as, for the most part, literary productions.'

[43]See especially Gundry 1994: 617-20 (whence these quotations), following J. Kürzinger; so also S. McKnight, *DJG*, 527-28; and Carson (1984: 13) leans in this direction. As Gundry notes, all six instances of *dialektos* in Acts, including the three references to the Hebrew or Aramaic language, carry the definite article. One naturally speaks of '*the* [not *a*] Hebrew language,' and of '*a* [not *the*] Hebrew way of presenting Jesus.' For *dialektos* as 'discourse, debate' and 'style' (as well as 'speech, language') see LSJ s.v.; for the matching verb *dialegomai* as 'reason' or 'argue' (as well as 'use a dialect or language'), ibid., s.v. On Matthew's debates, see VI. below.

possess, and we cannot know for certain whether a Hebrew (or Aramaic) original ever existed.[44] Yet whatever material Papias has in view, he associates Matthew's name, and no other, with it. Moreover, even if Papias is speaking of a Semitic original, nothing in his testimony precludes Matthean authorship of the Greek version as well.

Conclusion

The testimony of the early church, insofar as it is available to us and speaks to the matter, is unanimous in its judgment that the apostle Matthew wrote this gospel.

This ascription is the more noteworthy when we consider that his name *Matthaios* appears only five times in the NT (in one account of his call and in four lists of the twelve), his name *Leui* only three times (in two accounts of his call and in one account of the dinner he hosted thereafter), and neither name in John's gospel.[45] It is hard to imagine the church's attributing the gospel to this relatively obscure member of the twelve – to him and no other, as far as we can tell – unless he were in fact its author, or at least the person principally responsible for its existence.

How critical is this decision? Does our appreciation for this book, or our trust in its reliability, or our understanding of its contents, increase with our confidence that the apostle Matthew was its author? With these questions in view, we turn to Matthew itself.

B. The Testimony of the Book

As noted, Matthew is anonymous. But it will be of interest to examine certain of its texts in light of the early church's witness.[46]

---

[44]Cf. Hendriksen 1973: 90-91. Gundry 1994: 618 considers it 'extremely odd that Papias's elder should have talked about a collection of OT passages fulfilled by Jesus, or a collection of Jesus' sayings, or a loose body of materials concerning Jesus' deeds and sayings, or an Aramaic gospel, yet not about our Greek gospel, the only one of those to survive, let alone achieve canonicity.'

[45]For *Matthaios,* see Matthew 9:9; 10:3; Mark 3:18; Luke 6:15; Acts 1:13. For *Leui,* see Mark 2:14; Luke 5:27, 29; all other instances of *Leui* refer to OT figures. If Matthew is included in the list of John 21:2, it is only as one of 'two others of his disciples.'

[46]As noted in remarks about 'the storyteller' (pp. 23-24), in some literary works we can, from knowing about the author in advance, detect his

Matthew 9:9-13

Jesus commands a man named *Matthaios* to follow him (Matt. 9:9). The Greek spelling transliterates the Aramaic *Mattay* or *Matti'y*, probably an abbreviation of the Hebrew *Mattan^eyāh*, which means 'gift of Yahweh.' The parallels in Mark 2:14 and Luke 5:27 speak instead of *Leui*. I conclude that both names belong to the same person, *Leui* being his tribal name and *Matthaios* his personal name; that his father's name is *Alphaios* (Mark 2:14); and that the use of the personal name is natural if the author is referring to himself.[47]

Thereafter, relate Mark and Luke, Jesus dined with a crowd of people 'in his [Levi's] house.' Matthew says that Jesus was reclining 'in *the* house' (Matt. 9:10), a natural way to speak of one's own home.[48] Jesus here eats with 'many tax collectors [*telōnai*] and sinners [*hamartōloi*]' (9:10, 11). The tax collectors are mentioned as notorious representatives of the latter group. As one who sits 'at the tax office [*telōnion*]' (9:9), Matthew himself is a 'tax collector [*telōnēs*].' That in turn makes him a 'sinner [*hamartōlos*],' the very kind of person Jesus came to call (9:13).[49] The passage also identifies Matthew as a man of some wealth; cf. Luke 5:29: 'Levi gave a great banquet.'

---

personal traits and experiences in his characters. Yet it would be arguing in a circle to examine Matthew with the assumption that the early church's testimony proves Matthean authorship, and then to use evidence from Matthew to establish the truth of the church's testimony.

[47]Nehemiah 11:17, 22 speak of a Levite named *Mattan^eyāh* (Mattaniah); and 1 Chronicles 9:31 of a Levite named *Mattith^eyāh* (Mattithiah), which means the same as *Mattan^eyāh*. Cf. Gundry 1994: 166; also references to *Matthat* (similar to *Matthaios*), son of Levi, in Luke 3:24, 29. The name 'Levi' never appears in Matthew. Mark 2:14 alone reveals that Levi's father is named Alphaeus. The only other Alphaeus mentioned in the NT is the father of the apostle James, who is hereby distinguished from James the son of Zebedee (e.g., Matthew 10:2-3; Mark 3:17-18).

[48]The Greek is *en tē oikia* in Matthew 9:10; and *en tē oikia autou* in Mark 2:15 and Luke 5:29 (a verse that expressly identifies Levi as the host). In the Matthean phrase the definite article *tē* implies possession: 'in the [i.e., in his – Matthew's] house' (cf. *GGBB*, 215). No prior instances of *oikia* in Matthew suggest that Jesus' own dwelling may be in view.

[49]Of the prior instances of *kaleō* ('call') in Matthew, the closest in meaning to 9:13 is 4:21 (Jesus' call to the fishermen James and John). In the language of 9:2, Jesus has come to forgive Matthew's sins (*hamartiai*). See further the comments on 9:9-13.

Matthew 10:2-4

We next meet the name *Matthaios* in the list of the twelve apostles. The parallels in Mark and Luke also use 'Matthew'(rather than 'Levi,' as before);[50] but in Matthew alone he is called 'the tax collector' (9:3). The other five surnames in the present list serve to distinguish certain persons from others whose names are spelled the same.[51] Yet in this case there is no such need, for the NT never speaks of another *Matthaios*.[52]

If the author is speaking of himself, he may deliberately use the self-identification 'the tax collector [*ho telōnēs*]' to recall the condition out of which Jesus called him.[53] In any case, when reading that 'the Son of Man came eating and drinking,' and that he was accused of being 'a glutton and a drunkard, a friend of tax collectors and sinners' (11:19), we are to think of Matthew among others – indeed, of Matthew especially, since the only prior references to a dinner party and to 'tax collectors and sinners' occur in 9:10-13. We are likewise to recall Matthew's former life when reading the disparaging words about tax collectors in 5:46 and 18:17. It is also possible that among 'the tax collectors and the prostitutes' who believed the preaching of John the Baptist (21:31-32), was the tax collector Matthew.[54]

It was stated above that Levi is the man's tribal name, and Matthew his personal name. It is possible, I think probable, that he acquires the latter from Jesus after his call. Here in Matthew 10:2 the author speaks of 'Simon, who is called Peter [*ho legomenos*

---

[50]Mark 3:18; Luke 6:15 (and Acts 1:13).

[51]'Simon [*Simōn*] called Peter' is distinguished from 'Simon [*Simōn*] the Zealot' (Matt. 9:2, 4); 'James [*Iakōbos*] the son of Zebedee' from 'James [*Iakōbos*] the son of Alphaeus' (9:2, 3); and 'Judas [*Ioudas*] Iscariot' from 'Judas [*Ioudas*] not Iscariot' (9:4; John 14:22).

[52]Judas' successor is *Matthias* (Acts 1:23, 26), and he is given no surname. Appearing in the genealogy of Matthew 1 is the name *Matthan* (v. 15); and in that of Luke 3, the names *Matthat* (24, 29), *Mattathias* (Matt. 1:25, 26), and *Mattatha* (1:31).

[53]Cf. 1 Timothy 1:15, whose language is reminiscent of Matthew 9:13b.

[54]Luke, but not Matthew, reports that tax collectors came to be baptized by John (Luke 3:12-13). The terms used in Matthew 3:1, 5 to describe the places of John's activity appear to encompass territories well south of Capernaum, Matthew's home (cf. Hendriksen 1973: 196). Yet Jesus came to the Jordan from Galilee (3:13). Perhaps Matthew did as well; if so, and if he is the author, some of the teachings in Matthew 3:1-17 may be personal recollections.

Petros]'; the same phrase appears in the account of Peter's call (4:18). The same participle appears in 9:9, Jesus 'saw a man... called Matthew [*Matthaion legomenon*]' – which suggests (though it does not prove) that Jesus conferred *Matthaios* on Levi, as he had *Petros* on Simon (16:18, cf. John 1:42). This would help to explain why *Leui* occurs only in accounts of his call (in Mark and Luke), and *Matthaios* everywhere else. This name – 'gift of Yahweh' – would indeed be a fitting choice, since both the tax collector's Master and the salvation he imparts are presented in Matthew as such gifts.[55]

The twelve apostles are named within the context of their receiving authority from Jesus to participate in his mission to 'the lost sheep of the house of Israel' by casting out demons, healing the sick and proclaiming the dawn of the kingdom (10:1, 5-8). This gospel's record of just such a manifold ministry, and its thoroughly Jewish character, accord with this commission. If Matthew is the author, his book represents an extension of his earlier work.

Matthew 13:52

This verse comes at the close of a collection of parables about the kingdom of heaven. After telling certain parables to his disciples and explaining others spoken to the crowd as well, Jesus asks: 'Have you understood all these things?' To the disciples' 'Yes' (Matt. 13:51), Jesus replies: 'Therefore every scribe [*pas grammateus*] who has been discipled [*mathēteutheis*] for the kingdom of heaven is like a householder who brings out of his treasury things new and old' (13:52).

The disciples' response to Jesus' question shows that they have indeed 'been discipled.'[56] It is 'therefore' (*dia touto*)

---

[55]Writes Gundry 1994: 166: 'Or "Matthew," because it means "gift of Yahweh,"...is a name given to Levi when he became a disciple.' For another instance of this present participle to denote a surname, see Matthew 1:16, 'Jesus, who is called Christ [*ho legomenos Christos*]' (again in 27:17). Yet in some instances this participle is used otherwise: e.g., 2:23; 26:3, 14, 36; 27:33.

[56]*Mathēteutheis* is an aorist passive participle of *mathēteuō*, which occurs four times in the NT, three of them in Matthew. The passive forms (here and 27:57) mean 'to be discipled,' 'to be instructed'; the active forms (28:19 and Acts 14:21), 'to make disciples,' 'to instruct.' Cf. BAGD s.v. A related verb is *manthanō*, 'learn.' The noun for 'disciple' is *mathētēs*.

their responsibility, says Jesus, to impart to others what they have learned. (Cf. Jesus' words at the earlier commissioning: 'Freely you received, freely give;' 10:8.) While speaking to the disciples in the awareness of their present condition, Jesus challenges them all ('*every* scribe') to master his teachings, to understand the theological realities of the kingdom, and thus to be equipped to 'make disciples of all nations' (28:19).[57] One purpose of the whole enterprise is to counteract and eventually to foil the designs of another company of *grammateis*, namely those who oppose Jesus and his message of the kingdom.[58] To that end, in 23:34 Jesus implicitly commissions his scholars to address the opposition directly: 'I am sending to you [*pros hymas* – the 'scribes and Pharisees' of 23:29] prophets and wise men and scribes [*grammateis*].'[59] So the ongoing mission to 'the lost sheep of the house of Israel' (10:6) entails confronting the nation's leaders with the gravity of their sins – as relentlessly catalogued in chapter 23 – and calling them to repentance (4:17) before judgment falls.[60]

Thus verse 52 is potentially applicable to all the disciples Jesus addresses. But a particular representative of the twelve may also be in view. The words aptly describe an erstwhile tax collector – a secular scribe – who became a follower of Jesus; that the statement is peculiar to Matthew

---

[57]Hagner 1993: 401 rightly says that Jesus 'has in mind the disciples whom he has been teaching (and not specialist theologians...).' But in response to Jesus' challenge some of the disciples might well *become* such scholars. Consider what three men from among the twelve – Simon Peter, John and Matthew – contributed to the writings of the NT.

[58]The noun *grammateus* appears twenty-two times in Matthew. Of these, twenty are plural (*grammateis*); and of these twenty, all but one (23:34) refer to Jesus' enemies. The one instance of the singular besides 13:52 is 8:19; whether this *grammateus* became Jesus' disciple is uncertain. Jesus' words about 'things new and old' 'may include a dig at the *Jewish* scribes, who could produce only what was old!' (France 1985: 231).

[59]The *grammateis* of Matthew 23:34 are not primarily 'Christian scholars of the Torah' (see Hagner 1993: 402), but persons schooled in *Jesus'* teachings (13:52; 28:19-20; and Matthew *passim*) who are thereby granted understanding of the Torah (see e.g., 5:17-48; 22:37-40).

[60]Like Jesus, John identifies Israel's leaders (in this case, Pharisees and Sadducees) as a 'brood of vipers' and calls them to repentance in face of imminent judgment (Matt. 3:2, 7; cf. 23:33).

also encourages us to think the author is writing about himself. While C. F. D. Moule distinguishes the author of Matthew from the tax collector, his oft-quoted words about this verse are very suggestive: 'The writer of the Gospel was himself a well-educated literate scribe in this [secular] sense. But so must also have been that tax-collector who was called by Jesus to be a disciple. Is it not conceivable that the Lord really did say to that tax-collector Matthew: You have been a "writer"...; you have had plenty to do with the commercial side of just the topics alluded to in the parables – farmer's stock, fields, treasure-trove, fishing revenues; now that you have become a disciple, you can bring all this out again – but with a difference.'[61]

One task of a Jewish *grammateus* might be literally to inscribe words on a page: Matthew's doing so would serve to clarify and reinforce what he had learned as a member of the twelve. What 'things new and old' he would take from his treasury as he wrote his gospel, we shall consider presently. Suffice it here to say that the commission implicit in Matthew 13:52 is discharged in this very book (whoever its author); and that of 23:34 (that Christian scribes should directly address their Jewish antagonists), in Matthew 23 itself.

Matthew 28:16-20

As the gospel closes, the remaining eleven members of the twelve meet the risen Jesus in Galilee. Here, as in chapter 10, he commissions them by virtue of his stupendous authority.[62] Now that they have 'been discipled [*mathēteutheis*]' (Matt. 13:52), they are to 'make disciples [*mathēteusate*]': only now Jesus tells them to go, not just to Israel (10:5-60), but to 'all the nations,' Israel included,

---

[61]Moule 1964: 73-74. A word play may be intended between the verb *mathēteuō* in Matthew 13:52 and an implied *Matthaios* (but Hagner 1993: 401-2 thinks the idea 'far-fetched') – and similarly between the *Matthaios* of 9:9 and the noun *mathētēs* of 9:10-11 (Brown 1997: 209, n. 82, considers this 'possible').

[62]*Exousia* ('authority') in Matthew 28:18, appeared also in 10:1.

(28:19a). Moreover, the stress now is upon teaching (*didas-kontes autous*; 28:20), whereas in the earlier commission it was upon working miracles.[63]

The content of Matthew is no less harmonious with this commission than with that of chapter 10. This gospel, for all its Jewishness, has much to say about Gentiles and much hope to offer them, as we shall see. Furthermore, while Matthew contains notable accounts of miraculous healings and exorcisms (e.g., in chs. 8–9), it accentuates Jesus' teachings – as is especially evident from the five great discourses.[64] If Matthew is the author, the book is his most notable achievement in response to the risen Christ's commission, and it remains one of the chief means by which Jesus' teachings are imparted to disciples from among the nations – including readers of this sentence.

C. Conclusion

Having considered the superscription, the testimony of Papias and passages from the book itself, I restate my belief that the author is Matthew, a Jewish tax collector also named Levi, who became a disciple of Jesus, a member of the twelve and a commissioned apostle. Let us now address the questions posed at the close of section A.: How critical is this decision? Does our appreciation for this book, or our trust in its reliability, or our understanding of its contents, increase with our confidence that the apostle Matthew was its author?

Whoever its author, the gospel we possess was ordained by God the Father, authorized by the risen Christ and inspired by the Holy Spirit. It has therefore always been authoritative for the church. Since in the wisdom of the Holy Trinity the gospel has come to us as an anonymous work, understanding and appropriating its teachings does not depend on identifying the author.[65]

---

[63]In chapter 10 there is much greater stress on working miracles (10:1, 8) than on preaching (10:7). The implicit commission of 23:34 – referring as it does to prophets, wise men and scribes – anticipates the accent on teaching in 28:20a.

[64]On these discourses, see III. below. Note, e.g., the use of the verb *didaskō* ('teach'), and the emphasis on this aspect of Jesus' ministry, in the summaries of Matthew 4:23; 9:35; 11:1.

[65]Stonehouse 1964: 47 writes that 'the inspiration and authority of these anonymous writings [the four gospels] ultimately do not depend upon

Yet as we have seen, the early church attributed this gospel to Matthew; so far as we can tell, there were no competitors for this honor. Evidence thus far considered from the gospel itself is consistent with that judgment. Some have argued that the book is the product of a Matthean *community* or a Matthean *school*.[66] If it were demonstrable that these teachings were first imparted by the apostle Matthew (perhaps both orally and in writing) and then collected and edited by his followers and published as our gospel, the book would still be authoritative for the church, and it would still be valid to ascribe the work to Matthew. However, that the gospel is the product of such a communal or scholarly enterprise is not demonstrable.[67] To be sure, there is nothing in Matthew to match Luke 1:3, where we learn that the book is written by an individual ('it seemed good to me also'). But neither is there anything in Matthew to correspond to John 21:24, where followers of 'the disciple whom Jesus loved' let their voice be heard ('we know that his testimony is true'). On this matter the evidence of the book itself is inconclusive, so it is preferable to join the external witnesses in identifying the gospel as the work of Matthew himself.[68] We will have occasion to test the validity of this judgment at certain points hereafter; I believe the evidence yet to be considered (both in this introduction and in the commentary itself) supports rather than discredits belief in Matthean authorship.

As noted, understanding and embracing this book's teachings does not require certainty about the author's identity. Yet discovering what appear to be (so to speak) fingerprints of the apostle Matthew heightens our appreciation for the book – as would be true if we were to learn that the Epistle to the

---

the identification of their human authors but upon the activity of the Holy Spirit in the process of redemptive revelation.'

[66]For the first, see Kilpatrick 1946; for the second, Stendahl 1968.

[67]For criticisms of Kilpatrick and Stendahl, see, e.g., Guthrie 1990: 50-52.

[68]Stonehouse 1964: 46-47 rightly says both 'that the apostolic authorship of Matthew is as strongly attested as any fact of ancient church history' and that we 'should not elevate this testimony of tradition to the level of the Scripture and so regard it as a dogma of the Christian faith' (similarly France 1989: 79). Guthrie 1990: 53 judges 'that there is no conclusive reason for rejecting the strong external testimony regarding the authorship of Matthew.'

Hebrews was written by Apollos, or that a favorite painting was the work of Rembrandt. Moreover, evidence that the author was a personal companion of Jesus, a member of the twelve and a commissioned apostle, bolsters our confidence that this is a reliable account of Jesus' words and works. Such evidence does not increase the authority of the book, but instead discloses one way in which Christ and the Spirit invested the document with authority.[69]

---

[69]On the importance of eyewitness testimony in the purpose of Christ and the Spirit, see, e.g., Luke 1:1-4; Acts 1:1-8; John 14:25-26; 15:25-26; 21:24; 1 John 1:1-3; Hebrews 2:3; as well as Matthew 28:16-20.

III.
THE SCRIBE

'Therefore every scribe [*pas grammateus*] who has been discipled for the kingdom of heaven is like a householder who brings out from his treasury [*ekballei ek tou thēsaurou*] things new and old,' says Jesus (Matt. 13:52). What are these 'things new and old'? How did Matthew come to possess them? By what process did he 'bring them out from his treasury'? How did his skills as a scribe assist him in doing so? We start with the last question.

A. Designing the Gospel
Matthew's work 'has more of careful design than any other of the gospels.'[1] So complex is the structure that no single description does justice to the whole.[2] Yet some features of the design are readily discernible.

Progress in Time and Space
The words *Apo tote Iēsous ērxato*, 'From that time Jesus began...' identify two critical junctures in Matthew. The first is Matthew 4:17, where Jesus began to preach (*kēryssein*) God's coming rule. The second is 16:21, where, after Peter's confession (16:16), Jesus began to show (*deiknuein*) his disciples that he must go to Jerusalem, and there suffer, die and be raised. On that basis, Matthew may be divided into three major sections, each marked by progress in time (i) and in space (ii). The first, *1:1–4:16*, (i) links Jesus to OT times

---

[1]Guthrie 1990: 39.

[2]Gundry 1994: 11 rightly concludes that Matthew is 'structurally mixed'; similarly, Hagner 1993: l-liii. France 1989: 153 notes that 'to single out any one of these narrative techniques as in itself an adequate pointer to the total intended structure of the book is to miss the crucial fact that Matthew's account of Jesus is not a static and symmetrical structure, but a powerful drama with a dynamic force of its own.' Cf. 'The Story,' pages 18-24 above.

(through the genealogy of 1:1-17, e.g.) and takes us from his
birth to the threshold of his public ministry; and (ii) proceeds
from Bethlehem and Jerusalem to Egypt to Nazareth to the
Judean wilderness to Capernaum by the Sea of Galilee. The
second, *4:17–16:20*, (i) takes us from the beginning to the
close of Jesus' Galilean ministry, or from the spring of A.D.
28 to the spring of 29; and (ii) traverses a host of places in
and around Galilee, the last being Caesarea Philippi. The
third, *16:21–28:20*, (i) also encompasses about a year, from
the spring of 29 to Jesus' death and resurrection in the spring
of 30;[3] and (ii) progresses from Caesarea Philippi and the
Mount of Transfiguration to Judea and the climactic events
in Jerusalem, and then – following Jesus' resurrection – to a
mountain in Galilee.[4]

It is clear what times are most momentous for the evangelist
Matthew: the period of Jesus' birth and infancy; his year of
ministry in Galilee (the three decades between his birth and
baptism having been passed over in silence); and the following
year, especially the events of its last eight days, beginning
with Jesus' entry into Jerusalem and culminating with his
resurrection from the dead – events to which Matthew devotes
eight chapters (Matt. 21:1–28:15).[5]

We likewise learn what places are important to Matthew.
The story begins in Judea – in Bethlehem and Jerusalem,
both names associated with Jesus' ancestor King David. The
opening section also features the Judean wilderness: here
Jesus receives John's baptism and is tempted by the devil,

---

[3]For these dates, see the suggested chronology of Jesus' ministry in
Appendix B.

[4]The one other instance of *apo tote* in Matthew appears in this third section
(Matt. 26:16), where Judas' resolve completes the plot to destroy Jesus and
prepares for Matthew's account of the Passion itself, beginning with the
Last Supper (26:17-30). For this threefold division, see Kingsbury 1975: 7-25.
Cf. Blomberg's outline (1992: 49): I. Introduction to Jesus' Ministry (1:1-4:16);
II. The Development of Jesus' Ministry (4:17–16:20); III. The Climax of Jesus'
Ministry (16:21–28:20).

[5]For the chronology of Passion Week, see Appendix B in Volume 2. All
four gospels devote a disproportionate amount of space to these eight days.
In the words of Kähler 1988: 80, n. 11, 'one could call the Gospels passion
narratives with extended introductions.'

both of which events take account of Jesus' kingship. The section that opens with Jesus' prophecy of events in Jerusalem (Matt. 16:21) is the longest in the gospel. As Jesus enters the city, he is acclaimed 'the Son of David'; at his death he is identified as 'the King of the Jews'; and following his resurrection his kingship is recognized to be universal in scope.[6] But Galilee is notable as well. The close of the first section (4:12-16) stresses Jesus' choice to live and work in 'Galilee of the Gentiles'; and the section devoted to Jesus' work in and around Galilee (4:17–16:20) is nearly as long as the concluding section.[7] At the end of the story (28:16-20), Jesus draws his disciples back to Galilee, and to the very mountain where he earlier taught them (5:1).

Progress in Narrative and Teaching

As an aid to readers, Matthew interlaces narratives and teachings. The most conspicuous feature of this plan is that the scribe embeds into his narrative framework five major discourses of Jesus: the Sermon on the Mount (chs. 5–7), the Charge to Missionaries (ch. 10), the Parables of the Kingdom (ch. 13), Relationships in the New Community (ch. 18), and the Judgment in Store for Israel and the Nations (chs. 23–25).[8] As evidence of Matthew's intention to set these discourses apart, each is followed by the words *Kai egeneto hote etelesen ho Iēsous*, 'And it happened when Jesus had finished....' This formula is followed in turn by 'these words' (7:28); 'giving instructions to his twelve disciples' (11:1); 'these parables' (13:53); 'these words' (19:1); and 'all these words' (26:1) – the 'all' (*pantas*) a fitting addition to the closing of the final

---

[6]Matthew 21:9; 27:37; 28:18.

[7]This period is yet longer when we consider that it is not until Matthew 19:1 that Jesus 'departed from Galilee and went into the region of Judea....' The third section of Matthew consists of 523 verses; the second contains 467 verses.

[8]Some (e.g., Morris 1992: 593) limit the fifth discourse to chapters 24–25. But the common theme of judgment binds chapters 23–25 together (Blomberg 1992: 338-39; Gundry 1994: 453; Keener 1999: 37). In several ways, chapters 23–25 balance chapters 5–7; see the commentary on chapters 23–25.

discourse.[9] Perhaps one purpose of this arrangement is to recall the Five Books of Moses.[10]

Those discourses are by no means exhaustive: each portion of the narrative framework contains further teachings of Jesus. Matthew 1–4 records his replies to John the Baptist and to the devil, and his first public pronouncement.[11] Sayings of chapters 8–9 are prompted, e.g., by his mighty works, or by questions about table fellowship and the practice of fasting.[12] The teachings of chapters 11–12 focus on Jesus' relationship to John the Baptist, God the Father, the Sabbath command and demonic activity; on the judgment precipitated by Jesus' presence and power; and thus on the need of being rightly related to God

---

[9]The formula in these five verses is especially striking since (i) this (Semitic) construction, *kai egeneto* followed by a main verb, appears only once more in Matthew, in 9:10 ('And it happened that...many tax collectors and sinners came and reclined with Jesus'); and (ii) the verb *teleō*, in the sense 'finish,' occurs elsewhere in Matthew only in 10:23. Cf. France 1985: 60.

[10]This view is attractive, since Matthew's portrait of Jesus often recalls Moses (e.g., 2:13-18; 4:2; 5:1, 17-48); cf. Davies 1964: 25-93 ('New Exodus and New Moses'), 93-108 ('Mosaic Categories Transcended'). The OT Psalter provided a precedent if, as is probable, its division into five books was inspired by the Torah (Gen.– Deut.). Bacon 1930 argues that Matthew as a whole is 'a Christian Pentateuch.' Each of these 'Five Books of Matthew against the Jews' consists (as did the Five Books of Moses) of narrative (n) and discourse (d): Book 1, *Discipleship* (n, chs. 3–4; d, 5–7); Book 2, *Apostleship* (n, 8–9; d, 10); Book 3, *the Hiding of the Revelation* (n, 11–12; d, 13); Book 4, *Church Administration* (n, 14-17; d, 18); Book 5, *the Judgment* (n, 19–22; d, 23–25); with the flanking Prologue (1–2) and Epilogue (26–28). But Bacon goes too far: (i) Matthew's formula (7:28, etc.) applies strictly to *discourses*; (ii) narrative, not discourse, determines the structure of Matthew as a whole; and (iii) chapters 26–28 are no mere epilogue but the dramatic peak of the whole gospel (cf. section I. above). Cf. Davies and Allison 1988: 58-61; France 1985: 60-61; Hagner 1993: li; Keener 1999: 37-38; and Gundry 1994: 11 (who notes both that the fivefold arrangement found in Matthew 'had become customary because of the great authority of the Pentateuch,' and that 'we look in vain for similarities in the contents of Moses' five books and Jesus' five discourses'). Bacon's outline itself remains attractive and those of Brown (1997: 172) and Carson (1984: 51-57) are very similar to his. Yet their headings are a better guide to contents than are Bacon's: e.g., 'The Kingdom Extended Under Jesus' Authority' (Carson for 8:1–11:1); 'Christology and Ecclesiology' (Brown for 13:53–18:35); and 'Climax: Passion, Death, and Resurrection' (Brown for 26:1–28:20).

[11]Matthew 3:15; 4:4, 7, 10, 17.

[12]Matthew 8:4, 10-13; 9:2, 4-6, 12, 15-17, 22, 29.

through him.[13] Chapters 14–17 contain teachings related, e.g., to Jesus' mighty works, to debates with religious authorities, to Simon Peter's confession of faith, and to Jesus' approaching death and resurrection.[14] In chapters 19–22 Jesus teaches about divorce and about little children, answers questions raised by a rich young man and by representatives of Israel's leadership, gives instructions about his entry into Jerusalem, interprets his cleansing of the temple and his cursing of the fig tree, again foretells judgment, and speaks of Messiah's relationship to David.[15] In Matthew 26–28 the number and the length of Jesus' utterances decrease markedly. Yet their very brevity, together with their content and the momentous events to which they are joined, gives a special poignancy to these words – e.g., Jesus' reminder of his imminent death; his clarification of the anointing at Bethany; his sayings at the Last Supper; his prophecy of Peter's denial; his prayers in Gethsemane and his words at the scene of the arrest; his answers to Caiaphas and to Pilate; his cry of dereliction; and his final instructions to the disciples following his resurrection.[16]

We have thus discerned eleven blocks of material – the five discourses of chapters 5–7, 10, 13, 18 and 23–25, and the enclosing six narratives of chapters 1–4, 8–9, 11–12, 14–17, 19–22 and 26–28. Let us now observe how Matthew joins these sections to one another.[17]

---

[13]Matthew 11:4-19, 21-30; 12:3-8, 11-13, 25-50. While these chapters consist largely of Jesus' sayings, they lie outside the discourses of chapter 10 (cf. 11:1, 'When Jesus had finished *instructing his twelve disciples...*') and chapter 13 (cf. 13:53, 'When Jesus had finished *these parables...*').

[14]Matthew 14:16, 18, 27, 29, 31; 15:3-20, 24, 26, 28, 32, 34; 16:2-4, 6-11, 13, 17-19, 23-28; 17:7, 9-12, 17, 20, 22-23, 25-27.

[15]Matthew 19:4-12, 14, 17-30; 20:1-16, 18-19, 22-28; 21:2-3, 13, 16, 21-22, 24-44; 22:1-14, 18-21, 29-32, 37-40, 42-45.

[16]Matthew 26:2, 10-13, 21-29, 31-34, 36-46, 52-56, 64; 27:11, 46 (the single word from the cross recorded in Matthew); 28:10, 18-20.

[17]C. H. Lohr detects in these eleven blocks a chiastic scheme (cited in Davies and Allison 1988: 60): Birth and beginnings, 1–4, Narrative [a]; Death and rebirth, 26–28, Narrative [a']. Blessings, entering the kingdom, 5–7, Discourse [b]; Woes, coming of the kingdom, 23–25, Discourse [b']. Authority and invitation, 8-9, Narrative [c]; Authority and invitation, 19–22, Narrative [c']. Mission discourse, 10, Discourse [d]; Community discourse, 18, Discourse

1. The close of the first section relates that Jesus went throughout Galilee teaching and preaching the good news of the kingdom, and healing various diseases and maladies (Matt. 4:23), thus preparing for the preaching and teaching of chapters 5–7 and the mighty works of chapters 8–9.

2. The Sermon on the Mount was delivered with singular authority (*exousia*; Matt. 7:29), which is further evident – both verbally and visibly – in the miracles of chapters 8–9.[18]

3. The conclusion of the second narrative section (Matt. 9:35-38): (a) serves with 4:23-25 to enclose the teachings of chapters 5–7 and the mighty works of chapters 8–9 (the language of 9:35 is almost identical to that of 4:23); and (b) refers to Jesus' compassion for the crowds and the need for harvesters, the twin basis for the ensuing charge to the twelve.

4. The Mission of the Twelve, chapter 10, is founded on that of Jesus himself, chapters 5–9. He now grants the disciples his 'authority' (Matt. 10:1, *exousia*, as, e.g., in 7:29; 9:6, 8) to 'cast out' demons (10:1, *ekballō*, as e.g. in 8:16; 9:33), to 'heal every kind of disease and every kind of sickness' (10:1, the very wording of 4:23 and 9:35), and to 'proclaim' the kingdom of heaven (10:7, *kēryssō*, as in 4:23 and 9:35) to 'the lost sheep of the house of Israel' (10:6, cf. 9:36, 'as sheep not having a shepherd').

5. From Jesus' concluding words in that discourse (Matt. 10:40-42), it is plain that the disciples represent Jesus; that Jesus represents God the Father; and that being rightly related to God and receiving his approval at the Last Judgment depends on heeding the words and works of Jesus and his disciples. This is the very issue that confronts John the Baptist (11:2-6), as well as those Israelites whom God has addressed through John and Jesus (11:7-24).[19]

[d']. Rejection by this generation, 11–12, Narrative [e]; Acknowledgment by disciples, 14–17, Narrative [e']. Parables of the kingdom, 13, Discourse [f]. I think it doubtful that Matthew was consciously designing such a chiasm; but portions of the scheme are suggestive (e.g. reading chs. 26–28 in light of chs. 1–4). See our further discussion.

[18]'Authority' (*exousia*) recurs in Matthew 8:9; 9:6, 8.

[19]Note how the judgment of Matthew 11:24 echoes that of 10:15.

6. The opening of the next section (Matt. 11:1) returns to Jesus' own ministry in Galilee, specifically to his teaching (*didaskein*) and preaching (*kēryssein*). This is noteworthy, since the previous summaries (4:23 and 9:35) join speaking to miracle-working, as do Jesus' instructions to the disciples (10:1, 6) and his reply to John (11:4-6). Yet that accent on verbal witness is anticipated in the foregoing chapters: Jesus' public ministry begins with proclamation (4:17); the summaries of 4:23 and 9:35 speak of teaching and preaching before healing; and the Sermon on the Mount (chs. 5–7) precedes the miracle stories (chs. 8–9). Consistent with this is the small chiasm in 11:4-5: 'the things you *hear* [a] and *see* [b],' cures for the blind, the lame, the leprous, the deaf and the dead [b'], the preaching of good news to the poor [a'].[20]

7. In radically redefining 'family' at the close of that section (Matt. 12:46-50), Jesus draws together three strands from his earlier teaching: submission to God's rule requires becoming Jesus' disciple; doing the heavenly Father's will shows that discipleship is genuine; and such a commitment inevitably causes divisions in human relationships.[21] This paragraph prepares in turn for the parables of chapter 13, where Jesus depicts the might of the kingdom's advance, the varied human responses, and the resultant twofold division brought to light at the Last Judgment.

8. That division is illustrated at the close of chapter 13, where the disciples' understanding stands opposed to the unbelief in Jesus' hometown (Matt. 13:51-58). Moreover, this rejection of the prophet Jesus by his townspeople has a counterpart in the execution of the prophet John, as recounted at the opening of the next block of narrative (14:1-12).[22] That the herald of the kingdom and of the Messiah should be so treated, makes us wonder what is in store for Jesus.[23]

---

[20]Almost all these miracles are represented in chapters 8–9. The close of the summary, 'and the poor are evangelized,' recalls 'the gospel of the kingdom' (4:23; 9:35); and the first beatitude (5:3; note the 'blessed' of 11:6). The summary also embraces the disciples' mission.

[21]See e.g. Matthew 4:17-22; 5:1-12; 7:21-27; 8:18-22; 10:32-42; 11:12-30; 12:28-32.

[22]The noun 'prophet' (*prophētēs*; Matthew 13:57) recurs in 14:5.

[23]Hostility to John was already evident in Matthew 4:12; 11:2, 12-19. Before the present block of narrative concludes, Jesus makes it plain that a similar end awaits him (16:21; 17:11-13).

9. That narrative section concludes with a miracle through which Jesus provides the temple tax for himself and Peter, lest they offend the authorities (Matt. 17:24-27). That same verb, *skandalizō* 'offend, cause to stumble' – recurs three times at the beginning of the next discourse, where Jesus sternly warns his followers against causes of stumbling.[24] Matthew thus argues from the lesser to the greater: if disciples are to avoid giving offense to the guardians of Israel's traditions, should they not devote far more care to safeguarding members of the new community, the rightful heirs of Israel's true King – these 'little ones who believe in' Jesus (18:6)?[25]

10. The parable concluding that discourse (Matt. 18:21-35) depicts both God's readiness to forgive the disciples' enormous debts (18:27) and the peril of their withholding such mercy from fellow disciples (18:35). Likewise we learn from the opening of the next block of narrative (19:1-12) that the advance of God's kingdom – wherein he shows his favor as never before – calls for unprecedented fidelity and mercy between disciples joined in marriage.

11. The close of that narrative section (Matt. 22:41-46) concerns David's relation to Messiah. Jesus stresses that David acknowledged Messiah to be his Lord, and that God has promised this One a place of singular honor and also the conquest of all his enemies. This paragraph well introduces chapters 23–25. For in this his final discourse, Jesus – the One whom Matthew early declares to be both Messiah (*Christos*) and Lord (*Kyrios*)[26] – speaking with the very authority that has silenced his interrogators (22:46), pronounces woes upon his enemies; prophesies judgments both imminent and ultimate; and promises that on that final Day he himself – God's appointed *Kyrios* – will preside as Judge, to reward the faithful and punish the unbelieving.[27]

---

[24]*Skandalizō* is found in Matthew 17:27; 18:6, 8, 9; the noun *skandalon* occurs three times in 18:7.

[25]Such an argument – *qal wachomer*, 'light and heavy' – was a common rabbinic device.

[26]For *Christos*, see Matthew 1:1, 16-18; 2:4, etc. for *Kyrios*, 7:21-22; 8:2, 6, 8, 21, 25, etc.

[27]No fewer than nineteen times in Matthew 24-25 Jesus is identified, directly or indirectly, as the *Kyrios* to whom persons are accountable at the Last Judgment.

12. That discourse concludes with a parable about that Day of Judgment, on which 'all the nations' are gathered before 'the Son of Man,' i.e., 'the King,' Christ the Lord, and are separated as sheep from goats (Matt. 25:31-46). Immediately thereafter, at the opening of the final block of narrative, Jesus prophesies that 'the Son of Man' is soon to be crucified (26:1-2). From this juxtaposition, together with the sequel in chapters 26–28, we learn: (a) that the man about to be executed is the very One destined to reign and judge; (b) that the nations are to receive 'the gospel of the kingdom' before they face the judgment;[28] (c) that the major events of this closing narrative – Jesus' death and resurrection – will stand at the very center of that gospel;[29] and (d) that 'the brothers' in the parable (25:40) are the men Jesus will commission to 'make disciples of all the nations' (28:19).[30] The close of the final narrative (28:18-20) thus harks back to the close of the final discourse. It also recalls Matthew's opening narrative, especially its testimony about the coming of Immanuel and the inclusion of Gentiles in his saving purpose.[31]

Intramural Patterns
We perceive the foregoing features of Matthean architecture when viewing his edifice as a whole. Within those larger blocks (inside the house, so to speak) there is further evidence of careful design, notably the presentation of material according to numbers (not surprising in the work of a former tax collector), especially two, seven and (most often) three.

---

[28]See Matthew 26:13 (with 24:14); 28:18-20.

[29]This is clear from the basic design of Matthew (considered earlier) – itself a proclamation of the gospel to the nations. There is a hint of this too in Jesus' anointing at Bethany (Matt. 26:6-13).

[30]The only instance of 'brothers' (*adelphoi*) in Matthew after 25:40 comes in 28:10, which anticipates 28:16-20. See the commentary on 25:31-46.

[31]See Matthew 1:2-16 (which includes the names of Gentiles), 23 (cf. 28:20); 2:1-12 (Gentile magi pay homage to Jesus); 4:15 (Jesus lives in 'Galilee of the Gentiles'). For further affinities between chapters 1–2 and 28, see Davies and Allison 1988: 60, n. 27. Cf. C. H. Lohr's chiastic scheme (n. 17 above), linking chapters 26–28 to chapters 1–4.

Matthew expressly speaks of Simon and Andrew as 'two brothers,' and of James and John as 'two other brothers' (4:18, 21), whereas the Markan parallel lacks the numerals.[32] Matthew records the cure of two demoniacs (8:28) and of two blind men (20:30), whereas the parallel accounts speak in each instance of one; he reports that disciples bring two animals for Jesus' entry into Jerusalem (21:2), while Mark and Luke mention only one; and he speaks of two false witnesses at Jesus' trial (26:60), where the parallel speaks of 'certain ones.'[33] Matthew 22:40 speaks of 'these two commands,' a numeral absent from the parallels in Mark and Luke.[34]

Matthew 12:45 speaks of 'seven other spirits'; 15:34-37 refers to seven loaves and seven baskets; 18:21-22 mentions forgiving another 'up to seven times'; and 22:25 tells of seven brothers. Matthew 13:1-52 records seven parables;[35] and 23:13-33 details seven woes.

Matthew is especially fond of triads.[36] The genealogy is divided into three sections (1:17). Jesus faces three temptations in the desert (4:1). He speaks of three marks of piety in 6:1-18; the Lord's Prayer contains a threefold petition (6:9-10), followed by three others (6:11-13). Jesus' charge to the missionaries contains a threefold 'do not be afraid (10:26-31);

---

[32]Cf. Mark 1:16-19. The same holds true for Matthew 20:24 ('concerning the two brothers'; cf. v. 21, 'my two sons') and its parallel in Mark 10:41 ('concerning James and John'); and for Matthew 26:37 ('the two sons of Zebedee') and its parallel in Mark 14:33 ('James and John').

[33]With Matthew 8:28, compare Mark 5:2 and Luke 8:27; with 20:30 (and 9:27), Mark 10:46 and Luke 18:35; with 21:2, Mark 11:2 and Luke 19:30; with 26:60, Mark 14:57.

[34]Cf. Mark 12:31 and Luke 10:27-28.

[35]Some (e.g., France 1985: 215) view verse 52 as an eighth parable. I would rather say Jesus tells seven parables about the kingdom – which call for a certain response from the disciples (13:51-52; so too Gundry 1994: 250, 280). The question of 13:51 is the only one Jesus puts to his followers in the whole chapter (the questions of Mark 4:13 have no Matthean parallel); and Matthew 13:52 says 'a *scribe* is like...,' whereas previous verses say 'the *kingdom of heaven* is like...' (13:31, 33, 44, 45, 47).

[36]Davies and Allison speak of 'the pervasiveness of triads in the gospel' as a phenomenon that 'has yet to receive just treatment' (1988: 62, with n. 32; for their examples, see 62-68, 86-87). Most of my examples are selected from the list in Allen 1912: lxv.

and a threefold 'is not worthy of me' (10:37-38). His 'three days
and three nights' in the heart of the earth are likened to Jonah's
'three days and three nights' in the belly of the fish (12:40).
The first three parables in chapter 13 speak of sowing seed
(13:1-32); the yeast is hidden in three measures of flour (13:33).
A hungry crowd has been with Jesus for three days (15:32).
He takes three disciples onto the mountain, where three tents
are needed for him, Moses and Elijah (17:1, 4). In chapter 18,
Jesus thrice speaks of 'one of these little ones' (18:6-14); and
twice of 'two or three witnesses' (18:16, 20). Three parables
of judgment are drawn together in 21:28-22:14, and another
three in 25:1-46. Three questions are put to Jesus in 22:15-40.[37]
He prays three times in Gethsemane (26:36-46). Peter disowns
him three times (26:69-75). Jesus' enemies twice quote his
prophecy about rebuilding the temple 'in three days' (26:61;
27:40); and once his prophecy about rising again 'after three
days' (27:63). Jesus three times predicts that he will be killed
and 'be raised on the third day' (16:21; 17:23; 20:19).[38]

Section A. has considered some features of this scribe's
literary artistry. Yet the gospel's design serves a purpose
beyond itself: it is the setting wherein Matthew displays the
'things new and old' brought forth from his treasury (13:52).
How did he become equipped for this enterprise?

B. Approaching the Task

Jesus made Matthew a disciple (*mathētēs*) so that he might
become an apostle (*apostolos*; Matt. 10:1-2). By the same token,
having 'been discipled [*methēteutheis*] for the kingdom of
heaven,' Matthew is newly equipped to be a scribe (*grammateus*;

---

[37]About paying taxes to Caesar, life in the resurrection and the greatest
commandment.

[38]The first two texts speak of Jesus' being killed (the verb *apokteinō*), the
third of his being crucified (the verb *stauroō*). All three use the aorist passive
of *egeirō*, 'be raised.' Allen 1912: lxv, discerns three triads in Matthew 8–9:
miracles of 'healing' (8:1-15), of 'power' (8:23-9:8) and of 'restoration'
(9:18-34). But these miracles cannot be so easily divided; those labels are
not mutually exclusive (a leper, e.g., is healed and restored by an act of
divine power). Moreover, if the calming of the storm is included, these
chapters record ten miracles and not nine.

(13:52) – which proves to be this particular apostle's premier vocation. Conversely, his written record will acquaint us with the character of his education, his aptitude as a student and his response to the Master's commission.

Matthew, the Studious Disciple
As Jesus chose Matthew to be a 'disciple' (*mathētēs*), then to be one of 'the twelve disciples,' it is instructive to consider this scribe's own usage of the term.[39] Of the seventy-three instances of *mathētēs* in Matthew, sixty-nine speak of Jesus' disciples.[40] Such references are scattered throughout the gospel, appearing in twenty-one of the twenty-eight chapters. Disciples are present at the major turning points in the narrative; and it is they – or they together with the crowds – who hear Jesus' five great discourses.[41] Indeed the presence of a disciple or disciples is expressly stated, or implied, for nearly all the events, miracles and teachings recorded in Matthew from 4:17 to 28:20.[42]

Matthew is among them, whether they be 'the twelve' (or, after Judas' departure, 'the eleven') or 'the disciples' generally, for the twelve were chief among the latter. Matthew is there personally to receive all five of Jesus' discourses;[43] to witness

[39]Matthew, whose call is recorded in 9:9, is among the 'disciples' mentioned in verses 10-11. For 'the twelve disciples,' see 10:1; 11:1; 20:17; cf. 'the eleven disciples,' 28:16. These twelve are also called 'the twelve apostles,' 10:2; but this is the sole instance of *apostolos* in Matthew.

[40]The two instances of Matthew 10:24-25 are included; they occur in a proverbial saying, but in context clearly denote Jesus' disciples. The four exceptions: references to disciples of John the Baptist (9:14; 11:2; 14:12) and of the Pharisees (22:16).

[41]In light of earlier comments on the book's 'progress in time and space' (pp. 49-51), see Matthew 4:18-22 (the call of the first disciples) in relation to 4:17; and note that in 16:21 Jesus discloses forthcoming events to 'his disciples.' For the disciples' reception of the five discourses, see 5:1-2; 9:37-38; 10:1-5; 13:10, 36, 51-52; 18:1; 23:1; 24:1-3.

[42]For explicit references to *mathētai*, see, e.g. (besides those already mentioned) Matthew 8:23; 9:14, 19; 12:1, 49; 14:15, 22; 15:12, 23, 32; 16:5, 13; 17:6, 10, 19; 19:10, 13, 23; 21:1, 20; 26:1, 8, 18, 36-37. The *mathētai* as a company are conspicuously absent between 26:56 (where 'all the disciples abandoned [Jesus] and fled') and 28:16 (where 'the eleven disciples went to Galilee'). Peter is present in the story but distant from Jesus (26:58, 69-75). Judas (27:3-5) has ceased to be a disciple. Joseph of Arimathea had become a disciple, but

his miracles; and to surrender to his authority. Summoned by the One 'in whom are hidden all the treasures of wisdom and knowledge,' Matthew himself is like a man who finds a 'treasure in a field,' or a 'pearl of great value.'[44] So there is no doubt who fills the 'treasury' of Matthew 13:52. It is Jesus who imparts the 'new things' to Matthew, by that means granting him access to 'things old' as well.

Matthew was probably one of the more studious members of the twelve. Given his prior experience as a secular scribe, it is likely (though not demonstrable) that he began during Jesus' ministry to keep a written record of what he was witnessing. Such notes, even those informal and fragmentary, would help to assure that things placed in the treasury remained there for later use. That record might also aid others, including members of the twelve, responsible for propagating the truth about Jesus.[45]

---

he appears only briefly between Jesus' death and resurrection (27:57-60), and is identified not by the noun *mathētēs* but by the verb *mathēteuō* (27:57). The faithfulness of Jesus' female followers during this period is therefore all the more striking: it is they who appear at the scenes of the crucifixion and the burial (27:55-56, 61); and it is they who first learn of Jesus' resurrection and who first see him (28:1-10). These women, however, are not expressly called 'disciples.'

[43]Including that of Matthew 5–7, although his call is not recorded until chapter 9; for Matthew's arrangement of material is not strictly chronological but thematic as well. See later discussion.

[44]Colossians 2:3; Matthew 13:44, 45. The noun *thēsauros* can mean both 'treasure' (Col. 2:3; Matt. 13:44) and 'treasury' (Matt. 13:52; 2:11).

[45]Gundry offers 'the hypothesis that the Apostle Matthew was a note-taker during the earthly ministry of Jesus and that his notes provided the basis of the apostolic gospel tradition. The use of notebooks which were carried on one's person was very common in the Graeco-Roman world. In ancient schools outline notes [*grammata hypomnēmatika*] were often taken by pupils as the teacher lectured. The notes became the common possession of the schools and circulated without the name of the lecturer. Sometimes an author would take this material as the basis for a book to be published [*grammata syntagmatika*]. Shorthand was used possibly as early as the fourth century B.C. and certainly by Jesus' time.... Rabbinic traditions were transmitted by the employment of catchwords and phrases which were written down in shorthand notes. Thus, from both the Hellenistic side and the Judaistic side it is wholly plausible to suppose that one from the apostolic band was a note-taker – especially since the relationship of Jesus to his disciples was that of a teacher, or rabbi,

So already there is good reason to expect that this book will record much of what Matthew himself saw and heard.[46]

Matthew, the Commissioned Apostle

As we have seen, Matthew was one of twelve apostles whom Jesus authorized to evangelize Israel (10:1-8); and one of eleven whom he commanded to disciple 'all the nations' (28:18-20). As these closing verses make plain, it is not Matthew but Jesus who defines this writer's duty: 'All authority [exousia] in heaven and on earth has been given to me [by the Father]. Therefore [oun] ...make disciples of all the nations, baptizing them... teaching them to keep all that I commanded you ....'

According to this commission, Matthew's task is not to be innovative but faithfully to report and apply what Jesus said and did: 'teaching them to keep all that *I commanded you*.' His record is also to be comprehensive: 'teaching them to keep *all* that I commanded you.' It is therefore of interest to observe: (i) that the Greek text of Matthew contains approximately 18,300 words, about 7,000 more than Mark, 3,000 more than John, and only 1,000 fewer than Luke;[47] and (ii) that of the 1,068 verses in Matthew, 641 contain words of Jesus, the highest proportion (60 percent) of all four gospels.[48] In the language

---

to his pupils' (1967: 182-83, with documentation). The reasoning that brings Gundry to this view: *1*. A study of OT quotations and allusions in Matthew, together with those in Mark and Luke, reveals Septuagintal (Greek), Hebrew and Aramaic elements in all three gospels. *2*. That linguistic mixture points to a common tradition employed by all three evangelists, one most likely to have been provided by a note-taker among the twelve disciples. *3*. Matthew, unlike some members of the twelve (Acts 4:13), was admirably suited for such a task, for he was a former tax collector accustomed to keeping records and able to use Greek as well as Hebrew and Aramaic; and he was perhaps a Levite (cf. Matt. 9:9, Mark 2:14) 'whose background would have given him acquaintance with the OT in its Semitic as well as [its] Greek forms' (ibid., 183). On Matthew's use of the OT, see further below.

[46]In other words, to expect that the words about John's witness would apply with equal validity to this member of the twelve. See John 19:35; 20:30-31; 21:24; 1 John 1:1-3.

[47]According to Morgenthaler (1982: 164), Luke contains between 19,404 and 19,428 words; Matthew, between 18,278 and 18,305; John, between 15,416 and 15,420; and Mark, between 11,229 and 11,242. According to Stein 1987: 48 (following J. B. Tyson and T. R. W. Longstaff), Mark contains 11,025

of Luke 1:2, Matthew, having been an 'eyewitness' (*autoptēs*), becomes a 'servant [*hypēretēs*] of the Word.' He writes his book as an act of obedience to the risen Lord; and he does so in the confidence that Immanuel will equip him for the task (Matt. 28:20b).

Matthew, the Bearer of Tradition

Matthew, having been a follower and student of Jesus, is entrusted with a sacred tradition.[49] This tradition he is to preserve and protect, but it is not to remain his private possession: as the magi opened up their treasure chests to offer gifts to Jesus, so Matthew is to bring forth goods from his treasury to instruct his readers.[50] Doing so is his foremost calling. To put it in the terms Jesus used when commissioning him and the rest of the twelve (Matt. 10:27), Matthew is bringing merchandise out of the darkness of a storage room into the daylight of a marketplace, and converting private instruction into public proclamation.

Given the character of that 'merchandise,' and the personal transformation Matthew has experienced as a follower of Jesus, the words of Matthew 12:35 also serve to describe his scribal activity: 'The good [*ho agathos*] man brings out [*ekballei*] from his good treasury [*ek tou agathou thēsaurou*] good things [*agatha*].' Being explains doing; doing reveals being. Now that Matthew is a new person – a 'good man' – he may be entrusted with 'good things,' and be trusted not to hoard them in a 'good' safe place but to impart them, complete and unalloyed, to his readers. Conversely, what he writes will testify to the kind of person he has become, because 'from the overflow of the heart the mouth speaks' (12:34) – or, we might say, 'the pen

---

words; Matthew, 18,293; and Luke, 19,376. The numbers vary owing to differing judgments about textual variants.

[48]Of Luke's 1,149 verses, 583 (or 51%) contain words of Jesus; of John's 866, 428 (or 49%); of Mark's 661, 279 (or 42%). As noted in sec. A., the narrative blocks of Matthew contain much of Jesus' teaching.

[49]Jewish scribes (*grammateis*) likewise had their received tradition (*paradosis*; Matt. 15:1-6).

[50]In Matthew 2:11 and 13:52, *thēsauros* is a place where treasures are stored (BAGD s.v., 1).

records.' Moreover, his is a most serious responsibility, for on the Day of Judgment men will be held accountable for 'every careless word they have spoken' (12:36) – or, we might say, 'they have written.'[51]

C. Drawing Out 'Things New'

It might be thought more appropriate to start with the 'old things,' in accord with the order of events and the progress of redemption. Yet, when studying Matthew, it is correct to start with the 'new things,' because it was with these that Matthew's own Christian experience began, and through these that he gained access to the 'old things.' The word order of Matthew 13:52b – 'things new and old' (*kaina kai palaia*) – agrees with this, as does Jesus' summary of the history of salvation in 11:12 ('From the days of John the Baptist until now...') and 11:13 ('For all the prophets and the law prophesied until John').

The process by which the 'things new' come into Matthew's keeping and then find their way out of his treasury and onto the pages of his gospel, is illustrated in Figure 1 (on the following page), and it will be helpful to keep this picture in view as we proceed.

As already stated, Jesus is the Source of all these 'new things.' It is out of his *life, words and works* (the upper part of Figure 1) that all else flows; the 'things new' that Matthew records have their origin in actual events of history, beginning with Mary's conception in Matthew 1, and concluding with the commission of Matthew 28. Observe that all four arrows pointing to 'the

---

[51]Whether Matthew consciously applied Matthew 12:35 to his scribal activity, we cannot say. But given the verbal links with 13:52, it is appropriate to use the verse, together with its immediate context, illustratively. Moreover, the contrast between 'the good [*agathos*] man' and 'the evil [*ponēros*] man' in 12:35, together with the contrast in 12:33 between 'the good [*kalon*] tree and fruit' and 'the bad [*sapron*] tree and fruit,' recalls the contrast in 7:16-20 between 'the good [*agathos*] tree' that bears 'good [*kalous*] fruits' and 'the bad [*sapron*] tree' that produces 'evil [*ponērous*] fruits.' Matthew, Jesus' appointed scribe, is like 'a good tree' that brings forth 'good fruit' – a 'doing' that both nourishes his readers and testifies to the 'being' of the tree, i.e., to the changes that Jesus has effected in the writer himself.

FIGURE 1

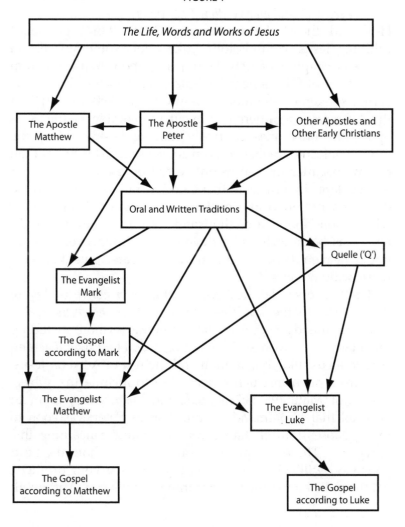

Evangelist Matthew' can ultimately be traced to the top of the picture. We now focus on the period between the close of Jesus' earthly ministry and the writing of Matthew's gospel.

The Progress of Oral and Written Traditions

How did those eleven disciples (Matt. 28:16) go about fulfilling Jesus' commission? Luke offers some answers in the early chapters of Acts. Here Jesus, about to ascend from the Mount of Olives near Jerusalem, underscores his words earlier spoken on the mountain in Galilee (Acts 1:8, 12).[52] Of the 120 persons gathered to await the coming of the Holy Spirit, the only ones expressly named, besides Mary the mother of Jesus, are these eleven apostles (1:13-15).[53] Less than two weeks after the ascension, Peter (representing the other ten) declares in Jerusalem that God has raised Jesus from the dead and provided in him the forgiveness of sins (2:14-40), whereupon 'about three thousand' become believers, 41. As Peter has been addressing devout Jews 'from every nation under heaven' (2:5), there is now far greater potential for a worldwide witness.[54]

The first essential, however, is that new converts devote themselves 'to the apostles' teaching' [didachē; Acts 2:42 – teaching already begun in the foregoing sermon, including the 'many other words' (2:40) not recorded by Luke; teaching sure to focus (like that sermon and the rest of Acts) on Jesus. Moreover, such instruction was sure to include the subject matter of Matthew 28:20a: 'teaching [didaskontes] them to keep all that I commanded you.' For, as Peter was soon to recall, Moses himself had given command concerning this Lawgiver: 'There is a prophet, one like me, whom the Lord your God will raise up for you from among your brothers; you must listen to him, to everything he tells you. And it will

---

[52]The angels' words ('Men of Galilee...' Acts 1:11) recall the scene of Matthew 28:16-20.

[53]Joseph and Matthias are soon to be named as well (Acts 1:23-26).

[54]With Acts 2:5, 'from every nation' (apo pantos ethnous), compare 1:8, 'to the end of the earth,' and Matthew 28:19, 'make disciples of all the nations' (panta ta ethnē).

happen that anyone who refuses to listen to that prophet will be utterly destroyed from among the people' (Acts 3:22-23), a text that helps to account for the stern words of judgment against Jesus' enemies in Matthew.

What Jesus 'began to do and to teach [*poiein te kai didaskein*]' during his earthly ministry (Acts 1:1), he will now continue through his apostles. As he was empowered by the Spirit for his mission, so are they.[55] While the apostles continue to accentuate Jesus' death and resurrection, they also acquaint listeners with his public ministry, from John's baptism onwards.[56] They recount Jesus' mighty works and ascribe to him their own miraculous powers.[57] What he disclosed about the kingdom of God, they impart to others.[58] In short, the word (*logos*) declared by the apostles and others from Pentecost onwards focuses on 'the life, words and works of Jesus' (the top of Figure 1) – especially on his death and resurrection – by virtue of which the Scriptures are being fulfilled, the Holy Spirit is being poured out, and sins are being forgiven. In other words, materials later incorporated into the gospels are propagated from the very first.[59]

---

[55]See, e.g., Matthew 3:11, 16; 10:20; 12:18, 28; Luke 3:22; 4:18; John 1:32-33; 3:34; 14:26; 15:26-27; 16:13; 20:21-22; Acts 1:2, 5, 8; 2:4, 16-21; 4:8; 10:38; 11:16.

[56]This is explicit in Peter's address to the gathering in Cornelius' home (Acts 10:34-43), where 'good news of peace' commences with Jesus' ministry (10:36; not, as in Ephesians 2:17, with his resurrection). It is implicit, I think, in Luke's reference to Peter's 'many other words' in Acts 2:40. Note that material summarized in 10:37-38 is itself summarized in 2:22. For Peter's accent on Jesus' death and exaltation, see (besides Acts 2:23-36 and 10:39-41) 3:13-15, 26; 4:2, 10; 5:30-32.

[57]See Acts 2:22 ('Jesus of Nazareth...made known to you through miracles, wonders and signs'); 10:38 ('how he went about doing good and healing all who were oppressed by the devil'); with 3:16; 4:8-10; 5:12-16; 9:34 ('Jesus Christ heals you'), 40-42.

[58]Matthew 4:17, 23; 9:35; 10:7; Acts 1:3, 6; 8:12; Paul later takes up the theme (Acts 14:22; 19:8; 20:25; 28:23, 31). Since Christ serves as King in the Kingdom of God (Matt. 2:2; 5:35; 21:5; 25:34, 40; 27:37), the history of Jesus (Matt. 24:14; 26:13) and his being exalted to reign from God's right hand (Acts 2:32-36), are themselves manifestations of God's Rule.

[59]Note the use of *logos* in Acts 2:41; 4:4, 29, 31; 6:2, 4, 7; 8:4, 14, 21, 25. Those declarations of the *logos* therefore draw heavily upon materials later included in the writer's 'first account [*logos*],' Acts 1:1, i.e., the Gospel

As the church spread into new areas, and encountered a growing number of persons whose knowledge of Jesus was scanty or distorted or non-existent, there was ever greater need for disseminating that manifold tradition. Newly planted churches needed it for catechizing converts; for learning about worship; for evangelizing non-believers; and for addressing those who challenged or opposed Christian beliefs.[60] As time went on, sayings, speeches and parables of Jesus were joined together – as were 'pronouncement stories' (in which an action of Jesus paved the way for his climactic utterance on a given subject), miracle stories and other narratives – for distribution, both orally and in writing, between and within churches.[61]

The apostles and other early Christians would assist one another in propagating the truth about Jesus: see the horizontal arrows near the top of Figure 1.[62] As stated above, notes taken

according to Luke. For the outpouring of the Spirit as a consequence of Jesus' exaltation, see Acts 2:32-33; John 7:39. For the fulfillment of Scripture in these events, see, e.g., Acts 2:16-21, 24-32, 34-36; 3:17-26.

[60]Cf. Bruce 1970b: 58-71. He rightly concludes that 'the ministry of Jesus [was] the original life-setting of the gospel tradition, while all the activities of the early church – preaching, controversy, worship and instruction – provided settings for its preservation, shaping and transmission' (71).

[61]'Form criticism' (German Formgeschichte, 'form history') studies ingredients of the tradition and makes judgments about their history prior to their incorporation into the gospels: see C. L. Blomberg's fine discussion of the subject in DJG, 243-50. His six major 'forms': individual sayings; pronouncement stories; parables; speeches; miracle stories; and other historical narratives (243-44). Ryken 1987: 35-40 discusses ten categories within the gospel narratives, including 'annunciation or nativity stories,' 'calling or vocation stories,' 'encounter stories,' 'conflict or controversy stories,' 'miracle stories' and 'passion stories.' For support of the view that such traditions were transmitted both orally and in writing, see, e.g., Guthrie 1990: 1043; Gerhardsson 1979: 23-24; Paul's letters (e.g., 1 Cor. 11:23-26; 15:3-7); and earlier comments on Matthew as a note-taker during Jesus' ministry.

[62]'All the sources from early Christianity indicate that already in its first stages certain leaders and teachers occupied positions of authority in the congregations and that these men were in contact with one another,' says Gerhardsson (1979: 79), who goes on to speak of 'the central authority' vested in the twelve. Ellis 1991: 46 notes that the NT contains evidence that 'the transmitters of Jesus-traditions did not work as separate and individual authorities but as part of a corporate or group endeavor.'

by Matthew during Jesus' ministry would be of help to others in the church. By the same token, Matthew need not have relied exclusively upon his own recollections when bearing his witness and (in time) writing his gospel. Why should he not freely receive as he has freely given? There were those who could assist him, especially persons instructed with him during Jesus' ministry and commissioned with him after Jesus' resurrection: as noted, 13:52 applies potentially to all members of the twelve. Why should Matthew, even as an eyewitness, not employ methods chosen by Luke the evangelist (Luke 1:1-4) and later by Papias (*HE* 3.39)? Did not Christ encourage such interdependence among his followers?[63] This is in fact what we find: that Matthew, in drawing from his treasury 'new things' about Jesus, depends both upon his own remembrances and upon those of other believers. Thus, in Figure 1, three of the four arrows drawn to 'the Evangelist Matthew' illustrate his indebtedness to others. Before pursuing this subject, however, we must place it within a larger context.

The Synoptic Gospels

Figure 1 refers to the evangelists Matthew, Mark and Luke, and also to the gospels that bear their names. These three books are commonly called the Synoptic Gospels. The term *synopsis*, 'seeing together,' describes both the evangelists' and the readers' perspectives.[64] Placing the three texts in parallel columns, we may examine them together. Doing so, we discover that they share many features in common with each other, but not with John's gospel. This holds true for the *events* they record;[65] for

---

[63]Matthew 20:25-28; John 13:12-17. Cf. Paul's counsel in 1 Corinthians 12:12-31.

[64]'Synopsis' is applied to the writers' perspective by J. Julius Scott, Jr., 'The Synoptic Gospels,' *EBC*, 1: 501; and to the readers' by Brown 1997: 111.

[65]E.g., the plucking of grain on the Sabbath and the healing that follows (Matt. 12:1-15; Mark 2:18-3:6; Luke 6:1-11); the healing of the Gerasene demoniac (Matt. 8:28-34; Mark 5:1-20; Luke 8:26-39); and Jesus' conversation with the rich young man and the teaching that follows (Matt. 19:16-30; Mark 10:17-31; Luke 18:18-30).

the *language* they use;[66] and for the *order* in which they present material.[67]

It is ultimately the work of the Holy Spirit that explains those similarities and differences among the Synoptic Gospels, and between them and John. Still, it is proper to inquire into the Spirit's chosen ways of bringing these documents into being.[68] One such way was testimony from participants in the events. All three Synoptists had *direct* access to such evidence: Matthew was himself an eyewitness; according to Papias (as noted earlier) Mark records Peter's reminiscences of Jesus' ministry; Luke states his reliance on persons who 'from the beginning became eyewitnesses and servants of the word' (Luke 1:1-4).[69] In addition, all three had *indirect* access to eyewitness testimony through oral and written traditions assembled and transmitted during the period between Jesus' ministry and the writing of the gospels – traditions that would underscore, amplify or augment testimony the evangelists had received directly.[70] Thus, in Figure 1, arrows are drawn directly from 'Oral and Written Traditions' to all three of the Synoptics.

Some believe the above to be an adequate account of the matter: *similarities* among the Synoptic Gospels bolster our confidence that these writers have all remained true to received tradition and have reported accurately the events of Jesus' life; the *differences* show that the writers have access to

---

[66]E.g., compare (i) Matthew 19:13-15 with Mark 10:13-16 and Luke 18:15-17; (ii) Matthew 22:23-33 with Mark 12:18-27 and Luke 20:27-40; and (iii) Matthew 24:4-8 with Mark 13:5-8 and Luke 21:8-11. Linguistic affinities extend to parenthetical remarks (see, e.g., Matthew 9:6, 'then he says to the paralytic,' with Mark 2:10 and Luke 5:24) and to quotations from the OT, even when the wording common to all three differs from both MT and LXX (see, e.g., Matthew 3:3, with Mark 1:2 and Luke 3:4). For these and other examples, see Stein 1987: 30-33, 37-42; ibid., 'Synoptic Problem,' *DJG*, 784-85.

[67]See, e.g., (i) Matthew 12:46-13:58; Mark 3:31-6:6; Luke 8:19-56; (ii) Matthew 16:13-20:34; Mark 8:27-10:52; Luke 9:18-51 and 18:15-43; (iii) Matthew 21:1-28:10; Mark 11:1-16:8; Luke 19:29-24:12. Cf. Stein 1987: 34-37.

[68]On the work of the Holy Spirit in the producing of the gospels, see E. below.

[69]The fourth evangelist was also an eyewitness: see John 19:35; 21:24; 1 John 1:1-3.

[70]Similarly, Papias was instructed both by John the presbyter (apostle) and by John's followers; cf. II. A. above.

testimonies and traditions which supplement each other and enlarge our understanding of Jesus. Yet those similarities have persuaded others, myself included, that some sort of literary relationship exists among the documents themselves, even as those differences make it plain that such a relationship cannot fully account for the documents' contents.[71]

Just *how* the three are related literarily has been – and is still – much debated. According to one view Matthew appeared first, Mark used Matthew, then Luke used Mark.[72] A second is that Matthew wrote first; that Luke used Matthew; and that Mark employed both Matthew and Luke.[73] A third is that Mark, largely through Peter, drew upon a (possibly Semitic) form of Matthew, and that Luke wrote with a knowledge of both Matthew and Mark.[74] A fourth view has more to commend it.

Matthew's Use of the Gospel according to Mark
In my judgment, the most satisfactory explanation for those similarities among the Synoptics – the so-called 'triple tradition' – is that both Matthew and Luke employed Mark's gospel as a source for their own writings.[75] Thus, in Figure 1, arrows are drawn from the Gospel of Mark to the Gospels of Matthew and Luke. For evidence, I focus on five matters.

---

[71]Some evangelical scholars argue that the Synoptic Gospels are literarily independent of each other; others (the majority) that they are related literarily. Cf. the debate between Grant Osborne, who defends the latter view (1999: 193-210; 2000: 113-17), and Robert Thomas, who defends the former (2000: 97-111). While Wenham argues that verbal similarities and differences among the Synoptists are 'best explained by independent use of the primitive form of oral instruction,' he also contends that '[g]enre and order are best explained by a literary relationship' (1991: 243).

[72]Stein, *DJG*, 786, ascribes this interpretation to Augustine. Thomas contends (2000: 97) that Augustine, while sharing the view (common at the time) that Matthew was the first gospel to be written (cf. p.34, n. 30 above), considered the Synoptic Gospels to be literarily independent.

[73]This was argued by J. J. Griesbach (1783 and 1789) and more recently by W. R. Farmer (1964). Cf. Stein, *DJG*, 786.

[74]This is the view of Wenham 1991: 115, 198-216. On the other hand, few if any argue that Matthew consulted the Gospel according to Luke.

[75]Material common only to Matthew and Luke is considered later.

1. Length

Mark's gospel is the shortest: as noted earlier in section B., Mark contains about 7,000 fewer words than Matthew, and about 8,000 fewer than Luke. If Mark employed Matthew (or Matthew and Luke), why did he omit so much material? On the other hand, if Matthew and Luke used Mark, it is easy to understand both why they incorporated so much of his material (i.e., about 97 percent of Mark is found in Matthew, and 88 percent in Luke), and why – given Mark's brevity – they chose to supplement Mark with so much material from elsewhere (i.e., about 40 percent of Matthew and about 53 percent of Luke have no parallel in Mark).[76]

Some suggest that Mark chose for pastoral reasons to abridge Matthew (or Matthew and Luke). Yet for many episodes reported by all the Synoptists, Mark's account is the longest.[77] If his overall purpose is to provide a reader's digest of one or both of the others, why does he repeatedly expand so many of their accounts while disregarding so much else? A better explanation for those differences is that Matthew and Luke – whose writings are without question literarily superior to Mark's – have polished or condensed the Markan prose.

2. Language

As Mark's Greek is of a poorer quality than Matthew's (and Luke's), the latter's improving Mark's grammar is easier to understand than Mark's impairing Matthew's. Certain colloquialisms and Aramaic terms in Mark have no parallels in Matthew and Luke; better to say that the latter have removed those expressions than that Mark has added them – especially when addressing Greek-speaking readers. Numerous Markan redundancies are lacking in Matthew and Luke; that the latter authors, given their literary sensibilities, eliminated them is far more likely than that Mark manufactured them while being aware of Matthew's and Luke's formulations. Certain features of Markan style – the adverb *euthys* (*eutheōs*), 'immediately,'

---

[76]Writes Styler 1962: 231: '[G]iven Mk, it is easy to see why Matthew was written; given Matthew, it is hard to see why Mk was needed.'

[77]This is strikingly evident in Stein's table of fifty-one episodes (1987: 50).

and the explanatory conjunction *gar* ('for') – appear in Matthew almost exclusively in material shared with Mark.[78]

Mark and Matthew are frequently in verbal agreement against Luke, as are Mark and Luke against Matthew; yet seldom do Matthew and Luke agree against Mark. The best explanation for these phenomena – once Luke's use of Matthew and Matthew's use of Luke have been excluded – is that both Matthew and Luke have employed Mark.[79] Moreover, some of Matthew's expressions are more readily explained by his indebtedness to Mark than by the Matthean context.[80]

3. Order

As noted above, the Synoptists often arrange their materials in the same way. Where they do not, we find evidence like that of the preceding paragraph: sometimes Mark and Matthew agree in order against Luke, as do Mark and Luke against Matthew; but where Matthew and Luke depart from Mark's order, they never do so in the same way. It is true that this phenomenon could be otherwise explained, for example by Luke's use of Matthew and Mark's use of both Matthew and Luke. Yet here, as in other respects, Matthew's and Luke's divergences from Mark's order are more intelligible than would be Mark's from theirs.[81]

---

[78]For discussion of these matters, see Stein 1987: 52-62, 81-83.

[79]For support of these points see Stein 1987: 67-69, 91-103; ibid., *DJG*, 790. In Figure 1 (p.65 above), there is no arrow from 'the Gospel according to Luke' to 'the Evangelist Matthew,' nor from 'the Evangelist Matthew' to 'the Gospel according to Luke.'

[80]E.g., (i) Matthew 9:2b, 'Jesus, seeing their faith' (= Mark 2:5a), although Matthew says nothing about their removing the roof and lowering the paralytic (Mark 2:4); (ii) Matthew 19:17b, 'There is only one who is good' (par. Mark 10:18b, 'No one is good except God alone'), although *agathos* in Matthew's preceding question is neuter ('Why do you ask me about what is good?' 19:17a) rather than masculine, as in Mark 10:18a ('Why do you call me good?'); and (iii) Matthew 20:22a, 'You do not know what you [pl.] are asking' (= Mark 10:38a), words addressed to James and John, though in 20:20-21 Jesus is speaking with their mother. For these and other examples, see Stein 1987: 70-76; Styler 1982: 293-98. But see also my comments on those passages.

[81]See Stein 1987: 69-70, including his comments on the so-called 'Lachmann fallacy.'

Given the design of Matthew (A. above), it is noteworthy that Matthew's departures from Markan order generally serve his purpose of gathering together materials of the same kind.[82] This accords with a conclusion earlier drawn (II. A.) from Papias' testimony – namely, that Matthew writes with Mark's gospel in view, and with the intention of presenting 'the oracles' in a more orderly fashion than Mark had done.

4. Teaching

While for many an episode reported by all the Synoptists Mark's account is the longest (as noted earlier), his gospel is on the whole the least explicit theologically. Is not Matthew 16:16 ('You are the Christ, the Son of the living God') more likely to have been written in face of Mark 8:29 ('You are the Christ') than vice versa? Another name, 'Lord' (*Kyrios*), is applied to Jesus only six times in Mark but thirty times in Matthew (those six together with another twenty-four, of which fifteen appear in material found also in Mark.[83] Places where Matthew identifies Jesus as 'Son of David' but Mark does not are better explained as Matthean additions than as Markan deletions, given the primacy of this motif in Matthew (1:1, etc.). The same holds true for references to the OT prefaced by the verb 'fulfill' (*plēroō*). There are at least twelve such instances in Matthew, seven (or eight) of which appear in material shared with Mark; yet only once (or twice) does the Markan parallel contain this verb. That Mark

---

[82]Thus Guthrie 1990: 151. Kümmel 1975: 58-60 observes that Matthew, where having material in common with Mark 6:7 onwards, practically never deviates from Mark's sequence; and that Matthew, where having material in common with Mark 1:1-6:6, diverges from the Markan order in two ways: (i) miracle stories separated in Mark (1:29-34; 4:35-5:43) are more closely joined in the collection of Matthew 8–9 (8:14-17, 23-34; 9:18-26), while, conversely, the inclusion of debates about table fellowship and fasting (Matt. 9:9-17) in a section otherwise dominated by miracles, shows Matthew's fidelity to Mark's order (2:1-22, par. Matthew 9:1-17); and (ii) Mark's account of the call of the twelve (3:13-19) is brought forward in Matthew to 10:2-4, to introduce the discourse that follows the collection of miracle stories ('brought forward,' since the material of Mark 2:23-3:35 is otherwise paralleled in Matthew 12:1-50).

[83]Cf. Stein 1987: 84-86; Guthrie 1990: 152.

omitted the formula is again less likely than that Matthew added it – Jesus' fulfillment of the Old Testament being a major theme of his gospel.[84]

It is often noted, in favor of Markan priority, that certain of Mark's statements thought to place Jesus or his disciples in an unfavorable light are absent from the Matthean (and Lukan) parallels. Thus Mark sometimes speaks with greater candor than does Matthew about disciples' lack of understanding or faith or charity or humility.[85] Markan expressions that might suggest limits to Jesus' healing power are absent from Matthew,[86] as are a report of Jesus' anger and a puzzling reference to a former high priest.[87] In Mark 10:18, Jesus asks the rich man, 'Why do you call me good?' whereas in Matthew 19:17 the question reads, 'Why do you ask me about what is good?' It is not to be inferred from those comparisons that the only source available to Matthew for such accounts was the Gospel according to Mark. I am also aware that such comparisons often lead to erroneous conclusions. Yet it would be premature at this stage to plunge into exegesis. For now, suffice it to say that Matthew's amending of Mark offers a better explanation for those differences than does Mark's altering of Matthew.[88]

In none of the above do I mean to insinuate that Mark's theology is inferior to Matthew's, or that Matthew is solely responsible for the distinctive features of his teaching. See the later parts of the present discussion, together with my commentary on the passages concerned.

---

[84]The twelve (of sixteen) instances of *plēroō* in Matthew are 1:22; 2:15, 17, 23; 4:14 ; 8:17; 12:17; 13:35; 21:4; 26:54, 56; 27:9. Those in material parallel to Mark are 8:17 (par. Mark 1:34); 12:17 (Mark 3:12); 13:14 (Mark 4:12), 35 (Mark 4:34); 21:4 (Mark 11:3); 26:54 (Mark 14:47), 56 (Mark 14:49), and possibly 4:14 (Mark 1:15). But only two of the Markan passages contain *plēroō*: 1:15 and 14:49. For more on 'Son of David' and 'fulfill,' see Stein 1987: 77-81.

[85]See Mark 4:13 (and Matt. 13:18); 4:40 (and Matt. 8:26); 6:51-52 (and Matt. 14:32-33); 10:14 (and Matt. 19:14); 10:35-37 (with Matt. 20:20-21).

[86]See Mark 1:32-34 (and Matt. 8:16); 3:9-10 (and Matt. 12:15); 6:5-6 (and Matt. 13:58).

[87]See Mark 3:4-5 (and Matt. 12:12); 2:25-26 (and Matt. 12:3-4).

[88]For matters discussed in this par., see Stein 1987: 62-67; Guthrie 1990: 151-52.

5. Authority

For some interpreters, evidence that the writer of Matthew employed the Gospel according to Mark is also evidence against the Matthean authorship of Matthew. It is argued that an eyewitness and apostle would not depend so heavily upon an author who was neither.[89]

Yet the testimony of an eyewitness and apostle undergirds Mark's account. Writing from 'Babylon' (i.e., Rome), Peter speaks of 'Mark my son' (1 Pet. 5:13). We learned from Papias how 'the presbyter [i.e., the apostle John] used to say, "Mark, who had been Peter's interpreter, wrote down carefully... all that he remembered of the Lord's sayings and doings."'[90] In this light, it is interesting to observe the kinship between the structure of Mark's written *euangelion* (1:1) and Peter's preaching, especially as recorded in Acts 10:34-43.[91] Accordingly, in Figure 1, there is an arrow drawn directly from 'the Apostle Peter' to 'the Evangelist Mark.' It is not in the least surprising that Matthew should consult a document whose main human authority was one of the other ten commissioned in Matthew 28. Why should Matthew imagine

[89]Brown (1997: 210) considers that 'if canonical Matthew drew on canonical Mark, the idea that Matthew, an eyewitness member of the Twelve, would have used as a major source a non-eyewitness, Greek account (Mark) is implausible.' So too Stanton 1989: 79.

[90]*HE* 3.39.15; cf. the discussion of 3.39 under II. A. above; and Hagner 1993: lxxvi. For a careful and positive assessment of Papias' testimony about Mark, see Gundry 1993: 1026-43. He concludes 'that the Gospel of Mark contains Peter's reminiscences of Jesus' words and deeds, that John Mark wrote it, that he wrote it in Rome while Peter was still preaching there and before two years of Paul's Roman imprisonment [ca. A.D. 60-62] came to an end' (1043). Whether Mark was himself a follower of Jesus is debatable: cf. Mark 14:51-52 (vv. peculiar to Mark and thought by some to be the author's personal reminiscence); *HE* 3.39.15.

[91]The connection was noted long ago by Dodd 1936: 27-28, 46-52. Peter's recounting of prophetic fulfillment (Acts 10:43), of John's ministry (10:37), of good news for Israel through Jesus (10:36, *euangelizomai*), and of his anointing with the Spirit (10:38), all have counterparts in Mark 1:1-15. The reference to Jesus' practice, beginning in Galilee, of 'doing good and healing all who were dominated by the devil' (Acts 10:37-38) aptly summarizes Mark 1:14-8:30. Like Acts 10:39-40, Mark 8:31-16:8 is mainly occupied with Jesus' activity in Judea and Jerusalem, his death, and his resurrection. Cf. comments on 'the progress of oral and written tradition' on pages 66-69 above.

that he could recall, or that he had recorded, 'all that [Jesus] commanded'? Knowing that the document is undergirded by Peter's authority and filled with Peter's reminiscences would help to explain why Matthew is on the whole 'remarkably faithful to Mark, almost as a scribe copying his source.'[92] Moreover, Matthew's consulting of Peter is consistent with what Matthew 16:16-18 discloses about this apostle.

Mark may also have been indirectly dependent on Matthew. As indicated by the horizontal arrow at the top of Figure 1, Peter's early preaching about Jesus may have been indebted to Matthew, particularly if the latter possessed written memoranda. Furthermore, Mark probably had access to 'oral and written traditions' besides those supplied by Peter; and Matthew's contribution to those traditions may have been considerable (see those arrows). Some have even suggested that Mark drew upon an earlier, Semitic version of the Gospel according to Matthew – in which case Matthew, by consulting Mark when writing his Greek gospel, also consults himself![93]

Taken together, the arguments offered under those five headings provide a very strong case for Matthew's use of Mark. While this must remain an hypothesis (i.e., absolute proof in such a case is unattainable), it is to my mind a very satisfactory one and it is presupposed in all that follows.[94] But there are other matters related to 'the Synoptic problem' still to be considered.

---

[92]Brown 1997: 204; but he denies the apostolic authorship of Matthew (ibid., 208-12).

[93]Cf. Gundry 1967: 184. As noted earlier (II. A.), even if Papias is speaking in *HE* 3.39.16 of a Semitic original, nothing in his testimony precludes Matthean authorship of the Greek version as well.

[94]'Even if the Marcan hypothesis is not without its own problems, it is generally maintained to be most probable on the grounds that the theory which solves a greater number of the difficulties is more likely to be correct' (Guthrie 1990: 153). Robert Stein argues strongly that 'the best available hypothesis for explaining the Synoptic Problem is that Matthew and Luke used Mark in the composition of their Gospels,' while acknowledging that 'the Synoptic Problem must always remain open to a better hypothesis if one should become available' (*DJG*, 790).

Matthew's Use of 'Q'

Besides material common to all three Synoptic Gospels (the 'triple tradition'), there is a substantial amount – between 231 and 241 verses – absent from Mark but shared by Matthew and Luke (the 'double tradition'). In Figure 1, in accord with scholarly parlance, this material is designated 'Q' (for *Quelle*, the German word for 'source').[95] I now seek to clarify and to defend the view reflected in that figure.

1. Rejecting the case against Q

The Q material commences with words of John the Baptist and accounts of Jesus' temptations.[96] Thereafter Q consists almost entirely of Jesus' sayings, beginning with beatitudes and concluding with an assurance of coming glory.[97] Sometimes there are striking verbal agreements between the Matthean and Lukan versions of those sayings; other texts, though clearly devoted to the same subject, exhibit impressive verbal differences.[98] By the same token, while Matthew and Luke sometimes present Q material in the

---

[95]Scholars have thus used the term for over a hundred years (G. N. Stanton, 'Q,' *DJG*, 644). Whether certain verses and words belong to Q is a matter of ongoing debate. Brown's table of Q's contents, in the Lukan order (1997: 118-119), contains 231 verses or parts of verses from Luke, and 241 from Matthew. (Stein 1987: 89, notes that 4,290 words in Matthew have parallels in Luke but not in Mark, and that 3,559 words in Luke have parallels in Matthew but not in Mark.) The material tabulated by Brown provides the main basis for our discussion.

[96]Matthew 3:7b-12 / Luke 3:7-9, 16-17; and Matthew 4:2b-11a / Luke 4:2-13.

[97]Matthew 5:3, 6, 4, 11-12 / Luke 6:20b-23; and Matthew 19:28 / Luke 22:38, 30. An exception is Jesus' healing of the centurion's servant, Matthew 8:5a-10, 13 / Luke 7:1-2, 6b-10; but both accounts, especially Matthew's, feature Jesus' words.

[98]For such agreements, see, e.g., Matthew 3:7b-12 / Luke 3:7-9, 16-17; Matthew 4:2b-11a / Luke 4:2-13; Matthew 6:24 / Luke 16:13; Matthew 11:2-11, 16-19 / Luke 7:18-28, 31-35; Matthew 11:25-27 / Luke 10:21-22; Matthew 23:37-39 / Luke 13:34-35. For such differences, see e.g. Matthew 7:21, 24-27 / Luke 6:46-49; Matthew 10:34-36 / Luke 12:51-53; Matthew 25:14-30 / Luke 19:11-27. In some passages agreements and differences are equally in evidence: e.g., Matthew 6:9-13 / Luke 11:2-4; Matthew 7:7-11 / Luke 11:9-13; Matthew 23:4, 6-7, 13, 23, 25-27, 29-32, 34-36 / Luke 11:39-52. All these examples come from Stanton, *DJG*, 645; and Stein 1987: 89-90, 97-99.

same order, at other times they arrange it very differently.[99] Examining these texts also reveals that certain sayings from this 'double tradition' closely resemble sayings from the 'triple tradition.'[100]

Some contend that those phenomena are adequately explained by Luke's use of Matthew, or of Matthew together with Mark, and that there is thus no need to posit the existence of a source such as Q.[101] But this hypothesis is dubious for several reasons.

The Lukan order

Of the 241 verses identified as Q material in Matthew, 156 (or 65 percent of the total) appear in the five great discourses, most notably in chapters 5–7 (64 verses), 10 (29 verses), and 23-25 (51 verses).[102] Yet those sixty-four verses in Matthew 5–7 are spread over six chapters of Luke.[103] The twenty-nine verses in Matthew

---

[99]So, e.g., while Matthew's parallels to the Q material of Luke 11 accord (with one exception) with Matthew's own order (texts from Matthew 6, 7, 12 and 23), Matthean parallels to the Q material of Luke 12 appear in a very different order (texts from Matthew 10, 6, 24, 10, 16 and 5). See the table in Brown 1997: 118-119.

[100]Examples of such 'doublets': (i) In the 'triple tradition,' Mark 4:25 ('for the one who has will be given more') and Matthew 13:12; Luke 8:18; in the 'double tradition,' Matthew 25:29 ('for whoever has will be given more') and Luke 19:26. (ii) In the 'triple tradition,' Mark 8:34 ('if anyone wants to come after me, let him deny himself and take up his cross and follow me') and Matthew 16:24; Luke 9:23; in the 'double tradition,' Matthew 10:38 ('he who does not take his cross and follow me') and Luke 14:27. Cf. Stanton, *DJG*, 645; Stein 1987: 107-8.

[101]The second and third views mentioned at the close of the section on 'The Synoptic Gospels.'

[102]By contrast, there are only five Q verses in Matthew 13, and seven in Matthew 18.

[103]Luke *6*:20b-23 (Matt. 5:3, 6, 4, 11-12), 27-30 (Matt. 5:44, 39b-40, 42), 31 (Matt. 7:12), 32-33, 35b-36 (Matt. 5:46-47, 45, 48), 6:37a, 38c (Matt. 7:1-2), 41-42 (Matt. 7:3-5), 43-45 (Matt. 7:16-20), 46-49 (Matt. 7:21, 24-27); *11*:2-4 (Matt. 6:9-13), 9-13 (Matt. 7:7-11), 33-35 (Matt. 5:15; 6:22-23); *12*:22-31 (Matt. 6:25-33), 33-34 (Matt. 6:19-21), 58-59 (Matt. 5:25-26); *13*:24-27 (Matt. 7:13-14, 22-23); *14*:34-35 (Matt. 5:13); and *16*:13 (Matt. 6:24), 17-18 (Matt. 5:18, 32).

10 are scattered over five chapters of Luke,[104] as are the fifty-one verses in Matthew 23-25.[105] It may be added that the eighteen Q verses in Matthew 11 are spread over three chapters of Luke,[106] as are the twenty-one Q verses in Matthew 12.[107] Would Luke so frequently disturb Matthew's established order, especially that of his great discourses?[108]

The Lukan content

If Luke used Matthew, we might understand his altering 'forgive us our *debts*' (Matt. 6:12) to 'forgive us our *sins*' (Luke 11:4); or 'how much more will your Father *who is in heaven give good things* to those who ask him' (Matt. 7:11) to 'how much more will the Father *give the Holy Spirit from heaven* to those who ask him' (Luke 11:13).[109] Not so intelligible would be Luke's abbreviating Matthew's versions of the Beatitudes (Matt. 5:3-12/ Luke 6:20-23) and of the Lord's Prayer (Matt. 6:9-13/Luke 11:2-4); and his eliminating over one-third of the Sermon on the Mount.[110] The Q material of Luke 19:12-27 is in some respects

[104]Luke 6:39-40 (Matt. 10:24-25a); 10:2-16 (Matt. 10:7-16, 40); 12:2-9, 11-12 (Matt. 10:26-33, 19-20), 51-53 (Matt. 10:34-36); 14:26-27 (Matt. 10:37-38); 17:33 (Matt. 10:39).

[105]Luke 11:39-44 (Matt. 23:25-26, 23, 6-7a, 27), 46-48 (Matt. 23:4, 29-31), 49-52 (Matt. 23:34-36, 13); 12:39-40, 42-46 (Matt. 24:43-44, 45-51); 13:34-35 (Matt. 23:37-39); 17:23-24, 37 (Matt. 24:26-28), 26-27, 30 (Matt. 24:37-39), 34-35 (Matt. 24:40-41); 19:12-27 (Matt. 25:14-30). To those fifty-one verses might be added Matthew 25:11-12 (cf. Luke 13:25b).

[106]Luke 7:18-28 (Matt. 11:2-11), 31-35 (Matt. 11:16-19); 10:13-15 (Matt. 11:21-23), 21-24 (Matt. 11:25-27); 16:16 (Matt. 11:12-13).

[107]Luke 6:43-45 (Matt. 12:33-35, akin to Matt. 7:16-20); 11:14-15, 17-23 (Matt. 12:22-30), 24-26 (Matt. 12:43-45), 29-32 (Matt. 12:38-42); 12:10 (Matt. 12:32).

[108]Stein asks concerning the Sermon on the Mount: 'Why would Luke, who was by no means an inept writer, choose to break up this masterpiece and scatter its material in a far less artistic fashion throughout his Gospel?' (1987: 96).

[109]See Stein 1987: 96-99. Among his other examples in which the Q material of Matthew 'appears more primitive' than that of Luke: Matthew 5:17-18/ Luke 16:16-17; Matthew 5:44/Luke 6:27-28; Matthew 5:46-47/Luke 6:32-35; Matthew 7:1-2/Luke 6:37-38 (ibid., 99, n. 9).

[110]Lacking Lukan parallels are Matthew 5:5, 7-10, 14, 16, 17, 19-24, 27-31, 33-38, 41, 43; 6:1-7, 14-18; 7:6, 15, 19, 28-29 (= forty-four verses, or about 4 per cent of the 111 comprising the Sermon on the Mount). Even Luke 6:20-49, which contains many sayings similar to those of Matthew 5–7, and in roughly the same order, lacks much that the Matthean discourse includes.

quite different from that of Matthew 25:14-30; and the flanking parables of Matthew 25 (vv. 1-13 and 31-46) are absent from Luke. Indeed there are many Matthean texts, including several other parables and virtually all of Matthew 1–2, without Lukan parallels.[111]

The Lukan sources

If Luke employed both Matthew and Mark, he treated them very differently. Whereas Luke usually retains the Markan order, he often departs from that of Matthew.[112] While Luke shows great respect for Mark's record of Jesus' sayings, very seldom does he adopt a Matthean supplement to those sayings. For example, compare Peter's confession of faith in Mark 8:29 ('You are the Christ') to those of Matthew 16:16 ('You are the Christ, the Son of the living God') and Luke 9:20 ('You are the Christ of God'). Or observe that while Mark 2:23-28, Matthew 12:1-8 and Luke 6:1-5 are quite close to each other, Jesus' words in Matthew 12:5-7 are absent from Mark and Luke.[113]

The above evidence, besides confirming the earlier conclusion that both Matthew and Luke employed the Gospel according to Mark, strongly suggests that Luke wrote without

---

[111]On these Matthean texts (the so-called 'M' material), see the later discussion.

[112]As seen above. The Q materials of Matthew 4:1-11 and Luke 4:13 are placed in the same Markan context (Mark 1:12-13). Never again is that the case. 'If Luke has used Matthew, then he has carefully removed every non-Markan (Q) saying from the Markan context it has in Matthew and placed it in a different context!' (Stanton, *DJG*, 648). For example, he separated the Markan and non-Markan portions of Matthew 24–25; included the former in Luke 21; and isolated the latter for inclusion in Luke 12, 13, 17 and 19 – 'a tortuous explanation of Luke's methods, to say the least' (ibid., 647).

[113]For other examples, see Stein 1987: 91-95. There exist minor agreements between Matthew and Luke against Mark, both in order (e.g., Matt. 27:55-56/ Luke 23:49 and Mark 15:40-41) and in content (e.g., Matt. 12:3-4/Luke 6:3-4 and Mark 2:25-26), which M. D. Goulder, e.g., takes as evidence that Luke used Matthew as well as Mark. But why then has Luke 'ignored numerous *major* Matthean additions or modifications to Mark which would have suited his purposes' (Stanton, *DJG*, 648)? And how then can Goulder insist 'that in Markan contexts Luke makes it his policy *not* to keep turning up Matthew to see what he has added' (ibid.)?

access to the Gospel according to Matthew. We are therefore ready to consider another alternative.

2. *Affirming the existence of Q*

In my judgment, the most reasonable explanation for the 'double tradition' is that both Matthew and Luke drew upon the collection of Jesus' sayings identified as 'Q' in Figure 1. Support for this view may be summarized as follows.

The order

This hypothesis satisfactorily explains why Matthew and Luke sometimes arrange Q materials in the same way. It accounts for the many differences by positing that the original order of Q is better reflected in Luke than in Matthew; that (in other words) Matthew disrupted the order more often than did Luke; and that his main reason for doing so is that the Q material admirably served his purpose of gathering Jesus' sayings into those five – especially those three – discourses.[114]

The content

On the one hand, this view accounts for the striking verbal agreements that came to light. On the other hand, it offers one or more explanations for such differences as were noted above: (i) Sometimes Matthew, and sometimes Luke, altered or augmented the Q material to a greater degree than did the other. The same can be said about their usage of Mark.[115] (ii) The two evangelists had access to distinctive and complementary versions of the Q material. F. F. Bruce, for example, considers it probable 'that "Q" was translated into Greek from Aramaic and that Matthew and Luke sometimes use the same translation

---

[114]Read independently of Matthew, the Q material in Luke is anything but scattered and disorderly. Of the sixty-five verses in Luke 6:20–7:35, forty-nine contain Q material. Almost all the rest of Q in Luke appears in 9:51–19:27 (the 'travel narrative'), most of it in blocks of verses: e.g., Q material occurs in twenty-three of the thirty verses in 9:57–10:24; in forty of the fifty-four verses in chapter 11; in thirty-eight of the fifty-nine in chapter 12; in thirteen of the eighteen in 13:18-35; in thirteen of the twenty in 14:16-35; and in nine of the eighteen in 17:20-37.

[115]Stanton, *DJG*, 645.

and sometimes different ones.'[116] Even if Q first appeared in Greek, distinctions might arise as the original was duplicated for ever wider distribution.[117] (iii) Both evangelists drew upon traditions of Jesus' sayings besides those identified as Q. Thus in Figure 1, arrows are drawn to 'the Evangelist Matthew' and 'the Evangelist Luke,' not only from 'Q' but also from the 'Oral and Written Traditions' out of which Q itself sprang. Given the duration of Jesus' ministry, and his manifold skill as a teacher, it is highly probable that he presented the Beatitudes on numerous occasions and in various formulations; that he taught more than one version of the Lord's Prayer, in part to discourage a magical use of its words; and that he himself supplemented his parable of the pounds (Luke 19:12-27) with that of the talents (Matt. 25:14-30), and his parable of the great dinner (Luke 14:16-24) with that of the marriage feast (Matt. 22:1-14).

The source
Taking account of the above discussion, including the observations of the preceding paragraph, I offer the following hypothesis: (i) Q originally existed as a *written* collection of Jesus' sayings, whether in Aramaic or in Greek.[118] Its manifest purpose was to augment accounts of Jesus' mighty works and the events of Passion Week.[119] (ii) In duplicating and

---

[116]In 'Gospels,' *IBD*, 2: 584. As noted earlier, T. W. Manson took Papias' statement in *HE* 3.39.16 to mean that 'Matthew compiled the oracles [*ta logia*] in the Aramaic language,' and identified this work as the Q in modern scholarship.

[117]Whatever one thinks of the Q hypothesis, the sayings in question evidence such distinctions: e.g., the Greek of Matthew 7:12 is similar, but not identical, to that of Luke 6:13. For arguments that Greek was the original language of Q, see Kloppenborg 1987: 51-64.

[118]Viewed as a whole, the Q material evidences both a unity of subject matter (the sayings of Jesus) and – especially when viewed in the Lukan order – a natural progression (from John's ministry and Jesus' temptations to the teachings of Jesus during Passion Week). For strong arguments that Q was a written document, see Kloppenborg 1987: 41-88.

[119]Cf. earlier remarks on 'the progress of oral and written traditions.' Discovered in 1945 was the *Gospel of Thomas*, a collection of 114 sayings of Jesus. On the one hand this document is distant from Jesus both theologically

distributing this material to meet the churches' ever growing needs, the early Christians were careful to safeguard Jesus' actual teachings and to impart them accurately. As it was transmitted, the Q material was frequently joined to other written records and to oral traditions of the same or a similar kind.[120] (iii) In time, this writing or collection of writings disappeared, in part because most of it had been incorporated into Matthew and Luke.[121]

The above remains an hypothesis, of course, like the earlier case for Markan priority. Here, as there, certainty is unattainable; indeed, this hypothesis must be offered more tentatively than that one, for the simple reason that the document Mark exists and a document Q does not.[122] Still, of all the explanations for the Q material offered to this point the above is to my mind the best one available, and it is presupposed in all that follows. Yet my interpretation of the evidence (beginning with the following summary of content) could just as easily rest upon the view that Q existed throughout its history in both written and oral forms.[123]

(it is strongly Gnostic in character) and historically (it probably dates from no earlier than the end of the first century). On the other hand, its existence supports the idea of an earlier such written collection, which, in Q's case, would consist exclusively of Jesus' authentic sayings. Indeed, the *Gospel of Thomas* may have been partially inspired by and dependent upon such a collection. See R. J. Bauckham, *DJG*, 286-87; Stein 1987: 109.

[120]We should thus not be surprised to find overlappings between Markan and Q materials – e.g., between Mark 3:22-27 and Matthew 12:22-30/ Luke 11:14-15, 17-23; and between Mark 4:30-32 and Matthew 13:31-32/ Luke 13:18-19. Cf. Stein 1987: 110, 124-25, 136. Keener 1999: 10 judges that 'Matthew's community certainly had other Palestinian traditions besides Mark and Q, and these traditions had undoubtedly been interacting with Mark and Q long before he wrote his Gospel.'

[121]On this view, the writing of Matthew is comparable to the writing of 1–2 Chronicles. Matthew's indebtedness to Mark is like the Chronicler's to Samuel and Kings. As the Chronicler relied on royal and prophetic writings, which later disappeared, so Matthew drew on Q materials. Matthew handled his sources as carefully as did the Chronicler. Cf. Pratt 1998: 11-12.

[122]Having offered impressive arguments for the position I have adopted, Stanton observes: 'Even the strongest supporters of Q accept that the hypothesis is less securely established than Markan priority' (*DJG*, 646).

[123]CMM, 36, concludes: 'A source like Q remains the best explanation for the agreements between Matthew and Luke in non-Markan material.

3. Exploring the contents of Q

What instruction did this collection of sayings offer to the early Christians, both for their own growth in understanding and for their witness to the non-believing world? We may summarize the teachings of Q under four headings.[124]

Christ

Jesus dominates the Q material. John's opening testimony (3:7-12) sets the tone for what follows. All subsequent sayings come from Jesus. Q elucidates his understanding of Messiahship, and acclaims him to be the Son of Man in both his present humiliation and his future exaltation.[125] Jesus inaugurates the kingdom of God, imparts its blessings and executes its judgments.[126] Q makes it plain that being rightly related to God requires knowing and obeying his Son.[127]

Crisis

That manifold disclosure of Christ, and the ineluctable advance of the kingdom, calls for swift and decisive action.[128] Would-be citizens of the kingdom must pledge their highest

---

Almost certainly some, if not a substantial portion, of Q was in written form. But we must probably allow for more than one written source, and some mixture of oral traditions as well.' Brown likewise argues for the existence of Q but cautions against 'extravagant hypotheses based on this hypothetical document' (1997: 116-22, especially 122). So does Stein 1987: 109-112.

[124]The following takes account of all the references in Brown (1997: 118-19), but only summarizes their content lest we too much anticipate later sections of the Introduction and the commentary itself. (I did not include a comparable summary of the contents of Mark, since they are more readily discernible.) For extended commentary on the contents of Q, see Catchpole 1993 and Edwards 1976; for a more concise statement, see Stanton, *DJG*, 648-50.

[125]On the character of Jesus' Messiahship, see Matthew 4:2-11; 11:2-11. On Jesus as the Son of Man, see 8:19-22; 11:16-19; 24:26-28, 37-39.

[126]Jesus inaugurates the kingdom (Matt. 11:12-13; 12:38-42; 13:16-17; 16:2-3); mediates its blessings (5:3, 4, 6, 11-12); and executes its judgments (7:21-27; 23:37-39; 24:37-41; 25:14-30).

[127]See Matthew 6:9-13, 24; 7:7-11; 10:40; 11:25-27; and texts in the preceding note.

[128]See 5:25-26; 7:13-14; 22:1-10.

allegiance to Jesus and serve him at whatever cost.[129] The centurion's trust in Jesus provides a model for others.[130] As the coming of Messiah represents the ultimate expression of God's saving grace, the prospect for those who reject and oppose that witness is perilous indeed.[131]

Conduct

Whether one has really embraced Jesus' teachings and has genuinely chosen to follow him will become apparent in one's conduct (Matt. 7:16-20). Q offers much guidance for living in the new community, and for relating both to fellow believers and to non-Christians.[132] One mark of serious discipleship is a willingness to proclaim Jesus' gospel of the kingdom, even amid threats of deprivation and persecution.[133]

Consummation

One of the strongest incentives to holy living is recognizing that God's kingdom will surely be consummated.[134] On the one hand a Day of Judgment is coming, on which the condition of one's heart will be brought to light and the character of one's service appraised. But there is also the assurance that all who truly belong to Jesus will receive a heavenly reward, share in his rule, and enter into fullness of fellowship with him and the heavenly Father.[135]

Matthew's Use of 'M'

Alongside the material shared with one or both of the other Synoptics, there is much that appears in Matthew alone. This material, termed 'M' in scholarly circles, includes: (i)

---

[129]See 10:24-25a, 32-39.

[130]See 8:5-10, 13; 17:20.

[131]See 11:21-23;12:22-30, 32, 43-45; 15:14; 23:4, 6-7, 13, 23, 25-27, 29-31, 34-36.

[132]See 5:13, 18, 32, 39-40, 42, 44-48; 7:1-5, 12; 18:7, 12-15, 21-22.

[133]See 5:15; 9:37-38; 10:7-16, 19-20, 26-33.

[134]Another strong incentive, of course, is the salvation accomplished in Jesus' death and resurrection, events which the Q material presupposes.

[135]See 6:9-13, 19-23, 25-33; 8:11-12; 13:31-33; 19:28; 24:43-51. For further references to the Day of Judgment, see the preceding notes.

the Infancy Narrative (Matt. 1–2); (ii) an exchange between Jesus and John the Baptist (3:14-15); (iii) many portions of the great discourses, as well as each one's closing formula;[136] (iv) equally momentous utterances and parables of Jesus in the intervening blocks of narrative;[137] (v) some miracle stories;[138] and (vi) several passages in the Passion Narrative of chapters 26–28.[139] Other texts peculiar to Matthew will be considered in due course.[140]

How did Matthew obtain this material? I think it highly probable that he recalled most of it from his days as Jesus' studious disciple. Matthew may be writing thirty or forty

---

[136]Some notable texts peculiar to Matthew: (i) in chapters 5–7: the Beatitudes of 5:5, 7-10; most of 5:13-48; and all of 6:1-18 except for the Lord's Prayer; (ii) in Chapter 10: restricting the mission to Israel, 5b-6 (also 15:24); being like serpents and doves, 16; relating the mission to the coming of the Son of Man, 23; welcoming a prophet and a righteous man, 41; (iii) in chapter 13: the parables of the wheat and weeds, 24-30, 36-43; the treasure, 44; the pearl, 45-46; the net, 47-50; and the saying in 51-52 about the well taught scribe; (iv) in chapter 18: sayings about the little ones, 4, 10, 14, and about reconciling a sinful brother, 16-20; the parable of the unmerciful servant, 23-35; (v) in chapters 23–25: about half of chapter 23 (the woes upon scribes and Pharisees); and the parables of the ten virgins, 25:1-13, and of the Last Judgment, 25:31-46, to which might be added the parable of 25:14-30 (the talents), which differs in many respects from that of Luke 19:12-27 (the pounds). On the discourses' recurrent closing (e.g., Matthew 7:28, etc.), see section A. above.

[137]Examples of such utterances: Matthew 9:13 and 12:7 (valuing mercy over sacrifice); 11:14 and 17:13 (identifying John as Elijah); 11:28-30 (offering rest to the weary); 12:36-37 (warning that words will be judged); 16:17-19 (granting Peter blessing and authority). The parables: the workers in the vineyard (20:1-16); and the two sons (21:28-32); to which might be added the parable of 22:1-10 (the wedding banquet), which in important ways differs from that of Luke 14:16-24 (the great dinner).

[138]The healing of two blind men (Matt. 9:27-31) and of a mute demoniac (9:32-34); Peter's walking on the water (14:28-31) and his finding the coin in the fish's mouth (17:24-27).

[139]See, e.g., Matthew 26:44 (the third prayer in Gethsemane), 26:52-54 (at the scene of the arrest); 27:3-10 (the end of Judas), 27:19 (the dream of Pilate's wife), 27:24-25 (Pilate's handwashing), 27:43 (words of mockery), 27:51b-53 (signs and wonders associated with Jesus' death and resurrection), 27:62-66 (guarding the tomb); 28:2-4 (an earthquake, and the angel's appearance), 28:11-15 (bribing the soldiers) and 28:16-20 (the commissioning of the eleven in Galilee).

[140]The M material is conveniently listed in Davies & Allison 1988: 122-24.

years after receiving the commission of Matthew 28; but
the contribution of his *memory* to his work, even at that
distance, should not be underestimated. Given (i) Jesus'
authority and skill as a teacher, including his repetition of
important subjects; (ii) the inherently impressive character
of his miracles; (iii) the stupendous impact of his death and
resurrection; (iv) the magnitude and mystery of his being;
and (v) his manifestly transforming effect upon Matthew, can
there be any doubt that much from 'the life, words and works
of Jesus' became permanently engraved upon the mind of 'the
Apostle Matthew,' thereafter to be recollected ('drawn from
the treasury') and employed by 'the Evangelist Matthew'
(Figure 1.)?[141] That is to say: the explicit testimony about the
writing of the Fourth Gospel (John 19:35; 21:24), captures
Matthew's intent as well.[142]

Here too, in all probability, Matthew was indebted to 'oral
and written traditions' to underscore or amplify or augment
his personal recollections – in other words, to serve him as
Mark and Q had done.[143] Such traditions may have supplied
Matthew with knowledge of events in which he did not
personally participate, such as those of chapters 1 and 2. Yet,
such knowledge may also have come directly from Jesus or
from eyewitnesses to those events.[144]

---

[141]On those five points, see, e.g., (i) Matthew 7:28-29; 6:9-13 (with
Luke 11:2-4); (ii) Matthew 8:28-34; 21:18-22; (iii) the disproportionate
amount of space devoted to Passion Week in Matthew; (iv) 11:28-30; 14:33;
16:16; and (v) 9:9-13; 13:52; and the whole of Matthew. On the Holy Spirit's
work in this process, see E. below. Written notes (considered earlier) would
aid, but not entirely explain, Matthew's recollections. To this day, I vividly
remember two events from about forty years ago – the deaths of President
John F. Kennedy in November 1963, and of Sir Winston Churchill in January
1965 – memories aided by, but not totally dependent upon, preserved press
clippings. The effect of those events on me is, of course, not worthy to be
compared with the effect of Jesus on Matthew.

[142]See also John 20:30-31; 1 John 1:1-3. By the same token, in *HE* 5.20.6-7,
the church father Irenaeus recalls how Polycarp, having conversed 'with
John and with the others who had seen the Lord, ...repeated their words
from memory'; and how he himself had 'listened eagerly' to Polycarp's
words, 'not committing them to writing but learning them by heart.'

[143]See Figure 1. 'M' possibly includes portions of Q which Luke chose
not to record.

All this M material, however Matthew came to possess it, is traceable to 'the life, words and works of Jesus,' and faithfully represents them, as Mark and Q had done.[145] At the same time, attentiveness to texts peculiar to Matthew helps to illuminate the author's identity and special interests.[146] We have already found this to be true: see section I. ('The Apostle'), especially the comments on Matthew 13:52. Consistent with my earlier conclusion that Matthew was written by a former tax collector is the focus on money in several M passages.[147] Also of interest, since Matthew resided in Capernaum by the Sea of Galilee and did business with Gentiles as well as Jews, are references in M to 'Galilee of the Gentiles' and to the Gentile mission.[148] Further evidence from M of Matthew's special concerns may be summarized in terms of his Christology. Jesus is (i) the One in whom the Scriptures are fulfilled; (ii) the Son of God in a unique sense; (iii) the founder of the new community, the Church; (iv) the One uniquely authorized to discern God's will and to expound God's law for the members of that community; (v) the One appointed to expose and to judge those who disobey and dishonor that Law; and (vi) the One who discloses

---

[144]Jesus, in turn, would have learned of the events of Matthew 1–2 (and Luke 1–2) from his parents (Luke 2:40, 52). Similarly, how would Matthew and other members of the twelve have learned of the temptations in the desert (Matt. 4:1-11 and pars.), if not from Jesus (or Jesus and the Spirit)? As a member of the twelve, Matthew was not as dependent as Luke was upon others' eyewitness testimony (cf. Luke 1:1-4).

[145]See Figure 1. Having seen that Matthew, when working with Mark and Q, makes 'conservative changes in a scribal manner' (Brown 1997: 206), we have reason to expect that he was equally scrupulous when using M materials.

[146]So too the Chronicler's additions to (and deletions from) Samuel and Kings disclose his theological and pastoral purposes. Cf. Pratt 1998: 101, 124, 147, et passim.

[147]See Matthew 17:24-27; 18:23-35; 20:1-16; 27:3-10; 28:11-15 (also 25:14-30, which in several respects differs from Luke 19:11-27); and Gundry 1994: 620.

[148]Capernaum was the residence of both Jesus and Matthew (Matt. 4:13; 8:5; 9:1, 9). See especially the M material of 4:13-16, 23-25; 28:16-20. Cf. Gundry 1994: 620, who notes that the choice of 'Gadarenes' at Matthew 8:28 in place of the 'Gerasenes' of Mark 5:1 (cf. TC at both verses) 'may show familiarity with the region around Galilee, since Gadara was both smaller, less well known, and closer to the lake than Gerasa.'

the character, exercises the power, oversees the progress and foretells the consummation of God's Kingdom.[149]

Matthew's Scribal Artistry

I expect some readers will judge the foregoing discussion of Matthew's sources to be hopelessly complex or dangerously critical or utterly useless, or all three. If one or more of those expressions describe your response, but you are nonetheless reading this paragraph, you are to be commended for your perseverance! To such readers I offer several comments.

i. The entirety of section C. (Drawing Out 'Things New') is prompted and governed by the actual content of the Gospel according to Matthew, when viewed together with that of Mark and Luke. If readers find my proposals unacceptable, they are of course free to offer alternatives; but let them be sure to take full account of the actual texts of the Synoptic Gospels as they do so.

ii. That whole discussion has sought to shed light on the methods chosen by Matthew for writing his account of Jesus. That method in turn illuminates the work of the Holy Spirit: Matthew's scrupulous use of sources (whether oral or written or personal), and his talents as a scribe, were means whereby the Spirit brought this inspired document into being.

iii. The actual transmission of those oral and written traditions about Jesus – all of it under the Spirit's direction – was probably far more complex than our best theories.

iv. The value of the foregoing discussion will become more apparent within the commentary itself. There we shall discover – as we have already begun to do – that the theological and pastoral concerns of Matthew are illuminated by a comparison with the other Synoptic Gospels.

v. As that point implies, this commentary's main purpose is *to expound Matthew's proclamation of Jesus the Messiah.* Exploring

---

[149]See respectively (i) section D. below; (ii) Matthew 14:33; (iii) 16:17-19; (iv) 5:13-43; 6:1-18; 18:3-4, 10, 14, 16-20, 23-35; 23:8-10; (v) 23:1-3, 5, 15-22, 24, 28, 32-33; 24:10-12; (vi) 9:27-36; 10:5-8, 16b, 23; 13:24-30, 44-50; 17:24-27; 21:28-32; 25:1-13, 31-46. On the Christology of M, see F. W. Burnett, 'M,' *DJG*, 511-12.

Matthew's sources is useful, but must not be allowed to obscure his own splendid achievement.[150] Matthew is indeed a well-trained scribe; but he is not merely recording data about Jesus as he would have formerly entered tax receipts into a ledger. Nor is he merely a 'scissors-and-paste' editor collating and arranging materials from his oral and written sources; as is already clear from our study of the gospel's design (A. above), Matthew employs those materials in the service of his own literary and theological craft.[151] If we may express it so, Matthew uses his sources as Rembrandt used oil paints – to produce a masterpiece of his own.

We will presently have more to say about Matthew as an evangelist and a theologian and a pastor-teacher. But there are other aspects of his scribal activity yet to be considered.

D. Drawing Out 'Things Old'

'Therefore every scribe who has been discipled for the kingdom of heaven is like a householder who brings out from his treasury things new and old,' says Jesus in Matthew 13:52, the point of departure for this lengthy section (III.) on Matthew the Scribe. Jesus, by depositing all those 'things new' into Matthew's 'treasury,' granted him access to 'things old' as well. These 'old things' are to be found in the Holy Scriptures.

---

[150]'It may be academically useful to detect the sources he employed, but to concentrate on the compositional background and miss the impact of the final product is to miss the beauty of the forest while counting the trees' (Brown 1997: 208).

[151]France 1985: 21 observes that 'all who have studied Matthew's Gospel in detail have been impressed by the care and literary artistry involved in its composition.' Writes Carson (1984: 17): 'In sections very difficult to interpret (e.g., Matt 24), it is sometimes argued that the evangelist has sewn together diverse traditions that by nature are incapable of genuine coherence. Failing to understand the material, he simply passed it on without recognizing that some of his sources were mutually incompatible. There are so many signs of high literary craftsmanship in this Gospel that such skepticism is unjustified.'

Jesus, the Scribe and the Scribes

The language in Matthew 13:52 harks back to 13:35, where a quotation from Psalm 78:2 explains Jesus' use of parables: 'I will open my mouth in parables, I will declare things hidden since the foundation of the world.'[152] Jesus possesses unequaled wisdom to *understand* the Scriptures, and unique authority to *expound* them. Moreover, he is the One in whom the Scriptures are *now being fulfilled*. Thus he differs in two respects from the 'teachers of the law.' Whereas they are occupied exclusively with 'things old,' Jesus imparts 'things new' as well. But even with respect to 'things old,' those teachers have failed: they have nullified the divine Word for the sake of their ancestral traditions; and even when they have correctly taught that Word to others, they have not obeyed it themselves. Jesus, by contrast, honors God's ancient revelation, interprets it aright to his listeners and personally submits to its instruction.[153] So it is his teachings that Matthew the scribe records, not those of the official scholars.[154]

Jesus and the OT illuminate one another; neither is intelligible apart from the other. Nowhere is this plainer than in the Gospel according to Matthew – testimony to how strongly Jesus' own use of Scripture influenced his apostle.

Old Testament Quotations and Allusions in Matthew

Matthew contains more OT quotations than any other gospel, and scores of allusions besides. Gundry finds forty 'formal quotations' in Matthew and 108 'allusive quotations.' Davies and Allison list forty-two 'quotations' and 107 'possible allusions.'[155] According

---

[152]On the link between Matthew 13:52 and 13:35, see France 1985: 231.

[153]On these two matters, see, e.g., Matthew 7:28-29; 15:1-9; 22:34-40; 23:1-36.

[154]This choice would be even more impressive, had Matthew himself been a scholar of the law or even a rabbi before becoming Jesus' disciple (cf. the sources cited in Blomberg 1992: 44). But as we saw in II. B., all the evidence points to his having been a *secular* scribe.

[155]See Gundry 1967: 9-150 (summary on 147-50); Davies and Allison 1988: 34-58. Gundry's forty 'formal quotations' are the very same as the forty-two 'quotations' in Davies and Allison: the latter arrive at the higher number by counting Hosea 6:6 twice (since it is quoted in Matthew 9:13 and 12:7), and by viewing the material in Matthew 11:10 (Exod. 23:20 and Mal. 3:1) as

to *GNT*, there are fifty-two 'quotations' and 160 'allusions and verbal parallels.'[156] Joined together, these scholarly judgments maintain that Matthew quotes or alludes to all but four OT books (Obadiah, Nahum, Ecclesiastes and Song of Solomon). Further attention to the allusions is reserved for the commentary; for now we focus on the quotations. My list of fifty-three quotations, Appendix C, is almost identical to that of *GNT*.[157]

According to my list, there are sixty-four OT texts cited, from fifteen books.[158] Those books most often quoted are Deuteronomy (thirteen), Isaiah (eleven), Psalms (nine) and Exodus (seven). In some instances a single quotation has more than one OT source; in others two quotations are joined together under a single heading.[159] Sometimes the OT writer is identified by name: David (once), Moses (twice), Jeremiah (twice) and Isaiah (six times). At least one quotation appears

---

two quotations rather than as a composite quotation. Similarly, the choice of 'possible allusions' in the latter largely matches Gundry's 'allusive quotations,' though each source includes texts not found in the other.

[156]*GNT* lists quotations on pages 888-89; allusions and verbal parallels on pages 891-901. According to Hagner 1993: liv, 'Matthew contains well over sixty explicit quotations from the OT (not counting a great number of allusions), more than twice as many as any other Gospel.' As the above numerical differences show, what some interpreters call quotations, others call allusions; and some find allusions where others find none.

[157]My one addition to *GNT* is Matthew 2:23. Gundry (1967: 9, n. 1) comments: 'The distinction between formal and allusive quotations is not always easily made. I have tried to judge by whether the quoted words flow from and into the context (allusive) or stand apart (formal).' But some quotations Gundry calls 'allusive' stand out in the text (e.g., Deut. 24:1 in Matt. 19:7); and some he classifies as 'formal' certainly flow into the context (e.g., Isa. 7:14 in Matt. 1:23). Of the OT texts Gundry deems 'formal quotations,' my list excludes only one (Exod. 23:30 in Matt. 11:10); and my list includes several of his 'allusive quotations' (e.g., Deut. 24:1, as noted).

[158]The figure sixty-four represents the total number of citations, not the total number of texts – some of which are quoted more than once (e.g., Lev. 19:18 and Hosea 6:6).

[159]For the former, see, e.g., Matthew 5:21 (Exod. 20:13 and Deut. 5:17) and Matthew 5:27 (Exod. 20:14 and Deut. 5:18); for the latter, e.g., Matthew 1:23 (Isa. 7:14 and 8:8, 10); and Matthew 21:5 (Isa. 62:11 and Zech. 9:9). Other, more debatable, examples of the latter are taken up in the commentary.

in each of the eleven blocks of material identified earlier. Quotations are especially prominent in the first block of narrative, Matthew 1–4 (twelve), and in the fifth, chapters 19–22 (fifteen).

Matthew draws twenty-three of his fifty-three quotations from Mark, and six from Q.[160] The remaining twenty-four appear in Matthew alone. No fewer than thirty-six – or 68 percent of the total – appear on the lips of Jesus.[161] An additional twelve are contributed by Matthew, of which eleven are peculiar to this gospel.[162] The remaining five come, respectively, from the chief priests and scribes; the devil; the Pharisees; the crowd; and the Sadducees.[163]

The Introductions to the Quotations

The prefaces to the actual quotations are themselves illuminating. We may classify them according to the sources named above.

1. Introductions to quotations from Jesus

Sometimes Jesus prefaces a quotation with an exhortation: Matthew 9:13 ('Go learn what it is...'); 18:16 ('take with you one or two, in order that...'); and 19:17 ('keep the commands'). Sometimes an opening question tacitly reproves his listeners: 19:4 ('Have you not read...?'); 21:16 ('Have you never read...?'), 42 ('Have you never read in the Scriptures...?'); and 22:31, quoted below (and see 12:3, 5). At other times he is introducing a statement of fact: 10:35 ('For I came to turn a man against...'); 12:7 ('If you had known what it is...'), 40 ('For just as Jonah was...'); 23:39 ('from now on you will surely not see me until you say...'); 24:30 ('and they

---

[160]See Appendix C, starting with Matthew 3:3 (for quotations with parallels in Mark, and sometimes in Luke as well) and Matthew 4:4 (for quotations with parallels in Luke alone).

[161]Jesus utters the first of these in the wilderness (Matt. 4:4), the last from the cross (27:46).

[162]The first of the twelve occurs in Matthew 1:23, the last in 27:9-10. The one quotation not peculiar to Matthew is 3:3 (which is drawn from Mark).

[163]See, respectively, Matthew 2:5; 4:6; 19:7; 21:9; 22:24.

shall see...'); and 26:64 ('from now on you shall see...'). Two introductions supplied by Matthew are similar: 22:37 ('And he [Jesus] said to him...'); and 27:46 ('Jesus cried out with a loud voice, saying...').[164]

The remaining introductions are more formal and more expressive of scriptural authority. In responding to Satan, Jesus prefaces each of his quotations from Deuteronomy with the words 'it stands written [*gegraptai*]' (Matt. 4:4, 7, 10). He identifies John the Baptist as the one 'concerning whom it stands written [*gegraptai*]' (11:10); and again in 21:13 and 26:31 prefaces his quotations with *gegraptai*. This perfect tense of the verb *graphō* indicates that these OT texts have lost none of their authority, that they still remain in force: each one 'stands written.'[165] This is confirmed by Jesus' words in 13:14 ('With them indeed is being fulfilled [*anaplēroutai*] the prophecy of Isaiah which says...') and 15:7 ('Isaiah rightly prophesied *concerning you*, saying...'). In the introductions of 15:4 ('For God said...') and 19:5 ('And he [the Creator, 4] said...'), Jesus points to the Scriptures' ultimate source, and to the reason for their abiding authority. He does so again in the repeated formula 'You heard that it was said [*errethē*]' (Matt. 5:21 through 5:43); for this verb implicitly identifies the speaker as God.[166] This becomes explicit in 22:31, 'Have you not read what was spoken [*to rhēthen*] to you by God [*hypo tou Theou*], saying...?'[167] Jesus' question in 22:43 further explains how the Scriptures were revealed and how they came to speak

---

[164]Given the character of these introductions, Gundry understandably classifies several of the accompanying OT references as 'allusive quotations.'

[165]The *gegraptai* shows that the following quotation has 'present and binding authority' (*GGBB*, 576).

[166]*Errethē* (on which see the next note) is a 'divine passive.' Cf. Davies and Allison 1988: 510-11 (who claim that if the implied subject were human, he – e.g., Moses – would be named); Jeremias 1971: 9-14; *GGBB*, 437-38. In 5:21, 33, the formula is 'You have heard that it was said to those of old'; in 5:31, 'It was said.'

[167]*Rhēthen* (an aorist passive participle) and *errethē* (an aorist passive indicative) are forms of *eipon*, which serves as the second aorist of *legō* (see BAGD s.v. *eipon*).

with such authority about Jesus: 'How is it then that David by the Spirit calls him Lord, saying...?'[168]

2. Introductions to quotations from Matthew

All twelve of these contain a form of the aorist passive participle of the verb *legō*. The single instance of the masculine participle *ho rhētheis* ('the one spoken about') appears in 3:3, prefacing the quotation drawn from Mark. All the other formulae – i.e., those introducing quotations peculiar to Matthew – contain the neuter participle *to rhēthen* ('what was spoken'). We recall Jesus' use of the latter participle in 22:31, and of the aorist passive indicative *errethē* in 5:21-43. These prefaces from Matthew, like those from Jesus, identify God as the principal speaker.

All twelve include the phrase 'through the prophet' (*dia tou prophētou*) or the like.[169] While none of Jesus' introductory formulae contain this phrase, he sometimes speaks in equivalent terms: Matthew 13:14 ('is being fulfilled the prophecy of Isaiah which says...'); and 15:7 ('Isaiah rightly prophesied concerning you, saying...').[170] Furthermore, in each of the first two formulae, 1:22 and 2:15, Matthew states that an event occurred 'in order that what was spoken [*to rhēthen*] by the Lord [*hypo Kyriou*] through the prophet [*dia tou prophētou*] might be fulfilled, saying....' The preposition *hypo* followed by the genitive case denotes *source*; the preposition *dia* followed by the genitive denotes *agency*. The phrase 'by the Lord' makes explicit what each instance of 'through the prophet' implies: the Source of the spoken word is God, the inspired prophet is truly but merely his chosen channel. Thus

---

[168]That the phrase *en pneumati*, (Matt. 22:43), means not 'in spirit' (*NRSV* mg.) but 'by the Spirit' (*NRSV* text), is clear from the parallel in Mark 12:36, *en tō pneumati tō hagiō*, 'by the Holy Spirit.' Cf. 2 Peter 1:20-21.

[169]For 'through the prophet,' see Matthew 1:22; 2:15; 13:35; 21:4. For 'through Jeremiah the prophet,' see 2:17; 27:9; for 'through Isaiah the prophet,' 3:3; 4:14; 8:17; 12:17; for 'through the prophets,' 2:23.

[170]See also Matthew 12:40 ('For just as Jonah was...'); 22:43 ('How is it then that David by the Spirit calls him Lord, saying...'); and 24:15 ('what was spoken through Daniel the prophet...,' introducing an allusion to Daniel 9:27, etc.).

here, at the opening of his gospel, Matthew makes it plain
(as Jesus had done before him, 22:31) that these biblical texts
come from God; and it is likely that the evangelist intends
for all subsequent citations from Scripture to be read in this
light.

Conspicuous by its absence from all these formulae is the
verb *gegraptai*, 'it stands written,' which appears in several of
Jesus' introductions. The absence of *graphō*, together with the
presence of *legō* (noted above), suggests that in these prefaces
Matthew wishes to stress that Scripture records God's *spoken*
utterances. Especially does this appear to be the case in 3:3,
where Matthew's *ho rhētheis* ('the one spoken about') replaces
the *gegraptai* of Mark 1:2.

The most notable feature of introductions to the eleven
quotations peculiar to Matthew is that each contains the verb
plēroō, 'fulfill' – which is the more striking because no other
OT quotations in Matthew are prefaced by this term.[171] The
closest approach is Jesus' use of the compound verb *anaplēroō*
(likewise 'fulfill') when introducing the quotation from Isaiah
6 in Matthew 13:14.[172] There can thus be no doubt that one of
Matthew's major interests is the fulfillment of Scriptures in
Jesus, a subject to which we shall soon return (V. below).

3. *Introductions to quotations from other sources*
The first of these five appears on the lips of the priests and
scribes, as a preface to their quotation from Micah: 'for thus
it stands written [*gegraptai*] through the prophet [*dia tou
prophētou*]' (Matt. 2:5). This formulation underscores the above
points about *gegraptai* (Micah's prophecy would stay in force
until fulfilled) and *dia tou prophētou* (the prophet received the
word from God and wrote at his direction). It may be noted
that apart from the twelve quotations contributed by Matthew,

---

[171]The aorist passive subjunctive *plērōthē* appears in Matthew 1:22
(introducing 23a and 23b); 2:15, 23; 4:14; 8:17; 12:17; 13:35; 21:4; the aorist
passive indicative *eplērōthē* in 2:17 and 27:9.

[172]This is the sole instance of *anaplēroō* in Matthew It is noteworthy
that almost all of 13:14-15 is peculiar to Matthew; most of Mark 4:12 and
Luke 8:10 is paralleled in Matthew 13:13.

this (2:6) is the only one prefaced by the phrase 'through the prophet' or the like; and that this one too, like eleven of those twelve, is peculiar to Matthew.

In the second (4:6), Satan himself brazenly employs *gegraptai* for his own malevolent purpose. A third introduces a statement of fact (21:9; 'The crowds... cried out, saying...').

The remaining two come from Pharisees (19:7; 'Why then did Moses command...?) and Sadducees, 22:24 ('Moses said....'). Himself invoking Scripture in these passages, Jesus each time tacitly rebukes his adversaries: 'Have you not read...?' (19:4; 22:31). Moreover, Jesus speaks in the former passage of what *the Creator* did and said (19:4-5); and in the latter of what *was spoken to you by God* (22:31). Nowhere does Jesus, or Matthew, preface a quotation with an explicit reference to Moses – itself testimony that the Law comes ultimately from God.[173]

The Language of the Quotations
Sometimes the wording of a quotation is identical, or very close, to that of the LXX. This is especially true in quotations drawn from Mark or Q, though there are some examples among quotations peculiar to Matthew.[174] In other places a quotation (a) combines Septuagintal and non-Septuagintal features; or (b) is closer to the MT than to the LXX; or (c) differs in some ways from both MT and LXX. These phenomena are especially evident in quotations peculiar to Matthew.[175]

That varied evidence calls for several observations. (i) Matthew's OT quotations indicate that he is capable of employing both Hebrew and Greek, and also of paraphrasing

---

[173]In 5:21-48, Jesus is constantly interacting with the Mosaic Law; but his chosen introductory formula is 'You heard that it was said [by God]' (5:21- 43). But see also Jesus' references to Moses in 8:4; 19:8; and 23:2.

[174]See passages marked * in Appendix C, e.g. (among quotations drawn from Mark or Q), Matthew 3:3; 4:6, 7; 15:4b, 8-9; 19:4; 21:13, 42; 22:39, 44; and (among those peculiar to Matthew) 5:21, 27, 38, 43; 21:16. In some of these instances the LXX closely follows the MT; in others, it differs in some respects from the MT.

[175]Examples of (a): Matthew 4:15-16; 5:33; 12:18-21; 13:35; 21:5. Examples of (b): 2:15, 18; 8:17. Examples of (c): 1:23a; 2:6; 4:10; 11:10; also 26:31, following Mark 14:27.

OT texts in the manner of the Aramaic targums.[176] (ii) In every case Matthew chooses the reading that best serves his theological and pedagogical purposes. (iii) That a gospel written in Greek should quote from the LXX is quite understandable.[177] That these are especially prominent in material shared with Mark and Luke, accords with earlier conclusions about Matthew's sources.[178] (iv) Matthew's quoting from the LXX where it differs from the MT, or from the MT where it differs from the LXX, may indicate that the chosen reading better preserves the original meaning than does the alternative. (v) That departures from both the MT and the LXX are especially evident in quotations peculiar to Matthew does not mean that the evangelist has freely and arbitrarily altered existing readings. In some instances he may be drawing on a Hebrew or a Greek text unknown to us.[179] A more likely explanation – which, however, is compatible with that one – is that Matthew himself, by the Spirit's direction, has sometimes altered the wording of quotations *in light of the coming of Jesus, the One about whom the Scriptures testify and in whom they reach their appointed goal.*[180]

---

[176]The targums were 'interpretive renderings of the Hebrew Bible in Aramaic for use in synagogue worship' (B. D. Chilton, 'Targums,' *DJG*, 800). For the practice's point of departure, see Ezra 4:7. Gundry 1967: 147-50 cites evidence of such paraphrasing in both the 'formal quotations' and the 'allusive quotations' of Matthew. Some of this paraphrasing appears in quotations on Jesus' lips – evidence that Matthew's practice follows that of Jesus.

[177]See France 1989: 172-73.

[178]On Matthew's use of Mark and Q, see pages 71-86.

[179]The LXX was fairly standardized by Matthew's day; but there remained variations, as would arise in the transmission of the NT. Maarten J. J. Menken argues, in a series of essays, that several quotations peculiar to Matthew depended on 'a revised LXX.' See, e.g., Menken 2000: 106-25. Other articles consider the quotations in Matthew 2:15; 4:15-16; 8:17; 12:18-21; 13:35; 21:5 (ibid., 107, n. 3). Gundry offers 'evidence that the LXX and the NT rest on a Hebrew text possibly used by Jesus himself (if he did not use the LXX)' (1994: 305; cf. idem 1967: 14-16).

[180]Notable examples are the quotations of Isaiah 7:14 in Matthew 1:23, and of Zechariah 13:7 in Matthew 26:31. To these may be added the quotation of Micah 5:2 (by chief priests and scribes) in Matthew 2:6, and of Malachi 3:1 (by Jesus) in Matthew 11:10. See the commentary on those passages; also France 1989: 173-74 (speaking of those quotations – peculiar to Matthew – prefaced by the verb 'fulfill').

E. Depending Upon the Holy Trinity

Jesus commissioned his followers to baptize new believers 'into the name of the Father and the Son and the Holy Spirit' (Matt. 28:19b). That 'name' (*onoma*) – a sign of the holy Trinity's *presence* and *power* – likewise accompanied the eleven 'disciples' (*mathētai*), including 'Matthew' (*Matthaios*), who went forth to 'disciple' (*mathēteuō*) the nations.[181] In that presence and by that power the scribe Matthew did his work.

Depending upon the Father

The authority Christ imparted to his followers for fulfilling their mission, and to Matthew for writing this gospel, came from the Father.[182] Matthew was one of those 'infants' to whom the Father chose to reveal truth about his Son (11:25). For knowing Jesus to be 'the Messiah, the Son of the living God,' Matthew was just as dependent as Peter on the Father's teaching (16:16-17).[183] By the Father's design, the One he acclaims as his 'beloved Son' at the baptism and on the mount of transfiguration (3:17; 17:5), stands at the center of Matthew's story (section I.).

By employing the prayer of 6:9-13, the author voices his submission to, and reliance upon, the 'Father in heaven.' His entreaty, 'Your will be done on earth...,' is matched by personal obedience: in writing this book Matthew 'does the will of [Jesus'] Father who is in heaven' (Matt. 7:21). The publishing of Matthew will prove to be a principal means by which God's rule is established, and his name hallowed, among all the nations (24:14). Matthew itself is one of those 'good works' Jesus challenged his disciples to produce: by 'seeing' – by reading and understanding – this work, recipients would

---

[181]See Matthew 28:16, 19a; 10:3. For OT Israel the Name of Yahweh signaled his 'invocable presence' and his 'accessible power' (Pratt 1998: 180, 178). Matthew 28:18 speaks of Jesus' universal authority, 28:20 of his abiding presence.

[182]The verb *edothē* ('was given'; Matthew 28:18) is an instance of the 'divine passive.' On another occasion the risen Christ says to the remaining members of the twelve (and perhaps to other disciples as well): 'As the Father has sent me, so I am sending you' (John 20:21; cf. v. 24; 21:1-2).

[183]Likewise, in John 6, the Father draws pupils into his presence to teach them about his Son (6:44-45), then presents them to the Son (6:37).

honor not the author but the heavenly Father (5:16). Matthew here 'confesses [Jesus] before men,' which assures that the Son will honor him before the Father (10:32).

Depending upon the Son

As noted, it was Jesus who filled up the 'treasury' from which Matthew the scribe would draw out 'things new and old' (13:52). In one way or another, the whole of Matthew relies upon Jesus.[184] Not only is the book filled with his works and words: Immanuel attends the apostle as he writes, and invests the entire enterprise with his stupendous authority (28:18-20).

The broad design of Matthew is ultimately determined, not by the structure of Mark but by the actual course of Jesus' life. Had these events – from Jesus' birth and infancy to his death and resurrection – not occurred in history, what authority would there be in the Matthean record, and how could its very existence be explained? Matthew reports that Jesus 'went about Galilee, teaching in their synagogues, preaching the gospel of the kingdom and healing every disease and every sickness among the people' (4:23, cf. 9:35). Had Jesus not actually imparted such teachings and accomplished such miracles, there would be no adequate basis for Matthew's account.

All that Matthew teaches about God's dawning rule, and its implications for human belief and behavior, he learned from Jesus. It was Jesus who taught him at what cost salvation from sins would be secured.[185] If Matthew knew the Son because of revelations from the Father, he was likewise dependent on the Son for knowing the Father (11:27), as is clear from countless texts in Matthew, including those cited in the previous section. Similarly, Jesus provided access to events beyond Matthew's and the other disciples' personal experience, such as the angel's announcement to Joseph, the visit of the magi, the baptism at the Jordan and the testings in the wilderness.

---

[184]Cf. Figure 1 (p.65). It is Jesus, the divine Messiah, 'who alone can account for the origin of the gospel tradition and its final inscripturation in the Gospels,' including Matthew (Stonehouse 1964: 176, with 192).

[185]See Matthew 16:21; 17:22-23; 20:18; 20:28; 26:28, with 1:21.

Matthew was indebted to Jesus for his method as well. Jesus' speech helps to explain Matthew's manifest facility in Hebrew, Aramaic and Greek.[186] In the same regard, Matthew's use of the OT is deeply indebted to that of Jesus.[187] The alternating of discourse and narrative reflected Jesus' own practice (4:23-25, anticipating chs. 5–7 and 8–9). The scribe's professional past and literary proclivities help to explain his fondness for design, but the chief inspiration lies in Jesus' way of teaching. It was he who first pronounced beatitudes before expounding law, and joined together the three pillars of Jewish piety; and he who first fashioned a manifold charge to missionaries, taught a series of parables about the kingdom, drew together instructions about life in community, pronounced woes upon scribes and Pharisees, and combined prophecies about the near and distant future.[188] The same can be said for Matthew's use of numbers: most of the evidence for Matthew's love of triads, for example, comes from Jesus' own teaching and practice.[189]

---

[186]M. O. Wise judges 'that Jesus certainly spoke a dialect of Aramaic... that Jesus probably knew both the H[igh] and one or more L[ow] forms of Hebrew, and that he had at least a minimal competence in Greek' ('Languages of Palestine,' *DJG*, 442, 443).

[187]As noted, thirty-six of the fifty-three quotations in Matthew appear on Jesus' lips. For Jesus' influence on the evangelists' use of the OT, see Luke 24:27, 44-48; Dodd 1952: 109-110; France 1971: 223-26. Dodd writes: 'To account for the beginning of this most original and fruitful process of rethinking the Old Testament we found need to postulate a creative mind. The Gospels offer us one. Are we compelled to reject the offer?' (p. 110). France responds 'that we not only can but must accept the offer. The source of the distinctive Christian use of the Old Testament was not the creative thinking of the primitive community, but that of its founder' (p. 226).

[188]See Matthew 5:3-48; 6:1-18; 10:5-42; 13:3-50; 18:1-35; 23:13-36; 24:4-51. Supporting the view that such arrangements go back to Jesus are (i) the presence in Mark of such clusters of teachings, notably the parables in chapter 4 and the discourse about the future in chapter 13; and (ii) the agreement of Luke 6:20-49 with the order of Matthew 5:2–7:27. I do not wish to minimize Matthew's personal contribution to the gathering of teachings into discourses (our discussion of 'Q' suggested that it was considerable), only to stress that the primary impetus for his doing so came from Jesus. See further the commentary on the respective discourses, especially the Sermon on the Mount.

[189]See pages 57-59.

Depending upon the Holy Spirit

The risen Jesus promised that the Holy Spirit who had equipped him for service would likewise endow his apostles. Exercising the same authority by which he commissions them, Jesus pours out the Spirit's power upon them. Matthew becomes an evangelist the same way Jesus did – through anointing by the Spirit of God.[190] The Spirit, no less than the Father, is responsible for the centrality of Jesus in Matthew. The Spirit enables Matthew the scribe to magnify Jesus, to recall the events of his life, to recount his teachings clearly and accurately, and to interpret him correctly and effectively for his readers.[191] The cruciality of the Spirit's work for producing the Gospel according to Matthew cannot be overestimated.[192]

We have now considered Matthew's scribal endeavors (III.): the design of his work (A.), his approach to the task (B.), his practice of drawing out 'things new and old' from his treasury (C. and D.), and the direct involvement of all members of the Godhead in the process (E.). Before that we spoke of the author as an apostle (II.). 'Apostle' expresses the writer's authority, and 'scribe' his mode of expression. But another term better expresses the character of his message.

---

[190]See Matthew 3:11, 16; 10:20; 12:18, 28; 28:18-20; Luke 4:16-21; 24:45-49; John 7:37-39; 20:21-22; Acts 1:8; 2:33. The history of Jesus 'is intelligible... only as we grasp the fact that the divine Messiah, who was endowed with the Spirit of God in a unique fashion, himself qualified his spokesmen and representatives with an enduement of the Spirit from on high that they might bear faithful witness to him' (Stonehouse 1964: 192).

[191]See John 14:26; 15:26-27; 16:13. Matthew 10:20 – 'For you are not the ones who speak; on the contrary, it is the Spirit of your Father who speaks in you' – well applies to Matthew, who wrote in face of such hostility as is described in 10:16-23.

[192]Donald Guthrie speaks of 'the impossibility of explaining the origins of the gospels apart from the activity of the Holy Spirit' (1990: 1041). He affirms further that the Spirit 'controlled the traditions' which Matthew and the other evangelists employed; and that 'the gospel material was found to be ideally suited to the needs of the communities because of the sovereign direction of the Spirit in the selection of the material' (1041, 1043). On the work of Christ and the Spirit in producing the gospels, see Ellis 1991: 27-28.

IV.
The Evangelist

The NT never calls Matthew or any other apostle an 'evangelist' (*euangelistēs*).[1] Yet the name is rightly used of him, because declaring good news stands at the heart of his apostolic and scribal calling. He writes not merely from a sense of duty: given the character of what he has seen and heard, he cannot keep the news to himself (cf. Acts 4:20). The primary focus of Matthew's evangel has been in view from the start of section I. Some of its major themes will be explored in sections V. and VI. For now our main interests are linguistic, literary and aesthetic.

A. The Fourfold Gospel

As we saw when discussing the superscription for Matthew (II. A.), it is proper to speak not of 'the four gospels' but of *the gospel* according to Matthew, Mark, Luke and John respectively. There is only one gospel – the good news about Jesus the Messiah – a reality not to be obscured even when for convenience we speak of 'the gospels' or 'the gospel of Matthew.'

Mark, to whose writing Matthew is indebted, identifies his whole book as gospel (1:1, *euangelion*), a record that begins with the activity of the Messianic herald and the appearance of Messiah himself, both in fulfillment of OT prophecy (Matt. 1:2-15). As we have seen, the Gospel according to Mark is greatly indebted to Peter. Yet the chief inspiration for Mark's identifying his book as *euangelion* is not the apostolic preaching but Jesus' own use of this language.[2]

---

[1]The term appears three times in the NT. In Ephesians 4:11, 'evangelists' are expressly distinguished from 'apostles' and others. Acts 21:8 speaks of 'Philip the evangelist,' in part to distinguish him from Philip the apostle. Paul urges Timothy to 'do the work of an evangelist' (2 Tim. 4:5), but the NT never calls Timothy an apostle.

[2]*Euangelion* appears on Jesus' lips in Mark 1:15; 8:35; 10:29; 13:10; and 14:9 (16:15 is textually doubtful). Given Mark's association with Paul (Acts

Matthew does not expressly call his book a *euangelion*, but the term captures his intention.[3] Does he not record 'the gospel [*euangelion*] of the kingdom' that Jesus proclaimed throughout Galilee (Matt. 4:23; 9:35)? 'The poor are being evangelized [*euangelizontai*]' (11:5): does not Matthew tell us, as early as 5:3, what Jesus was saying to them? Moreover, by writing this book in obedience to Jesus' commission (28:18-20), Matthew helps to fulfill Jesus' prophecy that 'this gospel [*euangelion*] of the kingdom [i.e., the very gospel Jesus proclaimed] will be preached in the whole of the inhabited world as a witness to all the nations' (24:14).[4]

While the Gospel according to Luke never uses the noun *euangelion*, the verb *euangelizomai* appears here ten times (as compared to one in Matthew and none in Mark) – to denote Gabriel's message to Zechariah, the angel's announcement to the shepherds, the preaching of John the Baptist and especially the preaching of Jesus, together with his disciples.[5] It is Luke's purpose, following the example of these disciples and other 'servants of the word,' to impart this very story to Theophilus and others (9:6; 1:1-4). The good news of the kingdom orally

---

13:5, 13; 15:37-39; Col. 4:10; Philem. 24; 2 Tim. 4:11), Paul's fondness for *euangelion* (it appears sixty times in his letters) helps to explain Mark's. Moreover, Mark's accent on Jesus' death (especially from 8:31 onwards) reflects the influence of Paul, in whose *euangelion* the cross is central (cf. 1 Cor. 1:18-2:5; Rom. 1:16-17; 3:21-26; Martin 1973: 117-20). Mark also supplements Paul. Paul's letters focus on Jesus' birth and especially on his death and resurrection, and disclose little about his earthly career (note too how Paul's sermon in Acts 13:23-31 moves directly from Jesus' birth and John's preaching to Jesus' death and resurrection); Mark provides an extensive account of Jesus' public ministry in Galilee and Judea. On Mark as a supplement to Paul, see Martin, ibid., 156-62.

[3]Matthew 1:1a (*Biblos geneseōs*) does not apply to Matthew as a whole (see comments on that verse). Even if it did, *biblos* would tell us nothing about the book's *character*.

[4]Cf. Matthew 26:13a: 'wherever this gospel is preached in the whole world....' The demonstrative pronoun 'this' (*touto*) here and in 24:14 draws attention to the earlier instances of *euangelion* in 4:23 and 9:35, i.e., to Jesus' own preaching. Matthew helps to fulfill the prophecy of 26:13 (cf. 26:6-12) no less than that of 24:14.

[5]Luke 1:19; 2:10; 3:18; 4:18, 43; 7:22; 8:1; 9:6; 16:16; 20:1.

announced by John the Baptist and Jesus is now proclaimed
in writing by Luke.[6]

Euangelion and *euangelizomai* never occur in the Fourth
Gospel. Yet the reality is there, and the ancient superscription
'Gospel according to John' is as fitting as the other three.[7]
Conversely, John's statement of purpose (20:30-31) well applies
to the Synoptics.

All the evangelists want their readers to understand the
verities of which they speak, to embrace their gospel, and to
share their experience of Christ and his salvation. It is therefore
impossible for them to write in a literary or cultural vacuum;
which brings us to the next subject.

B. The Gospel Genre

David Aune defines a genre as 'a group of texts that exhibit
a coherent and recurring configuration of literary features
involving a form (including structure and style), content,
and function.'[8] So, to what genre, or category, of literature
do Matthew and the other gospels belong? The question has
been much debated in recent years.[9] A full inquiry would
include the Gospel according to John. But in keeping with
section III., and to avoid too broad a discussion, we will
focus on the Synoptic Gospels. Recalling what has already
come to light about the form, content and function of these
documents, we compare them to similar writings in the
ancient world.

---

[6]See Luke 16:16, where 'since then' (*apo tote*) embraces the ministry
of John the Baptist. Luke's proclamation continues into the Book of Acts,
where *euangelizomai* denotes preaching about both Jesus and the kingdom
of God (e.g., 5:42; 8:4, 12; 10:34-43).

[7]Answering to the Synoptists' gospel -terminology is John's usage of
martyria ('witness') and *martyreō* ('bear witness'). The noun occurs in John
fourteen times (compared to four in the Synoptics) and the verb thirty-three
times (compared to two in the Synoptics).

[8]Aune 1987: 13. Talbert 1977: 6, 133-35, proposes 'structure, function and
attitude' as the three criteria for determining genre. But *content* is critical,
and *function* and *attitude* may be combined; so Aune's triad is preferable.

[9]See Guelich 1991: 175-94; L. W. Hurtado, 'Gospel (Genre),' *DJG*, 276-82;
France 1989: 123-27.

The Synoptic Gospels and Other Ancient Literature
Some have contended that the gospels belong to the genre of Graeco-Roman biography. It is pointed out that ancient concepts of biography differed markedly from those of the modern period; that the gospels' portrayals of Jesus, with respect to form, content (both what is accentuated and what is omitted), and function, have counterparts in Graeco-Roman biography; and that differences among the Synoptics, and between the Synoptics and other ancient biographies, witness to the flexibility and diversity characteristic of the genre as a whole.[10]

Others have stressed the relationship between the gospels and the OT. It is pointed out that the story of Jesus brings the story of Israel to its great climax, and that here many an OT promise is fulfilled, many a question answered, and many a tension resolved.[11] Correspondingly, it is maintained that Israel's literature has helped to determine the gospel genre – its form (teachings presented within a narrative framework), its content (the authoritative words and mighty works of Yahweh's chosen representative) and its function (good news from God for his covenant people). Willard M. Swartley concludes that a 'narrative-compositional study of each Synoptic Gospel [reveals] a significant sequential use of the exodus, conquest, temple, and kingship traditions within the structure and emphases of the Gospels' respective sections....'[12]

---

[10]See especially Aune 1987: 17-76; and Burridge 1992. The latter concludes 'from an analysis of many generic features that both the four canonical gospels and Graeco-Roman [bios] exhibit a clear family resemblance. The genre of [bios] is flexible and diverse, with variation in the pattern of features from one [bios] to another. The gospels also diverge from the pattern in some aspects, but not to any greater degree than other [bioi]; in other words, they have at least as much in common with Graeco-Roman [bioi] as the [bioi] have with each other. Therefore, the gospels must belong to the genre of [bios]' (p. 258).

[11]See Wright 1992: 373-403, especially 396-403.

[12]Swartley 1994: 254; see 254-59. Kline 1975: 172-203 finds a model for Mark in the Book of Exodus.

A New Literary Genre

While acknowledging the value of both those viewpoints, and of literary criticism in general, for interpreting the Synoptics, we must stress that the main explanation for them is not literary but historical and theological. The writers' prime motivation was to record the actual story of Jesus as unfolded in history and as proclaimed by the apostles, and to bring that good news of salvation to bear upon the lives of their readers both within and beyond the Christian community. Matthew 'was a historian-biographer and interpreter and not just a storyteller.... [His] basic genre suggests historical *intention*.'[13] Matthew and the other evangelists 'were by no means simply patterning their narratives after genres of contemporary literature.... [T]he major reason biography-like accounts of Jesus appeared is that the early Christian message from the first was focused on Jesus as the personal vehicle of revelation and redemption.... The impetus, basic contents and general narrative complexion of the Gospels reflect primarily the Jesus-centered proclamation of early Christianity.'[14] This helps to explain why the gospels do not expressly identify their authors, 'contrary to the frequent literary practice of the Greco-Roman era.'[15]

It is indeed true that these records, Luke especially, share features in common with Graeco-Roman biography. This is not in the least surprising. Some similarities are to be expected between works of the same period and language whose common purpose is to celebrate the life and achievement of a distinguished individual. Moreover, these literary affinities are one indication that the gospels were not written in a literary vacuum, and that they were written for the precise purpose of communicating their message effectively to the inhabitants of the Graeco-Roman world of the first century.

---

[13]Keener 1999: 23, 24. While Matthew unfolds as a drama (cf. the summary of 'the plot,' section I.), it is not 'historical drama' in the sense of Shakespeare's *Macbeth*; rather, it is 'dramatic history' (R.M. Frye's term, quoted by Combrink 1983: 65).

[14]Hurtado, *DJG*, 278-79.

[15]Ibid., 279. Cf. Guelich 1991: 207; Aune 1987: 18, 29. The superscriptions were added later, as we saw in II. A.

Yet these documents have no exact literary precedent in the Graeco-Roman world.[16]

There are the closest connections between the gospels and the OT – as expressed in the strongest terms throughout Matthew. With the coming of Jesus the story of Israel reaches its appointed goal.[17] OT counterparts may be found for the form and content of many texts within these writings. Yet nowhere is the genre of a gospel *as a whole* anticipated in the literature of the OT. 'None of the forms of canonical literature which appear in the Old Testament offers an exact parallel to the New Testament Gospels. In spite of the great variety with which the Hebrew canon shaped its material...there is nothing which can be considered as a direct analogy.'[18]

The Synoptic Gospels have literary antecedents and arise in a literary context. Nevertheless, we meet here a phenomenon that has no exact literary precedent, that has (so to speak) burst the seams of antecedent genres. Under the impact of Christ, Mark and his successors offer the church and the world a new literary genre, the *euangelion*.[19] One writer calls a gospel a 'theological biography.'[20] I would rather say 'biographical *evangel*' as compared to the epistolary evangel of Paul or the apocalyptic evangel of Revelation.

---

[16]See Guelich 1991: 173-208; Hurtado, *DJG*, 276-82. The later apocryphal gospels 'attempt to satisfy "biographical" curiosity about Jesus' (Stanton 1989: 30).

[17]Mark 1:14; Luke 4:18-21; Matt 11:12-13. Cf. Galatians 4:4; 1 Corinthians 10:11; Hebrews 1:1-2.

[18]Childs 1984: 154-55.

[19]'The Gospels are a literary genre whose form and content consist of, to use Mark's words, the "gospel of Jesus Messiah, Son of God"' (Guelich 1991: 208). A comparison of Matthew with other 'biographical' writing of his day will show, not that the author works in a literary world of his own, but 'that he and the other gospel writers have produced something which has in significant ways broken new ground in terms of literary genre' (France 1989: 127).

[20]Blomberg 1991: 511.

C. The Synoptic Gospels: Portraits of Jesus

These documents offer us, not photographs or abstract paintings, but *portraits* of Jesus.[21] By the Spirit's design, Jesus
sits for each portrait. Each portrays the real Jesus; each one
faithfully and accurately depicts aspects of his manifold
splendor. At the same time, and again in accord with God's
purpose, the paintings are produced by three artists, not just
one.[22] Nor are the three, so to speak, working in the same
studio on the same day and viewing Jesus from the same
position.

The Artists and Their Subject

A portrait is both *like* and *unlike* its subject: a good portrait
captures, and well represents, the character of the person;
yet a portrait by its very nature is distinct from the one being
depicted. Roger Lundin's words about the biographer's task
may be applied to the gospels: "'An interpretation as such
is different from and yet also the same as what it interprets.
Unless it is both, it is not an interpretation." If an interpretation is not in some sense the same as what it interprets, then it
is not an interpretation but an entirely new text.... Yet, at the
same time, if an interpretation is not in some sense different
from its object, then it "is not an interpretation of the text
but a copy of it."... Attention without creative understanding
makes for a lifeless recitation of facts; creative understanding
without attention to facts produces mere fantasy.'[23]

The Synoptists do not strive to be original. '"Originality"
in the New Testament is quite plainly the prerogative of God
alone.'[24] Nor do they seek fame for the brilliance of their prose:
as noted, their singular purpose is not literary but historical
and theological. Or, more precisely, it is *christological*: to tell
the story of Jesus, to impart to others what they have learned

---

[21]Guelich 1981: 117-25.

[22]As when George Washington, in 1795 and 1796, sat for three portraits
by Gilbert Stuart.

[23]In *Books & Culture* 2 (July/Aug 1996): 12, including quotations from Joel
Weinsheimer.

[24]Lewis 1967: 6.

about him. Put another way, each evangelist seeks, not to bring beauty or wisdom into existence but 'to embody in terms of his own art some reflection of eternal Beauty and Wisdom.'[25] These writers are therefore not mere conduits of revelation; on the contrary, the truth they have received renews their minds and activates all their literary and rhetorical powers.[26] To persuade readers, they employ these powers to the full.[27] As artists who value something – Someone – more than themselves and their work; who are not self-consciously striving to produce the ancient equivalent of 'best sellers'; and who want above all to depict the glory and grace of Christ, they produce documents of artistic merit. Donald Hagner with good reason calls Matthew 'a masterpiece.'[28] What C. S. Lewis says about Christian writing in general applies to the gospels: 'When Christian work is done on a serious subject there is no gravity and no sublimity it cannot attain. But they will belong to the theme.... [I]t is not hard to argue that all the greatest poems have been made by men who valued something else much more than poetry.... The real frivolity, the solemn vacuity, is all with those who

---

[25]Ibid., 7. In Lewis 1946: 73, an inhabitant of heaven addresses a ghost who had been an artist on earth: 'When you painted on earth – at least in your earlier days – it was because you caught glimpses of Heaven in the earthly landscape. The success of your painting was that it enabled others to see the glimpses too.' Jesus accounts for the gospels' *unity*, and also for their *multiplicity* (which the richness of his work requires): see Hengel 2000: 164-68.

[26]The Synoptists, having meditated on the truth about Jesus, are like fruit-bearing trees (Ps. 1:2-3). Kidner 1973: 48 writes that 'the tree is no mere channel, piping the water unchanged from one place to another, but a living organism which absorbs it, to produce in due course something new and delightful, proper to its kind and to its time.'

[27]The worldview underlying these documents 'is profoundly true for the authors. So true that the Gospels are attempts to lead readers to affirm or reaffirm belief in such a world. The Gospels may then be called narrative rhetoric, and a literary approach will give attention to the means utilized... to appeal to the reader' (E. V. McKnight, 'Literary Criticism,' *DJG*, 480).

[28]Hagner 1993: xi. Wilder 1964: 38, says that 'none of our four evangelists writes as a *self-conscious* literary craftsman' (italics added). Matthew is a 'literary craftsman' (cf. III. A.). But it is his preoccupation with Christ, not with his craft, that explains his book's masterful design.

make literature a self-existent thing to be valued for its own sake.'[29]

Diversity in Unity

The joining of the Synoptic Gospels together in the NT canon testifies both to the *unity* of their genre and to the recognition of *diversity* within the genre. On the one hand the church brought the Synoptics and John together, not as 'the four gospels' but as 'the fourfold gospel.' In the process Luke was separated from Acts, evidence that Luke was thought to have a closer affinity to the other Synoptics than to its companion volume.[30] On the other hand, the church refrained from fusing the Synoptics and John into one book. A Syrian Christian named Tatian did compose such a document soon after A.D. 150 – the *Diatessaron* ('harmony of four') – which proved to be very popular among Syriac-speaking Christians, but whose use the church eventually forbade.[31] The value of each writer's distinctive witness to Jesus was recognized. 'From a canonical perspective it is fully legitimate and indeed mandatory that the integrity of each single Gospel be maintained. The canonical ordering neither fused the Gospels nor subordinated one to another.'[32]

As all three Synoptists are depicting the same figure, and serving the same word, their writings display many common features – as would portraits of Winston Churchill by three different painters. Each is written in the common (*koinē*) Greek of the time.[33] Each is indebted to Jesus' own artistry as a teacher.[34] Within the broad literary framework common to all, all three arrange material sometimes topically, sometimes

---

[29]Lewis 1967: 10.

[30]On the forming and canonizing of the fourfold gospel, see F. F. Bruce, *DJG*, 94-100; Childs 1984: 144-56. The distinctive literary features of Luke–Acts are impressive; cf. Marshall 1993: 179-80. But attention to genre justified placing Luke with the other gospels and separating it from Acts (see Burridge 1992: 243-47).

[31]Cf. G. L. Carey, 'Tatian,' *DJG*, 952; and R. E. Nixon, 'Diatessaron,' *DJG*, 296-97 (in face of its popularity, 'steps had to be taken in the fifth century to abolish its use,' 297).

[32]Childs 1984: 153. Cf. Kingsbury 1979: 363-75.

[33]On the Greek of the NT, see Bruce 1963a: 58-73.

chronologically. Their portrayals of Jesus complement each other; each is reminiscent of the other two. Many an episode from Jesus' life is recorded in all three books, often in similar or identical language.[35]

But while all the Synoptists employ the common Greek, their styles are distinctive. Each contains material absent from the other two. No two of them arrange their material (whether topically or chronologically) in exactly the same way. In parallel reports of the same episode, differences in wording and emphasis are often evident.[36]

As three different men are at work, each addressing his own set of readers and pastoral needs, each writing displays an artistic grace and a theological potency all its own. The practice of *redaction criticism* seeks to understand a gospel's particular theology and setting by studying the way the author has employed his received traditions and fashioned them into a unified whole.[37] Each writing's distinctive qualities are obscured if we join the three together, as would happen if we combined paintings of Jesus by Raphael, Rembrandt and El Greco.[38] Just as we may profitably compare such paintings to each other, so we will frequently have occasion to compare Matthew to Mark and Luke. But in this, as in the commentary as a whole, the main object is a deepened appreciation for Matthew's magnificent portrait of Jesus the Messiah.

---

[34]On Jesus' pedagogical powers, including his 'total mastery of poetic forms,' see Ryken 1974: 291-314. See also R. Reisner, 'Teacher,' *DJG*, 807-11; and pages 101-2 above, on Matthew's indebtedness to Jesus.

[35]Cf. pages 69-77, on the Synoptic Gospels and on Matthew's use of Mark.

[36]Evidence presented under III. C. supports every sentence of this paragraph. For each Synoptist's Greek style, see *GNTG* 4: 11-63.

[37]See G. R. Osborne, 'Redaction Criticism,' *DJG*, 662-69. For a survey of earlier such studies, see Rohde 1968; works on Matthew are considered on pages 46-112.

[38]Burridge, renewing a practice in the early church, uses the symbols of Ezekiel 1:5-10 and Revelation 4:7 – lion, face of a man, ox and flying eagle – to characterize Mark, Matthew, Luke and John respectively. He hopes hereby 'to change our perceptions away from the unthinking harmonized amalgam to the four gospel portraits of the one Jesus' (1994: 32). The aforementioned *Diatessaron* is not nearly so exciting to read as any one of the four gospels.

Artistic Selectivity

No Synoptist offers an exhaustive account of Jesus' life; each is highly selective in what he records. Moreover, upon examining all three books (together with John), we discover that much about Jesus remains undisclosed. We are not certain in what year he was born, or exactly at what age he died, although Luke relates that he was about thirty when his ministry began (Luke 3:23). Most of those thirty or so years are hidden from view. Almost all the attention is devoted to his public ministry and to the last week of his life. We are told that Jesus grew in wisdom, but his mental state is not explored. His bodily growth is noted, but his physical appearance is not described. We learn that he grew in favor with God and other people, but the writers do not reflect upon his relational skills. Jesus' emotions are not subjected to close scrutiny: only rarely are we expressly told that he loved another person, or that he was angry or sad or anxious, though the presence of these qualities is often strikingly clear from the events recorded.[39]

The evangelists are *deliberately* selective. Their overriding purpose is not negative but positive – not to omit but to proclaim certain evidence about Jesus, and to do so clearly and pointedly. Each one knows what he is doing: from start to finish the work proceeds in accord with the writer's evangelical purpose and under his direction.[40]

---

[39]Jesus clearly showed his indignation in driving the money changers from the temple (Matthew 21:12-17 and pars.); but no Synoptist expressly says he was angry. Never are we told that Jesus smiled or laughed; but what reader of the parables could doubt that Jesus possessed wit and humor? Jesus' manifold growth is described in Luke 2:52 (if *hēlikia* here denotes advance in age, then his physical growth is stated indirectly). Of the Synoptists, Mark alone records that Jesus 'loved' the rich young man (10:21). Nowhere in Matthew or Luke is Jesus expressly said to love another person; but who could doubt that the love expressed by the woman in Matthew 26:6-13 or the woman in Luke 7:36-40 (where *agapaō* occurs three times) is a response to Jesus' love for her? (In John, by contrast, Jesus is expressly said to love John, Lazarus and Peter.) Mark 3:5 (but neither parallel) records Jesus' anger and grief over his accusers. Luke 19:41 (but neither parallel) states that Jesus wept over Jerusalem; Mark 14:33-34 and Matthew 26:37-38, that he suffered anguish in Gethsemane (Luke 22:44, peculiar to Luke, expressly speaks of his *agōnia*).

Form and Substance

With respect to the actual content – the substance, the matter – of Jesus' words and works, the Synoptists refrain from artistic creativity. But when casting that substance into a particular form, each writer employs his artistic and literary skills to the full – as is evident from the aforementioned linguistic and structural differences among the Synoptic Gospels.

Consider Matthew in particular. As we have seen, his task as a commissioned apostle and disciplined scribe is faithfully and correctly to transmit the tradition about Jesus. But as we have also seen, Matthew is highly resourceful when giving shape to that substance. His chosen structure is unlike that of any other gospel. In fashioning his great discourses, he draws together sayings of Jesus scattered over several passages in Luke. Such shaping extends, furthermore, to the terms Matthew chooses for translating an utterance of Jesus or describing an event, particularly when his terms differ from those of the other Synoptists. Yet in all those cases the substance is fashioned without being falsified. Giving the matter a certain form does not alter its nature.[41] The *ipsissima vox* of Jesus – his 'very voice' – is to be heard even in places where his *ipsissima verba* – his 'very words' – cannot be ascertained.[42] Moreover, the same Spirit who preserves the substance prompts Matthew and the other evangelists to give it a certain shape.

---

[40]For a kindred selectivity joined to an evangelical purpose, see John 20:30-31; 21:25. From a literary perspective, 'the narrators of the Gospels are third person, omniscient and intrusive' (McKnight, *DJG*, 480) – like the director of a film.

[41]Notes Keener (1999: 31-32): 'Had Matthew wished to create teaching material for Jesus (apart from minor transitions), the importance of his work's literary unity would have provided him plenty of incentive to do so. But the evidence of Matthew's text suggests not merely his freedom to rearrange sayings but also his conservatism in reporting rather than inventing them.'

[42]I say 'cannot be ascertained' chiefly for two reasons: (i) Utterances of Jesus in Aramaic cease in a sense to be his 'very words' when Matthew translates them into Greek – just as we do not retain Matthew's 'very words' when translating from Greek into English. (ii) In places where the Synoptists report the same episode but phrase Jesus' utterances differently,

D. The Synoptic Gospels: Holy Scripture

Matthew's outlook is theocentric. He believes that God exists, and that he is the source and revealer of truth. If there were no God, and if truth were therefore relative, a writer's disclosure of his own existential reality, and of his psychic and emotional state, would be no more or less valid, or meaningful, than a writing that sought to speak about objective matters. But if Christian theism is true, then a writer's highest calling is to become a window that directs attention not to itself but to the objective and transcendent realities that lie on the landscape beyond.[43]

The meaning of the Synoptics is discovered neither within the story exclusively (as in 'narrative theology') nor apart from the story (as though the gospel were confined to the story's interpretation), but rather in the purpose of God as unfolded within the story, and (conversely) within the story as illuminated by the divine Word.[44]

The Synoptists recount Jesus' personal history – from his birth (Matthew and Luke) or his baptism (Mark) to his crucifixion and resurrection. The particular historical setting

---

it is not always easy to determine precisely what words Jesus used. For example, according to Mark 10:18, Jesus asks the rich man 'Why do you call me good?' whereas, according to Matthew 19:17, he asks 'Why do you ask me about what is good?' Do we choose between these formulations, or combine them? Answers to such questions are reserved for the commentary. The present point is that Matthew's Greek (i. above) is unfailingly faithful to Jesus' 'very voice'; and that both formulations cited under ii. are essential for determining Jesus' 'very voice' during that conversation. For kindred comments concerning Jesus' *ipsissima vox* and *ipsissima verba*, see Carson 1984: 110, 422-23.

[43]Cf. Lewis and Tillyard 1939: 1-30. Randel Helms, *Gospel Fictions* (Amherst, NY: Prometheus, 1988), by maintaining that 'the Gospels are self-reflexive,' and that 'they are not about Jesus so much as they are about the writers' attitudes concerning Jesus' (from the jacket), exemplifies the 'personal heresy.' In a review of A. K. M. Adam's book *What Is Postmodern Biblical Criticism?* (Minneapolis: Fortress, 1995), D. A. Carson observes that 'Adam offers no word on how postmodern Biblical criticism might be affected if there is a sovereign/transcendent and omniscient God out there who...chooses to disclose himself to his finite image-bearers in *their* language...[or on] how postmodern criticism might be forced to change if the Bible's metanarrative [i.e., the story that unites the whole] is true' (*JETS* 40 [March 1997]: 147).

is identified by references genealogical (Matt. 1 and Luke 3), geographical (Jerusalem, Judea and Galilee), political (the Herods, Caesar and Pilate), religious (Pharisees, Sadducees and Caiaphas the high priest) and architectural (the temple as a place for praying, paying taxes and offering sacrifice).

Even though all these things are absolutely true, those data alone do not account for the character of these documents. Each Synoptist becomes an evangelist precisely by joining Jesus' redemptive significance to his personal history. Mark, depending upon Peter, accurately reports Jesus' works and words; as these words make plain, the works are not bare data but full of theological import.[45] Moreover, focusing as he does on the period from John's ministry to Jesus' resurrection, Mark does not allow his account to be flooded with post-resurrection theology.[46] Matthew, already accustomed to keeping careful records, is if anything more scrupulous after his conversion. For he is now under orders from Christ the King; and it is for a theological reason – namely, propagating 'the gospel of the kingdom' – that the scribe determines to offer a trustworthy account of what Jesus actually said and did.[47] Luke's carefully formulated prologue (1:1-4) voices his intent to be a reliable historian, to the end that readers may grasp more firmly his message of salvation.[48]

Each Synoptist's theological interpretation of Jesus is integral to the story, and cannot be removed without violating the story's function and spoiling the story itself.

---

[44]Bloesch 1994: 212-13 puts the matter in a slightly different way.

[45]See, e.g., how Jesus explains his exorcisms in Mark 3:23-29; and his death in 10:45.

[46]Chamblin 1997: 31-40, especially 37-39, on Mark as an historian and artist of integrity.

[47]France states 'that Matthew, for good theological reasons, took the historical dimension of his task seriously, that he was interested in recording for his church the events of the life and teaching of Jesus in which he saw fulfilment as having come. To have a theology of "fulfilment in Jesus" is not incompatible with, but indeed rather demands, the careful recording of history' (1989: 201-2; see further 201-5).

[48]Stein (1992: 67) comments: 'For Luke the main purpose of the prologue [1:1-4] was to establish his credibility as a historian...[but he also] stated [1:4] that his goal in writing was to help his readers come to a cer-

In the Synoptic Gospels, story and significance are fused; history and theology are inextricably bound together.[49] 'In the gospel there is no antithesis or disjunction between history and revelation.... The gospel witness concerning the divine Messiah who came to effect the redemption of his people... is a revelation in history and a history that is truly revelatory.'[50] Robbed of the gospel of redemption, the history would cease to be gospel. If the Jesus of Classical Liberalism or of the 'Jesus Seminar' were the real Jesus, it is highly doubtful whether Matthew and the others would have written these books – or at any rate identified their contents as *euangelion*.[51] To strip away the revelatory in an attempt to recover the purely historical, would be like peeling an onion: nothing would be left in the end.[52] Conversely, without the history of Jesus the message of salvation has no basis in reality and therefore no authority.[53] In reaction against certain nineteenth-century 'lives of Jesus,' Rudolf Bultmann and other form critics rightly emphasized the evangelical, or kerygmatic, character of the

---

tainty of the truthfulness of the gospel teachings the readers had been taught.' Writes Marshall (1978a: 35): 'Of all the Evangelists he is the most conscious of writing as an historian, yet throughout his work the history is the vehicle of theological interpretation in which the significance of Jesus is expressed.'

[49]Stanton 1989: 5-6, 29.

[50]Stonehouse 1964: 191.

[51]On Liberalism, see Machen 1946, especially chapter 5 ('Christ') and chapter 6 ('Salvation'). On the Jesus Seminar, see Johnson 1996; Wilkins and Moreland 1995; and Witherington 1995: 42-57 ('this seminar Jesus will not preach, did not come to save and likely will not last,' 57).

[52]Hoskyns and Davey 1958 concluded that no strand of gospel tradition reveals a purely historical Jesus devoid of redemptive significance. Writes Allan Bloom, *The Closing of the American Mind* (New York: Simon & Schuster, 1987), 374-75: 'A teacher who treated the Bible naively, taking it at its word, or Word, would be accused of scientific incompetence and lack of sophistication. Moreover, he might rock the boat and start the religious wars all over again, as well as a quarrel within the university between reason and revelation, which would upset comfortable arrangements and wind up by being humiliating to the humanities. Here one sees the traces of the Enlightenment's political project, which wanted precisely to render the Bible, and other old books, undangerous.... The best that can be done, it appears, is to teach "The Bible as Literature," as opposed to "as Revelation," which it claims to be.'

gospels.[54] Bultmann's error was to loose the evangel from its historical and biographical moorings.

I herewith record my belief that the accounts and interpretations of Jesus' life presented in the Synoptic Gospels are trustworthy and infallible; that they supplement and elucidate each other without contradicting and overruling each other; that the triune God is ultimately responsible for both their unity and their diversity, for both their form and their substance; and that these documents are to be received and read as Holy Scripture.[55]

---

[53]See Blomberg, 1987, and his article on the subject in *DJG*, 291-97. Bruce 1963b: 338 states that a gospel is not a gospel when 'it is detached from the Jesus of history.'

[54]See Talbert 1977: 1-6.

[55]'God's Spirit, who appointed the Evangelists as recorders, deliberately controlled their pen, so that all should write in complete agreement, but in different ways' (Calvin 1994: 82). Cf. 'Depending on the Holy Trinity,' above, pages 100-103. Osborne rightly says that respect for the doctrine of inspiration demands attention to each Synoptist's distinctive witness, and that (conversely) 'redaction criticism has enabled us to rediscover the Evangelists as inspired authors' (*DJG*, 668). I concur with 'The Chicago Statement of Biblical Hermeneutics,' article 17 (in *JETS* 25 [December 1982]: 400), as it applies to the Synoptic Gospels: 'WE AFFIRM the unity, harmony, and consistency of Scripture and declare that it is its own best interpreter. WE DENY that Scripture may be interpreted in such a way as to suggest that one passage corrects or militates against another. We deny that later writers of Scripture misinterpreted earlier passages of Scripture when quoting from or referring to them.' Cf. *WCF* 1.9.

V.

THE THEOLOGIAN

Matthew the apostle, scribe and evangelist is also a theologian. From start to finish, his book contains 'a message [*logos*] about God [*Theos*].' Some major themes of this message are here introduced, with a view to exploring them more fully in the commentary.

A. The Purpose of God

All that Matthew records happens 'according to the purpose of him who accomplishes all things in accord with the counsel of his will' (the language of Ephesians 1:11). That manifold purpose is disclosed both in the life of Jesus and in the Hebrew Scriptures. From Matthew's perspective, neither the OT nor Jesus can be understood apart from the other.[1] Equally clear is that Matthew began to acquire such understanding, not by studying the OT but by following Jesus; through the 'new things' disclosed in him Matthew gained access to 'things old.'[2] Matthew's approach is not strictly chronological but thoroughly christological. From the very outset he rivets our attention upon the One in whom God's saving purpose reaches its appointed goal and finds its fullest realization – 'Jesus Christ, the Son of David, the Son of Abraham.'[3]

Jesus the Fulfillment of the Old Testament
The cruciality of this theme for Matthew is evident from his use of the verb 'fulfill,' *plēroō*. Ten of the sixteen instances appear

---

[1]Cf. John 5:39-40. 'The new is in the old concealed [or *latent*]; the old is in the new revealed [or *patent*],' a saying attributed to Augustine.

[2]See above, III. C. and D. 'The essential key to all Matthew's theology is that in Jesus all God's purposes have come to fulfilment' (France 1985: 38).

[3]Matthew 1:1. Matthew's OT 'quotations have as their foundation christological convictions – they are, indeed, christocentric. They take as their *starting point* that Jesus is the One promised by the OT Scriptures'

in introductions to OT quotations supplied by Matthew and peculiar to Matthew, evidence which (as already noted) is the more striking because no other OT quotations in Matthew are prefaced by this term.[4] These quotations are applied to Jesus' conception in Mary's womb (Matt. 1:23); to his return from Egypt (2:15); to Herod's slaughter of the innocents (2:18); to Jesus' being a 'Nazarene' (2:23); to his dwelling in Capernaum (4:15-16); to his healing miracles (8:17); to the character and intent of his service (12:18-21); to his teaching in parables (13:35); to his triumphal entry (21:5); and to the disposal of the money paid to Judas (27:9-10). For the OT sources, see Appendix C.

Four of the other six instances are pertinent as well: 1. Jesus' declaration that 'it is right for us [himself and John] in this way *to fulfill* all righteousness' (3:15) indicates that he will take the path appointed for the Servant of Isaiah 42–53. 2. 'Do not suppose,' says Jesus, 'that I came to abolish the Law or the Prophets; I did not come to abolish but *to fulfill*' (5:17). His later references to 'the Law and the Prophets' show that he both *underscores* the Scriptures (7:12; 22:40) and *surpasses* them (11:12-13). 3. Knowing that the Father could spare him the ultimate test, Jesus asks, 'How then would the Scriptures *be fulfilled*, which say that it must happen this way?' – namely, by his going to the cross (26:53-54). 4. Shortly thereafter Jesus addresses his own question by asserting that 'all this has happened in order that the writings of the prophets *may be fulfilled*' (26:56).

Such statements as Matthew 5:17 and 26:56 indicate that Jesus fulfills not only specific predictions but also broader patterns of OT revelation.[5] Moreover, the foregoing evidence – especially that of the eleven quotations introduced by 'fulfill' – shows that Jesus both *carries forward* OT realities and *goes beyond* them.[6] He cannot be confined to OT categories – just as a piece of unshrunk cloth cannot be safely attached

---

(Hagner 1993: lvi). Sailhamer 2001: 5-23 considers the Messianic hope to be the very *raison d'être* for the writing of the OT.

[4]See 'Drawing Out Things Old,' pages 91-99 above.

[5]So France 1985: 40. Cf. 2 Corinthians 1:20.

[6]The remaining two instances of *plēroō* illustrate the point. Matthew 13:48a, 'when it [the net] *was full*,' one process (gathering fish, 13:47) ended, and another (sorting fish, 13:48b) began. Matthew 23:32, '*Fill up*, then, the

to an old garment, or new wine poured into old wineskins
(9:16-17). But as refraining from those two actions preserves
both the old and the new (9:17b), so honoring the distinction
between 'the Law and the Prophets' and the dawn of God's rule,
(11:12-13), assures that both the OT and the Gospel according to
Matthew will bear the witness that God intends.[7]

The OT now bears a more eloquent witness than before.
Many an OT text invoked by Matthew contains a *sensus plenior*,
a 'fuller meaning' – one not perceived by the original author,
yet intended by God from the first, and now brought to light
by Jesus' life and teachings. In fulfillment of prophecy, Jesus
brings to light 'things hidden since the creation of the world'
(13:35), many of them having been 'hidden' – or buried – by
God in the OT Scriptures. The *sensus plenior* does not *depart
from* but *develops from* the text's original meaning – just as
an oak tree, already *there* in the acorn though not visibly so,
retains its 'oakness' throughout its growth (never becoming an
elm instead) and, upon reaching maturity, fulfills the purpose
intended for the acorn. Or, to change the figure, the 'fuller
meaning' is not discovered by digging *beneath* the original sense
but by digging further *into* it: Matthew is a gardener for whom
the soil itself is important, not a prospector who removes the
soil in search of mineral deposits.[8] This brings us to a further
way of describing the relationship between Jesus and the OT.

measure of your forefathers,' indicates that the sins of Jesus' contemporaries
will both *duplicate* and *surpass* their ancestors' murderous acts.

[7]The 'both' of Matthew 9:17d speaks of the new wine and the old – not
the new – wineskins. For the effect of putting new wine into new wineskins
(9:17c) is that the old skins are not 'destroyed' (9:17b), but 'preserved'
(9:17d). See comments on 9:14-17.

[8]To approach Scripture as Matthew does 'is to recognize the dimension of an
ongoing and consistent divine purpose, which may invest a text with a *sensus
plenior*, to be perceived by those who come to it in the light of further experience
and revelation' (France 1989: 183). Hagner 1993: lvi, speaks of 'a fuller or deeper
sense within the quoted material not understood by the original author but now
detectable in the light of the new revelatory fulfillment.' Raymond E. Brown
defines the *sensus plenior* as 'that additional, deeper meaning, intended by God
but not clearly intended [I would rather say *not fully perceived*] by the human
author, which is seen to exist in the words of a Biblical text...when they are
studied in the light of further revelation or development in the understanding
of revelation': quoted by LaSor 1978: 270 (see 260-77).

Typology in the Gospel according to Matthew

Matthew, like the other evangelists, 'employs typology to demonstrate recurring patterns of God's activity in salvation history.'[9] Typology recognizes: (i) that God's purposes for his people remain unchanged but become increasingly clear as history progresses; (ii) that certain NT persons, events and institutions have their counterparts in the OT; and (iii) that features of these OT 'types' help to illuminate and interpret their NT 'antitypes.'[10]

We begin with the marks of typology, as suggested by certain instances of *typos* in the NT.[11] In that light we can better discern evidence of typology in Matthew's portrait of Jesus.

1. The marks of typology[12]

Historicity

'Only historical facts – persons, actions, events, and institutions – are material for typological interpretation.'[13]

---

[9]Blomberg 1992: 30.

[10]Similarly France 1971: 40; C. A. Evans, 'Typology,' *DJG*, 862. Virkler 1981: 184 calls typology 'a preordained representative relationship which certain persons, events, and institutions bear to corresponding persons, events, and institutions occurring at a later time in salvation history.'

[11]In the NT (according to BAGD s.v.), the noun *typos* may denote (i) a *'visible impression* of a stroke' (the 'marks' of the nails in Jesus' hands; John 20:25); (ii) *'that which is formed, an image* or *statue'* ('the images which you made to worship'; Acts 7:43); (iii) *'form, figure, pattern'* ('form of teaching'; Rom. 6:17; 'a letter having this form' Acts 23:25); (iv) *'(arche)type, pattern, model'* both 'technically *design, pattern'* ('according to the pattern which was shown to you on the mountain'; Heb. 8:5) and 'in the moral life *example, pattern'* ('become an example to the believers'; 1 Tim. 4:12); and (v) 'the *types* given by God as an indication of the future, in the form of persons or things' ('a type of the one to come'; Rom. 5:14). Whether the *typos* of 1 Corinthians 10:6 (with the *typikōs* of 10:11) belongs to iv. or to v. is debatable; see below. The term never occurs in Matthew; but note the cognate verb *typtō* in 24:49 and 27:30, both corresponding to usage i. above (cf. 2 Cor. 3:7, where the verb *entypoō* is used of *carvings* on stone). The term *antitypos* appears twice in the NT, in Hebrews 9:24 (the holy place in the temple is a *copy* of the heavenly original; cf. iv. above) and in 1 Peter 3:21 (baptism *corresponds to* the flood waters in the days of Noah); cf. BAGD s.v.

[12]These four marks of typology are drawn from Currid 1994: 118-121.

[13]Goppelt 1982: 17-18.

Adam, a *typos* of Christ (Rom. 5:14), is not a mythical figure but an historical individual (cf. Luke 3:23-38). Israel's actual experiences in the wilderness offered *typoi* for the instruction of the NT Church (1 Cor. 10:6; cf. v. 11, *typikōs*). Whereas for allegorical interpretation the reported history of the biblical story is incidental or unimportant, for typology history is essential.[14]

Theology
Lamech is an historical individual – father of Noah and ancestor of Jesus, (Luke 3:36). But that does not suffice to make Lamech a *typos* of Christ: for he is not *theologically* joined to Jesus as is his ancestor Adam (Luke 3:38). The Israel whose history is recalled in 1 Corinthians 10 is a theological counterpart to the church Paul addresses; 'Israel of God' applies to the latter as to the former (Gal. 6:16). Moreover, those Israelites 'were all baptized into Moses,' and they 'all ate the same spiritual food and all drank the same spiritual drink' (1 Cor. 10:3-5). That *language* is clearly meant to remind the Corinthians of baptism and the Lord's Supper. But those *experiences* are not OT 'types' of the Christian sacraments: that distinction is reserved for circumcision and the Passover.[15] Rather, the fact that ancient Israel incurred devastating judgment for her theological apostasy and moral declension provided an *example* – a solemn *warning* – for the

---

[14]Evans, *DJG*, 862. According to G. W. H. Lampe, writing on 'the reasonableness of typology,' in Lampe and Woollcombe (1957: 31), the allegorist 'has to penetrate through the shell of history to the inner kernel of eternal spiritual or moral truth.' In keeping with imagery used in our discussion of the NT fulfillment of the OT, we affirm that for typology the 'kernel' is no less historical than the 'shell.'

[15]In the case of the sacraments, we move from OT *types* (circumcision and Passover) to NT *antitypes* (baptism and the Lord's Supper); see, e.g., Colossians 2:11-12; 1 Corinthians 5:7; cf. *WCF* 7.5-6. In 1 Corinthians 10, Paul begins with NT *realities* (the two sacraments) and goes back to the OT for *illustrations*. In this passage, 'the apostle's gaze moved from the situation of the community to the prior work of God in history, where he found light for the present' (Leonhard Goppelt, *TDNT* 8: 251). In 1 Peter 3:21 (noted earlier), while baptism is said to be an *antitypos* of the floodwaters, the latter is not expressly said to be a *typos*.

Corinthians, much of whose behavior emulated that of their forebears.[16]

Intensification

Those historical, theological realities 'are to be interpreted typologically only if they are considered to be divinely ordained representations or types of future realities that will be even greater and more complete.'[17] Not only is Christ *like* Adam; he is far *greater*. Whereas Adam transgressed God's command in the hour of crisis, Christ went to the cross in utter obedience to the Father. Moreover, by that act he reversed the effects of Adam's disobedience (Rom. 5:12-21; 1 Cor. 15:21-22). The Corinthian Christians for whom Paul invokes Israel's example are among those 'on whom the ends [*telē*] of the ages have come' (1 Cor. 10:11).[18]

Revelation

A final feature of typology is that 'there must be evidence that the type was designed and appointed of God to represent the thing typified.'[19] So while Rahab's 'scarlet cord' (Josh. 2:18, 21) is instrumental in her family's salvation (Josh. 6:23-25), this cord

---

[16]All the sins described in 1 Corinthians 10:7-10 have recurred in the Corinthian church. Ancient Israel too had its 'sacraments'; but they were not talismans protecting them against Yahweh's judgments. *Israel herself* is a *type* of the church (v. in the earlier list); but her *experience* of sin and judgment provides a frightening *example* to the church (iv. in that list). This reading of the *typos* of 10:6 agrees with Fee 1987: 450-58, against Goppelt, *TDNT* 8: 251-52.

[17]Goppelt 1982: 18.

[18]Cf. the Gospel according to John, where Jesus (i) teaches that the foremost purpose of the OT is to point beyond itself to the greater reality of Christ (5:39-40); (ii) turns water into wine and cleanses the temple (ch. 2), thus dramatically demonstrating that the old order has been superseded by a greater one; (iii) feeds a multitude in the wilderness, and so interprets the event as to make it plain that God's present gifts far exceed his provisions during Israel's years of wandering (6:26-58); and (iv) declares during the Jewish Feast of Tabernacles, in chapters 7–8, that those ceremonies are now being superseded by virtue of his presence, his coming glory and the imminent outpouring of the Holy Spirit.

[19]Terry 1961: 247. As noted, Virkler defines a type as 'a *preordained* representative relationship,' and Goppelt limits the study to '*divinely ordained* representations or types' (the italics are added).

is not a 'type' of the blood of Christ, for there is no evidence that it was 'designed and appointed by God to represent the thing signified.' On the other hand, it is clear from Paul and John that the Passover sacrifice is a type of Christ's death (cf. John 19:36; 1 Cor. 5:7). Similarly, Paul's teachings about Adam in Romans 5 and about Israel in 1 Corinthians 10 are ordained by the Spirit.

In that light, we turn to Matthew. The following is illustrative, not exhaustive; states positions to be developed and defended in the commentary; and concentrates on the first and third marks of typology – *historicity* and *intensification* – because the *theological* connections are either self-evident or better pursued in the commentary, and the *revelatory* character of the Matthean evidence was affirmed in previous sections.[20]

2. Persons as types and antitypes

Matthew relates Jesus to Abraham, David, Jonah, Moses and Solomon; to a child born in Isaiah's day; to the Servant of Isaiah; to Daniel's Son of Man; and to an OT *Nazōraios*.[21] Similarly, John the Baptist is related to Elijah and to the unnamed voice of Isaiah 40:3.[22] Each of those figures is *historical*. This holds true whether the OT figure (i) is distinguished from the NT counterpart (e.g., David and Jesus); or (ii) embraces persons in both OT and NT (one view of Isaiah 7:14); or (iii) denotes a NT figure exclusively (another view of Isaiah 7:14).[23] At every turn *intensification* is evident. Abraham received covenantal promises; Jesus brings them to fulfillment. The child born to

---

[20]See II. ('Apostle'), III. ('Scribe'), especially E. ('Depending upon the Holy Trinity'); and IV. ('Evangelist'), especially D. ('The Synoptic Gospels: Holy Scripture').

[21]Abraham (Matt. 1:1, 17; 3:17); David (1:1, 6, 17, 20; 2:4-6; 9:27; 12:3, 23; 15:22; 20:30-31; 21:9, 15; 22:42-45); Jonah (12:39-41; 16:4); Moses (4:1-11; 5:1 [with 23:2], 17-48; 17:3-4; 19:7-8; 22:24); Solomon (12:42); the child (1:22-23); the Servant (3:17; 8:17; 11:5; 12:17-21); the Son of Man (16:13, 15; 24:30, etc.); the *Nazōraios* (2:23).

[22]Elijah, 3:4; 11:7-15; 17:10-13; cf. 14:1-12. (Jesus himself is associated with Elijah in 16:14 and 17:3-4.) The voice, 3:3.

[23]John the Baptist is both *reminiscent of* the historical Elijah (3:4; 14:1-12), and *identified as* the latter-day Elijah (11:7-15; 17:10-13).

Mary not only betokens God's presence; he himself is 'God with us.' Jesus is David's son, but also David's Lord and God.[24] Jesus' authority far surpasses that of Moses. Moses mediated the fourth command, but Jesus is 'Lord of the Sabbath.'[25] Jesus imparts wisdom as Solomon had done, and calls listeners to repentance as Jonah had done; yet in Jesus 'something greater' than Jonah and Solomon has appeared.[26] The Servant of Isaiah and the Son of Man of Daniel, and the Elijah of Malachi are no longer predicted; they have arrived on the scene.

3. Events as types and antitypes

Messiah's conception has a counterpart in Isaiah's day. Herod's attempt to murder Jesus recalls Pharaoh's threat to Moses, Babylonian tyranny over Judah, and the revolt against the Davidic king in Psalm 2. Jesus' return from Egypt recalls the Exodus; he, like Israel, is tested in the wilderness. Like Elisha, Jesus feeds many people on little food and raises a child from the dead. The present generation's resistance to Jesus' teaching recalls Israel's response to Isaiah, and compares unfavorably to the effects of Jonah's preaching and Solomon's wisdom upon Gentiles. Judas' pact with the chief priests is reminiscent of evils in the days of Jeremiah and Zechariah. Jesus' resurrection from the dead corresponds to Jonah's rescue from the sea monster. The glorious coming of the Son of Man is likened to the cataclysm in Noah's day.[27]

---

[24]These two sentences are based especially on Matthew 1:1-23; 22:41-46. Bethlehem, thought to be insignificant even after David's time, is now – as Jesus' birthplace – 'by no means least among the rulers of Judah' (2:6, with Micah 5:2 and 2 Samuel 5:2). By the same token, if the material needs of David's men overruled tabernacle ceremonial, how could the followers of Jesus – who offers 'something greater than the temple' – be denied their daily bread? See the comments on Matthew 12:1-8.

[25]See 5:17-48 (including 'You heard that it was said... but I say to you'; 5:21, etc.); 7:28-29; 12:1-8; 13:35; 28:18. On Jesus as the New Moses, see Davies 1964: 25-108; France 1989: 186-89; Baxter 1999: 69-83.

[26]See 12:41, 42; France 1989: 189-91.

[27]See Matthew 1:22-23; 2:14-18; 3:17; 4:1-11; 9:23-26; 12:38-42; 13:11-17; 14:15-21; 24:37-39; 26:14-16; 27:6-10.

In each case both OT type and NT antitype are *historical*: this holds true for Jonah's rescue from the fish and Jesus' resurrection from the dead as surely as for Solomon's imparting of wisdom and Jesus' teaching in parables. *Intensification* is again much in evidence. The child of Isaiah's day was conceived in the normal way; Mary remained a virgin till her son was born. The murder of God's Messiah would be far more catastrophic than the slaying of Moses; for the One called from Egypt (2:15) is God's Son in a way that Israel was not, and the Exodus he inaugurates is far more momentous than that of Moses' day.[28] The stakes are far higher in 4:1-11 than when Israel was tested in the wilderness. Elisha fed a hundred men with twenty loaves (2 Kings 4:42-44), but Jesus feeds 5,000 men with only five loaves; raising the dead was more laborious for Elisha (2 Kings 4:32-35) than for Jesus. Consequences for those who reject Jesus' witness are far more severe than for their OT counterparts (Matt. 11:20-24); the judgment attending the glorious appearance of the Son of Man will be even more catastrophic than that of Noah's day (24:37-51). Plots against OT prophets pale by comparison to the conspiracy bent on destroying Jesus. Whereas Jonah remained alive during his sojourn in the fish's belly, Jesus is raised from among the dead.

4. Institutions as types and antitypes

Jesus' words and works recall the institutions of the Covenant (as made by God with Abraham, and thereafter with Moses and David), the Passover and the temple.[29]

---

[28]A sermon by Chrysostom (a fourth-century churchman) expounded Matthew 2:16 as follows: 'The fact that only the children two years old and under were murdered while those of three presumably escaped is meant to teach us that those who hold the Trinitarian faith will be saved whereas Binitarians and Unitarians will undoubtedly perish' (Lampe and Woollcombe 1957: 31-32). This interpretation, while honoring Matthew's Trinitarian theology (3:16-17; 28:19), is to be rejected because: (i) it finds no support in the text itself, and (ii) intrudes upon Matthew's clearly intended historical and theological purpose.

[29]Covenant (Matt. 26:28), together with references to Abraham (1:1, 17; 3:9; 8:11; 22:32), Moses and Mosaic law (5:21-48; 8:3-4; 12:1-14; 15:1-6; 17:3-4, 24-27; 18:15-20; 19:1-12, 16-21; 22:24, 37-40) and David (e.g., 1:1, 6, 17, 20; 22:41-46). Passover (26:1-30). Temple (12:5-7; 21:12-17, 23).

The Covenant, the Passover and the temple all apply to particular and successive periods of OT *history*, as do the corresponding realities from Jesus onward. Again there is an unmistakable *intensification*. Jesus comes to inaugurate a *new* covenant, which both incorporates and surpasses that manifold OT covenant.[30] Jesus does not merely reiterate promises made to Abraham about Jews and Gentiles; he actually accomplishes their salvation.[31] Jesus comes not to destroy but to fulfill the Mosaic law; at the same time, in light of the grace that attends God's dawning rule, he places greater demands upon his hearers than did Moses. Moreover, obedience to God now requires allegiance to Jesus; lasting rest is found, not in the fourth command but in the 'Lord of the Sabbath.'[32] In the very act of keeping Passover, Jesus foretells the atoning sacrifice by virtue of which the Passover celebration will be replaced by a richer covenantal sign. By the same token, in Jesus 'something greater than the temple' has appeared on the scene. Although he is a descendant of Judah, not Levi, his conduct reveals him to be 'Lord of the temple.'[33]

---

[30]See Matthew 26:28, with Luke 22:20; 1 Corinthians 11:25; Jeremiah 31:31-34; Hebrews 8:1-13; 10:1-18. For progress within the covenant of redemption, from 'the covenant of commencement' (Adam) through 'the covenant of preservation' (Noah), 'the covenant of promise' (Abraham), 'the covenant of law' (Moses) and 'the covenant of the kingdom' (David), to 'the covenant of consummation' (Christ), see Robertson 1980. Christ is 'the personal embodiment of the new covenant. In him is found the fulfillment of all God's covenant purposes' (ibid., 63).

[31]See Matthew 1:21; 20:28; 28:19; and E. below, on 'the People of God.'

[32]See the comments on 5:17-48; 19:18-21; 11:28-12:8; also France 1985: 48-50.

[33]See Matthew 1:1-2, 16; 11:10 (with Mal. 3:1); 12:6; 21:12-17; 26:28; cf. 1 Corinthians 5:7. As when the Lord's Supper is compared to Passover, Christian baptism (Matt. 28:19) testifies to covenantal grace more powerfully than does circumcision (the sign of the Abrahamic covenant): baptism causes no pain; females as well as males may receive it. But Matthew never speaks of circumcision.

B. The Son of God

The figure of Jesus so dominates the Gospel according to Matthew that it may rightly be called 'Christology in narrative form.'[34] How does Matthew identify him?[35]

Jesus is the Messiah

Of the seventeen instances of *Christos* in Matthew, almost one third appear in the opening two chapters, starting with the opening verse – evidence of the term's importance for the evangelist.[36] Simon's confession – 'You are the Christ...' (16:16) – comes at a crucial turning point in the gospel, forms an inclusion with 1:1 and is echoed in the high priest's question (26:63).[37] *Christos*, the Greek equivalent of the Hebrew *Māšîach*, declares Jesus to be a person whom God anoints for special service. As in the OT, three kinds of service are in view: Jesus the Messiah is prophet, priest and king.[38] In Matthew, as in the OT, the three are joined in the closest way – distinguishable, but inseparable, functions.

1. Jesus the Prophet

Like OT prophets, Jesus is anointed by the Spirit of God for proclaiming the word of God. He preaches the gospel of God's dawning rule, calling listeners to repentance and faith. With equal authority he expounds the law of God, requiring of his followers personal holiness and social righteousness. He foretells events both near and distant.[39]

---

[34]Burridge 1994: 8, speaking of the other three gospels as well.

[35]'Jesus' (*Iēsous*) – the name Matthew most often gives to his central figure – is itself significant; but attention to this name is better reserved for later (see sec. D.).

[36]See Matthew 1:1, 16-18; 2:4 (a total of five).

[37]16:21 was earlier (III. A.) identified as a major turning point in the gospel.

[38]This does not mean that Matthew stresses the three to the same degree. The statement in *WCF* 8.1 that it 'pleased God...to choose and ordain the Lord Jesus...to be the Mediator between God and man, the Prophet, Priest, and King...' is grounded in part in Matthew See also *WSC*, nos. 23-26. For examples of OT anointing, each including the verb *māšach* ('to anoint'), see Isaiah 61:1 (prophet), Exodus 29:7 (priest), and 1 Samuel 10:1 (king).

[39]See, e.g., Matthew 3:16-17; 4:17, 23; 5:1–7:29; 9:35; 12:15-21; 19:16-21; 24:1-51. Of the thrity-seven instances of 'prophet' (*prophētēs*) in Matthew, only three refer to Jesus (13:57; 21:11, 46). The rest refer to OT prophets, John the Baptist and Jesus' own followers.

As a faithful prophet, Jesus also submits to the word of God. Unlike the nation's leaders whom he denounces (Matt. 23:3), he practices what he preaches. His whole life is one of unswerving obedience to the Father's will. He who teaches followers to be merciful, forgiving and steadfast amid persecutions, himself embodies those qualities. Before appointing others to be missionaries, he has been one himself. He, more than any other, shows by his conduct what it means to love God and neighbor. Indeed, Jesus' own fidelity to the revealed and preached word helps to explain the great authority of his utterances.[40]

2. Jesus the Priest

Jesus prays for himself and intercedes for others. Like OT priests and Levites, he instructs Israel – crowd, authorities and disciples – on various subjects, prayer included. Some of this teaching takes place in the temple, together with healings and the response of praise appropriate to the place. Shortly before his death, he takes action to restore the temple to its proper function.[41]

Yet, in some respects, Jesus' priesthood is vastly different from that of Aaron and his successors. He does not merely assist sinful human beings in securing forgiveness from God; he himself forgives sins (Matt. 9:1-8). The Jewish high priest had to 'offer sacrifices for his own sins as well as for those of the people'; Jesus, the sinless one, need only address the sins of others.[42] Moreover, he saves his people from their sins, not by slaying goats and calves and lambs, but by sacrificing his own life and pouring out his own blood. Once exalted to

[40]See, e.g., 5:7, 10-12; 6:12, 14-15; 7:28-29; 8:14-17; 9:1-7, 10-13; 9:35–10:1; 11:28-30; 12:1-14; 18:21-35; 20:26-28; 22:37-40; 26:36-46; 27:33-50. Precisely because of his utter obedience to the Father, Jesus does *not* share his listeners' need of repentance.

[41]See Matthew 11:25-26; 14:19, 23; 15:36; 26:26-27, 36-44; 27:46 (Jesus' prayers); 4:23; 5:1–7:29, etc. (his teachings); 21:12-17; 21:23–23:39; 26:55 (Jesus in the precincts of the temple to teach, heal and purify); 2 Chronicles 17:7-9; 19:8; 35:3; Nehemiah 8:7-9 (priests and Levites as teachers).

[42]See Hebrews 5:3; 7:26-28; 4:14-16. Jesus fully identifies with sin without becoming sinful. As his ministry begins, he receives a baptism designed for the repentant, but he is not said to confess his own sin (Matt. 3:6, 11-17). Cf. 2 Corinthians 5:21; Romans 8:3.

his Father's right hand, he exercises his universal authority
(28:18) by interceding for his people (cf. 18:19-20).[43]

3. Jesus the King

The name 'Christ' is directly joined to the title 'son of David'
in Matthew 1:1. David is a pivotal figure in the genealogy to
follow (1:17); of all the kings in 1:6-11, he alone is expressly
called *basileus* ('king'; 1:6). Jesus is called 'son of David' seven
more times in Matthew; apart from the reference to Joseph in
1:20, this term is applied to Jesus alone. By the same token,
while Matthew employs *basileus* in a variety of ways, only
Jesus is called 'king of the Jews' or 'king of Israel.'[44]

Jesus proclaims the dawn of the kingdom (*basileia*) of God, in
which Messiah reigns by God's appointment (cf. Luke 1:32- 33).
Jesus is born 'king of the Jews' (Matt. 2:2). At his baptism,
the Father identifies him with words drawn from a royal
psalm (3:17). His coming is a frontal assault upon tyrannies
both human and demonic. His disciples become his subjects,
destined to share in his reign. This king, seated on his glorious
throne, will execute final judgment.[45]

Yet the Father also describes his royal Son with words from
a Servant song (3:17). This king is 'gentle and humble in heart'
(11:29). Far from tyrannizing his subjects as do other rulers, he
exercises his authority by serving them. His choice of mount
for entering Jerusalem represents not a rejection of kingship

---

[43]See Matthew 1:21; 20:28; 26:26-28; Hebrews 9:11-28; 10:1-18; 12:24;
13:11-12, 20. Jesus, by applying Psalm 110:1 to himself (Matt. 22:41-46),
implies that he is 'a priest forever, according to the order of Melchizedek,'
Psalm 110:4, a link fully explored in Hebrews 5–7.

[44]For Jesus as 'son of David,' see Matthew 9:27; 12:23; 15:22; 20:30, 31; 21:9,
15 (v. 5 speaks of 'your king'); cf. 22:41-46. For 'king of Israel,' see 27:42; for
'king of the Jews,' 2:2; 27:11, 29, 37. God the Father is depicted as a king in
18:23-35 and 22:1-14, and, by implication, in 17:24-27. The language of 5:35
– 'the city of the Great King' – originally referred to Yahweh (Ps. 48:2), and
so might rightly be applied to God the Father or to Jesus the Messiah, or to
both.

[45]See Matthew 2:1-23 (Jesus' threat to Herod and Archelaus); 12:25-28
(Jesus and Beelzeboul); 19:28 (the Son of Man enthroned, and his disciples
on 'twelve thrones'); 25:31-46 (the Son of Man, the King, judges 'the sheep
and the goats'). Cf. 14:1-12, where John, another herald of God's rule (3:2),
challenges the illicit powers of Herod Antipas.

but a deliberate and visible departure from popular messianic expectations. It is indeed as 'the King of the Jews' that he hangs upon the cross, here achieving his ultimate triumph through defeat.[46]

4. The commands to silence

In his opening verse, Matthew declares Jesus to be the Messiah. Jesus affirms his own Messiahship – but only once, and there indirectly (26:63-64). Never does he repudiate the title; on the contrary, when Peter confesses him to be 'the Messiah, the Son of the living God,' Jesus pronounces him 'blessed' and calls his confession a revelation from the Father (16:16-17). Yet, three verses later, 'he ordered his disciples to tell no one that he was the Christ' (16:20). Similarly, a leper is charged to tell no one about his cure (8:4), as are two blind men (9:30). Why are these commands to silence given?

One reason is that recognizing Jesus to be Messiah does not depend upon his, or someone else's, using the *term* 'Messiah.' For those who, granted insight by the Father, rightly interpret Jesus' words and works, the *reality* of his Messiahship will be abundantly clear apart from this language.[47] Another reason is that Jesus' *concept* of Messiahship was very different from popular notions – as becomes strikingly clear in the aftermath of Peter's confession (Matt. 16:21-23). Even apart from Jesus' use of the name 'Messiah,' false expectations were easily aroused among those who witnessed his mighty works; his habitual use of the name would only have made matters worse.

Yet, in the end, Jesus was rejected, not because he was hard to understand but because he was hard to accept. In time his exposition of Messiahship became all too clear. Moreover, he made it plain that the submission, sacrifice and service that marked Messiah himself, were to be true for his followers too. In Matthew 20:25-28, 'we have the messianic task clearly and simply defined. It is and remains a secret until after the

---

[46]See Matthew 20:25-28; 21:1-11; 27:37. In Sayers (1943: 54) Balthazar, one of the magi, predicts that the newborn king 'will be victor and victim in all his wars, and will make his triumph in defeat.'

[47]See Matthew 11:2-6; 13:11-17; 16:16-17.

Crucifixion and Resurrection, simply because no secret is ever so well kept as that which no one is willing to discover.'[48] See the comments on 12:15-21.

Jesus is the Son of Man

This expression helps to explain Jesus' understanding of Messiahship.[49] 'The Son of Man' (*ho huios tou anthrōpou*) appears thirty times in Matthew, always on Jesus' lips. In each instance the definite article *ho* is used. Jesus always speaks of the Son of Man in the third person, but he is clearly referring to himself. For example, compare his question in 16:13 ('Who do people say the Son of Man is?') to that in 16:15 ('Who do you say that I am?'). Furthermore, the majority of instances (twenty-one out of thirty) appear later in Matthew than 16:13 (near the major turning point of 16:21).

1. The Old Testament background: Daniel 7

The consistent use of the definite article indicates that Jesus has a particular figure in view: '*the* Son of Man' – indeed, '*that* Son of Man,' namely the one spoken of in Daniel 7.[50] Daniel 7:9-10 describes a scene of judgment over which Yahweh, 'the Ancient of Days,' presides. Then Daniel beholds 'one like a son of man [Aramaic *kᵉbar 'enāš*], coming with the clouds of heaven' (7:13). He is like a human being. He is also divine: he comes 'with the clouds' (cf. Ps. 104:3; Isa. 19:1) and receives universal worship (Dan. 7:14).[51] At the same time, he is distinguished from the figure seated on the throne (7:9): the 'one like a son of man' approaches 'the Ancient of Days' (7:13), who grants him 'authority, glory and sovereign power' (7:14). Thus endowed, he will conquer the kingdoms represented by the four beasts of Daniel's dream (7:1-8). 'His dominion,' unlike

---

[48]Manson 1955: 220, on the parallel in Mark 10:42-45. Cf. Matthew 18:1-5; John 6:60-71.

[49]Cf. John 12:34, where the crowd's response to Jesus indicates that at least some of his contemporaries equated the figures of 'Messiah' and 'the Son of Man.' Cf. Scott 1995: 313-14.

[50]Moule 1977: 11-13.

[51]For further references to clouds in OT theophanies, see A. Oepke, *TDNT* 4: 905.

theirs, 'is an everlasting dominion that will not pass away, and his kingdom is one that will never be destroyed' (7:14). By his victories, 'the saints of the Most High will receive the kingdom and will possess it forever...' (7:18), and will together serve their Liberator and King (7:14).[52]

2. The humanity and suffering of Jesus

In Matthew, in accord with OT texts, including Daniel 7:13, the term 'the Son of Man' testifies to Jesus' true humanity.[53] The Son of Man enjoys the company of other people: unlike John, he comes 'eating and drinking' (Matt. 11:19). But he also experiences deprivation: he 'has nowhere to lay his head' (8:20). Worse than that, the Son of Man will 'suffer many things' and be crucified at the hands of the authorities. Yet, those events accord with his own prophecies and with his and the Father's saving purpose.[54]

3. The exaltation and kingship of Jesus

In Matthew, as in Daniel 7:14, the Son of Man is granted 'authority, glory and sovereign power.' As Jesus predicted, the Son of Man who suffered and died was raised from among the dead, exalted to a place of singular honor at God's right hand, and given authority to reign universally.[55] Jesus also prophesied that the Son of Man would one day return to earth

---

[52]The 'something like the figure of a man' in 2 Esdras 13:3, and 'the Son of Man' in the Parables of 1 Enoch (chs. 37–71), presuppose Daniel 7. 'It is evident that the Enochic Son of man is preexistent, heavenly, and majestic. He possesses dominion and will judge all humankind and angels' (Scott 1995: 313). See further ibid., 311-14.

[53]Cf. Psalm 8:4 ('what is man..., the son of man...,' an instance of synonymous parallelism); Ezekiel 2:1 (where Yahweh calls Ezekiel 'son of man,' as frequently in this book).

[54]See Matthew 12:40; 17:12, 22-23; 20:18-19, 28; 26:2, 24, 45. 'The Son of Man is going just as it is written about him' (26:24; cf. Mark 9:12; 14:21). Daniel 7 does not expressly say the Son of Man will suffer (though this might be inferred from his identification with God's oppressed people). But for Jesus, this figure and the Suffering Servant (Isa. 42–53; Matt. 3:17; 8:17; 12:17-21, etc.) are one and the same. Bruce 1968 suggests (with Matthew Black) that 'from the first the "one like a son of man" was a re-presentation of the Servant of Yahweh' (29-30; cf. 96-99). The suffering of Ezekiel, the 'son of man,' also prefigures that of Jesus (Eichrodt 1970: 73).

[55]See Matthew 16:21; 17:9, 23; 20:19; 22:44; 26:64; 28:18, together with Daniel 7:14.

in great power and glory, to gather his people, to judge the nations and to establish his rule.[56]

4. *The deity and divine sonship of Jesus*

In accord with Daniel 7:13-14, Jesus is a divine being – Immanuel, 'God with us' (Matt. 1:23). Thus the Son of Man is 'Lord of the Sabbath' (12:8) and has 'authority on earth to forgive sins' (9:6). He is sovereign over the mission that brings the kingdom to consummation (13:37); and it is his angels who are sent forth to execute final judgment (13:41). Furthermore, as Daniel 7 affirms both the deity of the 'one like a son of man' and his distinction from the Ancient of Days, so Matthew declares the Son of Man to be 'the Son of the living God' (16:16, with v. 13), the one who 'is going to come in the glory of his Father' (16:27). As the Father's beloved Son and appointed King (3:17), Jesus both mediates the Father's authority and exercises an authority of his own.

5. *The people of Jesus*

As in Daniel 'the saints of the Most High' are freed from the beasts by the sovereign might of the 'one like a son of man,' so Jesus comes to liberate persons from tyrannies human and demonic, and to bring them under God's righteous and merciful rule.[57] The Son of Man deliberately dines with the disreputable; as 'Lord of the Sabbath' he offers rest to the weary and wholeness to the afflicted.[58] Henceforth, the people of God are those loyal to the Son of Man. He shows his loyalty in turn by giving his life as a 'ransom for the many,' for Gentiles as well as Jews. Returning 'on the clouds of heaven,' he will gather his elect from all over the world. Then, seated on his glorious throne and joined by his twelve apostles, he

---

[56]See Matthew 10:23; 13:41-43; 16:27-28; 19:28; 24:27-31, 37-44; 25:31-46; 26:64. Both 24:30 and 26:64 quote from Daniel 7:13.

[57]See Daniel 7:13-18; Matthew 4:17, 23-25; 12:28. That Jesus' message is termed 'good news' (4:23; 9:35; 11:5; 24:14; 26:13) testifies to the benevolence of the divine rule.

[58]See Matthew 9:9-13; 11:19, 28-30; 12:9-13.

[59]See 8:18-22; 16:24-28; 19:27-30 (with 10:2-4); 20:28; 24:30-31; 25:31-46; 26:28.

will judge the nations, and thereafter usher his people into the kingdom long prepared for them.[59]

6. The parable of Jesus

'The Son of Man' is a concise parable – which helps to explain why Jesus always speaks of this figure in the third person.[60] As with other parables, responses will differ. Some will conclude that Jesus is thus describing himself as a man (cf. Ps. 8:4) or at most a prophet (like Ezekiel). Others, discerning the link with Daniel 7, will assume that Jesus is speaking of a person other than himself, or else – rightly interpreting the parable – will oppose Jesus the more strongly. Others, perceiving that Jesus is identifying himself as the Son of Man prophesied in Daniel, will embrace the fact and thereafter be granted deeper insight into the reality.[61]

Jesus is Lord

Kyrios appears eighty times in Matthew. Fewer than half of those instances – twenty-eight – refer directly to Jesus.[62] But the other fifty-two are pertinent for understanding Matthew's Christology, and we begin with them.

1. Preface: related instances of Kyrios

Nineteen of these fifty-two apply to Yahweh, the God of Israel. Matthew speaks of 'the angel of the Lord,' or states that a quotation 'was spoken by the Lord through the prophet,' or

---

[60]The NKJV of 16:13b, 'Who do men say that I, the Son of Man, am?' is to be rejected in favor of the NIV's 'Who do people say the Son of Man is?' Cf. *TC*, 34.

[61]Some modern scholars think Jesus (though not the evangelists) spoke of the Son of Man as a figure other than himself. For evidence that hostility toward Jesus increases as truth about him is progressively revealed, see comments on Matthew 12:22-32. For evidence that believing responses to truth are rewarded with further enlightenment, see comments on 13:10-17. In the Gospel according to John, twelve of the thirteen instances of 'the Son of Man' appear in 'the Book of Signs' (John 1:19-12:50), and only one in 'the Book of Glory' (13:1–20:31) – which suggests that the term is *itself* a sign – akin to its being a parable. On the Son of Man in the Synoptics, see Guthrie 1981: 270-82; Ladd 1993: 143-57; I.H. Marshall, *DJG*, 775-81.

[62]These counts include Matthew 20:30, 'Have mercy on us, Lord [*Kyrie*], Son of David!' which is in some doubt textually. See *TC*, 43.

quotes an OT passage that mentions 'the Lord.'[63] The same holds true for Jesus' use of the term when quoting from or alluding to the OT, or when referring to God the Father.[64] Another thirty-two appear in Jesus' parables and metaphors to denote an 'owner' or 'master.'[65] In one instance (27:63) where Pharisees are addressing Pilate, *kyrios* may be translated 'your excellency' or 'sir.'

2. Jesus the master

Kyrios can express Jesus' mastery over physical afflictions, demonic powers and the elements of nature.[66] By the same token, in accord with biblical prophecy and the Father's will, he foresees and oversees the events culminating in his death and resurrection.[67] With this name, disciples voice their allegiance to Jesus, and their respect for his authority as leader and teacher.[68] Jesus is also depicted as an owner: since he is 'the Lord,' a pair of donkeys are supplied for him without question; and since he is 'Lord of the Sabbath,' he has the right to determine how the day shall be spent.[69]

3. Jesus the Master

Some of those instances grant us insight into Jesus' very being. Who but *Yahweh* can rightly declare himself to be 'Lord of the

---

[63]Not surprisingly, this is true for all the instances in Matthew 1–2 (1:20, 22, 24; 2:13, 15, 19). See also 3:3; 27:10; 28:2.

[64]See 4:7, 10; 5:33; 9:38; 11:25; 21:42; 22:37, 44 (the first instance); 23:39 (the language of the crowd in 21:9).

[65]See 6:24; 10:24-25; 13:27; 18:25, 27, 31, 32, 34; 20:8; 21:30, 40; 24:42, 45, 46, 48, 50; 25:11 (twice), 18, 19, 20, 21 (twice), 22, 23 (twice), 24, 26, 37, 44. A Canaanite woman uses such a metaphor in 15:27.

[66]See 8:2, 6, 8, 25; 14:28, 30; 15:22, 25, 27 (the first instance); 17:15; 20:30, 31, 33.

[67]In view of Jesus' prophecies of his death and resurrection (16:21, etc.) and such texts as 26:24, 39-46, 53-54, Matthew's report of the Pharisees' statement to Pilate is filled with irony: 'Your excellency [*Kyrie*], we remember that when he was still alive, that deceiver said, "After three days I will rise." Give orders, therefore...' (27:63-64a) – as though Pilate were master of the situation, and as though his actions could prevent that prophecy's fulfillment.

[68]See 7:21-22; 8:21; 16:22; 17:4, 15; 18:21; 26:22. Cf. 10:24-25.

[69]See 21:1-3; 12:1-8.

Sabbath'? Who but Yahweh can still the storm and calm the sea? Who but Yahweh has the right to determine who shall enter the kingdom of heaven?[70] Especially instructive in this regard is Matthew 22:44, where Jesus quotes from Psalm 110:1, 'The Lord [*Kyrios*] said to my Lord [*Kyriō*], "Sit at my right hand..."' Jesus thus identifies the Messiah as a divine being, worthy of worship and of the name *Kyrios* – which the LXX uses to translate *Yahweh*. At the same time, the linguistic distinction in the Hebrew of Psalm 110 between *Yahweh* ('the LORD') and *'ādōnî* ('my LORD') honors the ontological distinction between the Father and the Son.[71] In this light, it is also clear that some instances of *Kyrios* in the parables and metaphors of Jesus reflect his divine sovereignty, just as others reflect that of God the Father.[72]

Jesus is God the Son

It is thus clear that the terms 'Lord' and 'the Son of Man' testify to Jesus' divine sonship. So does Matthew's usage of 'Messiah.' The *Christos* of Matthew 1:1 is a divine being who has become human to save his people (1:21, 23). David and Solomon, Jesus' ancestors, were rightly called 'sons of God' by virtue of their kingly office, but they remained mere men.[73] Peter's confession – 'You are the Messiah, the Son of the living God' (16:16) speaks not only of Jesus' function but of his being. This ascription is anticipated in 14:33, where the disciples 'worshiped [Jesus], saying, 'Truly you are the Son of God.' It is also echoed

---

[70]See 7:21; 8:25; 12:8; 14:28, 30. In view of Jesus' mastery of the storms, Matthew intends for the *Kyrios* in 8:25; 14:28, 30, to be read as expressive of Jesus' deity. In the latter passage, this may be Peter's intent as well; cf. 14:33.

[71]In light of the quotation of Malachi 3:1a in Matthew 11:10 (cf. 3:1b: '"Then suddenly the Lord [*ha 'ādôn*] you are seeking will come to his temple; [he]...will come," says the LORD [*Yahweh*] Almighty.' In both Psalm 110:1 and Malachi 3:1, LXX employs *Kyrios* for both *Yahweh* and *'ādôn*. See also the comments on Matthew 11:10 and 22:41-46.

[72]For Jesus as *Kyrios*, see 10:24-25; 13:27 (cf. v. 37); 24:42, 45, 46, 48, 50; 25:11, 18-24, 26, 37, 44 (cf. v. 31). For the Father as *Kyrios*, see 6:24; 18:25, 27, 31, 32, 34 (cf. v. 35); 20:8; 21:30, 40 (cf. v. 37).

[73]Psalm 2:7 originally applied to David and his successors on the throne. Cf. 2 Samuel 7:14, where Yahweh says of Solomon, 'I will be his father, and he will be my son.'

in 26:63-64, where Jesus acknowledges that he is 'the Messiah, the Son of God.' The high priest, rightly perceiving this to be a claim of deity, judges Jesus to be worthy of death (26:65-66). Yet Jesus' crucifixion, far from disproving his divine sonship, is the very end to which the Father appointed him, and from which the devil sought to deter him.[74] Significantly, a confession of faith akin to Peter's is offered just after Jesus has died: 'Truly this was the Son of God!'[75]

Other instances of 'son' (*huios*) are to be understood in the same way. Upon Jesus' return from Egypt, and later at his baptism and his transfiguration, God speaks of him as 'my Son.'[76] Correspondingly, Jesus identifies himself as 'the Son' whose relationship to God the Father is unique: this is plain from his words about the Father's and the Son's knowledge of each other; from certain of his parables; from his question whether Messiah is David's son; from his discourse on the future; and from his closing reference to the Holy Trinity.[77] The phrase 'my Father' is frequently found on Jesus' lips; and while he often stresses that God is Father of the disciples, never does he place himself with them under the heading 'our Father.'[78] Moreover, while Matthew identifies Jesus as Mary's son, and Mary as his mother, never does he speak of Jesus as Joseph's son, or of Joseph as Jesus' father.[79]

---

[74]See Matthew 3:17; and Satan's and the demons' use of 'son of God' in 4:3, 6; 8:29.

[75]Matthew 27:54, nasb. Within Matthew's proclamation this utterance ascribes deity to Jesus, whatever may have been the centurion's meaning. See the comments *ad loc.* In contrast to the centurion, others at the cross use 'son of God' to mock and tempt Jesus (27:40, 43).

[76]See Matthew 2:15; 3:17; 17:5.

[77]See 11:25-27; 21:37-38; 22:2, 41-45 (where Messiah's divine sonship is implied); 24:36; 28:19.

[78]For 'my Father,' see 7:21; 10:32, 33; 11:27; 12:50; 15:13; 16:17, 27; 18:10, 19, 35; 20:23. For 'your Father' or 'our Father' applied to disciples, see 5:16, 45, 48; 6:1, 4, 6, 8, 9, 14, 15, 18, 26, 32; 7:11; 10:20, 29; 13:43; 18:14; 23:9. For disciples as 'sons of God,' see 5:9, 45.

[79]For Mary as Jesus' mother, see 1:18; 2:11, 13, 14, 20, 21; 13:55; cf. 12:46-50. For Jesus as Mary's son, see 1:21, 23, 25; 13:55.

In short, throughout his book Matthew presents Jesus as a divine being who is worthy to receive the worship due God alone.[80]

C. The Kingdom of God
This theme stands at the heart of Matthew's 'message about God.' Anticipating the present discussion are earlier remarks about the centrality of the kingdom in Jesus' gospel, and about Jesus' manifold exercise of kingship.

The Dawn of God's Rule
In Matthew the first public declaration from both John the Baptist and Jesus is that 'the kingdom of heaven [*hē basileia tōn ouranōn*] has drawn near [*ēngiken*]' (3:2; 4:17). The parallel to 4:17 in Mark 1:15 – 'the kingdom of God [*hē basileia tou Theou*] has drawn near' – describes the same reality. This is clear from Matthew itself, where the phrase 'the kingdom of God' appears four (or perhaps five) times; of special note is 19:23-24, where Jesus speaks of 'entering into the kingdom of heaven,' then of 'entering into the kingdom of God.'[81]

Yet, no fewer than thirty-three times in Matthew we meet the phrase 'the kingdom of heaven'; that it occurs nowhere else in the NT makes Matthew's usage the more striking. By thus avoiding a direct reference to God and speaking instead of his habitation, the evangelist honors the sensibilities of his Jewish readers.[82] Yet Matthew also shows his reverence for God by *employing* his name: the word *Theos* ('God') appears in

---

[80]See Matthew 2:2, 11; 28:9, 17. For a discussion of the Synoptic Gospels' christological titles, see Guthrie 1981: 219-321, together with the section 'Jesus, God and Man,' 401-07.

[81]The language of 19:23, *eiseleusetai eis tēn basileian tōn ouranōn*, is very close to that of 24, *eiselthein eis tēn basileian tou Theou*; the future indicative *eiseleusetai* and the aorist infinitive *eiselthein* both come from the verb *eiserchomai*. The other instances of 'the kingdom of God': 12:28; 21:31, 43; and a *v.l.* at 6:33. Cf. 13:43, 'in the kingdom of their Father.'

[82]To this day many a Jew, seeking to obey the third commandment (Exod. 20:7), renders the *Tetragrammaton*, the sacred covenantal name of Israel's God, not as 'Yahweh' but as 'Adonai.'

his gospel fifty-eight times (including the noted instances of 'the kingdom of God'). The phrase 'the kingdom of heaven,' besides showing deference to Jewish piety, expresses one of Matthew's favorite motifs, 'the majesty of God's universal dominion.'[83] Moreover, for 'heaven' as God's dwelling place Matthew mostly uses plural forms of *ouranos*, whereas he much prefers the singular when speaking of 'the heavens' as God's creation.[84]

The Greek word for 'kingdom,' *basileia*, primarily denotes God's rule, and secondarily the realm over which he rules, and into which one may enter. John and Jesus announce the dawn of God's kingdom. In one sense, God's reign is both eternal and universal. 'Yahweh reigns.... Your throne is established from of old' (Ps. 93:1-2). Yahweh's 'kingdom rules over all' (Ps. 103:19). 'Your kingdom is an everlasting kingdom' (Ps. 145:13). 'You [Yahweh] rule over all the kingdoms of the nations' (2 Chron. 20:6). Yet God's laws are flagrantly disobeyed, and wickedness is rampant in the earth, as Matthew itself shows (see, e.g., Matt. 2 and 27). John and Jesus declare that God is now unleashing powers to make what is his by right (*de jure*) to be altogether his in fact (*de facto*). 'The kingdom of God has come [*ephthasen*] upon you,' says Jesus in 12:28; his ministry marks the inauguration of God's final rule. 'The kingdom of heaven has drawn near [*ēngiken*],' says Jesus in 4:17 (and John in 3:2); now that the kingdom has dawned, its consummation (6:10) is assured.[85]

---

[83]Gundry 1994: 43. In Daniel 4:26 (MT, 4:23) 'heaven' is probably a surrogate for God (see Goldingay 1989: 89); the whole chapter celebrates the majesty of God's universal dominion.

[84]See BAGD s.v. *ouranos*, 2. and 1. For references to God's dwelling, all with plural forms of *ouranos*, see, e.g., Matthew 3:2; 5:3; 6:9; 7:11, 21; for instances of the singular, see 6:10, 20; 18:18. For the created heavens, all with singular forms of *ouranos*, see, e.g., 5:18; 11:25; 24:35; 26:64; the plural of 24:31 is a rare exception. 'The kingdom of heaven [singular *tou ouranou*]' never occurs in the NT. Since 'the heavens' usually suggests a part of the universe (as, e.g., in Gen. 1:1 and Ps. 8:3), every instance in Matthew of a plural form of *ouranos* for God's dwelling is translated as a singular to avoid confusion: so, e.g., 3:2 ('the kingdom of heaven') and 6:9 ('Our Father in heaven').

[85]Cf. Ridderbos 1962: 40-41; BAGD s.v. *phthanō*, 2. ('arrive, come'); s.v. *engizō* ('approach, come near'); comments on Matthew 4:17 and 12:28; and below ('the already and the not yet').

God's Rule and God's Son
These two are distinguishable but quite inseparable. The
message Jesus declares is not 'the gospel of Christ,' but 'the
gospel of the kingdom of heaven.' Jesus proclaims God's rule
and submits to God's rule; but he is not equated with God's
rule.[86] At the same time, it is because Jesus has come that
God's rule has dawned. John the Baptist is a herald of the
kingdom; Jesus is both herald and the one through whom
God's rule will actually be established.[87] Jesus' preaching,
unlike John's, is accompanied by miracles; and while Jesus'
assault on Satan's dominion is in some ways comparable
to acts of other Jewish exorcists, it is unique and decisive
in its effects. Who but God incarnate – one equipped as
no other to exercise divine authority – could achieve the
destruction of Satan's kingdom? Who but the Son of Man
has the right to decide who enters the Father's kingdom?
Upon whom but God the Son will God the Father bestow
singular honor when the kingdom is consummated?[88]

Because the Son's work is vital for the coming of God's rule,
he is fiercely assaulted from his birth onwards by rival kings
both human (Matt. 2) and demonic (Matt. 4). The death of John,
the kingdom's herald, foreshadows what is in store for Jesus.
In commissioning his followers to spread the good news of
the kingdom, Jesus describes the perils that await them. His
final reference to 'this gospel' is closely joined to the day of his
death.[89] But the event by which Jesus' foes sought to eradicate

---

[86]Matthew does not present Jesus as *autobasileia* ('the kingdom itself'),
a term Origen used when expounding Matthew 18:23 (see *TDNT* 1: 589).

[87]As noted, John's opening declaration (Matt. 3:2) is identical to that
of Jesus (4:17). Yet nowhere does Matthew expressly call John's preaching
'good news' (but cf. Luke 3:18). Reserving this term for the proclamation of
Jesus and his followers (4:23; 9:35; 24:14; 26:13) is one way Matthew shows
Jesus' work to be more crucial than John's for the kingdom's coming.

[88]See 4:23; 9:35; 10:7-8 (where Jesus' preaching of the kingdom is closely
joined to acts of healing); 12:27-28 (where it is precisely Jesus' exorcisms
which prove that the kingdom has dawned); 22:2 (where the kingdom is
likened to a king's hosting a wedding banquet for his son), 44 (where the
Father puts Messiah's enemies under his feet); 25:31-46 (where the Son of
Man determines who enters the kingdom prepared by the Father).

[89]For this link between John and Jesus, see 4:12-17; 14:1-12; 17:10-13. For
Jesus' warnings to apostolic witnesses, see 10:2-23; 24:4-14. In 26:12-13, Jesus

the threat of God's rule, assures its triumph. By virtue of his dual triumph in death and resurrection, Jesus is given universal dominion.[90] Now we can better understand why the devil early sought to deter him from the path to the cross (4:1-11).

The Already and the Not Yet

The kingdom of God has *truly* come with Jesus, but not yet *fully*. God's rule has been inaugurated, but it is not yet consummated.

As we just saw, Messiah's presence and preaching and miraculous powers testify to the advent of the kingdom. Yet in some respects God's rule is now being exercised covertly rather than overtly, as we learn from the parables of the mustard seed, the yeast and the hidden treasure. Let listeners beware lest the kingdom's present *hiddenness* blind them to its present *reality*. Let them 'see with their eyes' (Matt. 13:15) what is happening: the mustard plant is already growing, the yeast is already permeating the dough, and the treasure is already being joyously discovered. Members of the community being gathered around Jesus are already submitting to God's rule and producing fruit accordingly. God's truth has already begun to affect societies and to transform cultures.[91]

God mightily displayed his rule in Jesus' death and resurrection. Yet neither here nor in the fall of Jerusalem (A.D. 70) does his kingdom come in its fullness; that awaits the glorious return of the Son of Man. Till then Jesus' servants are faithfully to preach his gospel and teach his commands; they will be sorely tried and fiercely opposed, but those who endure to the end will surely be saved. Then God's will shall be done on earth as in heaven, and his rule will be fully realized. All rival kingships will have been destroyed; justice and peace

---

promises that the preaching of the kingdom will recall his being anointed in advance for burial.

[90]See 28:18-20 (also 1 Cor. 15:20-28). In Matthew 26:26-29, at the very time he speaks of his imminent death, Jesus anticipates the day of final victory in his Father's kingdom.

[91]See Matthew 13:3-23, 31-33, 44; 7:17-20; and 'The Kingdom and the Church' under E. below.

will finally be established throughout his realm. The D-Day of Jesus' first advent assures the V-Day of his second![92]

D. The Salvation of God

The noun *sōtēria* ('salvation') never appears in Matthew, and nowhere is God the Father or Christ the Son expressly called *Sōtēr* ('Savior'). But the verb *sōzō* ('save') occurs fifteen times, all but one of which have God's work in view, and most of which speak of Jesus' achievements.[93] We first meet the term in Matthew 1:21, in the angel's words to Joseph: 'She [Mary] will bear a son, and you shall call his name Jesus [*Iēsous*], for he himself will save [*sōsei*] his people from their sins.'

The Gravity of Sin

Jesus 'will save his people *from their sins*.' All whom Jesus later addresses are in need of such rescue, for sin (*hamartia*) infects and enslaves them all. 'Wicked thoughts, murder, adultery, fornication, theft, perjury, slander – these all proceed from the heart' and defile everyone (Matt. 15:19; REB). Those who receive God's law stubbornly and wilfully disobey it: all are 'workers of lawlessness [*anomia*]' (7:23). The house of Israel consists of 'lost sheep' (15:24). Some are publicly recognized as 'sinners' (*hamartōloi*) because of flagrantly immoral lives or dishonorable occupations. But Jesus also exposes the manifold sin and hypocrisy of Israel's religious leadership – those who are recognized to be, and who recognize themselves to be, 'the righteous.'[94]

---

[92]See 5:3-12; 6:9-13; 10:5-23; 13:24-30, 36-43, 47-50; 16:24-28; 24:3-51; 25:1-46; 26:64; also the reference in Hebrews 12:28 to God's 'unshakeable kingdom.' On 'the already and the not yet' of the kingdom in Jesus' teachings, see Beasley-Murray 1986; Ladd 1974; Ridderbos 1962. Cullmann 1962: 84 likened Jesus' death and resurrection to D-Day, and the kingdom's future consummation to V-Day (the original German was first published in 1946).

[93]The one exception is Matthew 16:25: 'whoever wants to save his life....' Jesus' deliverance from the cross would be ascribed to God or to his agent Elijah (see 27:40, 42, 49). Both *sōtēria* and *sōtēr* are applied to Jesus in Luke and John.

It is therefore urgent that Israel embrace Jesus' gospel (4:23). Those who reject the grace attending the dawn of God's rule and the advent of Messiah are at far greater risk than those who disobeyed the Mosaic law. The hour is critical; when the kingdom fully arrives, judgment will be swift, decisive and severe. Jesus warns that punishment, anguish and destruction await the wicked, and – worst of all – exclusion forever from the presence of God and his Messiah.[95]

Jesus the Savior

'You shall call his name Jesus [*Iēsous*],' says the angel, 'for he himself will save [*sōsei*] his people from their sins' (1:21). The latter part of the statement expounds the meaning of *Iēsous*, the Greek equivalent of the Hebrew Joshua, 'Yahweh is salvation.'[96] The name God chooses for the child concisely expresses the singular purpose of his mission. This opening instance of *sōzō* will prove to be foundational for all further references to Jesus' saving works.

'He will save his people from their *sins*,' says the angel – not 'from their enemies,' nor 'from every social ill or physical affliction or mortal peril.' God does establish his rule by destroying all rival and tyrannical kingdoms.[97] Just as surely, forgiving sins and healing disease are distinguishable but inseparable aspects of Jesus' mission. Forgiveness can be described as 'healing'; and the language of 'saving' can be applied to a physical cure and to rescue from threatened drowning.[98] Moreover, Jesus speaks of the gospel's social, political and economic implications.[99] But all those problems – including physical death – are symptomatic of a deeper

---

[94]For 'sinners' (or 'tax collectors and sinners') in the technical sense, see Matthew 9:10, 11, 13; 11:19. For Jesus' exposure of 'the righteous' as 'the sinful,' see e.g. 5:20; 6:1-18; 9:12-13; 12:30-42; 15:1-20; 16:1-4; 23:1-36; 26:45.

[95]See, e.g., 3:2-12; 7:13-14, 21-23; 11:20-24; 12:24-45; 13:24-30, 36-43, 47-50; 22:1-14; 23:13-36; 24:36-51; 25:1-46. Cf. Hebrews 10:26-31.

[96]In the LXX of Joshua, the title figure's name is written *Iēsous*, for *yēšûa'*, a contracted form (used e.g. in Nehemiah 3:19) of the earlier *yĕhôšua'* (Josh. 1:1, etc.).

[97]See above on 'the Kingdom of God.' Cf. Luke 1:32-33, together with 1:46-55, 67-79.

[98]See Matthew 9:2-7 (the paralytic), 20-22 (the woman with internal bleeding; *sōzō* appears three times in 21-22); 8:25 and 14:30 (where the

malady. Being murdered is not nearly as tragic as having both soul and body destroyed in hell on account of sin (Matt. 10:28). It is precisely in face of that ineluctable judgment that Jesus comes, proclaiming 'the gospel of the kingdom.' The very God whose wrath is coming, acts to save his people from it. God's Rule is *radical*; recognizing the root of human misery, God sends Messiah to free persons from bondage to their sins. That the one appointed to judge the nations is the very one sent to save people from destruction, discloses how amazing is the divine grace. Once liberated, and once captivated by that grace, those people can more effectively address sins' effects upon themselves and others.[100]

The theological and evangelical significance of *Iēsous* helps to explain its frequency. Applying the angel's command to himself, Matthew 'calls him *Iēsous*' 150 times – far more often than any other name.[101]

The Cost of Forgiveness

In 9:5, Jesus poses a question to his critics: 'Which is easier, to say "Your sins are forgiven," or to say "Arise and walk"'? For us the first would be easier: the effectiveness of a pronouncement of forgiveness could be neither proved nor disproved, but the failure of a paralytic to 'arise and walk' at my command exposes me as a fraud. For Christ the matter is different: when we come to the cross we discover that it is infinitely easier for him to cure paralysis than to forgive sins. There is no mistaking the centrality of Jesus' death in Matthew's story; for this event all else from the incarnation

---

imperative *sōson* – 'save!' – voices the desperation of men threatened by drowning); and 13:15 (where the repentant are 'healed'; in the parallel of Mark 4:12, they are 'forgiven'). Given its use in 1:21, it is perhaps significant that *sōzō* is applied to a healing miracle only in 9:21-22. By contrast, Matthew uses the verb *therapeuō* sixteen times.

[99]For the effects of 'the gospel of the kingdom' in these areas, see, e.g., the comments on 4:3-4; 5:3-10; 6:2-4; 15:1-9; 17:24-27; 19:16-24; 22:15-22; 25:31-46.

[100]For pictures of grace's magnitude, see, e.g., the parables of 18:23-35 and 20:1-16.

[101]By comparison, 'son' occurs eighty-nine times (many of which do not refer to Jesus); *kyrios*, eighty times (many of which do not refer to Jesus); 'God' (*Theos*), fifty-one; 'Son of Man,' thirty; *Christos*, seventeen.

onwards has prepared (see sec. I.). To liberate his people from bondage to sin, Jesus must offer his own life as the ransom (Matt. 20:28). To secure their forgiveness, he must pour out his own blood (26:28). If they are to escape the divine disapproval, he himself must drink 'the cup' of God's wrath. No wonder he pleads in Gethsemane that he may be spared doing so (26:39). The only saying from the cross that Matthew records is Jesus' cry of dereliction (27:46). Now bearing the sins of his people, the beloved Son is abandoned by the Father. At the cross Jesus' enemies mocked him, saying 'He saved others, he cannot save himself' (27:42). In truth, it is because he chose not to save himself that he saved others.[102]

Jesus 'will save *his people* from their sins' (Matt. 1:21). They are indeed his people, for he is their Davidic Messiah and their God incarnate. 'You shall call his name *Iēsous*,' says the angel to Joseph. But those whom he saves 'will call his name *Emmanouēl*..."God with us"' (1:23). The one who atones for sins must be both human and divine, as Anselm recognized: 'If, then, it be necessary that the kingdom of heaven be completed by man's admission, and if man cannot be admitted unless... satisfaction for sin be first made, and if God only *can*, and man only *ought* to make this satisfaction, then necessarily One must make it who is both God and man.'[103] Let us inquire further into the identity of these people whom Jesus came to save.

E. The People of God
The noun *laos* ('people') appears in Matthew fourteen times, starting with 1:21. All remaining thirteen instances speak of the people of Israel, whether as (i) those whom the nation's leaders represent, and whose unrest they fear; or (ii) the

---

[102]On this 'cup' of God's wrath, and on the link between the agony in Gethsemane and the cry of dereliction, see comments on the pertinent texts and Morris 1965: 42-49.

[103]*Cur Deus Homo?* ('Why God a Man?'), Book II, in Bettenson 1970: 139. Cf. the *Heidelberg Catechism*, nos. 16 and 17. Given Matthew's accent on the cross, his restraint in expounding the *theology* of the cross testifies to his integrity as an historian. The full *exposition* of the cross awaits Jesus' death; Matthew leaves that task to those (such as Paul and Peter) who are writing from a post-resurrection perspective.

special objects of God's and Messiah's favor; or (iii) those who stand under judgment because they have resisted and disobeyed God.[104] How does the *laos* of 1:21 relate to that threefold usage?

Israel and the Nations

Some texts in Matthew depict Israel as the object of God's favor to the exclusion of Gentiles. Others announce blessings for Gentiles and threaten to exclude Jews. Scholars have long been intrigued by this diversity; one calls the co-existence of such passages 'probably the major puzzle' in Matthew.[105] While some think that Matthew does not try to solve the puzzle but only lays out its several pieces, I believe that a solution may be found by examining the texts in question.[106]

From its opening verse, Matthew is thoroughly Jewish. Jesus honors the law of Moses, commends those who teach it and censures those who break it. He declares that he has been sent only to 'the lost sheep of the house of Israel,' and tells his apostles to avoid Gentiles and Samaritans. He likens persons excluded from the church to pagans, and on one occasion appears reluctant to heal a Gentile.[107] Yet it is already clear from the opening genealogy, and from the magi's visit to the infant Jesus, that Gentiles are numbered among Messiah's 'people.' Jesus first proclaims his gospel in 'Galilee of the Gentiles.' Israel's Servant is the Gentiles' hope. Even as he focuses on 'the lost sheep of the house of Israel,' Jesus serves Gentiles, as had Jonah and Solomon. He commends two Gentiles for their extraordinary faith. More than once he enters Gentile territory, where he expels demons, heals the sick, feeds a multitude and promises Gentiles a share in the

---

[104]See (i) Matthew 2:4; 21:23; 26:3, 5, 47; 27:1, 64; (ii) 2:6; 4:16, 23; and (iii) 13:15; 15:8; 27:25.

[105]Hagner 1993: lxvii.

[106]'In the Gospel of Matthew, K. Tagawa finds "quite contradictory attitudes concerning the problem of the Gentiles and the Jews," and concludes that Matthew has no worked-out theological understanding of the question' (France 1989: 206), a judgment well refuted by France (ibid., 206-41). See also Hagner 1993: lxv-lxxiii.

[107]See Matthew 1:1; 5:17-20; 10:5-6; 15:24-26; 18:17; 23:2-3.

kingdom of heaven. The request for healing which he first seemed to rebuff, he grants.[108]

In time, Jesus announced that he would give his life as a ransom 'for many' (*anti pollōn*; Matt. 20:28), and that his blood is to be poured out 'for many' (*peri pollōn*; 26:28). Messiah dies not just for 'the few' – Israelites – but for Gentiles too. Once he has paid that price, he commands his apostles to spread the news of accomplished redemption to all the nations (28:19). We now understand why Jesus devoted most of his time to evangelizing and discipling Jews: it was to prepare them for evangelizing and discipling Gentiles – which would bring to fulfillment a host of OT promises.[109] Both Jesus' mission to Israel and his vicarious death 'took place *in order that* the incorporation of the Gentiles into the Kingdom of God might be possible.'[110]

The Jewish tenants of God's vineyard will be condemned for rejecting and killing his Son, and the vineyard leased to tenants who will produce the expected harvest (Matt. 21:33-41). But Jews are not hereby excluded from the kingdom; despite the infidelity of Israel, especially her leaders, there remains a faithful remnant. While Jesus' words in 23:39 do not revoke his preceding judgment on unbelieving Israel, they do hold out hope of Israelites' future repentance.[111] The apostles' earlier mission to Israel (10:1-23) is not ended, only expanded. The 'other tenants' of 21:41 stand for a 'nation' (*ethnos*; 21:43) drawn from 'all the nations [*ethnē*]' (28:19) – a 'people' (*laos*; 1:21), that includes Gentiles as well as Jews, Jews no less than Gentiles.[112]

---

[108]See 1:2-16; 2:1-12; 4:13-16; 8:5-13, 28-34; 12:15-21, 41-42; 15:21-39.

[109]See Genesis 12:1-3 (Matt. 1:1); Leviticus 19:18, 34 (Matt. 5:43-44; 22:39); Psalm 2:7-12 (Matt. 1:1; 3:17); Isaiah 9:1-2 (Matt. 4:14-16); 42:1-4 (Matt. 3:17; 12:18-21); 49:1-6 (Matt. 28:19); 56:4-8 (Matt. 21:13); Daniel 7:13-14 (Matt. 26:64); Zechariah 9:9-10 (Matt. 21:5).

[110]Jeremias 1958: 73. Simeon joins Israel's glory to her mission to Gentiles (Luke 2:32), then alludes to Jesus' death (2:35) as the precondition of that mission. Compare and contrast 'intertestamental Jewish attitudes toward Gentiles' as set forth in Scott 1995: 335-52.

[111]See France 1989: 237-38; and my comments *ad loc*. For the 'faithful remnant' in OT and NT, see *TDNT* 4: 196-214; *ISBE* 4: 130-34. Cf. Luke 1–2; and comments on Matthew 1:18-25.

As Peter and Matthew were called by Jesus' sovereign initiative, so it is with all citizens of that *ethnos*, of that *laos*. They are all his 'elect' (*eklektoi*): he saves them from their sins; he and the Father disclose to them the secrets of the kingdom; he protects them amid tribulation and false teaching; and he will gather them from all the nations upon his return.[113]

The Messianic Community

At a critical juncture of his ministry Jesus declares: 'I will build my church' (16:18). This 'church' (*ekklēsia*) consists of 'his people,' the very ones whom he saves from their sins (1:21). As each of these persons belongs to him, so naturally does the community into which they gather – further testimony to his divinity and to the authority the Father has granted him.

The future tense 'I will build' is notable: the commencing of the project awaits Jesus' glorification and the outpouring of the Holy Spirit (cf. John 7:39; Acts 2:33). Yet that *ekklēsia* stands in continuity with the OT people of God, just as the new covenant brings to fulfillment promises made to Abraham, Moses and David. Moreover, the new community is already being gathered around Messiah during his ministry. The company of disciples is a genuine family – one whose obligations surpass those of an earthly family.[114] Jesus deliberately chooses *twelve* apostles, corresponding to the twelve tribes of Israel – a sign that the people of God are being newly constituted around his person. Just as significantly, Jesus does *not* choose eleven, making himself the twelfth: for while he will be with his people, and

---

[112]According to Richardson 1969: 189, 'The two most important titles of Israel [*Israēl* and *laos*] are, in Matthew, never taken over by the Church.' I believe this holds true for *Israēl* but not for *laos*. Israel is the object of Messiah's favor, and he saves many a 'lost sheep' in Israel (2:6; 10:6; 15:24). But neither Jesus nor Matthew applies *Israēl* to the church as a whole (so too Childs 1984: 78). Some think 'the twelve tribes of Israel' in 19:28 is to be so understood; but Jesus here more likely speaks of national Israel as the object of divine judgment (see those comments). As for *laos*, we saw that 'his people' in 1:21 embraces Gentiles as well as Jews.

[113]See Matthew 1:21; 11:25-30; 13:10-15; and (for the four instances of *eklektos*, all in the plural) 22:14; 24:22, 24, 31.

[114]See 10:34-39; 12:46-50; 20:20-28.

while they are to be intimately joined to him, he also stands over them and is distinguished from them as Lord from subject.[115]

A Loyal People

Because Jesus is Lord, disciples are to pledge their supreme allegiance to him alone.[116] The noun *mathētēs*, 'disciple,' occurs seventy-three times in Matthew, but the related verb *manthanō*, 'learn,' only three times.[117] On the other hand the verb *akoloutheō* – 'follow' – occurs twenty-five times, at least thirteen of which relate that certain disciples followed Jesus or that Jesus commanded persons to do so.[118] The primary requirement for Jesus' disciples is that they *follow* him, that they be committed to *him*. Following Jesus provides the basis for receiving his teaching and obeying his commands. 'Come to me,' he says, then 'learn from me' (Matt. 11:28-29).

These people first express their allegiance by embracing Jesus' gospel of the kingdom, repenting of their sins and purposing to do the Father's will, (6:10). Rescued by Jesus from the tyranny of legalism, and rejoicing over God's grace to 'the poor in spirit,' they readily receive and obey God's law now being expounded by Jesus the New Moses, and commit themselves to 'the way of righteousness' (*dikaiosynē*; 21:32) i.e., to doing good works (5:16). Their fruitful lives and their self-forgetful service testify that they truly belong to Messiah.[119]

---

[115]See Matthew 28:18-20; 23:8-10; also John 15, on the vine and the branches.

[116]See Matthew 10:34-39; 16:24-25; 23:8-10.

[117]In 11:29 and 24:32, Jesus exhorts his disciples to 'learn.' In the third instance, 9:13, it is principally if not exclusively the Pharisees whom Jesus commands to learn.

[118]See 4:20, 22; 8:22, 23; 9:9; 10:38; 16:24; 19:21, 27, 28; 20:34; 27:55; probably 8:10 as well. Most of the other instances speak of crowds' following Jesus (e.g., 4:25).

[119]See Matthew 7:15-23; 13:3-23; 25:31-46. For freedom from legalism, see 11:28-30; 12:1-8. For Jesus' gospel as the foundation for law-keeping, see 4:23-25; 5:3-12 (with 5:17-48; 6:1-18); 9:12-13; 22:1-14. 'The grace of the kingdom and the demands of the law as interpreted by the messianic king stand in dynamic tension throughout [Matthew], but it is clear that the former precedes the latter' (Hagner 1993: lxiii). 'The true righteousness [*dikaiosynē*] Matthew writes about gives evidence of genuine discipleship, but does not deserve salvation' (Gundry 1994: 82); cf. Psalm 24:4-5; 119:166; Hosea 10:12 (those called to *tsᵉdāqâ*, holy conduct [10:12a] must yet depend on the gift of Yahweh's saving *tsedeq* [10:12b]). The *dikaiosynē* of Matthew 5:20

The Kingdom and the Church

As Christ and the kingdom are distinguishable but inseparable (C. above), so are the kingdom and the church. As we saw, *basileia* primarily denotes the *rule* of God inaugurated by Jesus; and *ekklēsia*, God's *people* who are joined to Jesus. As also noted, *basileia* implies a realm over which God reigns – whether it be earthly or heavenly, (6:10; 11:25). The realm presently designed for those who submit to God's rule on Jesus' terms is *the church*. The apostles and their successors go forth proclaiming 'the gospel of the kingdom' (24:14; 26:13). By using 'the keys of the kingdom' (16:19), they grant to those embracing the gospel the right to enter the church, to receive Christian baptism and to learn what Jesus taught (28:19-20a). Fidelity to that instruction ('to *keep* all that I commanded you'; 28:20a) evidences their submission to God's rule.

When God's people keep Jesus' commandments – for example, those set forth in the first and the fourth discourses (Matt. 5–7, 18), together with the foundational command of 22:37-40 – the effects within the new community are profound and far-reaching. But as the one granted universal authority (28:18), Jesus exerts his rule beyond the church as well. Love for one's neighbor (22:39) is not limited to those within the community. Jesus' disciples are 'the salt of the *earth*' and 'the light of the *world*' (5:14-16), persons whom he equips to influence the surrounding culture.[120] The 'gospel of the kingdom' is addressed, initially at least, to those outside the church; that they are commanded to repent and submit to God's rule shows Jesus' authority over them. They only escape 'the wrath to come' (3:7) by obeying Christ's command, pledging their allegiance to him and entering the Messianic community. By this means that which belongs to Christ by right (*de jure*)

---

is closer to Philippians 1:11 (where 'the fruit of righteousness' means 'holy living') than to Romans 3:21 (which speaks of God's saving righteousness). See BAGD s.v., 2. and 3.; and the comments on Matthew 3:15; 5:20; 6:1, etc.

[120]In the church 'the gifts and powers of the *basileia* are granted and received' (Ridderbos 1962: 356). The church is the kingdom's witness and instrument (Ladd 1993: 111-14). Instructed by the church, individual Christians can begin to bring societal structures under the dominion of Christ (O. Palmer Robertson, 'The Kingdom and the Church,' unpublished MS., 3, 7-9).

becomes his in fact (*de facto*). The worship accorded him within the church anticipates the universal acclaim which he will receive at the kingdom's consummation.

For now the true – the invisible – church is not to be equated with the kingdom. It may rightly be said that 'the visible church... is the kingdom of the Lord Jesus Christ, the house and family of God, out of which there is no ordinary possibility of salvation.'[121] But this 'visible church' is a mixed multitude consisting of both true and false disciples.[122] At the end, the angels, by order of the Son of Man, 'will weed out of his kingdom everything that causes sin and all who do evil' (Matt. 13:41, NIV). Thereafter the invisible church – that is, 'the whole number of the elect' – and the citizenry of the kingdom of heaven will be seen to consist of the same company of people.[123]

---

[121]*WCF*, Ch. 25, 'Of the Church,' sec. 2.

[122]See the parables of 13:24-30 (and 36-43), 47-50; 22:1-14; 25:1-46. 'Thus,' writes Ladd (1993: 111), 'entrance into the Kingdom means participation in the church; but entrance into the church is not necessarily synonymous with entrance into the Kingdom.'

[123]Cf. *WCF* 25.1, 'The catholic or universal church, which is invisible, consists of the whole number of the elect, that have been, are, or shall be gathered into one, under Christ the Head thereof....'

VI.
THE TEACHER

Frequently in Matthew, Jesus is called 'teacher' (*didaskalos*) and is said to 'teach' (*didaskō*).[1] Correspondingly, foremost in his followers' task of discipling the nations is 'teaching them' (*didaskontes autous*) what Jesus commanded (Matt. 28:20). The book before us is the fruit of obedience to that commission. The apostle, scribe, evangelist and theologian is a masterful teacher.

What Matthew teaches has been in view from the survey of his story (I.) through the summary of his theology (V.). Our present focus is upon his classroom, so to speak. For whom does he write? How, in what circumstances, and for what purposes do he instruct them? Two things are already clear: what Matthew teaches, he has first learned; and as he teaches, he remains a pupil of the master Teacher, and a brother to the students under his care (28:18; 23:8).

A. The Intended Audience

Where was Matthew written, and when? For whom was it intended? Matthew does not directly answer any of these questions. Given the subject of his book, the setting which he most illuminates is not the one within which he writes but the one within which Jesus lived and taught. This is a story *about Jesus*. Yet it is also a story *for Matthew and his readers*; and we may be sure that the apostle selects his material in light of his readers' pastoral and catechetical

---

[1] Ten of the twelve instances of *didaskalos* in Matthew refer to Jesus (e.g., 8:19; 9:11); he is included in the other two (the proverbial sayings of 10:24-25). Of the fourteen instances of *didaskō*, nine refer to Jesus' teaching (e.g., 4:23; 5:2), and five to that of others (e.g., 5:19; 15:9). The two nouns for 'teaching,' rarely occur – *didaskalia* once, and *didachē* three times.

needs.[2] So it is appropriate to ask those three questions. It is the third on which Matthew itself sheds the most light; so we begin here. We shall then be better able to address the first two.

In keeping with his chosen subject, Matthew makes clear *Jesus'* intended audience: it consisted mainly of the crowds, his disciples and his chief antagonists, Israel's religious leaders. Judging by what Matthew records of Jesus' instructions to his followers, there were counterparts to all three in Matthew's day. The same 'gospel' which Jesus declared to 'the crowds,' is to be taken to 'all the nations.'[3] Those who embrace this message are 'made disciples': they receive Christian baptism and begin to learn the very commands Jesus gave his first disciples (Matt. 28:19-20). Furthermore, warns Jesus, those who follow him are sure to be opposed as he himself was.[4]

As Jesus' closing commission embraces both Jews and Gentiles, and as Matthew contains good news for both, we may reasonably conclude that Matthew wants his book to be read by both – wherever and whenever they live. This gospel is intended not only for members of 'the crowd' in the apostle's time and place but also for those scattered throughout the world (24:14; 26:13) and for those living to the close of the age (28:20). This means that Matthew may serve as an evangelistic tract for both Jews and Gentiles in our day as surely as in his.[5]

In accord with the universality of the gospel, Jesus' church (16:18) consists of both Jewish- and Gentile-Christians. The

---

[2]On 'artistic selectivity,' see pages 114-15. 'Matthew emphasized those features of his tradition that best addressed the pastoral situation of his readers' (Keener 1999: 42). Still, as a conscientious scribe and historian he may have recorded material which he did not perceive to be immediately applicable to his readers. We may also agree that Matthew 'writes as an ancient churchman concerned to adapt Jesus' words and deeds to the situation current at the time of writing' (Gundry 1994: 604), if 'adapting' is not taken to mean 'altering' or 'distorting' (cf. pp. 110-19 above).

[3]See Matthew 4:17, 23; 9:35-38; 24:14; 26:13; 28:19. About three-fifths of the instances of *ochlos* ('crowd') in Matthew are in the plural.

[4]See 10:16-39; 16:21-26; 20:17-23; 23:33-36; 24:9-13.

[5]Matthew 24:14; 26:13; and 28:18-20 suggest that Matthew expects his book to have an impact beyond his own time and place. Cf. John 17:20; Luke 24:46-49; Acts 1:7-8.

entirety of Matthew is a means of instructing both, wherever and whenever they live. As Jesus' gospel is intended for Gentiles as well as Jews, so is his law. His exposition in 5:17-48 is rooted in Mosaic legislation; but 28:19-20 makes it plain that these commands are for Gentile believers as surely as for Jewish. The strongly Hebraic character of Matthew naturally suggests a Jewish-Christian audience and it may be these who are principally addressed. But the book is meant for Gentile-Christians too, and it does not somehow alter its character for their sake. That would violate the very nature of what Matthew reports; for the salvation these Gentiles receive, the laws they obey and the Jesus they worship, are *themselves* thoroughly and uncompromisingly Hebraic.[6]

Jesus warned his followers of opposition from both Jews and Gentiles (Matt. 10:17-20). But in Matthew the persons most hostile to Jesus are Israel's religious leaders, particularly the scribes, Pharisees and chief priests. To judge from the frequency of such texts, including some peculiar to this gospel, the apostle and his intended readers have witnessed or experienced opposition and oppression of a kindred sort.[7] Since, according to the NT, Christians at various times and places were objects of such hostility, Matthew's teachings are again shown to be applicable to the church at large – and to her antagonists, particularly those among the Jews.[8]

---

[6]A judgment shared by the apostle to the Gentiles: cf. e.g., the pervasive use of OT texts and imagery in Romans, Galatians and Ephesians.

[7]All three terms – 'scribe' (*grammateus*), 'Pharisee' (*Pharisaios*), and 'chief priest' (*archiereus*) appear more often in Matthew than in any other gospel. For their opposition to Jesus, and his censure of them, see Matthew 5:17-20; 6:1-18; 9:11, 34; 12:2, 14, 24-45; 15:1-20; 16:1-12, 21; 19:3-12; 20:18; 21:15, 23-46; 22:15-22, 34-46; 23:1-36; 26:3-4, 47; 27:1, 12, 20, 41, 62.

[8]For strong arguments that Matthew and the other gospels were intended not just for their local communities but for the church at large, see Hengel 2000: 106-15; Bauckham 1998: 1-7 *et seq*. In support there is evidence that the early Christians were 'a network of communities in constant, close communication with each other' (ibid., 2); cf. pages 66-69 above, on 'the progress of oral and written traditions' in the early church. 'The question of genre is obviously relevant; and many have commented on the difference between a Gospel, with a relatively open horizon, and a letter, with a considerably more restricted horizon' (Barton 1998: 181). 'We should stop supposing that [Matthew] reflects the evangelist's close relationship

B. The Place of Origin

Where was Matthew written? We cannot say with certainty. Combining this with the above conclusions about the intended audience, we might think the question impractical. However, at least considering the possibilities may give us a sharper understanding of the milieu in which Matthew writes, and of his purpose for writing. (The same applies to the question of dating, to be considered shortly.) Two suggestions deserve special mention.

Arguments for Jerusalem, or Elsewhere in Palestine

1. Matthew's story is set in Palestine; we last meet him in Jerusalem (Acts 1:13; cf. 8:1; 15:2-4).

2. Matthew is thoroughly Hebraic, deeply rooted in the OT and highly respectful of Mosaic law. The book recounts Pharisaic teachings and practices; includes Aramaic words without translation; and refers to Jewish customs without explanation. Some of the Greek is strongly Semitic.

3. This case is yet stronger if Matthew was first written in Hebrew or Aramaic. Thus did patristic writers understand Papias' reference to Matthew's 'Hebrew dialect.' Moreover, both Jerome and the Anti-Marcionite Prologue to Luke expressly state that Matthew was written 'in Judea.'[9]

4. While a Palestinian setting becomes far less likely after Jerusalem's destruction in A.D. 70, Matthew can be reasonably dated before that (see below).[10]

---

with one group of Christians in one house church in one particular urban geographical location.... Surely Matthew's carefully crafted, very full account of the [*bios*] of Jesus was not written for such a small group of people: ...we should envisage a loosely linked set of communities over a wide geographical area' (G. N. Stanton, quoted in Barton 1998: 181-82). The author 'may have been more itinerant than usually assumed; and out of such a ministry he may have written his Gospel to strengthen and inform a large number of followers and given them an evangelistic and apologetic tool' (Carson 1984: 21-22).

[9]See *Evidence from Papias*, pages 28-40 above; France 1989: 60-62, 91. Jerome's claim that 'the Hebrew text [of Matthew] is still preserved to this day in the library at Caesarea' contributes to B.T. Viviano's belief that Matthew originated in this coastal Palestinian town (ibid., 62, 94).

[10]For some of these points, see Davies and Allison 1988: 139-40; France 1989: 91-94.

Arguments for Antioch, or Elsewhere in Syria

1. Since its founding in 300 B.C. Antioch had become the third largest city in the empire (after Rome and Alexandria) with a population estimated at 500,000, many of whom were Jews. According to Acts, Jewish-Christians fleeing persecution in Jerusalem brought the gospel to Antioch; many were converted, and a church consisting of both Jews and Gentiles was established – which in turn sponsored a westward mission to both Jews and Gentiles.[11] In accord with that evidence, Matthew reports that Christ authorized missions to both Jews and Gentiles (Matthew 10 and 28), and that Christ's *laos* (1:21) – his *ekklēsia* (16:18) – includes both.

2. The church of Antioch, given its location and the fruitful missions within and beyond its borders, became a major center of early Christianity. The origin of Matthew in such a center would help to explain its early prominence and influence.[12]

3. The Christians who brought the gospel to Antioch had already experienced persecution at the hands of Jews (Acts 11:19-20). It is probable that this church too, once established, encountered opposition from within the city's

---

[11]Acts 11:19-26; 13:1-3; etc. In 11:20b *Hellēnistas*, not *Hellēnas*, is likely original (*TC*, 340-42). It 'means strictly "one who uses Greek [language or customs]"; whether the person be a Jew or a Roman or any other non-Greek must be gathered from the context' (*TC*, 342). In the two other NT instances (Acts 6:1 and 9:29), the term denotes 'Grecian Jews' (NIV) among believers and non-believers respectively. In view of 11:19 – 'to no one but Jews [*Ioudaiois*] alone' – *Hellēnistas*, 20, at least embraces Gentiles and may refer to Gentiles exclusively. In any case, both Acts 15:22-23 and Galatians 2:11-12 show that the church in Antioch included Gentiles.

[12]Streeter 1924: 500-01 argues (i) that the unknown author of Matthew incorporated into his book a document known to come from Matthew (Streeter thought the document was 'Q'); (ii) that the whole of Matthew thus came to be viewed as apostolic; (iii) that Matthew 'would not have been generally accepted as Apostolic unless it had been backed by one of the great Churches'; and (iv) that the great Church in question was Antioch. I contend, on the contrary, (i) that Matthew was written by the apostle Matthew, and that it was very early viewed as apostolic because it *was* apostolic; and (ii) that no matter where Matthew originated, its *inherent qualities* chiefly explain its early impact on Christianity. See my earlier discussion, especially II. A. and B., III. E., IV. D.

large Jewish community.[13] But those very Christians, who had fled from persecution in Jerusalem, *evangelized* Jews in Antioch. Correspondingly, Israelites are depicted in Matthew as both adversaries and potential converts.

4. There were intramural battles too. Both Galatians 2:11-14 and Acts 15:1-5 testify to conflicts that arose in the church of Antioch because of its racial and cultural diversity. Both these texts address the relationship of gospel to law, or of justification to sanctification. (Galatians 2:11-14 also relates to Acts 10:1–11:18 and Matthew 15:1-20.) This subject is in view throughout Matthew as well; and while its teaching is especially close to James' (both at the apostolic council and in his epistle), it is also compatible with Galatians and Paul generally.[14]

5. As a Hebrew or Aramaic document would favor a Palestinian source, so a document in Greek – the original language of our Matthew – favors a Greek-speaking populace like that of Antioch.[15]

6. Ignatius was a bishop of Antioch martyred in Rome between A.D. 98 and 117. Letters he wrote to various churches during his journey to Rome contain notable references to Matthew, evidence of his acquaintance with this gospel during his bishopric.[16] There are further such references in the

---

[13]As Stanton notes (1989: 79), 'it is not hard to envisage in Antioch the tensions which seem to be reflected in Matthew between dominant Jewish synagogues and Matthew's smaller mixed Jewish and Gentile Christian community.'

[14]See pages 145-54; comments on Matthew 5–7; 15:1-20, etc. At the apostolic council, James' testimony is decisive (Acts 15:13-21). Apostles (*apostoloi*) also participated in these deliberations, (15:2, 4, 6, 22, 23). If, as is probable, Matthew was among them, both he and Paul assented to the letter of 15:22-29. The first to receive it were the Christians in Antioch (15:30-35). Affinities among Matthew, the apostolic decree and the epistle of James are explored by Scott 1969: 361-96.

[15]See above on *Hellēnistas* in Acts 11:20. Kümmel 1975: 119 says 'it is certain that the author of Mt lived in a Greek-speaking area and wrote for Greek-speaking Christians most of whom were of Jewish origin.' On the view that Matthew was first written in Greek, the case for Palestine is not greatly weakened; for many first-century Palestinians, Matthew included, spoke Greek.

[16]On Ignatius, see D. F. Wright, in *DCC*, 498-99. Streeter 1924: 505-06 detects about fifteen such references. E.g., in his letter to the church at Smyrna, 1:1, Ignatius says that Jesus 'is truly of the race of David according

Didache, which may have appeared in Syria as early as about A.D. 100 .[17]

I think the arguments for Antioch and Syria are stronger than those for Jerusalem and Palestine. But (to repeat) certainty is impossible. 'Antioch was by no means the only city with well-established Jewish and Christian communities,'[18] and thus not the only place where conflicts could arise between church and synagogue – which accords with my earlier contention that Matthew is intended for the church at large. The main value of the foregoing discussion (as of the following) is gaining a better sense of the environment within which Matthew arose.[19]

C. The Date of Composition

The destruction of Jerusalem and the temple in A.D. 70 'forms a natural boundary between the possibilities of an early date and a late one for the writing of Matthew.'[20] A majority of scholars think Matthew was written between A.D. 70 and 100; yet many of them allow for a range of ten or twenty years. A weighty minority, including several recent commentators,

---

to the flesh, but Son of God of the Divine Will, truly born of a virgin and baptized by John that all righteousness might be fulfilled in him' (ibid., 506); cf. Matthew 1:1, 23; 3:15. Ignatius' references do not prove that Matthew originated in Antioch. The gospels began to circulate among the churches from the earliest days (cf. pp. 25-28, 66-69 above). Nor do we conclude from Ignatius' indebtedness to John and the Pauline Epistles that these writings arose in Antioch (cf. Carson 1984: 21).

[17]On the *Didache*, see R. E. Nixon, in *DJG*, 297-98. For the references to Matthew, see Streeter 1924: 507-11; he concludes, 511, that both Ignatius and the *Didache* 'stand to Matthew as the preacher to his text.'

[18]Stanton 1989: 79.

[19]France 1989: 94-95 thinks that 'the geographical location in which [Matthew] originated is probably the least significant [introductory question] for a sound understanding of the text.' For some, including Gundry 1994: 609, (i) the 'Syria' of 4:24, in place of the 'Tyre and Sidon' of Mark 3:8; Luke 6:17, 'suggests that Matthew writes at some place in Syria besides Tyre and Sidon'; and (ii) the coin called a 'stater' in 17:24-27 'equals two double drachmas, as only in Damascus and Antioch in Syria.' But France 1989: 92-93 considers the latter point very questionable. For most of the above points, and some others, in favor of Antioch, see Streeter 1924: 500-523; Davies and Allison 1988: 143-47 (who also discuss, 139-43, other suggested places such as Alexandria, Phoenicia and Transjordan); Brown 1997: 212-16.

[20]Gundry 1994: 599.

argue for the period before 70; but here too a range of dates is commonly suggested. Many on both sides offer their conclusions tentatively; and some consider both views to be about equally defensible.[21]

Arguments for a Date After A.D. 70
1. Matthew employs Mark, which was written close to A.D. 70, so Matthew must be later.[22]

2. Certain texts indicate that Jerusalem has already fallen, among them Matthew 21:13 (which excludes the words 'for all the nations,' Mark 11:17, since there is no longer a temple to which Gentiles may come); Matthew 22:7 ('the king...set their city on fire'); 23:38 ('your house is left to you desolate'); 24:2 ('there will by no means be left here a stone upon a stone that will not be thrown down'), 15 ('when you see the abomination of desolation...standing in the holy place'); 27:25 ('his blood be

---

[21]Of the fifty-three scholars listed in Davies and Allison 1988: 127-28, to illustrate the 'spectrum of opinion,' forty-two choose dates between A.D. 70 and 110 ; and most of these (twenty-six of forty-two) allow a range of ten years (A.D. 70–80, 80–90, or 90–100) or twenty (A.D. 80–100, or 85–105). (So too Brown 1997: 172: '80–90, give or take a decade.') Of the eleven who opt for dates before 70, seven allow a range of ten years or more (A.D. 40–50, 50–60, 50–64, 60–70, or, atypically, 65–75). Among recent commentators who cautiously favor a date before A.D. 70 are Blomberg 1992: 42 ('a very slight preponderance of weight favors a date from ca. 58–69.... But we dare not be dogmatic; the evidence is simply too slim to come to any secure conclusion'), Carson 1984: 21 ('While surprisingly little in the Gospel conclusively points to a firm date, perhaps the sixties are the most likely decade for its composition'); France 1985: 30 ('there is certainly a good case to be made for a date in the sixties for the final "publication" of Matthew. It must be recognized, however, that [given various factors, including the link between Matthew and Mark]...any "publication date" can be advanced only very tentatively'); and Hagner 1993: lxxiv ('The inclination toward an early date taken here...is just that and no more'). Just as cautious from the other side is Keener 1999: 44 ('I...guess that Matthew was written in the late 70s').

[22]Kümmel (1975: 98) thinks Mark was written ca. A.D. 70. Given 'Mt's dependence on Mk...a date before 70 is excluded' (ibid., 119). Cf. Brown (1997: 217): 'Probably the best argument for a post-70 date is the dependence of Matt or Mark, a Gospel commonly dated to the 68–73 period.' Estimates vary on how much time was needed for Mark to come into Matthew's hands; and judgments about the date of Matthew rest also on matters yet to be considered.

upon us and upon our children,' implying a day of reckoning for a later generation).[23]

3. The phrase 'to this day' (Matt. 27:8; 28:15) 'would be very inappropriate if Matt was written only two or three decades after A.D. 30/33.'[24]

4. Texts such as Matthew 4:23 ('*their* synagogues'[25]), 10:14-39 (Jewish hostility towards Jesus' followers; cf. 23:34-37), 21:43 ('the kingdom of God will be taken away from you [namely, from 'the chief priests and the Pharisees,' 45] and given to a nation...'), 23:13-32 (seven woes upon scribes and Pharisees), and 24:24 (the rise of 'false messiahs and false prophets'), indicate that the *ekklēsia* (16:18) has become separated from Judaism. This evidence suggests a date for Matthew near A.D. 85; for at about this time a council at Jamnia introduced into the synagogue liturgy – specifically into the twelfth of the 'Eighteen Benedictions' (the *Shemoneh 'Esreh*) – the 'Benediction against Heretics' (*Birkath ha-Minim*). The version probably in use at the end of the first century reads as follows: 'And for apostates let there be no hope; and may the insolent kingdom be quickly uprooted, in our days. And may the Nazarenes [i.e., Christians] and the heretics [*minim*] perish quickly; and may they be erased from the Book of Life; and may they not be inscribed with the righteous. *Blessed art thou, Lord, who humblest the insolent.*'[26] Moreover, Matthew's preoccupation with the Pharisees accords with their ascendancy once the old Sanhedrin (consisting of chief priests and elders) collapsed with the destruction of the temple, and a 'new Sanhedrin' (consisting of scholars and champions of the law) was established at Jamnia.[27]

---

[23]Most of these texts are cited in Brown 1997: 217. Cf. Kümmel 1975: 119.

[24]Brown 1997: 217.

[25]For this phrase, see also Matthew 9:35; 10:17; 12:9; 13:54 (cf. 23:34).

[26]As quoted in Schürer 1979: 461; for the full Palestinian version, see 460-61. In the later and longer Babylonian version, 456-59 (the one still in use today), the twelfth benediction is not so specific: 'and let all who do wickedness quickly perish' (p. 457). Cf. Scott 1995: 366-67.

[27]The old Sanhedrin, whose members were primarily drawn from the priestly nobility, ceased to function with the temple's destruction. Thereafter 'a new Sanhedrin of doctors of the law was established,' with the Romans' permission, at Jamnia in western Judea under Johanan ben Zakkai, a foremost rabbi (Bruce 1971: 384). The Pharisees were now 'the

5. That Matthew represents a relatively late stage in the church's life and thought is evident from its *ecclesiology* (the concept of the church is well developed [16:18]; a well-organized church under established leaders is assumed [ch. 18]), *Christology* (Jesus is 'the Son of God' in the fullest sense; 28:19 'is the most advanced NT step in a Trinitarian direction and easier to understand as coming at the end of the NT period'),[28] and *eschatology* (the closing [28:20] stresses Jesus' abiding presence rather than his second coming).[29]

Arguments for a Date Before A.D. *70*
These arguments correspond to those presented above.

1. There is good reason to think that Matthew employed Mark (III. C.). Yet once we place the writing of Mark at around A.D. 65, and recognize that documents of such merit were readily circulated among the churches and their leaders, it is not hard to envisage Matthew's obtaining a copy of Mark within a year.[30]

2. References to Jerusalem's destruction are perfectly intelligible as prophetic utterances of Jesus, given all that Matthew discloses about him. Indeed, it is precisely as his *predictions* of God's judgment against a recalcitrant people that these texts possess such power.[31] Moreover, there are several

---

only party in Jewry equal to the task of reconstituting the national life, and they accomplished it' (ibid., 81); rabbis at Jamnia promoted Pharisaic traditions exclusively (Scott 1995: 102).

[28]Brown 1997: 217.

[29]Brown 1997: 217. Other evidence said to reflect a period towards the close of the first century: (i) a heightened reverence for Jesus, shown, e.g., in the change from Mark 6:5 (Jesus 'could not do') to Matthew 13:58 (he 'did not do'); and (ii) a heightened sense of the supernatural and miraculous, seen, e.g., in 27:19 (the dream of Pilate's wife) and 27:52-53 (the raising of many bodies from the tombs), texts peculiar to Matthew (reported, not endorsed, by France 1989: 87).

[30]'But even if Mark is as late as 65, there is no reason based on literary dependence why Matthew could not be dated A.D. 66. As soon as a written source is circulated, it is available for copying' (Carson 1984: 20). Cf. CMM, 78. In this instance, the document may well have been sent from one major church (at Rome, the likely source of Mark) to another (at Antioch). Some of the earlier remarks about Matthew's 'intended audience' are relevant here as well.

passages whose impact on Matthew's original audience is strengthened if the temple is still standing – e.g., 5:23-24 (offering a gift at the altar); 12:5-7 (the priests' eating the consecrated bread); 17:24-27 (paying the temple tax); 23:16-22 (swearing by the temple and its altar); 26:60-61 (predicting the temple's destruction).[32]

3. Is not a span of thirty years sufficiently long for the phrase 'to this day' to become appropriate? Do not Americans speak 'to this day' of events leading to President Nixon's resignation some thirty years ago (cf. 28:15), and identify them 'to this day' as 'Watergate' (cf. 27:8)?

4. *a.* The main conflicts described in Matthew occur *during Jesus' life* and culminate in his trial and execution. These conflicts recall those of the OT (in Jeremiah e.g.) between Yahweh's servants and Israel's alleged leaders, and anticipate those between Jesus' followers and their enemies; but these surpass all the others in gravity and intensity. Whenever Matthew wrote, the main reason for his preoccupation with Pharisees is not their influence in his own day but their virulent opposition to Jesus himself. Moreover, even before the crucifixion Pharisees ban a man from the synagogue because of his allegiance to Jesus (John 9:34).

b. In Matthew, the really crucial ban is pronounced not by Jews against Jewish-Christians but by *Jesus* against Jewish leaders (Matt. 21:43, 45), words inseparable from his

---

[31]On the Son of God's prophetic powers, see pages 130-31. The judgment that predictive prophecy is impossible is philosophical, not exegetical or historical – a judgment imposed on the text, not drawn from it (noted by Lewis 1967: 158). If the Synoptic texts (Mark 13, Matt. 24, etc.) are 'prophecies after the event,' they show remarkable restraint, lacking as they do many details from the actual history of Jerusalem's destruction. See further CMM, 76-77; France 1989: 83-85; Gundry 1994: 599-600, 603; Robinson 1976: 13-30 (who makes passages about the city's fall the point of departure for his argument that all the Synoptics were written before 70).

[32]Cf. Gundry 1994: 604, 606. Even if he is writing after A.D. 70, Matthew might choose to include these teachings about the temple as a matter of historical record. But if the temple still stands, his *selecting* them from a host of teachings is all the more understandable. On the absence of the phrase 'for all the nations' from Matthew 21:13, see comments *ad loc.*

prophecies of judgment, whose authenticity was affirmed above.

c. All of Paul's letters were written, and all the events in Acts occurred, before A.D. 70. It is clear from both sources that Jesus' predictions of false prophets and phony saviors, and of conflict between his disciples and other Jews, and between church and synagogue, find fulfillment well before A.D. 70. Paul himself, before his conversion, typified ongoing Pharisaic opposition.[33]

d. Those conflicts during Jesus' life are *intramural* in character: all the combatants are Israelites *within Israel*. But such are the disputes that an unmistakable *separation* has begun to occur within the walls: Jesus and his enemies occupy (so to speak) different quarters within the same house, whence they emerge for doing battle in a common room.[34] Paul and Acts describe an ever deepening rift between Jewish-Christians and non-Christian Jews, but also indicate that the warring parties still spend at least some of the time in the same house. The relationship is like that of a husband and a wife who are increasingly hostile to each other and alienated from one another, who sometimes live apart and sometimes together, but who are not yet divorced. Such are the tensions depicted in Paul and Acts, and reflected in Matthew. Had the separation signaled by the *Birkath ha-Minim* already occurred,

---

[33]See Matthew 10:16-23; 23:34; 24:5, 11, 24; Acts 4:1-3, 18; 5:17-18; 6:8–8:25; 9:1-2, 13-14, 21-29; 12:1-4; 13:6-12, 45-50; 14:2-5, 19; 17:5-9, 13; 18:6-17; 19:9-16; 20:3, 19; 21:11-13, 27-36; 22:3-5, 19; 23:12-15; 24:1-9; 25:1-7; 26:9-11; Romans 15:31; 1 Corinthians 15:9; 2 Corinthians 11:13-26; Galatians 1:13; 2:4; Philippians 3:2-6; Colossians 4:11; 1 Thessalonians 2:14-16; 1 Timothy 1:3-4, 13; Titus 1:10. Pharisees 'became the Christians' chief antagonists from the start. Josephus clearly states that in Judaism the Pharisees enjoyed dominance before A.D. 70' (Gundry 1994: 601). Given the argument that Matthew's accent on Pharisees reflects a post-Jamnian period, note that opposition to Sadducees is very strong in Matthew (*Saddoukaios* occurs seven times in Matthew, only once each in Mark and Luke and never in John), although they lost influence after A.D. 70 (all five instances of *Saddoukaios* in Acts reflect the time before A.D. 70). See further Gundry 1994: 600-602.

[34]References to 'their synagogues' (4:23; 10:17) reflect such a separation.

we would expect *less* tension than this – just as, once divorce ends a marriage, tension (if not sadness) often subsides.[35]

e. It is also clear from Paul and Acts that a principal reason for that Jewish opposition and the resultant conflicts is the church's ongoing mission to Israel, a mission fully in accord with Jesus' instructions to his apostles in Matthew.[36] While Matthew, like Paul, teaches that the mission to Israel will continue till Jesus returns, a concerted evangelistic outreach to Israel is more intelligible before the *Birkath ha-Minim* than afterwards.[37]

5. *a.* Why should the three instances of *ekklēsia* in Matthew be considered evidence of a late date, when the term frequently describes communities of Christians living well before A.D. 70?[38] How can Matthew be said to reflect a

---

[35]According to Robinson 1976: 103, the matters addressed in Matthew (e.g., food laws and fasting; temple sacrifices and Sabbath; marriage and divorce; attitudes toward Samaritans and Gentiles) 'reflect a period [namely A.D. 50 and 64] when the needs of co-existence force a clarification of what is the distinctively Christian line on a number of practical issues which previously could be taken for granted. It corresponds to the period when the early Methodists were compelled by events to cease to regard themselves as methodical Anglicans, loyal to the parish church and its structures as well as to their own class meetings.... But uneasy co-existence does not necessarily imply an irrevocable break: indeed John Wesley claimed that he lived and died a priest of the Church of England.' See D. below. Gundry 1994: 607-9 notes that Matthew reflects persecutions instigated by Jews; that comparisons with other writings suggest a date 'in A.D. 65–67'; and that 'for lack of data we cannot pinpoint the particular Jewish persecution during which Matthew wrote' (though Gundry favors Syria over Rome) – which may indicate that Matthew, intended as it is for the church at large, has more than one persecution in view.

[36]See, e.g., Acts 1:8; 2:1–3:26; 9:20; 13:5, 14-46; 17:1-4; 18:4; 28:17-24; Romans 1:16-17; 2:1-29; 9:1–11:36; 1 Corinthians 1:22-24; 9:19-23; 12:13; Galatians 3:28; Colossians 3:11. Again note Matthew 10:16-23: the 'coming' of verse 23 is the Son of Man's glorious return (see those comments).

[37]The longer a majority of Jews resisted the gospel, 'the more Christian evangelism shifted from the Jewish sphere' (Gundry 1994: 605). Yet even in the face of such resistance, Israel is to be evangelized till the end comes: see 10:23; 19:28; 24:14; 28:19-20; Romans 9:1–11:32.

[38]There are twenty-three instances of *ekklēsia* in Acts and sixty-two in Paul (and in eleven of his thirteen letters). The concept is rooted in the OT and in Jesus' own usage (Matt. 16:18; 18:17). For Jesus to foretell the building of his *ekklēsia* (16:18) accords fully with his self-understanding, his gathering of disciples, his appointing of twelve apostles and his prophetic powers.

relatively advanced church order, when documents describing conditions before 70 reveal much more about the complexion of church leadership?[39]

b. Paul's Christology is just as advanced as that of Matthew; and Paul too joins Father, Son and Holy Spirit together.[40]

c. Matthew affirms *both* Jesus' abiding presence with his people till the end of the age (28:20) *and* his glorious return at the end (24:27-31). Similarly, while Paul's letters increasingly stress believers' present union with the exalted Christ, the certainty of Christ's return is affirmed in letters both early and late.[41]

These arguments are in my judgment much stronger than those for a date after A.D. 70 ; so I favor the earlier period with more confidence than have some others. Yet, as noted earlier, the chief value of this discussion (as of that concerning the place of origin) has been to gain a better understanding of the circumstances within which Matthew wrote, and therefore of his purpose for writing.[42] How then did he address his threefold audience (A. above)?

D. Instructing Believers

Matthew writes for Jewish- and Gentile-Christians within and beyond his own community. Intent upon teaching them in the most effective way, he has produced a carefully designed and

---

[39]See Acts 13:1-3; 14:23; 15:1-4; 20:28; 1 Corinthians 12:28; Ephesians 4:11; Philippians 1:1; 1 Timothy, 2 Timothy and Titus, *passim. Diakonos* in Matthew 20:26 and 23:11 denotes a function; in 1 Timothy 3:8, 12, an office as well. Jesus is often called *didaskalos* in Matthew; not so disciples (23:8; contrast Acts 13:1; Eph. 4:11). The *presbyteroi* of Matthew are always Jewish, never Christian (as, e.g., in Acts 14:23; 1 Tim. 5:17). Matthew never uses *episkopos*, 'overseer' (Acts 20:28; Phil. 1:1).

[40]See, e.g., Romans 1:3-4; 8:3; 1 Corinthians 12:3-6; 2 Corinthians 13:14; Galatians 4:4-6; Ephesians 4:4-6; Philippians 2:6-11; Colossians 1:15-20; Titus 2:13; 3:4-6.

[41]See 1 Thessalonians 4:13-18; 2 Thessalonians 1:7-10; 1 Corinthians 15:51-57 (early letters); 1 Timothy 6:14-15; 2 Timothy 4:1; Titus 2:13 (late letters). For believers' union with Christ in the heavenlies, see Colossians 3:1-4 (which also affirms Christ's return); Ephesians 1:3; 2:6.

[42]A date before A.D. 70 accords with apostolic authorship (II.); but we recall an early tradition that the Fourth Gospel was written by the apostle John about A.D. 90 (cf. Carson 1984: 17).

well-organized textbook, a kind of catechism for the church's leaders and members. Let us think of Matthew not as the *product of* a school, but as a *curriculum for* a school, prepared by the authorized scribe and teacher; not as 'a theology *of* the Matthean churches' but as 'a theology *for* the churches,' imparted by the inspired apostle in the hope that it will become theirs.[43]

The Life and Teaching of Jesus

Jesus authorized and oversaw the writing of Matthew, and in every way accounts for its existence. He now employs the book for teaching his ever widening circle of disciples. Matthew's task is to enable all these learners to do what he himself did: sit at the feet of the master Teacher.

As we have seen repeatedly, the whole of Matthew is dominated by Jesus the Messiah, God incarnate. The fundamental lesson for all these Christians – now as at the time of their baptism (28:19) is that they are the servants of Christ the Lord, committed to following him, worshiping him and obeying him at whatever cost. Given Jesus' identity, his words are to be taken with utmost seriousness. In accord with the commission of 28:19-20, Jesus' teachings – beginning with the five great discourses – occupy much space in Matthew. All who study the book – Jewish and Gentile pupils alike – are responsible for 'keeping' – i.e., for obeying – all these teachings (28:20), indeed for honoring 'the whole purpose of God' (cf. Acts 20:27) as set forth in these twenty-eight chapters. Moreover, just as Jesus gave special attention to the twelve chosen from among the larger circle of disciples, so some of Matthew is directed particularly to persons given leadership in the new community. By the same token, Matthew by its very nature calls for submission

---

[43]Stein, speaking thus of Mark, compares Paul: 'Is the theology of Galatians the theology of the Galatian community? If it were, Paul would not have written Galatians. Paul wrote Galatians to change the theology of the Galatian community to that of his letter' (1987: 111). 'Matthew probably expected his audience to hear his Gospel more than once' (Keener 1999: 15).

to the authority Jesus has vested in his apostles and those who propagate the apostolic teaching.[44]

By presenting those teachings within the framework of a narrative, Matthew directly relates what Jesus *says* to what he *does*. Jesus' teaching gains its authority in part from its consistency with his conduct. Not only does he talk about gentleness and humility (e.g., in Matthew 5:3-10); he himself embodies these qualities (11:29). He calls sinners to repentance but also shares meals with them. He who sends forth apostles is himself a missionary. He teaches on prayer but also prays. The one who summons followers to service and sacrifice, himself provides the supreme example of both. He does not merely talk about giving his life 'as a ransom for many'; he goes to the cross. It is he who perfectly fulfills the twofold command to love God and neighbor (22:37-40).[45] Let the readers of Matthew therefore become 'doers of the word' they have studied. One loves God and neighbor by exertions of the *will*. Obeying Jesus' teachings both demonstrates and deepens understanding.[46] Let readers learn from Jesus how to preach and pray; how to condescend to the lowly and care for the needy; how to relate to fellow believers, to non-believers and to the church's enemies. Jesus' behavior shows church leaders how to join justice and mercy, firmness and gentleness, in their exercise of authority; the apostles' obedience to Jesus likewise encourages church members to obey him by adhering to apostolic teaching. When Christians are reviled and persecuted and betrayed, and their very lives are at risk, let them recall how Jesus endured such trials and how he remained faithful unto death – and let them then willingly take up their own crosses and follow him.[47] Seeking to follow Jesus' example would surely cause conscientious followers to despair, were it not for the three great realities upon which those exhortations are based: believers' redemption from the

---

[44]See Matthew 10:1-42; 18:1-20; 19:23–20:28; 26:17-30; 28:16-20.

[45]See 9:9-13; 9:35–10:1; 14:23; 16:21-26; 20:24-28; 26:36-44.

[46]See 7:15-27; 19:16-22; cf. Colossians 1:9-10; James 1:22-25.

[47]See Matthew 16:21-25; 26:1–27:56. The call of 16:24, far from calling into question the uniqueness of Jesus' atoning sacrifice, presupposes that event (20:28).

guilt of sins; their baptism into the name, and therefore the power, of the Holy Trinity; and Jesus' presence with them through all their days.[48]

Gospel and Law

Matthew teaches Christians that gospel and law are both distinguishable and inseparable, and that both are vitally important for their personal and corporate growth.

All these readers need to 'preach the gospel to themselves every day.'[49] Let Jewish-Christians never forget that they needed 'the gospel of the kingdom,' and the forgiveness of sins, as surely as Gentiles did; that they are therefore to keep the law not *as* the basis, but *on* the basis, of their acceptance before God; and that Jesus offers rest and refuge for those still enslaved to the law and laden with guilt as law-breakers. And let Gentile-Christians never forget that the Jewish Messiah came to save Gentiles as well as Jews; that he forgave them the vilest and most destructive sins of their lawless past; and that they became privileged members of the Messianic community by the gracious and sovereign initiative of Israel's God.[50]

Those same readers also need to be instructed in the law every day. Let Jewish-Christians recognize that Messiah's commands are more demanding than were those of Moses. Let Gentile-Christians find here a place of stability, directions

---

[48]See Matthew 1:21; 26:28; 28:19-20; cf. Philippians 2:1-11. Keener 1999: 4 notes (i) that ancient narrators 'regularly sought to teach morals...through their narratives,' and praised the virtuous 'to spur others to imitate them'; and (ii) that the gospels similarly illustrate 'the early Christian use of Jesus as a moral example,' and that 'Matthew probably provides the clearest example of this purpose.' L.W. Hurtado rightly says, 'The Evangelists were mainly concerned to show Jesus' significance in the divine purpose, not his virtues' (*DJG*, 279). My point is that Jesus' virtues are disclosed precisely in his fidelity to the Father's saving purpose. (It is interesting to observe that the figures of Acts – e.g., Peter, Stephen and Paul – often behave like Jesus in Luke.) McGrath 1991: 295 says that 'Jesus has moral authority on account of who he is,' and thus that a 'nonincarnational or [purely] exemplarist Christology' is too weak a basis for faith and life.

[49]See Bridges 1994: 45-60. In 'the pursuit of holiness,' nothing is more important than 'learning to preach the gospel to yourself every day' (60).

[50]Cf. the argument of Romans 1:18–3:20 (showing Jews' and Gentiles' bondage to sin [3:9] as preparation for declaring the gospel [3:21-31 *et seq.*]).

for living, a remedy for the laxity and aimlessness of their pagan past. Let them all learn that Jesus' abiding presence keeps those commands from being burdensome; and that the grace of the gospel provides the best hope for law-breakers and the strongest incentive for law-keeping.[51]

A Crisis of Identity

All of Matthew's Christian readers face an identity crisis. How could it be otherwise for persons who have decided to follow Jesus – he whose being and words are 'essentially subversive of established arrangements and ways of thinking'?[52]

Gentile-Christians have not ceased to be Gentiles; but as they learn the mind of Christ and adhere to his commands, they become increasingly different from other Gentiles. Both their beliefs and their behavior are being dramatically affected (cf. Eph. 4:17-24). They have joined a community unlike any they have known before. Some former associations will end; others, which continuing, can never be quite the same. Joined to Christ, they have gained a new identity.

Matthew, himself a Jew, is acutely aware of the crisis Jewish-Christians face. They are both like and unlike their non-Christian Jewish neighbors; they are both inside and outside contemporary Judaism. They are not being called upon to deny their Jewishness; on the contrary, their fidelity to Jesus – himself a Jew – deepens their understanding of their Jewish heritage. At the same time, as followers of Jesus the New Moses they cannot remain what they were; and they now belong to a community which in important ways is distinguishable from

---

[51]See 5:17-48; 7:15-27 (which could serve as a warning to persons flirting with prophecy and other charismatic phenomena as substitutes for the rigors of law-keeping; cf. 24:23-24); 11:28-30 (with 1 John 5:3); 28:20. Cf. Bolton (1964: 71): 'The law sends us to the Gospel that we may be justified; and the Gospel sends us to the law again to inquire what is our duty as those who are justified.' Both clauses must be affirmed. To stress law without gospel (as some Jewish-Christians might be tempted to do) is neo-nomian; to stress gospel without law (an imbalance to which some Gentile-Christians might be especially susceptible) is anti-nomian. See above on 'the Salvation of God' (pp. 145-48) and 'the People of God' (pp. 148-54).

[52]Willard 1998: xiii.

Israel, not least in the breadth of its appeal to Gentiles. Not surprisingly, therefore, many of their fellow Jews – including some to whom they were once bound in the closest way – have reviled and rejected them, and betrayed and oppressed them. Joined to Jesus, they too have gained a new identity.[53]

In face of that manifold crisis, Matthew does not counsel Christian individuals and communities to isolate and insulate themselves from the outside world. Did not Jesus command them to love their neighbors, including those outside the church (Matt. 22:39)? Did he not commission his followers to take his teachings into that very world (28:19-20)?

E. Addressing Non-Believers
By writing this gospel, Matthew obeys both those commands and exhorts Christian readers to do the same. Taking what they have learned from studying this book, let them enter the world, and there address both Jews and Gentiles; there declare and defend the gospel of the kingdom; and there confront the church's adversaries, both seeking to win them and warning them that it is Jesus' foes, not his followers, whose lives are most imperiled.[54]

Good News for Jews and for Gentiles
Matthew is not only a catechism for Christians but a missionary tract for non-Christians and for Christians wanting to evangelize them.[55] By 'preaching the gospel to themselves every day,' Matthew's Christian readers will be better equipped to impart it to outsiders.

---

[53]See Matthew 10:16-39; 19:29; France 1989: 98-108; Hagner 1993: lxx-lxxi; Keener 1999: 48-49.

[54]Matthew 'seems designed as an apologia, to be used by Christians in reply to curious or critical Jews' (Moule 1982: 93). Matthew offers instruction, 'certainly for believers in the first instance, but with special reference to unbelievers: [an aid] to Christians in explaining their faith and defending it when occasion offered' (ibid., 122; cf. 122-28). Writes Keener (1999: 51): 'Matthew probably functions as a discipling manual, a "handbook" of Jesus' basic life and teaching, relevant to a Jewish-Christian community engaged in the Gentile mission and deadlocked in scriptural polemic with their local synagogue communities.' I would rather say: 'relevant to communities of Jewish- and Gentile-Christians engaged....'

[55]See Hagner 1993: lviii-lix.

Let Jews hear the good news: Jesus is your long-awaited Messiah; he the Son of Abraham in whom God's ancient covenantal promises are fulfilled; he the Son of David destined to rule in justice and mercy; he himself the God of Israel come in the flesh; he therefore the only one who can save you from your sins. So recognize yourselves to be among those 'lost sheep of the house of Israel' whom he came to save. Do not be deceived by Jesus' enemies – by those who portray him as violator of the law and destroyer of the temple, as a man who served Satan and blasphemed God, as a failure who died an accursed death and never rose from the dead as his followers claim. Beware too of Messianic pretenders who seek to use truth about Jesus to exalt themselves and seduce the gullible.[56] In our own day, there is a danger that Christians who long to affirm and embrace Jews, will sacrifice Christ's centrality and uniqueness, and refrain from presenting him as Matthew does – as both God and man, and as the sole Hope of all nations, Israel included.[57]

Let Gentiles hear the good news: the Jewish Messiah came to seek and to save the lost among the nations. As an infant, Jesus received homage from Gentiles in the face of Jewish indifference, and a foreign land offered him escape from danger in Judea. Consider his mercy to a Canaanite woman and a Roman centurion – representatives of Israel's enemies past and present. Join those Roman soldiers in contemplating the event of his death, and understand that the people whom he thus forgives and ransoms from manifold bondage include Gentiles. Take note too of his closing commission to his Jewish apostles. Heed his call, entrust your lives to him, worship and serve him, enter his church. Jesus does not begrudge Caesar

---

[56]See Matthew 12:24-42; 21:23-27; 24:11, 23-24; 26:57-68; 27:62-66; 28:11-15; Gundry 1994: 605.

[57]Lauren F. Winner (herself a Jewish-Christian), 'God of Abraham – and Saint Paul,' *Books & Culture* (Jan/Feb 2001): 10-11, remarks that 'Christians who led the way in Jewish-Christian relations in the 1970s' sacrificed 'the central and unique role of Christ in order fully to embrace Jews. In other words, they fudged on the very claims that got Christianity started in the first place.' Cf. 1 Corinthians 1:18-31.

the tribute due him. But he, not Caesar, is your true Lord and God; he will govern you as no emperor could or would.[58]

These Jewish- and Gentile-Christians are in a unique position. Standing as they do between the Jewish and the Gentile worlds, and appealing to both on behalf of Jesus – Messiah of Israel and Lord of the nations – they play a crucial role in reversing the cultural and racial disintegration and alienation that have occurred from the tower of Babel onwards.[59]

Confronting the Opposition

Let the church's adversaries seek better to understand what they are opposing by listening – not just to fellow adversaries but to the church's testimony concerning itself. Better still, let the church's enemies *read for themselves* the Gospel according to Matthew, in the process being attentive to the full length and breadth of its witness.

All you enemies – Jewish and Gentile alike – pay close attention to Jesus' gospel of the kingdom! Could it be that you find Christian teaching opaque or offensive or both, because you have not repented of your sins, because you have resisted rather than welcomed this gospel?[60] Could it be that this message is actually the 'hidden treasure,' the 'pearl of great value,' for which you have searched all your life? Could this Jesus whose people you harass be the answer to your heart's deepest longings? Does your opposition signal your fear that he is closing in on you? Is your very hostility an attempt to deny his claims upon you?[61]

---

[58]See Matthew 2:1-15; 8:5-13; 15:21-28; 20:28; 22:15-22; 26:28; 27:54; 28:19; cf. Luke 2:1-12; Isaiah 9:6-7; 11:1-9.

[59]Cf. Ephesians 2:11–3:13; 1 Peter 2:4-10. Billie Davis, 'The 150% Person,' *Books & Culture* (Nov/Dec 2000): 45, reflects on Everett Stonequist's *The Marginal Man – A Study in Personality and Culture Conflict.* The marginal man stands between two or more social worlds. He is 'the key personality in the contacts of cultures.... He is the crucible of cultural fusion.' So, in a sense, were the Christians in the churches Matthew addresses. In Ephesians 1–3 Paul teaches that the unity of Jews and Gentiles in Christ foreshadows the unifying of all things under him.

[60]See Matthew 4:17, 23; 9:35; and especially 13:10-17, with comments.

[61]See 5:3-10; 11:28-30; 13:44-46.

All of you, pay close heed as well to Jesus' exposition of the law! If he is what Matthew claims, are not his directives to be taken seriously? Do we not ignore them to our own loss and ruin? And if you have caught a glimpse of the grace of his gospel, can you imagine that he will use his law to tyrannize you?

But all of you, be warned as well! You are responsible for all that you have seen and heard and read concerning Jesus. This is a message about the rule of God and his Messiah: are you so foolish as to imagine that you can impede its ineluctable advance, or that you can somehow domesticate the Messiah-King and usurp his powers for your own ends (cf. Psalm 2)? This is also a message about the supreme manifestation of God's grace in history, so you reject it to your peril. If you choose to persecute his followers, realize (from your reading of Matthew) that Jesus has anticipated the worst you can do to his people; that he has prepared them for it; and that in the end they will be delivered and their enemies punished.[62]

You enemies within Israel, recognize what dangers beset you! You are exceptionally privileged recipients of divine revelation. Yet you have supplanted God's law with human traditions. In opposing Jesus you show that you are ignorant of, or indifferent to, your own Scriptures' witness to him; in rejecting his claims, you repudiate the supreme disclosure of God's 'grace and truth' (cf. John 1:14). In accusing Jesus of serving Satan and blaspheming God, you are in danger of committing sins unpardonable. In pursuing Jesus' followers, you persecute him; in having his people crucified, you crucify Messiah afresh. In seeking to bar persons from confessing him, and in assaulting those who do, you risk eternal damnation. Take seriously, then, the 'woes' that Jesus pronounced against such people as you. Your condition is grave indeed, and your prospects are hopeless. Yet recognize that 'woes' are not pronouncements of irreversible judgment, but urgent warnings to jolt you into perceiving your dire condition and into heeding the gospel before it is too late. Your capital and your temple stand under judgment. Lay down your arms; embrace the Messiah you have opposed, so that upon his

---

[62]See Matthew 4:17; 9:35; 10:5-39; 13:24-30, 37-43, 47-50; 16:21-28; 24:26-25:46.

return you may welcome him with joy, receive his blessing and be welcomed into his kingdom rather than banished from him forever.[63]

F. Reading Matthew Today

Some students of contemporary culture tell us that 'the true measure of reading ability is the ease and accuracy with which a person can understand *diverse* kinds of writing.'[64] The challenge before us is to comprehend a document from the ancient past that is in some respects different both from the other three gospels and from other writings of the period (as we saw in section IV.), and that is very different from those of our own day. Adding to our difficulty is a widespread and deeply rooted 'chronological snobbery' that considers works of earlier generations to be outdated, untrue and irrelevant.[65] But has not the above discussion already shown that Matthew's message is quite intelligible (although it remains unfathomable); that it is startlingly relevant to today's church and culture (although 'relevance' is not its prime motivation); and that it is very much worth our while to press forward to deeper understanding, whatever the barriers?

Discerning the Message

Jesus made it clear that today's readers are among the intended recipients of Matthew. For its writing was one of

---

[63]See 5:20; 11:4-30; 12:24-45; 15:1-9; 21:33-46; 23:13-39; cf. 3:7-10; Acts 9:4-5; Hebrews 6:6.

[64]E.D. Hirsch, Jr., Joseph F. Kett and James Trefil, *The Dictionary of Cultural Literacy*, 2[65] ed. (Boston: Houghton Mifflin, 1993), xii.

[65]On 'chronological snobbery,' see Kreeft 1994: 11-19. C. S. Lewis 'knew that in every field progress is made only by those who ignore the Zeitgeist and simply tell the truth' (17). In Lewis 1953: 139, Screwtape writes to Wormwood: 'The Historical Point of View, put briefly, means that when a learned man is presented with any statement in an ancient author, the one question he never asks is whether it is true.' Lewis 1961: 70-71 speaks appreciatively of children's indifference to literary fashion: 'What we see in them is not a specifically childish taste, but simply a normal and perennial human taste, temporarily atrophied in their elders by a fashion. It is we, not they, whose taste needs explanation.' In this regard, consider children's unfailing interest in stories from the gospels.

his authorized means for discipling the nations till the close of the age (28:18-20; cf. John 17:20). It follows that Matthew's message to his original audience is the very one addressed to us. So the better we understand his intent for those early Christian communities as he writes from Antioch (or some such place) in about A.D. 65 to 67 (or a time close to that period), the better we can appropriate his message for ourselves and our contemporaries.[66] Encouraging us in this effort is the knowledge that we have before us Holy Scripture; that the Father still delights to bear witness, through the apostle, to his beloved Son; that the Christ who authorized and oversaw the writing of Matthew, directs and controls us as we read it; and that the Holy Spirit who employed Matthew and inspired these pages, enlightens us as we study.[67]

To understand the Gospel according to Matthew, the reader must endeavor to enter as far as possible into the perspective of the writer (which is different from psychoanalyzing the writer himself), to see the world and life from his point of view, and to discover why he has written this kind of book.[68] My first responsibility is not to determine what a text means to *me*, but rather what the writer wanted his original readers to know – which in turn requires some awareness of

---

[66]Barth 1965: 7 observes 'how energetically [John] Calvin, having first established what stands in the text, sets himself to re-think the whole material and to wrestle with it, till the walls which separate the sixteenth century from the first become transparent!' Said the NT scholar C. H. Dodd: 'The ideal interpreter would be one who has entered into that strange first-century world, has felt its whole strangeness, has sojourned in it until he has lived himself into it, thinking and feeling as one of those to whom the Gospel first came, and who will then return into our world, and give to the truth he has discerned a body out of the stuff of our own thought' (*The Present Task in New Testament Studies: an Inaugural Lecture* [Cambridge: University Press, 1936], 40-41).

[67]'The key to unlocking the mystery of the text...lies in being grasped by the Spirit of God, the ultimate author of the text, as he speaks through the text clarifying its original meaning ....' (Bloesch 1994: 277). 'Only the Spirit can plumb the depths of...the mystery of Christ and his gospel' (71). See above, pages 100-03, 116-19.

[68]In this regard, compare the opening lines of William Butler Yeats' 'The Scholars': 'Bald heads forgetful of their sins/ Old learned, respectable bald heads/ Edit and annotate the lines/ That young men, tossing on their beds/ Rhymed out in love's despair....'

the book's historical, cultural and literary setting. Much of this Introduction has been devoted to such matters. While attention to critical scholarship is essential for understanding Matthew,[69] the present work is not primarily an exercise in criticism. My indebtedness to scholarly judgments, both within and beyond my Reformed Evangelical tradition, will be evident everywhere. My approach is not *non*-critical or *anti*-critical; but it is *post*-critical. We shall pass *through* criticism, for it provides invaluable insight into Matthew, and boundaries to be respected in interpreting it. But we seek to go beyond critical study, in the belief that it alone is inadequate for fully appropriating the text.[70]

What C. S. Lewis says about viewing a painting applies (*mutatis mutandis*) to reading Matthew: 'We must not let loose our own subjectivity upon the pictures and make them its vehicles.... We sit down before the picture in order to have something done to us, not that we may do things with it. The first demand that any work of any art makes upon us is surrender. Look. Listen. Receive. Get yourself out of the way.'[71] In this endeavor, the reader should be cautious about employing the canons of modern literary theory – in particular those of reader-response criticism, which 'finds the meaning of the text in how the reader is affected more than in what motivated the original author.'[72] Merely to peer into the well of Jesus' story is to see only the reflection of my own face – to discover no one but myself. 'The reader at the well, in order to be nourished, must draw from and drink of the text.'[73] By so doing I will – to my surprise and dismay – discover a great deal about myself.

---

[69]So too Ladd 1967: 37-38, answering the question, 'What is criticism?'

[70]'Faith goes through criticism, for its object is beyond criticism' (Bloesch 1994: 205).

[71]Lewis 1961: 18-19.

[72]Bloesch 1994: 200. '"Radical" reader-response critics...privilege the ideology or position of the reader rather than that of the text. The text becomes the opportunity for the reader to pursue his or her own interests and agenda' (Vanhoozer 1995: 307).

[73]Vanhoozer 1995: 325. The image of the well comes from Albert Schweitzer.

Pondering the Message

Discerning the message of Matthew requires serious study. But that study is not an end in itself, only a beginning: it prepares for *meditation upon the text*. 'Blessed is the man,' says Psalm 1:1-2, who delights in the *torah* of Yahweh, and meditates upon it day and night. This instance of *torah* is usually translated 'law' (so, e.g., NIV and NRSV); but *torah* is basically 'instruction,' and here it denotes 'divine revelation in general.' In other words, *torah* embraces gospel as well as law.[74] The noun *torah* comes from the verb *yarah*, which means to *throw* something so that it hits its mark. The words of *torah* – both gospel and law – are like javelins hurled at us from the mind of God. They pierce through our defenses, they begin to change us from the inside out.[75] Thus are we to be affected as we ponder Yahweh's *torah* as set forth in Matthew – his gospel and his law, these distinguishable but inseparable dimensions of his revelation.

The man of Psalm 1 '*meditates* on Yahweh's *torah*.' This Hebrew verb, *hagah*, on the one hand means *to think or muse or meditate*; on the other, *to murmur or mutter or speak*. Meditation begins with *thought*: we ponder, reflect upon, the text. Then thought finds expression in *speech*: 'This book of the *Torah* shall not depart out of *your mouth*,' said Yahweh in Joshua 1:8. Speech helps to engrave the Word on the memory, whence it may be repeatedly drawn for reflection. It is possible to study Matthew yet remain detached from it. Critical scrutiny of the text may become a useful and subtle device for keeping it at a distance. We may even enter Matthew on a spiritual quest but reject its understanding of spirituality. Meditation embraces the text, welcomes its truth, enters into it, feeds upon both its gospel and its law. Meditation, writes Richard Foster, 'centers on internalizing and personalizing the passage.' Its purpose 'is not so much to study the passage as to be initiated into

---

[74]W. Gutbrod, *TDNT* 4: 1046. The first five books of the Hebrew Bible (the ones called *Torah*) record gospel (Yahweh's saving acts) as the foundation for law (Yahweh's commands), both evidence of Yahweh's love (*chesed*) for his covenant-people (e.g., Exod. 20:1-17; 34:5-7). The forthcoming Psalter likewise celebrates both gospel and law: see, e.g., Psalms 19 and 136.

[75]Cf. Peterson 1991: 25.

the reality of which the passage speaks.'[76] Or we might say that we have not adequately studied a Matthean passage until we enter into that reality. Such an approach takes much time: Richard Baxter speaks of persons who 'teach too hurriedly what can only be rendered holy by meditation.'[77]

Meditation on God's *torah* is meant to flow into meditative prayer – into communion with God.[78] Psalms 1 and 2 are not cast into the form of prayer; but the *torah* meditation of Psalm 1 and the Messiah expectation of Psalm 2 prepare us for prayer. The opening verses of Psalms 3–10 are all addressed to God. Psalm 119 is a lengthy written meditation on one theme – the *torah* of God. Its opening verse is reminiscent of Psalm 1: 'Blessed are they whose ways are blameless, who walk according to the [*torah*] of the LORD.' But no less than 172 of the remaining 175 verses are addressed *to God*. 'Oh, how I love your law! I meditate on it all day long' (119:97). Reflecting upon God's words and works leads inevitably to God himself: 'O God, you are my God, earnestly I seek you; my soul thirsts for you.... On my bed I remember you; I meditate upon you through the watches of the night' (Ps. 63:1, 6).

Our appropriation of the Gospel according to Matthew is incomplete if, having studied and meditated upon it, we do not transpose its teachings into meditative prayer; use these texts as material for our prayers of praise, thanksgiving, intercession and petition; and contemplate the wonders of the Holy Trinity – especially those of God the Son – that are disclosed in this gospel. Does not the Lord's Prayer of Matthew 6:9-13, incorporating as it does themes from Jesus' teaching, offer us a superb model? Does not the absolute centrality of Jesus the Messiah in Matthew encourage us to sing our great Redeemer's praise? The 'Torah meditation'

---

[76]Foster 1992: 146, 149. 'When your words came [Yahweh], I ate them; they were my joy and my heart's delight,' says Jeremiah 15:16. Psalmists meditate on Yahweh's mighty works (Ps. 77:12); on his statutes (119:99) and on his promises (119:148) – i.e., on both gospel and law.

[77]1974: 87. I invoke Baxter in part to justify how long it has taken me to write this commentary!

[78]So it was in the old *lectio divina* (divine reading): see Foster 1992: 149-50.

of Psalm 1 flows into the 'Messiah expectation' of Psalm 2.[79] Jesus, that royal Messiah now come, is the very embodiment of Torah. Meditating upon him, we discover that there is always more to explore, that his riches are inexhaustible (cf. Eph. 3:9). As Jesus accounts for the existence and character of Matthew, he is the key to our understanding it.[80] Interpreting Matthew aright requires that I receive God's love as offered in his Son, and love God in return by honoring his Son. 'This is the reason why it is saints, not scholars, who understand the Bible.... Scripture is a love letter, not a manual of scholastic theology. And only a lover understands a love letter.'[81]

Obeying the Message
In meditation and meditative prayer 'God is always addressing our will.'[82] The man of Psalm 1, having meditated upon the *torah*, 'prospers in all he does,' verse 3. Says Yahweh to Joshua, 'Meditate on [this *torah*] day and night, so that you may be careful to do everything written in it' (Josh. 1:8). The same holds true for students of Matthew. The people whom Jesus gathers from among the nations are to be taught to *keep – to obey – all that he has commanded* (Matt. 28:20).

We obey Jesus by repenting in view of the coming kingdom, and by believing his gospel of the kingdom. Matthew and the other gospels are 'written expressions of profound encounters with the divine, intended to mediate those experiences to others as the basis for faith, repentance and new life.'[83] I may have correctly identified the genre of Matthew, but I will not comprehend the *euangelion* until I begin to experience salvation myself. If Matthean spirituality is fundamentally 'knowing and being known by God, on the one hand, and responding with

---

[79]Cf. Peterson 1991: 23-32.

[80]So Burridge 1992: 256-58.

[81]Kreeft 1992: 175-76. Augustine says that growth in love for God and neighbor (Matt. 22:37-40) is the test whether we have understood Scripture: see *On Christian Doctrine* 1.36.

[82]Foster 1992: 149.

[83]Barton 1992: 3. The gospels 'are shaped through and through by a sense of the presence of God in Christ, and they are deeply serious attempts to re-envisage the whole of life in response' (ibid., 2).

the whole of life, on the other,' then true spirituality begins with believing Matthew's gospel of salvation.[84] And doing that is inconceivable apart from an encounter with, and a personal commitment to, the One through whom that salvation is provided (1:21; 20:28). I submit myself to God's rule precisely by entrusting myself to the Lordship of Jesus the Messiah.

Jesus commands those who have received his gospel to obey the law he expounds, from Matthew 5:17 onwards; to put his words into practice and do his Father's will (7:21-27).[85] At the heart of that law is the twofold command to love God and neighbor (22:37-40). Loving God with one's whole 'heart' employs all one's faculties; for in Hebrew thought the heart has rational, emotional and volitional properties.[86] It is especially important that the enlightening of the mind and the stirring of the emotions bear fruit in actions prompted by the will. Loving God, moreover, finds expression in love for other people, beginning with fellow members of the *ekklēsia*. Here we are together taught to seek first the rule of God (6:33), not our own; to exercise responsible dominion under Christ's authority (28:18; cf. Gen. 1:26-28); to help others to exercise the rule God has granted them, not to impose our rule upon them. 'We will then enjoy individualized "reigns" with neither isolation nor conflict.'[87] By all such acts of obedience my theological understanding is deepened: John Calvin goes so far as to say that 'all right knowledge of God is born of obedience.'[88]

One path of obedience for a person who has received truth from God is to impart it to others – following the example of Matthew and the other evangelists, together with prophets and psalmists before them. We can use the very teachings Matthew has recorded to address a threefold audience akin

---

[84]Barton 1992: 1. Cf. the commentary on 13:10-17.

[85]See the quotation from Samuel Bolton, page 172, n. 51. Cf. Psalm 119:32 ('I run in the path of your commands, for you have set my heart free') and 45 ('I will walk about in freedom, for I have sought out your precepts'). 'The "challenge" of the kingdom that put stern demands on people should not be rephrased away' (Brown 1997: 220).

[86]See Johannes Behm, *TDNT* 3: 611-13. On reading and applying Scripture holistically, see Houston 1996: 148-73.

[87]Willard 1998: 27. Cf. Matthew 20:24-28; 23:8-12.

[88]Calvin 1960: 72. Cf. John 7:17; 8:31-32; Col. 1:9-11; Psalm 119:100.

to his own: Jewish- and Gentile-Christians; non-Christian Jews and Gentiles who may be receptive to the gospel; and persons who dispute or oppose the claims of Christ. For all three audiences the message of Matthew is extraordinarily and mightily relevant. Especially is this true for the church – the *ekklēsia* – Jesus came to build. 'Wherever the church has grown large and mixed, wherever the church is polarized between the extremes of latitudinarianism and sectarianism, wherever the church feels drawn to accommodation with forces that oppose the gospel, wherever the church loses its vision of worldwide evangelism, wherever the church lapses into smug religiosity with its attendant vices of ostentation, hypocrisy, and haughty disdain for its underprivileged and correspondingly zealous members – there the Gospel of Matthew speaks with power and pertinence.'[89]

It is probable that you have taken up this commentary, and are reading these words as a person responsible for teaching other Christians. You may be a pastor or an elder or a Sunday school teacher or a seminary professor or student. But whoever you may be, you may have hardly begun to realize what there is for you to learn from Jesus through the apostle Matthew. In any case, such has been my experience since beginning this protracted exercise of meditating upon this book. I fervently hope that this commentary will aid rather than hinder your own explorations into the marvels of this masterpiece and its magnificent portrayal of the King of kings.

---

[89]Gundry 1994: 10. See France 1989: 242-78, on 'Matthew's Gospel and the Church,' especially 251-60 ('The Pastoral Function of the Gospel'), and 260-78 ('Matthew's Vision of the Church'). Cf. above, pages 148-54, 168-73. Wise counsel for interpreting biblical texts today is offered by Eugene H. Peterson, *Eat This Book: A Conversation in the Art of Spiritual Reading* (Grand Rapids: Eerdmans, 2006).

* * * * *

Our Father in heaven, we thank you for the Gospel according to Matthew. How impoverished, how benighted, how desperate, we would be without it. Thank you for the truth it records, for the salvation it declares and for the Christ it discloses. Grant us attentiveness and discernment as we read. Speak to us, confront us, convict us, console us, challenge us according to our need. By your sovereign mercy, and through your enlightening Spirit, enable us to behold the grace and glory of Christ, to grasp the truth he revealed, to experience the salvation he accomplished and to submit to his Lordship. In the writing of this commentary, may I assist rather than impede your working in the hearts of those who read. In the name of Jesus the Christ we pray, Amen.

Section 2

'O Come, O Come Emmanuel'[1] (Matt. 1:1-25)

In the opening verse Matthew introduces us to the central figure of his book – 'Jesus Christ, the son of David, the son of Abraham.' These are the three most notable names in the following genealogy (1:2-17). The importance of the name 'Jesus Christ' (*Iēsous Christos*) for Matthew is further evident from its recurrence at the close of this section ('Jesus, who is called Christ' (1:16; 'until the Christ,' 1:17) and at the beginning of the next ('the birth of Jesus Christ happened in this way'; 1:18). *Iēsous*, the first name to appear, is also the closing word of the chapter (1:25). Why this name is so significant will soon be explained (1:21). Indeed, there is much disclosed about Jesus in this first chapter that makes us long for his appearance on the scene.

---

[1]The opening words of a Latin hymn (from 1710), translated by John Mason Neale in 1851.

I.
'LATE IN TIME BEHOLD HIM COME'[1]
(1:1-17).

The language of the first verse draws us back into OT history and not just to the times of David and Abraham, but to the very beginning. The opening phrase, *biblos geneseōs*, occurs twice in the LXX. The first (Gen. 2:4) denotes the 'record of the origin' of the heavens and the earth; the second (Gen. 5:1) the 'book of the genealogy' of Adam. Correspondingly, here in Matthew the phrase may introduce 'a record of [Jesus'] *genealogy*' (1:2-17)[2] or 'an account of [his] *origin*,' whether the term encompasses 1:2-25 (*genesis* recurs in v. 18, 'the birth of Jesus Christ'), or 1:2–2:23 or even 1:2–4:16.[3] Yet here in the opening section of Matthew we meet themes – as in the overture to an opera – that will recur throughout the book, and that the author considers crucial for our understanding of Jesus.[4]

---

[1]Words from 'Hark! The Herald Angels Sing,' by Charles Wesley (1739).

[2]So most translations, e.g., ESV, NASB, NIV, NKJV, NRSV; cf. Keener 1999: 77, n. 17.

[3]As noted on page 49, 4:17 marks a major turning point in Matthew. For both 'origin' and 'genealogy' as translations of *geneseōs*, (1:1), see BAGD s.v. Davies and Allison, and others they cite (1988: 149-55), argue that *biblos geneseōs* describes the whole of Matthew as the 'book of the history,' or the 'book of the genesis' (or 'of new creation' on the analogy of Genesis 2:4), of Jesus Christ. But the language of Matthew 1:1 seems an overly subtle way to express this: why not simply 'the book of Jesus Christ,' or 'the book about new creation [*kainē ktisis*] in Jesus Christ'?

[4]Writes Green (1997: 189): 'As a literary form, genealogies are concerned as much with theological and apologetic issues as with historical; in them resides remarkable social power' (cf. Keener 1999: 77). This is surely true of the long genealogy at the opening of 1–2 Chronicles (1 Chron. 1–9); cf. Pratt 1998: 62-63. Chronicles, considered as one book, closes the canon of the Hebrew OT (cf. Matt. 23:35), so that the documents that link the two testaments both open with genealogies – Chronicles and Matthew being the only canonical writings that do so.

A. The Christ of God

Christos, the Greek equivalent of the Hebrew *Māšîach*, 'anointed one,' identifies Jesus as one whom God appoints for special
service.[5] The stress on the term at the close of the opening section (*Christos* occurs twice in 1:16-17) witnesses to the importance of the concept for Matthew. For what work God anoints
Jesus, and to what end, will become plain as the book unfolds;
but already there are clues.

Jesus: Son of David, Son of Abraham

The name 'Christ' is directly joined to the title 'son of David'
in Matthew 1:1. David is a pivotal figure in the genealogy to
follow (1:17). As David's ancestor, Judah is the only son of Jacob
who is mentioned by name (1:2; 'Judah and his brothers').[6] Of
all the kings listed in 1:6-11, David alone is expressly called
king (*basileus*; Matt. 1:6). Seven more times in Matthew Jesus
is called 'son of David'; apart from the reference to Joseph in
1:20, this term is applied to Jesus alone.[7] The numerical value
of the Hebrew name for David is 14, which probably accounts
for Matthew's structuring the genealogy, and selecting its
names, according to this number (1:17).[8]

---

[5]On Jesus as Messiah, see pages 130-34.

[6]Three of David's ancestors – Judah (Matt. 1:2-3) and his offspring
Perez (1:3) and Ram (1:3-4) – are prominently featured in the genealogy of
1 Chronicles 1–9 (see 2:3–4:23).

[7]By the same token, while Matthew employs *basileus* in a variety of
ways, only Jesus is called 'king of the Jews' or 'king of Israel' (see p. 132).

[8]The list of Judean kings is not exhaustive ('generations are skipped in
biblical genealogies without notice,' Pratt 1998: 72): missing, e.g., are the
names of Joash, Amaziah, Jehoiakim and Zedekiah (son of Josiah and uncle
of Jehoiachin, i.e. of Jeconiah; Matthew 1:11-12). Suggested ways to reckon
Matthew's numbers: 1. Abraham through David = 14 (1:2-6); David through
Jeconiah = 15 (1:6b-11); Jeconiah through Jesus = 14 (1:12-16). 2. Abraham
through David = 14; *Solomon* through Jeconiah = 14; *Shealtiel* through Jesus =
13. 3. Abraham through David = 14; Solomon through Jeconiah = 14; Shealtiel
through Joseph *and Mary* and Jesus = 14. 4. Abraham through David = 14;
David through *Josiah* ('the father of Jeconiah and his brothers at the time of
the exile to Babylon') = 14; *Jeconiah* through Jesus = 14. In support, note the
wording of 1:17: 'fourteen from David to the *exile* to Babylon, and fourteen
from the *exile* to the Christ.' Unless we opt for #4, we must conclude that
Matthew is not concerned about perfect *consistency* (cf. 1-3), or strict *precision*

The genealogy of Luke 3:23-38, unlike that of Matthew 1, begins with Jesus and concludes with Adam (rather than with Abraham). The names between Abraham and David are virtually identical in the two accounts; for the generations between David and Jesus, Luke's genealogy differs markedly from Matthew's. Puzzlement in face of these differences must not obscure the fact that the main purpose of each genealogy is to affirm Messiah's Davidic ancestry.[9]

Jesus is further identified in Matthew's opening verse as 'son of Abraham,' the other pivotal OT figure in the genealogy (1:17). In tracing Jesus' ancestry all the way back to Abraham, Matthew places Jesus firmly within the history of Israel and identifies him as a true Hebrew (cf. 3:9, 13-17). While not himself a king, Abraham would be progenitor of kings (Gen. 17:6), of whom David and Jesus were the most notable. We are also being prepared for Matthew's presentation of Jesus as the one in whom OT history reaches its appointed goal; about whom the Law (starting with the Book of Genesis) and the Prophets testify; and in whom God's ancient covenantal promises for both Israel and the Gentile nations are being fulfilled.[10]

(i.e., three exactly parallel reckonings of 14). His main concern, in any case, is to present Jesus' ancestry in three sections, according to a number (14) derived from David's name. 'The symbolic value of the fourteens is of more significance than their precise breakdown' (Carson 1984: 68). According to Keener (1999: 74, n. 8), Jewish interpreters of genealogies 'did not expect numerical exactitude.'

[9]For Jesus as Son of David in Luke, see also 1:27, 32-33, 69; 2:4. On the two genealogies, see the fine discussion by D. S. Huffman in *DJG*, 253-59. He mentions four 'plausible solutions to discrepancies': (i) Matthew gives Joseph's natural lineage; Luke, his legal lineage; (ii) Matthew gives Joseph's legal lineage; Luke, his natural; (iii) Matthew gives Joseph's ancestry; Luke, Mary's; (iv) Matthew gives Mary's ancestry; Luke, Joseph's (see p. 258 for details). I find the second solution the most attractive: cf. Zechariah 12:12-13; Keener 1999: 75-76; Calvin 1994: 57 ('though [the Messiah] was not of Solomon's natural descent, He may be reckoned his son in legal order, as He took His origin from the kings'). Yet we must admit, with Marshall (1978a: 159), 'that the problem caused by the existence of the two genealogies is insoluble with the evidence presently at our disposal.' In this connection, Calvin (1994: 58) cites Titus 3:9, which speaks of useless questionings about genealogies.

[10]Genesis 12:1-3; 18:18; 22:18; 26:4; Matthew 4:15-17; 8:11 11:12-13; 22:32; 28:18-20. See pages 120-29 on 'the Purpose of God'; Keener 1999: 77-78.

Jesus: Son of Mary
The genealogy concludes at Matthew 1:16, where the closing words 'Jesus, who is called Christ,' form an inclusion with the 'Jesus Christ' of 1:1.

Matthew 1:16 begins 'Jacob begat [*egennēsen*] Joseph,' in accord with the formula consistently used in 1:2-15. But in 1:16b, Matthew's language changes abruptly: 'Joseph, the husband of Mary, *of whom* [*ex hēs*, a feminine singular relative pronoun] was born [*egennēthē*, an aorist passive of *gennaō*] Jesus, who is called Christ.' This peculiar form of expression 'cries out for the explanation provided in the ensuing verses.'[11]

Luke's genealogy does not mention Mary; but its statement that Jesus 'was the son – so it was supposed – of Joseph' (3:23) recalls the explanation provided in 1:26-38. Accordingly, Luke affirms that Jesus is 'son of Mary,' 'son of David' and 'Son of God,' but never that he is 'son of Joseph.'[12]

B. The Wonders of God
The segments of Matthew's genealogy (1:1-17) are like stanzas of a hymn in praise of Israel's God.

Yahweh's Grace
In Matthew's genealogy the names of five women appear: Tamar (1:3); Rahab and Ruth (1:5); 'the wife of Uriah' (Bathsheba; 1:6); and Mary (1:16). The mention of women in a Hebrew genealogy is remarkable.[13] The list in Genesis 5, for example, consists entirely of men (though several are said to have had daughters). So does the parallel to Matthew in Luke 3:23-38 (though the evangelist Luke shows the highest respect for women). Only men are named in the genealogy at the close of Ruth (4:18-22); these ten – Perez through David – reappear in Matthew 1:3-6, but now the names of Rahab and Ruth are added.

---

[11]Carson 1984: 68.

[12]See, e.g., Luke 1:13, 31, 32, 35; 2:7; 3:31; 20:41. Apart from 3:23, 'son of Joseph' appears only in 4:22 (the Nazarenes' question about Jesus). Matthew agrees: see page 140 and II. A. below.

[13]Such is the case in 1 Chronicles 7:14-19, where women are mentioned five times in the record of Manasseh's descendants.

More remarkable are the women Matthew chose to include. Conspicuous by their absence are the patriarchs' wives: Sarah, mother of Isaac; Rebecca, mother of Jacob; and Leah, mother of Judah (see Matthew 1:2). At least two, and perhaps four, of the five were Gentiles: Rahab was a Canaanite, and Tamar may have been. Ruth was a Moabitess; and Bathsheba, like Uriah, may have been a Hittite.[14] Sexual irregularities are associated with at least three of the five. Tamar was involved in an illicit sexual liaison with her father-in-law Judah (Gen. 38). This Rahab is almost certainly the prostitute of Joshua 2 *et seq.*, although nowhere does the OT indicate that Boaz's mother was named Rahab. Bathsheba was involved in an adulterous union with King David (2 Sam. 11). (It is possible, but I think improbable, that Ruth 3:1-14 describes a sexual encounter between Ruth and Boaz.)[15]

Yahweh's amazing grace is further evident in the reference to Jeconiah, to his son Shealtiel and to his grandson Zerubbabel (1:11-12). Yahweh had declared through Jeremiah that Jeconiah, king of Judah (and also known as Jehoiachin), would be taken captive to Babylon, a prophecy fulfilled in 597 B.C. Furthermore, said Yahweh, 'none of his offspring shall succeed in sitting on the throne of David, and ruling again in Judah.'[16] Yet where Jeconiah's sin increased (2 Kings 24:9), Yahweh's grace abounded all the more (Rom. 5:20-21); in wrath Yahweh remembered mercy (Hab. 3:2). In time Jeconiah was released from prison and elevated to a place of honor in Babylon. More importantly, Yahweh reversed his curse upon the king by re-establishing his royal house. While Zerubbabel did not occupy the throne of David, he governed in Jerusalem

---

[14]Keener 1999: 79 thinks both Tamar and Bathsheba were Gentiles. Yet as Hagner rightly notes (1993: 10), it is 'not fully clear' that either is. Even if Bathsheba is Jewish, she takes on Gentile status through marriage to Uriah, repeatedly designated a Hittite (Gundry 1994: 15).

[15]Some think the Hebrew idiom 'to uncover the feet' (Ruth 3:4, 7) is euphemistic for exposing the sexual organs. For strong arguments against this view, see Bisson 1999: 81-94.

[16]Jeremiah 22:30b (NRSV), with 22:24-30; 2 Kings 24:8-17.

after the exile and became the focus of hopes for a restored Davidic monarchy.[17]

Already at the beginning of Matthew, we learn that God deals with *actual* people, not ideal ones. He enters into covenant with the *fallen* and the *guilty*, terms applicable to all of Jesus' ancestors, Mary included. To be sure, Mary is different from the other four women, in that she is neither flagrantly immoral as some of them were, nor a Gentile. Yet she, like them, receives saving grace: Gabriel addresses her as one 'graciously favored' by God (Luke 1:28); Mary herself speaks of 'God my Savior' (Luke 1:47). God sends his Son to save these very persons – including both those of OT times and his own mother – from their sins (Matt. 1:21; Rom. 3:25-26). To that end Jesus will identify with them in the closest way. To find him linked with prostitutes in his genealogy is not nearly so shocking as to discover him actually eating with them (Matt. 9:10-11). Moreover, some of the kings featured in the genealogy were guilty of great evils – Ahaz for example (2 Kings 16:1-4), and Manasseh (2 Kings 21:1-6). And the most distinguished king from whom Jesus is descended, and the one with whom he is most closely associated, was an adulterer and murderer.[18] Every sordid deed and sinful practice to which this genealogy alludes, served God's mysterious purpose. The sins are acknowledged, so that the divine grace that forgives them may be magnified (cf. 1 Cor. 15:9-10).

Yahweh's Faithfulness
Yahweh never forgets or abandons his promises to Abraham and to David, but brings them through the course of history to their appointed goal. Jesus the seed of Abraham has come,

---

[17]Pratt 1998: 73. On Jeconiah, see 2 Kings 25:27-30; Jeremiah 52:31-34; on Zerubbabel, see Haggai 1:1; 2:2, 23 (contrast Jeremiah 22:24); Zechariah 4:1-14. In Matthew 1:12, Zerubbabel's father is Shealtiel (so too Ezra 3:2, 8; Nehemiah 12:1; Haggai 1:1); in the MT (though not the LXX) of 1 Chronicles 3:17-18 the father is Pedaiah and Shealtiel an uncle (on this matter, see Pratt, ibid.). The crisis of the Exile confirmed the need not just for a Davidic, but for a *divine,* Messiah (Robertson 1990: 19-20).

[18]On David as a real (not ideal) person and redeemed sinner, see Peterson 1997a.

the One in whom the covenant of grace will be fulfilled. From the seed of David, Messiah has come, the One through whom David's throne will be established forever.[19]

That covenant of grace promises Gentile salvation. As this genealogy reports – and as the story of Ruth and Boaz (1:5) charmingly attests – already in OT times certain Gentiles are 'being blessed through Abraham' (Gen. 12:3) and incorporated into God's covenant-people.[20] Matthew's genealogy guards us against applying the words 'his people' (Matt. 1:21) to Jews exclusively. If God can raise up children for Abraham out of stones (3:9), how much more from among the Gentiles. Some expected that the Davidic Messiah, once enthroned, would destroy the Gentiles. Matthew shows that Christ uses his regal authority to oversee a saving mission to the Gentile nations (28:18-20). Gentiles united to Christ will themselves become the seed of Abraham and heirs of the covenantal promises.[21]

Yahweh's Power
The genealogy speaks four times of the 'deportation to Babylon' (*metoikesia Babylōnos*; 1:11, 12, 17), a critical juncture in Israel's history. Yet the people are indeed deported – not eradicated – at the time of Nebuchadnezzar's assault on Jerusalem (2 Kings 25). Nor do they lose their national identity in Babylon: see Jeremiah 29. Nor is the exile permanent. The people are restored to the land, liberated from bondage by the hand of Yahweh's servant Cyrus (Isa. 45:1). OT writers of the post-exilic period, notably Zechariah and the Chronicler, avow that God will restore the Davidic kingship.[22] Moreover,

---

[19]Gen. 12:1-3; Galatians 3:16; Romans 1:3; 2 Samuel 7:16; 23:5; 1 Kings 11:39 ('I will afflict the offspring of David...but not forever'); Psalm 89; Luke 1:33. The Davidic covenant presupposes, and keeps alive, the promises of the Abrahamic covenant. See Robertson 1980: 28-41, 243-52.

[20]Cf. the genealogy of Ruth 4:18-21. On the presence of Gentiles in the genealogy of 1 Chronicles 1–9, see Pratt 1998: 19.

[21]Galatians 3:16, 26-29. On Jesus as Savior of the world – of non-Jews as well as Jews – see also John 3:16-17; 4:42; 12:47; and pages 148-54, on 'the People of God.'

[22]See Zechariah 9:9 (with Matthew 21:4-9); and 1–2 Chronicles *passim*, with Pratt 1998: 10-11 (on the post-exilic setting), 24-25 (on the necessity of re-establishing David's throne).

as Matthew 1:12-16 indicates, the royal lineage is kept intact after the exile even though there are no descendants of David reigning from Jerusalem.[23] All those facts testify to the sustaining and protecting might of Israel's sovereign God.

A yet greater manifestation of the divine power underlies the language of 1:16b. Mary is like the other women in the genealogy, in that through them all God does unusual and unexpected things to achieve his saving purpose. Yet, in other respects, Mary's experience is very different from theirs, as we are about to learn.

---

[23]See the above comments on Jeconiah and his successors. We recall that the royal Messiah was to arise from the stump of a felled tree (Isa. 11:1-9). Cf. Ezekiel 19, which laments the apparent extinction of the Davidic dynasty.

II.
'YE SERVANTS OF GOD, YOUR MASTER PROCLAIM'[1]
(1:18-25).

This passage records a manifold testimony – all of it traceable to God – about the nature of Jesus' conception, and about his names as disclosures of his identity and mission. The passage is joined to verses 1-17 in several ways. (i) The introductory *Tou de Iēsou Christou hē genesis* ('the birth of Jesus Christ'; 1:18, echoes *Biblos geneseōs Iēsou Christou* (1:1).[2] (ii) *Gennaō* (1:20) recalls the genealogy, where this verb appears forty times. But the phrase of 1:20, *en autē gennēthen* ('conceived in her') has a special link with 1:16b, *ex hēs egennēthē* ('from whom was born'), these being the only two places in the chapter where the passive voice of the verb is used.[3] (iii) In accord with 1:16 Mary is called Jesus' mother (18). In keeping with the major emphasis of the genealogy, Joseph is expressly called 'son of David' (20).

A. God's Mighty Initiative

This section contains the first instances of *Kyrios* ('Lord') in Matthew. Here, and in chapter 2, the term consistently denotes Yahweh, the God of Israel.[4] *Theos* ('God') also appears here for the first time. Both *Kyrios* and *Theos* witness to the saving initiative

---

[1] The opening words of a hymn by Charles Wesley (1744).

[2] See comments on verse 1. Some MSS. read *gennēsis* instead of *genesis* in Matthew 1:18. But the latter is much better attested; and as Bruce Metzger notes (*TC*, 7), copyists would tend to replace the broader term *genesis* ('origin, birth, genealogy') with the narrower *gennēsis* ('birth'), especially since *gennēsis* corresponds more closely to the verb *gennaō*, so frequent in the genealogy of 1:1-17.

[3] In all the other thirty-nine instances of 1:1-17, the verb is active: 'he begat.' The indicative of *gennaō* (1:16b) is translated 'was born,' and the participle (1:20) 'conceived,' in accord with the respective prepositional phrases '*from* whom' and '*in* her.' So BAGD s.v.

[4] See Matthew 1:20, 22, 24; 2:13, 15, 19; also page 138.

of Israel's sovereign God, but Matthew's use of the second term supplements his use of the first in a most significant way.

The Angel of Yahweh

While Joseph was sleeping, having resolved to take the action described in 1:19 ('behold [*idou*], an angel of the Lord [*angelos Kyriou*] appeared to him in a dream'; 20a); compare 1:24, '*the* angel [*ho angelos*] of the Lord,' namely, the one introduced in 1:20. On the two other occasions in Matthew when a single angel appears – significantly, following Jesus' birth and resurrection (chs. 2 and 28) – the figure is again identified as *angelos Kyriou* – a servant and messenger of Yahweh.[5] The opening *idou* prepares readers for the startling and the significant; this will be true to a yet greater degree in 1:23: 'Behold [*Idou*, for Hebrew *hinēh*] the virgin will conceive....'

In this passage, the angel is the only servant of God whose speech is directly reported. He addresses Joseph by name, and identifies him as 'son of David' (1:20). Then the angel discloses the manner of Mary's conception, together with the name and the mission of the child she will bear.

The Holy Spirit

Both Matthew and the angel declare that this child is conceived in Mary's womb by a power 'from the Holy Spirit' (*ek pneumatos hagiou*; 1:18, 20). Lest it be thought that the Spirit is cooperating with a human father (as in the case of John the Baptist), the evangelist expressly says that this conception occurred before Mary and Joseph 'came together' (1:18); i.e., before they began to live together and consummated their marriage sexually.[6] Joseph figures prominently in the section;

---

[5]See 2:13, 19 (both recalling 1:20); 28:2, 5. The *angelos* of 11:10 is John the Baptist. All other instances are plural: once it is angels who serve the devil (25:41), elsewhere those who serve God the Father (e.g., 26:53) and the Son of Man (e.g., 24:30-31). On linguistic grounds, one may interpret *angelos Kyriou* in 1:20 as '*the* angel of the Lord': see GNTG 4: 180; GGBB, 252.

[6]Luke 1:23-24 clearly indicates that John's mother Elizabeth became pregnant by her husband Zechariah. But given the couple's advanced age and Elizabeth's barrenness (1:7), together with the angel's promise that John would be 'filled with the Holy Spirit while still in his mother's womb; (1:15), we may infer that the Spirit was extraordinarily active in John's conception.

but neither here nor elsewhere does Matthew call him Jesus' father.[7]

The simplicity of Matthew's explanation is matched by Luke's: 'The Holy Spirit will come upon you, and the power of the Most High will overshadow you,' says Gabriel to Mary (1:35). That is all we need to know; our curiosity about the exact manner of the Spirit's work is not satisfied. The evangelists' reticence reflects their sense of wonder before a holy and impenetrable mystery.[8]

By the Spirit's power, human life is created in Mary's womb – an act that recalls the Spirit's activity in creation (Gen. 1:2; Ps. 33:6) and offers promise of new creation with the dawn of the kingdom of God. As the coming of Jesus occurs not by the will of the flesh but by the divine initiative exclusively, so God's kingdom is to be established by a divine invasion rather than through human progress and social reform.[9] Moreover, the present passage reveals that the Spirit who will empower Jesus for inaugurating the kingdom (Matt. 3:16; 12:28) is at work from the moment of his conception, protecting him from the threat of evil and the pollution of sin. The term 'immaculate conception' may rightly be applied to that of Jesus, but not to that of his mother.[10]

---

[7]See page 140. Joseph's name appears four times in Matthew 1:18-25, and only three times elsewhere in Matthew (1:16; 2:13, 19). Significantly, it is the skeptical people of Jesus' hometown who ask, 'Is not this the carpenter's son?' (13:55, with vv. 54-58).

[8]To suggest that the Spirit 'mated' with Mary, as the gods did with humans in the pagan myths, and as 'the sons of God' did according to one view of Genesis 6:1-4, has no basis in the record, reduces God in the most blasphemous way, and converts a holy mystery into an absurdity. For a brilliant and reverent study of Jesus' virginal conception, see Machen 1932. 'One cannot deny testimony for a miracle by dismissing it on the grounds that miracles cannot happen' (Keener 1999: 84). As Lewis says (1955: 59), '[A]ny modern man who believes in God can accept the miracle as easily as St. Joseph did.'

[9]See Matthew 4:3-4, 17. Like his people, Jesus 'was born...neither by the will of the flesh nor by the will of a man [*anēr*, which can also mean 'husband'], but of God' (John 1:13).

[10]The papal bull *Ineffabilis Deus*, issued by Pius IX in 1854, declared 'that the most Blessed Virgin Mary in the first instant of her conception... was preserved free from all stain of original sin,' and that this is 'a doctrine revealed by God' as early as Genesis 3:15. As G. W. Bromiley notes, 'The claim

Jesus the Savior

The angel tells Joseph that Mary 'will bear a son, and you shall call his name Jesus [*Iēsous*], for he will save his people from their sins' (1:21). The latter part of the statement expounds the meaning of *Iēsous*, the Greek equivalent of the Hebrew *yᵉhôšua'* ('Joshua'), 'Yahweh is salvation.' The name God chooses for the child captures the singular purpose of his mission.

'He will save his people from their *sins*,' says the angel; and 'from *their* sins,' not those of others. Cf. Luke 1:77, 'to give knowledge of salvation to his people in the forgiveness of their sins.' We are not told that the Son of David, the warrior king, will rescue Israel from her Gentile enemies; nor that the latter-day Joshua will lead a crusade patterned after his forebear's war against the Canaanites. To be sure, the dawn of God's rule (Matt. 4:17) assures that the foes of Messiah's people will be defeated (Luke 1:74). But we already know from Matthew 1:1-17 that Gentiles are to be numbered among his people. Indeed, the angel's declaration (1:21) may allude to God's promise to Abraham concerning Isaac (Gen. 17:19), the one whose birth would keep the promise to Gentiles alive, and whose near-sacrifice would point forward to Messiah's atoning death.[11]

'He will save *his* people,' says the angel. But do not they belong to Yahweh? And does not Yahweh alone have authority to forgive sins (Matt. 9:1-8)? Let us consult an OT writer for light on these questions.

B. Isaiah the Prophet

'All of this happened in order that what had been said by the Lord through the prophet might be fulfilled: "Behold, the virgin will conceive and will give birth to a son, and they will call his name Immanuel" – which is, being interpreted, "God

---

to divine revelation is odd in view of the silence of Scripture and the late promulgation of the doctrine in Christian history' ('Mary,' in *ISBE* 3: 72).

[11]Cf. the references to Abraham in Matthew 1:1, 2, 17, and to Isaac's birth in 1:2. Erickson 2000: 44-49 highlights seven features of 1:18-25 (most notably the angel's words in 21) which suggest that Matthew is deliberately alluding to the story of Abraham in Genesis 12–17. If Matthew 1:21a alludes to Genesis 17:19, then 1:21b may allude to Messiah's atoning sacrifice (Genesis 22:8-14; Matthew 20:28; 26:27-28; Romans 8:32; and see comments on Matthew 3:15, 17). For more on 1:21, see pages 145-48.

with us"' (1:22-23). In the events he has just foretold through
his angel (20-21), God will fulfill the word he formerly spoke
through his prophet in Isaiah 7:14; thus declares God's
evangelist.[12] Understanding the meaning of this prophecy
– for Matthew no less than for Isaiah – calls for attention to
Isaiah 1-12.[13]

Ahaz: The Hour of Decision

As Assyria asserts its power under Tiglath-Pileser, Aram and
Israel seek to unite their neighbors against the common foe.
When Judah refuses to cooperate, Rezin of Aram and Pekah of
Israel lead their armies against Jerusalem to overthrow Ahaz
and enthrone their own man, the son of Tabeel (Isa. 7:1-2,
6; 2 Chron. 28:5-8). But Yahweh, through Isaiah, assures the
terrified king and people that the fierce anger of Rezin and
Pekah is about to be snuffed out (Isa. 7:3-7). Judah's greatest
need is to trust in Yahweh their God: 'If you do not stand firm
in your faith, you will not stand at all' (7:9b).

Yahweh even condescends to Ahaz's weakness and
offers to give him a *sign* – of whatever sort the king might
wish (7:10- 11). 'But Ahaz said, "I will not ask; I will not test
Yahweh"' (7:12). This sounds pious but is actually impious –
expressive of national unbelief. 'Then Isaiah said, "Hear now,
O house of David! Is it too little for you to try the patience of
men? Will you try the patience of my God also?"' (7:13). In
refusing the sign, Ahaz refuses the word to whose reliability
the sign would point; if the sign were given, there would be
less excuse for rejecting the word. In face of the threat Ahaz
trusts instead in the king of Assyria (2 Kings 16:7-18).

---

[12]'By [*hypo*] the Lord through [*dia*] the prophet' (Matt. 1:22) accords with
Isaiah 7, which states that Yahweh's message comes to Ahaz both through
Isaiah (7:3-9, 13-17) and directly from Yahweh (7:10). See the discussion of
Matthew's OT quotations on pages 92-99.

[13]Chs. 1–5 prepare for Isaiah's call in chapter 6. Chs. 7–12 comprise a
unit built on chapter 6. Thereafter come the oracles about the nations (chs.
13 *et seq.*). For our present purpose, it is sufficient to focus on Isaiah 1–12,
chapters crucial for understanding 7:14.

Yahweh: Judge and Savior

From the very opening of Isaiah 1–12, Judah is depicted as rebellious against Yahweh, forgetful of his saving actions, disdainful of his law's righteous demands. Under their inept and corrupt leaders, and their kings' sins of omission and commission, the people have become thoroughly iniquitous, a brood of idolaters and evildoers laden with guilt. Yahweh's choice vineyard has yielded nothing but bad fruit. Judgment is therefore inevitable. Already Yahweh spurns the people's prayers and sacrifices. Soon their material prosperity will end; soon the fruitless vineyard will be overrun and devastated by foreign armies. Ahaz's response to the offer of a sign recalls the history of Judah's unbelief and disobedience, and exhausts Yahweh's patience. Assyria, the very power on which Ahaz relies, will become the rod of Yahweh's wrath against king and people, and reduce them to servitude.[14]

Through those same chapters, and precisely in face of imminent judgment, there resounds the promise of salvation. So grievous is the sin that the remedy must be radical; if the people are to be saved at all, their Judge must become their Savior. And it is indeed Yahweh who, amid the opening indictment, offers cleansing from sin (1:18), an atonement Isaiah personally experiences at the time of his call (6:6-7). Destruction is 'decreed upon the whole land,' but a remnant of those struck down 'will return to the mighty God' (10:20-23). Amid devastation and loss, Yahweh will exert his recreative and redemptive might. On the Day of Yahweh the Gentiles whose armies once executed God's judgment on Judah, and who were themselves judged for their ruthless arrogance, will call on Yahweh's name and rejoice in his salvation (11:10–12:6).

---

[14]See Isaiah 1:2-31; 2:6–4:1; 5:1-30; 6:9-13; 7:16–8:22; 9:8–10:4. The first two kings mentioned in 1:1 – Uzziah and Jotham – 'did what was right in the eyes of Yahweh' yet allowed pagan worship to continue (2 Kings 15:3-4, 34-35). But Ahaz, Jotham's son, 'did not do what was right in the eyes of Yahweh' (see 2 Kings 16:2-4); when he became 'servant and vassal' to Assyria's king, his iniquities increased (16:7-18).

The Davidic Messiah
Yahweh's chosen instrument, for both judgment and salvation, is an offspring of David. Just when the royal lineage appears to have been eradicated, 'a shoot will come up from the stump of Jesse; from his roots a Branch will bear fruit. The Spirit of Yahweh will rest on him' (Isa. 11:1-2a) – he being the 'Prince of Peace' appointed to reign from David's throne forever (9:6-7). The glory of his kingship will penetrate pagan darkness (9:1-2). 'In that day the Root of Jesse will stand as a banner for the peoples; the nations will rally to him' (11:10, NIV). Gentiles will stream to Yahweh's holy mountain, there to receive his teaching, walk in his light, and be trained in the way of peace (2:2-4; 11:6-9).

Integral to Messiah's saving work is a process of judgment. 'In that day the Branch of the LORD will be beautiful and glorious' for 'those who are left in Zion' – that is, for the faithful remnant who have survived the judgment through faith and repentance (4:2-6; 10:20-23). *Shalom* is established on Yahweh's holy mountain, because Messiah has granted justice to the meek of the earth, and has slain the wicked with the breath of his lips (11:1-9). His authority surpasses that of David; for this Prince of Peace is himself the 'Mighty God' come to dwell with and to rule over his people forever (9:6-7).[15]

The Promise of Immanuel
Ahaz refuses to ask for a sign, but a sign will nonetheless be given: 'Therefore Yahweh himself will give you a sign: Behold, the virgin [*hā 'almâ*] is pregnant and giving birth to a son; and she will call his name Immanuel' (7:14, MT). The prophecy is directly addressed to king and people: 'Yahweh will give *you* [plural] a sign.' The closing term consists of two words in Hebrew, *'Imānnû 'ēl*, 'God with us' (a translation provided in Matthew 1:23). The context discloses that 'God is with' king and people in the two ways indicated above.

On the one hand, the birth of the child will testify to approaching *judgment*. The sign is given precisely in face

---

[15]'The case for the expectation of a divine Messiah is strong in the Old Testament.... Isaiah foresaw the birth of the divine son of David...' (Motyer 1993: 85, 86).

of Ahaz's and Judah's unbelief: thus the opening 'therefore' (*lākēn*). Judgment will fall swiftly, 'before the boy knows enough to reject the wrong and choose the right' (7:15-17); the 'boy' (*na'ar*) of 16 is clearly to be identified with the 'son' (*bēn*) of 14.[16] Having enlarged upon that warning in 7:18-25, Isaiah reports: 'I went to the prophetess, and she conceived and gave birth to a son. And the LORD said to me, "Name him Mahar-shalal-Hash-Baz. Before the boy knows how to say 'My father' or 'My mother,' the wealth of Damascus and the plunder of Samaria will be carried off by the king of Assyria"' (8:3-4). The proximity of 8:3-4 to 7:10-17, and the linguistic affinities between the two texts, indicate that with the birth of Isaiah's son, Yahweh keeps the promise of 7:14 and verifies the imminence of catastrophe.[17] Underscoring this warning is the name God chooses for Isaiah's son (8:3): 'Quick to the plunder, swift to the spoil' (NIV mg.).

Yet in the same passage Isaiah declares that God is 'with us' in *grace*. Even amid calamity, he is a sanctuary to those who trust in him (8:11-22). The prophet and his sons are 'signs' (*'ōtôt*; 8:18) that this is so – which recalls the 'sign' (*'ôt*), and in turn the *'Immanû 'ēl* of 7:14.[18] And what of the vaunted Assyrians? They conquer Aram and Israel, and deport their inhabitants (2 Kings 16:9; 17:6); but when they invade Judah they are turned away by a mighty act of Yahweh (Isa. 31:4-9; 37:1-38:6). It is Babylon, not Assyria, which will send the Judeans into exile.

---

[16] Against Calvin's view that 7:14-15 refer to one child and 7:16 to another, see Oswalt 1986: 208.

[17] Isaiah 7:14 and 8:3-4 have in common the verbs *hārāh* ('conceive'), *yālad* ('give birth to'), and *qār'ā* ('call'); and the nouns *bēn* ('son') and *shēm* ('name'). 'The prophetess' (*han'bi'â*; 8:3), recalls 'the virgin' (*hā 'almâ*; 7:14). The opening of 8:4, 'for before the boy knows' (*kî b'terem yēd'a hana'ar*) is identical to that of 7:16. Damascus and Samaria (8:4) are capitals of the countries mentioned in 7:16. Both 7:17 and 8:4 close with a reference to 'the king of Assyria' (*melek 'asshûr*).

[18] The only places *'ôt* occurs in Isaiah prior to 8:18 are 7:11 and 14. Also harking back to 7:14 are the instances of *'Immanû 'ēl* in 8:8, 10. Nowhere is Isaiah's son expressly called 'Immanuel'; but neither does the NT apply the term to Jesus beyond Matthew 1:23.

So the birth of Isaiah's son signals but fleeting hope. The reign of Hezekiah, son of Ahaz, indeed brings restoration and revival (2 Kings 18:3-8); but it is an act of Hezekiah that evokes Isaiah's prophecy of Babylonian captivity (Isa. 39; 2 Kings 20:12-21) some 100 years before the fall of Jerusalem and the close of the Davidic monarchy (2 Kings 25). Yet in the very place he records the birth and name of his son, and describes the mounting Assyrian threat, Isaiah speaks of a more powerful and more durable kingship (8:5-10). Of special note are verses 8 and 10, the only instances of 'Imannû 'ēl in Isaiah beyond 7:14. 'Its [Assyria's] wings will cover the breadth of your land, O Immanuel!' (8:8). Then: 'Devise your strategy, but it will be thwarted; propose your plan, but it will not stand, for God is with us' (8:10). This description of Immanuel as owner and ruler of the land, as one in whom God is personally present, and therefore as one far mightier than the hostile nations, anticipates the prophecy about the One who is to reign from David's throne forever (9:6-7).[19] Isaiah 8 in turn links Isaiah 9 to Isaiah 7. The 'son' of 9:6 is the very 'son' of 7:14; the 'Immanuel' of 7:14 is the 'Mighty God' of 9:6.[20]

I have deliberately refrained from saying that the birth of Isaiah's son *fulfills* the promise of 7:14. Given the language of Matthew 1:23 ('might be fulfilled,' the passive of *plēroō*), this verb is to be reserved for Jesus' birth. The birth of Isaiah's son foreshadows or adumbrates Messiah's coming. The earlier event is a – not *the* – realization of the promise; it offers a pledge and assurance that Messiah will come at Yahweh's appointed time.[21]

---

[19]'Ultimately, Immanuel is the owner of the land, the one against whom Assyria's threats are ultimately lodged, the one upon whom deliverance finally depends. That cannot be Isaiah's son, nor even some unknown son of Ahaz. It can only be the Messiah, in whom all hope resides' (Oswalt 1986: 227). Cf. Isaiah 9:1 (with its phrase 'in the future'); Matthew 4:14-16. Messiah is his people's 'everlasting Father,' Isaiah 9:6, because he governs, protects, guides and loves them forever (cf. 9:7b): 'father' describes Messiah's (and thus Jesus') *function*, not his *being*.

[20]So too Motyer 1993: 86. The noun *bēn* ('son') appears in both 7:14 and 9:6, as does the verb *yālad* ('give birth to').

[21]'The OT passages are not treated as mere predictions but as anticipations.... Matthew's idea of fulfillment says, in effect, that the event that the Jews thought was significant turns out to be only an anticipation of an event of a similar kind but ultimately more significant in God's purposes

In light of the above, we turn to Isaiah's chosen term for the mother of 7:14 – *'almâ*. This Hebrew noun basically means 'a young woman of marriageable age.'[22] In ancient Hebrew society it is assumed that such a woman would be a virgin – which explains why the LXX translates the *'almâ* of 7:14 *parthenos*, 'virgin,' rather than *neanis*, 'young girl.'[23] On the one hand, *'almâ* is appropriate in a prophecy about a child to be miraculously conceived in the womb of a virgin before her marriage has been consummated.[24] But on the other hand *'almâ* does not *require* that meaning; it is also rightly applied to a woman who, once married, conceives a child in the usual way (8:3). Given the dual intent of the prophecy of Isaiah 7:14, *'almâ* is eminently the right choice.[25]

Yet precisely because of the ambiguity of *'almâ*, it is not until we come to Matthew 1 that we learn assuredly that Messiah will be miraculously conceived in the womb of a virgin by the power

---

for the salvation of mankind. It is in this sense that the latter fulfills the former' (R. Schippers, 'Fullness,' etc., *DNTT* 1: 737). A comparison with Matthew 2:15 is instructive, as we shall see. Cf. pages 120-22 above, 'Jesus the Fulfillment of the Old Testament.'

[22]Oswalt 1986: 210, citing the lexicon of Koehler and Baumgartner. There is no instance of *'almâ* in the OT or beyond that clearly refers to a married woman (ibid.; Motyer 1993: 85).

[23]Oswalt 1986: 210. *'Almâ* 'presumes rather than states virginity' (Derek Kidner, *NBC: R*, 596).

[24]It is often argued that, had Isaiah intended to refer to a virginal conception, he would have used the noun *bᵉtûlâ* (BDB, 'virgin'). But *bᵉtûlâ*, like *'almâ*, denotes 'a girl of marriageable age' whose virginity is assumed. Affirmations of virginity are supplied (if at all) by the contexts, not by the term itself. Thus Genesis 24:16 says that Rebekah 'was...a virgin [*bᵉtûlâ*]; no man had ever lain with her'; verse 43 calls her 'a maiden ['almâ],' which clearly harks back to verse 16. In the LXX, both the *bᵉtûlâ* of 24:16 and the *'almâ* of 24:43 are translated *parthenos*, as in Isaiah 7:14. Only in the Christian era is there clear evidence that *bᵉtûlâ* has become a technical term for 'virgin.' Cf. Motyer 1993: 84-85 (following G. J. Wenham), who thinks *'almâ* actually comes closer to expressing *virgo intacta* than does *bᵉtûlâ*.

[25]In the judgment of Oswalt 1986: 210-11, 'while the prophet did not want to stress the virginity, neither did he wish to leave it aside.... In fact, he may have used this term ['almâ] precisely because of its richness and diversity.... Ahaz's sign must be rooted in its own time to have significance for that time, but it also must extend beyond that time and into a much more universal mode if its radical truth is to be any more than a vain hope. For such a twofold task ['almâ] is admirably suited.'

of the Holy Spirit. Once Matthew declares that historical reality, we perceive with greater clarity that Isaiah already, 'without linguistic impropriety, opens the door to such a meaning.'[26]

C. The Coming of Immanuel

'All of this happened in order that what had been said by the Lord through the prophet might be fulfilled' (Matt. 1:22). The promised *Christos* is about to be born. Verse 23a, 'Behold, the virgin will conceive and will give birth to a son,' exactly quotes the LXX of Isaiah 7:14. In agreement with the MT, it is '*the* virgin' (*hē parthenos*) who will conceive.[27] Her child will prove to be, in the fullest sense, the 'sign' promised to the house of David centuries earlier.[28] Unlike Isaiah's wife, this maiden does not lose her virginity in conceiving her son: on the contrary, before she and Joseph come together, she is found to be pregnant by a power from the Holy Spirit (Matt. 1:18, 20). Moreover, in accord with the prophecy that '*the virgin...will give birth to* a son,' Joseph has no sexual relations with Mary until after Jesus is born (1:25).[29]

The Identity of the Child

We do not know from what tribe Isaiah came, nor is there proof that his son was of royal blood.[30] But Mary's son is assuredly of the tribe of Judah, a descendant of David, and the One through whom David's throne will be established forever.[31]

---

[26]Motyer 1993: 85. Isaiah 'laid the foundation for the understanding of the unique nature of [Messiah's] birth' (86).

[27]The corresponding term in the MT is *ha 'almâ*: this denotes the particular maiden through whom the prophecy will be fulfilled (*GHG*, par. 126r, p. 408).

[28]Cf. Isaiah 7:14a: 'Therefore the Lord himself will give you [plural, referring to the house of David, v. 13] a sign [*'ôt*]....' This *'ôt* is translated *sēmeion* in the LXX. Cf. Luke 2:12: 'And this will be a sign [*sēmeion*] for you: you shall find an infant....'

[29]That Joseph and Mary had sexual relations thereafter is evident from the reference to Jesus' brothers and sisters in Matthew 13:55-56. There is no biblical basis for the idea of Mary's perpetual virginity. See the discussion in Bruner 2004a: 48-52.

[30]Oswalt (1986: 82) says 'the claim for Isaiah's royalty is without any objective evidence.'

[31]Romans 1:3; 2 Samuel 7:16; Luke 1:33. It is therefore vital that Joseph – Jesus' *legal* (though not biological) father – be a descendant of David (Matt. 1:16); a 'son of David' (1:20). Cf. Luke 2:3-4.

This child is both human and divine. He is miraculously conceived but truly conceived: Jesus' humanity is as genuine as that of his ancestors Abraham and David (Matt. 1:1-17). But this very child is to be called *Emmanu ēl*, a transliteration of the Hebrew term that Matthew translates 'God with us' (1:23b). God was assuredly with Israel during the reign of David, but David was not a divine being.[32] The birth of Isaiah's son signaled Yahweh's presence with Judah during the Assyrian crisis, yet the prophecy of Isaiah 7:14 was not fulfilled at that time. But now, with the appearance of Mary's Son, Yahweh – the very One who dwelt in the midst of the sons of Israel (Exod. 29:45) – will be with his people in an unprecedented way. This child not only witnesses to God's presence, he embodies it. Jesus himself is God – now come to abide with his people forever (cf. Matt. 28:20).

Jesus has a human mother but a divine Father. Matthew often speaks of Mary as Jesus' mother; and throughout his book the evangelist identifies God as Jesus' Father, and Jesus as the Son of God. The connection between Jesus' being conceived by the Spirit of God and his being identified as the Son of God should not be overlooked. Says Gabriel to Mary, 'The Holy Spirit will come upon you, and the power of the Most High will overshadow you; therefore the child to be born will be called holy, the Son of God' (Luke 1:35).[33]

Moreover, given Matthew's witness to Jesus' deity, we must also be attentive to his usage of *Kyrios*. This is the LXX's chosen translation of Yahweh, the sacred covenantal name of Israel's God. Thus to be understood are the three instances of *Kyrios* in Matthew 1: 'angel of *the Lord*' (1:20, 24); 'what was spoken by *the Lord*' (1:22). It would be consistent with the evidence of Matthew 1 for the evangelist to apply *Kyrios* to Jesus in light of that OT usage – that is, to identify Jesus himself as Yahweh; and this is indeed what we find.[34]

---

[32]'Unlike other ancient Near Eastern cultures, Israel did not believe her king was divine or shared in divinity' (Pratt 1998: 154).

[33]See 'Jesus is God the Son,' pages 139-41.

[34]See 'Jesus is Lord,' pages 137-39.

The Mission of the Child

Three times in this passage, in quick succession, the Greek noun *onoma* ('name') appears: 'you shall call his name Jesus' (1:21); 'they will call his name Immanuel' (1:23); 'he called his name Jesus' (1:25). In the OT, for Israel's sake, the high and holy God placed his Name in their midst; by virtue of that Name his people were blessed and sustained.[35] The joining of 'name' to 'Immanuel' in Matthew 1:23 expresses the divine presence with exceptional force, just as the collocation of 'name' and 'Jesus' signals a stupendous outpouring of saving power.

Whereas for the post-exilic writers the restoring of an earthly Davidic kingship would testify to Yahweh's heavenly reign, the appearance of Jesus the Messiah 'represents the conjoining of the divine and human thrones.'[36] As both Yahweh and David were mighty warriors, so Jesus as both Yahweh incarnate and Son of David is the One through whom God's Rule will be established by the conquest of all his and his people's enemies.[37] Yet as we have seen (sec. A.), the primary purpose of that conquest is not to destroy but to save. '*He* [*autos*] will save his people from their sins,' declares the angel (1:21) – he and no other. He, their Davidic king and their God incarnate, is indeed mighty to save; and he, the One sent to atone for their sins, is both human ('the son of David') and divine ('God with us').[38]

The Hebrew of Isaiah 7:14 reads, 'Behold, the virgin is pregnant and giving birth to a son; and *she* will call his name Immanuel.'[39] According to the LXX, '*you* [singular] will

---

[35]Pratt 1998: 30. Yahweh's Name signaled his 'invocable presence' and his 'accessible power' (ibid., 180, 178).

[36]Ibid., 25. 'With the re-establishment of the Davidic throne in Christ, the reign (Kingdom) of God was re-established' (ibid., 154).

[37]That Jesus' life is to be a scene of titanic conflict is apparent already in Matthew 2:13-20 and 4:1-11. Matthew declares both that Jesus is mightier than Satan (4:1-11; 12:28-29) and that he will achieve his ultimate triumph through defeat (Matt. 26–28). On the joining of David's human army to Yahweh's heavenly army, see 1 Chronicles 11–12 and Pratt 1998: 114-21.

[38]See 'The Cost of Forgiveness,' pages 147-48. The *autos* in Matthew 1:21b makes the subject (already stated in the verb *sōsei*) emphatic: cf. BAGD s.v., 2.; Bengel 1873: 114; Morris 1992: 29-30.

[39]As noted in NIV mg., Isaiah in the Dead Sea Scrolls reads, '*and he* or *and they*.'

call....'[40] But in the quotation of Matthew 1:23, '*they* will call his name Immanuel' – 'they' being, in this context, 'his people,' the ones he saves from their sins (1:21). On their lips 'God is with us!' is an exclamation of praise and thanksgiving for Jesus, their divine and incarnate Redeemer. This verb *kalesousin*, 'they will call,' is all the more striking in view of the angel's command to Joseph: 'you will call' (1:21, *kaleseis*, as in the LXX of Isaiah 7:14).[41]

D. Joseph the Husband of Mary

Joseph, whose name occurs four times in verses 18-25, is another faithful servant of God.

In that day, a Jewish marriage began in two stages. First came betrothal: the man and the woman, standing before witnesses, gave their formal consent to marry one another and thus 'became engaged' (*mnēsteuō*; Matthew 1:18a). Henceforth they could rightly be called husband and wife; so the NIV of verse 19 renders *anēr* as 'husband' and *apolyō* as 'divorce.' It was usually another year before the second stage was reached. During the interval the girl (who may have been thirteen or fourteen years old) continued to live with her parents. Then came the bridegroom with his friends to the bride's home, whence the party returned in festal procession to the home of the bridegroom's parents for the wedding banquet (cf. the parables of 25:1-13 and 22:1-14). Afterwards, the man and the woman 'came together' (*synerchomai*; 1:18b), and consummated their marriage sexually (1:25).[42]

[40]The Greek verb *kaleis* ('you will call') translates the Hebrew *qārā'ta*, whose consonants are the same as the Hebrew behind 'she will call' (*qārā't*).

[41]Gabriel's earlier words to Mary, (Luke 1:31, 'you will conceive *in your womb and you will bear a son and you shall call his name Jesus*'), both recall Isaiah 7:14 (see also *parthenos* in Luke 1:27) and anticipate the angel's message to Joseph (Matt. 1:21). Luke 1:28b ('the Lord is with you') echoes the promise of Isaiah 7:14 for Isaiah's day but also brings to mind the richer sense that 'Immanuel' will bear once Mary's son is born. Cf. the angel's message to the shepherds in Luke 2:11: 'because today there has been born *for you [hymin]* in the city of David, a Savior [*sōtēr*, the nominal counterpart to *sōzō*, the verb used in Matthew 1:21] who is Christ [cf. Matt. 1:1, 16-18]....'

[42]The language of Matthew 1:25, 'he did not know [*eginōsken*] her,' recalls Genesis 4:1, 'Adam lay with [literally, knew; LXX, *egnō*] his wife Eve....' Both verbs are forms of *ginōskō*. See C. S. Keener, 'Marriage,' *DNTB*, especially 683-87 ('Beginning Marriage').

During the period of betrothal Joseph learns of Mary's pregnancy and concludes that she has had sexual relations with another man – itself testimony to Joseph's own fidelity to the seventh commandment.[43] In response Joseph, 'being righteous and not wanting [*dikaios ōn kai mē thelōn*] to subject her to public disgrace, planned to divorce her secretly' (Matt. 1:19). Some take this to mean that Joseph, *although* righteous (i.e., committed to upholding the Mosaic law concerning adultery), was yet unwilling to expose Mary.[44] It is preferable to view *mē thelōn* as an explanation of *dikaios ōn*: Joseph is righteous and *therefore* does not want to disgrace Mary; his righteousness seeks expression in an act of mercy.[45] Jesus too would teach that longing for righteousness (*dikaiosynē*) and showing mercy are twin traits of character (5:6-7; cf. Mic. 6:8).

There are further tokens of Joseph's righteousness. We have already noted how 1:25a shows his respect for the precise wording of Isaiah 7:14. He also honors God's word as mediated by the angel. 'Having arisen from his sleep, Joseph did as the angel of the Lord had commanded him, and took her to be his wife' (1:24). Moreover, in accord with the angel's command ('you shall call [*kaleseis*] his name Jesus'; 1:21), 'he called [*ekalesen*] his name Jesus' (1:25).[46]

This singular form of the verb *kaleō* is no less important than the plural of 1:23: 'they shall call.' The preceding

---

[43]'Sources as early as the Mishnah [codified A.D. 90–200] do not exclude the possibility of sexual contact between betrothal and marriage' (Scott 1995: 250). Joseph's contemplated action (Matt. 1:19) 'indicates he knew he was not the father of Mary's child' (ibid., n. 39).

[44]E.g., Hagner 1993: 18; Calvin 1994: 62 ('Joseph in his zeal for righteousness condemned what he took to be a crime in his wife; at the same time, his mind was disposed to humanity and restrained him from applying the full rigour of the law'). In this case the participle *ōn* is concessive, '*although* righteous.' Cf. Luke 1:6, where the 'righteous' (*dikaioi*) are persons blameless in their obedience to God's commands.

[45]E.g., Schweizer 1975: 30-31; Keener 1999: 92 ('Joseph models the principle of justice tempered by compassion'). On this view the conjunction *kai* is rendered 'and,' as most often in the NT. On the first view, *kai* means 'but,' a permissible but much less common usage.

[46]Erickson 2000: 38 argues that 'Matthew 1 presents Joseph in the role of Abraham' (38): e.g., Joseph is 'righteous' (1:19; cf. Gen. 15:6); is commanded not to fear (1:20; cf. Gen. 15:1), and names his son (1:25; cf. Gen. 21:3).

genealogy has strongly affirmed Joseph's descent from David (6-16). The angel addresses him as 'son of David' (1:20). While Joseph is not Jesus' biological father, he is assuredly his legal father. For Mary the true mother of Jesus to have bestowed this name upon him would have accorded with the Hebrew of Isaiah 7:14 ('she shall call'). That the angel grants Joseph – not Mary – the authority to confer the name, certifies that Jesus is a true, legal descendant of King David. The following chapter will provide further evidence that this is so.[47]

---

[47]For a helpful discussion of lessons from Joseph's obedience, see Keener 1999: 87-95.

Section 3

'By Prophet Bards Foretold'[1]
(Matt. 2:1-23)

The word 'prophet' (*prophētēs*) occurs four times in this chapter, always with reference to OT prophets. Having introduced us to Isaiah in chapter 1, Matthew now draws upon Micah, Hosea and Jeremiah, while continuing to show his indebtedness to Isaiah. Nor, as we shall see, is that the extent to which OT texts illuminate these verses.

---

[1]Words from the hymn 'It Came upon the Midnight Clear,' by Edmund H. Sears (1850).

I.
'ONCE IN ROYAL DAVID'S CITY'[1]
(2:1-12)

'When Jesus was born in Bethlehem of Judea in the days of Herod the king, behold magi from the east arrived in Jerusalem, saying: "Where is he who has been born king of the Jews? For we saw his star in the east [or, at its rising] and have come to worship him"' (2:1-2).

A. The Unfolding Story

These two verses join the present narrative to what has preceded and heighten our anticipation of what is to come. The opening words, 'When Jesus was born [*gennēthentos*]...,' and the magi's question, 'Where is he who has been born [*techtheis*]...?' recall language about Jesus and Mary in Matthew 1.[2] In using the name *Iēsous*, Matthew honors the angel's command as Joseph had done (1:21, 25). The One declared to be 'Son of David' (1:1) is now said to have been born 'in Bethlehem of Judea,' David's hometown.[3] He is also called 'king of the Jews' (1:2), which reminds us that David alone is expressly called 'king' in the genealogy (1:6). Further disclosing the identity of the king is the ensuing inquiry about 'where the Messiah [*ho Christos*] is to be born [*gennatai*]' (1:4). Both titles – King and Messiah – belong to Jesus. The *basileus* of 1:2 joins the *Christos* of 1:4 to the *Iēsous* of 1:1; that both

---

[1]The opening words of a hymn by Cecil Frances Alexander (1848).

[2]Both *gennēthentos* (from *gennaō*; 2:1) and *techtheis* (from *tiktō*; 2:2), are aorist passive participles to denote an event which has already occurred. *Gennaō* is very frequent in chapter 1; but forms of the aorist passive occur only in 1:16 and 20, where Mary is said to have conceived and given birth to Jesus. Forms of *tiktō* occur in 1:21, 23 (in the quotation from Isaiah 7:14), 25.

[3]The name *Bethleem* occurs in 2:1, 5, 6, 8, 16, and nowhere else in Matthew. For Bethlehem as David's home, see 1 Samuel 16:1-13; John 7:42. 'Joseph, son of David' (Matt. 1:20) also has ties with Bethlehem (Luke 2:3-4).

these names are subjects of the verb *gennaō* strengthens the connection – which in turn recalls the close association of the two names in 1:1, 16 and 18.

But now Matthew introduces a third ruler – Herod, who is here three times called 'the king' (*ho basileus*; 2:1, 3, 9), and who is elsewhere called 'Herod the Great.'[4] Between David and Jesus, there is no room for rivalry and conflict, only for promise and fulfillment. But the juxtaposing of 'Herod the king' (2:1) and 'king of the Jews' (2:2) arouses tension in the reader. With the advent of the new king, what place will there be for Herod, who is not himself a Jew, but an Idumean (a descendant of Esau, not of Jacob)? How is the magi's announcement (2:2), which leaves no room for their worshiping the king now reigning in Jerusalem, going to affect him? His immediate response to the news is recorded in verse 3: he was 'troubled, frightened, terrified,'[5] which makes us wonder how he will act upon his fear.

B. The Magi

'Behold [*idou*], magi [*magoi*] from the east arrived in Jerusalem, saying: "Where is he who has been born king of the Jews?"' (2:2a). As in 1:20, 23, *idou* introduces the startling and significant. Matthew calls the visitors *magoi*, whence the Latin *magi*. Among Medes and Persians, a *magus* was a wise man or seer who interpreted dreams.[6] In Greek texts of Daniel, *magos* translates the Aramaic *'āshaf*, 'conjurer, enchanter,' and denotes persons associated with magicians, sorcerers, astrologers, wise men, diviners and interpreters of dreams in the Babylonian court.[7] 'In later centuries down to NT times, the term loosely covered a wide variety of men

---

[4]For the ancestry and impressive achievements of Herod the Great, who was born in about 73 B.C., and ruled in Judea from 37 to 4 B.C., see H. W. Hoehner, *DJG*, 317-22.

[5]BAGD s.v. *tarassō*, the verb used here. That 'all Jerusalem' was troubled too (Matt. 2:3) may mean that they, a people long accustomed to trials, 'feared the change, in case it brought them to the beginning of further disaster' (Calvin 1994: 84). Similarly Keener 1999: 102.

[6]LSJ, s.v. *magos*; and Brown 1993: 167.

[7]See LXX and Theodotion (a second century A.D. Greek translation based on the LXX) of Daniel 1:20; 2:2, 10, 27; 4:7; 5:7, 11, 15.

interested in dreams, astrology, magic, books thought to contain mysterious references to the future, and the like.'[8] *Magos* appears in only one other NT passage, where it means 'magician' (Acts 13:6, 8).

Matthew's 'magi from the east' have come in response to the sighting of the 'star' of a Jewish king (2:1-2), evidence that they have joined astronomy and astrology to the study of the Hebrew scriptures; which in turn makes it likely that they have journeyed westward from Babylon rather than from Persia or the Arabian desert.[9]

Later Christian tradition elevated the magi to royal status, reflecting the influence of prophecies (such as Isaiah 60:1-6 and Psalm 72:10-11) that Gentile kings would come to the brightness of Israel's dawn, and pay homage to an Israelite king with two of the very gifts mentioned in Matthew. The variety of gifts – 'gold, frankincense and myrrh' (2:11) – explains how the church came to speak of '*three* kings.'[10] Given Matthew's indebtedness to those very prophecies (see below), his *not* calling the magi 'kings' is remarkable. Moreover, considering the sequel we might have thought them more deserving of the name than Herod. But Matthew knows better. *Magoi* are not themselves kings; here, as in Babylon, they *serve* a king. Indeed, says Matthew, the singular purpose of their mission is to pay homage to the one true King. To call *them* kings would undercut the evangelist's very reason for

---

[8]Carson 1984: 85. Similarly, BAGD s.v. *magos*.

[9]The three possibilities are discussed in Brown 1993: 168-70. The history of the term *magos* (*magus*) might favor a Persian origin; and Isaiah 60:6 and Psalm 72:15 associate gold and frankincense (Matt. 2:11) 'with the desert camel trains coming from Midian (NW Arabia) and from Sheba (the kingdom of the Sabeans in SW Arabia)' (ibid., 169). But Babylon is the location 'most favored by the astrological implications of the rising of the star.... Moreover, after the Babylonian Exile in the sixth century, a large colony of Jews had remained on, so that Babylonian astrologers could have learned something of Jewish messianic expectations and might have associated a particular star with the King of the Jews' (ibid.). Cf. Daniel's references, noted above, to *magoi* as members of the Babylonian court – the only instances of *magos* in LXX and Theodotion.

[10]See Brown 1993: 197-200, on 'the Magi in Subsequent Christian Piety'; cf. Carson 1984: 85.

telling the story.[11] Nor does Matthew tell us how many magi there were, just as he does not tell us their precise place of origin. All his stress falls on the nature and the success of their mission.[12] But what prompts their quest in the first place?

C. Star of Wonder

That question is answered in verse 2: 'For [*gar*] we saw his star [*astēr*] in the east [or, at its rising], and have come to worship him.'

Identifying the Star

This is indeed a star of wonder, and for more than one reason. Long have readers of Matthew wondered what the magi beheld in the sky.

Some think it was a *supernova*, a faint or distant star that bursts forth with tremendous light and energy (so that it might be visible even in daylight) and then weeks or months later returns to relative obscurity. The phrase *en tē anatolē*, (2:2) 'in the east' in NIV, may indeed be translated 'at its rising' – or 'at its flaring up.' Yet, there is no corroborative evidence of such a star just before Jesus' birth.[13]

Others believe the magi saw a *comet*. The third-century apologist Origen wrote that the magi's star was to be classed with comets or meteors or 'bearded or jar-shaped stars,' a description suggested by the comet's luminous tail of gasses and dust. Centuries later it was calculated that the comet named for Edmund Halley (d. 1742) made an appearance in 12–11 B.C. Yet, that is long before Jesus' birth. Nor do we know whether Matthew would apply *astēr* to a comet, as Origen was to do. Moreover, whereas a comet was usually

---

[11]The verb *proskyneō*, '(fall down and) worship, do obeisance to' (BAGD s.v.) appears in both 2 and 11 (an *inclusio*), statements that accentuate Herod's hypocrisy in using the same verb ('that I too may come and worship him,' 8). Cf. comments on verse 11. Father Christmas honors the example of the magi and the intent of Matthew, when he exclaims about Aslan: 'Merry Christmas! Long live the true King!' (C. S. Lewis, *The Lion, the Witch and the Wardrobe* [London: Bles, 1950], 103).

[12]For further explorations, see Trexler 1997.

[13]Brown 1993: 171.

thought to presage disaster, the present phenomenon attends the birth of a Savior.[14]

Or does Matthew have in view a *planetary conjunction*? In their orbits around the sun, the planets Jupiter and Saturn pass each other every twenty years; on much rarer occasions Mars joins the two. The German astronomer Johannes Kepler (d. 1630) witnessed this threefold conjunction in 1604; he calculated that it occurs every 805 years, and thus that it had appeared in 7–6 B.C. It has also been determined that Jupiter and Saturn passed one another three times in 7 B.C. (a rare event indeed), before Mars came into the picture; and that the two planets were conjoined 'in the zodiacal constellation Pisces [fishes], a sign sometimes connected in ancient astrology with the Hebrews.'[15] According to Alfred Edersheim, 'Kepler...also noticed, that when [in 1604] the three planets came into conjunction, a new, extraordinary, brilliant, and peculiarly colored evanescent star was visible between Jupiter and Saturn, and he suggested that a similar star had appeared under the same circumstances in the conjunction preceding the Nativity.'[16] Given the dates suggested by Kepler, we may note that Herod the Great died in 4 B.C., and that he ordered the killing of 'all the boys...two years old and under, according to the time which he ascertained from the magi' (2:16), which explains why Jesus' birth is usually dated 6–4 B.C.

That third choice is attractive. Yet Matthew, speaking as he does of only one heavenly body, offers no hint of a planetary conjunction.[17] Kepler's suggestion that a supernova ('a new... brilliant...evanescent star') joined the conjunction of 7 B.C. remains speculative. Furthermore, none of those views accords well with the testimony of verse 9: that the very star the magi had seen in the east 'went before them until it came and stood above the place where the child was.' In light of this evidence, I conclude that the 'star' is a miraculous and mysterious

---

[14]Cf. 1:21; Brown 1993: 171-72.

[15]Carson 1984: 85. See also Brown 1993: 172-73 ('Pisces is a constellation sometimes associated with the last days and with the Hebrews,' 173).

[16]Edersheim 1956: 1.213.

[17]We have 'no contemporary evidence justifying the reference to such a conjunction of planets as a "star" or attaching a particular astrological effect to it...' (Brown 1993: 173).

phenomenon whose precise identity cannot be ascertained.[18] Yet, its purpose is clear: God provides it to herald the birth of his Son, and to bring into his presence those persons intent upon honoring him.

But why a 'star'?

Interpreting the Star

The magi tell of having seen 'his star' (*autou ton astera*), the one belonging to, or associated with, the newborn 'King of the Jews' (Matt. 2:2). As noted, this language shows that the magi had joined study of the stars to Hebrew thought and expectation.

An oracle of Balaam son of Beor, recorded in Numbers 24:17, declares that 'a star will come out of Jacob, a scepter will rise out of Israel.' In the LXX, the opening words are translated *anatelei astron*, 'a star will arise.' Appearing several times in Matthew 2:1-12 are *astēr* (a synonym of *astron*) and *anatolē*, the noun corresponding to the verb *anatellō*.[19]

Those words in turn bring to light similarities between Balaam's story and that of the magi. He too is a Gentile from the east, who may aptly be called a *magos*. The fear and hostility that Balak, king of Moab, shows toward the Israelites as they journey from Egypt to Palestine matches that of Herod toward Jacob's Son (Matt. 1:2) soon to journey to Egypt and back (2:15, 19-21). Truth revealed by God (about Israel and Israel's king respectively), both Balaam and the magi proclaim at whatever personal risk. Both parties return home once their mission is accomplished.[20] All these similarities,

---

[18]For a 'star' (i) to disappear at certain times and then suddenly to shine again, and (ii) to lead directly to Bethlehem and then to stand fixed over the house where Christ lay 'was not of the order of nature' (Calvin 1994: 83; he thinks a comet is the closest natural counterpart). Similarly, Chrysostom says that 'this was no ordinary star, for no other star had this capacity to guide, not merely to move but to beckon...' (*ACC* 1a: 26). Bruner 2004a: 59 is 'inclined to think that Matthew is depicting a *miraculous* star...that took on a natural star's form.' Cf. Kidger 1999.

[19]For *astēr* ('star'), see Matthew 2:2, 7, 9, 10; *astron* can denote a single star or a constellation (BAGD s.v.). *Anatelei* is a future form of *anatellō*, 'arise'; as the sun (i) rises (ii) in the east, *anatolē* (2:1, 2, 9) can bear both meanings.

[20]For Balaam's homeland, see Numbers 22:5; 23:7; for his practice of divination and sorcery, 22:7; 23:23; for Balak's reaction to Israel, 22:4-6; for

together with the aforementioned linguistic links, underscore the importance of Numbers 24:17 for the story of the magi. Moreover, the ancestry of the figure that Balaam calls a 'star out of Jacob' and 'scepter out of Israel,' was earlier disclosed more fully by Jacob (or Israel) himself: 'The scepter will not depart from Judah, nor the ruler's staff from between his feet, until he comes to whom it belongs and the obedience of the nations is his' (Gen. 49:10, NIV). Isaiah 60:3 ('Nations will come to your light, and kings to the brightness of your dawn') recalls both those texts, together with the prophecy of the Davidic Messiah in Isaiah 9:1-7 (compare 9:2 with 60:1-2).

Matthew writes in light of all those prophecies. He announces the birth of the king of the Jews (Matt. 2:2), the offspring of Judah and Son of David (1:1-2). The names he uses for region and people – 'Judea' and 'Jews' – bear their own witness; for both have their origin in the name 'Judah.'[21] The 'star' that for Balaam symbolized Messiah himself (Num. 24:17), is now Messiah's possession and herald, 'his star' (Matt. 2:2); but what matters is the close association between the two.[22] In Matthew's narrative the very first persons to pay tribute to Jesus come in response to his star. That they are also Gentiles from the east strikingly recalls the prophecies that nations would be drawn to light in Israel, and come under the rule of Israel's Messiah.[23]

Balaam's oracles, and pledges of fidelity to God's revealed Word, 23:3, 7-12, 18-26; 24:2-9, 12-24; for Balak's anger toward Balaam, 24:10-11; for his return home, 24:14, 25. For Herod's threat to the magi, and their return home, see Matthew 2:12, 16. Brown 1993: 193-96, was the first to direct my attention to links between Balaam and the magi. The importance of these connections is not much diminished by later judgments against Balaam (Num. 31:8; 2 Pet. 2:15-16; Jude 11; Rev. 2:14).

[21]For 'Judea' (*Ioudaia*), see 2:1, 5; for 'Jews' (*Ioudaioi*), 2:2. Cf. 'Judah' (*Ioudas*), 1:2-3; 2:6 (*bis*). Note the shift from 'Bethlehem of Judea [*Ioudaias*],' 2:5, to 'Bethlehem, land of Judah [*Iouda*],' 2:6.

[22]First-century Jews viewed Balaam's prophecy as Messianic (Brown 1993: 195). The 'shift [in the imagery of the star between Numbers 24 and Matthew 2] is quite intelligible once the king has been born' (ibid., 196). Similarly, the 'scepter' belongs to Messiah in Genesis 49:10, but symbolizes Messiah himself in Numbers 24:17.

[23]See Genesis 49:10 (one line of which might be rendered, 'until he comes to whom tribute belongs'; NIV mg.); Isaiah 60:1-6; Numbers 24:17-19 (the ruler's conquest of Moab and Edom); also Psalm 72:8-11 and the above

D. The Prophecy of Micah

In response to Herod's inquiry about Messiah's birthplace, the chief priests and scholars quote what 'has been written through the prophet: "And you, Bethlehem, land of Judah, are by no means least among the rulers of Judah; for from you shall come forth a ruler who will shepherd my people Israel,"' (Matthew 2:5-6, quoting Micah 5:2 [and alluding to 2 Samuel 5:2]). Introducing the quotation is the verb *gegraptai* ('has been written'), a perfect passive form of *graphō*. The passive voice, joined as it is to the phrase 'through the prophet,' reflects divine activity: the *source* of the prophecy is God, its *mediator* is Micah.[24] The perfect tense indicates that the prophecy has lost none of its authority – that it remains in force, that it 'stands written' until the time appointed for its fulfillment. In the case of the present prophecy, that time has now arrived (2:1).[25]

The Setting in Micah

In many ways Micah echoes his contemporary Isaiah (Mic. 1:1; Isa. 1:1). Judah is indicted for its flagrant violations of God's commands; idolatry and injustice abound. Princes and prophets have abdicated their responsibilities and have led the people astray. Yahweh will therefore judge the nation – as he did those peoples (including Israel, the northern kingdom) whose sins Judah has emulated. Judah too will be invaded by foreign armies and will eventually go into exile. Yet Yahweh will keep the promises he made to Abraham and to David. The salvation of a remnant presages national restoration under a Davidic king; and Gentile nations too will become objects of Yahweh's favor.[26]

---

survey of Messianic prophecies in Isaiah 1–12. The magi's origin, together with their quest for 'the King of the Jews,' identifies them as Gentiles. 'The God who sought servants from the pagan west like the Roman centurion [8:5-13] also sought previously pagan servants "from the east" [2:1; cf. Isa. 2:6] like the Magi [see 8:11]' (Keener 1999: 98).

[24]This concept of prophecy is expressed more plainly in the formulation 'spoken by the Lord through the prophet' (Matthew 1:22 and 2:15; cf. 2:17, 'spoken through the prophet'). See pages 94-98.

[25]*Gegraptai* is an intensive (or resultative) perfect, here denoting that prophecy is now being fulfilled (*GGBB*, 574-76). On *gegraptai* in Matthew, see page 95 above.

Micah 5 opens on an ominous note. Foreigners have besieged Jerusalem and 'will strike Israel's ruler on the cheek with a rod' (5:1).[27] Yet amid that very judgment there is renewed hope: 'But from you, Bethlehem Ephrathah, home of one of Judah's smaller clans, from you will emerge for me one who is to be sovereign over Israel, one whose origins stretch far back to days of yore (5:2).'[28] The focus is on Bethlehem, the place of David's origin, rather than on Jerusalem, the place of his reign; cf. John 7:42. Messiah will *not* be born in Jerusalem, a city now 'tainted by the corruption of power, immorality, foreign influences, and idolatry.'[29] Instead, like his forebear David, he will emerge from an obscure, insignificant town. Endowed with strength from Yahweh, he will eradicate the evils entrenched in Jerusalem. Under this Shepherd's righteous rule the flock of God will once again live securely. As the One who brings peace to the Gentiles by teaching them the way of Yahweh, his name will be honored to the ends of the earth.[30] This King's 'origins stretch far back to days of yore' (5:2b), for through his manifold work Yahweh confirms his covenantal promises to Abraham and David.[31]

'Therefore Israel will be abandoned until the time when she who is in labor gives birth' (5:3a) to the King described in verse 2. Only with his coming are lasting salvation and

---

[26]For coming judgments on Samaria and on Judah and its leaders, and for the sins that are to blame, see Micah 1:2–2:11; 3:1-12; 5:10–7:7. For Israel's rescue and restoration, and the Gentiles' salvation, see 2:12-13; 4:1–5:9; 7:8-20.

[27]The Assyrians would invade Judah (5:5; 2 Kings 18–19). But Micah 5:1 speaks principally of the Babylonians – who would reduce Jerusalem to rubble and exile the people, including Jehoiachin (= Jeconiah, Matt. 1:11-12) and Zedekiah (Jechoiachin's uncle), the last of the Davidic kings (Mic. 3:12; 4:10; 2 Kings 24–25).

[28]As translated by Allen 1976: 339.

[29]VanGemeren 1990: 156; see 154-59 for Micah 5 as a prophecy of the Davidic Messiah.

[30]Micah 5:4, with 2:12-13; 4:1-5; cf. earlier remarks on Isaiah 2:2-5; 11:1-9.

[31]Micah 5:2b refers 'to a time in finite history, i.e., the distant past' (Allen 1976: 343) – namely, to the time Yahweh established his covenant with Abraham. Cf. 7:20, 'You will be true to Jacob, and show mercy to Abraham, as you pledged on oath to our fathers in days long ago.' That covenant expressly included Gentiles (Gen. 12:1-3; 22:18). The Davidic Covenant (2 Sam. 7:14-16; Ps. 89:34-36) is founded upon, and helps to fulfill, the Abrahamic (see pp. 128-29 above). Gleason L. Archer, Jr., thinks that Micah

restoration achieved. Given the affinities we have already discovered between Micah and Isaiah 1–12, there is good reason to think that the mother whose labor is here described is the *'almâ* of Isaiah 7:14, whose Son will reign from David's throne forever.[32]

The Setting in Matthew

The experts report to Herod what Yahweh has revealed 'through the prophet' about the coming Messiah: 'And you, Bethlehem, land of Judah, are by no means least among the rulers [*hēgemosin*] of Judah; for from you shall come forth a ruler [*hēgoumenos*], who will shepherd [*poimanei*] my people Israel' (2:4-6).

The quotation adds weight to all that Matthew has proclaimed thus far about Jesus, 'the Son of David,' the Messianic King.[33] The allusion to 2 Samuel 5:2 – 'who will shepherd my people Israel' – strengthens the OT witness. There the people remind David of Yahweh's charge to him: 'You will shepherd [*poimanei*] my people Israel, and you will become their ruler.' 'The prophet' is still Micah, whose own language prompts the allusion to 2 Samuel.[34]

The MT of Micah 5:2 says that Bethlehem is 'small to be among the clans [literally, thousands] of Judah'; the LXX, that the town is 'too small to be among the thousands of

---

5:2b, besides tracing the ancestry and promises of Messiah to the earliest times, also views Messiah 'as pre-existing the actual date of His appearing' (*NBC: R*, 758). Cf. NIV mg., 'whose origins are from days of eternity.'

[32]See Isaiah 9:6-7, and comments on Matthew 1:22-23. 'The brief reference to...the woman *with child* [3], obviously the mother of the promised king [2], evidently alludes to a popular expectation too well known to require amplification. This expectation is doubtless to be related to Isaiah's mysterious promise of Immanuel's birth (Isa. 7:14) pronounced over thirty years earlier' (Allen 1976: 345).

[33]See above, pages 214-15, on 'The Unfolding Story,' as well as commentary on Matthew 1.

[34]In MT and LXX (whose verse numberings in Micah differ from the English versions), both Micah 5:4 and 2 Samuel 5:2 use the verb 'to shepherd' (Hebrew *rā'ah*; Greek *poimainō*, as in Matthew 2:6); and both Micah 5:1-2 and 2 Samuel 5:2 speak of one who will govern 'Israel.' The LXX of 2 Samuel 5:2 uses the participle *hēgoumenon*, from *hēgeomai*, 'to rule.' This verb does not occur in the LXX of Micah 5; but Matthew, in quoting Micah 5:2, does use it, and

Judah.'[35] But Matthew, using an adverb found in neither MT nor LXX, portrays Bethlehem very differently: 'you are *by no means* [*oudamōs*] least....' For between the prophecy of Micah and the writing of Matthew stands the actual birth of Jesus the Messiah. Even after David's rise, Bethlehem was apparently still considered inconsequential. But now this town has attained a distinction shared by no other. By appointing Bethlehem as the birthplace of the Davidic king, Yahweh exalts a place of lowly station.[36]

Yahweh chooses Bethlehem – not Jerusalem. Jerusalem is the place where Herod reigns (2:1, 3), and where 'the chief priests and scribes of the people' exert their authority (2:4), all of them being (as the sequel will show) contemporary counterparts to the corrupt leadership denounced in Micah. In accord with Micah's prophecy about Messiah, Jesus has come to challenge and eventually to end their rule. It is God's will both to exalt lowly Bethlehem and to dethrone the tyrant Herod.[37] Herod's gross injustice and cruelty (2:16-18) will be supplanted by Messiah's righteousness and mercy (cf. Mic. 6:8). It is he, says Yahweh, 'who will shepherd my people [*ton laon mou*] Israel' (Matt. 2:6) – he, and not those 'chief priests and scribes of the people [*tou laou*]' (4) who quote Scripture but do not believe it, and whose later actions against Jesus will show what a danger they are to persons under their care.[38] Only under the reign of King Jesus will the people of God find security and peace (cf. 9:36, and those comments; Mic. 5:4-5).

---

in its participial form *hēgoumenos* (for the Hebrew participle *mōshēl*, 'a ruling one,' rendered *archōn*, 'ruler,' in LXX), together with the corresponding noun *hēgemosin*, thus strengthening the link between Micah 5:2 and 2 Samuel 5:2.

[35]Both translations are from Brown 1993: 185.

[36]Calvin notes (1994: 85-86) 'that as often as the Apostles quote a testimony from Scripture, although they do not render it word for word, in fact may move quite a way from it, they adapt it suitably and appropriately to the case at hand.' Matthew's quotation here accords with the prophecy's 'real purpose.... Matthew intended, by this alteration, to praise God for His grace, that a slight and obscure little town had been made the birth-place of the supreme King.' Similarly Jenson 1995: 204-11. Cf. pages 120-22 above, on 'Jesus the Fulfillment of the OT.'

[37]Cf. Luke 1:52. Messiah's promised victory over Assyria (Mic. 5:5- 6) 'signifies his subjugation of all resistance to the rule of God on earth' (VanGemeren 1990: 157).

E. Journey's End

'When they saw the star, they rejoiced with very great joy. And entering the house, they saw the child with Mary his mother; and kneeling down, they paid homage [*prosekynēsan*] to him. Then opening their treasure chests, they presented to him gifts [*dōra*] – gold [*chryson*] and frankincense [*libanon*] and myrrh [*smyrnan*]' (2:10-11).

The magi have reached their goal; now at last they come into the presence of the One they have sought. The 'house' (*oikia*) they enter may be the very place where, according to Luke 2:7, Joseph and Mary found lodging.[39] As they recognize, this child is not just destined for kingship but 'has been born [*tektheis*] king of the Jews' (2:2). So they do not merely pledge to him their future loyalty but now pay him homage in accord with their original intent (2:2, 11) and in expression of their boundless joy (2:10).[40] Nor do they promise donations to Jesus for a future coronation: having come prepared, they open their treasure chests,[41] and offer him gifts of gold, frankincense and myrrh (2:11b).

Verses 10 and 11 allude to two OT passages. In the coming Redeemer, promised Isaiah, Yahweh's glory would be disclosed

---

[38]Cf. Brown 1993: 186. The *archiereis* ('chief priests') and the 'scribes' (*grammateis*) are two of the main parties responsible for having Jesus put to death (Matt. 16:21). Cf. the 'woes' against the *grammateis* in Matthew 23.

[39]The term used in Luke 2:7, *katalyma*, is usually translated 'inn' (so, e.g., NIV and NASB), but more likely means 'guest room,' as in 22:11 and Mark 14:14 (the only other instances in the NT). The word used in Luke 10:34, and properly translated 'inn,' is *pandocheion*. Green 1997: 129, opting for 'guest room' in Luke 2:7, notes 'that in peasant homes in the ancient Near East family and animals slept in one enclosed space, with the animals located on a lower level. Mary and Joseph, then, would have been the guests of family or friends [cf. 2:3-4], but their home would have been so overcrowded [owing to the census] that the baby was placed in a feeding trough.'

[40]The expression 'they rejoiced with very great joy' is exceptionally strong: the verb *chairō* ('rejoice') joined to the noun *chara* ('joy'), the adjective *megalē* ('great') and the adverb *sphodra* ('very'). This combination of terms occurs nowhere else in the NT.

[41]In this context the noun *thēsauros* means not 'that which is stored up, treasure' (BAGD s.v., 2.), but 'that place where something is kept...treasure box or chest' (s.v., 1.).

to Gentiles as well as to Israel (59:14–60:9): 'Nations will come to your light, and kings to the brightness of your dawn.... And all from Sheba will come, bearing gold and incense [LXX, *chrysion kai libanon*] and proclaiming the praise of the Lord' (60:3, 6, niv). Similarly, Psalm 72 says of the One destined to 'rule from sea to sea and from the River to the ends of the earth' (72:8): 'the kings of Sheba and Seba will present him gifts [LXX, *dōra*]. All kings will bow down [LXX, *proskynēsousin*] to him and all nations will serve him.... Long may he live! May gold [LXX, *chrysion*] be given him' (72:10-11, 15).[42] If the Queen of Sheba brought spices and gold to Solomon (1 Kings 10:2), how much more fitting that the royalty of Sheba and Seba and other nations bow before the incomparable successor to Solomon (Matt. 12:42) and present to him such gifts. The magi are not themselves kings, but kings will do well to follow their example.

While neither Isaiah 60 nor Psalm 72 mentions it, myrrh too is fit for a king: 'All your robes are fragrant with myrrh [LXX, *smyrna*] and aloes and cassia,' says Psalm 45:8 of the coming Messiah.[43] Associated as it was with kingly and marital celebrations, this spice serves as an apt expression of the magi's joy.[44]

The verb *proskyneō*, 'pay homage' in Matthew 2:11 and 'bow down' in Psalm 72:11 may also mean 'to worship' (so, e.g., esv and niv at 2:11).[45] The first two translations adequately

---

[42]As translated in niv. The portrait of the king in Psalm 72 'is so close to the prophecies of Isaiah 11:1-5 and Isaiah 60–62 that if those prophecies are Messianic, so is this,' says Kidner 1973: 254. Jews too came to view this psalm as Messianic (ibid.). On the allusions to Isaiah 60 and Psalm 72 in Matthew 2:11, see Brown 1993: 187-88; Gundry 1994: 32. See also Haggai 2:7.

[43]On the Messianic character of Psalm 45, see Kidner 1973: 170. Cf. the application of 45:6-7 to Christ in Hebrews 1:8-9.

[44]Myrrh is commonly thought to symbolize suffering, given its use in Jesus' crucifixion (Mark 15:23) and burial (John 19:39); 'but in the Old Testament it is rather a symbol of joy and festivity' (France 1985: 84). Besides Psalm 45:8, see Proverbs 7:17; Song 1:13; 3:6; 4:6, 14; 5:1, 5, 13. Some of these texts also refer to incense.

[45]Cf. BAGD s.v.: '(fall down and) worship, do obeisance to, prostrate oneself before, do reverence to, welcome respectfully.' *Proskyneō* is literally 'kiss [*kyneō*] toward [*pros*].'

describe the magi's action, for in all probability they consider the newborn child to be, for all his greatness, merely human. Yet for Matthew, recognizing the full identity of this child calls for nothing less than worship and adoration[46] – worship marked by a joy exceeding even that of the magi.[47]

The magi's mission, then, recalls a host of OT texts, not least prophecies that Gentiles would pay tribute to Israel's Messiah, in accord with both Abrahamic and Davidic covenants.[48] Indeed, in Matthew the magi are the only persons said to pay homage to (or to worship) the child Jesus. Matthew records nothing of such tributes from shepherds, or from devout Jews such as Simeon and Anna, or even from Mary and Joseph (contrast Luke 1–2). But he does starkly contrast the magi's behavior with that of the Jews in Jerusalem. The populace is 'disturbed' (3) by the rumor about a newborn king; but no action ensues, and no one follows the magi to Bethlehem. Neither chief priests nor scholars, having connected the rumor to Micah, take steps to see if perhaps the prophecy has come true. Herod (not himself a Jew) is apparently the only person in Jerusalem who takes the news seriously. He for one will respond: just how, we are about to discover.

The only explicit reference to 'Jesus' in Matthew 2 comes in the opening verse. No fewer than nine times in the chapter Matthew refers to him as 'the child' (*to paidion*); and in five of these, starting in verse 11, he speaks of 'the child and [or with] his mother.'[49] The latter phrase recalls the whole of 1:18-25, and testifies to the importance of Isaiah 7:14 (together with Micah 5:2-3) for Matthew. Given the frequency of the phrase, the absence of references to Joseph as Jesus' 'father' is especially notable (cf. p. 140).

---

[46]Cf. France 1985: 82.

[47]V. 10 expresses the magi's joy in the strongest possible terms. Worship and joy are joined in the answer to question 1 of *WSC*: 'to glorify God and to enjoy him forever.' Cf. Lewis 1958: 95, 'I think we delight to praise what we enjoy because the praise not merely expresses but completes the enjoyment....'

[48]Cf. Matthew 1:1, together with above discussions of OT texts quoted, or alluded to, in Matthew 1–2.

[49]For the nine instances of *paidion*, see Matthew 2:8, 9, 11, 13 (*bis*), 14, 20 (*bis*), 21.

II.
'THEN WARNING CAME OF DANGER NEAR'[1]
(2:13-23)

Verse 13 so links this section to the preceding that the tension already evident at the beginning of the chapter is greatly increased. As the magi were warned in a dream not to return to Herod (2:12), so 'an angel of the Lord appears to Joseph in a dream,' commanding him to flee from Herod (2:13). With the disclosure that the king 'is about to seek to destroy the child' (2:13), his earlier words – 'that I may come and worship him' (2:8) – have a chilling effect. A linguistic link between the two sections is provided by the verb *anachōreō*, applied to the magi in 2:12 ('they returned,' NIV) and again in 2:13 ('When they had gone,' NIV). In view of the perilous circumstances, the magi do not merely depart, or return, or retire; the verb signals that they are 'withdrawing' from danger and 'taking refuge' in another place. So too is the term used in 2:14 (where Joseph and his family flee by night to Egypt) and 2:22 (where Joseph, escaping Archelaus, moves to Galilee).[2]

A. Egypt: A Place of Refuge

As Egypt provided relief from famine for Jacob and his sons, so it provides Joseph and his family protection from Herod's murderous design. Not only have Gentiles instead of Jews paid homage to Jesus; in face of a dire threat from the king in

---

[1]Words from the hymn 'In Bethlehem a Newborn Boy,' by Rosamond E. Herklots (1969).

[2]NIV is better in Matthew 2:22 ('he withdrew') than in 2:14 ('and left'). Cf. BAGD s.v. *anachōreō*, 1. ('go away'); 2.a. ('return'); 2.b. ('withdraw, retire, take refuge'). Unlike them, I take all four instances of the verb in Matthew 2 in sense 2.b. (though 'retire' is not strong enough to match the other two verbs). In seeking to destroy Jesus (2:13), Herod is Satan's instrument (cf. Rev. 12:4).

Judea, it is a Gentile land that provides sanctuary for Israel's Messiah.[3]

As God raised up Moses to rescue Israel from bondage, so he has appointed Jesus to save his people from their sins.[4] As Pharaoh endangered the infant Moses, so Herod seeks to slay the child Jesus.[5] When Pharaoh later tried to kill Moses, he fled to a foreign land, Midian; and following the death of that Pharaoh, he returned to Egypt in obedience to Yahweh's commission. Similarly, Jesus escapes death by fleeing to a foreign country, Egypt; and once Herod dies, he returns to his own land to carry out his mission.[6] As Israel was redeemed by the death of a Passover lamb, so Jesus will give his own life as 'a ransom for many' (Matt. 20:28).

Joseph stayed with his family in Egypt 'until the death of Herod, in order that what had been said by the Lord through the prophet might be fulfilled: "Out of Egypt I called my son"' (2:15).[7] The very words that prefaced the quotation from Isaiah 7:14 (in Matthew 1:22) now introduce a quotation from Hosea 11:1b. Here too, two distinct but related events are in view. As Isaiah spoke initially (and prospectively) of the birth of his

---

[3]For Egypt as a haven for Jacob and his family, see Genesis 42:1-2; 43:1-2; 46:1–47:31. (As it was a Joseph who secured a place for Israel, so it is a Joseph who leads Israel's Messiah to safety.) Egypt 'was a classic land of refuge for those fleeing from tyranny in Palestine' (Brown 1993: 203). Cf. 1 Kings 11:40 (whose wording is similar to Matthew 2:14); Jeremiah 26:21. For links between Jesus' experience as a refugee and his later teachings, see Keener 1999: 109.

[4]Exodus 3:1–4:17; Matthew 1:21.

[5]Exodus 1:13–2:10; Matthew 2:13. Both Pharaoh and Herod, in ordering the death of Jews, act against a foreign people. Herod, an Idumean, is once called 'king of Judea' in the gospels (Luke 1:5) but never 'king of the Jews' or 'king of Israel.' Moreover, both rulers decree the death of male infants exclusively, Exodus 1:22; Matthew 2:16 (cf. Davies and Allison 1988: 264-65).

[6]Exodus 2:11-22; 4:18-31; Matthew 2:14-15, 19-23. The wording of Exodus 4:19 is very close to that of Matthew 2:20. 'Although Matthew mentions Herod's murder of the children, he notes Herod's own death three times [2:15, 19, 20] – indicating that God alone holds the ultimate power of life and death' (Keener 1999: 112).

[7]'I called my son,' *ekalesa ton huion mou* (2:15b) closely follows MT. LXX on the contrary reads, 'I called away [or called back] his [i.e., Israel's] children,' *metekalesa ta tekna autou*.

own son, Hosea speaks (retrospectively) of Yahweh's rescuing his own son from bondage. The identity of the son and the motivation for the father's act are stated in 11:1a, 'When Israel was a child, I loved him.' As Isaiah also foretold the coming of the Davidic Messiah, so too Hosea speaks of God's beloved Son, as Matthew 3:17 will make plain.[8] It is he who personally embodies the faithfulness expected from Israel; who will lead God's people on a new Exodus; in whom the divine grace so poignantly revealed in Hosea will be manifested as never before; and whose saving work will provide forgiveness for Israel's gravest iniquities. Corresponding to its usage in 1:22-23, the verb 'fulfill' (*plēroō*; 2:15) applies strictly to the person and work of Jesus, the Son of God and the New Moses now sojourning in Egypt.[9]

B. Bethlehem: A Place of Sorrow

Herod, enraged over having been outwitted by the magi, orders the death of 'all the male children in Bethlehem and in all the surrounding region who were two years old and under' (Matt. 2:16). 'Then was fulfilled what had been said through Jeremiah the prophet: "A voice was heard in Ramah, weeping and loud lamentation, Rachel crying for her children; and she would not be consoled, because they are no more"' (2:17, quoting Jeremiah 31:15).

Prophecy

Rachel was Laban's younger daughter and Jacob's favorite wife. During a journey from Bethel to Ephrath, she died giving

---

[8] At the Exodus, God calls Israel his 'firstborn' son – *prōtotokos* (Exod. 4:22, LXX). This term is applied to the incarnate Christ, both as son of Mary (Luke 2:7) and as Son of God (Heb. 1:6).

[9] Hosea mainly recites infidelities and iniquities in Israel and Judah, and warns of severe judgment: see 2:1-13; chapters 4–10, 12–13. Yet he also celebrates Yahweh's steadfast love (*chesed*, 2:19) and restorative power: see chapters 1 and 3 (the story of Hosea and Gomer); 6:1-3; 11:8-11; 14:1-9; and he relates future blessings to the Exodus in 2:14-23; 12:9; 13:4-5. Dan McCartney and Peter Enns, 'Matthew and Hosea: A Response to John Sailhamer,' *WTJ* 63 (2001), 103, argue that Matthew applies Hosea 11:1 to Jesus' call out of *Israel*: they note that Jesus' return from literal Egypt is stated later (2:21), and they cite Revelation 11:8 (which calls Jerusalem 'Egypt'). But Herod's death is already mentioned in 2:15; and the context speaks only of literal Egypt (2:13, 14, 19).

birth to Benjamin 'and was buried on the way to Ephrath (that is, Bethlehem'; Gen. 35:19). As Jacob later reports to Rachel's other son, Joseph: '"I buried her there beside the road to Ephrath" (that is, Bethlehem'); (48:7).[10] Ramah was close to Bethel, on the southern route to Bethlehem; and was about five miles (or eight kilometers) north of Jerusalem, matching Bethlehem's distance to the south. So the sadness of Rachel's final hours, and Jacob's own mourning for her, are associated with both Ramah and Bethlehem.[11]

Now, as Yahweh tells Jeremiah (Jer. 31:15), Ramah again hears the sound of Rachel's weeping. Rachel did not mother as many sons as did Leah, Laban's older daughter (Gen. 35:23-24); but now, as wife of Jacob, she mourns the loss of all his offspring. For her lament embraces the ten tribes of the northern kingdom, already exiled by the Assyrians, and the two tribes of the southern kingdom (Judah and Benjamin), soon to be exiled by the Babylonians. The place of Rachel's mourning – Ramah, in Benjamite territory – suggests that the Babylonian exile is mainly in view.[12]

Yet, immediately before the lament of Jeremiah 31:15 we read: 'He who scattered Israel will gather them.... For the Lord will ransom Jacob.... I will turn their mourning into gladness' (31:10, 11, 13). And immediately afterwards: 'This is what the Lord

---

[10]According to 1 Samuel 10:2, Rachel's tomb was located 'at Zelzah on the border of Benjamin.' The 'great tree of Tabor' (10:3) lies within Benjamite territory, and is to be distinguished from the Tabor of Joshua 19:22 and 1 Chronicles 6:77 (D. F. Payne, 'Tabor,' *IBD*, 1512). Verse 3 also speaks of three men who are 'going up to God at Bethel.'

[11]Rachel's sorrow is reflected in her chosen name for Benjamin – Ben-'ônî, 'son of my trouble,' (Gen. 35:18).

[12]Jeremiah's focus on the two southern tribes is evident from the very beginning. He is 'son of Hilkiah, one of the priests of Anathoth in the territory of Benjamin' (1:1). He began to prophesy in the thirteenth year of Josiah's reign in Judah (1:2), i.e., in 626 B.C., nearly a century after the fall of the northern capital Samaria (722 B.C.); and he continued to do so until the time when, during Zedekiah's rule, 'the people of Jerusalem went into exile' (1:3). Yet Jeremiah 31 is addressed to the house of Israel (or Ephraim) as well as to the house of Judah: see references to Israel, Ephraim and Samaria in verses 4-10, 18-21. Cf. Gundry 1994: 36; Carson 1984: 94. Jeremiah 40:1-2 speaks of Judah being taken into Babylonian exile, and also refers to Ramah.

says: "Restrain your voice from weeping and your eyes from
tears, for your work will be rewarded," declares the LORD. "They
will return from the land of the enemy. So there is hope for
your future," declares the LORD. "Your children will return to
their own land'" (vv. 16-17). A little later comes the promise
that Yahweh will make a 'new covenant with the house of Israel
and with the house of Judah.' He will forgive his people's sins;
grant them the deepest communion with himself; summon them
to renewed worship; build his law into them; and by all those
means restore the warring tribes to their lost unity (vv. 31-34).[13]
Rachel's mourning will be transposed into joy.

Fulfillment
King Herod's slaughter of perhaps twenty male children in and
around Bethlehem was not a novelty. 'The suspicion, scheming,
and cruelty [reflected in this passage] are in complete harmony
with what is known of his character from other sources.' He
'was given to fits of ungovernable rage and had three of his
own children put to death.' Caesar Augustus is reported to have
said, 'It is better to be Herod's pig [*hys*] than his son [*huios*].'[14]

To express the effects of Herod's act, Jeremiah 31:15 is
well chosen because of the pathos of the words themselves,
because of the association between Ramah and Bethlehem in
Rachel's final hour, and because such an act recalled cruelties
inflicted by Assyrian and Babylonian armies. The preface to
this quotation states, 'Then was fulfilled what had been said
through Jeremiah the prophet...,' whereas in the other three
instances of *plēroō* in Matthew 1–2 we are told that an event
occurred '*in order that* an OT prophecy (or prophecies) might

---

[13]All quotations in this paragraph are from the NIV. Once regathered, the
houses of Israel and Judah will again be united in common allegiance to
Yahweh, as at the time of the Sinaitic covenant (Jer. 31:31-32). For the joyous
worship evoked by the new covenant, see verses 12-14.

[14]The first quotation is from Scott 1995: 95. Herod was by nature 'wild,
passionate, harsh, arrogant, calculating, and ruthless' (ibid.). The other
quotations are from Brown 1993: 226. See also the evidence in Keener 1999:
110-11. 'In an era of many, highly placed political murders, the execution
of perhaps twenty children in a small town would warrant little attention'
(ibid., 111). See also Brown (ibid., 204-5) for estimates of the number of
children killed.

be fulfilled.'[15] That difference in wording is deliberate: the slaughter of the innocents was the effect of an evil purpose, whereas Jesus' virginal conception (1:22-23), his return from Egypt (2:15) and his going to Nazareth (2:23), all happen in precise fulfillment of God's saving purpose.[16]

That does not mean that the death of the male children in and around Bethlehem lay outside God's will. To say that it did raises more questions than it answers. This act of Herod (like all his other acts, however cruel), no less than Satan's assaults upon Job, God permits by his sovereign will and controls by his sovereign power. Jesus' rescue from Herod's treachery testifies to God's *marvelous* providence; the slaughter of the male children, to his *mysterious* providence.[17]

The mother of a son slain in Bethlehem would doubtless experience a grief equal that of a mother bereft of a child during Assyrian or Babylonian exile; and she might well find in the words of Jeremiah 31:15 a welcome avenue for her sorrows. Yet, in Matthew, as in Jeremiah, it is *Rachel* – representative of all Israel – who weeps. Herod's act causes her an anguish equal to that evoked by the acts of the Assyrian and Babylonian kings. Indeed, viewing the verb 'fulfill' (*plēroō*; 2:17), in light of its two previous occurrences in Matthew,[18] we may conclude that there is now cause for greater lamentation than before. For, as Jeremiah 31 itself declares, Assyrian and Babylonian captivities are not permanent: the people of God would be regathered, and granted unprecedented blessings. But the massacre in and around Bethlehem marks an attempt

---

[15]In Matthew 1:22 and 2:15, the conjunction *hina* is used; in 2:23, the synonymous conjunction *hopōs*. Cf. Brown 1993: 205.

[16]Perhaps for the same reason the language that expressly identifies the Source of the prophecy in 1:22 and 2:15 – 'by the Lord' (*hypo Kyriou*) – is absent from 2:17.

[17]The two kinds of providence are also evident in Exodus 1:15–2:10; the infant Moses is saved (as are some other Hebrews, by the midwives' cunning), others are drowned. In Jesus' atoning sacrifice, the two kinds coalesce; see Matthew 26:24; Acts 4:27-28. Reflecting upon his exile in Aberdeen, Samuel Rutherford wrote of God's 'deep and unsearchable providences' (1984: 317). The church father Chromatius (who died in 407) called the babies slain in Bethlehem 'the first martyrs of Christ' (*ACC* 1a: 35).

[18]See comments on Matthew 1:22 and 2:15.

by the cruelest of tyrants to destroy Messiah himself – the very One whom Yahweh has appointed to fulfill the promises of Jeremiah 31. Were those promises not kept, Israel's losses would be irreparable and Rachel's grief unending.

The Babylonian exile concludes the second segment of the Matthean genealogy (1:11). At this juncture all hopes associated with the Davidic dynasty appear to have been crushed, which helps to explain the lament of Jeremiah 31:15. But the exile also marks the beginning of the third and final segment of the genealogy (Matt. 1:12), which climaxes with the birth of Jesus the Davidic king. This event injects new life into all the promises to the House of David. Now that God has rescued the young Messiah from death, there is renewed hope that those promises will indeed be fulfilled. Matthew does not expressly quote the words of hope from Jeremiah 31. But his citing of verse 15 directs attention to its context; and this whole gospel is devoted to setting forth the fullest realization of that hope.[19]

C. Joseph: Faithful Servant

God earlier disclosed his will to Joseph through an angel in a dream (Matt. 1:20-21). He does so at least twice in the present passage; and on these occasions, as on that one, Joseph follows the angel's directives to the letter. Commanded to rise, to take the child and his mother, to flee to Egypt, and to stay there until further instructions are given, Joseph does precisely that (2:13-15).[20] When told, following Herod's death, to rise, to take

---

[19]Yahweh promised that with the establishing of the 'new covenant,' the knowledge of God would be marked by greater breadth and depth (Jer. 31:31-34). That promise is fulfilled in Jesus: for never before has God incarnate (Matt. 1:23) invited persons into fellowship with himself (11:25-30; where v. 28 may allude to Jer. 31:25); and only the shedding of Jesus' blood secures the forgiveness essential for reconciliation to a holy God (Matt. 26:28, alluding to Jeremiah 31:31, 34). Cf. the discussion of typology in Matthew, pages 123-29, especially 128-29; also Keener 1999: 111-12.

[20]Matthew's language shows how carefully Joseph obeys: about a dozen of the Greek terms used in the angel's command (2:13) recur in the description of Joseph's response (2:14-15). The magi responded similarly to a warning in a dream (2:12); but only Joseph is expressly said to have been warned by 'an angel of the Lord,' which suggests that as a Hebrew and son of David, he is especially favored. But see below on verse 22.

the child and his mother, and to go into the land of Israel, he again exactly obeys (2:19-21).[21]

We turn to verse 22: 'Having heard that Archelaus was reigning in Judea in place of his father Herod, he [Joseph] was afraid to go there. Having been warned in a dream, he withdrew into the district of Galilee....' The threat from Archelaus is real indeed. At Herod's death his kingdom was divided among his three sons. Archelaus was to rule in Judea–Samaria–Idumea; the other full brother, Herod Antipas, in Galilee–Perea; and the half-brother Philip, in the regions east and north of the Sea of Galilee. 'Archelaus was the least liked of the three because of his dictatorial ways. The Jewish deputies who went to Rome to protest against his becoming ruler stated that he had ushered in his reign with a massacre of three thousand people.... He persisted till his brutality became intolerable; and at the request of his subjects he was deposed by Rome in A.D. 6, thus enjoying the shortest reign of the three heirs....'[22] This verse does not expressly mention an angel; but the imparting of a warning *in a dream* in response to Joseph's *fear* in face of a threat reminiscent of Herod, strongly implies that an angel is again at work.[23] But in any case the warning comes from God: the aorist participle

---

[21]Again the description of Joseph's response (2:2) closely matches that of the angel's command (2:20). The language of 2:19-21 echoes that of 2:13-15. Whereas 2:15, 19 spoke only of Herod's death, 2:20 reports that 'those who sought [*hoi zētountes*] the life of the child have died.' (The same verb, *zēteō*, appeared in the angel's earlier warning about Herod [2:13].) The plural recalls both Yahweh's words to Moses in Exodus 4:19 (noted earlier) and Matthew's reference to Herod's counselors in 2:4. Perhaps some from among the chief priests and scholars have died; in any case, with Herod's death the present plot against Jesus' life has failed (cf. Brown 1993: 206). Herod the Great died in the spring of 4 B.C. Jesus may have been born close to that time, in December 5 B.C. or January 4 B.C. (so H.W. Hoehner, *DJG*, 118).

[22]Brown 1993: 207, with citations from Josephus. Luke 3:1 mentions both Antipas and Philip.

[23]In each instance of *angelos* in Matthew 1–2, the angel appears to Joseph 'in a dream' (*kat' onar*; 1:20, 24; 2:13, 19). The verb *phobeomai* ('be afraid'; 2:22) also occurs in 1:20, where the angel tells Joseph he need not fear taking Mary as his wife. From Joseph's expressed fear of Archelaus (2:22), we may infer that the angel addresses a kindred fear of Herod and others in 2:20.

chrēmatistheis ('having been warned') signals divine activity.[24]
Yahweh again protects and directs Joseph and his family.

Earlier in this chapter, the fidelity of Gentile magi is set in
contrast to the unbelief and perfidy of Jews in Jerusalem. But not
all Jews were like that, as the portrait of Joseph in Matthew 1–2
testifies. His faithfulness to God and scrupulous obedience
to his commands are the means whereby God protects the
newborn King from the tyranny of Herod and Archelaus.

In accord with the angel's instructions, Joseph took the child
and his mother 'and entered into the land of Israel [*eis gēn
Israēl*]' (2:21). Having been warned against returning to Judea
(and Bethlehem), 'he withdrew into the region of Galilee [*eis
ta merē tēs Galilaias*]' (2:22). And there in Galilee 'he came and
settled in a town called Nazareth [*eis polin legomenēn Nazaret*]'
(2:23a). This is the place from which Joseph and Mary originally
came (see Luke 1:26; 2:4). Following their visit to the temple, as
reported in Luke 2:22-38, Mary and Joseph returned with Jesus
to Galilee, 'to their own town of Nazareth' (2:39). The journey to
Egypt 'would have to be placed between Luke 2:38 and 2:39.'[25]

D. *Nazōraios:* A Notable Name

Matthew tells us that Joseph and his family resided in
Nazareth (*Nazaret*) 'in order that what was spoken through
the prophets might be fulfilled: "He shall be called a
Nazarene [*Nazōraios*]"' (Matt. 2:23b). Up to this point in
Matthew, the noun 'prophet' has appeared exclusively in the
phrase 'through the prophet' (*dia tēs prophētēs*),[26] so the use
here of the plural 'through the prophets' (*dia tōn prophētōn*) is
arresting. In each of the quotations ascribed to one prophet,
a single text was in view,[27] so the reference to 'the prophets'
suggests that Matthew has at least two OT texts in view.
Yet, unlike the previous quotations, the source of this one

---

[24]This passive participle (from *chrēmatizō*) is an instance of the 'divine
passive.' Another form of the same participle occurs in verse 12, indicating
God's protection for the magi.

[25]Stein 1992: 118.

[26]See Matthew 1:22; 2:5, 15, 17.

[27]Namely, Isaiah 7:14 (Matt. 1:23); Micah 5:2 (2:6); Hosea 11:1 (2:15); and
Jeremiah 31:15 (2:18).

– 'he shall be called a Nazarene [*Nazōraios*]' – is not readily discernible; and (to put it mildly) interpreters are not agreed on what text or texts Matthew has in view.

Recognizing 'the allusive wealth of the term' *Nazōraios*,[28] we may (I believe) detect in this quotation three meanings woven together. In the first place, there is obviously an intended link between the word *Nazōraios* and the name of the town, *Nazaret*, although *Nazarēnos* (Mark's chosen spelling) is closer than *Nazōraios* to *Nazaret*.[29] By Jesus' coming to this particular place, the prophetic word is 'fulfilled.' Jesus not only lives in a province that many Judeans view with contempt; he resides in a town that fellow Galileans despise. He is 'the Nazarene,' not 'the Jerusalemite' or even 'the Bethlehemite.'[30] One is reminded of certain features of Isaiah's portrait of the Servant of Yahweh (Isa. 49:7; 53:2-3), and it is possible that Matthew is alluding to them.[31] But the term *Nazōraios* does not itself point to such passages.

Secondly, *Nazōraios* recalls the Hebrew noun *nāzîr*, used of a person consecrated to Yahweh by such vows as abstinence from wine and the use of a razor. Laws governing the Nazirites' conduct are found in Numbers 6:1-21, where the words *nāzîr* ('a consecrated or separated person'), *nēzer* ('act of consecration') and *nāzar* ('to separate oneself,' 'to abstain from' certain practices) are frequent. The angel of Yahweh tells Manoah's wife that her son (Samson) is to be a *nāzîr*, 'set apart to God from birth' (Judges 13:4-7; one version of the LXX

---

[28]Brown 1993: 218-19.

[29]Matthew uses *Nazōraios* exclusively (2:23; 26:71), as does John (18:5, etc.); Mark, *Nazarēnos* exclusively (1:24, etc.); and Luke, both *Nazōraios* (4:34; 24:19) and *Nazarēnos* (18:37). Matthew thrice refers to the town, each time with a different spelling: *Nazaret* (2:23), *Nazara* (4:13) and *Nazareth* (21:11). Linguistically, the transition from *Nazaret* to *Nazōraios* is difficult (BAGD s.v. *Nazōraios*); cf. the discussion in Brown 1993: 207-10.

[30]For many a Jew, 'Galilee of the Gentiles' (Matt. 4:15) would be a term of derision. Cf. John 1:46 ('Can there be anything good from Nazareth?'); 7:41-42 (the Messiah will surely not come from Galilee but rather from David's town, Bethlehem), 52 (a prophet – or the prophet like Moses, Deuteronomy 18:15 – does not arise from Galilee). On Nazareth's political insignificance, see Keener 1999: 113. He and others judge that Nazareth had 'perhaps five hundred inhabitants' (ibid.).

[31]Strengthening the possibility is the quotation of Isaiah 42:1-4, the first Servant Song, in Matthew 12:18-21.

exactly transliterates the Hebrew, another uses *naziraion*).[32]
Hannah vows that, if given a son, she will 'give him to
Yahweh all the days of his life, and a razor will not touch
his head' (1 Sam. 1:11). Once Samuel is born, Hannah keeps
her word: 'Therefore I have given him to Yahweh. As long
as he lives, he is given to Yahweh' (1:28). Gabriel's command
to Zechariah concerning John (Luke 1:15) recalls both the
angel's instructions to Manoah's wife and Hannah's vow. Each
woman whose son is thus dedicated had no hope of becoming
a mother until Yahweh directly intervened.[33] Jesus did not
follow John's example of abstaining from wine (Luke 1:15):
on the contrary (Matt. 11:18-19)! Yet the singular purpose of
the Nazirite vow was to set the person apart to serve God, as
is clear from all four of those passages (i.e., Num. 6, Judg. 13,
1 Sam. 1 and Luke 1). Abstaining from wine and from using
a razor showed that the vow was being taken seriously. Thus
Jesus is a Nazirite in the deepest sense: a man consecrated to
serving God all his days, as the next chapter of Matthew will
attest. It should also be noted that Jesus' conception was yet
more miraculous than that of Samson or Samuel or John, as
Matthew 1 has already shown.

In a third way Matthew 'marries phonetics with Christology.'[34] *Nazōraios* alludes to Isaiah 11:1, 'A shoot will come
up from the stump of Jesse; from his roots a Branch [Hebrew
nētser] will bear fruit.'[35] That allusion in turn evokes the Isaianic
context, including the prophecy of 7:14, together with all that

---

[32]In Judges 16:17, Samson tells Delilah, 'I have been a Nazirite set apart
to God since birth.' In one version of the LXX *nāzîr* is rendered *naziraios*; in
another, *hagios* ('holy'), which basically means to be set apart to God. Brown
argues that Judges 16:17 is one of the main texts in view in Matthew 2:23
(1993: 223-25).

[33]Manoah's wife 'was sterile and remained childless' (Judg. 13:2, as
echoed in the angel's words, v. 3). Hannah had no children (1 Sam. 1:2),
'Yahweh had closed her womb' (v. 5, cf. v. 6). Zechariah and his wife 'had
no children, because Elizabeth was incapable of having children [*steira*] and
they both were well advanced in age' (Luke 1:7).

[34]Gundry 1994: 40.

[35]Cf. Keener 1999: 114, and the sources he cites. The other two instances
of *nētser* in Isaiah (14:19; 60:21) are not relevant. 'The Branch of Yahweh'
(Isa. 4:2) designates the same person (Motyer 1993: 65) as does the 'righteous

Isaiah 1–12 discloses about coming judgment and subsequent restoration through Yahweh's Messiah. On the one hand Jesus 'was a branch from a royal line hacked down to a stump and reared in surroundings guaranteed to win him scorn.'[36] Yet on the other hand, this is the very One destined to inaugurate the rule of God and to sit on David's throne forever. The closing verse of Matthew's infancy narrative thus forms an inclusion with the gospel's opening proclamation of 'Jesus the Messiah, the Son of David.'

We may observe, finally, that in the closing chapter of the Bible Jesus himself recalls more than one theme from Matthew's opening chapters: 'I am the root and the offspring of David, the bright morning star' (Rev. 22:16).

Branch' of Jeremiah 23:5 and 33:15; but in these three texts the Hebrew is not *nētser* but *tsemach*. Given the conceptual link between Isaiah 11:1 and 4:2, and between 'Nazirite' and 'holiness' (see above note on Judg. 16:17), Brown 1993: 223-24 judges that Matthew 2:23b alludes to Isaiah 4:3: 'Those who are left in Zion...will be called holy [*hagioi klēthēsontai*].'

[36]Carson 1984: 97. Cf. the above comments on Nazareth.

Section 4.

'Make Straight, Make Straight, the Highway of the King'[1] (Matt. 3:1-17)

Matthew has thus far traced Messiah's journey from Bethlehem to Egypt to Nazareth. His coming from Galilee to the Jordan to be baptized by John (Matt. 3:13) marks a further stage in his royal progress. The testimonies which John, the Spirit and the Father bear to Jesus' person and work on this occasion, prepare for his ordeal in the wilderness of Judea and the beginning of his Galilean ministry. See also Mark 1:2-11 and Luke 3:1-22.

---

[1]Words from the hymn 'Heralds of Christ, who bear the King's commands,' by Laura S. Copenhaver (1894).

I.

'Herald of Christ, who Bears the King's Command'[1]
(3:1-12)

The opening verse links this chapter to the foregoing narrative chronologically ('In those days'), conceptually (Jesus was a *Nazōraios*, John a *nāzîr*), and geographically ('in the desert of Judea').[2] The name of the John here introduced appears twenty-three times in Matthew. In seven of these, he is expressly called 'John the Baptist,' both to underscore a cardinal feature of his work, and to distinguish him from John the son of Zebedee.[3]

A. John and the Old Testament
In Matthew 11:13 Jesus will expressly relate the work of John to the testimony of the OT, i.e., to 'the Prophets and the Law.'[4] There are several ways in which the present record of John's ministry is illuminated by the OT.

John the Nazirite
It was stated, in comments on 2:23, that John was a *nāzîr* like Samson and Samuel. Like other Nazirites, John is set apart for special service to God. Like Samuel, he attends to Yahweh's voice and declares Yahweh's word.[5] Introducing John,

---

[1]Adapted from the opening lines of the hymn cited on page 241.

[2]On *Nazōraios* see comments on 2:23. *Ioudaia*, (3:1), appeared in 2:1, 5, 22, and recurs in 3:5, 'all Judea.' 'Q' began with John's ministry (see pp. 78-86). So do Mark (1:1-11) and the apostolic preaching in Acts 10:37 and 13:24-25. In this regard, note the weighty historical preface in Luke's account, (3:1-2). Cf. Keener 1999: 116.

[3]The seven instances of *Iōannēs ho baptistēs*: Matthew 3:1; 11:11, 12; 14:2, 8; 16:14; 17:13. Cf. 21:25, 'the baptism of John.' Jesus' disciple is simply called 'John' (17:1) or identified as the brother of 'James the son of Zebedee' (4:21; 10:2).

[4]This reverses the usual order (cf. 5:17); see comments on 11:13.

[5]Cf. 1 Samuel 3:10 ('Then Samuel said, "Speak, for your servant is listening"') and 3:21 ('Yahweh continued to appear at Shiloh, and there

242

Matthew makes no direct reference to his practice of baptism but speaks exclusively of his verbal witness: 'John the Baptist appeared, preaching [*kēryssōn*] in the desert of Judea, saying [*legōn*]:...' (3:1b-2a).[6] Apart from his pronouncement about God's rule (3:2b), his baptism makes no sense. John is primarily 'a voice crying out in the desert' that people must prepare for the imminent coming of Yahweh (3:3).

In keeping with the place – the *erēmos* ('desert') – John's diet is Spartan (3:4). It is also fitting that a holy person – a Nazirite set apart to serve Yahweh – should choose rations 'devoid of flesh from which blood has had to be drained (hence locusts) and devoid of wine (hence honey).'[7]

Samson and Samuel became Nazirites amid political and religious crises (Judg. 13:1, 5; 1 Sam. 3:1, with 2:12–3:21). Matthew's earlier portrayal of 'the chief priests and scholars of the people' (2:4), and the references to dangerous kings in Judea (Herod and Archelaus), together with the present indictment of Pharisees and Sadducees (3:7), reflect both religious and political decline. We are now to learn that the nation faces the greatest crisis in its history, and that for this very reason God has summoned John to preach. John's message makes it clear that God's rule is dawning at a time of spiritual barrenness and moral declension in Israel; and that, in face of the judgment that is sure to fall with the coming of that rule, it is urgent that the children of Abraham – and especially those appointed to lead them – repent of their manifold sin.

---

he revealed himself to Samuel by his word'). John, like Samuel, is to be dedicated to God's service all his days (see Luke 1:15-17, 76, 80).

[6]Behind 'appeared' is *paraginetai* (from *paraginomai*), an historical (or dramatic) present (*GGBB*, 526-32). With 3:1 contrast Mark 1:4 (NIV), 'And so John came, baptizing [*baptizōn*] in the desert region and preaching [*kēryssōn*] a baptism....' Like Matthew, Luke 3:2-6 accentuates John's receiving and imparting revelation from God ('the word of God came upon John in the desert'; 3:2). Yet Luke 3:3 ('preaching a baptism of repentance...') follows Mark 1:4, and thus does not distinguish John's preaching from his baptizing as sharply as does Matthew 3:2-3.

[7]Gundry 1994: 45. Again note Luke 1:15. 'John lived simply – with only the barest forms of necessary sustenance' (Keener 1999: 119). Pierre Bonnard, *L'Évangile selon Saint Matthieu*, 2nd ed. (Neuchâtel: Delachaux & Niestlé, 1970), 34, says of the locust: 'cet insecte était très prisé comme nourriture, soit à l'eau

John and Elijah

Matthew's stress on John's preaching continues into verse 4: 'This very John [*Autos...ho Iōannēs*, i.e. the one identified in vv. 1-3] wore clothing made from camel's hair, with a leather belt around his waist; and his food was locusts and wild honey.'

The first part of this description recalls 2 Kings 1:8, where Elijah is identified as 'a man with a garment of hair and a leather belt around his waist.'[8] We know from 1–2 Kings that Elijah was a miracle-worker as well as a preacher. But 'John did no miracle' (John 10:41) and Elijah did no baptizing. It is forceful and fearless speech that unites the two prophets. When in Matthew 11 Jesus identifies John as 'the Elijah who was to come,' it is John's preaching that he emphasizes: 'from the days of John the Baptist until now the kingdom of heaven has been forcefully advancing' (cf. 3:2); 'all *the prophets* and the law *prophesied* until John...he who has *ears*, let him *hear*.'[9]

John's courage in addressing Pharisees and Sadducees at the Jordan (Matt. 3) recalls that of Elijah when confronting the prophets of Baal on Mount Carmel (1 Kings 18). While Jesus' mighty works remind Herod Antipas of John the Baptist (Matt. 14:2), there is no evidence that John ever worked a miracle to win Herod's (or anyone else's) favor. On the contrary, it is because he preaches God's law – and condemns the adulterous union between Herod and Herodias – that he is imprisoned and eventually put to death (Matt. 14:1-12). Similarly, Elijah

---

et au sel comme nos crevettes, soit séché au soleil et confit dans du miel ou du vinaigre, soit réduit en poudre et mélangé à de la fleur de farine sous forme de galette' ('this insect was highly valued as food, whether in water and salt like our shrimp, or dried in the sun and preserved in honey or in vinegar, or reduced to powder and mixed with flour to form a pancake').

[8]The MT describes Elijah as 'a possessor [*bā'al*, literally 'master'] of hair,' which might mean 'a hairy man' (so LXX, *anēr dasys*) or 'a man with a garment of hair' (so NIV). Favoring the latter are the parallel reference to 'a leather belt' (2 Kings 1:8b) and Zechariah 13:4, which speaks unambiguously of 'a prophet's garment of hair.' The Greek behind 'leather belt around his waist' in Matthew 3:4b is almost identical to the LXX of 2 Kings 1:8b. Cf. Gundry 1994: 45.

[9]Matthew 11:12-15. In stressing that John did not wear fine clothes (11:8), Jesus alludes to 3:4, and implies a contrast with Herod Antipas (cf. 14:1-12). See comments on 11:7-19.

pronounces Yahweh's judgment upon Ahab and Jezebel for killing Naboth and stealing his vineyard (1 Kings 21).[10] One can as easily think of John as the Sanhedrin's or Herod's dutiful servant, as to think of Elijah as one of Ahab's court-appointed prophets (1 Kings 22:6; Matt. 11:7-9).[11]

Yet Jesus does not compare John to Elijah as we might compare Micah to Isaiah. Yahweh had promised through the last of the writing prophets: 'Behold, I will send you Elijah the prophet before the coming of the great and dreadful day of Yahweh' (Mal. 4:5 [MT, 3:23]). Jesus equates this prophet with the 'messenger' of Malachi 3:1, the one Yahweh appoints to prepare for his own coming; and announces that this prophet has come in the person of John the Baptist. In thus declaring John to be 'the Elijah who was to come,' Jesus underscores the truth of John's own message (Matt. 3:2).[12] The historical Elijah stood within the time of promise, and was followed by a kindred figure, Elisha. John, the latter-day Elijah, stands within the time of fulfillment, and heralds the coming of its central figure, whose work and whose being are very different from his own.

Nowhere in Matthew or in any other gospel does John identify *himself* as Elijah. Indeed, in John 1:21, he positively *denies* that he is Elijah. John concentrates on the one who will follow him, and is not in the least concerned to make a name for himself. He calls himself merely 'the voice of one crying out in the desert...' (John 1:23, quoting Isa. 40:3) – which accounts for Matthew's use of this prophecy in Matthew 3:3.

John and Isaiah
Jesus will later call John 'a prophet...and more than a prophet' (11:9). But in Matthew 3, the only person expressly termed a

---

[10]Herod and Herodias violate the seventh commandment (Exod. 20:14); Ahab and Jezebel, the sixth and eighth (Exod. 20:13, 15), as well as the ninth and tenth (Exod. 20:16, 17). See 1 Kings 21:1-16; and the comments on Matthew 14:1-12.

[11]Contrast the prophetic ministry of Nathan during David's reign; see, e.g., 2 Samuel 12. Cf. Keener, 118.

[12]See Matthew 11:10-15 (v. 10 quotes Mal. 3:1, and v. 14 alludes to Mal. 4:5); 17:10-13 (11 alludes to Malachi 4:5-6); and comments on those passages. Gabriel's prophecy about John (Luke 1:17) alludes to Malachi 4:6.

prophētēs – and the only OT person besides Abraham identified by name – is Isaiah: 'For this is he who was spoken of through Isaiah the prophet, saying: "A voice crying out in the desert: Prepare the way of the Lord, make straight his paths"' (3:3, quoting Isa. 40:3). Now we understand why John went into the desert and stayed there.[13]

The voice of Isaiah 40:3 summons the people of Jerusalem to prepare for the coming of Yahweh. That voice belongs to John the Baptist: 'This is he' of whom Yahweh spoke through Isaiah, says Matthew. Significantly, the verb 'fulfill,' present in earlier introductions to quotations from the OT,[14] is absent from Matthew 3:3. For there is no OT person or event antecedent to John's appearance in the desert (such as we found in examining 1:23 and 2:15). As the one who heralds Yahweh's coming, John occupies a unique position.[15] Here, in the desert, he urges people from Jerusalem, and other places too, to get ready, for Yahweh is about to judge the nation and to establish his Rule.[16]

The quotation of Isaiah in Matthew 3:3 recalls those in 1:23 (Isa. 7:14; 8:8, 10); and it anticipates those in 4:15-16 (Isa. 9:1-2); 8:17 (Isa. 53:4); and 12:18-21 (Isa. 42:1-4), to go no further.[17] Does not Matthew intend for this quotation of Isaiah 40:3 (a text clearly important in his presentation of John, and the only OT quotation in ch. 3) to be a pointer to those passages about the Servant of

---

[13]See Luke 1:80 (which uses the plural *erēmois*). By connecting the phrase 'in the desert' with 'crying out,' Matthew 3:3 follows the LXX of Isaiah 40:3 (as do Mark 1:3 and John 1:23). The MT of 40:3 is accented so as to read: 'A voice of one *calling*: "In the desert *prepare*..."' (NIV). Jewish interpreters (including the Targum and the Peshitta) follow the LXX; and the MT may not be original. See Ottley 1906: 2.297; and Gundry 1994: 44.

[14]Matthew 1:22; 2:15, 17, 23. The verb *plēroō* recurs in 3:15.

[15]The verb *plēroō* is also absent from Matthew 11:10, where Malachi 3:1 is applied to John. John is to 'prepare a people made ready for the Lord' (Luke 1:17); he is to be 'a prophet of the Most High,' to 'go on before the Lord to prepare his ways' (Luke 1:76, alluding to Isaiah 40:3; Luke 3:4-6 interprets John's ministry by quoting Isaiah 40:3-5).

[16]That 'Jerusalem and all Judea went out' to John (Matt. 3:5) accords with Isaiah 40: for 'Jerusalem,' see 40:2, 9; for 'the towns of Judah,' 40:9.

[17]For later quotations from Isaiah, see Matthew 13:14-15; 15:8-9; 21:5, 13. In six of the nine instances, the prophet is identified by name (3:3; 4:14; 8:17; 12:17; 13:14; 15:7).

Yahweh in Isaiah 42 and beyond (texts clearly important in his presentation of Jesus)? Do not the closing verses of Matthew 3 indicate this to be so (see below on vv. 15 and 17)?

B. John and Yahweh

The name of his predecessor is John's confession of faith as well: 'My God is Yahweh,' the meaning of the Hebrew for Elijah, *'ēliyyāhû*. As Isaiah 40:3 declares, John's singular mission is to prepare the way for Yahweh.

The Rule of God

'Repent, for the kingdom of heaven has drawn near' (Matt. 3:2). These are John's first words in the gospel. Matthew differs from Mark and Luke 'in this respect, that he sums up John's teaching in John's own words, while they do it in their own.'[18] This opening declaration stands out all the more because the remainder of John's preaching is reserved for verses 7-12, after Matthew has quoted from Isaiah, described John and summarized his baptizing activity (3:3-6). We may infer that the declaration of verse 2 is foundational for all that follows, both in John's actual ministry and in the evangelist's record of it.

John announces that 'the kingdom of heaven [*hē basileia tōn ouranōn*] has drawn near.' Jesus' opening declaration (4:17) is identical. The Greek word for 'kingdom' (*basileia*) primarily denotes God's rule, and secondarily the realm over which he reigns. John announces the imminent dawn of this rule. In one sense, God's reign is both eternal and universal (see, e.g., Ps. 3:1-2). Yet God's laws are flagrantly disobeyed, and wickedness is rampant in the earth, as Matthew 2 has shown. John declares that God is about to make what is his by right (*de jure*), altogether his in fact (*de facto*). When God's perfect will is done on earth as it is done in heaven, then and there his kingdom will have come in its fullness (6:10), and justice will finally be established throughout his realm (5:6). In other words, John's prophecy is eschatological in character: the final reign of God is at the door. See the discussion on pages 99-102.

---

[18]Calvin 1994: 114, speaking of 3:2 (cf. Mark 1:4; Luke 3:3).

The Call to Repentance

'Repent [*Metanoeite*], for [*gar*] the kingdom of heaven has drawn near (3:2). John's first recorded word is a command, a present imperative of *metanoeō*. His use of the corresponding noun *metanoia* in 3:8 ('fruit in keeping with repentance') and 3:11 ('I baptize you with water for repentance') underscores the importance of such action. What makes it urgent is the nearness of God's eschatological rule (3:2; note *gar*, 'for') and the certainty of his judgment (3:7. Like his precursors, the OT prophets, John is commanding Israelites to 'turn' or to 'return' to God.[19]

Genuine repentance begins in the heart. In Hebraic thought, the heart (Hebrew *lēb*, *lēbāb*) is 'the integrating center of man as a rational, emotional, volitional being.'[20]

Metanoia means, literally, 'a change of mind.' The reason is affected; persons who take John's preaching seriously are reoriented in their thinking.[21] Their whole outlook is changed once they understand and believe what he says about the nearness of God's rule and its attendant demands.

But the people are not said to engage in theological discussion. Instead, they actually confess their sins as they are being baptized (Matt. 3:6), which indicates that they have been affected emotionally as well as intellectually. Confession of sin is the effect of 'a broken and contrite heart' (Ps. 51:17). To be sure, repentance is more than remorse; but neither is repentance complete without it.

---

[19]See, e.g., Isaiah 31:6; 45:22; Jeremiah 3:7, 10; Ezekiel 14:6; 18:30; Hosea 12:6; 14:1-2; Joel 2:12-13; Zechariah 1:3-4; Malachi 3:7. For these and other references, see Keener 1999: 120.

[20]Dunn 1988: 100. So also Johannes Behm, *TDNT* 3: 612. The Greek word for 'heart,' *kardia*, does not appear in Matthew until 5:8; but the heart's three basic functions are in view in chapter 3. Cf. 2 Chronicles 30, where seeking God with one's heart (*lēb*, 30:12; *lēbāb*, 30:19) entails fixing one's mind on Hezekiah's letter (30:6-9); confessing and abandoning the sins of the past (30:11, 14); and coming to Jerusalem to celebrate Passover (30:13, 15-27). These marks of repentance are again evident during Josiah's reform (2 Chron. 34:14-33; note the references to the heart in vv. 27 and 31). See also page 183 above.

[21]As *metamorphoō* (*meta* + *morphoō*, 'to form'),17:2, means 'to change the form,' so *metanoeō* (*meta* + *noeō*, 'understand'), 3:2, means 'to change the

In genuine repentance, the rational and emotional dimensions of the heart do not act independently of the volitional. Obeying the command in Matthew 3:2 requires an exercise of will. Whether a true renewal of the mind has occurred, and whether one's contrition is real, will become apparent in what one chooses to do. Receiving John's baptism (3:6) is one such choice, a decision which for some Israelites would demand great humility and strength of will, given this rite's resemblance to a baptism required of *Gentiles*.[22] But being baptized is just the beginning: 'Produce fruit in keeping with repentance,' exhorts John in verse 8, an aspect of his preaching which is more fully developed in Luke 3:10-14. Cf. Yahweh's call to repentance in Isaiah 1:16-17.

Addressing Pharisees and Sadducees
That exhortation is directed to 'many of the Pharisees and Sadducees' (3:7). Both names – *Pharisaioi* and *Saddoukaioi* – appear here for the first time in Matthew. The Pharisees are expressly mentioned twenty-eight more times; the Sadducees, six. These 'many' who come to the Jordan represent the two leading religious sects within Judaism. Who these people are, what they believe, what places they occupy within the culture, and how John and Jesus understand them, will become plainer as we proceed.[23]

Both groups come 'for his baptism [*epi to baptisma autou*]' (3:7). If this phrase means they came 'to where he was baptizing' (NIV), they may be no more than observers – who come not to be baptized but to make official inquiry

---

mind.' For Pauline expressions of this transformation, see Romans 12:2 and Ephesians 4:23.

[22]In accord with John's mission, his baptism is unique and thus not to be equated with the 'proselyte baptism' required of Gentiles entering the Jewish community. At the same time, given John's acute awareness of Israel's grievous sins – including misplaced national pride (Matt. 3:9) – and his consequent call to national repentance (3:2), he may well have considered that Jews wanting to enter the new, eschatological community must humble themselves *like Gentiles* wanting to enter the old community. For this line of thinking, see Keener 1999: 121-22, with sources he cites.

[23]On Pharisees and Sadducees, see Appendix A.

into John's activities.[24] But those words are more naturally rendered 'for his baptism – i.e., to have themselves baptized by him.'[25] John's statement in verse 11 – 'I baptize you with water for repentance' – reflects the purpose of their coming to the Jordan. Yet the placement of this section (3:7-12) after the summary of 3:6 leaves open the question whether they received John's baptism. It is probable that both Pharisees and Sadducees reversed their intention and returned home unbaptized – lest by letting John baptize them, they appear to endorse his devastating assaults on their spiritual and national pride (3:7-9). See 21:31-32; Luke 7:30.

'You brood of vipers [*Gennēmata echidnōn*]! Who warned you to flee from the coming wrath?' (3:7b). For divine wrath as a dominant feature of the coming Day of Yahweh, see, e.g., Amos 5:18-20; Zephaniah 1:14-18; Romans 2:5; 1 Thessalonians 1:10.

John begins by depicting his listeners as poisonous snakes rapidly slithering away from a grass fire.[26] The metaphor aptly expresses his belief that these persons are dangerous and destructive. Not only are their own hearts poisoned; so powerful is their combined influence, that they have infected and endangered the whole populace.[27] Accordingly, John's opening words to the sectarians in Matthew 3:7 are the very ones he addresses to the 'crowds' (*ochloi*) in Luke 3:7.

John then issues a twofold command (Matt. 3:8-9a): 'Therefore [*oun*: i.e., in light of the coming wrath; 3:7b] produce [*poiēsate*] fruit in keeping with repentance, and do not presume [*mē doxēte*] to say to yourselves, "Our father is Abraham."'[28]

---

[24]For such inquiries, see John 1:19-28. Cf. Gundry 1994: 46.

[25]Cf. ESV; NASB; and BAGD s.v. *epi*, 1.

[26]Gundry 1994: 47. Do they think the waters of the Jordan will quench the fire? *Echidna* usually denotes a poisonous snake (BAGD s.v.), hence 'viper.' The more general term for 'snake' is *ophis*, used of disciples in Matthew 10:16. In 23:33, Jesus applies both *echidna* and *ophis* to scribes and Pharisees. For beliefs about vipers in antiquity, see Keener 1999: 122-23.

[27]We may apply to Matthew 3:7 a comment on Nah. 3:4 (in Robertson 1990: 102): 'By coarse, insulting language the Holy Spirit through the prophet tears away these pretenses and lays bare the moral degradation of the inner recesses of the heart.'

[28]*Poiēsate* is an aorist imperative of command (from *poieō*), *mē doxēte* an aorist subjunctive of prohibition (*dokeō*, with the negative particle *mē*). ESV's

One of the listeners' deepest convictions, and a source of great assurance, is that they are children of Abraham – the heirs of God's unshakeable promises to the patriarch. Yahweh indeed did a mighty work in fulfilling his promises to Abraham: 'Look to the rock from which you were cut...; look to Abraham, your father.... When I called him he was but one, and I blessed him and made him many' (Isa. 51:1-2, NIV). Yet, says John, other stones could serve that saving purpose: 'I tell you that God is able from these stones to raise up children for Abraham; (Matt. 3:9b). 'The close similarity of the Hebrew words for *stones* and *children* completes a devastating play on words.'[29]

That John enjoins them to 'produce fruit in keeping with repentance' implies that they have already, to their own satisfaction, both (i) repented of sin and (ii) produced good works that testified to the reality of the repentance and confirmed their Jewish pedigree.[30] It is precisely that manifold

---

'do not presume' captures the sense of the latter. The words expressive of the listeners' thought occur in the order *Patera* [father] *echomen* [we have] *ton Abraam*. The first and third terms form a double accusative: *ton Abraam* (direct object) and *Patera* (predicate object). The statement is usually rendered, 'We have Abraham as our father' (e.g., NIV). But the stress falls on *patera* (the predicate object is placed first in the clause); thus my translation. Bruner 2004a: 94 warns against a kindred trust in Protestant traditions.

[29]France 1985: 92. The Hebrew for 'son' is *bēn*; for 'stone,' *'eben*.

[30]Longenecker 1964: 78, rightly distinguishes between *acting legalism* and *reacting nomism* in the Pharisaism of Jesus' and Paul's day. The former is 'an ordering of one's life in external and formal arrangement according to the Law in order to gain righteousness and/or appear righteous.' The latter means 'the molding of one's life in all its varying relations according to the Law in response to the love and grace of God.' Both kinds of Pharisaism may have been represented in the group at the Jordan. In any case it would be wrong to suggest that *either* legalism *or* nomism, as defined above, fully represents first-century Pharisaism. Cf. the debate (prompted by the writings of E. P. Sanders and others) over the understanding of law in Paul (a former Pharisee); and in that light see the comments of Scott 1995: 273-77; F. Thielman, 'Law,' *DPL*, 529-42; Keener 1999: 125-27; Chamblin 1988: 367-68 (n. 88). As Longenecker says elsewhere (1990: 95), in Galatians 2:15-21 'Paul deals with both "legalism" (i.e., the attempt to gain favor with God by means of Torah observance) and "nomism" (i.e., the response of faith to a God who has acted on one's behalf by living a life governed by Torah).' Paul assaults *both* a Jewish 'national self-righteousness' (cf. Matt. 3:9) by which Gentiles could be excluded from God's favor, *and* a Jewish, or for that matter a Gentile, 'personal self-righteousness' by which one might expect to win God's favor (the Pharisee in the parable of Luke 8:9-14 well illustrates the latter).

assurance of salvation that John's severe language seeks to demolish. True repentance begins with the reasonings of the heart. So let the Pharisees and Sadducees consider what John's chosen name for them – 'brood of vipers' – reveals about their true condition. Let them comprehend that they themselves are objects of a judgment about to fall: 'Who warned *you* to flee from the coming wrath?... Already the axe is laid at the root of the trees,' (Matt. 3:7b, 10a). Let them perceive that, given the condition of their hearts, their vaunted achievements are not 'good fruit' at all; that they themselves are barren trees fit only to be consumed by fire (3:10b). Let them therefore recognize that their Jewish ancestry will not suffice to win vindication from the holy God. And let all those deliberations – and the attendant disillusionment – bring them to true and thorough repentance.

Although John does not expressly describe his listeners as 'hypocrites,' it is this condition that he uncovers – one in which outer appearances contradict and conceal inner realities. Jesus will apply the term *hypokritai* to persons who give alms, pray and fast, not to glorify God but to impress others (6:1-18); who honor God with their lips but whose hearts are far from him (15:7-9); and who keep the lesser requirements of the law but neglect its weightier matters (23:23-24). That the principal objects of Jesus' accusations are Pharisees, and that he describes them in language reminiscent of John's (see 23:33), suggests that John's view of the religious leadership helped to shape Jesus' own.[31] Even receiving John's baptism offers hypocrisy a dual opportunity. One might be ostentatiously baptized by John without truly repenting. And even a confession of sin can be used to impress other people, and bolster the pride that gives birth to hypocrisy.[32]

---

[31]Usually it is Pharisees together with scribes that Jesus denounces (Matt. 15:1, 7-9; 23:1-36); in 22:15-18, it is disciples of the Pharisees together with the Herodians. Jesus does not identify the 'hypocrites' of 6:1-18. But Pharisees and scribes are named in 5:20, and 'righteousness' (*dikaiosyne*; 5:20) recurs in 6:1 – which suggests that these people have inspired the portrait of the hypocrites in chapter 6. See those comments.

[32]See the comments on 6:1-18. One can imagine a confession of sins' being incorporated into the Pharisee's prayer in Luke 18:11-12, without its changing the character of the prayer.

No, says John! Apart from genuine repentance, baptism with water is an empty and meaningless – and dangerous – rite. So whether the Pharisees and Sadducees are baptized or not, their condition is grave indeed. In view of God's imminent wrath, John seeks to jar them out of their false sense of personal and national security. The best news for a person asleep in a burning building, is to hear someone shout, 'There's a fire [cf. 3:12]! Flee for your life [cf. 3:7]!' Cf. Ezekiel 33:1-9.

C. John and Jesus
In verses 11-12 John introduces the One through whom God's Rule will be established and his judgment executed.

Jesus the Baptizer
John is to be followed by another baptizer: 'I [*egō men*] baptize you with [or, in] water for repentance; he who is coming [*ho de...erchomenos*] after me is mightier than I, whose sandals I am not worthy to carry. He will baptize you with the Holy Spirit and fire' (3:11).[33] This figure is also depicted as a farmer who is about to winnow his harvested grain, to gather his wheat into the barn and to consign the chaff to unquenchable fire (3:12).[34]

Like John, the coming one will serve the people of Israel: 'I baptize you.... He will baptize you....' But the latter event is of far greater consequence. It is the very judgment whose nearness John has been predicting: the picture of the farmer ready to use his winnowing fork (Matt. 3:12) matches that of

---

[33]The particle *men* and the conjunction *de* mark a contrast. In accord with John's prophecy of the kingdom's imminent coming, 'he who is coming after me' (*ho...opisō mou erchomenos*; 3:11) is not to be understood spatially (as though John were referring to one of his disciples) but temporally; the participle *ho erchomenos* is a futuristic present (as confirmed by its recurrence in 11:3). *En hydati* may be local ('in water') or instrumental ('with water'); see NASB and NIV texts and mgs. The preceding phrase 'in [*en*] the Jordan River' (3:6) favors the former. The immediate context favors the latter, because the better translation of *en Pneumati Hagiō* is '*with* the Holy Spirit.' Matthew may intend for *en hydati* to bear both nuances.

[34]Cuttings that have been threshed (flailed, thrashed) are tossed into the wind with a winnowing fork (*ptyon*). By this means the chaff (*achyron*) is separated from the grain (*sitos*), and the farmer clears (*diakathariei*) his threshing floor (*alōna*). These are the terms of verse 12.

the woodsman whose ax is about to fell the tree (3:10). The one to come will baptize Israel 'with the Holy Spirit and fire' – a twofold description of a refining and purifying process that affects the whole nation.[35] How individuals are affected by that all-encompassing judgment, depends on their response to John's preaching. Those who truly repent will be personally refined – cleansed from all unrighteousness (cf. 1 John 1:9) – and be like 'wheat gathered into the barn.' Those who do not, will experience the coming wrath and be like chaff consumed 'with unquenchable fire.'[36]

Jesus the Messiah
Who is this figure of John's expectation? That he wears sandals (Matt. 3:11) identifies him as a human being. Yet he is mightier than John – so much greater, in fact, that John considers himself unworthy to render him even the lowliest service.[37] God endows him with authority surpassing that of John. He alone has the right to baptize Israel with the Holy Spirit and fire. The imagery of 3:12 suggests that the nation in

---

[35]As noted, the coming baptism affects the very ones whom John baptizes – 'you' (Matt. 3:11), i.e., Israel, represented in those baptized in the Jordan (3:6). For a kindred process of judging and purging in Israel, see Isaiah 4:4. The Greek phrase *en pneumati hagiō kai pyri* – 'with the Holy Spirit and fire' (Matt. 3:11b) – is a *hendiadys* (literally 'one by two'), a twofold expression of one reality. Indicative of this is that one preposition, *en*, governs both *pneumati hagiō* and *pyri*. So John is not saying that some will be baptized 'with the Holy Spirit,' and others 'with fire.' This, Israel's baptism, is not to be confused with Christian baptism: see further below.

[36]Even starker than this contrast between wheat and chaff is that of Psalm 1, between a tree and chaff. The imagery of a farmer's clearing a threshing floor (Matt. 3:12) sheds light on the nature of the coming baptism (3:11b). For the redeemed, this prophecy is fulfilled when the ascended Christ pours out the Holy Spirit on his people at Pentecost (Acts 2:33, 38; cf. 2:3, 'tongues as of fire.' This outpouring of the Spirit awaited Jesus' glorification (John 7:39) – which explains the language of John 4:1-2 (with 3:26): the disciples' baptizing is an extension of John's, whereas Jesus' own baptizing work is yet to come. In Christian baptism, it is not the Spirit who baptizes; rather, in accord with John's prophecy, *Messiah* baptizes with or in the Spirit (1 Cor. 12:13).

[37]'A Rabbi's disciple was expected to act virtually as his master's slave, but to remove [then carry, *bastazō*, 3:11] his shoes was too low a task even for a disciple' (France 1985: 93).

some sense belongs to him: 'he will clear *his* threshing floor, and gather *his* wheat.'

John foretells the coming of Messiah. The title *ho Christos*, introduced in 1:1 and last seen in 2:4 (in Herod's inquiry), does not appear in Matthew 3. Yet, its very next occurrence recalls and elucidates this passage. John, 'having heard in prison about the works of the Messiah [*ta erga tou Christou*]'; 11:2,) sends disciples to ask Jesus (11:3): 'Are you the coming one [*ho erchomenos*, as in 3:11], or are we to look for someone else?' The testimony of the Baptist in John 3:28 provides corroborative evidence: 'I am not the Messiah [*ho Christos*], but have been sent ahead of him.' The earlier inquiry (John 1:19-28) places the Messiah alongside the latter-day Elijah and the prophet like Moses – which indicates that *ho Christos* denotes the Davidic Messiah.[38]

Yet according to Isaiah 40:3, quoted in Matthew 3:3, John is to prepare the way for Yahweh. We do not conclude from this that John (the latter-day Elijah) precedes Jesus (the Davidic Messiah), who in turn paves the way for Yahweh's own coming. Rather, John is to be followed by Jesus the Messiah, in whom Yahweh is actively present. More than that, Jesus is himself God incarnate. He is the Son of God – God the Son – who is just as surely entitled to the name Yahweh as is God the Father.[39] We cannot be certain whether John believed the person of 3:11-12 to be God incarnate or (instead) a man in whom Yahweh was to be uniquely active. But *Matthew* assuredly presents Jesus as a divine being – as *Emmanouēl*, 'God with us' in the full ontological sense (1:23). In this regard, 11:10 is instructive. In the MT of Malachi 3:1a, Yahweh declares: 'See, I will

---

[38]For the latter-day Elijah, see Malachi 4:5-6; for the prophet like Moses, see Deuteronomy 18:15, 18. For both John and his interrogators, 'Messiah [*ho Christos*],' 'Elijah' and 'the Prophet' are parallel strands of expectation. For confirmation that John is to be followed by a *Davidic* Messiah, see Luke 1:32-33, 69; 2:4, 11.

[39]On Jesus as the Son of God, see above on Matthew 2:15 and below on 3:17; and the discussion on pages 139-41. In light of Luke 2:9 – 'the glory of the Lord [*ho Kyriou*, i.e. of Yahweh] shone around them' – see 2:11, 'a Savior who is Christ the Lord [*Christos Kyrios*].'

send my messenger, and he will prepare the way before my face [for this last phrase the LXX has *pro prosōpou mou*].' Yet Matthew quotes the latter clause to read: 'he will prepare your [*sou*] way before you [*sou*]'. God the Father (Yahweh) now addresses his Son (Yahweh) concerning John the Baptist (Yahweh's messenger).[40]

Jesus the Savior

In accord with the prophecy of Isaiah 7:14, the divine Messiah offers grace amid judgment. In the coming holocaust he will refine his people and gather them like wheat into a granary (Matt. 3:11-12). So John, the very one who foretells swift and severe judgment, is rightly termed a bearer of glad tidings (Luke 3:18, *euangelizomai*). The prophet who chooses language least likely to win his listeners' favor, offers them the best possible news for a critical hour. For by 'crying out in the desert' that Yahweh is about to invade Israel in holy and terrible splendor (Isa. 40:3), and that the people must therefore repent of their sin, John marks the way out of servitude and punishment, and into the experience of Yahweh's tenderest consolations (Isa. 40:1-2). And the Messiah who will precipitate the coming judgment is the very One appointed to save his people from the wrath to come.[41] John *proclaims* 'a baptism of repentance for the forgiveness of sins [*eis aphesin hamartiōn*]' (Mark 1:4). But the *provision* is made by Messiah

---

[40]For the language of Matthew 11:10, see also Mark 1:2 and Luke 7:27; all three texts cite Exodus 23:20 as well as Malachi 3:1 (see comments on 11:10). The change in language testifies to the progressive character of biblical revelation.

[41]See Matthew 1:21; 1 Thessalonians 1:10. 'For it is not true...that repentance is put in first place [Matt. 3:2], as though it were the cause of the remission of sins, or came before God's starting to be well-favoured towards us, but men are told to repent that they may perceive the reconciliation that is offered to them' (Calvin 1994: 115). Cf. Chamblin 1963: 7-15. As Yahweh called the Nazirite Samuel in the face of priestly corruption (1 Sam. 2:12–3:21), so he anoints the Nazirite John, both of whose parents are descended from Aaron (Luke 1:5), to prepare for Jesus the *Nazōraios* (Matt. 2:23), who 'will purify the sons of Levi' so that acceptable offerings may again be brought to Yahweh, (Mal. 3:2-4). See comments on Matthew 21:12-17.

himself, whose own blood will be 'poured out for many for the forgiveness of sins [*eis aphesin hamartiōn*]' (Matt. 26:28).[42]

---

[42]John exhorts the people to repent, says Ridderbos 1962: 212, 'so that those who obey may forthwith hear the definitively exonerating sentence of acquittal out of the mouth of the coming One who is mightier than John.' For Jesus' words of acquittal, see, e.g., Matthew 9:2b.

II.
'GOD IN THREE PERSONS, BLESSED TRINITY'[1]
(3:13-17)

Matthew now describes an event in which all persons of the Godhead participate. Jesus' commission that believers be baptized 'in the name of the Father and of the Son and of the Holy Spirit' (28:19) recalls the present scene.

'Then Jesus came from Galilee to the Jordan...' (3:13a). The name *Iēsous* appears for the first time since 2:1, and reminds us of the angel's command to Joseph (1:21). That he comes 'from Galilee' recalls 2:22-23, including the term *Nazōraios*. Jesus 'came [*paraginetai*]...to the Jordan.' He appears for the first time as an adult; we are reminded of the appearance of the magi in Jerusalem (2:1) and of John in the desert of Judea (3:1), the only other instances of the verb *paraginomai* in Matthew.[2] That Jesus comes to the Jordan presupposes all that Matthew has told us about John's activity at the river (3:4-6).

A. Jesus and John

Jesus comes 'to John in order to be baptized by him' (3:13b). 'But John tried to prevent him, saying: "*I* [*egō*] have need to be baptized by *you* [*sou*] – yet *you* [*sy*] are coming to *me* [*me*]?"' (3:14).

John's statement reveals his awareness that this Jesus is the figure of his expectation (Matt. 3:11-12). It is probable that instruction received from his parents Zechariah and Elizabeth helped John to make this identification. At the same time, it is virtually certain that John and Jesus meet for the first time here

---

[1]Words from the hymn 'Holy, Holy, Holy!' by Reginald Heber, published posthumously in 1827.

[2]*Paraginetai* in 3:13 is an 'historical present,' as in 3:1 (see those comments).

at the Jordan.[3] Knowing Jesus to be the Messiah, John cannot imagine his receiving 'a baptism of repentance,' so he tries to dissuade him.[4] Interpreted in light of John's question, the first part of his statement means not that he wishes to be baptized with the Holy Spirit and with fire,[5] but that it is *he*, not Jesus, who needs John's kind of baptism. It is indeed to be expected that John – believing his message about the coming kingdom to be true – would repent of his own sin before calling upon other Israelites to do so.[6]

But Jesus insists: 'Let it be so now; for it is right for us in this way to fulfill all righteousness' (3:15). By receiving John's baptism Jesus, by an exercise of his unique authority, validates John's whole ministry.[7] But Jesus' main reason for seeking baptism lies elsewhere.

John baptizes 'with water for repentance' (Matt. 3:11a). Astonishingly, Jesus the Savior submits to – indeed, insists on – receiving a baptism thus defined. At the very threshold of his Messianic career, he identifies in the closest way with the sinners whom he has come to save (1:21).[8] It is most significant, however, that Jesus is *not* said to confess his sins – as the others who come for baptism are expressly

---

[3]Cf. Luke 1:80; and John's words in John 1:31a ('I did not know him'), with verses 29–34.

[4]The verb *diekōlyen*, from *diakōlyō*) is a conative imperfect, so not 'he prevented' but 'he tried to prevent' (cf. NASB, ESV). On the grammar, see *GGBB*, 550.

[5]Such an individualizing of that baptism seems out of place, if (as suggested above) it signals the refining of the whole nation.

[6]For John thus to heed his own command, would of course strengthen the authority of his preaching. However, we are never expressly told that John received his own baptism.

[7]Conversely, there is evidence that John's preaching helped to shape that of Jesus (it is even possible that Jesus sat under John's teaching for a time): Jesus' opening proclamation (Matt. 4:17) is identical to that of John (3:2). We earlier noted that John and Jesus shared convictions about Israel's religious leadership.

[8]In Sayers 1943: 324 (play 12), Mary Magdalene says: 'The Master's the only good man I ever met who knew how miserable it felt to be bad. It was as if he got right inside you, and *felt* all the horrible things you were doing to yourself.'

said to do (3:6). The NT forcefully affirms both that Jesus is the sin-bearer and that he himself is not guilty of committing sin.[9]

Jesus declares that it is 'right [*prepon*] for us [*hēmin*, Jesus and John] in this way [*houtōs*, i.e., in Jesus' baptism] to fulfill all righteousness [*plērōsai pasan dikaiosynēn*].' These closing words indicate that by participating together in this event John and Jesus shall be obedient to all that God requires, to all that he has determined to be right, for this occasion – namely, that Jesus receive a baptism intended for sinners, be anointed by the Spirit and be consecrated by the Father, at the inception of his public ministry.[10] Thus understanding *dikaiosynē* accords well with Jesus' later use of the noun in Matthew.[11] Yet this instance of the term is richer still. The words of the Father, about to be quoted (Matt. 3:17), allude to Isaiah 42:1, which opens the first of the Servant songs. The major work the Father requires of the Son – that which above all else is 'right' for the Son to do and which will entail his utter submission to the Father's will – is that he, Yahweh's righteous Servant, should save his people from their sins by himself bearing their iniquities (Isa. 53:11). That climactic event – Jesus'

---

[9]Paul carefully states that God sent his own Son 'in the likeness of sinful flesh' (Rom. 8:3) – not 'in the likeness of flesh' or 'in sinful flesh.' See also 2 Corinthians 5:21; 1 Peter 2:22, 24; John 8:46; Hebrews 4:15. For strong arguments against the view (associated with Edward Irving and others) that the incarnate Christ assumed a *fallen* human nature, see Donald Macleod, 'Christology,' *DSCHT*, 172-77.

[10]The adjective 'all' (*pasan*), viewed within the immediate context, suggests this manifold understanding. Tasker 1961: 51 paraphrases Matthew 3:15b, 'It becomes us to comply with all that God requires of us.' 'By having Himself baptised by John Jesus fulfils a requirement of the divine will manifest to him' (G. Delling, *TDNT* 6: 294). Jesus underwent baptism 'to offer His father full obedience' (Calvin 1994: 130).

[11]For these instances, see 5:6, 10, 20; 6:1, 33; 21:32. This last verse – 'John came to you in the way of righteousness [*en hodō dikaiosynēs*]' – harks back in part to 3:15, and follows a statement about doing 'the will of the father' (21:31). Matthew 6:33 is likewise to be joined to 6:10; 7:21. 'For Matthew, the "way of righteousness" means "doing the will of the Father"' (Stanton 1989: 71).

atoning sacrifice – is foreshadowed here at the Jordan
River.[12] The belief that Matthew 3:15 alludes to Isaiah 53
is strengthened by the presence of *plēroō*, because at
least thirteen of the other fifteen instances of this verb in
Matthew denote the fulfillment of OT writings.[13]

John, like Joseph before him, precisely obeys. Once Jesus
commands, 'Let it be so [*aphes*] now' (Matt. 3:15a) and gives the
reason for the command, 'for [*gar*] it is right...' (3:15b), John 'lets
[*aphiēsin*] him' (3:15c).[14] Does not John 1:29 – 'Behold the Lamb
of God who takes away the sin of the world!' – indicate that
John grasped the implications of Jesus' words in Matthew 3:15?

B. Jesus and the Spirit

In this record of Jesus' meeting with John, there is nothing
to match the statement that the people 'were baptized in

---

[12]Isaiah 53:11b, 'by his knowledge my righteous servant will justify
many, and he will bear their iniquities' (NIV), is a construction 'unique in
the Old Testament' and 'one of the fullest statements of atonement theology
ever penned' (Motyer 1993: 441, 442). See also Psalm 65:3, 5; Matthew 20:28;
26:28; John 1:29 (words of John the Baptist); Romans 3:21-26. In Mark 10:38-39
and Luke 12:50, Jesus calls his approaching death a *baptisma*: he will be
engulfed and drowned. Here too, 'the way of righteousness' entails 'doing
the Father's will' (Matt. 26:42). Morris 1965: 41 says of Matthew 3:15 that
'at this moment Jesus set Himself to fulfil that righteousness that meant
justifying sinful men.' Cf. Ladd 1993: 184 ('The righteousness he would
fulfill is probably that of Isaiah 53:11'); France 1985: 95.

[13]For the thirteen, see 1:22; 2:15, 17, 23; 4:14; 5:17; 8:17; 12:17; 13:35; 21:4;
26:54, 56; 27:9. One of the remaining two, 13:48, refers to filling a net with fish.
In the other, 23:32, Jesus tells his hearers to 'fill up the measure of their fathers'
– i.e., to bring to full measure their ancestors' sins against the OT prophets – so
that this usage approaches that of the first thirteen. Concerning 3:15, Keener
says (1999: 132): since 'Jesus sometimes "fulfilled" the prophetic Scriptures
by identifying with Israel's history and completing Israel's mission,' this
baptism 'represents Jesus' ultimate identification with Israel at the climactic
stage in her history.... Jesus' baptism, like his impending death..., would be
vicarious, embraced on behalf of others with whom the Father had called
him to identify.'

[14]*Aphes* is an aorist imperative, and *aphiēsin* a present indicative (and
historical present), of the verb *aphiēmi*. Blomberg 1992: 86, n. 82, calls attention
to the use of the same verb in Matthew 4:11a ('Then the devil left [*aphiēsin*]
him'): 'Though the verb...is used in two different ways, the two passages
are parallel in that both John and the devil, wittingly or unwittingly, were
trying to deter Jesus' appointed course but failed.'

the Jordan River by him' (Matt. 3:6).[15] Matthew focuses on what happens before and after Jesus' actual baptism. In the preceding verses he has explained the character of the event. He now reports: 'Jesus, having been baptized [*baptistheis*], came up [*anebē*] immediately from the water; and behold [*kai idou*], heaven [*hoi ouranoi*] was opened [to him], and he saw the Spirit of God coming down [*katabainon*] as a dove and coming upon him [*erchomenon ep' auton*]' (3:16).[16]

The descent of God's Spirit recalls Genesis 1:2, where God, in causing his Spirit to hover over the waters, begins to fashion cosmos out of chaos. That the Spirit descends in the likeness of a dove recalls God's sending a dove to Noah to mark the end of the flood and the return of order.[17] The dawn of God's rule signals not just the end of an old order but new creation, not only judgment but rescue from judgment. The arrival of God's Messiah – 'the prince of peace [*šālôm*]' (Isa. 9:6) – promises restoration and wholeness to the people of God.[18]

The Spirit by whose power Jesus was conceived in Mary's womb (Matt. 1:18, 20), now anoints him for his manifold mission – including the imminent ordeal in the desert (4:1). Just as 'the Spirit of Yahweh came mightily upon David' from the day Samuel anointed him (1 Sam. 16:13), so now the Spirit anoints

---

[15]Contrast Mark 1:9: 'Jesus came...and was baptized in the Jordan by John.'

[16]Like Matthew, Luke 3:21 uses an aorist passive participle: 'Jesus, having been baptized' (*Iēsou baptisthentos*, a genitive absolute), better represented in ESV than in NIV. In keeping with Matthew 3:2, the plural *hoi ouranoi* is translated as a singular. *Anebē* and *katabainon* come from matching verbs, *anabainō* ('go, come up') and *katabainō* ('go, come down'). The phrase 'to him' (*autō*) is textually doubtful. On *kai idou*, see below on 3:17.

[17]See Dunn 1970: 27, together with the sources he cites; and Keener 1999: 132-33. Is Jesus' emergence 'out of the water' (3:16a) meant to recall the deliverance from the flood? Observes Farrer 1965: 28, 'Jesus' baptism, in being a new *beginning*, recalls the Creation; in being a *new* beginning, it recalls the days of Noah.'

[18]'The presence of the [S]pirit is a sign of the dawn of the time of salvation. Its return means the end of judgment and the beginning of the time of grace. God is turning towards his people' (Jeremias 1971: 85).

the Son of David to equip him for service.[19] The Spirit not only comes down from heaven: he 'comes upon' Jesus. And there he stays: John the Baptist testifies in John 1:32, 'I have beheld the Spirit coming down as a dove out of heaven, and he remained upon him.'[20] Not only so: according to Mark 1:10, the Spirit entered 'into' Jesus.[21] The endowment is not merely external: to equip him for service, the Spirit's power floods Jesus' whole being. So Isaiah had prophesied concerning the Branch (*nētser*) that would spring forth from the root of Jesse: 'The Spirit of Yahweh will rest upon him' (Isa. 11:2), upon the child conceived in the womb of a virgin (7:14), upon the divine Messiah destined to reign forever from David's throne (9:6-7). And thus Isaiah had prophesied concerning the Servant of Yahweh: 'I will put my Spirit on him' (42:1), which Matthew quotes in 12:18 and alludes to in the verse about to be considered.[22]

C. Jesus and the Father

'And behold [*kai idou*], a voice out of heaven [*ek tōn ouranōn*] saying: "This is my Son [*ho huios mou*], the Beloved [*ho agapētos*], in whom I take delight [*en hō eudokēsa*]"' (3:17). Here, as in verse 16, the opening *kai idou* prepares for a dramatic event.[23]

---

[19]See Luke 4:18 ('the Spirit of the Lord is upon me, because he anointed me...'); Acts 4:27; 10:38 ('Jesus from Nazareth, how God anointed him with the Holy Spirit and power...'). The verb *chriō* ('anoint'), used in all those verses, never occurs in Matthew.

[20]Matthew 3:16, Luke 3:22 and John 1:32 report that the Spirit came, or remained, *ep' auton* ('upon him'). John 3:34 testifies that God 'gives the Spirit without measure' to the One he has sent. Luke stresses how substantial that endowment is: 'in bodily form [*sōmatikō*] upon him.'

[21]BAGD renders the closing three words of Mark 1:10 – *katabainon eis auton* – '*come down* and enter *into him*' (s.v. *katabainō*, 1.).

[22]Cf. comments on Matthew 1:23 and 2:23. Calvin, noting Isaiah 42:3, 'a bruised reed he will not break [etc.]' (quoted in Matthew 12:20), thinks the Spirit's descent in the form of a dove signals 'Christ's gentleness in calling sinners in kind and soft tones to hope for salvation' (1994: 131).

[23]*Idou*, as an aorist middle imperative of *eidon* ('Look!'), takes a circumflex accent. When used as a demonstrative particle, as here, it takes an acute accent. Like the Hebrew *hinēh*, the particle often anticipates the disclosure of something significant or startling or splendid. Thus in Matthew 1–2, *idou* prefaces appearances by an angel of the Lord (1:20; 2:13, 19); the announcement of a virginal conception (1:23, where it translates

From the heaven which opened for the Spirit's descent the Father now speaks, adding his testimony to that of John and of the Spirit.[24] The Father has been testifying about his Son from the beginning of the gospel – by means of his prior disclosures in the Hebrew Scriptures. See, e.g., the comments on the genealogy (Matt. 1:1-17); on the quotations from Isaiah 7:14 (1:23), Micah 5:2 (2:6) and Hosea 11:1 (2:15); and on *Nazōraios* (Matt. 2:23).[25] Now, with further allusions to those disclosures, the Father speaks directly and audibly about the One of whom he spoke indirectly in 2:15 ('Out of Egypt I called my Son').

The Royal Son
The opening words – 'This is my Son' – recall Psalm 2. To the king whom he has established on Zion (3:6), Yahweh declares: 'You are my son; today I have begotten you' (3:7, NRSV). These words echo those of 2 Samuel 7, where Yahweh promises to establish the kingdom of David's offspring: 'He is the one who will build a house for my Name, and I will establish the throne of his kingdom forever. I will be his father, and he will be my son.... Your house and your kingdom will endure forever before me; your throne will be established forever' (7:13-14a, 16, NIV). This promise embraces Solomon (who built the temple) and his successors in the kingdom of Judah (all of whom will sin; 7:14b). Yet, it is only through the coming of the Messiah that David's 'throne will be established forever.' It is ultimately Jesus whom Yahweh addresses in Psalm 2:7.[26] It is

---

MT's *hinēh*); the announcement of the magi's arrival (2:1); and the report of the star's progress (2:9). Cf. BAGD s.v. *idou*.

[24]In Matthew 3:17, as in verses 16 and 2, the plural of *ouranos* is used. On the relation of the Father's voice to the *bath qol* ('daughter of a voice') in rabbinic literature, see Keener 1999: 133-34.

[25]On the OT as revelation from the Father through the Spirit, see 2 Timothy 3:16 (including the word *theopneustos*, 'inspired by God,' or 'God-breathed') and 2 Peter 1:21 ('men carried by the Holy Spirit spoke from God').

[26]For the NT's application of these texts to Jesus, see Luke 1:32-33 (2 Sam. 7:12-16), Acts 13:33 (Ps. 2:7), Acts 4:25-27 (Ps. 2:1-2), and Hebrews 1:5 (both Psalm 2:7 and 2 Samuel 7:14). The closing words of Psalm 2:7 – 'today I have begotten you' – are applied in Acts 13:33-34 to Jesus' resurrection, and in Hebrews 1:3-5 to his ascension. Both applications accord well with the coronation scene reflected in the psalm; significantly, those words are absent from Matthew 3:17 and even from 17:5.

therefore not at all surprising to find 'the kings of the earth' – Herod and Archelaus – taking their stand against Jesus, Yahweh's Anointed (Psalm 2:1-2 and Matthew 2).[27]

In accord with the psalm, the parallels to Matthew 3:17 in Mark (1:11) and Luke (3:22) employ the second person: 'You are my Son.' Matthew's third person, 'This is my Son,' is addressed both to John (to enlarge his understanding of Jesus) and to Jesus' disciples (as is the Father's identical affirmation in 17:5), i.e., to Matthew's readers.[28] In newly declaring Jesus to be his Son in the wake of the baptism, God ratifies all that Matthew 1 and 2 have disclosed about Jesus as the Davidic Messiah and King of the Jews. Moreover, God's fidelity to the Davidic covenant serves to fulfill his covenant with Abraham: through Jesus, the son of Abraham (1:1), God will raise up children for the patriarch (Matt. 3:9) – daughters as well as sons, Gentiles as well as Jews.[29]

---

[27]Currid 1994: 124 notes that 'the plotting and revolt of the heathen nations against the Davidic king in Psalm 2 [prefigure] the scheming of Herod and others to kill the Son of David, the true king of Israel.' Cf. again Acts 4:25-27.

[28]Cf. Gundry 1994: 53. In John 1, the Baptist testifies that his ignorance about Jesus (1:31) was dispelled when he saw the Spirit descend upon him (1:32-33) and (it is implied) when he heard the Father's voice (1:34). I take this passage to mean, not that John receives public confirmation that Jesus is the Messiah, but that the baptism and the voice from heaven reveal to him that the Messiah is divine, 'the Son of God' (1:34b). Cf. Calvin 1994: 130. Such a verse as this also makes it clear that Jewish opponents of Matthew's churches 'could not reject Jesus and simultaneously please God the Father, as they claimed' (Keener 1999: 135); cf. 'Confronting the Opposition,' pages 175-77 above.

[29]The closing words of Matthew 3:9 are *tekna tō Abraam*. *Tekna* ('children') embraces both males and females; *tō Abraam* is a dative of advantage ('for Abraham's benefit'). In the allusion to 2 Samuel 7:14 in 2 Corinthians 6:18, the original promise has been broadened to include all Christians as 'sons and daughters' of God. The inclusion of Gentiles in God's Covenant of Grace is already plain from the genealogy (Matt. 1:1-17) and the visit of the magi (2:1-12), and will become plainer as the book progresses. For Gentiles as heirs of the promises to Abraham, see also Galatians 3:6-29. Cf. the discussion of 'the People of God,' pages 148-54 above.

The Beloved Son

The latter part of the Father's declaration – 'the Beloved [*ho agapētos*], with whom I am well pleased [*en hō eudokēsa*]' – alludes to Isaiah 42:1. Matthew's own indebtedness to the Father for this statement is clear from 12:17-21, where he quotes Isaiah 42:1-4 to explain that Jesus' ministry to the sick is perfectly in accord with his concept of Messiahship (Matt. 12:15-16). The wording of 12:18a – 'Behold [*idou*] my Servant whom I have chosen, my Beloved [*ho agapētos mou*], in whom I take delight [*eis hon eudokēsen hē psychē mou*]' – confirms that Isaiah 42:1 is indeed in view in Matthew 3:17.[30] The remainder of the quotation (12:18b-21) sounds two further themes from Matthew 1–3: Jesus' anointing by the Spirit and the salvation of the Gentiles.

By thus joining Isaiah 42:1 to Psalm 2:7 in Matthew 3:17, the Father expounds the character of Jesus' kingship. He is the Servant-King, a regal figure so secure in who he is – the Father's beloved Son – that he is free to serve rather than tyrannize his subjects, and to deal gently rather than harshly with the lowliest and the weakest of them (Matt. 12:20; 11:25-30). Astonishingly, it is by the very means of his lowly service that all earthly tyrants will be subdued, and all nations made his possession.[31]

Just as the first Servant song (Isa. 42:1-4) prepares for the fourth (52:13–53:12), so Matthew 3:17 and 12:18-21 prepare for 20:28 and 26:26-28, where Jesus speaks of the Son's ultimate obedience and of the Servant's supreme sacrifice. Given that progression, together with the foreshadowing of Jesus' death in

---

[30]Behind the *agapētos* of Matthew 12:18 and 3:17 is the Hebrew *bāchîr*, for which a more common translation is *eklektos* (so LXX at Isa. 42:1). Matthew's *psychē* (= LXX) renders the Hebrew *nepeš*, and is better rendered 'I' (NIV) than 'soul' (NASB), so bringing 12:18 into closer conformity to 3:17. The verb *eudokēsa* (*eudokēsen* in 12:18), a timeless aorist based on the Hebrew stative perfect *rātsāh* ('be pleased with, favourable to,' BDB), is properly translated by a present tense, 'in whom I delight.' The view that Matthew has converted the *eudokēsa* of 3:17 from a timeless aorist into an 'historical aorist referring to God's pleasure in the baptism of Jesus' (Gundry 1994: 53) is possible but (given the recurrence of the term in 12:18) improbable.

[31]The Servant's kingship which Yahweh affirms by joining Isaiah 42:1 to Psalm 2:7 (and thus to the whole psalm; see especially 2:8) is evident in the Servant song itself. See the quotation of Isaiah 42:1-4 in Matthew 12:18-21; cf. the portrait of Messiah in Isaiah 11:1-5. Yahweh likewise established Jesus' ancestor David as king so that he would serve Israel (see 2 Samuel 5:12;

his baptism, I think it highly probable that the *agapātos* of 3:17 alludes not only to Isaiah 42:1, but also to Genesis 22:2. Here God instructs Abraham: 'Take your son, your only son Isaac, whom you love [LXX, *ton huion sou ton agapēton, hon ēgapēsas, ton Isaak*], and go to the land of Moriah, and offer him there as a burnt offering....'[32] Matthew's wanting to include Genesis 22 would help to explain his choosing *agapētos* instead of *eklektos* in citing Isaiah 42:1.

Both Isaac and Jesus were sons of Abraham (Matt. 1:1-2). Yet, whereas Isaac's life was spared (Gen. 22), Jesus' would not be (Matt. 27). Already, at the Jordan, it is clear to the Father and the Son, though not to the Baptist, 'that it would need something thicker than Jordan water to bind the New Israel together, that the New Covenant that would create the New Israel must be sealed in Messianic blood.'[33]

The Father's love for his Son, his only Son – 'the Beloved, in whom I delight' – finds expression in the gift of the Spirit. 'I will put my Spirit on him,' Yahweh promised concerning his Servant (Isa. 42:1), echoing 11:5, 'The Spirit of Yahweh will rest upon him.' And so it has come to pass (Matt. 3:16). The Father's voice, together with the descent of the Spirit, affords a glimpse, but only a glimpse, into the inexhaustible depths of the intimate, joyous and perpetual fellowship within the Holy Trinity.[34] But the Father's words are also spoken in light of what Jesus has just done: he has received John's baptism and embarked upon the appointed path to the cross. The Father's

---

Davis 1999: 55-56). Yet David, unlike Jesus, proved to be a flawed servant (see 2 Samuel 11; Davis, ibid., 118-20). Likewise 1 Kings 10:9 better applies to Jesus than to Solomon; cf. Matthew 12:42.

[32]ESV. LXX's *ēgapēsas* is an aorist of *agapaō* ('love'), for the Hebrew *'āhab*. LXX's choice of *agapēton* ('beloved') for the Hebrew *yāchîd* ('only') is understandable, given a parent's special love for an only son.

[33]Manson 1977: 47. Romans 8:32a, 'he who did not spare his own Son but delivered him up for us all,' probably alludes to Genesis 22.

[34]Cf. Matthew 11:25-30; 1 Corinthians 2:6-16; John 1:18; 1 John 4:8b ('God is love,' indicating that there must be at least two persons in the Godhead – as confirmed e.g. in John 3:35). Earlier theologians used the Greek term *perichōrēsis* ('mutual enfolding') to describe love among the persons in the Godhead. See Lewis 1952: 134-38. For Augustine's reflections on the disclosure of the Holy Trinity in Matthew 3:16-17, see *ACC* 1a: 54.

words of affection and approval will undergird the Son for the ordeal that awaits him in the desert, and indeed for the duration of his ministry.

The love between the Father and the Son, while incomparable, is not exclusive. It is love for the fallen world that causes the Father to send his Son upon his mission; and the Son goes to the cross because he loves the sinners he came to save.[35]

---

[35]These realities – most fully expressed in John's writings (e.g., John 3:16; 13:1, 34; 1 John 4:9-10) – are also evident in such passages as Matthew 11:25-30; 20:28; 26:26-28.

Section 5

'The Saviour of the World is here'[1]
(Matt. 4:1-25)

Having come to the desert to be baptized by John at the Jordan, Jesus is now 'led up into the desert' (4:1) – i.e., from the river (which is below sea level) onto higher ground.[2] Having defeated the devil, and hearing of John's arrest, Jesus returns to Galilee (4:12; cf. 3:13). But he chooses to live, not in Nazareth but in Capernaum (4:13). Here he begins to preach (4:17); here he chooses his first disciples (4:18-22); and from here he travels over the whole of Galilee, drawing crowds from this region and beyond, including places whence people had come for John's baptism (4:23-25).[3]

---

[1]Words from the hymn 'Lift Up Your Heads, Ye Mighty Gates!' by Georg Weissel (1642); translated by Catherine Winkworth (1855).

[2]John was 'in the desert [*en tē erēmō*]' (Matt. 3:1, 3). Jesus 'was led up into the desert [*eis tēn erēmon*]' (4:1), probably to 'a wilder part' than that of 3:1 (Bengel 1873: 148).

[3]With 4:25, 'huge crowds from...Jerusalem and Judea and beyond the Jordan,' compare 3:5, 'Jerusalem and all Judea and the whole area around the Jordan.'

I.

'THE SON OF GOD GOES FORTH TO WAR'[1]
(4:1-11)

'Then Jesus was led up into the desert by the Spirit to be tested by the devil' (4:1). The opening 'Then' (*Tote*) and the references to Jesus and the Spirit join the ensuing episode to Jesus' baptism. The devil is here named for the first time in Matthew.[2] See also Mark 1:12-13 and Luke 4:1-13.

A. The Devil

Matthew speaks of 'the devil,' *ho diabolos*, four times in this passage (4:1, 5, 8, 11) and only twice more in his gospel (13:39; 25:41). *Diabolos*, the source of our word 'devil,' is related to the verb *diaballō*, 'to charge with hostile intent, to slander,' and to the noun *diabolē*, 'slander.'[3] So a *diabolos* is a slanderer, a falsifier. Three times in the NT the term denotes a slanderous human being.[4] All but one of the remaining thirty-four occurrences denote the devil; and, in twenty-nine of the thirty-three, the definite article is included.[5] He is *ho diabolos*, '*the* slanderer,' a liar without peer (John 8:44), 'the ancient serpent, who is called the devil...the accuser of our brothers' (Rev. 12:9–10).

---

[1]The opening words of a hymn by Reginald Heber, published posthumously in 1827.

[2]The name 'Jesus' appeared nine times in Matthew 1–3, most notably in 1:21. For previous references to the Holy Spirit, see 1:18, 20; 3:11, 16.

[3]See BAGD s.v. *diaballō* and *diabolē*. 'Devil' is traceable through the Middle English *devel*, the Old English *dēofol* and the Late Latin *diabolus*, to the Greek *diabolos*.

[4]All appear in the Pastoral Epistles, and in the plural: 1 Timothy 3:11; 2 Timothy 3:3; Titus 2:3.

[5]That one exception is John 6:70, 'one of you is a devil,' Jesus' description of Judas, the devil's instrument (cf. Luke 22:3; John 13:2, 27). The definite article is absent from Acts 13:10; 1 Peter 5:8; Revelation 12:9; 20:2, for grammatical, not conceptual, reasons.

In 4:10, Jesus addresses the devil as *Satanas*, which transliterates the Hebrew *śātān*, 'adversary,' usually *ha Śātān*, 'the Adversary' (as in Job 1:6–2:7; and Zechariah 3:1-2, where the matching verb *Śātan* also occurs). All thirty-six instances of *satanas* in the NT denote the devil; accordingly, twenty-nine of the thirty-six include the definite article. He is 'the Satan' (*ho Satanas*), 'the Adversary.'[6] In the desert and beyond, he is Jesus' arch-enemy. So too will he be to Jesus' followers: 'Your adversary [*antidikos*], the devil, goes about as a roaring lion seeking someone to devour' (1 Pet. 5:8).[7]

Matthew also calls him 'the tempter [*ho peirazōn*]' (4:3); cf. Luke 4:13, 'And when the devil had finished every temptation [*peirasmos*]....' Yet, the matching term in Matthew 4:1, *peirasthēnai*, was translated 'to be *tested*.'[8] Why this difference?

B. Testing and Temptation

The verb *peirazō* may be used in a favorable sense. In John 6:6, Jesus 'tests' Philip, and, in the LXX of Genesis 22:1, this verb is used of God's testing of Abraham (Hebrews 11:17, recalling this event, uses the same verb). Likewise, the Spirit brings Jesus into a place of testing for a good purpose. But when the devil tests, his motive is always malevolent, his designs are always destructive and his singular purpose is always to separate persons from God. Especially will this be so in his assaults upon Jesus, who poses the gravest threat to his dominion (Matt. 12:25-29).[9] It is true that Jesus is led up into the desert 'by [*hypo*] the Spirit.' But he is 'to be tested by [*hypo*] the devil' (4:1). The devil is the source, not merely the instrument, of

---

[6]Cf. Matthew 12:26, 'If the Adversary [*ho Satanas*] casts out the Adversary [*ton Satanan*]....' The *Satana* of 4:10 and 16:23 is vocative, so the absence of the article is expected.

[7]Peter knew this well from his and the other disciples' personal experience. Says Jesus: 'Simon, Simon, behold Satan has asked to sift you [plural] like wheat...' (Luke 22:31). In Revelation 20:2, 'the ancient serpent' is called both *Diabolos* and *ho Satanas*.

[8]*Peirazōn* is a present participle, and *peirasthēnai* an aorist infinitive, of the verb *peirazō*.

[9]Here in the desert 'the sole object of [Satan's] game is for Christ to move away from God' (Calvin 1994: 137). It will be the same for Christ's followers. In Lewis 1953: 64, Screwtape counsels Wormwood: 'But do remember, the only thing that matters is the extent to which you separate the man from the Enemy.'

testing as temptation.[10] At the same time, the Spirit's action makes it clear that Jesus' ordeal is to serve God's own purpose.[11] God the Father and God the Spirit, both of whom met with Jesus at the Jordan, will now test his resolve to be and to remain God's Servant-King (Matt. 3:17). God seeks to strengthen that resolve by testing; Satan, to weaken or destroy it.

We learn from Hebrews 4:15 that Jesus 'has in every respect been tempted [*pepeirasmenon*] as we are, yet was without sin.'[12] Theologians have responded to such evidence with three formulations: 1. Jesus was able to sin (*posse peccare*). But we have no evidence that he sinned; this verse declares the contrary. What proof then do we have that he was able to sin? 2. Jesus was not able to sin (*non posse peccare*). But in this case, how can Jesus truly be

---

[10]Cf. BAGD s.v. *peirazō*, 2. '*try, make trial of, put to the test*': b. 'in a good sense of God or Christ'; d. 'in a bad sense...of enticement to sin, *tempt.*' Whereas *dia* with the genitive denotes means ('through'), *hypo* with the genitive denotes source. E.g., Isaiah 7:14 is spoken 'by [*hypo*] the Lord through [*dia*] the prophet' (Matt. 1:22). Cf. James 1:13, 'Let no one say when he is tempted [*peirazomenos*], "I am being tempted by God [*apo theou*, literally "from God"]." For God cannot be tempted to do evil [*apeirastos estin kakōn*], nor does he himself tempt [*peirazei*] anyone [to do evil: so the preceding clause indicates].' The phrase *apo theou* signals that the preposition *apo* is beginning to take over the functions of *hypo*; thus Davids 1982: 82. See also the comments on Matthew 6:13.

[11]As did the testings of Job: see 1:6-27, with chapters 38–42. The Spirit's action is expressed more strongly in Mark 1:12, if the verb *ekballō* as used here means not 'send out' but 'drive out' (cf. BAGD s.v., 1. and 2.). The dual account of David's census in 2 Samuel 24 and 1 Chronicles 21 is *unlike* Matthew 4:1-11 in that Satan (1 Chron. 21:1) is the instrument of Yahweh's *wrath* against Israel (2 Sam. 24:1), and in that Satan's temptation incites David to *sin* (2 Sam. 24:10; 1 Chron. 21:8). That account is *like* Matthew 4:1-11 in that Satan's tempting of David paves the way for Yahweh's mercy and salvation (2 Sam. 24:16, 25; 1 Chron. 21:15, 26-27).

[12]Brown 1982: 307 notes that some, including Augustine, relate the three temptations in the desert to the three enticements of the world (*kosmos*) in 1 John 2:15-16 – 'the desire of the flesh' (Matt. 4:3), 'the desire of the eyes' (4:8-9) and 'the pride of life' (4:5-6). Both these passages have been linked to Genesis 3:5-6 (see *ACC* 1a: 62; Marshall 1978b: 146, who judges that the correspondence 'is not especially close'). Brown 1997: 177, n. 11, detects kindred temptations in John 6:26-27 (par. Matt. 4:3), John 6:15 (par. 4:8-9), and John 7:1-9 (par. 4:5-6).

tempted? The affirmation of Hebrews 4:15 gains its force from the reality, the power and the seductiveness of the temptations. 3. He was able not to sin (*posse non peccare*). This to my mind is the most satisfactory formulation. Jesus, by constant reliance upon the heavenly Father and upon the Spirit of power (Matt. 3:16-17) steadfastly resists and repels the temptations of the devil, as the present passage will show. He therefore knows far more about the power of temptation than do we who repeatedly succumb to it by sinning (just as a current's force is felt more by those swimming against it than with it), and is therefore 'able to sympathize with our weaknesses' (Heb. 4:15a) and 'able to help those who are tempted' (Heb. 2:18).

We know *that* Jesus was sorely tempted, but we cannot say precisely *how*. Did the devil come to him visibly, or in human form? Was his voice audible? Was Jesus actually transported to the temple (4:5) and to a high mountain (4:8), or were these visionary experiences? Favoring the latter alternative are (i) the impression from Mark's concise report (1:12-13) that Jesus is in the wilderness for the entirety of his ordeal, (ii) Ezekiel's antecedent vision of the Jerusalem temple during his Babylonian exile, and (iii) the physical impossibility of beholding 'all the kingdoms of the world' from a single mountain, and (Luke 4:5) 'in a moment of time.'[13] With T. W. Manson, we may regard this passage 'as spiritual experience of Jesus thrown into parabolic narrative form for the instruction of his disciples.'[14] Yet the mystery of how these events occurred must not obscure the stark reality and the enormous appeal of the temptations.[15]

---

[13] For Ezekiel's vision, see Ezekiel 8:1-3; 11:24. Cf. France 1985: 99; Calvin 1994: 140; Hendriksen 1973: 232.

[14] Manson 1977: 55. Similarly Bruner 2004a: 134.

[15] Peterson 1991: 101-2 writes: 'We are easily duped by evil. Evil almost never looks like an enemy in its presenting forms. There was nothing in the wilderness temptations of Jesus to indicate that anything evil was involved – provide bread for hunger, furnish a miracle to encourage belief, acquire power that could be used to establish a just world society.'

C. Prelude to Temptation

Jesus, 'having fasted forty days and forty nights, afterwards became hungry' (4:2).

Here, as in Matthew 2:13-15, we are reminded of the Exodus. Jesus' forty days and nights of fasting recall the Israelites' forty years of wandering in the wilderness: cf. the reference to the forty years in Deuteronomy 8:2, immediately before the verse quoted in Matthew 4:4. Moreover, Jesus will be tempted to dishonor God in the very ways the Israelites did: to fret about food, to put God to the test and to succumb to idolatry.[16] There is also a parallel with the personal experience of Moses, who fasted 'forty days and forty nights' on Sinai, both before receiving the original stone tablets (Deut. 9:9-10), and before receiving the replacements for those he had broken (Deut. 9:18; Exod. 34:28). We also remember that Yahweh appointed Joshua – LXX, *Iēsous* – to lead Israel out of the wilderness at the end of the forty years: cf. Matthew 2:15, with 2:13-23.

Moses says of his second stay on the mountain: 'Then, as before, I lay prostrate before Yahweh for forty days and forty nights' (Deut. 9:18a). Compare Exodus 34:28, 'Moses was there with Yahweh....' So too, we may infer, the singular purpose of Jesus' fasting was to commune with, and to wait upon, the heavenly Father.[17]

Whereas Moses testifies that he 'ate no bread and drank no water' during either of those forty-day periods, we are told that Jesus 'became hungry [*epeinasen*],' and that Satan urged him to provide loaves of bread for himself (Matt. 4:2-3), which may indicate that he abstained from food but not from

---

[16]Jesus' quotations (Matt. 4:4, 7, 10) come from Deuteronomy 8:3 (which recalls the grumbling about food in Exod. 16:3); from Deuteronomy 6:16 (which recalls Israel's testing God at Massah when they had no water, Exod. 17:2, 7); and from Deuteronomy 6:13 (which prefaces a warning [6:14] against worshiping other gods). Kindred temptations beset the church at Corinth (1 Cor. 10:1-22).

[17]Foster 1988: 54 rightly says of the Christian practice: 'Fasting must forever center on God. It must be God-initiated and God-ordained.' Having communed with the Father for 40 days and nights, Jesus saw through the devil's 'polite and plausible offers. His prayers had given him discernment' (Peterson 1991: 102).

water.[18] In any case, it is not in the least surprising that Jesus was hungry after a forty-day fast: this is about as long as the human organism can last without food.[19] Nor is it surprising that precisely at this point of perceived weakness the devil makes his first assault.

D. The First Test (4:3-4)
In view of what happened at the Jordan, this test, like the two to follow, is related both to Jesus' *identity* and to his *mission*.

The Devil
'And having come, the tempter said to him: "If you are the Son of God, tell these stones to become loaves of bread"' (4:3).

The devil harks back to Jesus' experience at the Jordan, and to the Father's declaration, in order to make the temptation the more tantalizing. Satan is aware of Jesus' divine Sonship (see 8:29); but his language is manipulative, not worshipful. Within the grammar of temptation, the Sonship is 'assumed to be true for the sake of argument.'[20] 'If you are in fact the Son of God, prove it to me by taking this action.' The tempter seeks to draw Jesus away from filial obedience and willing submission to the Father, into an independent exercise of his status and power. The devil tempts him 'to rely on that sonship in

---

[18]For Moses' absolute fasts, see Deuteronomy 9:9, 18; Exodus 34:28; cf. Esther 4:16; Jonah 3:7. The verb *peinaō* ('hunger') – sometimes joined to *dipsaō* ('thirst'), as, e.g., in Matthew 5:6 and 25:35 – stands alone in 4:2.

[19]'Anywhere between 21 and 40 days or longer, depending on the individual, hunger pains will return. This is the first stage of starvation and the pains signal that the body has used up its reserves and is beginning to draw on the living tissue. The fast should be broken at this time' (Foster 1988: 59). 'Since the human body cannot go without water much more than three days,' Moses must have been miraculously sustained during his 'absolute fasts' (ibid., 49). The same would hold true for Jesus, if he abstained from water as well as food (but Foster, ibid., thinks he fasted from food alone).

[20]The devil's words are cast in the form of a first class conditional sentence, one mark of which is the conjunction *ei* ('if') in the protasis (or 'if-clause'). On this kind of conditional sentence see *GGBB*, 690-694, which cautions against translating the protasis 'Since you are....' The devil uses the conditional clause of verse 3 to 'manipulate' Jesus (ibid., 704).

self-serving ways that would lead him disobediently from the path of the cross.'[21]

Moreover, Satan tempts Jesus to choose the material over the spiritual – to address his acute physical need by exerting his own will instead of awaiting the Father's will. Perhaps the tempter also seeks by this means to convert Jesus into a social reformer preoccupied with human beings' physical and material needs rather than their need to be reconciled to God (1:21). It is far easier to crusade for human rights than to atone for human sins.

Jesus
'But he answered and said: "It stands written, 'It is not on bread alone that a man shall live, but on every word that goes forth from the mouth of God"'' (4:4).

Here, as in response to the other temptations, Jesus quotes from Deuteronomy, which reflects at length on Israel's years of wandering in the wilderness. In accord with Yahweh's command to Jesus' OT counterpart Joshua, 'this Book of the Law,' Deuteronomy, is literally on Jesus' lips as an impetus to obedience.[22] This first quotation comes from 8:3 (in wording almost identical to the LXX), a *word* from God which explains the *bread* from God. It is prefaced, as are Jesus' other quotations, by the verb *graphō*, in its perfect passive form *gegraptai* – which indicates that the words about to be quoted have lost none of their vitality, that they are just as true now as when God revealed them to Moses centuries earlier. Thus the translation, 'It stands written.'[23]

---

[21]Gundry 1994: 55.

[22]Said Yahweh: 'Do not let this Book of the Law depart from your mouth; meditate on it day and night, so that you may be careful to do everything written in it' (Josh. 1:8a, NIV), after which comes a promise of Yahweh's presence (1:9). On Deuteronomy as 'the book of the law,' see Deuteronomy 31:9-11, 24-26. Jesus' three quotations suggest that Deuteronomy was one of the main OT books on which he 'meditated day and night' during the 40 days.

[23]See comments on the *gegraptai* of Matthew 2:5, the one prior instance of the verb in Matthew.

Jesus personally applies the quotation: *he himself* is a man (*anthrōpos*) who lives 'upon every word [*epi panti hrēmati*] that goes forth' from God. It is these very words – doubtless including those of this very text – that have sustained him during the forty days, just as they did Israel during the forty years (Deuteronomy 8:2-4, with Joshua 1:8). By means of his words – including those of his prior revelation – the Father has communed with his Son, enlightened his mind and nourished his soul. By means of that same word, the Son does battle with the tempter. For Jesus, as for his people, 'the sword of the Spirit...is the word [*hrēma*, as in Matthew 4:4] of God,' which he (like them) uses together with the 'shield of faith.'[24] And it is the Father's word – not the devil's – that will determine when and how the Son breaks his fast. He who turned water into wine *could* have turned stones into bread; as the Son attentive to the Father and not to the devil, he *would* not.

Deuteronomy 8:3 also sheds light on the character of Jesus' mission (which, says John 4:34, is his *food*). From his reception of the word of God arises his proclamation about the kingdom of God (Matt. 4:17). Seeking first God's kingdom (6:33a) – i.e., submitting to his rule – requires obedience to all his words, including those imparted by his Son (7:24-29). It is precisely on that basis that one's physical and material needs are met (6:33b; cf. Deut. 8:8-10). Man does not live 'on bread alone' (4:4). Nor does he live 'on bread primarily': the prayer for daily bread is offered within a context of fidelity to a sovereign God (6:9-13). Efforts to improve the human condition on any other basis – whether socialism or capitalism or materialism or naturalism or scientism – is ultimately doomed to failure, in part because no such 'ism' provides the needed stability or expected satisfaction. On the other hand, God purposes to establish his rule over every sphere of life, and to bring every dimension of culture under his control. The agents of his rule are therefore responsible for addressing the physical and material needs of their neighbors (25:31-46). Moreover, his people discover that

---

[24]Wielding the (s)word effectively requires confidence in its truth and its power, trust in the God who gave it, and reliance upon the Spirit who inspired it and uses it. See Ephesians 6:17-18; Calvin 1994: 137.

setting their hearts on God deepens their love for other people (22:37-40); and that laying up treasures in heaven enhances rather than diminishes their appreciation for the Father's earthly provisions such as health and clothing and daily food (6:19-34).[25] By the same token, here in the desert the Son who refuses to obey the devil by turning stones into bread, can trust his Father to give him bread instead of stones (cf. 7:9).

E. The Second Test (4:5-7)[26]

His first temptation having failed, the devil becomes bolder. He, the unholy one, having first 'come to' the holy Son (4:3), now 'takes' him (which presumes a certain authority over Jesus) into the holy city. Here he issues another command, and has the audacity to buttress it with an appeal to Holy Scripture. In going with the tempter, Jesus exercises his liberty as the Son of God, and positions himself to win a battle.

The Devil

Having brought Jesus to Jerusalem, the tempter has him stand on 'the highest point of the temple,' i.e., on the wing or corner of Solomon's porch on the southeast corner of the temple complex, some 450 feet above the Kidron Valley.[27]

The devil then addresses Jesus: 'If you are the Son of God, throw yourself down; for it stands written: "He will command his angels concerning you," and "In their hands they will carry you, lest you strike your foot against a stone"' (4:6-7, quoting Psalm 91:11a, 12). Satan again places Jesus' claim to divine

---

[25]Cf. the comments on those passages; and Kuyper 1931: 23 ('Calvinism put its impress in and outside the Church upon every department of human life') *et passim.*

[26]The Matthean order of the second and third temptations is reversed in Luke 4:5-12. Matthew's order appears to be chronological (the temporal adverb *tote*, 'then' [4:5] is absent from Luke), and Luke's thematic (it climaxes with the scene at the temple, a favorite Lukan motif). Cf. Blomberg 1992: 84, n. 79; Hendriksen 1973: 228. On the other hand, Keener 1999: 142-43 thinks Matthew changed the original order (in Luke) so the reference to all the *kingdoms* of the world (Matt. 4:8) would be climactic, in anticipation of Jesus' opening proclamation (4:17) and his ultimate conquest of all earthly kingdoms (24:13; 26:13; 28:18-20).

[27]See Blomberg 1992: 84; and the closing paragraph of section B. above.

Sonship at the heart of the temptation (the 'if-clause' is identical to that of verse 3), and capitalizes upon the second-person singular pronouns of Psalm 91 to strengthen his appeal.[28] He says in effect: 'The promise of Psalm 91:11-12 still holds true: "It stands written." And if the people of God in general may rely on this promise, *how much more* does it apply specifically to *you* – who purport to be the Son of God in a unique sense. If this is indeed who you are, you may be sure that the Father will command his angels concerning *you* (*sou*), and thus publicly confirm his private testimony at the Jordan River.'

Satan suggests a basic shift in the direction of Jesus' mission. 'Since the wilderness would have provided many precipices for private capitalization on divine providence, the selection of the Temple implies the public display of a messianic sign.'[29] With only the relatively private experience of the Jordan behind him, Jesus is now invited to consider the effects of a public spectacle upon the Jerusalem populace, already primed for such a display by their notions of Davidic Messiahship. How better to assure a successful mission than to offer, at its very inception, irrefragable proof that Jesus is Yahweh's Anointed? The Son is being urged to use the 'right-handed' power that would assure Israel's dominion over her enemies by political or military conquest, instead of the 'left-handed' power that achieves victory through defeat. The devil will again assail the Son with this temptation at a critical juncture in his ministry (Matt. 16:21-23) and at the very time of his death (27:39-44).

Jesus

All of Jesus' responses to the devil are concise – itself a witness to his great authority – this one especially so: 'On the other hand it stands written: "You shall not put the Lord your God to the test"' (4:7, quoting Deuteronomy 6:16).[30] Here,

---

[28]The three singular forms: 'concerning you [*sou*],' 'they will carry you [*se*],' 'your [*sou*] foot.' In this and other respects, the quotation agrees with both the MT and the LXX of the psalm.

[29]Gundry 1994: 56.

[30]This response consists of only eight words in the Greek text, as compared to 16 in the first and 13 in the third.

as in verse 4, Jesus prefaces the quotation with *gegraptai*, 'it stands written.' But now Jesus speaks in light of Satan's use of the same term in verse 6; thus the opening adverb *palin* is translated not 'again' but 'on the other hand.'[31]

Deuteronomy 6:16 reads in full, 'You shall not test Yahweh your God as you tested him at Massah.' Moses is recalling the incident of Exodus 17:1-7, where Israel, lacking water, quarrels with Moses and puts Yahweh to the test (17:2; LXX, *peirazete*). Moses therefore calls the place *Massāh* ('testing'; LXX, *peirasmos*) and *Mᵉrîbah* ('quarreling'; Exodus 17:7). One reason the Israelites complain is that they have become accustomed to Yahweh's provisions, most recently the manna and quail of Exodus 16; another is that they have ceased to trust that Yahweh will remain faithful to them. They 'put Yahweh to the test' *both* by insisting that he act in accord with their wants, *and* by failing to believe that he will meet their needs. Nevertheless, Yahweh supplies them with water (17:6).

In Matthew 4:7, 'the Lord your God' is not Jesus but the Father. Jesus is not commanding the devil to cease from tempting him: that awaits verse 10. Rather, Jesus applies the command to himself; the quotation from Deuteronomy 6:16, like that from Psalm 91, uses second-person singular forms: '*you* shall not put to the test [*ekpeiraseis*],' 'the Lord *your* [*sou*] God.' Jesus says in effect: 'You [the Son] shall not put your Father to the test by falsely applying the promise of Psalm 91.' Jesus knows the Father intimately (Matt. 11:27) and therefore believes his word – the word spoken in Psalm 91 as surely as the one spoken directly from heaven (Matt. 3:17). And *believing* Psalm 91 to be true, Jesus need not *test* the promise to see if it is true. 'The deliberate throwing of oneself from a high perch does not correspond to accidental stumbling over a stone on one's path (as in the psalm).'[32] God protects Paul when he is accidentally bitten by a viper (Acts 28:3-6). But

---

[31]Thus BAGD s.v., 4; Meyer 1884: 97; NASB. That *palin* harks back to Matthew 4:6 rather than to 4:4 is supported by the absence of the adverb from Jesus' response in 4:10 (where its presence might suggest Jesus is recalling his other two quotations).

[32]Gundry 1994: 57.

thrusting one's hand into a cage of poisonous snakes would be disobedient to the sixth commandment ('You shall not murder'; Exodus 20:13), and perhaps also selfish (a way to win acclaim by a sensational act) and unbelieving (a proof for a promise – such as Psalm 91:13 or Mark 16:18 – not thought to be trustworthy by itself).

By refusing to test God in the way Satan recommends, Jesus reaffirms his commitment to be the Servant-King. In pursuing the mission appointed for him, he will be exposed to grave danger and murderous opposition, much of it from Satan's underlings; so he will constantly need the protection and deliverance promised in Psalm 91. The Son need not test the promise to see if it is true: it will prove itself to be true at the proper time. If Yahweh granted water to grumbling and doubting Israelites, he will assuredly supply the needs of his beloved and believing Son.[33] So we will discover before this passage concludes.

F. The Third Test (4:8-10)

Having twice failed, the devil shows himself to be a relentless foe. Again, he 'takes' Jesus (*paralambanei*, as in Matthew 4:5) with him, this time to an unidentified 'very high mountain' (4:8a). Whereas he formerly invited Jesus to exercise his own authority (4:3) and to invoke that of the Father (Matt. 4:6), the tempter now claims an authority of his own, and on that basis utters a promise of his own, the keeping of which is conditional upon his receiving Jesus' worship (4:8b-9). Demanding this is yet more brazen than quoting Psalm 91, perhaps a sign that Satan is weakening under Jesus' counterattacks. Jesus again goes with the devil by an act of his own will, and readies himself to win a decisive battle.

---

[33]In view of Matthew 3:17, 'This is my Son, the Beloved,' observe how Yahweh reinforces the promise of Psalm 91:11-12 in 91:14: 'Because he loves me, I will rescue him; I will protect him, for he acknowledges my name.' The Father's vindication of his Son includes, ultimately, the destroying of Satan, to which there may be an allusion in 91:13, 'You will tread upon the lion and the cobra; you will trample the great lion and the serpent.' Cf. Genesis 3:1: 'Now the serpent...' (though this Hebrew term is different from those in Psalm 91:13), 15; Romans 16:20; *ACC* 1a: 61 (Jerome).

The Devil

On the mountain, the devil shows Jesus 'all the kingdoms [*basileias*] of the world [*kosmou*] and their splendor [*doxan*].' Then he says: 'All these things I will give to you, if you will fall down and worship me' (4:8b-9).[34] Satan claims *both* an authority over all earthly dominions *and* the authority to grant that authority to Jesus. Unless the devil in fact reigns over 'all the kingdoms of the world,' the temptation is without force. And he is indeed 'the ruler of this world' (John 12:31), on account of whose reign the world rejects Jesus (John 1:10), and human beings love the world rather than God (1 John 2:15-16).[35] Satan now offers Jesus universal and absolute power. He says in effect: 'The splendor of the kingdoms is but a reflection of the glory that will be yours. Your glory will far surpass Solomon's (cf. *doxa* in 6:29), for you will rule the whole world.'

But Jesus must first bow down to worship Satan. Here we meet the very language used of the magi: as they fell down to worship Jesus as the king of the Jews (Matt. 2:11), so Jesus' doing so would acknowledge the kingship of Satan – which means that Jesus, while exercising universal authority, would himself remain under Satan's authority. And what of Jesus' allegiance to the Father? Is Jesus somehow to be answerable to *both* God *and* the devil henceforth? But since a person *cannot* be bound to two masters (Matt. 6:24), would not the practical effect of worshiping Satan be to cease worshiping God?

Jesus

Jesus answers: 'Be gone, Satan! For it stands written, "You shall worship the Lord your God, and him alone you shall serve"' (4:10, quoting Deuteronomy 6:13).

---

[34] The devil's challenge takes the form of a third-class conditional sentence: the protasis contains the conjunction *ean* and the aorist subjunctive *proskynēsēs* ('if you will worship'); the apodosis, the future indicative *dōsō* ('I will give'). Whether the act described in the protasis (and consequently the one described in the apodosis) is probable or possible or impossible must be determined from the context (*GGBB*, 696-97; BAGD s.v. *ean*, 1.).

[35] In these Johannine texts, as in Matthew 4:8, 'world' translates *kosmos*. Cf. 1 Corinthians 2:12; Ephesians 2:2; 6:12 ('the world rulers [*kosmokratoras*]

The devil has twice commanded Jesus to take action: 'tell [*eipe*] these stones' (Matt. 4:3); and 'throw [*bale*] yourself down' (4:6). Now Jesus issues a command of his own – 'Be gone [*hypage*], Satan!' – which he both explains and reinforces with his third quotation from Deuteronomy.[36] Again Jesus applies the text to himself: '*You* shall worship [the singular verb *proskynēseis*] the Lord *your* [*sou*] God, and him alone *you* shall serve [the singular verb *latreuseis*].'[37] As in his previous responses, Jesus rivets his – and the devil's – attention upon God: all three quotations contain the word *Theos*; this one, like the second, speaks of 'the Lord your God.' Jesus' later words to Peter are similarly motivated: 'Get behind me, Satan! You are a stumbling block to me; for you are not setting your mind on the things of God [*ta tou Theou*], but on the things of men' (16:23).

The command of Deuteronomy 6:13 is founded in turn upon those of Deuteronomy 5:6-7 ('I am the LORD your God.... You shall have no other gods before me') and 6:4-5 ('Hear, O Israel: The LORD our God is one LORD; and you shall love the LORD your God with all your heart, and with all your soul, and with all your might,' RSV).[38] For Jesus to divide his allegiance between God and Satan is both unthinkable and inconceivable.

The effect of this temptation is the very opposite from what the devil intended. In applying Deuteronomy 6:13 to himself,

---

of this darkness'); 2 Corinthians 4:4 ('the god of this age [*aiōn*]'); and BAGD s.v. *kosmos*, 7, on the world as ruined, depraved and hostile to God.

[36]This instance of *gegraptai*, unlike those of Matthew 4:4 and 7, is joined by the conjunction *gar* ('for, because').

[37]Both MT and LXX of Deuteronomy 6:13 speak of *fearing* and serving Yahweh. Jesus' language about *worshiping* God (also in Luke 4:8) opposes Satan's use of this verb, 9, and states the principal way fearing God comes to expression. The adverb 'alone' is absent from but implicit in Deuteronomy 6:13 (so NASB and NIV include 'only' at Matthew 4:10), and may allude to 1 Samuel 7:3. Cf. Gundry 1994: 58. When Jesus receives worship (note the use of *proskyneō* in Matthew 14:33; 28:9, 17; also in 2:2, 11), the truth that God alone is entitled to worship is not violated, only deepened.

[38]Deuteronomy 6:13, in turn, provides a basis for 6:16, the text Jesus quoted in Matthew 4:7.

Jesus not only repudiates the notion of worshiping Satan. In resolving anew to worship and serve the Father alone, he is, if anything, *better prepared than before* for his mission – the very purpose for the Spirit's taking him to the place of testing (Matt. 4:1). Far from allowing his kingship to become subservient to that of Satan, Jesus will inaugurate a kingdom destined to vanquish Satan's kingdom.[39] Those far-flung regions of the *kosmos* presently under the devil's tyranny are the very places Jesus' gospel of the kingdom is going to be proclaimed (Matt. 24:14; 26:13). In the end 'all the kingdoms of the world' will indeed belong to Jesus – not as a bequest from Satan (who, as the very embodiment of the lie, could not be trusted to keep the promise of 4:9) but as the Father's gift to his beloved Son (28:18-20).[40]

Alec Motyer has noted the following links between Israel in Exodus and Jesus in the early chapters of Matthew. As Israel, God's son, is called forth from Egypt to a mountain (Exod. 4:22-23; 3:12), so is God's Son (Matt. 2:15; 5:1). Coming to the waters of the sea, the Israelites grumble (Exod. 14:10-12); God's Son comes to the waters of the river to do all the Father's will (Matt. 3:13-17). In the desert, whereas Israel longed for water and food (Exod. 15:24; 16:2-3), the Son lives on the Word of God (Matt. 4:3-4); whereas Israel put Yahweh to the test (Exod. 17:2), the Son refused to do so (Matt. 4:7); and whereas Israel worshiped the golden calf (Exod. 32), the Son worships God alone (Matt. 4:10).[41]

G. Aftermath of Temptation

By quoting from the living word of Deuteronomy, Jesus has repelled all of Satan's commands – the direct ones

---

[39]See the usage of *basileia* ('kingdom') in Matthew 4:17, 23; 12:25-28.

[40]Cf. Philippians 2:9-11; Revelation 11:15. The Father earlier applied to Jesus words from Psalm 2:7 and Isaiah 42:1 (see comments on Matthew 3:17). Just as applicable are the attendant promises of Psalm 2:8 ('Ask of me, and I will make the nations your inheritance, the ends of the earth your possession,' NIV) and Isaiah 42:1, 4 ('he will proclaim justice to the nations... in his name the nations will hope,' as quoted in Matthew 12:18, 21).

[41]In a lecture at Reformed Theological Seminary, Jackson, Mississippi, on April 23, 1999.

of Matthew 4:3 and 6, and the indirect one of 4:9 ('if you worship me'). Ancient Israel repeatedly succumbed to such temptations, but Jesus has remained utterly loyal to his Father. Now the devil is reduced to silence; the one who has twice 'taken Jesus' to places of testing, now 'leaves him' in response to Jesus' sovereign command (4:11a). The truth of James 4:7 is exceptionally clear in Jesus' case: 'Submit therefore to God; resist the devil, and he will flee from you.'

Jesus wins this great battle, but the war is not over: the devil now leaves Jesus 'until an opportune time' (Luke 4:13). Having suffered a major defeat in the wilderness, Satan will the more assiduously marshal his demonic host for assaults upon Jesus during his ministry in Galilee and especially during his final week in Jerusalem.[42] By the same token, does not the outcome of the contest in the wilderness assure that ongoing fidelity to the Father and reliance on the Spirit will bring Jesus victory in the ensuing battles too, including the costliest one of all?

'And behold: angels came to him and served him' (4:11b). The opening two words (*kai idou* in Greek) set apart those to follow and attach great importance to the angels' ministry.[43] In sending his angels, the Father proves himself true to the very promise Satan had invoked in verse 6. Moreover, it is highly probable that these angels, like the one who aided Elijah, provide Jesus with food and drink to relieve his acute hunger (4:2).[44] The Son, long sustained on nothing but the

---

[42]See Matthew 4:24; 8:16; 9:33-34; 10:1, 8; 12:28, 43; 13:19; 16:23; 17:18; Luke 13:16; 22:3, 31, 53; John 12:31; 16:31.

[43]Note the use of *kai idou* in Matthew 2:9; 3:16, 17; and of *idou* in 1:20, 23; 2:1, 13, 19. The instances of 1:20; 2:13, 19 preface appearances by 'an angel of the Lord.'

[44]The verb *diakoneō* ('serve,' 4:11b) may denote services of various kinds – including food and drink (e.g., 25:44; Luke 17:8; Acts 6:2). 'The ministering of angels to Jesus includes the serving of food...' (Gundry 1994: 59). For the story of Elijah, see 1 Kings 19:6-8; note, in view of Jesus' experience in the desert, that Elijah – strengthened by the food and drink furnished by the angel – 'traveled forty days and forty nights to Horeb, the mountain of God' (19:8) – the very site of Moses' fasts. Both Elijah and Moses signal their fidelity to God and covenant; and both stand between Yahweh and covenant-breakers. See Childs 1974: 599-600 (on Moses); and especially Davis 2002: 257-75 (on Elijah).

word of God, now receives from the Father his needed bread. The Messiah who has vowed to serve God alone, now receives service from God through his ministering angels.

Most important of all, the presence of angels signals that the communion between Father and Son, which the devil has done his best to weaken or sever, remains intact. Indeed, given his experience of Satanic evil, could it be that the Son now values communion with the holy Father yet more than before?[45] Having now experienced, during a lengthy ordeal, the reality of both the Father's faithfulness and the Spirit's power (cf. 3:16-17), Jesus is ready to embark upon his mission. So too has many a servant of Jesus discovered that a protracted period in the desert – whether literal or figurative – is God's chosen way to prepare his children for service, and for the more effective use of the armor he provides.[46] Not only so: what happens between the Son and the Father in the desert will encourage disciples to offer the prayer Jesus is soon to give them: 'Your will be done on earth.... Give us today our daily bread.... Rescue us from the evil one.'[47]

---

[45]One can only put this in the form of a question. Joachim Jeremias says of this passage: 'The table-service of angels is a symbol of the restored communion between man and God' (1971: 70). Cf. Psalm 23:5.

[46]Cf. Ephesians 6:11-18. Amid a lengthy spiritual battle of his own, Samuel Rutherford writes: 'The devil is but God's master fencer, to teach us to handle our weapons' (1984: 290). Calvin comments 'that the Spirit of God presides in all our trials [as in this trial of Jesus, 4:1], that our faith may be the better tried' (1994: 135).

[47]See Matthew 6:10-11, 13. Unlike his followers, Jesus need not ask for forgiveness (6:12). Unlike Jesus, the devil hates the will of God. 'He refuses to stand "under" God. He only stands "on" the fact of God [4:3, 6]' (Thielicke 1958: 50). He tempts people to become like him. For the contribution of 4:1-11 to Matthew's apologetics (pp. 173-77 above), see Keener 1999: 136-44.

II.
'Joy to the Lands that in Darkness Have Lain'[1]
(4:12-25)

'When he [Jesus] heard that John had been arrested [*paredothē*], he withdrew into Galilee' (Matt. 4:12). Only later does Matthew reveal the reason for John's arrest and imprisonment (14:3-4); but already we learn how perilous it can be to preach as John has done (ch. 3). In face of threats in Judea, Jesus – following the example of Joseph and the magi – withdraws, or takes refuge, in Galilee.[2] When the right time comes, Jesus will deliberately go to Jerusalem and there will allow himself to be handed over to suffering and death. For now, he deliberately goes to Galilee to pursue the Messianic mission God has appointed for him.[3]

A. The Advance of God's Rule (4:12-17)
Having come into Galilee, Jesus returns to Nazareth, the place of his childhood. But whereas Joseph chose to reside there (2:23), Jesus leaves Nazareth to reside in Capernaum 'beside the sea in the region of Zebulun and Naphtali' (4:13).[4]

---

[1]Words from the hymn 'Hail to the Brightness of Zion's Glad Morning!' by Thomas Hastings (1831).

[2]Here, as in Matthew 2:12-14, 22, the verb is *anachōreō*. The closest parallel to 4:12 is 2:22, where Joseph, likewise in face of a threat in Judea, withdraws into Galilee.

[3]The verb *paradidōmi* (4:12) appears in Matthew thirty-one times, nineteen of which refer to Jesus' being 'handed over' by Judas and others to arrest, trial and crucifixion (fifteen of the nineteen occur in chs. 26–27). Jesus also uses the verb to describe the trials in store for his disciples (10:17, 19, 21; 24:9). Like him, they are to flee persecution in order to complete their mission (see 10:23; Acts 8:1; 9:23-25; 11:19-21).

[4]As Joseph 'came to dwell in [*elthōn katōkēsen eis*] a town called Nazareth' (Matt. 2:23), so Jesus 'came to dwell in [*elthōn katōkēsen eis*] Capernaum' (4:13), a linguistic parallel that suggests Matthew wants 4:13 to recall 2:23. The verb *katoikeō* occurs only twice more in Matthew.

The Coming King

The reason given for Jesus' action is neither social (to escape the wrath of his townspeople)[5] nor economic (to establish a carpentry business in a more promising place) nor esthetic (to live near the water), but *theological*: 'in order that [*hina*] what had been said through Isaiah the prophet might be fulfilled' (4:14). Then follows a quotation from Isaiah 9:1-2: 'Land of Zebulun and land of Naphtali, the way of the sea, beyond the Jordan, Galilee of the Gentiles: the people who sat in darkness have seen a great light, and upon those who sat in the region and shadow of death, light has dawned' (4:15-16).[6] John the Baptist, to be sure, was 'a burning and shining lamp' (John 5:35). But is it not significant that Jesus, 'the light of the world' (John 8:12) chooses to dwell not in the *desert* but in the *city*?[7]

Naphtali's territory lay along the western shore of the Sea of Galilee and extended northward; Zebulun's lay west and southwest of Naphtali. 'The way of the sea' denotes land lying between the Sea of Galilee and the Mediterranean.[8] Naphtali, the northernmost tribe of Israel, was the first to fall to Assyria; the deporting of her people presaged Assyria's conquest of Israel, the exile of other northern tribes, and the influx of a Gentile population into their territories.[9] Yet the name 'Galilee

[5]Jesus' rejection at Nazareth comes later: see comments on Matthew 13:53-58.

[6]MT and LXX of Isaiah 8:23–9:1. The quotation is slightly closer to MT than to LXX. As a rule, Matthew's OT quotations are closer to LXX when they have gospel parallels (e.g., the quotations from Deuteronomy, Matthew 4:4-10; cf. Luke 4:4-12) than when they do not (e.g., the quotations in Matthew 1–2). Cf. pages. 98-99; Blomberg 1992: 88, n. 85. The participial form of *yāšab* (MT 9:1) is rendered in LXX by a form of *katoikeō* ('dwell, reside'). Matthew 4:16b chooses a form of *kathēmai* ('sit'), even though *katoikeō* was used in 4:13 of Jesus' residing in Capernaum. Matthew 4:16a also uses *kathēmai*; closer to MT's *hālak* ('go, walk') is LXX's *poreuomai* ('go, proceed').

[7]In keeping with their respective callings, says Origen (in *ACC* 1a: 68), John 'preaches in the wilderness,' Jesus 'in the midst of the people.' Capernaum had a larger population than Nazareth, and was better known. From this town, 'news would spread quickly around the perimeters of the lake of Galilee' (Keener 1999: 145).

[8]Motyer 1993: 99-100. For Zebulun's allotment, see Joshua 19:10-16; for Naphtali's, 19:32-39.

[9]See 2 Kings 15:29; 17:1-41.

of the Gentiles' occurs here in a context of hope – hope vested in the coming 'Son,' the royal Messiah of David's line, the hope Isaiah had voiced to Judah during the Assyrian crisis (7:14; 9:6-7). Isaiah 9:1-2 declares, astonishingly, that this hope does not exclude but *embraces* foreigners: 'in the future [Yahweh] will honor Galilee of the Gentiles' (9:1). The Hebrew Messiah will extend his benevolent rule to the whole world. To be sure, the light will dawn upon Israel and Judah; but so great is the glory attending Messiah's advent, that it will dispel pagan darkness as well.[10] Matthew's quoting of Isaiah 9:1-2, together with his express reference to Isaiah in Matthew 4:14, underscores all that he has disclosed thus far about the fulfillment of Isaianic promises in Jesus.[11]

But it is Jesus, not Matthew, who first draws attention to Isaiah 9. Remaining in Nazareth, Jesus would still have been in 'Galilee of the Gentiles,' and also within the ancient borders of Zebulun. But the prophecy speaks also of the land of Naphtali and of 'the way of the sea' (4:15). Jesus chooses Capernaum as a place which, unlike Nazareth, is 'beside the sea' (*parathalassian*; 4:13), on the northwestern shore of the Sea of Galilee. Moreover, Capernaum lies within Naphtali's former territory; so that Jesus, by moving from Nazareth to Capernaum, in a sense joins Zebulun to Naphtali. By a deliberate act, Jesus visibly and geographically brings the prophecy of Isaiah 9:1-2 to its fullest realization.[12]

Jesus has assuredly 'been born king of the Jews' (Matt. 2:2), as made plain in Isaiah's reference to the northern tribes of Zebulun and Naphtali (4:15). The people (*ho laos*) who have been sitting in darkness and in the region of death, and upon whom the light has dawned, are Israel first and foremost. It is Jesus, born in Bethlehem, 'who will shepherd my people [*ton laon mou*] Israel,' promised Yahweh through Micah (Matt. 2:6). Moreover, the encircling darkness and the threatening death

---

[10]See pages 199-206 on 'Isaiah the Prophet'; Motyer 1993: 100; and Luke 2:28-32.

[11]See comments on Matthew 1:23; 2:11, 23; 3:3, 17.

[12]For the significance of the aorist passive forms of *plēroō* ('to be fulfilled') in prefaces to Matthew's quotations from the OT, see comments on Matthew 1:22; 2:15, 17, 23. For the ancient tribal boundaries, and their relation to the Galilean towns of Jesus' day, see a Bible atlas.

are fundamentally spiritual (not political) in character: this people's paramount need is to be saved from bondage to their sins (1:21, the first instance of *laos* in Matthew).

But the people of Jesus do not consist of Jews alone. Now that Isaiah's prophecy *is being fulfilled* by Jesus' taking up residence in Capernaum beside the sea in 'Galilee of the Gentiles' (4:14-16), the salvation of foreign nations is closer to becoming a reality. Indeed it has already begun to happen: the promised light dawned (*aneteilen*, 4:16) upon Gentile magi who saw Messiah's star *en tē anatolē* – 'in the east' or 'at its rising' – and came to worship him at Bethlehem.[13] Indeed, Jesus' gospel of the kingdom is about to spread to Gentiles living *outside* provincial Galilee – to those living 'beyond the Jordan' (*peran tou Iordanou*), i.e., east of the river (Matt. 4:15, 25).[14]

The Coming Kingdom

'From that time Jesus began to preach and to say, "Repent, for the kingdom of heaven has drawn near"' (4:17).

This is Jesus' first public utterance in Matthew; heretofore he has spoken only to John the Baptist (Matt. 3:15) and to the devil (4:4, 7, 10). These are words of great importance, as attested by Matthew's weighty introduction, 'From that time [*Apo tote*] Jesus began [*ērxato*] to preach [*kēryssein*] and to say [*legein*].' This is, moreover, Jesus' *only* public declaration in the chapter, which makes it stand out all the more vividly.[15]

---

[13]The noun *anatolē* appears in Matthew 2:1, 2, 9; see those comments. Its cognate verb is *anatellō*, which first occurs in Matthew in 4:16 (as an aorist indicative).

[14]For people of Jesus' day who lived in the province of Galilee (bordered on the east by the Jordan River and the Sea of Galilee), the land 'beyond [*peran*] the Jordan' was east of the river. One such district was called *Peraea*. That the *peran tou Iordanou* of 4:25 denotes an area distinguished from Galilee confirms that Matthew intends such a distinction between *peran tou Iordanou* and 'Galilee of the Gentiles' in 4:15. The 'Decapolis' (4:25) was a region of ten cities (*deka* + *polis*) east of the Sea of Galilee and the Jordan. Bounded on the north by Damascus, and on the south by Philadelphia, the Decapolis 'had a largely Gentile population' (Gundry 1994: 65).

[15]Hereafter, Matthew records Jesus' words to the fishermen (Matt. 4:18-22) and his own summary of Jesus' ministry (4:23-25). On the importance of 4:17 in the structure of Matthew, see pages 49-51.

Matthew places Jesus' words immediately after the quotation from Isaiah 9:1-2, so that 'from that time' (4:17a) means 'from the time Jesus took up residence in Capernaum by the sea' (4:13-16). That is, it is chiefly through Jesus' *preaching* that God's light will dawn upon Jews and Gentiles.

Jesus' opening words are identical to those of John the Baptist; so for the meaning of 'repentance' and 'the kingdom of heaven,' attention may be drawn to the comments on 3:2.[16] That connection demonstrates that John and Jesus are both prophets of God, whose messages are therefore harmonious rather than contradictory; and that both, for all their differences, are allies in a common cause (see 3:15; 11:7-19). Yet, it is only Jesus' proclamation of the kingdom that Matthew expressly calls 'gospel' (*euangelion*; 4:23); and while John confronts Herod with God's rule (14:1-12), that rule actually *comes* when Jesus assaults Satan's citadel (12:28-29, with the verb *phthanō*). Thus, while John and Jesus preach the same message, the establishing of God's rule – already near before John is arrested (4:12) – is *yet nearer* when Jesus' work begins (4:17, with the verb *engizō*).[17]

As used in Matthew 4:17, the verb *engizō* is to be understood *spatially* as well as *temporally*. Jesus, having returned to Galilee, 'has drawn near to,' and now resides in, Capernaum. In towns throughout Galilee he will verbally and visibly declare God's sovereign rule (4:23-25). By virtue of *his actual presence* in these places, God's kingdom advances chronologically.[18] Jesus is

---

[16] As noted, John's words in 3:2 (like those of Jesus in 4:17) stand out in splendid isolation. See also the discussion of 'the Kingdom of God' on pages 141-45.

[17] It is yet closer when Jesus sends the twelve on their mission (10:5-7), and closer still when Paul writes Romans 13:11-12 (both passages use *ēngiken*, the form of the verb in Matthew 3:2 and 4:17). One reason the breadth of Jesus' appeal surpasses even that of John (see 3:5; 4:25) is that Jesus is a miracle worker and John is not. But the frequent notice that Jesus was attended by 'crowds' (*ochloi*, Matthew 4:25; 5:1, etc.), a term Matthew never uses of John's following (contrast Luke 3:7, 10), accords with the fact that Jesus is the more crucial figure in the advance of God's rule.

[18] The verb *engizō* occurs seven times in Matthew. It denotes *spatial* nearness in 21:1 (Jesus' nearness to Jerusalem) and 26:46 (Judas' approach to Jesus); and *temporal* nearness in 21:34 (the approach of harvest time) and 26:45 (the hour of Jesus' arrest). In the remaining three, which speak of the

distinguished from the kingdom: Matthew never equates the two, as if to say Jesus is 'the kingdom itself' (*autobasileia*). At the same time, the two are quite *inseparable*: the advance of the kingdom is inconceivable apart from the presence of Jesus the Messiah. See pages 143-44.

B. The Authority of God's Son (4:18-22)

Jesus now walks 'beside the Sea [*para tēn thalassan*] of Galilee' (4:18a), language reminiscent of 4:13, 'Capernaum beside the sea [*parathalassian*].' The calling of these fishermen is especially noteworthy. All are later numbered among the twelve: they are the first four named in 10:2-4. Three of them – Peter, James and John – come to enjoy a special closeness to Jesus (17:1; 26:37). Simon Peter figures prominently in the momentous episode at Caesarea Philippi (16:13-20). Most important of all, it is to these men, together with the rest of the twelve, that Jesus will entrust his message of the kingdom (16:17), together with its attendant powers (16:19; see 10:7-8).

The Summons

Seeing Simon called Peter and his brother Andrew in the act of casting a fishing net into the sea, Jesus says to them: 'Come, follow me, and I will make you fishers of men' (4:19). These are the only words of Jesus recorded in the passage; they stand out all the more in the absence of speech from the four fishermen. He is not said to respond to either pair of brothers. They do not volunteer their services; the initiative is entirely his.[19] He calls them by a sovereign command. His right to do so has been plain from the beginning (see 1:23).

---

kingdom's nearness (3:2; 4:17; 10:7), the temporal idea is dominant but the spatial is present too. Chilton 1996: 60 thinks language about the kingdom's 'coming near' (*engizō*) fundamentally denotes 'physical movement from one location to another.' The crowning such movement is when the Son of Man brings his kingdom *from heaven to earth* (16:27-28); as this happens at the close of history, the temporal element is of course present as well. The antecedent manifestation of Yahweh's rule in 2 Samuel 8 likewise joins the temporal and the spatial: see Davis 1999: 89-96, on 'The Coming of the Kingdom.'

[19]Normally, would-be disciples took the initiative to attach themselves to a rabbi, an act reflected in Matthew 8:19; Luke 9:57, 61. Cf. Keener 1999: 150.

Jesus' authority is further expressed in his promise to
make Simon and Andrew 'fishers of men [*halieis anthrōpōn*]'
(Matt. 4:19). Matthew has just identified the brothers as
'fishermen [*halieis*]' (4:18b). Jesus says in effect: 'You have been
casting your net for *fish* [18]; I will empower you to catch *men*
instead.' Matthew implies that Jesus speaks the same words to
James and John: 'and he called them' concludes 4:21.

The 'net' (so to speak) which Jesus will provide for their
work is the immediately preceding message about the
kingdom of God (4:17). Some think the 'men' in question
are to be 'hooked' by God's coming wrath (cf. 3:7; Jer. 16:16).
But Jesus' proclamation is *good news* (Matt. 4:23a), as the
accompanying acts of mercy testify (4:23b-24). The men are to
be drawn out of darkness into light, and out of death into life
(4:16).[20] Perhaps the fact that these fishermen work in the very
sea beside which Jesus enacts the fulfillment of Isaiah 9:1-2
is meant to be an image of their own future ministry to both
Jews and Gentiles (Matt. 28:18-19).

Jesus will equip these fishermen to advance *God's* rule, not
their own. Later in Matthew we find them seeking to enthrone
themselves, or even using their powers to *oppose* God's rule.[21]
In the end, they will learn that God and his Messiah impart
power to human beings without relinquishing it; and that
they are to remain under Jesus' supreme authority all their
days (23:8-10; 28:18-20).[22]

The Response
So compelling is Jesus' call that all four men respond
'immediately' (*eutheōs*, Matt. 4:20, 22). Their decision entails

[20]In the parable of Matthew 13:47-50, the righteous are likened to good
fish; the bad fish represent those who reject the gospel of the kingdom. The
imagery of 'fishing for men' implies nothing seductive, deceitful or harmful
(Blomberg 1992: 91). So too Chamblin 1969: 62-65.

[21]On the ambition of James and John, see 20:20-28. On Peter's opposition
to Jesus, see 16:22-23; 26:31-35, 51-54, 69-75.

[22]Bruce Larson, *Living on the Growing Edge* (Grand Rapids: Zondervan,
1968), 51, notes 'that no time limit was implied in that original call. When
they left their businesses, their friends, their familiar surroundings, and
even their families to follow Jesus Christ, they could not have known it was
to be a lifetime call.'

a *leaving*: the verb *aphiēmi* (4:20, 22) denotes a decisive break with the past based on a firm commitment to Jesus. The form here – the aorist participle *aphentes* – views the action as a whole or as instantaneous.[23] All four leave their occupations, whether the 'nets' of Simon and Andrew, or 'the boat' of James and John; for the latter two, the decision means leaving their father as well (4:21-22).[24] The fishermen's response to Jesus is expressed positively as well. Simon and Andrew 'followed [*ēkolouthēsan*] him' (4:20); James and John 'went away after [*apēlthon opisō*] him' (4:22). Both verbs are aorist indicatives – the first from *akoloutheō*, the second from *aperchomai* – which characterize the response as *aphentes* had done.[25]

Jesus calls these men into discipleship. The noun *mathētēs*, 'disciple,' occurs seventy-three times in Matthew, starting with 5:1. The related verb is *manthanō*, 'learn.' Disciples indeed have much to learn and Jesus is about to start teaching

---

[23]For this kind of aorist, see *GGBB*, 557; *IB*, 10-11.

[24]Cf. Matthew 8:21-22; 10:37; 19:29; 23:9. Gundry 1993: 68 comments on the parallel in Mark 1:20: 'Not even the closest, most obligatory family tie can keep the brothers there, so powerful is Jesus' call.' (*Aphiēmi* can mean 'leave' in the sense of 'abandon': BAGD s.v., 3. But this is too strong a term here; cf. Matthew 15:3-9.) These fishermen were not among the wealthy, but neither were they peasants; they 'had much to lose economically by leaving their businesses' (Keener 1999: 152). While Jesus dwelled in Capernaum and often ministered within walking distance of the town, his broader circuit (4:23) 'required his disciples to be away from their homes and livelihoods for substantial periods of time.' Nor do the gospels indicate that spouses traveled with disciples during this period (ibid., 152-53); the women of Luke 8:1-3 are not so identified; and 1 Corinthians 9:5 applies to a later period. Do not such privations show just how priceless the kingdom is (Matt. 13:44-46)?

[25]John 1:35-51 reports that Jesus encountered Andrew and Peter in Judea prior to his return to Galilee (Matt. 4:12; John 4:3) – and John the son of Zebedee as well, if (as is probable) he is the unnamed disciple of the Baptist who now follows Jesus (John 1:35-39). This earlier meeting makes the immediacy and decisiveness of the fishermen's response in Mark 1:16-20 and Matthew 4:18-22 (which follows Mark) more intelligible, without diminishing in the least the authority of Jesus. If Luke 5:1-11 'gives a fuller and independent narrative' of the incident in Matthew 4 and Mark 1 (so France 1985: 103; also Marshall 1978a: 199), the miracle of Luke 5:4-9 helps to explain the immediacy of the fishermen's response (5:11; Matthew 4:22; so Carson 1984: 119). But the episode of Luke 5 may well be later: so, e.g., Hendriksen 1973: 245-46; Chamblin 1969: 51-52.

them (5:1-2 *et seq*). Yet *manthanō* appears only three times in Matthew, whereas *akoloutheō* occurs twenty-five times, at least thirteen of which (starting with 4:20) relate that certain persons followed Jesus or that Jesus commanded them to do so. The primary requirement for Jesus' disciples is that they *follow* him, and be committed to *him*, which provides the basis for receiving his teaching and obeying his commands.[26]

C. The Grace of God's Servant (4:23-25)
The close of the chapter reveals – to Jesus' first disciples and to Matthew's readers – the manifold might of God's advancing rule, and offers a glimpse of its coming universal breadth.

Preaching and Teaching
'And Jesus was traveling about the whole of Galilee, teaching [*didaskōn*] in their synagogues and preaching [*kēryssōn*] the good news of the kingdom...' (Matt. 4:23a). We are reminded that the nearness of the kingdom of God stands at the heart of Jesus' message (4:17). Declaring this news and unfolding its implications became his established habit in Galilee, as did his choice of the synagogue (*synagōgē*), a center of both religious and communal activity.[27]

Jesus is said both to *teach* and to *preach*; the two are distinguishable, but inseparable, aspects of one message. Jesus *preaches*, 'Repent, for the kingdom of heaven is near' (4:17, *kēryssō*, as in 4:23). He *teaches* in order to explain and amplify that proclamation to worshipers in the synagogues, and also to provide further instruction to persons who have repented in response to his preaching – i.e., to his disciples (5:2, *didaskō*, as in 4:23). Teaching gives understanding (see 13:1-23)

---

[26]Cf. Matthew 11:28-29, 'Come to me...learn from me'; and page 152, 'A Loyal People.' In our day, Matthew 4:18-22 applies well, but not exclusively, to ordained clergy: cf. Bruner 2004a: 142-43.

[27]The verb *periēgen* (from *periagō*), 4:23a, is an instance of the 'customary imperfect,' here expressive of a habit, 'a *regularly* recurring activity in past time...' (*GGBB*, 548). For Jesus' visits to synagogues, see also 9:35; 12:9; 13:54 (with Luke 4:16-30); on the features and services of the synagogue in Jesus' day, see E. Yamauchi, in *DJG*, 781-84. 'His teaching in the synagogues was public, but His preaching more public still' (Bengel 1873: 159).

and direction to members of the new community established around Jesus' person (cf. 28:20, 'teaching them to keep all that I commanded you').

Conversely, all that teaching occurs in view of Jesus' preaching of the kingdom, for it is indeed a *gospel* – a *euangelion* – that he declares. One reason God's coming kingdom is such good news is that it offers the repentant salvation from their sins (4:17; 1:21). Another is that people can now be ruled by *Jesus* rather than by themselves.

Is anything more destructive than self-rule? Rebecca Pippert rightly says that Jesus is 'the only one in the universe who can control us without destroying us.'[28] Followers of Christ (4:18-22) are now free to be obsessed with Christ rather than with themselves. Is anything more incessantly *boring* than self-absorption? Is anyone so boundlessly *interesting* as Jesus?[29]

Jesus' *teaching* includes imperatives (as Matthew 5–7 will show), but his *preaching* is pure indicative, an announcement of what God and his Messiah are doing in the world. To be sure, there is an attendant call to repent (4:17); but it is seeing oneself in the light of God's saving initiatives that provides the motive for doing so. For Jesus' disciples the great indicatives of the gospel will always furnish the strongest incentives for obeying his commands. That is why we must preach the gospel to ourselves every day.[30]

Healings and Liberations
This closing passage stresses that Messiah has come to restore persons being destroyed by all sorts of afflictions; to liberate persons being tyrannized by the devil; and thereby to furnish visible proof that God's rule is indeed advancing. Integral to Jesus' habitual work in Galilee is 'healing every kind of disease [*noson*] and every kind of sickness [*malakian*] among the people' (Matt. 4:23b). In verse 24 we are told that 'they brought to him

---

[28]*Out of the Salt-Shaker and into the World* (Downers Grove: InterVarsity, 1979), 64.

[29]'True spirituality...takes attention off of ourselves and focuses it on another, on Jesus' (Peterson 1997b: 8). Foster 1985: 126 says that 'God is our only legitimate obsession.'

[30]See page 171, including the quotation from Jerry Bridges.

all who had illnesses [*tous kakōs echontas*], those tormented by various diseases and severe pains [*nosois kai basanois synechomenous*], the demon-possessed [*daimonizomenous*], epileptics [*selēniazomenous*] and paralytics [*paralytikous*].' This is the weightiest, most comprehensive such report in Matthew, which makes the sentence's conclusion – 'and he healed them' (4:24b) – all the more impressive.[31]

This summary, together with that of 4:23a, anticipates the chapters to follow. Jesus, whose habit is to teach in the synagogues of Galilee, and out of doors to huge crowds as well, is about to teach his disciples from the mountain in the hearing of the crowds (Matt. 5–7).[32] Chapters 8–9 are largely devoted to mighty works: no fewer than nine of Jesus' miracles are recorded here (together with the summary of 8:16-17), including two of the kinds mentioned in 4:24.[33]

Jews and Gentiles

As the chapter closes, Matthew amplifies the prophecy of Isaiah 9 about the Messianic kingdom's geographical breadth. As Jesus 'was traveling about the whole of Galilee [*en holē tē Galilaia*],' proclaiming the kingdom and accomplishing stupendous miracles (Matt. 4:23), 'his fame [*akoē*] spread to the whole of Syria [*eis holēn tēn Syrian*]' (4:24a). Matthew probably means 'the regions neighboring Israel to the north and northeast, not the much larger Roman province of Syria.'[34] Its population would be largely Gentile. As noted in

[31]The verb *therapeuō* occurs in Matthew 4:23, 24. The constative (comprehensive) aorist indicative of 4:24b, *etherapeusen* ('he healed'), echoes the customary (habitual) present participle of 4:23b: *therapeuōn* ('healing'). In between, there are seven different terms (*nosos* occurs twice) for human afflictions.

[32]The verb *didaskō* ('teach') appears in 4:23 and 5:2. Plural forms of *ochlos* ('crowd') appear in 4:25; 5:1; and 7:28.

[33]For the liberating of the demon-possessed (4:24b), see 8:28-34; 9:32-34; for the healing of paralytics (4:24b), 8:5-13; 9:1-8. (The healing of an epileptic [4:24b], who is also demon-possessed, is reported in 17:14-18.) In addition, in 8:23-27 Jesus calms the storm and saves his disciples from the threat of drowning.

[34]France 1985: 105. The Roman province of Syria embraced all of Palestine except Galilee (see Carson 1984: 121). Did this news about Jesus travel as far as Antioch in Syria? It was argued earlier (pp. 159-61) that the Gospel according to Matthew may well have originated in Antioch or somewhere

the comments on verses 14-16, among the huge crowds that follow Jesus (4:25) are representatives of Gentile territories (i.e., the Decapolis and the land 'beyond the Jordan'), as well as Jewish.

Jesus has not yet ventured into those places; but their inhabitants are irresistibly drawn to him in Galilee. And when they come, he imparts the grace of the kingdom to them. Whereas the phrase 'among the people' (en tō laō; 4:23b), apparently embraces Jews alone, the report of 4:24b, coming as it does immediately after the reference to Syria, suggests that the afflicted who are brought to Jesus come largely, if not entirely, from that territory.[35]

Moreover, Jesus himself chose to live in 'Galilee of the Gentiles' (4:15); and even synagogues (4:23) were places to teach 'God-fearing' Gentiles and Gentile proselytes.[36] From the very inception of his mission, therefore, the Jewish Messiah is declared to be Savior of Gentiles as well. Already it is becoming clear that one day he will reign over 'all the kingdoms of the world' (4:8).

---

else in Syria. Given the character of Jesus' work, and his huge following (Matt. 4:25), the instance of akoē in 4:24 (like that in 14:1) is better translated 'fame' (ESV) than 'news' (NIV). Cf. BAGD s.v., 2.a.

[35]Cf. Smillie 2002: 86-89.

[36]On the proselytes, see Scott 1995: 342-46; on the God-fearers, ibid., 346-47. For Jewish interest in Gentile converts, see Matthew 23:15.

Section 6

'Go Tell it on the Mountain'[1]

(Matt. 5:1–7:29)

'Seeing the crowds [*tous ochlous*] he went up onto the mountainside [*eis to oros*]; once he sat down, his disciples [*hoi mathētai autou*] came to him. And opening his mouth, he began to teach [*edidasken*] them, saying...' (5:1-2). Thus Matthew introduces the first of the five great discourses.[2] While Jesus travels all over Galilee (4:23), Capernaum remains his residence (4:13). Shortly after descending the mountain he enters Capernaum (8:5). So it is probable that this 'mountainside' lies north of the town and overlooks the Sea of Galilee.[3]

Luke 6:17-49 reports the same event, or at least a very similar one. (i) The sayings of Luke 6:20-49 are arranged like their counterparts in Matthew 5–7. (ii) In both passages, Jesus addresses disciples in

---

[1]An African-American spiritual of unknown date.

[2]See 'Designing the Gospel,' pages 49-59, especially 51-53.

[3]France 1985: 107; Bruce 1970a: 16-17. The singular *oros* with the definite article *to* (Matt. 5:1; 8:1) suggests a particular locale (contrast 5:14, where *oros* lacks the article: 'a city set on *a hill*'). The other instances of *eis to oros* (14:23; 15:29; 28:16) may denote the same place as 5:1. The plural *ta orē* (18:12; 24:16) is broader: 'the hills,' 'the mountains.' Further identification of the present site is lacking; contrast references to 'the Mount [*to oros*] of Olives' (21:1; 24:3; 26:30). Also to be contrasted with the texts where *oros* denotes a hillside (5:1, etc.) are those where the *oros* is said to be 'high' (17:1) or 'very high' (4:8).

the hearing of a crowd (Matt. 5:1-2; 7:28-29; Luke 6:17-20; 7:1), although in Matthew he is seated (for teaching; 5:1), and in Luke he is standing (since he heals as well as teaches; 6:17-20). (iii) In Luke 6:12, Jesus went 'onto the mountainside' (*eis to oros*, as in Matthew 5:1); having come down, he stood 'on a level [*pedinos*] place' (Luke 6:17). For addressing a multitude, such a place was needed: both Matthew and Luke 'envisage a plateau in a hilly area.'[4] (iv) At the close of the Lukan discourse, Jesus 'entered Capernaum' (7:1).[5]

---

[4]Blomberg 1992: 97. Though 'we cannot determine exactly where Jesus delivered his message,' the 'traditional site on the northeast shore of Galilee, known as the Mount of Beatitudes, at least gives a good acoustical illustration of how a speaker could address a large crowd on a plateau in the hills overlooking the lakeside and be heard by thousands at once' (ibid.). Cf. Keener 1999: 163-64; Marshall 1978a: 241-42. The adjective *pedinos* (Luke 6:17) can mean 'level' as opposed to 'steep.'

[5]Carson 1984: 125-26 argues that Matthew 5–7 and Luke 6:20-49 report the same occasion.

I.
'Teach me Thy Way, O Lord.'[1]

Prior to chapter 5, Matthew has recorded only six short sayings of Jesus – one addressed to John the Baptist, three to the devil, one to the people of Galilee, and one to the fishermen.[2] We have just learned (4:23) that Jesus made a practice of teaching (*didaskōn*) in the synagogues of Galilee. Much of that teaching is about to be unfolded (5:2; with *edidasken*).

A. The Messiah
Jesus dominates these three chapters as he does the rest of Matthew. Except for the opening two verses and the closing two, the chapters consist entirely of his words. The weighty introduction (5:1-2) prepares both listeners and readers for matters of great importance.

As in 2:13-15 and 4:1-11, Matthew links Jesus to Moses. Jesus goes up onto a *mountainside*, where he *teaches* his followers (5:1-2), as he will again do at the close of the gospel (28:16-20).

Moses too ascended a mountain, Sinai, whence he delivered Yahweh's instruction (*Torah*).[3] Like Moses' officially recognized successors (23:2), Jesus sits down to teach (5:1; 13:1-2; 24:3; 26:55; Luke 4:20). Like Moses (Exod. 18:13), he will one day be seated to execute judgment (Matt. 19:28; 25:31).[4] On the mount

---

[1]The opening words of a hymn by B. Mansell Ramsey (1919).

[2]Each saying consists of one verse: Matthew 3:15; 4:4, 7, 10, 17, 19.

[3]The LXX often applies the verb *anabainō* ('to go up,' 5:1) to Moses' ascent of Sinai. Twice more in Matthew Jesus is said to *go up* onto a mountainside: in one instance, 14:23, it is a place to commune with God, as it had been for Moses (e.g., Exod. 34:29); in the other, 15:29, a place to heal.

[4]For links between Jesus and Moses in 5:1-2, see Gundry 1994: 65-66. For 'the mountain' as a place of divine revelation, see Davies and Allison 1988: 422-23. They say the place's significance is 'not geographical but mythological' (422); I would rather say 'geographical, historical and theological.'

of transfiguration, as the disciples behold Jesus conversing with Moses and Elijah, the Father says about his beloved Son: 'Listen to him!' (17:5) – words reminiscent of Moses' own command concerning 'the prophet like Moses' whom Yahweh would one day appoint (Deut. 18:15).[5] That prophet has arisen: having been appointed by the Father and anointed by the Spirit (Matt. 3:16-17), he is ready to speak. About to be fulfilled is Yahweh's promise concerning him: 'I will put my words in his mouth, and he will tell them everything I command him' (Deut. 18:18). He is like Moses and true to Moses, but he is also far greater than Moses (5:17-48). This prophet speaks with unparalleled and unprecedented authority (7:28-29).

Not only does Jesus deliver this teaching; he himself is the key to understanding and embracing it. 'Above all else, the Sermon on the Mount makes a *christological* statement.'[6] Apart from the person and work of Jesus the Messiah, the blessings here promised are not available, and the obedience here required is not attainable.[7]

B. The People

'Seeing the *crowds* he went up onto the mountainside; once he sat down, his *disciples* came to him. And opening his mouth, he began to teach *them*' (5:1-2a). This is the first instance of *mathētēs* ('disciple') in Matthew. It identifies persons, represented by the four fishermen of 4:18-22, who have heeded Jesus' call and committed themselves to him and to his teachings (Jesus' sermon in Luke is prefaced by his choice of the twelve from a larger company of disciples; 6:13-16). From start to finish, this discourse is about discipleship and is addressed to all disciples.[8]

---

[5]Very close to Matthew 17:5b (*akouete autou*, 'Listen to him') is the LXX of Deuteronomy 18:15b (*autou akousesthe*, 'You shall listen to him').

[6]Guelich 1982: 27.

[7]Listeners' 'eternal destiny depends on their relation to him (7:21-23) and their response to his teaching (7:24-27)' (France 1985: 106). Cf. Davies 1964: 435 (the sermon 'compels us, in the first place, to ask who he is who utters these words'); Guelich 1982: 30-32, 38.

[8]On *mathētēs* in Matthew, see pages 59-61, 294-95. Since the Middle Ages, some have taught that the sermon is meant, not for ordinary Christians but for those pursuing exceptional holiness – e.g., those who take vows of

The noun *ochlos* (5:1a) here appears for the second time in Matthew. We have just learned not only that four fishermen 'followed' Jesus (*ēkolouthēsan*; 4:20, 22), but that huge crowds (*ochloi polloi*) did as well (*ēkolouthēsan*; 4:25). Jesus now teaches with the crowds in view. He ascends the mountain, not to escape them but to take a position from which he may effectively address a large gathering consisting of both disciples and the crowd. The conclusion to the discourse reports that 'when Jesus had finished these words, the *crowds* were amazed at his teaching, because he was teaching *them* as one having authority...' (7:28-29a).[9]

There is an unmistakable distinction in Matthew, as in the other gospels, between the 'disciples' and the 'crowd' (see, e.g., 13:10-17); but that line of distinction has not (or not yet) become a wall of separation. This sermon's teaching on discipleship is not meant for disciples exclusively. As he teaches disciples, Jesus exhorts persons in the crowd to become disciples – to convert their present following (itself a hopeful sign) into a more serious kind. This appeal is especially strong as the sermon begins (5:3-10) and ends (7:24-27).

C. The Apostle
Matthew was one of the disciples who originally received the teachings of these three chapters – and also one of the twelve whom Jesus selected as his special representatives just before the sermon commenced.[10] Moses was both a prophet and a

poverty and chastity and enter monastic orders. But Jesus addresses the entire sermon to 'his disciples' (Matt. 5:2), not to a select number among them (such as the twelve). See Blomberg 1992: 94-95; Schweizer 1975: 193-94; also G.N. Stanton, 'Sermon on the Mount/Plain,' *DJG*, 738, on Thomas Aquinas' distinction between the new Law's *commands* (necessary for gaining salvation) and its optional *counsels* (for those who strive for perfection).

[9]Like the rabbis, Matthew likes the plural *ochloi*; he uses it 31 out of 49 times (not counting 12:15; cf. *TC*, 26). But its difference from the singular is stylistic, not substantive; cf. 13:2; Davies and Allison 1988: 419. *Laos* ('people') in Luke 6:17 and 7:1 corresponds to *ochloi* in Matthew 5:1 and 7:28 respectively. Luke 6:17 also speaks of a 'large crowd [*ochlos*] of disciples.' 'All the crowd [*ochlos*],' (6:19), apparently embraces both the 'disciples' and the 'people' of 6:17.

[10]See Luke 6:13-16, with 17-20. Once Jesus chose the twelve, the other disciples of 6:13 presumably descended to the 'level place,' where they – the

scribe. Jesus, the anointed Prophet, here declares the word of God. Matthew, the appointed scribe (13:52), here records it. Just as Jesus addressed both disciples and crowd, so Matthew is both catechizing Christian believers and urging non-believers to submit to Jesus' authority and to the way of life he prescribes (see pp. 168-77).

Thus, in the first place, given (i) Matthew's commission to transmit Jesus' teachings faithfully and accurately, (ii) his personal reception of the words recorded here, and (iii) his fidelity to such tradition as received from other eye-witnesses, we may take this discourse as it stands (cf. the discussion on pp. 59-91). Its content is entirely Jesus' own: 'He began to teach them, saying' (5:2); 'these words of mine' (7:24, 26); 'When Jesus had finished these words' (7:28). Jesus himself taught and joined the very themes set forth here, and in this order.

Secondly, given (i) the presence of similar sayings at various places in Matthew and the other gospels, (ii) Jesus' authority, liberty and pedagogical skills, and (iii) a ministry that spanned all of Galilee for at least a year, we may conclude that Jesus presented the teachings of these three chapters on many occasions, with various formulations and in varying arrangements, all for the sake of impressing their truth upon his listeners.[11]

Thirdly, given (i) the matching collection of miracle stories (chs. 8–9), (ii) the degree of thematic unity evident in the other four discourses, and (iii) the brevity of the sermon (which can be recited in less than fifteen minutes), I conclude that Matthew here offers a digest of a much longer sermon, or a summary of themes selected from

---

'large crowd of disciples' of 6:17b – awaited Jesus' descent with the twelve (6:17a; Marshall 1978a: 238). Jesus here (6:13) appoints the twelve to be his specially authorized representatives (*apostoloi*): see ibid., 238-39; Green 1997: 258-59. Note that Matthew 10:1 presupposes Jesus' earlier choice of the twelve.

[11]See pages 78-86, on 'Matthew's use of Q.' For Synoptic sayings of Jesus akin to those in Matthew 5–7, see, e.g., Matthew 12:33; 18:8-9, 35; 19:9; 22:39-40; Mark 4:21, 24; 9:43, 47, 50; 10:11-12; 11:24-25; Luke 6:20-49; 8:16; 11:2-4, 9-13, 33; 12:22-31, 33-35, 58-59; 13:24, 26-27; 14:34-35; 16:13, 17, 18.

several sermons Jesus preached in this vicinity.[12] Attention to the texts peculiar to Matthew may illuminate the author's theological and pastoral concerns.[13] Yet, given the speaker's identity and authority, as well as this discourse's position in the gospel, there can be no doubt that Matthew believes the entirety of these chapters to be of utmost importance for all his readers.

Another apostle who shares that conviction is James, Jesus' half-brother (13:55) and author of the epistle that bears his name. Texts akin to those of Matthew 5–7 appear in all five chapters of James: 'the whole book exudes the Sermon on the Mount.'[14] James, like Matthew, recognizes the personal and social implications of 'the royal law' which Jesus expounds: one's response to the second great command ('Love your neighbor as yourself') will reveal one's response to the first.[15]

---

[12]See pages 51-57, on 'progress in narrative and teaching' in the design of Matthew. *Edidasken* (5:2), an ingressive (or inceptive) imperfect ('he began to teach'), stresses 'the beginning of an action, with the implication that it continued for some time' (*GGBB*, 544). Calvin 1994: 168 calls Matthew 5–7 'a short summary of the teaching of Christ, gathered from many and various discourses, of which this was the first.' Stott 1978: 23-24, like A. B. Bruce, considers Matthew 5–7 a condensed summary of Jesus' 'teaching from the hill,' teaching 'not of a single hour or day, but of a period of retirement.' Cf. Isaiah's method (e.g., in ch. 22) of fashioning a mosaic from oracles delivered at various points in his ministry (Motyer 1993: 187). Let us not forget that Matthew's catechetical method is indebted to that of Jesus (see pp. 101-2). As noted (p. 304), it is Jesus who first presents, joins and arranges the themes comprising this sermon. Jeremias 1961: 19 goes too far, however, when he says that 'the Sermon on the Mount [is] a composition of originally isolated sayings of Jesus.'

[13]See pages 86-90, on 'Matthew's use of M.'

[14]Davids 1982: 16. See, e.g., James 1:5 (Matt. 7:7), 1:17 (Matt. 7:11), 1:22-23 (Matt. 7:24, 26); 2:5 (Matt. 5:3, 5), 2:8 (Matt. 5:43), 2:10 (Matt. 5:19), 2:11 (Matt. 5:21-22), 2:13 (Matt. 5:7); 3:12 (Matt. 7:16), 3:18 (Matt. 5:9); 4:11-12 (Matt. 7:1); 5:2 (Matt. 6:19), 5:12 (Matt. 5:34-37). Cf. Davids 1982: 47-48; Davies 1964: 402-3.

[15]Matthew 5:43-48; 22:37-40; James 2:8, with 1:22-27; 2:1; 3:9-10; 4:4, 11-12. Foster 1998: 71 calls James 'a beautiful commentary' on this sermon's 'teaching on how right action flows from the wellspring of a right heart.' How Matthew and James illuminate each other will become plainer as we proceed.

D. The Kingdom

In keeping with the mission summarized in Matthew 4:12-25, Jesus in this sermon teaches about the kingdom of God. He will now explain more fully what makes this proclamation a *euangelion* (4:17, 23) and what is expected from persons who submit to God's rule on Messiah's terms (4:18-22).[16] The content may be outlined as follows: A. The Blessings of the Kingdom (5:3-16). B. The Righteousness of the Kingdom (5:17–7:12). C. The Two Alternatives (7:13-27).[17]

The Message of the Kingdom: Gospel and Law
In this sermon, as elsewhere in Matthew, gospel and law are distinguishable, but inseparable, aspects of Jesus' teaching.[18] Matthew 5:3-16 is dominated by gospel, but contains imperatives both veiled (e.g., Matt. 5:7, 9) and unveiled (5:12, 16). The exposition of law in 5:17–7:12 rests upon that good news, and itself refers to blessings from God (e.g., 5:45; 6:30-33; 7:7-11). The appeals and warnings of 7:13-27 presuppose all that the previous sections have taught about both gospel and law. Moreover, the whole sermon is to be viewed in light of what Matthew teaches elsewhere about the gospel of the kingdom (see below).

Each section reflects the centrality of the kingdom. The beatitudes of 5:3-10 open and close with the promise of 'the kingdom of heaven.' Entry into the kingdom, and honor within it, is reserved for those who obey the law as expounded by Jesus (5:19-20). As disciples pray for the coming of the kingdom,

---

[16]See pages 295-96. The kingdom is the sermon's 'unifying theme' (Carson 1984: 127).

[17]For the same division, see, e.g., Guelich 1982: 39; Stanton, 'Sermon,' 740.

[18]See pages 152, 171-72. In the sermon, as in Matthew as a whole, 'grace and demand are linked inextricably' (Stanton, ibid., 744). Jeremias 1961: 32 concludes that 'the Sermon on the Mount is not Law, but Gospel. For this is indeed the difference between Law and Gospel: the Law leaves man to rely upon his own strength and challenges him to do his utmost. The Gospel, on the other hand, brings man before the gift of God and challenges him really to make the inexpressible gift of God the basis for his life. These are two different worlds.' On the contrary, (i) in the sermon gospel and law are adjoining regions of the same country, to be occupied in this order; (ii) the challenge to make God's gift the basis of life is met by submission to his law; and (iii) the laws presented here call for strenuous effort but discourage self-reliance.

they devote themselves to its righteous requirements (6:10, 33). Toward the close, Jesus warns that entering the kingdom calls for *both* acknowledging his Lordship *and* doing the will of his heavenly Father (7:21).[19]

The Marks of the Kingdom: Love for God and Neighbor
Jesus later declares that 'all the Law and the Prophets' depend upon the commands to love God and neighbor (Matt. 22:37-40). Consider in that light how he begins and ends the central portion of the sermon: 'Do not suppose that I came to abolish the Law or the Prophets; I came not to abolish but to fulfill' (5:17); 'All things, therefore, as many as you want men to do for you, do the same for them; for this is the Law and the Prophets' (7:12). The 'therefore' (*oun*) of 7:12 embraces the whole preceding section.[20] 'The Law and the Prophets' forms an inclusion with 5:17. Matthew 7:12 is especially reminiscent of 5:43-48 (in Luke 6:27-36 'the golden rule' [6:31] appears amid sayings parallel to Matt. 5:39-48). Here, in the last of six paragraphs marked by similar openings (5:21-48), Jesus expounds the command about loving one's neighbor; forms of the verb *agapaō*, 'love,' appear four times in the paragraph. Jesus is telling his listeners, and Matthew his readers, that attitudes and actions of love are crucial for keeping the laws expounded in 5:21-48.

Conversely, all that Jesus teaches in this section about 'the righteousness of the kingdom' fosters love of God and neighbor (22:37-40). One shows love for God by serving him (6:24). When his people do his will, his kingdom advances and his name is hallowed (6:9-10). Love for God, moreover, finds expression in love for one's neighbors, both within and beyond the church (see pp. 183-84). God's rule advances when relationships among Christians are marked by respectful instead of disparaging speech; by reconciliation in place of alienation; by fidelity to wedding vows and other promises;

---

[19]This paragraph takes account of all eight instances of *basileia* ('kingdom') in Matthew 5–7. As Carson notes (1984: 127-28), they all occur at critical junctures in the sermon.

[20]Thus too Stanton, 'Sermon,' 743.

by humility rather than pride; by what James calls 'the wisdom from above,' which is 'first pure, then peaceable, gentle, willing to yield, full of mercy and good fruits, without a trace of partiality or hypocrisy.'[21]

Love embraces non-believing neighbors as well. Jesus identifies his people as 'the salt of the earth' and 'the light of the world' (5:13-16). They are therefore to keep promises made to non-Christians, and may freely give alms to them. Adversaries who threaten them with lawsuits, evildoers who assault them, persecutors for whom they pray, mostly come from outside the church. Thus (1.) let Christians not imagine that God's rule is confined to the church, and that evil societal structures and practices are to be deplored but not addressed. But let them not commit the opposite error (2.) of mistaking the kingdoms of this age for the kingdom of God, and of naively expecting the policies of the former to attain the reality of the latter. Rather (3.), by heeding Jesus' command to love non-believers, let them confront the fallen culture with Messiah's claims, and advance God's rule by obedience in their various places of responsibility.[22]

The Coming of the Kingdom: the Already and the Not Yet
Jesus announces the inauguration of the kingdom, and promises its consummation. By expelling demons, Jesus shows that

---

[21]James 3:17, NRSV. See Matthew 5:21-37; 7:1-12.

[22]O. Palmer Robertson, 'The Kingdom and the Church' (unpublished MS.), 5–7, calls these three views, respectively, (1.) *Conservative* (I would rather say 'Fundamentalist'), (2.) *Liberal*, and (3.) *Reformational* (I would rather say 'Reformed'). The Anabaptist-Mennonite reading of the sermon approximates the first view; classical Liberalism, the second (on these see Carson 1984: 126-27). Martin Luther spells out certain aspects of the third view. His expositions of Matthew 5–7 teach (i) that Christians live in two distinct (but inseparable) realms, the spiritual and the secular; (ii) that their life in the former realm (the church) calls for obedience to all the sermon's commands, whereas their responsibilities in the latter realm may call for different action, so that, e.g., a Christian who *personally* does not use violence to resist evil (5:39) may occupy the secular *office* of a policeman that requires him to do so; and (iii) that the Christian himself is not divided, so that, e.g., a Christian who holds the secular *office* of judge may *personally* grieve for a person upon whom he imposes the law's just demand of capital punishment. Cf. Stanton, 'Sermon,' 738; Guelich 1982: 16-17; also my remarks on 'Kingdom and Church,' pages 153-54.

God's rule is mightier than Satan's; yet evil persists, and will only be eradicated when the divine powers are fully unleashed at history's end. By the same token, the blessings announced in the beatitudes may now be experienced; but the poverty, sorrow and weakness depicted here, and the tyranny, injustice and oppression reflected here, will persist until Messiah's reign has eclipsed all others. See also the comments on pages 144-45.

Given the stupendous power and marvelous grace which mark the kingdom's inaugural, Jesus calls his disciples to radical obedience (Matt. 5:17–7:12). All these commands are to be taken as they stand. We must beware the temptation to make them less demanding or more manageable; or so to qualify and rationalize them that they become shades of their former selves. But in seeking to obey them, we must also keep in view the already and the not yet of the kingdom's coming. We are constantly beset by the evil one; we do not consistently and unfailingly do God's will. On the contrary, we often willfully and deliberately disobey his commands, and thereby show all too clearly that we are not fully submissive to his rule. We experience the struggle Paul describes in Romans 7:14-25. In Luther's language, we recognize ourselves – each one – to be *simul iustus et peccator* and *semper iustus et peccator*. So when we disobey Jesus' commands, whether by failing to do what he requires or by doing what he prohibits, we do not despair. We recognize that sinless perfection is not attainable in a fallen world; that we have been redeemed but not yet fully liberated from our fallen condition. At the same time, we grieve over sin and take action accordingly: we return to the gospel in the beatitudes; we ask the heavenly Father to forgive our debts and to hasten the end of spiritual warfare; and we turn from our sins and submit anew to God's rule – and to striving toward an elusive and seemingly unattainable goal.[23]

Furthermore, as we read the sermon 'already' given, we appropriate spiritual resources 'not yet' granted – but to be

---

[23]See Matthew 4:17; 5:3-12; 6:9-13. Manson 1956: 85 writes that the ethic of this sermon 'stands for the unattainable, which yet we are bound to strive to attain' (cf. 5:48; Phil. 3:12-16). See also Hunter 1965: 118-22. On the struggle of Romans 7:14-25, see Chamblin 1993: 170-76.

granted before Matthew concludes. The author obviously wants his book to be read *as an unbroken whole*. Our doing so puts us at a huge advantage: unlike Jesus' original listeners, we receive this sermon already knowing of Jesus' death and resurrection, the wondrous events at the gospel's close. So we have learned that Jesus by his redemptive death saved his people from their sins; that this sermon is intended for them; and that it is these very people whose repeated violations of his commands he forgives by virtue of his atoning sacrifice. Having newly experienced saving grace, the Savior's people are strengthened in their resolve to take up their own crosses and to obey Jesus' words at whatever cost.[24] A resource provided in addition to Jesus' redemptive death is the *Name* of the Trinity – that is, the presence and the power of the Father, the Son and the Holy Spirit – to aid us in keeping Jesus' commands.[25]

We now turn to the sermon itself, beginning with 'The Blessings of the Kingdom' (5:3-16).

---

[24]See Matthew 1:21; 20:28; 26:28; also 6:12, 14-15; 16:24-26; 18:21-35. The *gospel* in the sermon anticipates Jesus' redemptive death; the *law* in the sermon makes us grateful for salvation by that means, and becomes in turn a guide for showing gratitude. Cf. Martin Luther's reading of the sermon, as summarized in Guelich 1982: 16-17; Stanton, 'Sermon,' 738. A German Lutheran pastor much indebted to this sermon and to Luther's reading of it was Dietrich Bonhoeffer. Preparing to expound the Sermon, Bonhoeffer distinguishes 'cheap grace' from 'costly grace.' 'Cheap grace is grace without discipleship, grace without the cross, grace without Jesus Christ, living and incarnate' (1961: 36). 'Costly grace is the gospel which must be *sought* again and again, the gift which must be *asked* for.... Such grace is *costly* because it calls us to follow, and it is *grace* because it calls us to follow *Jesus Christ*. It is costly because it costs a man his life, and it is grace because it gives a man the only true life' (37). For a sketch of Bonhoeffer's life (including his martyrdom at the hands of the Nazis), and his adherence to the Sermon on the Mount, see Foster 1998: 72-82.

[25]See Matthew 28:18-20, with 11:28-30.

II.
'COME, YE SINNERS, POOR AND NEEDY'[1]
(5:3-12)

This first section opens with beatitudes (Matt. 5:3-12). This term comes from the Latin *beatus* ('happy' or 'blessed'), which translates *makarios*, the Greek adjective used here. In these verses, as also in 5:13-16, Jesus lays a foundation for 5:17–7:12. Furthermore, as we shall see, these beatitudes are as deeply rooted in OT teaching as is the following exposition of law.[2]

A. The Design Jesus Chooses
Here, as often in Matthew, the structure of the passage reflects both Jesus' artistic skill and his theological intention.

Each of the first eight beatitudes (Matt. 5:3-10) consists of one sentence, in which a main clause is followed by a subordinate clause. Each main clause begins with the predicate adjective *makarioi* ('blessed'), followed by the subject, each of which includes the definite article ('*the* poor in spirit,' *hoi ptōchoi*; '*the* mourners,' *hoi penthountes*, etc.). Each subordinate clause begins with the conjunction *hoti* ('for,' 'because'), followed by a pronoun in the third person ('theirs,' 'they'). The first and the eighth subordinate clauses are identical ('because theirs is the kingdom of heaven'); four of the remaining six conclude with a future passive indicative verb ('they shall be comforted,' 'they shall be satisfied,' 'they shall be treated mercifully,' 'they shall be called').[3]

---

[1]The opening words of a hymn by Joseph Hart (1759).

[2]In other words, the truth of 5:17 (that Jesus comes not to abolish but to fulfill 'the Law and the Prophets') is attested by what precedes as well as by what follows. On the OT in Matthew, see the discussions on pages 91-99 and 120-29.

[3]The four Greek verbs in order: *paraklēthēsontai* (5:4); *chortasthēsontai* (5:6); *eleēthēsontai* (5:7); *klēthēsontai* (5:9). Note the common ending *-thēsontai*, a mark of the future passive indicative.

There is also evidence for viewing the beatitudes as two sets of four: the fourth and the eighth main clauses refer to 'righteousness'; there are thirty-six words in verses 3-6, and thirty-six in verses 7-10; the subjects of verses 3-6 are alliterative (*ptōchoi, penthountes, praeis, peinōntes*: 'poor, mourning, meek, hungering'). These verses are a beautiful tapestry whose threads are inextricably woven together, and whose design must not be disturbed. Each portion of the design has a beauty of its own; but this will be most appreciated when we view the tapestry as a whole, and its parts in relation to each other.[4]

The ninth beatitude (5:11-12) differs from, but builds on, the first eight. On the one hand, it consists of two sentences instead of one; contains thirty-four (or thirty-five) words, whereas the longest of the others – verses 3 and 10 – contain twelve words each; employs the second person ('blessed are you') rather than the third; and expressly refers to Jesus ('on account of me'). On the other hand, it also begins with *makarioi*; each of its sentences contains a main clause ('blessed are you,' 'rejoice and be glad') followed by a subordinate clause ('whenever people insult you...' 'because great is your reward...'); and it builds on the eighth (both promise blessing to the persecuted).

Luke's opening is in some ways like Matthew's. Here too Jesus addresses his disciples in the hearing of the crowd (6:17-20; see p. 299-300), and makes eight pronouncements consisting of two sets of four (6:20-26). Here too Jesus begins with short beatitudes (6:20-21), whose grammatical features recall those of Matthew 5:3-10;[5] and he then utters a much longer one (6:22-23), which is very close to Matthew 5:11-12.

---

[4]Using another image, Kreeft 1992: 91 says that each beatitude, 'like an island in an archipelago, is connected to each of the others below the surface. Each is an outcropping of the same massive undersea mountain.' 'Each beatitude is connected with and implies every other one' (92). Green 2001: 181-251 classifies the beatitudes as four 'matched pairs': the poor and the meek; the merciful and the peacemakers; those who mourn and who hunger and thirst for righteousness; the pure in heart and those who are persecuted for righteousness' sake.

[5]Each of the beatitudes of Luke 6:20-21 consists of one sentence, in which a main clause opening with *makarioi* and joined to a subject with the definite article is followed by a subordinate clause beginning with *hoti*. So it is in Matthew 5:3-10 (see p. 311).

Yet in other respects, Luke's opening differs from Matthew's. Luke 6:20-26 consistently uses the second person ('you,' 'yours'), whereas Matthew mainly uses the third (5:3-10), then the second (5:11-12). Luke's first set of four consists of beatitudes, his second of matching woes: set in contrast are the poor and the rich (6:20, 24); the hungry and the well fed (6:21a, 25a); those who weep and those who laugh (6:21b, 25b); the rejected and the respected (6:22, 26); also prophets true (6:23) and false (6:26).[6] In the same regard, the four instances of the adverb 'now' (*nun*) in verses 21 and 25, all followed by verbs in the future tense ('you shall be satisfied,' etc.), affirm the coming reversal of present conditions in especially strong terms.

B. The Persons Jesus Portrays

We turn to the subjects of the main clauses in Matthew 5:3-10 ('the poor in spirit,' etc.). Recalling the passage's design, we will be attentive to each description, and especially to the ways in which the eight are arranged and joined. In accord with literary features noted above, we may view these subjects as two sets of four. The people portrayed in verses 3-6 know their need of God, depend on him, weep before him, long for him to establish his rule, and patiently wait for him to do so. Verses 7-10 describe persons who have received the grace of God's rule, experienced its powers and submitted to its commands. Yet all eight beatitudes remain connected to each other: the actions of 5:7 and 9 flow from the attitudes of 5:3-6; the activists stay focused on God (5:8); persecuted believers (5:10) will evidence the qualities of 5:3-6 to an exceptional degree.

Their Manifold Need
Jesus speaks first of 'the poor in spirit' (*hoi ptōchoi en pneumati*; 5:3). 'The poor' are likewise the first to be mentioned in the Lukan beatitudes (6:20) and in the Isaianic passage which Jesus applies to himself in the synagogue at Nazareth (Luke 4:18): 'The Spirit of the Lord is upon me, because he anointed me to proclaim glad tidings to the poor [*euangelisasthai ptōchois*]....'

---

[6]While starting his first discourse with a set of beatitudes, Matthew reserves a set of woes for the opening of his last discourse (chs. 23–25; cf. Gundry 1994: 69).

The phrase *hoi ptōchoi en pneumati* (Matt. 5:3) is rooted in the same passage, as is clear from Jesus' reply to John (11:5): 'the poor are evangelized [*ptōchoi euangelizontai*].' So understanding what Jesus means by 'the poor in spirit' calls for attention to Isaiah 61 and to other OT texts where such language is used.

Jesus applies Isaiah 61:1, as had the prophet himself, to Israel as a whole and to a variety of needs within the nation. Matthew 5:3 certainly includes the materially and physically needy. Jesus' miracles (4:23-24) show that he cares for the sick and the diseased. In replying to John, he closely joins the evangelizing of the poor to the healing of various afflictions (11:5). His appeal to the rich man (19:21) and his warnings about wealth (6:24; 19:23-24) reflect a concern for the economically poor. In the synagogue at Nazareth, Jesus proclaims recovery of sight to the blind and uses a famished widow and a leprous man as examples of 'the poor' (Luke 4:18, 25-27); and in the Lukan beatitudes he pronounces blessings over the poor and hungry and woes over the rich and well-fed (6:20-21, 24-25; cf. 1:53).[7] But 'poverty of spirit' has other causes too. One may view his paralysis as judgment for sin and thus long for a twofold deliverance (cf. Matt. 9:1-8). Not all victims of injustice and persecution are diseased and destitute; think of Jesus. People may grieve and crave for righteousness because they are burdened by the law and devastated by their repeated violations of its demands (cf. 11:28-30). In the OT too, people are 'poor and needy' for a variety of reasons: they are deprived and disadvantaged, oppressed and afflicted, weak and helpless, outraged by injustice and guilty of sin.[8]

The second Matthean beatitude speaks of 'those who mourn' (*hoi penthountes*; 5:4). Luke 6:21 is similarly addressed

---

[7]See also Jesus' commendation of the 'poor widow' (*chēra ptōchē*) in Mark 12:41-44. The original meaning of *ptōchos* was 'begging' (BAGD s.v., 1.).

[8]All these reasons, often in combination, are represented in the following. **1.** Instances of the Hebrew *'ānî* (BDB, 'poor, afflicted, humble') and *'ānāw* (BDB, 'poor, afflicted, humble, meek') translated in the LXX by *ptōchos* ('poor') or *ptōcheia* ('poverty'): 2 Samuel 22:28; Psalms 9:18; 12:5; 14:6; 22:24; 31:10; 34:6; 35:10; 40:17; 44:24; 69:32; 70:5; 72:2, 4, 12; 74:21; 86:1; 107:41; Isaiah 3:14-15; 29:19; 61:1. **2.** Instances of *'ānî* and *'ānāw* translated by *penēs* (BAGD, 'poor, needy'), *tapeinos* (BAGD s.v., 1: 'Of low position, poor, lowly, undistinguished, of no account') or *tapeinōsis* (BAGD s.v., 2:

to 'you who weep now' (*hoi klaiontes nun*).[9] Jesus is again indebted to Isaiah 61: the One anointed to evangelize the poor is also sent to bind up the brokenhearted (61:1) and to comfort all who mourn (61:2-3). That poverty of spirit and sorrow are thus joined from a literary standpoint corresponds to reality: all kinds of poverty identified in the preceding paragraph are cause for grief and anguish. Elsewhere in the NT, the verb of Matthew 5:4 (*pentheō*, 'grieve, be sad, mourn') and the matching noun (*penthos*, 'grief, sadness, mourning') are applied to persons who experience (i) the ruinous effects of their and others' sins; and (ii) suffering, loss and death as inhabitants of a fallen world or as objects of God's judgment.[10] The verb of Luke 6:21 (*klaiō*, 'weep') and the matching noun (*klauthmos*, 'weeping') are similarly used, sometimes alongside *pentheō* and *penthos*.[11] The corresponding Hebrew terms of Isaiah 61:1-3 are as broad in their application as the *ʿănāwîm* ('poor') of 61:1. So versatile is the Hebrew noun *lēb* ('heart') that *nishbᵉrê-lēb* ('brokenhearted'; 61:1) 'covers any and every human breakdown, from emotional prostration to conviction of sin.'[12] Verses 2 and 3 speak in quick succession of *kāl-ʾăbēlîm* ('all who mourn') and of *ʾăbēlê tsiyôn* ('those who mourn in Zion'). While Isaiah addresses all causes of grief in

---

'humility, humble station, humiliation'): Deuteronomy 15:11; 24:14-15; Psalms 9:18; 10:17; 18:27; 22:26; 25:18; 72:12; 74:19; 82:3; Proverbs 3:34; Isaiah 10:2; 11:4; 14:32; 49:13; 66:2; Zephaniah 2:3; Zechariah 7:10. 3. Instances where the Hebrew *'ebyôn* (BDB, 'in want, needy, poor') is closely joined to *'ānî* or *'ānāw* or both to accentuate the condition of the persons concerned: Deuteronomy 15:11; 24:14; Job 24:4, 14; Psalms 9:18; 12:5; 35:10; 37:14; 40:17; 69:32-33; 70:5; 72:4, 12-13; 74:21; 82:3-4; 86:1; 109:16, 22; 140:12; Proverbs 30:14; 31:9, 20; Isaiah 29:19; 32:7; 41:17; Ezekiel 16:49; 18:12; 22:29; Amos 2:6-7; 8:4. *'Ebyôn* is variously translated in the LXX, often by *ptōchos*, but most often by *penēs*.

[9]This is the third Lukan beatitude; the second (6:21a) speaks of 'the ones who hunger.'

[10]See (i) 1 Corinthians 5:2; 2 Corinthians 12:21; James 4:9; and (ii) Matthew 9:15; Luke 6:25; Revelation 18:7, 8, 11, 15, 19; 21:4.

[11]See, e.g., (i) Matthew 26:75; Luke 7:38 (where tears express joy over sins forgiven as much as sorrow over sins committed); 19:41; Philippians 3:18; James 4:9 (*); (ii) Matthew 2:18; 8:12; 13:42, 50; Mark 5:38-39; Luke 6:25 (*); 7:13; 23:28; John 11:31, 33; 16:20; 20:11; Acts 9:39; 20:37; 21:13; 1 Corinthians 7:30; Revelation 18:11(*), 15 (*), 19 (*). An * indicates places where *pentheō* or *penthos* also appears.

[12]Motyer 1993: 500. He compares Isaiah 57:15.

the nation, he chiefly has in view (i) individual and corporate sin, and (ii) personal and national calamities, including those identified as God's judgments upon sin.[13] Thus are *'ābēl* and its cognates used elsewhere in the OT, to which we may add (iii) mourning over the dead.[14]

Jesus speaks thirdly of 'the meek' (*hoi praeis*; 5:5). Taking account of the NT instances of this adjective (*praus*) and the matching noun (*prautēs*), and of terms closely joined to them, we conclude that such persons are (i) lowly and humble in heart; (ii) able to endure great wrong without responding in kind; and (iii) able to serve others, including wrongdoers, with gentleness, quietness and mercy.[15] As (i) suggests, 'the meek' further describes 'the poor in spirit.' Significantly, the *ptōchoi* of Isaiah 61:1 – the principal OT text behind Matthew 5:3 – and the *praeis* of Psalm 37:11 (LXX, 36:11) –

---

[13]Motyer 1993: 500 notes that the adjective *'ābēl* ('mourning'; Isaiah 61:2, 3) 'covers all the sadnesses of life,' but that 'mourning over sin [is] the primary thought' in view of the link with 57:17-19. As noted, he relates 'brokenhearted' (61:1) to the language of 57:15.

[14]See, e.g., (i) Ezra 10:6; Nehemiah 8:9; Hosea 4:3; (ii) Exodus 33:4; Numbers 14:39; 1 Samuel 6:19; 15:35; 16:1; Nehemiah 1:4; Esther 4:3; 9:22; Job 30:31; Isaiah 3:26; 19:8; 33:9; 60:20; 66:10; Lamentations 1:4; 5:15; Ezekiel 7:27; Daniel 10:2; Joel 1:9; Amos 5:16; 8:8, 10; Micah 1:8. (iii) Genesis 27:41; 37:34, 35; 50:10-11; Deuteronomy 34:8; 2 Samuel 11:27; 13:37; 14:2; 19:1, 2; 1 Chronicles 7:22; 2 Chronicles 35:24; Ecclesiastes 7:2; Jeremiah 6:26; 16:7. To these could be added (in light of Luke 6:21) many references to weeping (see n. 19 below).

[15]See (i) Matthew 11:29 (Jesus is *praus* and *tapeinos* – 'lowly, humble' – in heart); 21:5 (Jesus enters Jerusalem on a donkey); (ii) 2 Corinthians 10:1 (*prautēs* and *epieikeia* – 'forbearance' – are joined in Jesus); Galatians 5:23 (*prautēs* is joined to *egkrateia*, 'self-control,' and *makrothymia*, 'patience, longsuffering'); Ephesians 4:2 and Colossians 3:12 (*prautēs* is joined to *tapeinophrosynē*, 'humility,' *makrothymia*, and *anechomai*, 'endure'); Titus 3:2 (*prautēs* is joined to *amachos*, 'peaceable,' and *epieikēs*, 'forbearing'); James 3:13, 17 (*prautēs* born of wisdom is *eirēnikē*, 'peaceable,' *epieikēs* and *eupeithēs*, 'willing to yield'); ACC 1a: 83 ('The meek one is more content to endure an offense than to commit one,' said Chromatius, d. 407); (iii) 1 Corinthians 4:21 (*prautēs* in place of a chastening rod); Galatians 5:22-23 (*prautēs* is joined to *agapē*, 'love,' *chrēstotēs*, 'kindness,' and *agathōsynē*, 'goodness'); 6:1 (for restoring a sinful brother); 2 Timothy 2:25 (for correcting opponents); James 3:13, 17 (*prautēs* born of wisdom is also 'full of mercy and good fruits');1 Peter 3:4 (a wife's *praus* and *hēsychios* – 'quiet' – spirit, for effective witness to the husband, vv. 1-3), 16 (for effective witness in a hostile setting, vv. 15, 17).

the OT text to which Matthew 5:5 most plainly alludes – both translate the Hebrew *'anāwîm;* so REB uses 'humble' in both instances.[16]

Those depicted in Matthew 5:3-5 'hunger and thirst for righteousness [*dikaiosynē*]' (5:6). Persons tyrannized, exploited and ostracized by the wicked, the rich and the powerful, long 'to see right prevail' (REB). So do those who have steadfastly refused to return evil for evil, and have sought instead to overcome evil with good. Those dismayed by their own law-breaking, crushed by their guilt and weary of their struggle against sin, long 'to do what is right' (REB mg.). Those matters over which they mourn arouse such longings – which in turn bring their mourning to fuller expression.

Their Faith in God

Jesus speaks in Matthew 5:8 of 'the pure in heart' (*hoi katharoi tē kardia*). According to the witness of both OT and NT, these are persons (i) who love God with all their hearts, who trust him, thirst for him, devote all their hearts' powers (rational, emotional and volitional) to him, and offer such loyalty to no other; and (ii) who therefore long for worship that is free from ceremonial defilement, and for conduct that is free from moral stain.[17]

---

[16]Thus, receiving the kingdom (Matt. 5:3) and inheriting the earth (5:5) are two expressions of one reality. Cf. 25:34 ('inherit the kingdom prepared for you'); James 2:5, which states that the poor inherit the kingdom. As noted, Green 2001 considers 5:3 and 5:5 a 'matched pair.'

[17]See, e.g., (i) Hebrew *lēb,*or *lēbāb* ('heart'), in Deuteronomy 6:5; Psalms 12:2; 27:8 (with v. 4); 28:7; 33:21; 62:8; 84:2; 86:11; 119:10; Greek *kardia* ('heart') in Matthew 6:21; 22:37 (contrast 15:8); Ephesians 6:5 ('in singleness of heart, as you obey Christ,' NRSV); Colossians 3:16; (ii) Hebrew *tahôr* ('pure, clean') in Leviticus 7:19; 10:10; 11:47; Ezra 6:20; Psalm 51:10 (with *lēb*); Hebrew *bar* ('pure, clean') in Psalms 24:4; 73:1 (both with *lēbāb*); Hebrew *zākāh* ('be clean, pure') in Psalms 73:13 (with *lēbāb*); 119:9; Proverbs 20:9 (with *lēb*); F. Hauck, *TDNT* 3: 416-17, on laws of cleanness and uncleanness in OT worship; Greek *katharos* in 1 Timothy 1:5; 2 Timothy 2:22 (both with *kardia*); *hagnos* ('pure, holy') in James 3:17; *kardia* in James 4:8. On the heart as 'the integrating center of man as a rational, emotional, volitional being,' see page 248 above.

'The poor in spirit' (5:3), dismayed by their need and desperate in their extremity, cling to the covenant-keeping God and to his promises on their behalf. 'Purity of heart,' they recognize, is impossible apart from his creative power (Ps. 51:10). They implore God both to deliver them from, and to sustain them within, their troubles. Such faith also finds expression when the poor and needy seek help from Jesus the Messiah.[18]

Similarly, persons often mourn and weep (5:4) in God's presence to signal both their *confidence*, sometimes in the absence of human consolation, that he cares for them and is attentive to their need; and their *longing* for his deliverance in the face of sin, calamity, judgment and death. For the same twofold reason, sorrows are brought to God's Messiah.[19]

How are the 'meek' (Matt. 5:5) able to refrain from avenging themselves and from insisting on their rights? What enables them to show mercy to other people (5:7), including those who persecute them for doing what is right (5:10)? It is their assurance that the sovereign God will (i) judge and vanquish the wicked; and (ii) vindicate and reward his people, and thus will establish the righteous rule for which they 'hunger and thirst,' (5:6; cf. 6:10, 33). Psalm 37, which contains the text (v. 11) most plainly in view in Matthew 5:5, contains all these promises, together with appeals patiently to wait upon Yahweh to fulfill them.[20]

---

[18]For God as the trust of 'the poor,' see *'ānî* in 2 Samuel 22:28; Psalms 14:6; 25:18; 34:6; 40:17; 70:5; 72:12; 74:19, 21; 82:3; 86:1; 109:22; 140:12; Isaiah 66:2; Zephaniah 3:12; *'ānāw* in Psalms 9:18; 10:17; 22:26; 69:32; Zephaniah 2:3; cf. Mark 12:41-44 (the poor widow's offering). For appeals (explicit and implicit) to Jesus from the poor and needy, see Matthew 4:24; 8:2, 6, 16; 9:2, 10, 18-21, 27-28; 12:22; 14:13-14, 35-36; 15:22, 25, 30; 17:14-15; 19:13; 20:30-31; 21:14, 31-32. Cf. Rutherford 1984: 406: 'I have nothing, nothing to give Christ but poverty.'

[19]See e.g. Numbers 14:39-40; Judges 2:4-5; 20:23, 26; 21:2-3; 1 Samuel 1:10; 2 Samuel 12:16, 21-22; 2 Kings 20:2-3; 22:19; Ezra 10:1; Nehemiah 1:4; 8:9; Esther 4:3; Psalm 6:6-8; 39:12; 42:2-3; 56:8; Isaiah 38:2-3; Jeremiah 50:4; Lamentations 5:15 (with v. 1); Hosea 12:4; Joel 2:12-17; Matthew 15:22; Luke 2:25-26; 7:38; John 11:32-33. Cf. Jesus' own tears at Lazarus' grave (John 11:35) and over Jerusalem (Luke 19:41).

[20]See (i) Psalm 37:1-2, 9-10, 12-15, 17, 20, 22, 28, 34-36, 38; (ii) 37:3-6, 9, 11, 17-19, 22-29, 32-34, 37, 39-40; also the appeals of 37:1, 7, 34. Jesus, the meek one (Matt. 11:29) foresees the Day of Judgment (11:20-24). He who gently enters

Their Faithfulness to God

Persons who have faith in God are faithful to him and to his commands. Their obedience does not await the amelioration of their condition. As God abounds 'in love [*chesed*] and faithfulness ['*met*]' to them amid those conditions,[21] so it is precisely as the poor and needy, the mournful and the meek, the victimized and the persecuted, that they devote themselves to doing God's will (Matt. 6:10; cf. Zeph. 2:3). They respond to his faithfulness with a fidelity of their own: the 'pure in heart' (Matt. 5:8) serve God with wholehearted devotion, with 'undivided loyalty.'[22] Their love for God finds expression in love for neighbor (5:43-48; 22:37-40; cf. 1 Pet. 1:22). As those who have received the divine mercy and remain in constant need of it, they more readily show mercy to others (5:7).[23] Those to whom God grants *shālôm* become 'peacemakers' (5:9), one way their mercy finds expression, and one means by which their longing for justice (5:6) is satisfied.[24] One evidence that they do what is right – i.e., adhere to God's commands – is their experience of persecution (Matt. 5:10), not least from persons who love injustice and resist peacemaking (cf. Ps. 120:6-7).

Such is the behavior expected from Messiah's followers: (i) Themselves *poor in spirit*, they are to serve the impoverished,

---

Jerusalem on a donkey (21:5; Zech. 9:9) will rule universally (Zech. 9:10). Paul both invokes Christ's meekness (2 Cor. 10:1) and wields weapons for advancing Christ's rule (10:3-6). Those who bear witness with gentleness (1 Pet. 3:16) serve a Master who possesses supreme authority (3:22).

[21]The quotation comes from Exodus 34:6. See C. below.

[22]France 1985: 110. Cf. Keener 1999: 170 ('unmixed devotion to God'). For *'met* ('faithfulness') as a trait of God's people, see, e.g., Exodus 18:21; Joshua 24:14; Psalm 51:6. The related Hebrew noun *'mûnâ* can join 'faith' to 'faithfulness'; see, e.g., Habakkuk 2:4.

[23]Mercy (*eleos*) expresses love (*agapē*). The Hebrew noun *chesed* is so rich as to embrace both, as evidenced by both God (e.g., Num. 14:18-19; Ps. 136:1-26; Micah 7:18, 20) and his people (e.g., Josh. 2:14; Prov. 3:3; Hosea 6:6).

[24]For combating the disorder and evil produced by the earthly and demonic 'wisdom' (James 3:16), persons who receive wisdom from God are 'peace loving' and 'full of mercy' (3:17; as noted, Green 2001 matches Matthew 5:7 and 9). As in Matthew 5:6-7, so in the OT seeking justice (*mišpāt*) and loving mercy (*'met*) are joined together, in both God (Ps. 103:4-8; Jer. 9:24) and his people (Isa. 16:5; Micah 6:8; Zech. 7:9). By such means, God's people follow the Servant's example (Isa. 61:1-3; 58:6-7).

the afflicted and the oppressed. (ii) As those who *grieve*, they are to console and encourage one another. (iii) Like Jesus, let them be *meek*, gentle and forbearing. (iv) Since they *long for righteousness*, let them strive for social justice and personal holiness. (v) In accord with God's treatment of them, they are to be *merciful*. (vi) As they practice righteousness, let them remain *pure in heart* – loving and trusting God, undivided in their allegiance to him, and careful not to seek acclaim due him alone. (vii) As recipients of peace and as disciples of the Peacemaker, they are called upon to *make peace* between individuals and peoples. (viii) Manifesting the *righteousness* to which Messiah calls them, and which marks citizens of God's kingdom, they are sure to be *persecuted*.[25]

C. The Gospel Jesus Proclaims
To the people portrayed in the beatitudes, Jesus proclaims 'the gospel [*euangelion*] of the kingdom' (4:23; cf. 11:5; Luke 4:18). He declares them 'blessed' (*makarioi*) – recipients of blessing. What makes them so?

The Bestowal of God's Favor
All these benefactions come from God. By his authority, persons come under his sovereign, benevolent rule (Matt. 5:3, 10) and inherit the earth (5:5). To those who love him, he grants yet fuller disclosures of himself (5:8). By his covenantal initiatives, human beings become his children (5:9).

Four of the Beatitudes contain verbs in the passive voice – all instances of the 'divine passive': it is God who will comfort

---

[25]See, e.g., (i) Matthew 10:8; 25:35-36; Mark 14:7; Romans 15:26; 2 Corinthians 6:10; 8:2; James 2:1-6; (ii) 2 Corinthians 1:3-7; Galatians 6:1 10; 1 Thessalonians 5:14; (iii) 2 Corinthians 10:1; Colossians 3:12; Titus 3:2; James 3:13; 1 Peter 3:4; (iv) Matthew 5:20; 6:33; Romans 6:13; Philippians 1:11; 2 Timothy 2:22; Hebrews 11:33; (v) Matthew 18:21-35; Romans 12:8; James 2:13; 3:17; (vi) Matthew 6:1-24; 2 Corinthians 10:17-18; Ephesians 6:5; Philippians 4:2-3; Colossians 3:16-17; James 3:17; (vii) Matthew 5:44-45; Acts 9:26-27; Romans 12:17-21; 14:17, 19; Ephesians 2:11-18; 4:3; Philippians 4:2-3; Hebrews 12:14; James 3:17-18; 1 Peter 3:11; (viii) Matthew 5:11-12; 10:16-23; 24:9-13; John 15:18-21; Philippians 1:29; Colossians 1:24; 2 Timothy 3:12; 1 Peter 3:14; 4:14, 16.

those who mourn (5:4); he whose actions will fully satisfy those who long for righteousness (5:6); he who will grant mercy to the merciful (5:7); he who will declare peacemakers to be children of God (5:9). Here, as elsewhere in Matthew, *makarios* denotes a 'privileged recipient of divine favor.'[26]

In the OT too it is God who cares for the poor and the afflicted; consoles the grieving and the despairing; defends the victims of oppression and injustice; exalts the meek and the lowly; and shows mercy to the merciful, and to the guilty and contrite.[27] By the same token it is God who exercises his righteousness to save his people and to judge their enemies; establishes his just rule for his people's peace and prosperity; and enters with them into the joyous fellowship promised in his covenant with them.[28] The Hebrew counterpart to *makarios* is *'ašrê* ('How blessed...,' 'how happy...'), especially prominent in the Psalms.[29] Here it is invariably recipients of *God's* favor who are identified as *'ašrê* – as *makarioi*. 'How blessed' are persons whom God chooses for his own; to whom he grants

---

[26]BAGD s.v. '"Blessed" means "to be congratulated" in a deeply religious sense and with more emphasis on divine approval than on human happiness' (Gundry 1994: 68). Both here and elsewhere in Matthew (11:6; 13:16; 16:17; 24:46), blessings from God are pronounced by Messiah. The matching verb *makarizō* appears twice in the NT (Luke 1:48; James 5:11); here people recognize blessings God has bestowed, upon Mary and Job respectively.

[27]See, e.g., Numbers 22:28; Psalms 9:18; 12:5; 18:25; 22:24; 30:5; 34:6, 18; 35:10; 51:17; 69:32; 72:2, 4, 12; 103:3-14; 116:6; 136:23-24; 138:6; Isaiah 3:14-15; 29:19; 30:19; 35:10; 55:7; 57:15-19; 60:20-21; 61:1-3; 65:19; 66:10; Jeremiah 20:13; 31:13; Hosea 2:23; cf. 1 Corinthians 1:26-31.

[28]See, e.g., the instances of *tsedeq* and *tsᵉdāqâ* ('righteousness') in Psalms 5:8; 24:5; 65:5; 71:2, 15, 16, 24; 98:2; 103:6; Isaiah 45:8; 46:13; 51:5-6; 59:16 (with vv. 14-20); 61:10; Hosea 10:12b; the promise of God's (or Messiah's) rule and his people's inheritance in Psalm 37:9, 11, 29, 34; Isaiah 9:6-7; 11:1-9; 32:15-18; 60:15-22; Zechariah 9:9-10; and the covenantal promises in Genesis 17:1-22; Deuteronomy 7:9; 1 Chronicles 16:14-18; Isaiah 54:10; 55:3; 61:8-9; Jeremiah 31:31-34; 32:36-41; 50:4-5; Ezekiel 16:59-63; 37:24-28. The promises of Matthew 5:6, 8 are joined in Psalm 11:7, 'For the LORD is righteous [*tsaddîq*], he loves justice [*tsᵉdāqâ*]; upright men will see his face' (NIV).

[29]*'Ašrê* occurs twenty-six times in the Psalter; twenty-five are translated *makarios* or *makarioi* in the LXX. The exception is Psalm 144 (143):15, where LXX has *makarizō*, 'to call or consider blessed, happy' (cf. n. 26). In the OT the Hebrew noun *'ešer* (or *'āšār*) appears only as *'ašrê*, a plural construct. In the Psalms the form once appears with a suffix, *'ašreykhā*, 'how blessed you are' (128:2).

children, fruitful labor and material wealth; whose sins he forgives.[30] 'How blessed' are those who both fear God and delight in his presence, who meditate on his *Torah* and obey it with acts of justice and mercy;[31] who trust him, find in him their refuge and strength, and place their hope in him and his promised Messiah.[32] In short, 'how blessed the people whose God is Yahweh!' (Ps. 144:15b).

The Presence of God's Son

It is Jesus whom the Spirit of God anoints to proclaim good news to the poor (Matt. 11:5; Luke 4:18). The poor here addressed (Matt. 5:3) are *makarioi* because Jesus declares them to be so (cf. 11:6). His words are faithful and true because of who he is and what he does: he is the Servant king appointed to inaugurate God's benevolent rule; the beloved Son who mediates the Father's favor; and the incarnate God come to save his people from their sins, and to dwell with them forever.[33] Such is his authority (7:28-29) that his word *achieves* what it declares and commands, for the poor who are guilty (Luke 7:48) or afflicted (Matt. 8:16) or both (9:2, 6).

One reason Jesus utters the Beatitudes with such authority is that he embodies the qualities here described. He is *poor in spirit*: assailed by fierce and unrelenting evil, he trusts in God the Father for protection, deliverance and strength. He *mourns* – not over personal sins (for he has none), but over others' blindness of mind, hardness of heart, stubbornness of will, bondage to sin. He identifies himself as *meek* (11:29; cf. 21:5); God's Servant is not quarrelsome and clamorous, and he deals gently with the weak and vulnerable (12:19-20); when insulted

---

[30]See Psalm 32:1-2; 33:12; 65:4; 127:5; 128:2; 144:15a. Cf. Proverbs 20:7; Isaiah 32:20.

[31]See Psalm 1:1; 41:1; 84:4; 89:15; 94:12; 106:3; 112:1; 119:1-2; 128:1; 137:8-9. Cf. Proverbs 3:13; 8:32, 34; 28:14; Isaiah 56:2; also Proverbs 14:21 (where *'ašrê* is translated *makaristos*).

[32]See Psalm 2:12; 34:8; 40:4; 84:5, 12; 146:5. Cf. Deuteronomy 33:29; Isaiah 30:18; Daniel 12:12; also Proverbs 16:20 (where, as in 14:21, *'ašrê* is translated *makaristos*).

[33]See pages 301-02, 'the Messiah'; comments on Matthew 1:21-23; 3:16-17; 4:17; Willard 1998: 106.

and oppressed, he does not retaliate or threaten vengeance (1 Pet. 2:23; Isa. 53:7). Unlike fallen creatures who, appalled by their iniquity, crave to grow in holiness, Jesus *hungers and thirsts for righteousness* as one whose mission is to establish the just rule of God (12:18, 20) and to instruct his followers in the way of holiness (5:17-20 *et seq.*). Throughout his ministry, he is *merciful* to the helpless and needy. He, the Servant whose singular purpose is to know and to do the Father's will, is *pure in heart*; in him, faithful Israel is reduced to one person (Isa. 49:3; 50:5-8). As the one who supplants Satan's tyranny with God's gracious rule, atones for his people's sins and reconciles them to God, he is the *peacemaker* (cf. Isa. 9:6-7; 49:5-6; Eph. 2:14-17). As his life progresses, he is increasingly *persecuted for the sake of righteousness*.[34]

It is Jesus who accounts for the blessings promised here. He is the royal Messiah by whose presence and power the kingdom of heaven (Matt. 5:3, 10) is inaugurated and consummated; disciples who suffer on his account will be richly rewarded in heaven (5:11-12).[35] He, God's anointed Servant, fulfills Isaiah 61 by evangelizing the poor, healing the afflicted and proclaiming liberty (*aphesis*) to the captives (Luke 4:18-21) – especially those possessed by demons and enslaved by their own sins.[36] As he who saves from sins

---

[34]Matthew 5:10 is especially applicable to Jesus, for he is the supremely 'righteous one' (*dikaios*): see 27:19; Acts 3:14; 7:52; 22:14; 1 Peter 3:18; 1 John 2:1.

[35]Persecution 'for the sake of righteousness' (*heneken dikaiosynēs*; 5:10) and 'for my sake' (*heneken emou*; 5:11) are two expressions of one reality. For Jesus' decisive acts at the kingdom's consummation, and his right to decide who will enter the kingdom, see 5:19-20; 7:21-23; 8:11-12; 13:10-17, 37-43; 16:19, 27; 18:1-9; 19:13-30; 21:42-44; 24:27-31; 25:1-46; 26:64.

[36]The two instances of *aphesis* in Luke 4:18 describe 'release' for captives (as in Isaiah 61:1) and 'liberation' for the oppressed (as in Isaiah 58:6). That Luke here refers principally to the forgiveness of sins is suggested by the following: (i) in the other eight occurrences of *aphesis* in Luke–Acts, forgiveness of sins is expressly in view (as also in several instances of the matching verb *aphiēmi*); (ii) in Zechariah's prophecy God redeems his people, (Luke 1:68), both by rescuing them from their enemies, (1:71-74), and by forgiving their sins, (1:76-79; cf. 3:3); (iii) in Luke the manifold salvation promised in 4:16-30 (the inaugural of Jesus' mission) is primarily achieved through Jesus' death and resurrection (the climactic events in Luke),

(Matt. 1:21), who conquers Satan (12:28), whose words bring healing (9:22; 11:28-30; cf. Isa. 50:4), and who raises the dead (Matt. 9:23-26), he comforts those who mourn (5:4). Once the kingdom comes, his people will inherit the earth (5:5). By virtue of his reign from David's throne, righteousness and justice will be established forever (5:6).[37] To the needy and the helpless, to the guilty and the culpable, he imparts the divine mercy (5:7).[38] Joined to him, the Father's beloved Son, others will see God (5:8; cf. 2 Cor. 3:18; 4:6) and be acclaimed as his children (5:9; cf. 11:25-28).

Embodying as he does the qualities here commended, Jesus himself receives the blessings here promised. The coming kingship belongs to him (Matt. 5:3, 10). His hunger for righteousness (5:6) will be satisfied through his own just rule and through the sanctification and glorification of his people. The earth his people inherit (5:5) is his possession. When God raised him from the dead, he who had endured Gethsemane and Golgotha was consoled (5:4); he who had lain helpless in death was shown mercy (5:7). Exalted to 'the right hand of power' (26:64), Jesus beheld the Father (5:8), was newly acclaimed his Son (5:9), and received his own heavenly reward (5:12; cf. 28:18). Compare the victories won by the Servant by virtue of his atoning sacrifice (Isa. 52:13; 53:10-12).

---

a cardinal effect of which is the forgiveness of sins, (24:27; cf. 22:19-20); Jer. 31:31-34); and (iv) in Isaiah 61:1 the Servant declares 'release of every sort' (Motyer 1993: 500; cf. 42:1-7, where the Servant's manifold mission to Israel and the nations is described as freeing prisoners from a dungeon, v. 7). Israel's liberation from Babylonian captivity signals that the penalty for her sins has been paid (40:2) by virtue of the Servant's envisaged sacrifice (53:4-12). That Luke 4:18 also embraces release from demonic oppression is clear from ensuing passages (4:31-37; 8:26-39; 9:37-43; 11:17-20; 13:16).

[37]Cf. Isaiah 9:6-7; 11:1-9; 32:1; 42:1-4 (quoted in Matthew 12:18-21). For the justice and righteousness of David's rule, see 2 Samuel 8:15; for his prophecy about his greater Son, see 2 Samuel 23:3-4. Davis 1999: 246-47 speaks of the *attractiveness* of this king (in part because such rulers are so rare) and of 'the reviving, refreshing, renewing effects' of his reign. Only Jesus will perfectly fulfill the charge given to King Lemuel by his mother (Prov. 31:8-9).

[38]In Matthew, every time Jesus hears the plea, 'Have mercy' (*Eleēson*), he responds in kind (9:27-30; 15:22-28; 17:14-18; 20:30-34). For his, and

The Reality of God's Rule

Here is a further reason why the message of 5:3-12 is rightly called gospel (4:23). God's rule has already been inaugurated (4:17); so disciples' confidence about the future rests in part on present experience of the kingdom's blessings. Having submitted to Jesus' authority, they are already under God's benevolent rule (5:3, 10) and already receive rewards for their fidelity to him (6:4, 6, 18).[39] Because they belong to the Son of God, they are now God's children (5:9), privileged to address him as Father (6:9). As those whose sins are being forgiven (9:2), they are receiving the divine mercy (5:7); as those whose diseases are being healed (4:24), they now experience the divine consolation (5:4). By heeding Christ's commands about relationships within and beyond the church, they are beginning to see justice established (5:6) and the earth reclaimed (5:5). As those closely joined to Immanuel, in a real sense they already see God (5:8).

That kingdom is sure to be consummated (6:10). Disciples rejoice amid perils and persecutions (5:10-12), *because they know* present conditions will end; in the heavenly kingdom they will receive full consolation (5:4) and final reward (5:12).[40] Their longing for the conquest of evil, and for righteousness both social and personal, will be fully satisfied (5:6) when God's rule is fully established (5:3, 10) on a transformed earth (5:5).[41] As those who belong to God's Messiah, they will receive mercy at the Last Judgment (5:7). Thereafter, as God's glorified children, they will know his presence and behold his

---

the Father's, mercy to those with enormous debts of sin, see 18:21-35 (cf. 6:14-15); Luke 7:36-50; Ephesians 2:4; Titus 3:5.

[39]Cf. Matthew 19:29, which may speak of present as well as future rewards. See comments *ad loc.*

[40]Cf. 6:19-21; 25:21-23; Luke 6:23; James 1:12, beginning with *makarios*; 1 Peter 1:3-7.

[41]The promise of 5:5 embraces not just the *land* of Israel, but the whole *earth*; so too Jewish interpreters of Psalm 37:9, 11, 29 (Keener 1999: 167). Toward that end, the risen Messiah, given universal authority, commands that all nations of the earth be evangelized (Matt. 28:18-20). Cf. Yahweh's pledge to the Davidic king, (Ps. 2:8); see also Ephesians 1:10; 2 Peter 3:13; Revelation 21:1 *et seq.*

face forever (5:8, 9; cf. 1 Cor. 13:9-12). For all these reasons, Jesus calls his listeners to unceasing and unbounded joy.[42]

Living as they do between the 'already' and the 'not yet' of the kingdom, such persons are both satisfied and dissatisfied; they both rejoice and grieve; they have nothing but possess everything (cf. 2 Cor. 6:10). Witnessing present manifestations of divine power, they crave the final conquest of evil; adoring the wonders of divine grace, they are appalled by the tenacity of personal sin; knowing the kingdom has been inaugurated, they more fervently pray, 'Your kingdom come' (Matt. 6:10).

D. The Challenge Jesus Issues
Viewed in the light of Jesus' twofold audience and the remainder of the sermon, the Beatitudes offer a twofold challenge.

Acknowledge God
It must be thus, since all these benefactions come from him (pp. 320-22). There are probably many in the crowd (Matt. 7:28) who already trust and obey the God of Israel. It is also probable that the multitude includes many who, though unquestionably poor and needy, do not cling to God; whose desire is more for the kingdom's benefits than for God himself; who grieve over their afflictions and misfortunes but not over their sins and failures; who, utterly impoverished, are enslaved not to God but to the money they lack; who plot revenge against their oppressors instead of waiting for divine

---

[42]Romans 5:2-5 affirms that hope enables us to endure suffering and that suffering deepens hope; 2 Corinthians 4:17, that present troubles achieve future glory. Lewis (1962: 197) reflects upon such texts as Matthew 5:12 ('great is your reward in heaven'): 'If there lurks in most modern minds the notion that to desire our own good and earnestly to hope for the enjoyment of it is a bad thing, I submit that this notion has crept in from Kant and the Stoics and is no part of the Christian faith. Indeed, if we consider the unblushing promises of reward and the staggering nature of the rewards promised in the Gospels, it would seem that Our Lord finds our desires, not too strong, but too weak. We are half-hearted creatures, fooling about with drink and sex and ambition when infinite joy is offered us, like an ignorant child who wants to go on making mud pies in a slum because he cannot imagine what is meant by the offer of a holiday at the sea. We are far too easily pleased.'

retribution; whose efforts toward social justice and peace are for Israel's glory rather than God's;[43] who, in their desperation and extremity, are consumed by self-love rather than love for God and neighbor. The Beatitudes are overtures of grace to such persons: God is attentive to the lowliness of your condition and the acuteness of your need; he offers help to you whom others despise and ostracize; the injustice, disease and death you suffer, he will conquer; he alone can free you from the evils and the demons that enslave you; therefore repent of your sins, center your life upon God and submit to his rule (4:17). Even the adjoining woes of Luke 6:24-26 are expressions of grace to those addressed: you are enslaved to wealth and comfort, to security and pride; you have exploited or ignored the poor and needy; you are threatened with damnation; therefore repent of your manifold sin and surrender to God before it is too late.[44]

Also represented in the crowd, and doubtless among the disciples too, are (in James' language) the *double minded* – persons who strive to join meekness to assertiveness; or mercy to vengeance; or peacemaking to war making; or slavery to God and to money; or devotion to God and to self. Jesus challenges such persons to become 'pure in heart,' to love God with all their powers and to serve him with undivided loyalty.

Are there among Jesus' listeners persons whose very needs threaten to become *idols*, or virtues *entitling* them to God's blessing? Have some become *slaves to poverty* (as

---

[43]'For Christians, social justice concerns must always be rooted in profound spiritual realities' (Foster 1998: 279). Non-Christians may, in response to God's law inscribed on the heart (Rom. 2:14-15), honor the cardinal virtue of justice by working, for example, towards racial reconciliation. Such a virtue would be greatly strengthened – and radically transformed – by their being reconciled to God. Newly at peace with him through the forgiveness of sins (Matt. 1:21), they can now pursue peacemaking with far stronger motives, and with the primary aim of bringing persons, races and nations under the rule of God in Christ (6:33).

[44]Jesus offers a wealthy man 'treasure in heaven' (19:21) and affirms that the rich may, by God's saving power, enter the kingdom (19:23-26). James exhorts the rich to boast of their lowliness (1:10-11); better that they mourn now (5:1-6; cf. 4:7-10), than at the Judgment (Luke 6:25b). John the Baptist also evangelized by warning of imminent judgment (pp. 253-57).

others are slaves to money) and striven to become poorer (as others have striven to become richer) in expectation of greater recompense? Have some *sought after* sorrow instead of joy, or affliction instead of health, in hopes of gaining greater dividends? Has one *hungered and thirsted* for oppression and injustice, or *pursued* persecution and even martyrdom, in a calculated attempt to win the highest acclaim from men and the richest reward from God?[45] In face of such a mentality, real or potential, Jesus teaches that God blesses the poor because of what they lack, not what they have; that the basis for his benevolence lies nowhere but in his own nature;[46] that the genuinely poor in spirit trust not in their lowliness, afflictions and deprivations but in God; that the merciful receive not wages but *mercy* (Matt. 5:7);[47] that the truly virtuous are inattentive to their virtue (25:34-40) and to human acclaim (6:1-18) but preoccupied with God; that the pure in heart are, precisely because of their attentiveness to God, exceptionally aware of their sin and need of forgiveness;[48] and that good works, including martyrdom, are as nothing if motivated by self-love rather than love for God and neighbor (7:21-23; 19:16-22; cf. 1 Cor. 13:1-3).

---

[45]Willard 1998: 106 speaks of using the beatitudes to promote 'a new legalism.' For evidence of zeal for martyrdom, see Frend 1967: 220 (persons 'demanding execution'), 277 (martyrdom 'not merely to be suffered, but to be provoked'). Opposing such zeal, Clement of Alexandria invoked Jesus' command in Matthew 10:23; to court, rather than to flee, persecution makes us accomplices to evil (ibid., 263-64).

[46]Jesus speaks of reward (5:12) 'not in the sense of an earned payment... but of a freely given recompense, out of all proportion to the service' (France 1985: 112); cf. 19:29; 20:14-15; 25:21, 23; Luke 7:7-10; Calvin 1994: 173; Jeremias 1971: 215-17. The 'crown of righteousness' that Paul awaits is a gift from 'the righteous judge,' Christ the Lord (2 Tim. 4:8). In Ephesians 2:8, Paul declares that we are saved '*by* grace *through* faith [*dia pisteōs*]': never does he or any other NT writer say that we are saved 'on account of faith [*dia pistin*].'

[47]Mary acknowledges God to be her Savior (Luke 1:47), and herself and his other faithful servants to be recipients of his mercy (1:50, 54). It is because she has received the divine grace (1:28, *kecharitōmenē*) that others 'count her blessed' (1:48, *makariousin*).

[48]See, e.g., Psalm 24:3-6; Isaiah 6:1-7; 33:13-24; James 4:1-10; and comments on Matthew 9:13.

Follow Messiah

It cannot be otherwise, since God inaugurates his kingdom, and bestows its blessings, through his Servant-King (pp. 320-26). The opening and the close of the sermon (Matt. 5:3-12; 7:21-27) teach that these benefactions are secured by authority of the preacher, and that one submits to God's rule by heeding the words of his Son.[49] Only one beatitude (5:11-12) is directly addressed to Jesus' loyal followers; but in the end, the blessings of 5:3-10 are reserved for them as well.

So there is a challenge for the crowds. Those of their number who know the God of Israel can be expected to become Jesus' disciples. For Jesus is Immanuel (1:23), the Father's beloved Son (3:17), and the One in whom the Law and the Prophets reach their appointed goal (5:17) – and therefore the One whose disclosures of God will both perpetuate and surpass those of the OT. How could Israelites who embrace OT revelations of God fail to perceive those same qualities in Jesus? And will not persons who truly love the Father also love his Son and become his disciples? Those in the crowd who reject Jesus will thereby demonstrate that they do not know his Father, the God of Israel, and that they do not understand Moses and the Prophets.[50]

There is also a challenge for the disciples. How firmly they have grasped the grace of the gospel, how deeply they have repented, and how seriously they are committed to Jesus, will come to light in their responses to his radical commands (5:17–7:12) and in their resultant conduct (7:13-27).

Let all listeners pay the closest heed to the Beatitudes and the rest of the sermon, for at the Last Judgment, this speaker will determine who receives the kingdom's rewards (7:21-27;

---

[49]The cruciality of *following* Jesus is already evident in Matthew 4:18-22 (see pp. 294-95).

[50]Jesus later teaches that knowing the Father depends on disclosures from the Son (11:27); and knowing the Son, upon disclosures from the Father (16:17). In John, Jesus stresses that he reveals the Father (14:9; cf. 1:18); that those who honor the Father will honor him as well (5:23, 37-38; 6:45; 8:42); and that those who believe the Scriptures will believe him (5:39-47; cf. Luke 16:31). Following the third Servant song of Isaiah 50:4-9, we read: 'Whoever among you fears the LORD, let him obey his servant's commands' (50:10, REB; cf. Motyer 1993: 401).

25:1-46). As God's saving grace comes to supreme expression in Jesus' life and work, there is greater cause for joy than ever before – and also graver risk. *Makarioi* indeed are those who perceive Jesus to be the fulfillment of the Law and the Prophets; for whom he is not an obstacle to faith but an object of faith and worship; and who serve and obey him at whatever cost.[51] But woe to those (i) who reject, or who accept and then discard, the gospel of the kingdom; (ii) who fail to act upon, or grossly misread, the mercy shown in Jesus' miracles; (iii) who prove in the end to be false disciples; and (iv) who repudiate and kill the Son of God.[52]

The Final Judgment is postponed (the quotation of Isaiah 61:1-2 in Luke 4:18-19 stops short of 'the day of vengeance') – evidence of God's mercy to the recalcitrant and unrepentant (cf. 2 Pet. 3:9). But that Day will surely come – evidence of God's mercy to his sorrowing and longsuffering people. At the End, God will exercise his righteousness both to save his people and to judge the wicked; and he will accomplish both by means of his Servant-King (Matt. 12:18-21).[53]

---

[51]See Matthew 11:6; 13:16-17; 14:33; 16:16-17, 24-27; 18:6; 19:27-30; 28:17. *Makarios* occurs in 11:6; 13:16; 16:17, each confirming that it is the divine initiative, not the human condition, that make one 'blessed.'

[52]See, e.g., (i) 13:1-23; (ii) 11:20-24; 12:24-32; (iii) 7:21-23; 24:45-51; 26:14-16; John 6:60-71 (and note that it is members of the church whom Paul urges 'not to receive the grace of God in vain,' 2 Cor. 6:1; cf. 13:5); and (iv) 21:33-46; 22:1-14.

[53]Cf. pages 143-45. Note how the hope of salvation and judgment, as voiced by Mary and Zechariah, focuses on the coming Messiah (Luke 1:46-55, 68-79).

III.
'WE ARE GOD'S PEOPLE'[1]
(5:13-16)

These verses conclude the opening section of the sermon, 'The Blessings of the Kingdom' (5:3-16); pave the way for the following section, 'The Righteousness of the Kingdom' (5:17–7:12); and are to be interpreted in light of these surrounding verses.

A. Disciples

Jesus addresses disciples: '*You* are the salt of the earth.... *You* are the light of the world' (Matt. 5:13a, 14a).[2] He speaks of what they are, not of what they ought to be: 'You *are* the salt of the earth.... You *are* the light of the world.' Yet because nature and function are inseparable in both salt and light, the text also contains exhortations implicit (5:13b, 15) and explicit (5:16). What the disciples do discloses what they are: 'Salt salts because it is salt, and light illumines because it is light.'[3] As salt and light are eminently useful, so can the disciples be.[4] By the same token, if they do not function in accord with their nature, how can they justify their existence?

They evidence that nature and fulfill that function *as the persons described in 5:3-12* (and as identified on pp. 313-20). Verses 11-12, with seven instances of the second person plural (in verbs and pronouns), link verses 13-16 to the other beatitudes. The close of 5:16, 'your Father in heaven,' recalls the close of 5:9: 'they shall be called sons of God.' Included in

---

[1]The opening words of a hymn by Bryan Jeffery Leech (1976).

[2]Each verse begins, *Hymeis este*. Unlike the English 'are,' the Greek verb *este* (the second person plural of *eimi*) identifies the subject: 'you are.' The addition of the pronoun *hymeis* makes the expression emphatic.

[3]Franzmann 1961: 42. Cf. Matthew 7:15-20.

[4]'Nothing is more useful than salt and sunshine,' wrote Pliny in his *Natural History* (quoted in Carson 1984: 138).

the 'good works' of 5:16 are deeds of mercy (5:7), peacemaking (5:9) and righteousness (5:10).

The two metaphors also indicate that disciples affect persons beyond their own number: 'You are the salt of *the earth*.... You are the light of *the world*.' The disciples' witness therefore extends to those who exploit, oppress and persecute them (5:6, 10-12), as shall become plainer in Jesus' following exposition of the law (see 5:21-26, 38-48). It is also a witness that embraces all nations throughout the world, as Jesus shall explain in due course (24:14; 26:13; 28:18-20).

B. Salt

Salt (Greek *halas*) served many a practical purpose in the ancient world. Within the biblical context, the following uses are especially noteworthy: 1. Added to Israel's sacrifices, or to a polluted spring, salt was a sign or agent of *purification*.[5] 2. Salt was a desirable *seasoning* for food. By synecdoche 'to eat salt' meant to take a meal.[6] 3. Salt was an effective *preservative* for meats. Similarly, it helped to *protect* a newborn child from disease.[7] 4. Salt was used in small amounts as a *fertilizer*.[8] 5. Salt could signal the *covenantal bond* between God and his people, a usage related to the first three.[9] But salt that 'lost its taste'

---

[5]Exodus 30:35 ('salted, pure and holy'); Leviticus 2:13 (for the grain offering, salt is required but yeast is forbidden, v. 4); 2 Kings 2:19-22; Ezra 6:9; Ezekiel 43:24; cf. Mark 9:49.

[6]Job 6:6; Colossians 4:6. For the idiom 'to eat salt' see the Aramaic of Ezra 4:14 and the Greek of Acts 1:4 (if *synālizomenos* is original; cf. *TC*, 241-42).

[7]Writes Jacob Milgrom, *Leviticus 1–16* (New York: Doubleday, 1991), 191: 'Salt was the preservative par excellence in antiquity' (with extra-biblical references). In the *Babylonian Talmud* 'the salt of money' is 'diminution': i.e., charity preserves wealth (in Davies and Allison 1988: 472). At birth, a child was to be washed with water and rubbed with salt (Ezek. 16:4).

[8]The language of Matthew 5:13a – 'You are the salt of *the earth* [*tēs gēs*]' – may reflect such a usage: cf. the parallel to 5:13b in Luke 14:35, 'It is no longer useful for the soil [*gēn*] or for the rubbish heap; it is thrown out.' See Gundry 1994: 75.

[9]Given salt's durability, 'salt of the covenant' (Lev. 2:13) and 'covenant of salt' (Num. 18:19; 2 Chron. 13:5) signaled that Yahweh and his people were permanently bound to each other by covenant promises and obligations (Wenham 1979: 71). Sharing a meal, or 'eating salt' together, was a way of pledging fidelity to the provisions of a treaty or covenant (Ezra 4:14; Milgrom, *Leviticus*, 191; Wenham, ibid.; Davies and Allison 1988: 472). Salt's

(the verb *mōrainō*; 5:13b) or became 'unsalty' (the adjective *analos*; Mark 9:50) was good for nothing but disposal.[10]

Jesus' language in Matthew 5:13 cautions us against so *narrow* an interpretation of 'salt' that aspects of its meaning are omitted;[11] and against so *complex* an interpretation that the verse's primary lesson – salt's great usefulness and its potential uselessness – is obscured. What follows takes account of this twofold caution, of the above five uses, and of Jesus' other teachings.

1. Jesus' followers are a *preservative* in a fallen world, a *retardant* against a sinful society's otherwise rapid decline and decay. If the disciples are to fulfill this calling, it is vital that their own identity be safeguarded (that they not lose their saltiness), that they live as the persons described in verses 3-12, and that they not allow the surrounding culture to squeeze them into its own mold.[12]

2. As salt flavors as well as preserves meat, disciples are also a *seasoning* for the world. Not only do they resist the culture's evils: as Messiah's representatives in the world, they overcome evil with good (Rom. 12:21). Probably verbal

---

'preservative qualities made it the ideal symbol for the perdurability of a covenant' (Milgrom, ibid.).

[10]Matthew 5:13b; Luke 14:35b. 'Strictly speaking salt cannot lose its saltiness; sodium chloride is a stable compound. But most salt in the ancient world derived from salt marshes or the like, rather than by evaporation of salt water, and therefore contained many impurities. The actual salt, being more soluble than the impurities, could be leached out, leaving a residue so dilute it was of little worth' (Carson 1984: 138). Cf. Davies and Allison 1988: 473; Gundry 1994: 75-76.

[11]Given the various uses noted above, would not Jesus' listeners, and Matthew's original readers, have understood 'salt' in various ways? For cautions against too limited an application of the metaphor, see Davies and Allison, 1988: 473; Hagner 1993: 99.

[12]Cf. Proverbs 11:11; Romans 12:1-2 (J.B. Phillips transl.); Carson 1984: 139 (disciples are a preservative 'by conforming to kingdom norms'); Lloyd-Jones 1959: 158 (a Christian is 'a check, a control, an antiseptic in society, preserving it from unspeakable foulness, preserving it, perhaps, from a return to a dark age'); Tasker 1961: 63 (disciples can be 'a moral disinfectant... only if they themselves retain their virtue'); Mark A. Noll *et al.*, *The Search for Christian America* (Westchester: Crossway, 1983), 46 ('Christianity acts as a retardant against the natural tendencies of cultures built on sinful human nature to fall into decay. Such Christian influences are not always obvious, but they may be crucial'). Cf. 'Kingdom and Church,' pages 153-54 above.

testimony is especially in view, to match the visible one of
Matthew 5:14-16. While their witness will evoke violent
hostility from some (5:11-12), others will find it a life-giving
savor – as present believers can attest.[13] Let disciples beware
lest they 'become tasteless' (5:13). The Greek is *mōranthē*, a term
that primarily means 'to become foolish.'[14] When disciples fail
to embody and impart the wisdom Jesus has built into them,
they cease to attract and influence non-believers. Indeed, as
the foolish – and perhaps as those desperate to restore their
appeal and influence – they may become bearers of cultural
evil and peddlers of false teaching (cf. 7:15-20).[15]

3. As salt could fertilize the soil, so disciples are *good for
the earth* (*gē*; 5:13). For the One granted authority over the
whole earth (*gē*; 28:18) commissions them to bring all nations
under his benevolent rule (28:19-20; cf. Ps. 2:8; Isa. 11:1-9). The
gospel they proclaim (24:14; 26:13) is like seed, much of which
falls on good soil (*tēn gēn tēn kalēn*) and produces fruit (*karpon*;
13:8). The persons who welcome the gospel are themselves
like seed that is sown on good soil (*tēn kalēn gēn*) and bears
fruit (*karpophorei*; 13:23; cf. 7:16-20).[16]

---

[13]Colossians 4:6 ('Let your speech be always with grace, seasoned with
salt...'); 2 Corinthians 2:14-15 (Paul's witness is an aroma both 'from death
to death' and 'from life to life'); Titus 3:3-7 (the gospel's appeal to former
pagans). Calvin speaks of 'the salt of heavenly instruction' (1994: 175).

[14]The verb is *mōrainō*; cf. the cognate *mōros*, 'foolish'). The underlying
Hebrew-Aramaic *tpl* means both 'insipid' and 'foolish'; *tpl* and the Aramaic
tbl, 'salted,' would form a play on words (Black 1967: 166). Rabbinic texts
associated salt with Torah and with wisdom (F. Hauck, *TDNT* 1: 228, n. 2;
Davies and Allison 1988: 473).

[15]According to Luke 14, disciples become unsalty/foolish (14:34; *mōrainō*
again), and thus worthless (14:35) by failing to count the cost of becoming
Jesus' true disciples (14:25-33). Chromatius reflects that Judas 'deteriorated
into...useless salt,' no help to others 'and useless even to himself' (*ACC* 1a:
93). The wise disciple, whose allegiance to Jesus makes the strongest cultural
ties relatively unimportant (14:26; cf. Matt. 10:37), is actually the person
best equipped to serve within the family and other societal institutions. Cf.
Kuyper 1931, *passim*.

[16]Guelich 1982: 121, 126, stresses the link between Matthew 5:13 (discipleship) and 28:18-20 (mission). In the parable of the sower, the seed
is likened both to the message (13:19; cf. Mark 4:14) and to the listeners
(Matt. 13:20-23).

4. Mark 9:50a, which parallels Matthew 5:13b, is followed by a statement peculiar to Mark and reminiscent of OT references to salt as a sign of covenant: 'Have salt among yourselves, and be at peace with one another' (Mark 9:50b). Thus strengthening covenantal ties calls for putting to death the sins that threaten ruin, jeopardize community and prevent leaders from effectively serving the believers under their care (Matt. 9:33-37, 42-48).[17]

C. Light

The NT uses the term (Greek *phōs*) to denote literal light from (i) the sun, (ii) a fire, or (iii) an oil-burning lamp (*lychnos*), as here in Matthew 5:15. The OT also employs the language (Hebrew *'ôr* and *mā'ôr*) in those three ways.[18] Several figurative usages are notable in both testaments (as we shall see) – so that here, as with 5:13, we are cautioned against so *narrow* an interpretation that aspects of Jesus' meaning are omitted. And we are again cautioned against too *complex* an interpretation; for even though verses 14-16 are over twice the length of 5:13 (fifty-six Greek words to twenty-six), their central lesson is equally simple: the usefulness of light revealed, and the uselessness of light concealed.

1. The instances of *phōs* in 5:14 and 16 recall the two of 4:16 (the first in Matthew): here the words from Isaiah 9:2 announce, for dwellers in darkness and death, for Gentiles as well as Jews, the dawn of light by Messiah's appearing. By implication, disciples are 'the light of the world' because they belong to him who is 'the light [*to phōs*] of the world' (John 8:12). As he imparts light to mankind (John 1:4, 'the light of men,' *to phōs tōn anthrōpōn*), so do they (Matthew 5:16, 'before men,' *emprosthen tōn anthrōpōn*); cf. the words about John the Baptist in John 1:6-8.

---

[17]Cf. Gundry 1993: 515-16. Mark 9:49 – 'For everyone will be salted with fire' – serves a different purpose: linked by 'for' (*gar*) to 9:48, it underscores the reality and finality of judgment (a note implicit in Matthew 5:13b). Sowing a conquered city with salt to make it uninhabitable and unproductive (Judg. 9:45; cf. Deut. 29:23; Ps. 107:34; Jer. 17:6), in effect condemned it to death.

[18]See, e.g., (i) John 11:9; Revelation 22:5; Gen. 1:14-18 (light itself is created [1:3] before the sun); (ii) Mark 14:54; Luke 22:56; Exodus 13:21; (iii) Luke 8:16; 11:33; Revelation 18:23; 22:5; Exodus 35:14.

As Jesus, the Servant of Yahweh, brings light to both Jews and Gentiles, so do his people. In Matthew 5:14-16, as in 5:13, Jesus anticipates the commission of 28:19-20.[19]

2. The 'city built upon a mountain [*oros*]' (5:14b) may therefore mean 'not just any city – though cities commonly stood on hills for the purpose of easier defense – but the new Jerusalem, shedding the light of divine glory throughout the world during the messianic kingdom.'[20] Isaiah's prophetic vision of Gentiles streaming to Mount Zion and there learning, along with Israel, to 'walk in the light of Yahweh' (2:2-5), becomes a reality when disciples, by Messiah's own authority, impart his words – both gospel and law – to both Jews and Gentiles.[21]

3. As a gleaming city atop a mountain cannot be hidden (5:14b),[22] and as a lamp (*lychnos*) on a lampstand (*lychnia*) provides light in a house (5:15), so too when disciples function in accord with their nature they will surely be perceived as 'the light of the world.' (Revelation calls churches *lychniai*, 1:20; and the Lamb *lychnos*; 21:23.) Such recognition results from their total witness, which joins verbal and visible (as does Jesus; 4:23-25). But here the latter is accentuated: 'that *they may see* [*hopōs idōsin*] your good works [*ta kala erga*],' works that reveal

---

[19]Christians bear witness as 'lights in the world' (*phōstēres en kosmō*; Phil. 2:15). *To phōs tou kosmou* is common to Matthew 5:14 and John 8:12. Jesus' statement about himself, with its opening *Egō eimi*, is yet more emphatic than his statement about the disciples, with its opening *Hymeis*. For the Servant as light, see Isaiah 42:6; 49:6; for his people as light, Isaiah 55:5; 60:1-3; Acts 13:47 (and, for the effects on Gentiles, 1 Peter 2:9-10, 12). See comments on Matthew 4:12-17. The sun's light illustrates both the *universality* and the *durability* of the witness of 28:19-20.

[20]Gundry 1994: 77; cf. Betz 1995: 161-62; Carson 1984: 139-40. Cf. Isaiah 2:2, 'the mountain [MT, *har*; LXX, *oros*] of the house of Yahweh'; 3, 'the mountain of Yahweh'; also 4:4-6. The *oros* of Matthew 5:14 may also be translated 'hill' (so NASB, NIV, etc.). Perhaps here *oros* is both prophetic ('mountain') and proverbial ('hill').

[21]See Matthew 10:1-42; 24:14; 26:13; 28:18-20. In the OT, Yahweh himself is light for his people (Ps. 27:1; Isa. 60:19-20); that they may walk in his presence (Ps. 89:15), he imparts the light of his word (Pss. 43:3; 119:105, 130; Prov. 6:23; Isa. 2:2, 5). Jesus, Yahweh incarnate, discloses light both in his being (John 8:12; Matt. 11:25-30) and in his words (Matt. 5–7, etc.).

[22]'Often built of white limestone, ancient towns gleamed in the sun and could not easily be hidden' (Carson 1984: 139).

disciples' conformity to verses 3-12, and their obedience to Messiah's command (5:17–7:12). Jesus' sayings about light, as about salt, serve the same purpose as his teachings about bearing fruit.[23]

4. Jesus makes plain what is to be the disciples' objective: 'Let your light shine before men, that they may see your good works and glorify [*doxasōsin*] your Father in heaven' (5:16). Men will thus glorify God by repenting of their sins, submitting to his rule, and following his Son (4:17-25). Light (*phōs*) and glory (*doxa*) are very closely related: *doxa* often denotes 'brightness, splendor, radiance'; God is both light and glory to his people; Jesus, the light of the world, discloses the glory of God.[24] The light which the Son embodies, and which he imparts to mankind through his followers, by its very nature discloses the Father's glory and brings him honor. Therefore the singular calling of those who bear the light, as for those who behold it, is to glorify God.[25]

5. There is however a danger that disciples will abdicate that responsibility or impede that process. In view of the indicatives of Matthew 5:14, 15 ('You are the light,' 'cannot be hidden,' 'it gives light'), the opening imperative of 5:16 – 'Thus let your light shine' – stands out all the more prominently.[26] As worthless as unsalty salt, is light extinguished or concealed (5:15).[27] Disciples whose light fails to shine are of no greater

[23]In both Mark and Luke, the parallels to Matthew 5:15 immediately follow the parable of the sower: see Mark 4:20-21; Luke 8:15-16 (cf. John 15:8). See comments on salt, no. 3 (p. 334).

[24]See BAGD s.v. *doxa*, 1.; Isaiah 60:19-20, LXX; John 1:14; 8:12; 2 Corinthians 4:6.

[25]See BAGD s.v. *doxa*, 3. ('fame, renown, honor'); John 7:18; 15:8; 1 Corinthians 10:31; Ephesians 2:8 (with 1:6, 12, 14); Philippians 1:11 (cf. Matt. 5:6, 10); 1 Peter 2:12. As light and glory come from God and are mediated through the disciples, their good works (Matt. 5:16) are divine achievements (Calvin 1994: 178; Phil. 2:12-16). By the same token, disciples are to impart Jesus' teaching, not their own (Matt. 28:20a) and to honor him, the 'one Teacher,' rather than themselves (23:8-12).

[26]The verb *lampō*, a present indicative in Matthew 5:15 (*lampei*), recurs as an aorist imperative in 5:16 (*lampsatō*).

[27]The obvious place for a lamp is a lampstand: placing it under a *modios* (a bushel for measuring grain and holding about nine liters) would both conceal and extinguish the light. Cf. Mark 4:21; Luke 8:16; Jeremias 1963: 120-21; France 1985: 113.

value than non-disciples; indeed, lacking good works they are exposed as spurious disciples (7:24-27; 25:1-46). But if disciples without works are threatened with judgment, so also are those whose works are wrongly motivated: danger besets disciples who do 'acts of righteousness' for personal glory (6:1-18); apparently good works may be bad fruit (7:15-20); even mighty works done in Jesus' name do not assure entry into the kingdom (7:21-23). Doing the Father's will (7:21) includes letting one's light shine for the Father's glory (Matt. 5:16).[28] But let 'the men' – 'the crowds' – also be sure to take seriously what they have seen: blessed indeed are those who, having beheld and understood these good works, embrace the gospel of the kingdom and adhere to God's Messiah (Matt. 4:23; 5:3-12); but woe to those who flee from the light or seek to suppress it.[29]

---

[28]In both Mark and Luke, sayings parallel to Matthew 5:15 are followed immediately by warnings of judgment: see Mark 4:21-25 (and earlier comments on Mark 9:49-50); Luke 8:16-18. Cf. in this regard Matthew 6:23.

[29]See pages 329-30; John 3:19-21; and 1 Peter 2:11-12, where hostile pagans learn to glorify (*doxazō*, as in Matthew 5:16) God by seeing the 'good deeds' (*kala erga*, as in Matthew 5:16) of Christians who live as 'aliens and strangers' (i.e., as the persons described in 5:3-12).

IV.
'THE LAW OF GOD IS GOOD AND WISE'[1]
(5:17-48)

The sermon's opening section, 'The Blessings of the Kingdom' (5:3-16) paves the way for the second, 'The Righteousness of the Kingdom' (5:17–7:12). Jesus will now identify some representative 'good works' (5:16) whereby disciples can render thanks to God and his Messiah for those blessings; bring love for God and neighbor to practical expression; and bear the witness reflected in the beatitudes and in the metaphors of salt and light.[2]

This lengthy section's opening verses (5:17-20) are foundational not only for the exposition of 5:17-48, but for the rest of the Sermon on the Mount – and indeed for the rest of Matthew, all of which serves to show how Jesus fulfills 'the Law and the Prophets' (5:17). The noun *nomos* ('law') appears only in the preface (verses 17 and 18) – which, however, is crucial for understanding the exposition to follow.

A. Relating the Old to the New (5:17-20)

These four verses are conceptually joined together in the closest way, as is evident from the 'for' (*gar*) of 5:18a, the 'therefore' (*oun*) of 5:19a, and the 'for' (*gar* again) of 5:20a. Jesus' compact statement takes us from 'the Law and the Prophets' (5:17) and 'the Law' (5:18) to the consummation of God's purpose in 'the kingdom of heaven' (5:19, 20).

---

[1]The opening words of a hymn by Matthias Loy (1863).

[2]See 'Gospel and Law,' pages 171-72, including the quotation from Samuel Bolton; Psalm 119:32, NIV; Romans 8:1-4; Ephesians 2:8-10; Titus 3:3-8; Ridderbos 1958: 31 ('The Kingdom brings forth the gifts of love, and only secondly the demand of love'); and page 307 above, on Matthew 5:17 and 7:12 in relation to 22:37-40.

The Mission of Jesus

'Do not think [*Mē nomisēte*] that I came to abolish [*katalysai*] the Law or the Prophets; I came not to abolish [*katalysai*] but [*alla*] to fulfill [*plērōsai*]' (5:17).

Jesus' opening command and emphatic denial (with its repeated infinitive *katalysai*) warn the disciples against a certain mentality. On the contrary (the strong adversative *alla*), let the disciples recognize that his mission is nothing less than to fulfill (the matching infinitive *plērōsai*) the entire OT ('the Law' joined to 'the Prophets').[3] Jesus knows that some contemporaries will indeed think he purposes to sabotage the Scriptures; and that at least some such people – notably 'the scribes and Pharisees' (5:20) – will therefore bitterly resent his claim to fulfill the Scriptures and seek to destroy him.[4] True disciples may willingly heed the prohibition of 5:17a, yet be understandably slow to comprehend the claim of 5:17b. By all his words and works, including the following exposition, Jesus unfolds for his disciples the meaning and implications of that bold assertion.

Applied as it is to the whole of Scripture, *plērōsai* must be given the broadest meaning: *1.* Jesus brings the OT to its appointed *goal.* Let us think of Jesus as a builder who inherits a house under construction: far from demolishing it, discarding its plans and starting over, Jesus employs those plans and completes the edifice. Intelligently reading the Scriptures means recognizing that they are not complete in themselves; that they serve a purpose beyond themselves; that they point to a history beyond their own; that their promises are ultimately fulfilled beyond their pages; and that Jesus is the very One for whom the OT has prepared. *2.* Jesus *surpasses* the OT. As a completed house compared to one still under construction, so the epoch for inaugurating God's final rule and ratifying his

---

[3]As usual in such constructions, the opening prohibition employs the aorist subjunctive in the second person (cf. *GGBB*, 469). Both *katalysai* and *plērōsai* are likewise aorist. The adversative *alla* is stronger than *de*. For 'the Law' with 'the Prophets' to denote the OT Scriptures, see also Matthew 7:12; 11:13; 22:40; Romans 3:21.

[4]Cf. *katalyō* on the lips of Jesus' antagonists (26:61; 27:40); and the instances of *apollymi* ('destroy') in 12:14; 27:20.

new covenant is superior to prior generations. Not only so: as God incarnate, Jesus transcends the OT as does an architect his design. Or, to change the image, Jesus is the OT's goal in the sense that a mountain peak is the climber's: he stands not only beyond but above the OT; he and his work are the apex of biblical revelation. 3. In Jesus, OT patterns are fully *realized*. He is the great antitype of various OT types. He not only declares but enacts salvation. God's promises are fulfilled in his person. He, unlike any of his predecessors, perfectly embodies fidelity to God's commands. Altering the above images, we may say that in Jesus an OT *design* is for the first time realized in an *actual building*; and that he is the mountain whose huge shadow overlies OT history and literature.[5]

The Place of the Law

'For [*gar*] truly I say to you: until [*heōs an*] heaven and earth disappear [*parelthē*], by no means [*ou mē*] will the smallest letter or even the smallest stroke of a letter disappear [*parelthē*] from the Law until [*heōs an*] all things have happened [*genētai*]' (5:18).

Anticipating the exposition to follow, Jesus turns his attention to 'the Law' – the Torah (or Pentateuch) – and in particular to the 'commandments' (5:19) that God gave to Israel through Moses. He speaks both of 'the Law' and of its smallest members – the 'letter' (Greek *iōta*, for *yodh*, the smallest letter in the Hebrew alphabet) and the 'stroke' (Greek *keraia*, for the mark which, e.g., distinguished the Hebrew letter *beth* from *kaph*, or *daleth* from *resh*, or *cheth* from *he*). The opening 'For' links this verse to both the negative and the positive assertions of 5:17.

Verse 18, building on 17a, is not a warning against violating the law, whether by tampering with it (by removing some of its commands) or by transgressing it (by trampling its commands underfoot). Rather, Jesus here emphatically declares that the law *cannot* be violated, that even its smallest parts *will not* disappear 'until all things have happened' – i.e., until the kingdom is consummated.[6] On that Day, when the present 'heaven and

---

[5]For support of statements in this paragraph, see pages 120-29; Banks 1975: 207-10; France 1985: 113-14; Jeremias 1971: 83-85, 207.

[6]Gundry 1994: 79-80; Keener 1999: 178. The words *ou mē parelthē* (5:18b) are a subjunctive of emphatic negation, Greek's strongest way to express a

earth' are replaced by the new heavens and the new earth, the commandments will no longer be needed. But until that Day, one might as easily cause the universe to disappear as to remove the law's least commands.[7] So how foolish to think that the One who makes the authoritative pronouncement of 5:18 would, or could, seek to abolish the law (5:17).

But verse 18 also has in view the words *alla plērōsai* – that part of 5:17 with which the 'For' of 5:18a is most directly linked. The series of events by virtue of which 'all things' shall come to pass, has already begun; the kingdom whose consummation is envisaged (6:10) is being inaugurated (4:17). He who utters the words of 5:18 is the very One through whom that decisive shift in history is occurring. His ensuing exposition of the law is itself a means by which the Scriptures are being 'fulfilled.' Accordingly, verse 18 has in view the law as expounded *both* by Moses *and* by Jesus the New Moses. Jesus' interpretation of the law perfectly accords with the progress of God's saving purpose in history (11:12-13). For him to expound it differently would be quite impossible; by the same token, the law as he expounds it *cannot* be violated.[8]

The Call to Obedience

'Therefore, whoever breaks [*lysē*] one of these least [*elachistōn*] commandments and teaches men to do so, will be called least [*elachistos*] in the kingdom of heaven; but whoever practices

---

matter negatively (*GGBB*, 468-69). Here, as most often in such constructions, the negative particles *ou* and *mē* are followed by the aorist subjunctive (the future indicative is occasionally used, as in Matthew 26:35).

[7] As the repetition of *heōs an* and *parelthē* suggests, with the consummation of the kingdom (6:10) the present heaven and earth will pass away (cf. 24:35) and the law will no longer be needed (for in resurrected life believers will freely and fully love God and one another; cf. 1 Cor. 13:8-13). For 'the new heaven(s) and the new earth,' see Isaiah 65:17; 66:22; 2 Peter 3:13; Revelation 21:1.

[8] Cf. Banks 1975: 234 (the term 'fulfill' affirms 'the whole of the Law, yet only through its transformation into the teaching of Christ which was something new and unique in comparison with it'); Hagner 1993: 107 ('the law, as interpreted by Jesus, will remain valid until the close of this age'); Davies and Allison 1988: 492 (rabbis taught that the Torah, once future events made its meaning plainer, would be modified in some respects but remain immutable). Some of the law's commands, notably the Decalogue,

and teaches them, this one will be called great in the kingdom of heaven. For I tell you that unless your righteousness surpasses that of the scribes and Pharisees, you will by no means enter into the kingdom of heaven' (Matt. 5:19-20).

1. Law and kingdom

The law will not and cannot be abolished (5:17-18 – including the repeated verb *katalyō*; 5:17), but it can and will be broken, 19 (including the verb *lyō*).[9] This happens when people disregard or disobey its commands, or supplant them with human traditions (15:1-9). The law itself is not in jeopardy, but lawbreakers are. Verse 19, with its opening 'Therefore,' sounds a warning precisely in view of the law's inviolability (5:18). The law is like a concrete wall, the law-breaker like a man who beats on the wall; the wall suffers no damage but the man by repeated pounding will crush his fist.

Even the law's 'least commandments' are to be respected, because they come from God and are expounded by his servants Moses and Messiah. In the end God's judgments about his people will concur with their judgments about his law. To the person who treats even 'one of these least commandments' dishonorably (by breaking it and teaching others to do the same), God will assign a place of least honor in the kingdom (5:19a; note the repetition of the adjective *elachistos*). At the same time, God will confer high honor upon the one who honors such a command (by keeping it and teaching others to do so, 5:19b).[10]

Yet there is a graver danger than being dishonored within the kingdom of heaven, and that is being excluded from the kingdom altogether: 'you will by no means enter [*ou mē eiselthēte*]...' (5:20b).[11] The basis for this judgment, as for those

remain in effect until the kingdom's consummation. Others cease to function beyond the kingdom's inaugural: the atoning sacrifice of Jesus marks the appointed end of Levitical ceremony (see 26:28; 27:51; Heb. 10:1-18). Cf. WCF, chapter 19, 'Of the Law of God'; Chamblin 1988.

[9]John 5:18 (where the Jews falsely accuse Jesus of breaking the Sabbath law) uses *lyō* as does Matthew 5:19. The *lyō* of John 10:35 (where Jesus says the Scripture cannot be broken) matches the *katalyō* of Matthew 5:17.

[10]The repeated verb *klēthēsetai* ('shall be called'; 5:19), like the matching form of 5:9, is a 'divine passive.'

of 5:19, is one's attitude to God's commands: the opening 'For' (*gar*) of 5:20 links this verse to the preceding. The 'righteousness' (*dikaiosynē*) of 5:20 is that holiness of character and conduct – in other words, those 'good works' (5:16) – evident in persons faithful to those commands.[12] Moreover, in accord with preceding verses 'the way of righteousness' (21:32) calls for submission to God's law as mediated by both Moses and Messiah.

2. Scribes and Pharisees

In Matthew, Jesus censures 'the scribes and Pharisees' (5:20) for infidelity to revelation both old and new. They appear to take the Mosaic Law very seriously, but in fact take it too lightly. Although in many respects they expound the law correctly, they disobey their own teachings. They use their acts of righteousness to win people's acclaim. They accentuate the minutiae of the law but neglect its weightier matters. As those who nullify the divine commands for the sake of human traditions, they are in the profoundest sense antinomian.[13]

Worst of all, they reject the Prophet whom Moses foretold. By charging that Jesus violates rather than honors the Law, that his power comes from the prince of demons rather than the Spirit of God, and that he is a Messianic pretender deserving death, they betray their ignorance of Moses.[14] Disbelieving Jesus' message of the kingdom (4:17, 23), how can they pos-

---

[11]Here, as in Matthew 5:18, the two particles and the aorist subjunctive express strong negation.

[12]See page 152, n. 119 (on *dikaiosynē* in Matthew); and page 260 (on 3:15). Cf. Luke 1:74-75 ('to serve him in holiness and righteousness'); 1 John 2:29 ('everyone who does righteousness').

[13]See Matthew 15:1-9 (especially v. 6) and 23:1-36 (especially vv. 3, 5, 23, 28); and – in light of those passages – 5:21-48 and 6:1-18 (especially v. 1). Jeremias 1969: 254, taking note of 'scribes and Pharisees' in 5:20, thinks 5:21-48 is directed against the former (they being the ones who transmit and explain the received tradition; cf. 2:4-6); and 6:1-18 against the latter. He also finds such a distinction in chapter 23: verses 1-22, 29-36, against scribes; verses 23-28, against Pharisees (ibid.). It is preferable to say that both groups are in view throughout 5:21–6:18, as they are in 15:1-9 and in all seven woes of 23:1-36. On scribes and Pharisees, see Appendix A.

[14]See, e.g., Matthew 9:3, 11, 14, 34; 12:2, 14, 24; 15:1-2; 16:21; 19:3; 20:18; 21:45-46; 22:15; 26:57; 27:41-42, 62-63. For the fulfillment of Deuteronomy 18:15

sibly evidence the righteousness consistent with the dawn of
the kingdom (6:33)? Repudiating the words of God's Son, how
can they possibly do the will of his Father, the God of Israel
(7:21-27)?

3. Jesus and disciples

Jesus promises that, in the coming kingdom, God will honor
those who keep and teach the law's commands (Matt. 5:19b).
Jesus, and he alone, perfectly embodies fidelity to those
commands; and he expounds them to others with unparalleled
and unprecedented wisdom and authority, as the present
sermon demonstrates (see comments on 7:28-29). Accordingly,
the Father will not only 'call him great in the kingdom' but
will acclaim him the greatest of all: in the Father's kingdom,
the Son will reign as king.[15]

The immediate recipients of verses 19-20 are not the scribes
and Pharisees, or the crowds, but Jesus' disciples. As those
whom Jesus will commission to teach all the nations to keep
all his commands (28:19-20), they do well to heed both parts of
5:19. Let them beware lest they tamper with, or neglect or omit
or annul, any of those commands; let them honor and expound
OT law as Jesus has done; and let them be as scrupulous in
obeying all those commands as they expect others to be. With
5:19 we may compare 1 Corinthians 3:10-15, which affirms (i)
that at the Judgment some persons will be rewarded while
others suffer loss; but also (ii) that both kinds of persons will be
saved (i.e., inherit the kingdom; 1 Corinthians 6:9-10) because
they have built on the right foundation, namely Christ.[16]

---

in Jesus, see the quotations in Acts 3:22 and 7:37; the allusion in Matthew 17:5
and pars. ('Listen to him'); and references to '*the* prophet' in John 1:21; 6:14;
7:40, together with 5:39-40, 45-47.

[15]See, e.g., Matthew 16:28; 25:31; 26:29, with 28:18; and pages 132-33, on
'Jesus the King.'

[16]But the imagery of 1 Corinthians 3:10-15 differs from that of Matthew 7:24-27. Akin to 5:19 (there are different rankings in the kingdom) is
6:1 (the heavenly Father may withhold rewards from his children). These
verses must be balanced by other sayings of Jesus, including 11:11 ('the least
[*mikroteros*] in the kingdom of heaven is greater' than John); 20:26 (the 'great
[*megas*, as in 5:19]' disciple is the one who serves others); and 25:40 (service

The stern warning of verse 20 is likewise addressed to disciples: 'unless *your* righteousness surpasses...*you* will by no means enter....' Professed followers of Jesus who behave in the ways prohibited in verse 19 may be in danger of exclusion from the kingdom (again note the 'For' with which verse 20 begins). By what means, then, will disciples come to manifest that righteousness essential for entering the kingdom and for escaping the judgment which threatens scribes and Pharisees? They will do so primarily by recognizing Jesus as the One in whom the OT is fulfilled; by becoming and remaining his loyal followers; and by adhering to the law as he expounds it. By heeding that exposition, they will better understand OT law. The righteousness of 5:20 is the very conduct to which Moses summoned ancient Israel – a life of holiness in the presence of the holy God; so one learns about that righteousness, not by abandoning Mosaic law but by going more deeply into it. Its weightier matters, 'justice, mercy and faithfulness' (23:23), are the very qualities Jesus requires of his disciples (e.g., 5:6-10). Foundational for Moses no less than for Messiah is the twin command to love God and neighbor (22:37-40).

While all disciples are to heed the admonitions of verses 19 and 20, especially is this true for the twelve. Given their authority (10:1-4) and their commission (28:19-20), their position in the new community is comparable to that of the scribes and Pharisees within the old order, and they are therefore exceptionally vulnerable to the sins Jesus condemns in the others. Significantly, he denounces competitive pride both in 20:20-28 (where the point of departure is the ambition of James and John) and in 23:5-12 (where the point of departure is the behavior of scribes and Pharisees). Judas' sin against Jesus is as grievous as those of the scribes and Pharisees – indeed, more grievous in light of what Judas has witnessed.[17] While we can only imagine the weight of 5:19-20 and 28:19-20

---

to the 'least [*elachistos*, as in 5:19]' of Jesus' brothers is service to him). Cf. James 2:13b in light of 2:5-13a.

[17]By all indications, Judas was present for all five of the great discourses. See especially 13:10-17; and cf. Jesus' pronounced woe upon Judas at the Last Supper (26:23-24). Pertinent too is the third servant's exclusion from the kingdom in the parable of 25:14-30.

upon Matthew as he wrote his gospel, there is evidence that the evangelist was obedient to those words – and that he relied upon the presence of Christ and the power of the Spirit to complete so formidable and crucial a task.[18]

B. Expounding the Way of Righteousness (5:21-48)

Jesus now identifies some areas in which disciples can do the good works of 5:16, and thus bring to fruition the righteousness of 5:20.

The Section as a Whole

The passage consists of six paragraphs. At the opening of the first we meet the words, 'You have heard that it was said [*Ēkousate hoti errethē*] to the people of ancient times [*tois archaiois*].... But I say to you [*egō de legō hymin*]...' (Matt. 5:21-22). These very words are repeated at the beginning of the fourth paragraph, after an opening 'Again' (*palin*; 5:33-34). In the second, fifth and sixth paragraphs, the first part of the formula is shortened: 'You have heard that it was said.... But I say to you' (5:27-28, 38-39, 43-44). In the third paragraph, the first part is shorter still: 'And it was said [*errethē de*].... But I say to you' (5:31-32).

The presence of the full formula in paragraphs one and four suggests two pairs of three. Further evidence strengthens this suggestion. The *palin* of Matthew 5:33a occurs nowhere else in verses 5:21-48. In each of the first three paragraphs, the second part of the formula begins 'But I say to you that everyone who [*hoti pas ho*]' – words followed in each case by a present participle.[19] But in paragraphs four through six, those formulations are replaced by imperatives: 'But I say to you, do not swear... do not resist... love your enemies....'[20] But these are observations about the literary character of the

---

[18]See pages 59-64 (his approach to the task); pages 100-03 (his dependence on the Trinity).

[19]'Everyone who is angry [*orgizomenos*]' (5:22); 'who sees [*blepōn*]' (5:28); 'who divorces [*apolyōn*]' (5:32).

[20]The first two verbs are aorist infinitives (*omosai*, 5:34; *antistēnai*, 5:39) preceded by the negative particle *mē* in indirect discourse (cf. *GGBB*, 603). The third verb (*agapate*, 5:44) is a present imperative. Jesus' statements in verses 22, 28 and 32 are, of course, veiled imperatives.

passage. Theologically, all six paragraphs are bound together; to separate them into two sets of three would obscure, e.g., the important connection between paragraphs three and four, or between one and five.

I have deliberately refrained from speaking of six *antitheses*, a term which in my judgment expresses too strong a contrast, or the wrong sort of contrast, between the two parts of the opening formula.[21] The first part of each formula (i) speaks of law revealed by God (*errethē*, 'it was said,' is a divine passive)[22] through Moses to Israel ('to the people of ancient times'), and entrusted as well to subsequent generations, including Jesus' contemporaries ('You have heard'); and (ii) includes a specific command from the Mosaic law, in some instances together with an inference drawn from it. No instance speaks *directly* of violations and distortions of the law from Moses' day to the present – although, in accord with Matthew 5:19-20, such sins are in view throughout the section. Jesus' purpose in the second part of the formula is not to distance his teaching from that of the law. In each case, the milder adversative *de* is used, not the stronger *alla*. Instead Jesus, the divine Messiah appointed to inaugurate God's final rule, is accentuating his unique authority to interpret and apply God's ancient law: 'But *I* [*egō*] say to you....' In other words, this whole section is consistent with both verse 17 (Jesus has come not to abolish but to fulfill the law) and verse 18 (the law remains inviolable until it has fully served God's saving purpose). In accord with 5:17-20, the righteousness expounded in 5:21-48 'surpasses that of the scribes and Pharisees' in that it marks *both* a deeper obedience to OT law *and* an intensifying or escalating of obedience owing to the presence of Yahweh incarnate and the dawn of God's kingdom.[23] To illustrate we turn to Jesus' sixfold exposition.

---

[21]For the use of the term 'antithesis,' see, e.g., Hagner 1993: 110; Hendriksen 1973: 295. 'Unfortunately, the term "antithesis" designates the material incorrectly' (Gundry 1994: 83).

[22]*Errethē* is an aorist passive of *eipon*, the aorist for *legō*, the verb used in the second part of the formula. Cf. Romans 9:12 (*errethē*) and Galatians 3:16 (*errethēsan*), both divine passives.

[23]This reading of the introductory formulae is strongly supported by Davies and Allison 1988: 505-9; and Gundry 1994: 83-84. In Matthew 19:21,

Anger (5:21-26)

These verses form a coherent whole. The two parts of the opening formula share the expressions *hos d' an* followed by an aorist subjunctive verb ('whoever commits murder... whoever says... whoever says'; 5:21, 22); and *enochos estai tē krisei* ('shall be liable to judgment'; 5:21, 22 (*enochos estai* appears two more times in 5:22). Joining 5:22 to 23 are the conjunction *oun* ('therefore'; 5:23a) and the noun *adelphos* ('brother'), used twice in 5:22 and twice in 5:23-24 – indications that the 'something' which the brother holds 'against you' (*ti kata sou*) is one of the sins described in 5:22. Verses 23-24 prescribe one course of action in face of the warning of 22. Verses 25-26 prescribe another, which may well be needed in addition to the first.[24] The opening imperative *isthi eunoōn* ('Come to terms'; 5:25a) joins the four of 5:24 ('leave...go...be reconciled...offer'). The *antidikos*; (5:25) is, in this context, an 'opponent in a lawsuit.'[25] So offended is the brother by the slander (5:22) that he has decided to sue. Jesus urges the defendant to 'come to terms' with the plaintiff while both are *en tē hodō* – i.e. 'on the way' to court (5:25a; thus REB) – in order to avoid an adverse *krisis* ('judgment'; 5:22) from the *kritēs* ('judge'; 5:25b). With this analysis in view, we look more closely at the teaching of the passage.

1. Jesus first reminds listeners of OT teaching: 'You shall not murder [*Ou phoneuseis*]; whoever commits murder [*phoneusē*] shall be deserving of judgment' (Matt. 5:21). The first clause quotes the sixth commandment: the Greek is that of the LXX for the MT's *lō' tirtsāch* (Exod. 20:13 and Deut. 5:17).[26] The second clause acknowledges provisions in the Mosaic law for

---

Jesus calls the rich young man both to *renewed* obedience (the man has yet to honor the twofold command at the heart of the Mosaic law) and to *radical* obedience (loving God, and being *teleios*, now require submission to Jesus).

[24]This analysis accords with that of Davies and Allison 1988: 509-10.

[25]BAGD s.v. Cf. NIV ('your adversary who is taking you to court'); NASB.

[26]In the LXX, the sixth command appears in Exodus 20:15 (the seventh in 20:13, and the eighth in 20:14); and in Deuteronomy 5:18 (the seventh in 5:17). The words *Ou phoneuseis* literally render the Hebrew; this is an instance of the future indicative verb to express a command (so also in the quotations of Matthew 5:27, 33 and 43). Cf. *GGBB*, 452-53, 569-70.

bringing the murderer to justice by putting him to death.[27] In keeping with the singular forms of *phoneuō* in Matthew 5:21, the rest of the section focuses on individual responsibility and relationships between individuals. In this regard, the shift from the plural pronoun *legō hymin* in 5:21 to the singular *legō soi* in 5:26 is notable. The sixth commandment is foundational for the whole section: the gravity of actual murder is clear from Jesus' other sayings on the subject in Matthew.[28]

2. 'But I say to you [Jesus continues] that everyone who is angry with his brother shall be liable to judgment; and whoever says to his brother "Empty-head!" shall be answerable to the council; and whoever says "Fool!" shall be deserving of the Gehenna of fire' (5:22). This is a three-tiered statement, marked by the repeated *enochos estai*. Envisaged is a legal procedure in which a person liable to judgment (*krisis*) is brought before a council or court (*synedrion*), which rules that he deserves eternal punishment (*eis tēn geenna tou pyros*).[29] Since God alone has authority to decree

[27]KJV of Exodus 20:13, 'Thou shalt not kill,' is rightly changed to 'You shall not murder' in NKJV (so too NASB, NIV, etc.). The Hebrew verb in Exodus 20:13, *rātsach*, denotes willful murder. The execution of the murderer is normally expressed otherwise: cf. e.g. the forms of *mût* (Qal, 'die, be put to death'; Hiphil, 'kill, put to death'; Hophal, 'be killed, put to death') in Exodus 21:12, 14; Leviticus 24:17; Numbers 35:16-21 (v. 30 is exceptional in using *rātsach* of a murderer's execution). Accordingly, LXX employs *phoneuō* ('murder') at 20:13, but *apokteinō* ('kill') or *thanatoō* ('put to death') in these other passages. Cf. Childs 1974: 419-21.

[28]All such references in Matthew appear on Jesus' lips: *phoneuō* ('to murder'; 19:18; 23:31, 35); *phonos* ('murder'; 15:19); *phoneus* ('murderer'; 22.7). As Yahweh incarnate, Jesus perceives the horror of murder to a far greater degree than did Moses. Most horrifying of all is the murder of Jesus himself: see comments on 16:21.

[29]For these translations of *enochos*, see BAGD s.v., 2. *Krisis* might denote 'a local court' (BAGD s.v., 2.), and *synedrion* 'the high council' or 'Sanhedrin,' as in 26:59 (BAGD s.v., 2.); so NASB, 'the court...the supreme court.' But probably just one procedure is meant: by far the dominant sense of *krisis* is 'judging, judgment' (BAGD s.v., 1.); *synedrion*, even with the definite article, need not mean the Sanhedrin (the matching nouns in 22, *krisei* and *geennan*, also have the article; and cf. *synedria* in 10:17); and 5:25 has only one court in view. So NRSV for 22, 'liable to judgment...liable to the council'; cf. J. Jeremias, *TDNT* 6: 975. Verse 22 contains the first of seven instances of *geenna* in Matthew, all on Jesus' lips (the others occur in 5:29, 30; 10:28; 18:9; 23:15, 33). The

such an end, *synedrion* in this instance is either the heavenly court or an earthly court acting on its behalf.[30] That progression from *krisis* to *geenna* is matched by another. A person's anger (*ho orgizomenos*) finds expression in, and escalates into, abusive and destructive speech: 'Empty-head! [*Raka*]...Fool! [*Mōre*].' The second term reinforces the first: *raka* transliterates an Aramaic term whose meaning is virtually the same as the Greek *mōros*.[31] Cf. 15:19, where Jesus says that *blasphēmiai* ('slanders, defamatory words') arise from the heart. Why does Jesus threaten so severe a penalty for such sins, and how does 5:22 relate to 21?

a. Jesus alerts listeners to OT warnings against unrighteous anger and destructive speech.[32] To obey such teachings is to honor the sixth commandment, for *phonoi* ('murders') also arise from the heart (Matt. 15:19). So dealing with anger and its effects – and recognizing that vicious words *intensify* rather

---

term transliterates *gêhinnām*, Aramaic for Hebrew *gê hinnōm* ('Valley of Hinnom'), an abbreviation of *gê ben hinnōm* ('Valley of the Son of Hinnom'): see Joshua 15:8 for both forms, and 2 Kings 23:10 for 'Valley of the Sons [*bᵉnê*] of Hinnom.' Abominations in this valley (in south Jerusalem) evoked God's severest judgment (e.g., Lev. 18:21; 2 Kings 23:10; 2 Chron. 28:3; Jer. 7:30-34; 19:1-15). Given those associations, Gehenna came to denote the place of final punishment: thus do the gospels consistently use the term. For more details see J. Jeremias, *TDNT* 1: 657-58; J. Lunde, 'Heaven and Hell,' *DJG*, 310-11. *Hadēs* (Matt. 11:23; 16:18) likewise denotes the place of eternal punishment, not just the intermediate state of the wicked (*apud* Lunde, *pace* Jeremias). On the imagery of 'fire' (*pyr*), see comments on 18:8-9.

[30]Keener 1999: 184 thinks 'the Sanhedrin' in Matthew 5:22 is probably 'God's heavenly court.'

[31]Greek *raka* transliterates Aramaic *rêqā'* or *rêqâ*, 'fool, empty-head' (BAGD s.v.). *Mōros* means 'foolish, stupid' (BAGD s.v.). The absence of a translation for *raka* suggests that Matthew's audience already knew this term of abuse, and/or that Matthew counts on readers to recognize the parallel with *mōre* (cf. Davies and Allison 1988: 513).

[32]For warnings against anger, see Psalms 37:8; 50:19-20; Proverbs 14:17; 22:24-25; 27:4; 29:22; 30:33; against slanderous and destructive speech, Psalms 15:3; 101:5; Proverbs 6:16-19; 11:9; 12:18; 16:27-28;18:21; 30:11-14. *Sinful* anger is prohibited, not anger as such. The OT speaks much more often of Yahweh's anger than of man's: e.g., Exodus 4:14; Deuteronomy 7:4; Psalm 2:5; Hosea 8:5. So humans *ought* to be angry in face of evil: Exodus 11:8; 2 Samuel 12:5; Jeremiah 15:17 (Jeremiah is filled with Yahweh's own indignation); and Psalm 4:4a, which LXX (4:5a) renders *orgizesthe* [the verb used in Matthew 5:22] *kai mē hamartanete* ('Be angry but do not sin'), quoted in Ephesians 4:26.

than dispel anger – may prevent my taking another person's life.[33] Conversely, confining violations of the command to actual murder might have the tragically ironic effect that murder is committed because one failed to address feelings and words of rage toward the other.

b. If Israelites under Moses were to take those prohibitions seriously, *how much more* should Jesus' disciples. They are witnessing an outpouring of divine grace denied previous generations: God's rule is dawning, Messiah has come and the covenant community is being rebuilt around his person. By submitting to God's rule, following Jesus and receiving the salvation he promises, disciples are being gathered into a fellowship of unprecedented intimacy and intensity. The *adelphos* is not merely another creature, but a fellow member of this new community.[34] The behavior of Matthew 5:22, in violating the sixth command, also (i) spurns the manifold grace that first brought the two brothers together; (ii) shows lack of love toward a neighbor of the closest kind; (iii) fosters the spread of poisonous gossip in the community; and (iv) intimates that the other person is no true brother (for in Matthew, *adelphos* and *mōros* are incompatible), and thus questions Messiah's judgment about him – all of which (v) raises doubts about the speaker's own state.[35] His prospects seem graver still, once we recognize that his accusatory words have been heard and weighed in the heavenly court (cf. 12:36). Jesus' strong words help to explain why matters of speech figure prominently in apostolic instructions about Christian relationships.[36]

---

[33]'Anger that would generate murder if unimpeded is the spiritual equivalent of murder' (Keener 1999: 183). Cf. 1 John 3:15; and the sequence in Romans 3:13-15.

[34]For this use of *adelphos*, see especially Matthew 12:48-50; 18:15-20; 23:8; 25:40; 28:10.

[35]For (i) see 6:14-15; 18:23-35; for (ii), 22:37-40; 1 Corinthians 13:5 (love 'is not easily angered,' NIV); for (iii), Proverbs 11:9; 16:27-28; 18:8; 26:20-22; 1 Timothy 3:11; for (iv), Matthew 7:1-5; 23:8; James 4:11-12; *c.* below; and for (v), comments on Gehenna on pages 350-51. Matthew 5:22 joins the sins of *anger* and *contempt*: see the illuminating discussion in Willard 1998: 147-54.

[36]Besides Matthew itself, see James 3:1-9; 1 Peter 3:8-12; Ephesians 4:25-32; Colossians 3:8-9; and note in these two passages the sequence *orgē... blasphēmia* ('wrath...slander').

c. The speech condemned in 5:22 is itself an instance of 'foolish talk' (*mōrologia*; Eph. 5:4). Persons who repudiate the words and works of Messiah – whether by hostile opposition or by willful negligence – are rightly called 'fools': cf. Jesus' own use of *mōros* in Matthew 7:26 (the foolish builder); 23:17 ('foolish and blind' scribes and Pharisees); and 25:2, 3, 8 (the foolish virgins). But it is dangerously foolish for disciples to use such language unless it is known to rest on God's own judgment.[37]

3. Jesus mercifully prescribes for the wrongdoer two courses of action in face of threatened damnation. The first is set forth in verses 23-24, action the more urgent because anger has begotten anger: the offended brother now holds 'something against' the offender.

a. Jesus first envisages the wrongdoer's bearing a *dōron* ('gift') to the *thysiastērion* (5:23; i.e., to the altar of burnt offering in the temple courtyard). Varied sacrifices were made here for various purposes: see Leviticus 1–7.[38] While its nature is not specified, the gift is clearly important (*dōron* appears three times in 5:23-24); and it is about to be offered.

b. But, says Jesus, if at that point you remember your brother's resentment (over the sins of 5:21),'leave [*aphes*] your gift there before the altar and go [*hypage*]; first be reconciled [*diallagēthi*] to your brother...' (5:24a). Jesus thus affirms that the commands to love God and to love neighbor are inseparable (cf. 22:37-40); and that the moral dimension of the law (represented here by the sixth commandment) takes precedence over the ceremonial (here represented by directives for the altar of burnt offering). The three imperatives indicate that resolute action is required, however inconvenient.[39] Moreover, it is clear from the command to

---

[37]OT wisdom literature, notably Proverbs, makes abundantly clear what God judges to be foolish behavior. *Mōros* never appears in the LXX of Proverbs; but *aphrōn* ('foolish, ignorant') is very frequent (cf. Jesus' use of this term in Luke 11:40; 12:20).

[38]In the LXX of Leviticus 1–7, *thysiastērion* occurs fifty-three times.

[39]The difficulty in imagining listeners' exactly obeying this command – especially if it entailed a trip to Galilee and back – makes Jesus' words all the more arresting and shows how urgently reconciliation is needed. Cf. Keener 1999: 185; Davies and Allison 1988: 518.

'be reconciled' that a favorable response from the brother is expected. As the offender seeks to make peace (Matt. 5:9), so let the offended party show mercy (5:7), lest he be at risk for refusing forgiveness (6:14-15).[40]

c. 'And then, having come [back to the altar], present your gift' (5:24b). The ceremonial, far from being omitted, crowns the process (cf. Ps. 51:19, with 1-18). So important is the gift, that nothing must hinder God's receiving it. The gift is not identified; but the coherence of the passage, together with the content of Leviticus 1–7, strongly suggests that the worshiper, now appalled by his sin (22), seeks forgiveness from God through blood sacrifice.[41] For Christians guilty of such offenses and living in light of Matthew as a whole, the right response is clear: not to offer animal sacrifice to the Father but to invoke the merits of his Son's atoning death.[42]

4. The second course of action (Matt. 5:25-26) serves the purpose of the first. Since the 'opponent at law' is the alienated brother, 25 depicts one place for being reconciled to him; the road that leads to the court may also lead away from the temple.

a. Jesus calls for swift action – 'Come to terms with your adversary quickly [*tachy*]' (5:25a) – and thus underscores the

---

[40]Matthew 18:15-20 speaks of seeking peace with an *offending* brother; see those comments.

[41]Leviticus 1–7 prescribes five kinds of sacrifice: (i) burnt offering, 1:3-17; 6:8-13; (ii) grain (or cereal) offering, 2:1-16; 6:14-23; (iii) peace (or fellowship) offering, 3:1-17; 7:11-21; (iv) sin (or purification) offering, 4:1–5:13; 6:24-30; and (v) guilt (or reparation) offering, 5:14–6:7; 7:1-10. Four (all but ii.) entail the shedding of blood. In i. the animal dies in the sinner's place and ransoms him from death. In iii. the blood is a reminder that God's *shalom* depends on atonement for sin; according to Leviticus 3:5 this sacrifice is burned 'on top of the burnt offering.' In iv. the blood disinfects the sanctuary so the holy God may remain present with his people. In v. the sacrifice cancels sinners' accumulated debts to God. In the remaining offering, ii., sinners respond with thanksgiving for the forgiveness granted through i., and consecrate themselves to God as Savior and covenant King. For these points, see Wenham 1979: 71, 80, 111.

[42]See Matthew 20:28; 26:28; Romans 3:25; 5:9; Ephesians 1:7; 2:13; Colossians 1:20; 1 John 1:5–2:2; Hebrews 9:11–10:31. As Isaiah foresaw, the levitical sacrifices were not contradicted or modified but 'realized in the substitutionary death of the Servant' (Motyer 1999: 375).

urgency reflected in 5:23-24. Unless the matter is settled *now*, before the trial begins, it may never be.

b. As a spur to such action, Jesus describes for the offender what might otherwise happen (5:25b-26): you may well be sentenced to prison, where you are sure to stay until you have paid the fine in full. Ponder other costs as well: during that time you will be kept from going to the *thysiastērion* (in place of the *dōron* you freely offered there, your last *kodrantēs* will be forcibly extracted from you); and you will be isolated from the covenant community (so what hope can there be for reconciliation with the brother?).[43]

c. That horrible prospect mirrors a yet graver danger. The times are critical, says Jesus: given the dawn of God's rule and the prospect of its consummation, you must repent of sin before it is too late (4:17). Being cast into prison by a human judge for whatever length of time (5:25) is as nothing compared to experiencing the wrath of the divine Judge and being consigned by his irrevocable decree to an eternity in 'the Gehenna of fire' (5:22).[44]

Adultery (5:27-30)

A paragraph based on the seventh commandment naturally follows one based on the sixth (Jesus quotes the two in the same order in 19:18; cf. 15:19). The two sections are also linked by the kindred wording in the second part of the opening formula (noted earlier) and by the term *geenna* (5:29, 30, 22). Moreover, these verses, like 5:21-26, form a coherent whole. The verb *moicheuō* ('to commit adultery'; 5:27, 28) joins together the two parts of the opening formula. The phrase *ho ophthalmos sou* ('your eye'; 5:29) recalls *pas ho blepōn* ('everyone who looks at'; 5:28). The phrase *hē dexia sou* ('your right hand'; 5:30) reflects growing intimacy in the relationship. The last

---

[43]Imprisonment for debts was unknown to Jewish law, so Jesus appears to be 'deliberately referring to non-Jewish legal practice which his audience considered inhuman' (Jeremias 1963: 180). The *kodrantēs* was the smallest denomination in Roman currency (Latin *quadrans*); it was worth 1/64th of a *dēnarion*, a day's wage for a common laborer (Matt. 20:2).

[44]The divine Judge (5:22) stands behind the scenes in 5:25. Cf. 18:23-35; Luke 12:54-59; France 1985: 121; Jeremias 1963: 180.

two verses are closely parallel: twenty-five of the thirty-three words in 5:29 recur in 5:30, and in the same order. As before, the analysis is important for understanding Jesus' teachings.

1. Jesus again begins with the OT: 'You shall not commit adultery [*Ou moicheuseis*]'(5:27). The Greek is that of the LXX for the MT's *lō' tin'āp*, Exodus 20:14 and Deuteronomy 5:18.[45] In keeping with the singular *moicheuseis* of 5:27, every word beyond the plural *hymin* ('you') of 5:28a has the individual in view. The seventh command is foundational for the whole section: the gravity of actual adultery is clear from everything Jesus says on the subject, here and elsewhere.[46]

2. 'But I say to you [Jesus continues] that everyone who looks at a woman to satisfy lustful desire [*pros to epithymēsai autēn*], has already committed adultery with her [*ēdē emoicheusen autēn*] in his heart [*en tē kardia autou*]' (5:28).

a. Here, as in 5:22, Jesus seeks to awaken listeners to OT teachings. The closing command of the Decalogue itself shows that violations of the seventh command begin in the heart (*kardia*): 'You shall not covet...your neighbor's wife...or his female servant...or anything that belongs to your neighbor [which would include his daughter]' (Exod. 20:17).[47] For the Hebrew *chāmad* ('covet'), the LXX has *epithymeō*, the verb used in Matthew 5:28.[48] Not only do *moicheiai* ('adulteries') and *porneiai* ('fornications') come forth <u>ek</u> *tēs kardias* ('*from* the

---

[45]In the LXX, the seventh command appears in Exodus 20:13 (the sixth in 20:15, and the eighth in 20:14); and in Deuteronomy 5:17 (the sixth in 5:18).

[46]All such references in Matthew appear on Jesus' lips: beyond the present passage, see *moichaomai* ('commit adultery'; 5:32; 19:9); *moicheuō* ('commit adultery'; 5:32; 19:18); *moicheia* ('adultery'; 15:19). As with murder, Jesus perceives the horror of adultery to a far greater degree than did Moses (cf. 19:3-9).

[47]In Exodus 20:17, the neighbor's house is mentioned before his wife; in Deuteronomy 5:21, the wife comes first. Francis Schaeffer, *True Spirituality* (Wheaton: Tyndale, 1971), 7, stresses that coveting is 'entirely inward,' and that this command is broken before any of the other nine.

[48]Cf. the quotation of the tenth command in Romans 7:7. In 7:7-13 Paul recalls the period during which he became *bar mitzvah* ('son of the commandment'), a time – early adolescence – when strong sexual desires are commonly experienced. See Robert H. Gundry, 'The Moral Frustration of Paul before His Conversion: Sexual Lust in Romans 7:7-25,' in *Pauline*

heart'; 15:19); they also occur _en tē kardia_ ('_in_ the heart'; 5:28).[49] By honoring the tenth command, implicit in 5:28, I will honor the seventh. Dealing with lustful desires may safeguard me from physically committing adultery or fornication – and may also prevent a murder (5:21) from occurring.[50] On the other hand, the man who restricts transgressions of the command to physical acts may more readily commit the act for failing to reckon with his strong sexual desires.

b. If Israel under Moses was subject to those prohibitions, how much more are Jesus' followers (for reasons given in the discussion of 5:21-26). The disciple described in 5:28, by transgressing the seventh command, (i) wrongs his wife (if he is married), and the woman's husband (if she is married); (ii) violates the new community's covenantal bonds either by becoming unequally yoked to a non-believer, or by wronging a Christian _adelphē_ (as the man in 5:22 had wronged his _adelphos_) and exploiting the grace and intimacy of the new community for selfish ends; (iii) allows _agapē_ for his neighbor to be overruled by _erōs_; (iv) endangers others in the community, including the woman (if she is a fellow-disciple); and hampers his own witness to others, including the woman (especially if she is a non-believer) – all of which (v) raises doubts about the man's own spiritual condition.[51]

Studies, ed. Donald A. Hagner and Murray J. Harris (Grand Rapids: Eerdmans, 1980), 228-45.

[49]The articular infinitive _pros to epithymēsai_ may denote purpose (desire pursued) or result (desire fulfilled); cf. _GGBB_, 590-94. In either case, the lustful desire _constitutes_ adultery. 'Jesus refers not to _noticing_ a person's beauty, but to imbibing it, meditating on it, seeking to possess it' (Keener 1999: 189).

[50]The link between commands six and seven is not just literary. An adulterer may commit murder (2 Sam. 12:9); or he may be murdered by an enraged husband (Prov. 6:32-35). Anger and contempt (the sins condemned in Matthew 5:22) destroy sexual intimacy and help to account for the frequency of adultery and divorce in our culture: see Willard 1998: 163-64, 172.

[51]For (i) see Proverbs 5:15-20; 1 Thessalonians 4:3-6; for (ii), 1 Corinthians 7:39; 2 Corinthians 6:14-15; and for fellow believer as _adelphē_ ('sister'), Romans 16:1; 1 Corinthians 7:15; 9:5; James 2:15; for (iii), Matthew 22:39 (the verb _agapaō_); 1 Corinthians 13:1-13 (the noun _agapē_); and the argument in Lewis 1960, that _erōs_ must be ruled by _agapē_; for (iv), 1 Corinthians 5:1-11; and for (v), the repeated threat of _geenna_, Matthew 5:29, 30, plainer here than in 22 because of the reiterated 'your whole body [_sōma_].'

c. Persons guilty of those offenses are commanded to repent of their sin (Matt. 4:17) and to seek forgiveness in Messiah's atoning death (1:21; 20:28). Adulterers under Moses were to be stoned; they are now threatened with far severer punishment, but also offered hope of restoration.[52]

d. As the present subject is adultery, Jesus warns of *illicit* desires. Within the bonds of covenantal marriage, it is *good* that a husband should view his wife with passionate desire.[53]

3. As in the previous section, Jesus prescribes two closely related actions for dealing with the evil: 'If your right eye causes you to sin [*skandalizei*], gouge it out and throw it away.... And if your right hand causes you to sin [*skandalizei*], cut it off and throw it away' (5:29a, 30a, NIV).[54] These words demonstrate that severe measures are needed to combat such powerful sins; and they illustrate the radical obedience expected from persons who have experienced the powers and graces of the dawning kingdom. As ever, it is the *heart* that Jesus addresses: a disciple who loves God and Immanuel with all his heart (22:37) will want *nothing* to sully their holy Name (6:9) or to impede their saving mission (28:19-20), and will therefore resolve to do whatever Christ the Lord demands (7:24-27). One might (in another irony) take these words quite literally, yet remain enslaved (to his mind more excusably!) to the sin in question: there would still be an eye for leering at the woman, and a hand for caressing her.[55] We may apply

---

[52]See Leviticus 20:10; Deuteronomy 22:22; Matthew 5:29-30 (*geenna*; *blēthē*, 'be thrown' [5:29] is a 'divine passive'); 1 Corinthians 5:1-13; also John 7:53-8:11, which, while 'originally no part of the Fourth Gospel,' 'has all the earmarks of historical veracity' (*TC*, 188-89).

[53]See Song of Songs, *passim*; Proverbs 5:19; 1 Corinthians 7:2-5; Ephesians 5:25-28; and instances of *epitimaō* to express commendable desires, e.g., Matthew 13:17; Luke 22:15; 1 Timothy 3:1.

[54]The verb *skandalizō* means '*cause to be caught* or *to fall*; i.e., *cause to sin*' (BAGD s.v., 1.). As one might leave the temple (5:24) to meet the brother on the road (5:25), so (as noted) one might progress from viewing with the eye (5:29) to caressing with the hand (5:30). Contrast 18:8-9, where Jesus speaks first of cutting off hand or foot, then of plucking out an eye.

[55]If understood literally, Jesus' words in 19:12 about those who 'have made themselves eunuchs for the sake of the kingdom of heaven' speak of

the term *hyperbole* to these commands, so long as that does not become a subtle way to blunt their sharpness. Practical application might require unplugging a TV set and throwing it away (which could be more traumatic than losing an eye!), or ending a cherished relationship (which might be more painful than losing a hand!).[56]

Divorce (5:31-32)

This is understandably the shortest of the six sections, since this subject is addressed at greater length in Matthew 19:3-12 (present comments anticipate that discussion). The passage opens, *Errethē de*, 'And it was said' (5:31a). This is the shortest of the six openings, and the only one containing the conjunction *de*, here to be translated 'and' rather than 'but.'[57] Thus literarily this section is very closely joined to the preceding – which is fitting, given the close connection between the two subjects. For Jesus always relates divorce to illicit sexual practice, whether it is (i) a wife's 'sexual infidelity [*porneia*]' prompting a divorce (5:32; 19:9); (ii) a wife's adultery by marriage to

---

surgery more drastic than that of 5:29-30. But 5:29-30 is *prescriptive* and 19:12 *descriptive*. The latter act, while perhaps commendable (e.g., in Origen's case), might not succeed in curtailing the heart's lustful passions. According to the Stoic philosopher Seneca, one should rip out his heart if nothing else sufficed for banishing vice (cited in Keener 1999: 187). See further the comments on 19:12.

[56]Calvin 1994: 189 comments that 'it is not Christ's intention that we should mutilate our body to obey God.... Christ in hyperbole bids us prune back anything that stops us offering God obedient service, as He demands in His Law.' Colossians 3:5 may well have these verses in view (as Keener suggests, 1999: 188): Paul speaks of 'putting to death' one's 'members' (*melē*, as in Matthew 5:29-30), all five of which – 'sexual immorality [*porneia*], impurity [*akatharsia*], lustful passion [*pathos*], evil desire [*epithymia kakē*] and covetousness [*pleonexia*]' – could describe the sin of Matthew 5:28. Both Jesus and Paul appeal to the disciple's own will – as opposed to the practice in some Islamic societies of imposing the penalties of 5:29-30 from without. As Hilary of Poitiers (ca. 315–368) recognized, 'if the impulse of the heart is left unchanged, the cutting away of a member would be pointless' (in *ACC* 1a: 110).

[57]'Most common translations: *but*, when a contrast is clearly implied; *and*, when a simple connective is desired, without contrast...' (BAGD s.v. *de*). Given the subjects of sections two and three, the latter meaning is preferable here.

another man (5:32a);[58] (iii) a man's adultery by marriage to a divorced woman (5:32b); or (iv) a divorced man's adultery by marriage to another woman (19:9).[59] In other words, in Jesus' teachings divorce is hardly conceivable apart from violations of the seventh commandment.

1. As before, Jesus begins with a quotation from the OT: 'Whoever divorces his wife must give her a certificate of divorce' (Matt. 5:31). The Greek condenses, but conveys the sense of, Deuteronomy 24:1b according to both the MT and the LXX.[60] In keeping with the quotation, verse 32 focuses on individual responsibility and relationships between individuals, twice uses the verb *apolyō* ('divorce') and contains the phrase *tēn gynaika autou* ('his wife'). According to Deuteronomy 24:1-4, if a man divorces his wife, and she then marries another man who later divorces her or dies, the first husband is not permitted to remarry her. Only remarriage is expressly prohibited: the divorce(s) and the provision of certificate(s) are presupposed. As is clear from Jesus' quotation, the certificate was not optional: the husband 'must give [*dotō*]' one to the wife.[61] But as Jesus later makes equally clear, under Moses divorce itself was not commanded but permitted (Matt. 19:8; the verb *epitrepō*).

---

[58]The words 'causes her to commit adultery' (Matt. 5:32a) imply her remarriage, which Deuteronomy 24:2 expects (cf. Murray 1961: 24; France 1985: 123, n. 1).

[59]The *moicheuō* of 5:32a matches the instances in 5:27, 28 (the synonymous *moichaomai* appears in 5:32b and 19:9). So too the instances of *gynaika* (the accusative singular of *gynē*, 'woman, wife') in 5:31, 32 (and 19:9), match that of 5:28.

[60]The LXX of Deuteronomy 24:1b is very close to the MT. Both expressly speak of the husband's writing the certificate; Matthew 5:31 implies it. For the Hebrew behind 'a certificate of divorce,' LXX has *biblion apostasiou*, reproduced in Matthew 19:7 and abbreviated as *apostasion* in 5:31. For LXX's (= MT's) 'shall give [it] into her hand,' Matthew has 'let him give her.' For LXX's (= MT's) 'and he shall send her from his house,' Matthew has 'whoever divorces his wife'; LXX uses *exapostellō* ('to send away'), Matthew *apolyō* ('to dismiss, divorce').

[61]*Dotō*, from the verb *didōmi*, is an aorist imperative of command (*GGBB*, 485-86, including n. 97); cf. Matthew 19:7, 'Moses commanded [us] to give' it. This document granted the woman 'a certain protection under law from any further action by the man' (Craigie 1976: 305); and it stated her right to marry another man (R. H. Stein, 'Divorce,' *DJG*, 195).

2. Then Jesus, again exercising unique authority (*egō legō hymin*), declares that divorce virtually assures violations of the seventh commandment, and is therefore (by implication) itself forbidden.

a. The implicit becomes explicit in Matthew 19:6, where Jesus, having quoted Genesis 2:24, declares: 'Therefore what God yoked together, let man not separate [*mē chōrizetō*, an imperative of prohibition].' What Moses permits, Messiah prohibits.[62]

b. The words 'except for sexual infidelity [*parektos logou porneias*]' (5:32) are really no exception to that rule. For the *porneia*, whether an illicit act during betrothal or thereafter, has annulled the marriage (as would have happened with Mary and Joseph, had the angel not intervened; 1:18-25). The formal divorce simply acknowledges that a divorce has already occurred. Following a divorce for any other reason, the woman's sexual union with another man is adulterous (5:32b), because in God's sight she is still wed to her first husband.

c. In Jesus' day, the two major rabbinical schools differed in their interpretation of the *'erwat dābār* of Deuteronomy 24:1 – literally 'the nakedness of a thing.' The school of Shammai, pressing the word 'nakedness,' understood the term to mean strictly sexual sin. The more influential school of Hillel supposed that the provision was much broader, even including such things as the burning of the husband's food. Jesus assails such abuses, siding with the stricter view of the Shammaites.[63]

d. Jesus declares that the husband who takes unfair advantage of the Mosaic permission and divorces his wife for unjust cause, bears responsibility for her subsequent behavior: 'he causes her [*poiei autēn*] to commit adultery' (5:32).

e. In Jesus, the divine Messiah, we behold 'both the kindness and the severity of God' (a phrase from Romans 11:22). On the one hand, Jesus' teaching is more demanding than that of Moses. But on the other hand, the grace that attends the dawn of God's rule is unprecedented in its magnitude. Adulterers

---

[62]In overruling the Mosaic permission, Jesus appeals to foundational teachings of the *Torah* itself (in Matthew 19:4-5 he quotes Genesis 1:27 and 2:24) and thus 'penetrates to the deeper spirit of the law' (Hagner 1993: 112).

[63]Cf. Gundry 1994: 91.

and adulteresses, once condemned to die, may now be restored (as noted above). While *porneia* permits divorce, it does not require it: even a marriage torn asunder by such an act may be healed by the divine mercy.

Oaths (5:33-37)

As noted on page 347, the words of Matthew 5:33a suggest that a second set of three paragraphs is being introduced. At the same time, paragraphs three and four are closely joined, as already indicated by the opening *Palin* ('Again'; 5:33. How fitting that teaching about speaking truth and keeping one's word should follow examples of what happens when one fails to do so (5:32).[64] Moreover, one of the texts in view in 5:33 (Deut. 23:21) is near the one quoted in 5:31 (Deut. 24:1). It may also be observed that a later figure in Matthew – Herod Antipas – violates the teachings of all four paragraphs considered thus far: he is guilty of anger and murder (14:5, 10), of lust, adultery and divorce (14:3-4, 6), and of making a very foolish vow (14:7, 9).[65]

1. Jesus again starts with the OT: 'You shall not swear falsely [*Ouk epiorkēseis*], but you shall render [*apodōseis*] to the Lord [*tō kyriō*] your oaths [*horkous*]' (5:33). Several texts from Moses undergird this quotation.

a. Leviticus 19:12a: 'You shall not swear [*lô' tiššābe'û*] by my name with false intent [*lašāqer*],' Hebrew terms which 5:33 well renders *Ouk epiorkēseis*.[66] LXX has *ouk omeisthe ...ep' adikō*, 'you shall not swear unjustly,' this being the verb, *omnyō*, used in 5:34, 36 (and 23:16-22). The formulation 'to swear [*šāba'*] by

---

[64]The Jewish counterpart to our exchange of wedding vows occurred at betrothal. At this time 'the groom gave the bride money or something of value as a token of his intention. He also presented a written marriage contract listing his responsibilities and the amount of money she would receive at his death or in case of divorce' (Scott 1995: 250). Cf. the comments on 1:18-19, pages 209-11 above.

[65]See H. W. Hoehner, 'Herodian Dynasty,' *DJG*, especially 323-24 ('Antipas and John the Baptist'); Keener 1999: 189.

[66]The verb *epiorkeō* can mean both 'swear falsely, perjure oneself' and 'break one's oath' (BAGD s.v., 1. and 2.).

Yahweh' (*baYHWH*) – or 'by God,' or 'by his [or my] name' – is very common in the OT: Yahweh is hereby invoked as *witness* (that the oath is true) and as *guardian* (so that the oath may be kept). The phrase 'to swear, or make an oath, *to* Yahweh,' rarely appears.[67]

b. Numbers 30:2 (MT and LXX, 3): 'When a man makes a vow [*yiddōr neder*] to Yahweh, or swears an oath [*hiššāba' šᵉbu'â*]..., he shall not break his word; according to all that his mouth has spoken, he shall do.' LXX translates the first pair of words *euxētai euchēn*, using Greek cognates (the verb *euchomai*, the noun *euchē*) to match the Hebrew (the verb *nādar*, the noun *nēder*); neither Greek term appears in the gospels.[68] The second pair, also Hebrew cognates (the verb *šāba'*, the noun *šᵉbu'â*), LXX renders *omosē horkon*, closely joining the language of Matthew 5:33 (the verb *epiorkeō*, the noun *horkos*) to that of 5:34, 36 (the verb *omnyō*). In contrast to the rare usage of *šāba'* noted under a., the OT often speaks of vowing (*nādar*), or making a vow (*nēder*), '*to* Yahweh' (*laYHWH*).[69]

c. Deuteronomy 23:21a (MT and LXX, 22a): 'When you make a vow to Yahweh your God, you shall not delay to render it.' The language of the first part (in both MT and LXX) is like Numbers 30:2a. LXX (23:22a) well renders the second part *ou*

---

[67]For swearing (*šāba'*) 'by Yahweh' (*baYHWH*), or 'by God' (*bē'lōhîm*), or 'by my name' (*bišmî*), or 'by his name' (*bišmô*), or 'by the name of Yahweh' (*bᵉšēm YHWH*), see, e.g., Genesis 21:23; 24:3; Leviticus 19:12; Deuteronomy 6:13; 10:20; Joshua 2:12; 9:19; Judges 21:7; 1 Samuel 24:21 (MT, 22); 28:10; 30:15; 2 Samuel 19:7; 1 Kings 2:8, 23, 42; 2 Chronicles 36:13; Nehemiah 13:25; Isaiah 48:1; Jeremiah 12:16. See also Genesis 31:53; Jeremiah 4:2; 38:16; Hosea 4:15. For swearing (*šāba'*) 'to Yahweh' (*laYHWH*), see 2 Chronicles 15:14; Psalm 132:2; Zephaniah 1:5. Depending on the context, *šᵉbu'at YHWH*, 'oath of Yahweh,' may refer to Yahweh's own oath; or to swearing 'by Yahweh,' 'to Yahweh' or 'before Yahweh.' See the various translations of Exodus 22:11 (MT, 10); 2 Samuel 21:7; 1 Kings 2:43; also of Ecclesiastes 8:2, *šᵉbû'at ᵉlōhîm*, 'oath of God.'

[68]*Euchomai* means 'to pray' (James 5:16) and 'to wish' (Rom. 9:3); *euchē*, 'prayer' (James 5:15) and 'oath, vow' (Acts 18:18). Both terms are rare in the NT.

[69]Sometimes the verb *nādar* and the noun *nēder* are joined together, as in Numbers 30:2-3 (MT, 3-4). For other instances of the verb and/or the noun with *laYHWH* or the like, see Numbers 21:2; Deuteronomy 12:11; 23:21, 23 (MT, 22, 24); Judges 11:30; 2 Samuel 15:7; Psalms 50:14; 66:13; 76:11 (MT, 12); 116:14, 18; 132:2; Ecclesiastes 5:4 (MT, 3); Isaiah 19:21; Jonah 1:16.

chronieis apodounai autēn. The *autēn* ('it'), the direct object of the infinitive *apodounai*, refers to the *euchē* ('vow'); both terms are feminine singular. The indirect object is *kyriō tō theō sou* ('to the Lord your God'). This is the LXX's typical way of translating such passages.[70] The same verb, *apodidōmi*, appears in Matthew 5:33b. Here its indirect object is again *tō kyriō*, but its direct object is the accusative plural of *horkos* ('oath') – which never occurs as the object of this verb in the OT. The choice of *horkos* rather than *euchē* makes sense literarily; its cognate *epiorkeō* appears in 5:33a. It also makes sense theologically: in setting forth OT teaching, both Jesus and Matthew have a greater concern than making fine distinctions between *euchē* and *horkos*. The crucial factor in both swearing and vowing is *the use of Yahweh's name.* Swearing 'by Yahweh' and making a vow 'to Yahweh' are both solemn pledges to tell the truth or to keep one's word – and one might thus swear and thus vow at the same time for the same purpose.[71]

d. Underlying all those commands is the Decalogue's warning against misusing the name (*šēm*) of Yahweh, Exodus 20:7 and Deuteronomy 5:11 – which would include falsely swearing by his name, or giving false testimony against a neighbor while under such an oath, Exodus 20:16 and Deuteromony 5:20.[72] Oaths and vows are not banned; on the contrary, as is clear from many passages cited in the notes, it is honorable to make

---

[70]Cf. Psalms 50:14 (LXX, 49:14); 66:13 (65:13); 76:11 (75:12); 116:18 (115:9); Ecclesiastes 5:4 (3); Isaiah 19:21; Jonah 1:16. The use of both *kyriō* and *theō*, as in Deuteronomy 23:21(22), is exceptional.

[71]Numbers 30:2 (MT, 3) uses both verb and noun for both swearing and vowing; Psalm 132:2 uses both verbs. As noted, the OT speaks of 'swearing by Yahweh' and (though rarely) of 'swearing to Yahweh' – which seems equivalent to 'vowing to Yahweh.' On the question of distinctions between 'oath' and 'vow,' see Davies 1964: 240; Davies and Allison 1988: 534. To judge from the dictionaries, in English usage the terms overlap to the point of being basically synonymous.

[72]The term *laššāwᵉ'* – Exodus 20:7 (bis) and Deuteronomy 5:11 (bis) – speaks of using Yahweh's name *wrongfully* (cf. NIV, NRSV), and *worthlessly* (LXX, *epi mataiō*, 'for a useless purpose'; NASB, 'in vain'). One such use was to support *falsehood*: Exodus 20:16b, *'ēd šāqer*, 'false witness' (cf. Leviticus 19:12, quoted above); and Deuteronomy 5:20b, *'ēd šāwᵉ'*, 'vain witness' (cf. 5:11b; Exodus 23:1; Ps. 24:4). Another was to practice *magic* (Craigie 1976: 155-56).

a solemn vow to Yahweh or to swear an oath by his name. Indeed Yahweh *prescribes* such oaths to strengthen the people's devotion to him and dependence on him. Yet precisely because Israelites are thus privileged to utter the sacred name, their using it illegitimately is a serious offense indeed.[73]

2. 'But I say to you: "Do not swear at all [*mē omosai holōs*],"' begins 5:34.[74] After the opening 'to you' (plural *hymin*), Jesus again – in keeping with the singular verbs of 5:33 (*epiorkēseis, apodōseis*) – addresses the individual, (5:36): 'by your [*sou*] head...for you cannot [*ou dynasai*]' (singular pronoun and verb). Then, in the positive command of Matthew 5:37, he reverts to the plural: 'But let your [*hymōn*] speech....' Comments on 5:37 are reserved for 3.; for now we focus on 34-36.

a. Of the thirteen instances of *omnyō* ('to swear') in Matthew, twelve appear on Jesus' lips. In all twelve, one or more adjoining phrases indicate something *by* which one swears, or is not to swear: e.g., someone may swear *en tō ouranō* ('by heaven'; 23:22); but disciples are instructed not to do so, *mēte en tō ouranō* ('neither by heaven'; 5:34b).[75] The source of that idiom, *omnyō* + *en*, is the Hebrew OT, where its most notable usage is the one considered above – swearing 'by Yahweh' or 'by God' (or the like). Cf. the LXX of Judges 21:7 and 1 Kings 2:8.

b. Jesus' command in Matthew 5:34a is to be interpreted in light of those *en*-phrases. That is, the primary – or at least the initial – thrust of the words 'Do not swear *at all*,' is that disciples are to swear by *none* of the following – 'neither [*mēte*] by heaven...nor [*mēte*] by earth...nor [*mēte*] by [or toward] Jerusalem...nor [*mēte*] by your head' (5:34b-36).[76] As Moses

---

[73]See Deuteronomy 6:13; 10:20; Leviticus 19:12b; Andersen and Freedman 1980: 372 (at Hos. 4:15).

[74]The aorist infinitive *omosai*, preceded by the negative particle *mē*, forms an indirect command, 'I tell you not to swear' – here converted to direct speech. When the adverb *holōs*, from the adjective *holos* ('whole, entire'), is joined to *mē*, the sense is 'not at all.'

[75]For *omnyō* + *en*, see Matthew 5:34-36; 23:16, 18, 20, 21, 22. The *eis Hierosolyma* of 5:35b is usually translated '*by* Jerusalem' (e.g., ESV, NIV) to match the surrounding *en*-phrases; but this may mean '*toward* Jerusalem' (Davies and Allison 1988: 537). The imperative of James 5:12, *mē omnyete*, is followed by accusatives without prepositions; so too LXX, e.g., Gen. 21:23; 24:3.

[76]A point well made by Calvin 1994: 191.

instructed Israel to make oaths in Yahweh's presence (5:33), so all four of these realities witness to his glorious sovereignty: heaven is 'God's throne'; earth is 'his footstool' (cf. 11:25, 'Lord of heaven and earth'); Jerusalem is 'the city of the great King,' whether Yahweh or his Messiah (cf. Ps. 48:1-3); and it is not humans but God who controls the hairs on the head (cf. 6:27; 10:30). Thus one may violate the third commandment, and dishonor Yahweh, even when carefully avoiding his name. For, as Jesus makes explicit in 23:22, 'he who swears by [en] heaven swears by [en] the throne of God and by [en] the one who sits upon it.' So to view the oaths of 5:34b-36 as non-binding, or to imagine that they assure a desired outcome (see 36), or (worse still) to use such terms as a cloak for deliberate falsehood, is to employ God's own possessions illicitly and therefore to sully his name. To judge from 5:20 (which immediately prefaces these six sections), and from the matching passage in 23:16-22, it is especially the scribes and Pharisees whose teachings and practices Jesus is renouncing.

3. The section concludes with a positive statement: 'But let your speech [logos] be yes yes [nai nai], no no [ou ou]; whatever goes beyond these is from the evil one' (5:37). Clearly based on this saying is James 5:12b (as 5:12a is based on 5:34-35a): 'But let your yes be yes, and your no be no, lest you fall under judgment.'

a. Jesus does not expressly forbid swearing 'by God' (or a kindred expression): the name of God is conspicuously absent from the en-phrases of 5:34b-36. But neither does Jesus expressly command such an oath (as Deuteronomy 6:13 had done); on the contrary, he tacitly excludes it by saying 'Do not swear at all' (Matt. 5:34a), words underscored in James 5:12a: 'nor any other oath' (mēte allon tina horkon).

b. At the same time, Jesus upholds the truth at the heart of the Mosaic teachings summarized in Matthew 5:33: knowing that we stand perpetually in Yahweh's presence and under his scrutiny, we must tell the truth and keep our word. Here, as always, Jesus stresses the condition of the heart – just as Moses had done.[77] The person who loves God with all his heart, and

---

[77]In overruling the Mosaic injunction to swear by God's name (e.g., Deut. 6:13), Jesus appeals to foundational teachings of the Torah itself

his neighbor as himself (5:8; 22:37-40), 'speaks the truth from his heart,' and thus can be trusted to keep his word, and not to spread falsehood about his neighbor (Ps. 15:2-4). Such a person *need not* swear *by* anything (Matt. 5:5:34b-36); indeed he *need not* verbally swear *at all* (5:34a). Instead, says Jesus, 'let your speech be yes yes, no no' (5:37a).

The point here is not that the first 'yes' or 'no' must be reinforced by a second. For the person who tells the truth the single word is quite adequate; the second would be superfluous, or cast doubt on the sincerity of the first. The sense is, 'let your yes be yes, and your no be no,' as in James 5:12.[78] In other words, 'let your yes *mean* yes, and your no *mean* no.' The person of integrity whose heart has already willed, before God, to tell the truth or to keep a promise, need say only 'Yes' (I will keep my promise), or 'No' (I will refrain from falsehood). 'Whatever goes beyond these [i.e., this Yes and this No] is from the evil one' (5:37b). This 'whatever' is not confined to needless additions; indeed the main stress lies upon the use of 'yes' and 'no' themselves. One may say 'yes' though the heart has decided 'no'; the spoken 'no' may effectively conceal the 'yes' of the heart. Such deceptions and falsehoods, says Jesus, are inspired by the devil, the great deceiver and the father of lies.[79] By the same token James 5:12b – 'lest you fall under judgment' – warns both against buttressing one's 'yes' or 'no' with needless oaths, and especially against using these two terms falsely or deceptively.

(Deut. 6:5, Lev. 19:18, with Matt. 22:37-40). He did the same in Matthew 5:31-32; see those comments.

[78]'The repetition ['yes yes, no no'] is not a new formula, but a Semitic way of indicating that "Yes" and "No" are to be used (alone) on each occasion.... James 5:12...has correctly interpreted the meaning' (France 1985: 125). Cf. Jeremias 1971: 220. The imperative *ētō* (James 5:12b) is a colloquial form of *estō* (Matt. 5:37a).

[79]Christ calls for 'single-mindedness...where men have nothing on their lips that is not also in their hearts' (Calvin 1994: 192-93). There is 'Semitic evidence that the yes-yes, no-no formula means "let your word be (an outer) yes (which is truly an inner yes), etc."' (Davids 1982: 190, on James 5:12). (By contrast, the 'yes yes' and 'no no' of 2 Corinthians 1:17 reflect the charge that Paul *says* two different things.) For *ek tou ponērou* as 'from the evil one' (not 'from evil'), see comments on 6:13. For the devil as the deceiver,

c. The words 'yes' and 'no' are uttered in God's presence (the *en kyriō* of 5:33 is still in view), and they are therefore just as binding as OT oaths. Now, as then, better to refrain from words than, having uttered them, to fail to keep them (cf. Deut. 23:22). Indeed, given the graces attending the dawn of the kingdom, the radical obedience to which Jesus calls his disciples, and the character of life in the new community, the demand for truth telling is now greater than ever before. Yet for that need Christian disciples are granted stupendous powers: they are baptized into the *name* of the Holy Trinity, and *Immanuel* – the incarnation of truth – is with them all their days. Persons who cannot make even one hair white or black (Matt. 5: 36) are urged to depend on him who can, and who – as Lord of heaven and earth – can adequately equip them for every good work, including truthful speech.[80]

d. The disciple who submits to this teaching will refrain from making oaths, knowing them to be unnecessary. Yet he may, as an exercise of liberty, make an oath when required to do so by a properly constituted authority, for example in a court of law. His convictions remain unchanged: he knows that oath-taking does not assure truth-telling, and that he must tell the truth whether under oath or not. His own conscience is not violated: he knows that *he* requires no oath, even when a court requires it. The finest example is Jesus' response to Caiaphas in Matthew 26:63-64. Recalling Paul's willingness to abstain from meat for the sake of a weaker brother, a Christian can, in respect for a civil magistrate, relinquish his right to refrain from oath-taking. One mark of 'the wisdom from above' is its 'willingness to yield.'[81] We may further observe both (i) that

---

see 2 Corinthians 11:3; 1 Timothy 2:14; as father of lies, John 8:44. Cf. the comments on Matthew 4:1-11.

[80]As noted in remarks on Leviticus 19:12 (pp. 362-63), 'swearing by God' invoked him as guardian to assure fidelity to one's oath. Heeding 'the evil one,' a disciple might imagine that oaths, like prayers (Matt. 6:7-8), can be used to force God's hand (cf. comments on 4:1-11).

[81]See James 3:17, NRSV; and (on Paul and the weaker brother) 1 Corinthians 8:1-13. 'What Jesus emphasized...was that honest men do not need to resort to oaths; it was not that they should refuse to take an oath if required by some external authority to do so' (Stott 1978: 102).

Paul's letters never use the language of oath-taking, and (ii) that he several times invokes God as witness to the truth of his words, thus making explicit the truth underlying the present passage – that no words from the mouth and no intentions of the heart escape the divine scrutiny.[82]

Retaliation (5:38-42)
Contributing to the coherence of the paragraph are (i) the four pairs: two cheeks, two garments, two miles and two requests; and (ii) the alternate constructions *hostis se* (5:39, 41) and *tō thelonti soi, ton thelonta apo sou* (5:40, 42).[83] In this, the middle section of the second triad, the preface to the OT quotation is identical to that of the middle section in the first triad: 'You have heard that it was said' (5:38a, 27a). As parts two and three of the first triad are conceptually close (adultery, divorce), so are parts two and three of the second (relating to evil persons, loving one's enemies). Furthermore, 'the evil person' (*tō ponērō*) of 5:39a is distinct from, but closely related to, 'the evil one' (*tou ponērou*) of 5:37b.[84]

1. As before, Jesus quotes from the Torah: 'An eye for an eye, and a tooth for a tooth' (5:38). *Ophthalmon anti ophthalmou* and *odonta anti odontos* are the very phrases used in the LXX at Exodus 21:24; Leviticus 24:20; and Deuteronomy 19:21; and

---

Davids 1982: 190 notes that James 5:12 'prohibits not official oaths, such as in courts (for none of the sayings in Jewish or Christian sources touches on these...), but the use of oaths in everyday discourse to prove integrity.' WCF chapter 22, 'Of Lawful Oaths and Vows,' states that 'as in matters of weight and moment, an oath is warranted by the Word of God, under the new testament as well as under the old; so a lawful oath, being imposed by lawful authority, in such matters, ought to be taken' (par. 2). The motif of the two realms is apposite: see page 308, n. 22. Bruner 2004a: 234-46 well relates 5:33-37 to the history and theology of the church.

[82]See Romans 1:9; 2 Corinthians 1:23; 11:11; Galatians 1:20; Philippians 1:8; 1 Thessalonians 2:5, 10.

[83]*Hostis* is an indefinite relative pronoun: 'whoever.' *Thelonti* and *thelonta* are present participles (dative and accusative respectively) of *thelō*: 'I want, will.' *Se, soi* and *sou* are second singular personal pronouns (accusative, dative and genitive respectively): 'you.'

[84]The same is true of four Hebrew verbs repeated in Exodus 2:10-15; cf. Childs 1974: 29.

they well convey the sense of the MT.[85] This 'law of retaliation' (*lex talionis*) similarly stipulated that a hand be taken for a hand, and a foot for a foot; its most serious provision was that a life be taken for a life.[86] The injured party, however weak and lowly, was made in God's image and was entitled to just retribution; the guilty party, however high and mighty, was required to pay it. But the guilty person was also made in God's image, and was therefore to be treated justly, not vengefully: he was to lose *one* eye or tooth, not two.[87]

2. 'But I say to you [Jesus continues]: "Do not resist [*mē antistēnai*] the evil person"' (5:39a).[88] Then, again addressing the individual disciple and starting with the strong adversative *alla* ('on the contrary'), Jesus commands a very different set of actions (5:39b-42): *strepson* ('turn'), *aphes* ('give'), *hypage* ('go'), *dos* ('give') and *mē apostraphēs* ('do not turn away').[89]

a. Obeying this command begins with the recognition that the person in view is indeed *evil*: he is himself *ponēros* and under the influence of 'the evil [*ponēros*] one' (5:37). To resist

---

[85]In Exodus 21:24 and Leviticus 24:20, MT uses the preposition *tachat*, 'for, in place of, in exchange for'; in Deuteronomy 19:21, the preposition *bᵉ*, which in such a construction has the same meaning (BDB s.v., III. 3.).

[86]For these and other stipulations, see Exodus 21:23-25; Leviticus 24:19-21; Deuteronomy 19:21. The taking of a life for a life honors the laws of Genesis 9:5-6 and Exodus 20:13.

[87]For an instance of such vengeance, see Genesis 4:23-24. Applying as it did to all the people, the *lex talionis* prevented the rich and powerful from abusing or exploiting the poor and weak; cf. Matthew 5:3, 6. As it also applied to resident aliens, it prevented Israelites from taking advantage of gentiles; cf. Leviticus 24:22. The law also served as a deterrent (Deut. 19:20). See Childs 1974: 472; Wenham 1979: 283; Gundry 1994: 94.

[88]As in 5:34, an aorist infinitive (from the verb *anthistēmi*), preceded by the negative particle *mē*, forms an indirect command – 'I tell you not to resist,' here converted to direct speech.

[89]All five forms are second person singular. The first four are imperatives of command, the fifth is a subjunctive of prohibition (as *GGBB* notes, 469, n. 61, the NT never uses a second person imperative with the negative particle *mē*). The four forms in the aorist tense describe 'punctiliar' action; the one exception is *hypage*, which describes 'linear' action, a journey of two miles (5:41). See *IB*, 7, 10; and for cautions against viewing all aorists this way, *GGBB*, 557. The last verb in the series, *apostrephō* (here the aorist passive, 'turn away from') is a compound of the first, *strephō* (here the aorist active, 'turn').

this person in the sense here attached to the verb *anthistēmi* (5:39a) would be to repay evil with evil (Rom. 12:17)[90] and thus cause evil to increase – the devil's very design. The disciple who obeys the commands of 5:39b-42 appears to be succumbing to external powers and pressures, but is in fact effectively resisting the evil one and disclosing a power of his own to the evil person.[91]

b. Verses 39b-42 use singular terms exclusively: in every example one disciple relates to another individual.[92] The other person insults a disciple, or threatens to take his clothing, or presses him into service, or asks to borrow money. This accent on personal relationships is exceedingly important, given the imperative of 5:39a. There is no basis here for non-resistance to evil when my *neighbor* is affected in one of these ways; that would be to disobey what Jesus teaches elsewhere – starting with the Beatitudes – about loving other people. Jesus is *not* saying (e.g.), 'If a thug attacks your wife, let him assault your child too,' or 'If a powerful banker exploits one impoverished widow, let him cheat another as well.'

c. Nor do these verses undermine the truth that underlies the *lex talionis*: respect for the human body and for human life. On the contrary: that Jesus honors the image of God and the sixth commandment is already clear from verses 21-26. The examples in 5:39b-42 do not suggest serious threats to one's body, much less to one's life. Jesus does not quote the stipulation of the *lex talionis* that a life be taken for a life. The Pauline text which most illuminates the present passage (Rom. 12:17-21) is followed immediately by teaching about the governing authorities (13:1-7), whom God authorizes to wield the sword in opposing evil. The motif of the two realms is

---

[90]Romans 12:17 reads *kakon anti kakou* ('evil for evil'), the very construction found in the OT quotations of Matthew 5:38.

[91]Observe that the verb *anthistēmi* (5:39a) appears in the epistles in commands to *resist* the devil and the powers of darkness: see James 4:7; 1 Peter 5:8-9; Ephesians 6:13. In the language of Matthew 6:13, the actions of 5:39b-42 are ways of *deliverance* from the evil one.

[92]Here, as in previous sections, the singulars are the more notable after the plural of the opening *legō hymin*. By contrast, 5:43-48 uses plurals exclusively.

again pertinent. Jesus speaks of conduct which marks persons as members of the Christian community; so does Romans 12. Nothing in this passage prohibits a duly appointed civil magistrate (Rom. 13) from taking a life for a life – or a hand for a hand, or an eye for an eye. By the same token, the individual Christian would be disobedient, and extremely foolish, to take Matthew 5:39-42 to mean (e.g.) 'If an assailant chops off your right hand, let him chop off your left one as well,' or 'If he chops off your hand, let him chop off your head too.'[93]

d. Were Jesus merely applying the existing law (Matt. 5:38), we would expect him to say, 'If someone strikes you on the right cheek, strike him on the right and *only* on the right.' Were he simply teaching, 'Do not resist the evil person' (5:39a), we would expect him to say, 'If you are struck on one cheek, do not strike back *at all*'; or 'If someone sues you for your tunic, do not file a countersuit to prevent it'; or 'If a Roman soldier orders you to carry his gear for one mile, do not take flight.' Verses 39b-41 go beyond both exact retribution and non-resistance: 'turn to him the other also...give him your cloak also...go with him two.'[94] In each case the disciple (i) obeys *Jesus*, not the other party (again note the imperatives); (ii) exerts *his own will* to exceed the will of the other (who has chosen to slap only one cheek, or has sued for his tunic alone, or has dragooned him for only one mile); and (iii) upholds

---

[93]The wounds of Matthew 5:29-30, by contrast, are self-inflicted; see also page 328 (including n. 45) on fleeing, rather than courting, martyrdom. On the two realms, see page 308, n. 22; Calvin 1994: 193. As a civil authority is to protect the citizens of the realm, so a husband and father is to use his headship to safeguard the other members of the household (see example in b. above).

[94]In Matthew 5:40, faced with a lawsuit (the passive of *krinō*; BAGD s.v., 4.) that threatens the loss of his *chitōn* – 'tunic, shirt,' the garment worn next to the skin – the disciple offers also his *himation* – here 'cloak, robe,' the outer garment (his 'inalienable possession,' Exod. 22:26-27; Deut. 24:12-13; Gundry 1994: 95). The reversal of the terms in Luke 6:29 matches the order in which the garments would be removed, perhaps forcibly. In Matthew 5:41, an Israelite is ordered to carry a Roman soldier's equipment one *milion* (an originally Latin term), literally a thousand paces, then a fixed measure of about 4,854 feet (BAGD s.v.). In the other two NT instances of this verb, *aggareuō*, Simon of Cyrene is 'pressed into service' to carry Jesus' cross (27:32; Mark 15:21).

the *values* of the new community (disdain for insults; freedom
from anxiety over clothes; trust in God to rule the hours of
each day).[95] This is the radical obedience expected from
citizens of God's kingdom; this is love for neighbor freely and
extravagantly exercised. Its intent is to drain away the other's
malice; to shame him into repentance; in short, to overcome
evil with good (Rom. 12:21).[96]

e. Verse 42 is set apart from the preceding: the *kai* ('and')
used in 5:40a and 41a to join the first three examples together,
is absent from 5:42a. In each of those encounters the other
party is an aggressive adversary; here the other comes
with his need (whether real or apparent) and asks for help,
specifically for money.[97] The disciple who gives what is asked
is, as in the previous instances, responding primarily to Jesus'

---

[95]See Willard 1998: 178-81. 'A backhanded blow to the right cheek did
not imply shattered teeth...; it was an insult, the severest public affront to
a person's dignity' (Keener 1999: 197; cf. Gundry 1994: 95); the one who
turns the other cheek (Matt. 5:39) is secure in Christ and contemptuous of
insults. Knowing God will supply his needs, he need not bemoan the loss
of clothes; 5:40 does not endorse nudity or forbid all recourse to law, but
vividly depicts the prizing of God's rule above material things (6:25-34;
Keener 1999: 198; Calvin 1994: 195). Going a second mile offers opportunity
to advance God's rule (5:41; cf. 6:33).

[96]Romans 12:21 echoes Matthew 5:39. 'Do not be conquered by evil' (5:21a;
which happens when we resist evil in the wrong way; 5:39a); 'but [again
the strong adversative *alla*] conquer evil with good' (5:21b; which happens
when we take the actions of 39b-42). Giving an enemy food and drink 'heaps
burning coals' on his head (Rom. 12:20), an image not of judgment but of
'shame and remorse' or 'penitence.' See John R. W. Stott, *Romans* (Downers
Grove: InterVarsity, 1994), 336; Douglas Moo, *The Epistle to the Romans*
(Grand Rapids: Eerdmans, 1996), 788-89. This counsel was – significantly
– first given to Israel under Moses (Prov. 25:21-22) as a way to love one's
neighbor (Lev. 19:18). Loving others means refraining from certain acts, as
is clear from both Leviticus 19:18 and Romans 13:10. Still, formulating the
'golden rule' in a *strictly* negative way, as in Tobit 4:15 ('Do to no one what
you would not want done to you,' NJB), rather than in the positive way of
Matthew 7:12, could deter one from taking the positive steps of 5:39b-42.
See further the comments on 7:12. Believing that 'Christ is more worthy of
imitation than Caesar or Alexander,' we shall, when faced with 'stubborn
and stout and contemptuous' sinners, 'contend with charity, and not with
violence,' and shall 'overcome them with kindness' (Baxter 1974: 66).

[97]The parallel between 5:42a and 42b is typically Hebraic; 5:42b
reinforces and enlarges upon 42a (cf. Ps. 8:4). The structure of 5:40 is similar.

command rather than to the other person's request; and is freely exercising his will for his neighbor's sake (22:39). He is also behaving as one whose treasures are heavenly rather than earthly (6:19-21); who is slave to God rather than to money (6:24); and who would want to be treated the same way if the situations were reversed (7:12). In many instances the giver is being merciful (5:7) to the sorts of persons described in 5:3, some of whom are victims of the evils illustrated in 5:39-41. Such a disciple discovers that 'it is more blessed [*makarion*] to give than to receive' (Jesus' words in Acts 20:35) – one such blessing being that the heavenly Father gives to him at least as much as he has given to others (Matt. 6:33; Luke 6:38). Yet, some who ask for money may harbor evil designs equal to those of 5:39-41; there are always charlatans eager to exploit another's generosity, and some persons' alleged needs may not be real. So the disciple who is to be 'innocent as a dove' in the face of such requests (and to give the supplicant the benefit of the doubt), must also be 'sensible as a serpent' (10:16). Like his Master, let him willingly take risks in giving to others; but let him not be a 'gullible simpleton.'[98]

3. Viewing this paragraph within Matthew as a whole brings two further matters to light.

a. The evil here recognized will surely be judged – partially and imperfectly now by God's appointed magistrates, fully and flawlessly at the Last Judgment. The very one who commands 'Do not resist the evil person' will one day consign unrepentant and unredeemed evildoers to destruction.

Cf. Carson 1984: 156; Davies and Allison 1988: 547. The verb *aiteō* (5:42a) denotes an entreaty, not a demand; cf. its use in 6:8; 7:7-11.

[98]The phrase comes from a comment on 10:16 in France 1985: 182. For an example of Jesus' willingness to take risks in giving to the needy, see 14:13-21 and comments. On the one hand, for Christians universally to give to the needy until all their resources are depleted 'would be self-defeating: "there would soon be a class of saintly paupers, owning nothing, and another of prosperous idlers and thieves"' (France 1985: 127, quoting Leon Morris on the parallel in Luke 6:30; Carson 1984: 156-57, cites Proverbs 11:15; 17:18; 22:26). On the other hand, those who refrain from extravagant or reckless giving for fear of losing the power to be generous may be robbed of the blessing promised in Luke 6:38 (cf. Phil. 4:19). See comments on Matthew 19:21.

Compared to the punishments in store at the end, those stipulated in the *lex talionis* – including physical death – are almost as nothing.[99] In instructing Christians not to return evil for evil but to overcome evil with good, Paul quotes Deuteronomy 32:35: 'Retribution is mine, I will repay, says the Lord' (Rom. 12:19b). Thus, on the one hand, believers are not to avenge themselves but to 'leave room for the wrath' of God (12:19a; cf. 2 Tim. 4:14; Prov. 20:22; 24:29). And, on the other hand, a prime motive for their acts of love is that their adversaries may repent of sin and be saved from the coming retribution. Thus is God himself motivated: by his sovereign design the final judgment is postponed to allow for the worldwide proclamation of the gospel, and sinners' consequent repentance and faith.[100]

b. As that last statement suggests, the prime exemplars of the conduct commended in 5:39-42 are God the Father and God the Son. The Father responds to 'evil persons' by acts of kindness, in both creation (5:45) and redemption (3:17). The Son responds to the same kind of people by going to the cross for them. On the way, he is repeatedly and savagely insulted; he is twice taken to court and subjected to the worst injustice; and he is not only commandeered but brutalized and executed by Roman soldiers (cf. respectively 5:39b-41). Yet, through it all, he is obeying not his enemies but his Father, and trusting him for vindication; he is freely exercising his own will; and he is using those very evils to achieve the greatest good – the conquest of the evil one and the redemption of a people.[101]

---

[99]Cf. comments on Matthew 5:6, 22, 29-30; 10:28; and the parables of chapter 25. For God's retributive justice, see e.g. Psalms 9; 10; 21:8-13; Romans 2:5-11. Moses' personal act of vengeance, Exodus 2:11-14, however just, achieved nothing. Following the crucial encounter of 3:1–4:17, he announces and interprets *Yahweh's* acts of retribution against Pharaoh and the gods of Egypt.

[100]Matthew 24:14; 26:13; Acts 17:30-31; Romans 2:4; 2 Peter 3:15.

[101]See Matthew 1:21; 12:28-29; 16:21; 28:18. This is the conduct of the Servant of Yahweh: see Isaiah 42:1-4 (Matt. 12:17-21); 50:6 (Matt. 26:67; 27:30), 7-8 (vindication from Yahweh); 53:4 (Matt. 8:17), 7 (Matt. 26:63; 27:12, 14), 12 (Matt. 27:38; 20:28); also 1 Peter 2:21-24; Gundry 1994: 95. The Servant uses 'left-handed' power to overcome his enemies' 'right-handed' power.

Love (5:43-48)

A paragraph about loving one's enemies naturally follows
one about responding to evildoers. In this regard, note that
the preface to the OT quotation in Matthew 5:38a ('You have
heard that it was said') recurs in 5:43a; and that 5:45, like 5:39,
refers to 'evil persons.' These are now further identified as
'enemies' (*echthrous*; 5:44), 'persecutors' (*tōn diōkontōn*; 5:44)
and 'the unrighteous' (*adikous*; 5:45), to which might be added
'tax collectors' (*telōnai* 5:46) and 'Gentiles' (*ethnikoi*; 5:47).

Conversely, 5:39-42 indicates some practical ways to
obey the command of 5:44a. The present paragraph recalls
earlier teachings in Matthew 5 as well. Verse 11 warned that
people would persecute the disciples and utter all kinds of
evil against them.[102] The references to 'your Father in heaven'
(5:45) and 'your heavenly Father' (5:48) recall the language of
5:16 – which suggests that non-believers will come to honor
God through the disciples' obedience to 5:44.[103] In addition
5:45a, 'that you may be sons [*huioi*] of your Father...,' brings
to mind 5:9b, 'they shall be called sons [*huioi*] of God' – which
implies that loving one's enemies (5:44) is a way of making
peace (5:9a).[104] Joining the question of 5:46 ('What reward
[*misthon*] do you have?') to the promise of heavenly *misthos* in
5:12 (the only other instance of the term in ch. 5) suggests that
the reward for loving those who love us cannot compare with
the one in store for those who rejoice in face of persecution
and pray for their persecutors. The *dikaious* ('righteous
persons') of 5:45 (the only occurrence of this adjective in the
sermon) recalls the use of the matching noun *dikaiosynē* in
5:20 (as well as in 5:6 and 5:10); and the question 'What are
you doing more than [*perisson*] others?' (5:47b) recalls 5:20a:

---

[102]Within the sermon, *diōkō* ('persecute') occurs only in Matthew 5:10-12
and 44; and within chapter 5, *ponēros* occurs only in verses 11, 37, 39 and 45.

[103]Cf. 1 Peter 2:12. Within the sermon, 5:16 contains the only instance of
patēr prior to 5:45, 48. The phrase of 16, *ton patera hymōn ton en tois ouranois*,
is virtually the same as that of 5:45 (which has the genitive *tou patros...tou*
instead of the accusative, and lacks the article *tois*).

[104]These are the only two instances of *huios* in chapter 5. As noted, the
actions of 5:39b-41 can have the same effect; cf. again Romans 12:20, with
12:18b: 'be at peace with all men.'

'Unless your righteousness surpasses [*perisseusē*] that of the scribes and Pharisees,' verses which together indicate that loving one's enemies is a premier mark of the righteousness Jesus requires. Finally, we may note the reference in 5:47 to greeting 'your brothers [*adelphous*].' There are four previous instances of *adelphos* in the chapter, all in verses 5:22-24; given the subject of that paragraph, the greetings of 5:47 may well include brothers formerly alienated.

1. As in the five preceding paragraphs, Jesus begins by quoting from the Torah: 'You shall love [*agapēseis*] your neighbor [*ton plēsion sou*]' (Matt. 5:43a). These are the very words of the LXX at Leviticus 19:18b, and they accurately convey the Hebrew original. They are followed by the phrase 'as yourself' in both MT (*kāmôkā*) and LXX (*hōs seauton*), as also in the two other places in Matthew where Jesus quotes this verse (19:29; 22:39). By their present omission, a perfect balance is achieved between the quotation of 5:43a and the words of 43b: 'you shall hate [*misēseis*] your enemy [*ton echthron sou*].' The latter is nowhere expressly commanded in the OT; but it is easily inferred from such passages as Deuteronomy 23:3-6 (the exclusion of Ammonites and Moabites from Israel's blessings) and Psalm 139:21-22 ('Do I not hate those who hate you, Yahweh?... I count them my enemies').[105] In view of that evidence it is to be noted (i) that the 'neighbor' (Hebrew *rē'a*) of Leviticus 19:18b is a fellow Israelite (cf. 19:18a: 'the sons of your own people'); (ii) that even enemies among those neighbors are to be loved, by acts of omission (not taking vengeance; 19:18a) and of commission (restoring and rescuing the other's livestock; Exodus 23:4-5; providing him food and drink; Proverbs 25:21); (iii) that this love is to embrace resident aliens as well (Leviticus 19:34: 'you shall love him as yourself'); (iv) that in some passages 'to hate' means to withhold love, or to love someone less than another, rather than to exercise positive hatred;[106] and

---

[105]In the LXX of the latter text the verb of Matthew 5:43b, *miseō*, appears three times; and the noun, *echthros*, twice.

[106]See 6:24; 10:37 (with Luke 14:26); Romans 9:13 (with Mal. 1:2-3), where the subject is election; Genesis 29:30-31; France 1985: 128; Jeremias 1971: 213, n. 3.

(v) that the Torah does not exclude just retribution but leaves it to Yahweh (Deut. 32:35).[107]

2. 'But I say to you,' Jesus continues, 'love [*agapate*] your enemies [*tous echthrous hymōn*] and pray [*proseuchesthe*] for those who persecute you [*tōn diōkontōn hymas*]' (5:44). In the five previous paragraphs, Jesus addresses disciples individually, as the dominance of singular forms indicates. Now, drawing the section (5:17-48) to a close, he speaks to them collectively. Despite the singular terms in 5:43, all references to disciples in 5:44-48 are in the plural.

a. The first command of 5:44 joins the verb of 43a to the object of 43b. Jesus now expounds the *plēsion* of 43a (which does not recur in 5:44-48) by means of other terms. Included among one's neighbors are not only the good and the just but the evil and the unjust (5:45); not only friends and brothers (5:46, 47), but enemies and persecutors (5:44). On the one hand, addressing those who confine their love to selected Israelites, Jesus reaffirms the original meaning of Leviticus 19:18. *No* Jews are to be denied this love – not even unjust tax collectors, or notorious sinners, or hypocritical theologians, or those guilty of the evils described in Matthew 5:21-42.[108] God does not withhold common grace from such people, does he (5:45)? On the other hand, Jesus goes beyond Leviticus 19:18, and even beyond 19:34 (love for resident aliens). This love is also to embrace *the enemies of God's covenant people*, such as those described in Deuteronomy 23:5-6 and Psalm 139:21-22.[109] Does not the covenant God bestow sunlight and rainfall upon

---

[107]As noted, this verse is quoted in Romans 12:19. The Hebrew words translated 'take vengeance' in Leviticus 19:18 and 'vengeance' in Deuteronomy 32:35 are cognate forms from the root *nqm*. In view of the hatred expressed in Psalm 139:21-22, note verse 19a, 'Oh that you would slay the wicked, O God!' (ESV). Cf. David's words to Saul in 1 Samuel 24:12.

[108]In this sense, Jesus 'restores the true and original' meaning of Leviticus 19:18 (Calvin 1994: 198). On law-keepers' (especially Pharisees') contempt for 'tax collectors and sinners,' and for law-breakers generally, see, e.g., Matthew 9:10-11; 11:19; Luke 18:11; John 7:49. For hypocritical theologians, see Matthew 23:1-33.

[109]See France 1985: 128 ('There is a sweeping universality in the love Jesus demands which has no parallel in Jewish literature'); Banks 1975: 200-201.

pagans (Matt. 5:45; cf. Acts 14:17)? Luke 10:25-37 teaches the same lesson, but more shockingly: whereas the lawyer quotes Leviticus 19:18 and asks 'Who is my neighbor [*plēsion*]?' (Luke 10:29), Jesus tells of a Samaritan who *became* a neighbor (10:36, *plēsion*) to a helpless Jew.

b. Here, as before, Jesus' instructions are intended specifically for his own followers. The only persons from whom such radical obedience can be expected are those joined to Messiah, saved by his mighty works, and submissive to his and his Father's rule. For these Jewish disciples, fidelity to the commands of Matthew 5:44 calls for loving (i) other members of the new community, i.e., the 'brothers' (5:47a); (ii) Jews outside their number, including those who hate, persecute and kill them for obeying Jesus (10:17; 23:34), and who therefore become enemies of God's covenant people; and (iii) Gentiles (5:47b), including those whose malice matches that of the Jews (10:22; 24:9).[110]

c. *Agapē* for one's neighbor (here represented by four instances of the verb *agapaē* [5:43, 44, 46 *bis*]), like *agapē* for God, arises from the *heart* (22:37-40). Such love therefore marshals one's rational, emotional and volitional powers. Yet one's *will* is crucial: the love is *commanded*, both in 5:43 (*Agapēseis*) and in 44a (*agapate*); love does not come to fruition until there is action.[111] As in the previous paragraph, love means not only refraining from evil acts but taking positive action. Jesus again exemplifies the conduct he requires: he shows love for his enemies by dying for them; he prays for his executioners;

---

[110]So, even if Proverbs 25:21 originally spoke only of foes within Israel, as quoted in Romans 12:20, it includes people beyond the Christian community. The relationship between Jesus' disciples and other Jews progressed from intramural conflict to divorce between church and synagogue. See pages 165-67.

[111]The future indicative *agapēseis* (Matt. 5:43) voices a command: see page 349, n. 26. Stressing the action does not mean that emotions are disregarded or excluded (as Carson rightly notes, 1984: 158). On the heart's three dimensions, see page 248 above. Cf. 15:3-9 (failure to love one's parents reveals a heart estranged from God); 1 Timothy 1:5; 2 Timothy 2:22; 1 Peter 1:22. Pious words may conceal an unloving heart (Matt. 15:8); and loving words without loving deeds are empty (1 John 3:18). But words expressive of love from the heart are themselves a loving deed (Luke 6:28; Rom. 12:14; 1 Cor. 4:12; 14:3; Eph. 4:29).

and he befriends persons outside his own circle, including
telōnai and *ethnikoi*.[112] The Father whom Jesus invokes as
the disciples' model shows love not just by withholding
hurricane and earthquake but by causing the sun to shine
and the rain to fall (5:45; cf. Luke 6:35b). The verb *poieō*, 'do,'
occurs three times in 5:46-47 and again in related passages.[113]
Not only is a disciple to forbear from calling down curses
on Jewish or Gentile persecutors; he is to pray *for* them
(Matt. 44b). Likewise, an apostle, faced with false charges
in a Jewish or pagan court, should refrain from damning
his accusers and offer them the gospel instead (24:9-14; cf.
Paul in Acts). In each case, the Christian is fulfilling the
paradigmatic command of 7:12 (where *poieō* appears twice).
Moreover, as persons expected to be wise and discerning
(10:16), the disciples are to obey the commands of 5:44 in
the full awareness that the objects of their love are indeed
enemies, not just misguided friends; that they are *actually*,
not just apparently, evil and unrighteous (5:45; cf. comments
on 5:39). One use of persecution (5:44b) is to cure love's
blindness and naiveté.

d. Humans' recognition of the 'evil' and the 'unrighteous'
is as nothing compared to God's, ('send rain', Matt. 5:45);
and he will one day surely judge and condemn such persons (Ps. 1:5-6). So a prime motive for loving one's enemies
(Matt. 5:44a) is that they may repent of sin and be saved from
coming retribution.[114] Then comes a vital means of expressing
that love toward that end: 'and pray [*proseuchesthe*] for [*hyper*] those who persecute you' (5:44b). Using such language
for the first time in Matthew, Jesus commands disciples to

---

[112]On Jesus' death for his and his Father's enemies, see Romans 5:8-10;
Ephesians 2:14-16; Colossians 1:20-22. (Yet those for whom he dies are also
his friends; John 15:12-16.) He prays for his executioners in Luke 23:34. For
examples of his love towards tax collectors and Gentiles (Matt. 5:46, 47), see
9:9-13; 15:21-28.

[113]Cf. Luke 6:27, 'do good [*kalōs poieite*] to those who hate you' (words
later imported into Matthew 5:44; see NKJV; *TC*, 11-12); 6:35, 'love your
enemies and do good [*agathopoieite*].'

[114]So it was in Matthew 5:38-42; see the comments on pages 374-75. Cf.
Deuteronomy 30:7; the citation of Deuteronomy 32:35 in Romans 12:19 and
Hebrews 10:30; Calvin 1994: 198.

pray *for, in behalf of, for the sake of,* their enemies.[115] Many a disciple doubtless already prays *about* such people, asking God (as did the writer of Psalm 7:9) to end their violence, and (like the writer of Psalm 139:21-22) voicing to God his hatred. The latter prayer is commendable in that the hatred is flung toward God rather than into the face of the persecutors. Such language may even prompt intercessions on the others' behalf; indeed, unless this happens, persecutors remain in peril and disciples are endangered by their own hate.[116] Prayer for the persecutor implores God to save him through the One whose followers he is oppressing. Disciples who pray this way behave as God's *sons* (Matt. 5:45), the name earlier given to peacemakers (5:9); redeemed persecutors find peace – *shalom* – with God.[117] Who knows how many Christians thus prayed for Paul before Jesus confronted him on the Damascus Road. Who knows how often God has rescued the righteous, not by destroying their persecutors but, as in Paul's case, converting them. For the heavenly Father always loves his enemies more than his sons and daughters love theirs. One reason he lavishes his providential gifts on the evil and the unjust, both in Israel and among the nations (Matt. 5:45), is that they may seek *him*, the Giver, and be reconciled to him through the redemption he has provided. To that end he unfailingly and unceasingly causes the sun to shine and the rain to fall, and he postpones the Final Judgment.[118]

---

[115]This is the meaning of the preposition *hyper* when followed, as here, by the genitive case; see BAGD s.v., 1. NKJV includes words imported from Luke 6:28; cf. n. 113 above.

[116]Cf. Psalm 37:8, REB: 'Be angry no more, have done with wrath; do not be vexed: that leads to evil'; and *ACC* 1a: 120 (haters suffer more grievously than the hated). Peterson 1991 notes both that 'our hate needs to be prayed, not suppressed' (98) and that 'while hate provides the necessary spark for ignition, it is the wrong fuel for the engines of judgment; only love is adequate to sustain these passions' (102–3).

[117]Cf. 1 Peter 3:9-12, especially the commands to return good for evil (9) and to pursue peace (3:11); and the promise of God's attentiveness to the prayers of the righteous (3:12), as well as the connection earlier noted between 1 Peter 2:12 and Matthew 5:16, 44. See also 1 Timothy 2:1-7, where the appeal that prayers be made for (*hyper*) all men (2:1-3) is directly joined to news of salvation for all men through Christ the mediator (2:4-6).

[118]See Genesis 8:22; Acts 17:26-31; 2 Peter 3:8-9. The verbs *anatellei* ('cause to shine') and *brechei* ('send rain'), 45b, are instances of the customary, or habitual, present (*GGBB*, 521-22).

3. To underscore the commands of 5:44, Jesus discourages his listeners from emulating tax collectors (5:46) and Gentiles (5:47) – each a class of persons with whom even derelict disciples might favorably compare themselves. Instead, says Jesus, the disciples' model is to be their 'Father in heaven' (5:45), their 'heavenly Father' (5:48). Having considered 5:45, we turn our attention to verse 48: 'You therefore shall be perfect [*teleioi*], as your heavenly Father is perfect [*teleios*]' (5:48). Behind the words 'You shall be' are the verb *esesthe* (the future tense used as a command, as in 5:21, 27, 33 and 43) and the pronoun *hymeis* (used to emphasize the listeners' obligation): '*You* – you disciples – must be perfect....' What does Jesus mean?

a. *Teleios* is thoroughly Hebraic in character. With one exception, every instance of this adjective in the LXX translates one of two Hebrew word groups.[119] The first is *šlm*, which can attest (i) that a building project has been *completed*, (ii) that vows have been *fulfilled*, or (iii) that a person is *fully committed* or *wholeheartedly devoted* to Yahweh. The second, *tmm*, can denote (i) the *completion* of a task, (ii) a sacrifice *without blemish*, or (iii) a *blameless* person.[120] The *blameless* are, of course, not *sinless*. Persons identified by *šlm* and *tmm* submit to God's *torah*, which includes commands to offer sacrifices for personal sins. A chief reason for these people's utter devotion to God is the knowledge that they are sinners in perpetual need of his salvation.[121]

---

[119]It is of interest that the one exception appears in Psalm 139 (LXX 138): 22: 'I hate them with *perfect* [or *complete*] hatred.' Behind *teleios* is the Hebrew *taklît*.

[120]For *šlm*, see ,e.g., (i) 1 Kings 7:51; 2 Chronicles 5:1; 8:16; Nehemiah 6:15; (ii) Psalm 50:14; 61:8; 65:1; 116:14, 18; Ecclesiastes 5:4-5; (iii) 1 Kings 8:61; 11:4; 15:3, 14; 2 Kings 20:3; 1 Chronicles 28:9; 29:9, 19; Isaiah 38:3. For *tmm*, see, e.g., (i) Joshua 4:1; 2 Samuel 15:24; 1 Kings 7:22; (ii) Exodus 12:5; 29:1; Leviticus 1:3, 10; Numbers 6:14; (iii) Gen. 6:9; 17:1; Deuteronomy 18:13; 2 Samuel 22:24, 26; Job 1:1; Psalms 15:2; 18:23, 25; 37:18, 37; 84:11; 101:2, 6; 119:1, 80; Proverbs 2:21; 11:5, 20; 28:10, 18. Texts where LXX uses *teleios* are italicized; several others under *tmm* (iii) are rendered *amōmos* ('faultless, without blemish').

[121]Some psalmists declare their blamelessness and godliness even as they acknowledge their sin and need of salvation (e.g., Pss. 19:12-14; 26:11; 32:1-6; 38:18-22). See comments on Matthew 9:13.

b. Given its kinship with *šlm* and *tmm*, *teleios* as used in Matthew 5:48a well describes 'the pure in heart' (5:8) and, by extension, the persons portrayed in the other Beatitudes.[122] We earlier noted a link between 5:16 and 5:45, 48. Moreover, as those who exceed the norm (5:46-47) by loving their enemies (5:44), it is the *teleioi* who evidence the surpassing righteousness of 5:20, and whose holy lives reflect the character of the holy God.[123] Significantly, in Psalm 15, the person 'who walks blamelessly [*tāmîm*]' (15:2a; cf. Matt. 5:48), and 'does what is right [*tsedeq*]' (Ps. 15:2b; cf. Matt. 5:10, 20), manifests the very qualities Jesus requires of his disciples in 5:21-42.[124] Therefore verses 43-48, and especially 48, serve as a concluding summary for the whole chapter.[125]

c. Thus far, we have limited the application of *teleios*, and of *šlm* and *tmm*, to human beings. The same would hold true in Matthew 5:48b, were Jesus' chosen model could have been a figure such as Abraham or Moses or David or Daniel – each a sinful man yet also blameless in the above sense and worthy of emulation.[126] Instead, Jesus invokes the example of the heavenly Father – an application of *teleios* that both embraces and exceeds the first.[127] Verse 48b does not mean that disciples'

---

[122]See the discussion on pages 311-30, especially 317-18. A linguistic link between Matthew 5:45 and 5:9 was noted earlier.

[123]As France notes (1985: 130), Jesus' words in 5:48 echo both Deuteronomy 18:13 ('You shall be blameless [MT *tāmîm*, LXX *teleios*] before the Lᴏʀᴅ your God') and Leviticus 19:2 ('You shall be holy, for I the Lᴏʀᴅ your God am holy'; also 11:44-45; 20:26).

[124]With Matthew 5:21-26, cf. Psalm 15:3 ('does not slander with his tongue...nor takes up a reproach against his friend'), 4 ('honors those who fear the Lᴏʀᴅ'). With Matthew 5:33-37, cf. Psalm 15:2 ('speaks truth in his heart'), 4 ('swears to his own hurt and does not change'). With Matthew 5:38-42, cf. Psalm 15:3 ('does no evil to his neighbor'), 5 ('does not put out his money at interest'). All translations come from the ᴇsᴠ.

[125]Cf. France 1985: 129; Keener 1999: 205. The other two chapters of the sermon likewise call for wholehearted devotion (*šlm*) to God: see, e.g., 6:9-10, 24, 33; 7:21. A further indication that 5:43-48 are intended as a summary is the dominance of the plural, as compared to the singular in the five previous sections.

[126]We could add Paul's name: note how he describes his own behavior in 1 Thessalonians 2:10.

[127]If Matthew 5:48b shocks and dismays us, so too should the language of Leviticus 19:2, noted above.

love must be, like God's, flawless and sinless; they could never attain such a state in this life (among human beings, Jesus alone is blameless and sinless). Nor is the primary point that disciples' love must grow to maturity, or come to completion (on the analogy of certain instances of *šlm* and *tmm*); for God could not be said to be *teleios* in that sense (but see d. below). Rather, to judge from the immediate context, disciples are *teleioi* as the Father is *teleios*, when their love (i) knows no bounds but embraces all sorts of people, including their enemies, and (ii) is freely and lavishly bestowed upon all its objects.[128] In the closest parallel to 5:48 in the gospels, Jesus commands his disciples, 'Be merciful, as your Father is merciful' (Luke 6:36), a mercy that therefore includes enemies, the ungrateful and the evil (6:35). Significantly, in the only other instance of *teleios* in Matthew (19:21), Jesus makes it plain that being 'perfect' requires loving a neighbor as oneself (19:19; where Leviticus 19:18 is quoted).[129]

d. Given the nature of these commands – 'Love your enemies.... You shall be perfect' (Matt. 5:44, 48) – growth is essential. Who has ever loved as *God* loves, or as *Jesus* loves? What disciple could claim to have loved all his neighbors as he loves himself? Or to have consistently loved even a *single* person – even a close *friend*, let alone an enemy – this way? What husband has ever loved his closest neighbor as Christ loved the church (Eph. 5:25-28)? We are never, in fact, free from the huge indebtedness to love other people (Rom. 13:8-10). This 'surpassing righteousness' (Matt. 5:20) is thus a seemingly unattainable goal to which we must nonetheless strive. It is healthy for us to do so; for 'if we do not aim at the highest we shall certainly fall short of the utmost that we could

---

[128]REB renders Matthew 5:48, 'There must be no limit to your goodness, as your heavenly Father's goodness knows no bounds.' For the supreme expression of the Father's love for his enemies, see Romans 5:8-10; Colossians 1:21-22.

[129]See those comments. On 5:48 see Calvin 1994: 200; he also interprets this text in light of Luke 6:36. Allen 1997: 26 writes that 'to be perfect as God is perfect is to love as God loves.' His love is *complete* – not *partial* but *impartial*. Cf. 1 John 2:5, 'in him the love of God has truly been perfected [*teteleiōtai*],' and 4:18, 'perfect [*teleia*] love casts out fear,' in light of this letter's stress on loving other Christians.

achieve.'[130] Moreover, in thus striving we discover that the avenues for such love are limitless and the reserves of such love inexhaustible.[131] And when we do fall short – as shall inevitably and frequently happen – we are reminded of our poverty of spirit, we grieve over our sins and failures, and we flee to the loving Father for healing grace and restorative power.[132] And not to the Father alone: for all members of the Holy Trinity promise their presence and power (28:18-20), one proof of which is disciples' capacity to love their neighbors both within and beyond the church.[133]

---

[130]J. R. R. Tolkien, *The Letters of J. R. R. Tolkien*, ed. Humphrey Carpenter (Boston: Houghton Mifflin, 1981), 326. See also above, page 309, including n. 23; Hendriksen 1973: 317.

[131]Gregory of Nyssa (331-396) says that virtue is by nature *limitless*; and that evil by nature seeks to *limit* virtue's growth. Only God's love is free of this encumbrance. See excerpts from Gregory in Foster and Smith 1993: 155-157.

[132]Robert Murray M'Cheyne prayed, 'Lord, make me as holy as it is possible for a saved sinner to be': quoted in J. I. Packer, *Keep in Step with the Spirit* (Old Tappan, NJ: Revell, 1984), 120.

[133]'Into the *name*' (Matt. 28:19) signals both presence and power, as noted earlier. For *agapē* as a gift from one or more members of the Godhead, see Romans 5:5; 8:35, 39; 2 Corinthians 5:14; 13:13; Galatians 5:22; Ephesians 3:19; 2 Thessalonians 3:5; 1 John 2:5; 3:16-17; 4:9-10; Jude 21. Matthew 5:43-48 not only calls on disciples to love *their* enemies; it also 'requires the extremely difficult feat of loving even the enemies of *God*' (Bruner 2004a: 277, against Martin Luther).

V.
'LET US LOVE OUR GOD SUPREMELY'[1]
(6:1-18)

'The sermon's long middle section, 'The Righteousness of the Kingdom' (5:17–7:12), continues. This is the express subject of the present passage – doing righteousness, *dikaiosynē*, in one way and not in another. The noun occurs here only once, but it stands in verse 1 as a heading for the whole passage; and its use here shows that Jesus is still expounding the 'surpassing righteousness' of 5:20 (cf. 5:6, 10). His warning not to do righteousness 'before men [*emprosthen tōn anthrōpōn*]' (6:1) makes us wonder how this relates to his command in 5:16, where the same phrase appears. Other features of 6:1 closely connect the passage to the close of chapter 5: the verb *poieō*, 'to do' (cf. 5:46-47, and comments); the noun *misthos*, 'reward' (cf. 5:46); and the phrase 'your Father who is in heaven' (cf. 5:45, 48).

A. The Practice of Piety

Acts of righteousness (6:1) are represented here by almsgiving (6:2-4), prayer (6:5-15) and fasting (6:16-18). As we shall see, these paragraphs have several linguistic features in common, which accord with the conviction that the three practices belong together.[2] Jesus presupposes established habits, and

---

[1]From the hymn 'Brethren, We Have Met to Worship,' ascribed to George Atkins, a nineteenth century hymn-writer.

[2]For the joining of these practices, cf. Tobit 12:8 (in LXX of the apocrypha): 'Prayer [*proseuchē*] is good with fasting [*nēsteias*] and almsgiving [*eleēmosynēs*] and righteousness [*dikaiosynēs*].' This is the very language of Matthew 6: *proseuchomai* (six times in 6:5, 6, 7, 9); *nēsteuō* (four times in Matthew 6:16-18); *eleēmosynē* (three times in 6:2-4); and *dikaiosynē* (6:1). These practices are of course representative, not exhaustive. 'Another early teacher lists the three basic deeds as Torah observance [cf. 5:17-48], temple service, and charity...; still another, judgment, truth, and peace...; later teachers would list prayer, charity, and repentance' (Keener 1999: 207).

affirms their importance: 'Whenever you give alms' (Matt. 6:2); 'whenever you pray' (6:5); 'whenever you fast' (6:16).[3] He challenges his listeners to consider from what motives and for what purposes they practice their piety.

Examining Motives

As noted, the wording of Matthew 6:1 invites comparison with 5:16. 'Good works' there corresponds to 'doing righteousness' here. But whereas in 5:16 Jesus tells disciples to do such deeds in order that (*hopōs*) others may see them, here he commands them *not* to practice righteousness in order (*pros to*) to be seen by others. It may be said that 5:16 addresses disciples' cowardice (when they are tempted to *hide* what they should *show*), and 6:1 their pride (when they are tempted to *show* what they should *hide*).[4] Yet, the latter is in view in 5:16 as well. The burden of both verses is that the heavenly Father be glorified; and the main barrier to that is human pride. Jesus knows that fallen, congenitally proud persons will naturally do acts of piety in order to be seen, and acclaimed, by others. And the more virtuous the deed, the graver the temptation: the better the work on display (5:16), the greater the risk of boasting about it, and diverting glory from the Father to oneself.[5]

So strong is that temptation, and so destructive its effects, that Jesus repeats the warning of verse 1 in each section to follow. Unlike those who display their almsgiving 'in order that [*hopōs*] they may be glorified [*doxasthōsin*] by men [*anthrōpōn*]' (6:2; the very language of 5:16 to express the opposite motive), disciples' charitable deeds are to be done in secret (6:4). Unlike those who choose to pray in public where they can be seen (6:5), disciples should pray behind closed doors (6:6). Contrary to others' exhibitionism, they are to conceal the fact that they are fasting (6:16, 18).

---

[3]Each clause uses the temporal conjunction *hotan* ('when, whenever'), followed by a present subjunctive (*poiēs eleēmosynēn*, 2; *proseuchēsthe*, 5; *nēsteuēte*), the tense here indicating customary or habitual action (cf. *GGBB*, 521-22).

[4]See Stott 1978: 127, following A. B. Bruce.

[5]The Pharisees portrayed in Luke 18:11-12 and in Philippians 3:4-6 were genuinely pious men, and therefore more susceptible to pride.

There are two further shifts of emphasis between 5:16 and
6:1. Here it is not other people, but the disciples themselves
who glorify the Father by obeying his Son. And whereas in
5:16 it was others who saw the good works and glorified the
Father, here it is the Father – and he alone – who sees what
is done, and who honors – i.e., glorifies – obedient disciples
by rewarding them (6:4, 6, 18). Examining one's motives can
be dreadful and disgusting; but the ultimate effects can be
beneficial beyond belief. It should also be noted that Jesus
does not counsel disciples who detect false motives in their
hearts, to discontinue the practices; indeed, maintaining them
could be one way to purify their motives.[6]

Exposing Hypocrisy
At the start of each section, Jesus commands his followers not
to behave as do *hoi hypokritai* (Matt. 6:2, 5, 16). Of the seventeen
instances of *hypokritēs* in the NT, no fewer than thirteen appear
in Matthew.[7] Beyond the three present instances, particularly
striking are the six of chapter 23, in the woes upon the scribes
and Pharisees.[8] This latter evidence strongly suggests that
the *hypokritai* of 6:1-18 are principally, if not exclusively, the
scribes and Pharisees of 5:20, whose righteousness (6:1) Jesus
commands his disciples to surpass.[9]

The original sense of the matching verb *hypokrinomai*
was probably 'to explain' or 'to interpret,' whence the noun
hypokritēs came to denote an actor, one of whose arts was
rhetoric.[10] In Matthew, as in the LXX, the usage is uniformly
negative: the *hypokritēs* is a *play-actor* whose impressive speech
belies the condition of his heart (15:7-8; 22:18; 23:29-31); a

---

[6]Cf. Keener 1999: 207, n. 133, citing 1 Corinthians 4:3-5 and a rabbinic
source.

[7]The other four are in Mark and Luke; Mark 7:6 and Luke 6:42 have
Matthean parallels.

[8]See Matthew 23:13, 15, 23, 25, 27, 29. For the remaining four, see 7:5;
15:7; 22:18; 24:51.

[9]In this regard, note how closely 23:5a resembles 6:1a. In the sermon
Jesus speaks of scribes and Pharisees only in 5:20 (*grammateis* recurs in
Matthew's closing summary, 7:29); but 5:17-20 is foundational for the rest
of the discourse.

[10]See U. Wilckens, in *TDNT* 8: 559-61.

pretender whose outward appearance contradicts the inward reality, and whose apparent godliness conceals great evil (7:5; 23:25-28); and a *performer* who has the attention of the desired audience, and whose actions both reveal and conceal his true motives (6:1-18). Those under his influence are deprived of great truth (23:23-24), and threatened with the same condemnation that awaits him (23:13-15; 24:51).[11]

As already intimated, it is pride that fosters hypocrisy. Pride is by nature competitive: the persons Jesus depicts are not proud of being pious (that would be vanity), but of being – and of being thought to be – *more pious* than others. Appearances serve this purpose even when realities do not, or have ceased to do so. Since it is vital for pride's sustenance and survival to be *above* others, neither almsgiving nor prayer nor fasting is really done in God's presence (*coram Deo*). Because for the proud – and therefore hypocritical – person, the true and living God must *not* be brought into the picture; for he is the supreme threat to one intent upon establishing his own supremacy. Significantly, the hypocrites are said to do their righteous acts in order to be seen by men (6:2, 5, 16), not 'in order to be seen by God.' Furthermore, one way such a person establishes and maintains supremacy is by exerting power over those beneath him – which helps to explain Jesus' dire words of judgment.[12]

Expecting Rewards
By practicing each kind of piety, says Jesus, the hypocrites 'receive in full [*apechousin*] their reward [*ton misthon autōn*]' (Matt. 6:2, 5, 16). What they have sought – the praise of other people – they have won; and there is no further gain for them.[13]

---

[11]The portrayal of the hypocrites in chapter 23 begins in verse 1-12, though *hypokritēs* first occurs in verse 13. For the negative use of the terminology in the LXX, see Wilckens, ibid., 563-64.

[12]Again, note 23:13-15. On pride's character, competitiveness and use of power, see 20:20-28; Luke 18:9-14; Philippians 3:4-6; Lewis 1952: 94-99; Chamblin 1993: 111-29; and the devastating exposé in Baxter 1974: 137-46.

[13]In the active voice (as here), the verb *apechō* is a technical commercial term indicating that a sum has been received in full (BAGD s.v., 1.). 'God owes them nothing.... The transaction is ended and they can claim nothing more' (Plummer 1911: 91).

There is in each case a matching promise for the disciple who obeys Jesus: 'your Father [*ho patēr sou*] who sees [*ho blepōn*] what is done in secret [*en tō kryptō* or *en tō kryphaiō*] will reward you [*apodōsei soi*]' (6:4, 6, 18).[14] The language of verse 1b, 'reward [*misthon*]...from your Father,' remains in view throughout. The character of the reward will become plainer when we consider the paragraphs in turn. But let us note here (i) that these rewards are bestowed both now (when hypocrites too are rewarded) and hereafter (when hypocrites receive nothing); (ii) that among those so rewarded are persons viewed as the hypocrites' spiritual inferiors; and (iii) that the recipients' motivation – wholehearted devotion to God – leaves no room for selfish calculation in the practice of piety.[15]

B. Almsgiving (6:2-4)

The paragraph opens with two conjunctions: *hotan* ('when, whenever') and *oun*, 'then, therefore,' indication that the teaching of Matthew 6:2-4 (and of 6:5-18) builds and enlarges

---

[14]The Greek would be literally translated 'your Father who sees in secret' (thus ESV at Matthew 6:4, 6, 18). But NIV's 'who sees what is done in secret' (so too NASB) is preferable. *That* the Father sees in secret is already clear from the fact that he himself is in the secret place (see comments on vv. 6 and 18). The stress is upon *what* he sees – the hidden practice of piety (cf. 6:18a, 'that your fasting may be seen not by men but by your Father...'). The *en tō kryptō* of 6:4, 6 is synonymous with *en tō kryphaiō* (Matt. 6:18). Copyists later added the words *en tō phanerō* ('openly'; so NKJV) to all three verses to make the contrast more explicit; see *TC*, 12. Applied to the Last Judgment, 'openly' does no harm (cf. 1 Cor. 4:5). But applied to the present, it could feed the very pride Jesus is combating. If other people witness *both* my pious deeds *and* God's public ('open') approval of them, are they not sure to grant me the acclaim I crave?

[15]For i., see Matthew 5:11-12 (future reward); and 6:4, 6, 18 (all of which include present reward; see those comments). For ii., see 7:1-5 (on the plank and the speck); Luke 18:9-14. For iii., see Bruce Ellis Benson's discussion of Jacques Derrida in *Books & Culture*, Sept/Oct 2000, page 45. According to Derrida, some Christians have taken the promises of rewards in Matthew 6 to mean that 'if you avoid doing your good works publicly, you'll get an even *greater* reward. Such is the Nietzschean account of Christianity – that Christians peddle the sneakiest formula for selfishness precisely because "unselfishness" is used as a cover for "selfishness" of the most insidious sort.' But such thinking (however widespread in the church) totally misconstrues Jesus' teaching. On the subject of rewards, see also Chamblin 1993: 249-50.

on the exhortation of verse 1.[16] Then come the words *poiēs eleēmosynēn*. The first is a present singular subjunctive of the verb *poieō*. While all three paragraphs include admonitions to the individual disciple, only here is he or she in view from the opening clause.[17] The noun *eleēmosynē* occurs nowhere in Matthew outside this paragraph. Here it appears three times and identifies the main subject.

The Language of Mercy

We approach *eleēmosynē* by way of its cognates. In Matthew, the adjective *eleēmōn* appears only in 5:7: 'Blessed are the *merciful*.' This already suggests that persons who give in the way Jesus commands in 6:2-4, are among those chiefly commended in the beatitude.

All three instances of the noun *eleos* in Matthew appear in statements of Jesus opposing Pharisees, some of whom are prime exemplars of the hypocrisy exposed here. In 9:13 and 12:7, he quotes Hosea 6:6: 'I desire *mercy*'; in 23:23 (addressing scribes as well) he calls *mercy* one of the law's 'weightier matters.' Of the eight instances of the verb *eleeō* in Matthew, three are specially noteworthy. The first is in 5:7b, 'they shall *receive mercy*,' which helps to clarify what 6:2-4 teaches about rewards. The other two are in 18:33, where *having mercy* means cancelling a debt – one way of giving money to another person.[18]

We come to the language of Matthew 6:2-4. In nine of the thirteen places where the noun occurs in the NT, persons are expressly said to 'do' (*poieō*) or to 'give' (*didōmi*) *eleēmosynē*, or else to 'ask for' (*aiteō*) or to 'receive' (*lambanō*) it. The other four are not exceptions, since they appear together with the explicit usage.[19] Thus *eleēmosynē* invariably denotes a charitable deed,

---

[16]The absence of *oun* from the matching clauses of verses 5 and 16, suggests that the *oun* of Matthew 6:2 covers all of 6:2-18. In 2 Corinthians 9:9, giving to the poor is an act of righteousness (*dikaiosynē*).

[17]The other opening clauses use the plural verbs *proseuchēsthe* (6:5) and *nēsteuēte* (6:16).

[18]In the other five texts, the aorist imperative *eleēson* is an appeal for Jesus to 'have mercy' on the afflicted (9:27; 15:22; 17:15; 20:30-31).

[19]For *eleēmosynē* with *poieō*, see Matthew 6:2, 3; Acts 9:36; 10:2; 24:17; with *didōmi*, Luke 11:41; 12:33; with *aiteō*, Acts 3:2; with *lambanō* (and *erōtaō*, 'ask'), 3:3. For the other four, see Matthew 6:4; Acts 3:10; 10:4, 31.

an act of *eleos*, the practice of giving to the needy as evidence that one is *eleēmōn*. Taking such action is laudable: far better to *do eleēmosynē* than simply to talk about it.[20] And better to act now than to wait till one's intentions are above reproach: to disciples convicted over false motives Jesus offers not the slightest excuse for ceasing to be generous.

The Art of Giving
The hypocrites of 6:2 are skilled at giving alms for all to see: we might say they are artful and crafty. 'Do not sound a trumpet [*mē salpisēs*] before you,' says Jesus, as those people do in the synagogues and on the streets.[21] In the Judaism of Jesus' day, trumpets were blown to announce times for prayer and fasting (cf. 6:5-18), for worship and sacrifice, for feasting and celebrating.[22] There is no evidence, beyond that of verse 2, that almsgivers used real trumpets to summon the poor; and while there were horn-shaped chests in the temple and elsewhere for depositing offerings, the language of 6:2 does not suggest such an act.[23] The words, 'Do not sound a trumpet before you,' are in all probability a metaphor – one readily suggested by trumpets' actual usage (and perhaps also by the use of those chests), and well suited (once captured by the imagination) for showing how ludicrous such a performance is.[24] Yet some witnesses take

---

[20]See 7:21, 24-27; 23:3; James 2:13 (where *eleos* occurs twice), 14-17; 1 John 3:17-18.

[21]Here, as in 5:17 and often, the prohibition is expressed by the negative particle *mē* and an aorist subjunctive in the second person (*GGBB*, 469).

[22]For a summary of evidence from the OT and Judaism (including the trumpet's use in wartime), see G. Friedrich, *TDNT* 7: 76-85. In the LXX, *salpinx* ('trumpet') most often translates the Hebrew *šôpār* ('ram's horn').

[23]Friedrich, 7: 85-86, rightly rejects both the first view (held by Calvin 1994: 201) and the second (which is questionable on linguistic grounds, as also noted by Davies and Allison 1988: 579). According to Friedrich (7: 85), the offering chests in the temple were called *šôpārôt* 'because they were horn-shaped to prevent theft, narrow at the top and broad at the bottom.'

[24]No extant Jewish sources from that time use the very language of 6:2 (Friedrich, 7: 85). That prevents our saying that Jesus' language is *surely* figurative, since real trumpets may have been used in ways not reflected in our sources (Keener 1999: 208, n. 136). But that also means that *Jesus* may have been the first to use such language, in which case he is surely speaking

the display quite seriously, and bestow upon the actors the *doxa* – the glory and honor – they have sought.[25]

'But you [*sou*],' says Jesus, 'when you give alms, do not let your left hand know what your right hand is doing' (Matt. 6:3). The *sou*, standing first in its clause, is emphatic, to sharpen the contrast between the disciple and the hypocrites.[26] Whereas the latter act in order to (*hopōs*) be glorified by men (6:2b), the disciple purposes (*hopōs* again) to do his giving in secret (*en tō kryptō*; 6:4a). The gift is to be hidden not only from other people (starting with fellow disciples) but in a sense from the giver as well: 'let not your self (represented by the left hand) know what your self (represented by the right hand) is doing.'[27] Let the focus be instead on the needy person and on the God who commands such deeds. God needs no trumpet to call his attention to what is happening. 'Your Father who is in heaven' (6:1) is also 'your Father who sees what is done in secret [*en tō kryptō*]' (6:4b); he is both transcendent and

---

figuratively. The note of ridicule would be as evident here as in Matthew 23:24 (hypocrites strain out a gnat but swallow a camel). Some others who favor the metaphorical use are France 1985: 131; Keener 1999: 208; Davies and Allison 1988: 579. The latter think a word play on *šôpār* – both 'trumpet' and 'trumpet-shaped chest' – may be intended: if the receptacles 'could be made to resound when coins were thrown into them, thereby calling attention to the giver, our verse may have been a polemical barb at the practice and a call for silent and inconspicuous giving' (ibid.).

[25]*Doxa*, 'glory, honor,' is a cognate form of *doxazō*, the verb used in 6:2b: 'that they may be glorified [*doxasthōsin*] by men.' Friedrich, *TDNT* 7: 86, thinks it probable that exceptionally generous gifts were hailed in the synagogue by trumpet sounds, to commend donors to God and to spur others to similar acts, a practice which would nicely aid the hypocrites' quest for glory.

[26]Davies and Allison 1988: 583. The singular pronoun *sou* is in the genitive case, part of a genitive absolute construction. The same verb and object – *poieō* and *eleēmosynē* – appear in Matthew 6:2a; but there the pronoun is hidden in the verb.

[27]Here, as often, hands are identified by the adjectives *aristeros* ('left') and *dexios* ('right') alone; contrast 5:30, 'your right hand [*cheir*].' Behind the command 'do not let...know' are *mē*, a negative particle, and *gnōtō*, an aorist imperative (from *ginōskō*), third person singular; when a prohibition is expressed by the second person of the aorist tense, the mood is always subjunctive, as, e.g., in 6:2a (cf. *GGBB*, 723). Gundry 1994: 102 thinks verse 3 should probably be taken literally: 'a gift should be slipped unobtrusively

immanent, both omnipresent and omniscient, Lord both of
heaven and of earth (Matt. 11:25; cf. Isa. 57:15). Moreover,
the closing words of 6:4 ('he will reward you') indicate that
the Father has beheld not just the hidden action, but also
the hidden motives of the heart. Given the heart's capacity
for self-deception, one who gives secretively might compare
himself favorably to the ostentatious giver, and congratulate
himself for being the humbler of the two and therefore the
more deserving of divine favor. That the Father responds with
a reward, implies that the disciple's heart is not dominated by
pride; that his gift is prompted by love for his needy neighbor
(22:39; 1 Cor. 13:3); and that his giving is a genuinely righteous
deed.[28]

The Promise of Reward
'They receive in full their reward [*misthon*]' (Matt. 6:2b),
concerning which the comments under A. will suffice. We
focus on 6:4b ('your Father...will reward [*apodōsei*] you),'
together with 6:1b ('reward [*misthon*] from your Father in
heaven'). Compared to the reality of the Father's approval,
together with the nature and extent of his rewards, the praise
won from a multitude of men is as nothing.[29]

1. Present rewards
The Father first repays secretive almsgivers in the very act
of their giving: 'It is more blessed [*makarion*] to give than to
receive,' says Jesus (Acts 20:35). Or, in the language of Matthew

---

to the receiver with the right hand alone, not offered with both hands in a
fashion designed to attract the attention of others nearby.'

[28]It has been said that there are two kinds of people: the proud who think
they are humble, and the humble who know they are proud. A person who
detects pride in his heart and deplores it is less endangered than a person
who mistakes his pride for humility. For giving as genuinely righteous, cf.
Psalm 112:9, ESV: 'He has distributed freely; he has given to the poor; his
righteousness [LXX *dikaiosynē*, as in Matthew 6:1] endures forever.' Being
merciful (5:7) is one way to pursue righteousness (5:6). On the importance of
the heart's motives in giving, see also 2 Corinthians 9:7. On God's response
to mixed motives, see below.

[29]Let disciples 'be content to have the approbation of God alone for
their actions' (Calvin, 1994: 201). The verb is *apodidōmi*, 'render, reward,

5:7, almsgivers begin to receive God's mercy (*eleēthēsontai*) and blessing (*makarioi*) at the very time they show mercy (*eleēmones*) to others. It was in (not just after) contributing generously to the material needs of fellow Christians, that the Macedonians experienced the divine grace (*charis*; 2 Cor. 8:1-2). What reflective Christian could fail to see that his highest motive for giving alms is thanksgiving to God for grace received? What Christian with any degree of self-awareness could fail to see that unselfish motives are usually if not always mixed with (or exceeded by) selfish ones in his almsgiving? This being the case, could anyone ever doubt his need to be 'rewarded' with God's mercy and grace? and given the nature of the reward, could anyone but the benevolent God be congratulated for it?[30]

Secondly, in accord with the rule that 'whatever one sows, he will also reap,' (Gal. 6:7), the Father rewards his children with gifts in kind. As they have shown their allegiance to him by supplying their neighbors' material needs, so he in turn supplies theirs (Matt. 6:33). Nor could their benevolence to others ever match his to them (7:11; Luke 6:38).

2. Future reward

The Father's present approval anticipates the words which the obedient disciple will hear at the end, when the totality of his work is taken into account: 'Well done, good and faithful servant' (25:21). By the same token, while the sowing of gifts reaps benefits in this life, these pale by comparison to the full harvest yet to come: 'Great will be your reward in heaven,' Jesus assures his followers (5:12; cf. Gal. 6:9). Just as one sows what he reaps, so what one reaps now he will reap hereafter, though to a far greater degree: that is, the blessings in store for God's people in the restored paradise are as fully material as those – and if anything, more real than those – experienced in the paradise that was lost. Moreover, God's reward for

---

recompense' (BAGD s.v., 3.). Yet, incredible as it seems, some value honor from men more than honor from God (John 12:43).

[30]Jeremias 1971: 216-17 says of Jesus' teaching on the subject: (i) disciples are to detach themselves 'from striving for a reward,' and 'to forget the good deeds they have done' (Matt. 6:3-4); (ii) their recompense is based not on 'human achievement' but on 'God's faithfulness' (Luke 17:7-10); and (iii)

present service is not inactivity (such boredom is reserved for hell) but opportunity for greater service – service from which all threats of weariness and tedium, of selfishness and pride, will have been removed.[31]

C. Prayer (6:5-15)

This passage is anticipated in 5:44, where Jesus tells disciples to pray for their enemies; the verb used there, *proseuchomai*, occurs six times here (vv. 5, 6, 7, 9). The length of this section compared to the other two reflects prayer's central importance in Christian piety. The only place in the gospels where disciples ask for instruction on a subject comes in Luke 11:1 – 'Lord, teach us to pray' – in response to which Jesus gives a version of the Lord's Prayer (11:2-4).[32] In both this context and that one, teaching about prayer is joined to deeds of mercy (Matt. 6:2-4; Luke 10:25-37) and to study of revealed truth (Matt. 5:17-48; Luke 10:38-42). As with almsgiving, the critical issue is not *whether* one prays, but *how*. Verse 1 remains in view; as suggested earlier, the *oun* ('therefore') found in 6:2a but absent from 6:5a, covers 6:5-15 as well as 6:2-4.

Disciples and Hypocrites (6:5-6)

Linguistically and structurally, these verses are very close to Matthew 6:2-4. The opening *Kai* ('And') of 5 links this paragraph to the preceding. Verse 5, like verse 2, begins with the practice ('when you pray,' *proseuchēsthe*, another present subjunctive); warns against behaving 'like the hypocrites'; locates their acts in synagogues and streets; reveals their desire for human acclaim; and recognizes their reception of reward.[33] Verse 6, like verses 3-4, begins with the emphatic singular pronoun

their singular motive for serving and giving to others is 'gratitude for God's grace' (Matt. 13:44). Cf. 1 Corinthians 4:6-7.

[31]See comments on Matthew 25:14-30; also Revelation 21-22, in relation to Genesis 1–2.

[32]Marshall 1978a: 456. 'Prayer is beyond any question the highest activity of the human soul' (Lloyd-Jones 1960: 45). Says Calvin 1960: 850, 851 (3.20.1,2): Prayer is 'the chief exercise of faith.... Words fail to express how necessary prayer is, and in how many ways the exercise of prayer is profitable.'

[33]Of the 31 Greek words in Matthew 6:2, 17 recur in the same form and position in verse 5. Both verses speak of streets: the *rhymē* (6:2) was

'you'; reiterates the practice ('when you pray'); speaks of a hidden act; and promises recompense from the Father who sees what is done in secret.[34]

1. Hypocrites at prayer

The hypocrites 'like to pray standing in the synagogues and on the street corners' (6:5a), the places of their almsgiving (6:2; cf. 23:5-6, where Jesus says the scribes and Pharisees 'like [*philousin*, as in 6:5]...the places of honor in the synagogues and the greetings in the marketplaces'; and Mark 12:40, where he speaks of scribes who 'for pretense make long prayers'; cf. Luke 18:11-13; in the Greek text the Pharisee's prayer has twenty-nine words, the publican's six). Prayers in a synagogue 'were led by a member who stood at the front; to be invited to do so was presumably a mark of distinction in the congregation.'[35] Joachim Jeremias has suggested that the setting for the prayers 'at the street corners' was the hour of the afternoon sacrifice: 3:00 p.m. As a congregation prayed in the temple, loud trumpets were sounded thenceforth to mark the hour of prayer for persons out in the city. The hypocrites 'arranged things so that they happened to be in the midst of the crowds – apparently quite by chance – at the moment when the trumpets blew, and were thus compelled to pray before all eyes.'[36] They need not 'blow their own trumpets': those from the temple suffice. But their actions are almost as ridiculous as those of verse 2.

Whether in the synagogue or in the streets or (as in Luke 18:9-14) in the temple itself, the proud person uses the public occasion to pray ostentatiously. As prayer is by nature a spiritual exercise with limitless scope for expressing one's

relatively narrow; the *plateia* (6:5), relatively wide (the terms occur together in Luke 14:21).

[34]The emphatic pronoun is genitive in 6:3 (*sou*), and nominative in 6:6 (*sy*). The closing fourteen words of verse 4 are identical to the closing fourteen of verse 6.

[35]France 1985: 132.

[36]Jeremias 1971: 187. In Jesus' time it was customary for a devout Jew to offer prayer at three set times during the day: at dawn (cf. Ps. 5:3); at 3:00 p.m. (cf. Acts 3:1); and after sundown (cf. Ps. 141:2). Some people were doubtless not free to leave their work at 3:00 p.m. (see Matthew 20:5) to join the crowd in the temple and had to pray on the job (cf. Keener 1999: 211).

piety, it offers more hope than does almsgiving for winning the coveted reward – fame as an exceptionally holy person.

2. The disciple at prayer

'But you [*sy*], when you pray [*proseuchē*], go into your room [*eiselthe eis to tameion sou*], shut your door and pray...' (Matt. 6:6a). Having addressed disciples generally (6:5a, with its plural verb *proseuchesthe*) about a company of hypocrites (6:5b), Jesus now focuses on the individual. Each is commanded to enter (the aorist imperative *eiselthe*) his *tameion* – a private room, one with a door, perhaps the only room in the house so equipped.[37] Solitude offers a negative antidote to pride; by praying alone, the individual avoids the gaze of other people. The prayer is now 'that which is done in secret,' (6:6b), in stark contrast to the public prayers of 6:5. While Jesus was never guilty of pride, it is noteworthy that he chose solitude for his longest times of prayer.[38]

'Pray [*proseuxai*] to your Father...' (6:6b). The first command (*eiselthe*) serves this one (*proseuxai*, another aorist imperative);[39] seeking privacy is a means to an end – that the individual may focus upon God without distraction. The words 'pray to the Father' have no counterpart in Matthew 6:5, which implies that the hypocrites' attention is limited to themselves and other people.[40] The close of 6:6 states (as had 6:4b) that the Father 'sees what is done in secret.' But now Jesus also says: 'pray to your Father [*tō patri sou*] *who is in* the secret place [*tō en tō kryptō*]' (6:6b; note the repeated definite article *tō*). The

---

[37]The *tameion* of Matthew 24:26 (the only other instance in Matthew) is an 'inner room' (BAGD s.v., 2.); that of Luke 12:24 is a 'storeroom' (s.v., 1.). Isaiah 26:20 commands God's people to enter their closets (LXX, *eiselthe eis ta tameia sou*) and shut the doors to escape his wrath. In 2 Kings 4:33, Elisha shuts the door to a room before praying and raising a dead boy to life.

[38]See Matthew 14:23; 26:36-46; Mark 1:35; 6:46; Luke 5:16; 6:12; 9:18; 11:1.

[39]The two imperatives and the participle *kleisas* ('having shut') are all constative aorists: the *fact* of the actions is in view, not their *duration* (e.g., the length of the prayer). Cf. *GGBB*, 557-58.

[40]Luke 18:11a possibly means that the Pharisee stood and prayed 'to himself' (NASB); more likely that he stood and prayed 'about himself' (NIV); most likely that he stood by himself and prayed (ESV), or simply that he stood to pray (REB). See the commentaries.

'Father in heaven' (6:1, 9) is present in that private room; he has drawn near for communion with his child. If privacy serves as a negative antidote to pride, the surest positive antidote is preoccupation with 'the Lord of heaven and earth' (11:25), an attitude fostered by the theocentric prayer of 6:9-13. How can a person aware of being in the presence of the holy God be in the least impressed with what he himself is doing? Could he conceivably try to impress God, in hope of receiving a yet greater reward? How could he want to hallow his own name rather than God's?

Yet entering a prayer closet makes us vulnerable to a special kind of pride: comparing ourselves favorably to the hypocrites who crave acclaim, and reckoning ourselves – by virtue of our chosen place of prayer and our humble attitude – to be their spiritual superiors.[41] Probably for most of us, the usual problem here, as with giving, is *double-mindedness*: *both* longing for unimpaired fellowship with God *and* wanting to impress others. Discovering mixed motives, we do not stop praying. Rather, we ask the Father to forgive us these very debts (Matt. 6:12). Grieving over our pride, we humble ourselves before him and ask him to purify our hearts (5:8; James 4:1-10).

Matthew 6:5 does not prohibit public prayer, as is clear from Jesus' own practice: he offers the prayer of 11:25-26, e.g., in the hearing of the crowd (6:7). A disciple whose attitude has been shaped by private prayer may be the more trusted to pray in public. Public prayer may itself be a means of confessing and combating sinful motives; and such prayer may be, in time, one of those 'good works' for glorifying the Father (5:16).[42] By the same token, 6:6 does not limit the places for private prayer. The inner chamber is introduced as the best place for molding attitudes, not as the only correct place for private

---

[41]Says Screwtape to Wormwood, 'Your patient has become humble; have you drawn his attention to the fact?' (Lewis 1953: 71). See the rest of this letter (no. 14).

[42]Praying in others' presence, let one think of himself 'as though shut off in an inside room' with 'God as one's witness' (Calvin 1994: 203). Learning to pray *to* God *for* a congregation, rather than *to* a congregation *for* one's own sake, may take years rather than weeks.

prayer. I may pray as I mow the lawn or drive to work, as I walk a busy street or sit in a crowd at a public arena.

'Your Father...will reward you,' says Jesus (6:6c). The disciple receives recompense in the very practice of prayer: what higher reward could there be than communion with the heavenly Father? The reward for seeking him is finding him (cf. Heb. 11:6). As the communion deepens, the reward increases, as does one's assurance that the promises of 7:7-11 are true. In heaven too, the reward will lie within the prayer, never beyond it: for the essence of heaven is unceasing fellowship between God and his covenant-people.[43]

Disciples and Pagans (6:7-8)

The first word of verse 7, *proseuchomenoi*, is an adverbial participle of time – 'when you pray' – to match the opening clauses of 6:5a and 6a. It is also plural, like the *proseuchēsthe* of 6:5a (contrast the singular verb of 6:6a). For the remainder of his teaching on prayer (6:7-15), Jesus addresses the whole company of disciples. In 6:5-6, the practice of certain Jews was in view; here it is that of the Gentiles (*hoi ethnikoi*). Why does Jesus tell the disciples not to be like them (6:7a, 8a), and how does he tell them to pray instead?

1. Pagans at prayer

By all indications, these Gentiles are seriously and sincerely addressing the gods, or a god. Given the prominence of 'hypocrites' in the surrounding verses, its absence from Matthew 6:7-8 is notable. These people also expect the god or gods to give them a hearing (6:7b).[44]

---

[43]See Matthew 5:12; 6:19-21; Revelation 21:1-4; 22:3-5. The inner connection between the disciple's obedience (in this case, his praying) and the Father's reward, is again illustrated by the sowing of seed and the harvesting of a crop (Gal. 6:7-9). See further Chamblin 1993: 249.

[44]The verb *eisakousthēsontai*, 'they shall be heard,' is an instance of the 'divine passive.' C. S. Lewis observes that today's Christian is not so distant from those ancient Gentiles as from some of his contemporaries: 'Christians and Pagans had much more in common with each other than either has with a post-Christian. The gap between those who worship different gods is not so wide as that between those who worship and those who do not': from '*De Descriptione Temporum*,' in *They Asked for a Paper* (London: Bles, 1962), 14.

Exhorting disciples not to pray like Gentiles, Jesus says: *mē battalogēsēte* (6:7a, another subjunctive of prohibition). This is the sole instance of the verb *battalogeō* in the NT; its rarity makes its meaning harder to determine. Verse 7b, linked as it is to 7a, provides our best clue: 'for [*gar*] they think they will be heard because of their many words [*en tē polylogia autōn*].'[45] It is also likely that the Aramaic verb *bātēl*, 'speak idly,' contributes to the spelling of *battalogeō*.[46] Thus Jesus' command may be rendered, 'Do not heap up words in vain.' The point is not that Gentiles' prayers consist of unintelligible sounds, but that they are uselessly prolonged and perhaps also mindlessly repeated.

As 6:7b indicates, the pagans themselves believe their prayers to be eminently useful. A theological rationale underlies their practice, even if in some cases the prayers have degenerated into thoughtless repetitions. One reason, apparently, for the pagans' 'many words' is that they are bewildered polytheists searching for the right listener, or for the effectual name of the right listener.[47] Related to this is the worshiper's expectation that – once he has a hearing – he can wear down the resistance of the god or goddess by endlessly repeating his request.[48]

---

[45]Thus BAGD, s.v. *en*, III. 3. Note the kinship between the noun *polylogia* and the verb *battalogeō*, whose nominal counterpart would be *battalogia*.

[46]Cf. Ecclesiastes 12:3 (Hebrew *bātal*); BAGD s.v. *battalogeō*; Gundry 1994: 104. The verb *ballologeō* ('babble, use vain repetitions': LSJ s.v.) occurs in classical Greek but not in the NT.

[47]'The non-Christian, and non-Jew, thinks that by heaping up the names of God, of which he does not know the true and relevant one, he can include the deity which will grant his request....' (G. Delling, *TDNT* 1: 597). As a manipulative device, pagans might use as many names as possible for the deity being addressed, 'hoping at least one would be effective' (Keener 1999: 212-13). 'It was thought that knowing the name of a god and pronouncing it correctly gave a certain power to manipulate the god' (Gundry 1994: 104). Davis 1999: 218-19 contrasts the merciful clarity of Yahweh's response to David (2 Sam. 21:1-2) with the Babylonians' pathetic 'prayer to every god.'

[48]Delling, ibid. The idea is *fatigare deos*, 'to weary the god.' This may be one reason for the prolonged rantings of the prophets of Baal in 1 Kings 18:26-29. Such is often the motivation behind repeated appeals, e.g., to a parent, or to a church's General Assembly.

2. Disciples at prayer

Jesus condemns neither lengthy prayers as such (he himself prayed through a whole night [Luke 6:12]), nor repeated petitions (he himself prayed this way [Matt. 26:39-44]). Rather, he repudiates long or repetitious prayers based on false beliefs. Jesus uses pagans as his examples, but it is not pagans whom he addresses: he teaches Jews – and Christians – that prayer must be founded on truth and offered in faith.

Theology. 'Therefore [*oun*] do not be like [*mē...homoiēthēte*] them, for [*gar*] your Father knows what you need before you ask him' (6:8). As the language of 6:7a is elucidated by 7b (with its *gar*), so the command of 6:8a (another aorist subjunctive of prohibition) rests on the fact of 8b (*gar* again): 'Your Father' is the *one and only* God, 'the Lord of heaven and earth' (11:25); so there is no need to search for the right listener or for just the right name. He, the *omniscient* God, knows our needs and therefore needs no instructions about them (cf. 6:32). Because he is the *mighty God,* he *cannot* be manipulated: he gives by his own free choice, and he will not be coerced into answering prayers against his will (cf. 6:10b). Because he is the *loving Father,* he *need not* be manipulated: he knows his children's needs far better than they; and he is far more eager than they, to see those needs supplied (7:7-11; Ps. 103:13).

Trust. Whether disciples pray in faith (Matt. 21:22) will reveal how well they have grasped that theology. Endlessly repeating the same request may reflect lack of trust in the Father (cf. 6:7b); judging from Jesus' prayers in Gethsemane, a thrice-repeated petition on a given occasion is sufficient, given God's trustworthiness.[49] On the other hand, refraining from requests because of the Father's knowledge is misguided trust. The Father knows those needs 'before you ask him,' says 6:8b, not 'so do not ask him.' 'Therefore [*oun*] you [*hymeis*] pray [*proseuchesthe*] this way,' Jesus continues in 6:9a: the 'you' is emphatic; the verb is in the imperative mood; the command is based on the declaration of 6:8b (note the *oun*); and the prayer of 6:9b-13 is filled with requests. The

---

[49]Significantly, the Father responds to his Son's threefold petition (Heb. 5:7), as does Jesus to Paul's three prayers (2 Cor. 12:7-9).

children must voice to the Father needs of which he is already
aware, because such prayers are *good for them*. They are thus
reminded of their *dependence* on God, that they may 'become
accustomed in every need to flee to him as to a sacred anchor.'
And the Father's gracious answers to their requests evoke
their *gratitude and thanksgiving*.[50]

Thought. We may disregard the words of the Lord's Prayer
even while uttering them, so familiar have they become; and
we may forget that Jesus provides them as a guide for all our
praying. In contrast to the pagans' 'many words,' this prayer
is a model of brevity. Matthew's version contains fifty-seven
words in the Greek text, fifty-two in the translation of the ESV.
Luke's version is yet shorter: Thirty-eight words in the Greek,
thirty-six in the ESV.[51] Following this pattern calls for thoughtful
and disciplined language. A name for God – in this case, 'our
Father in heaven' – appears only in the address: is it not 'vainly
repeating' a divine name ('Father' or 'God' or 'Lord') to use it
in a prayer's every petition or every sentence?[52] This text also
encourages pointed and concise prayer: when devoting an
hour, for example, to interceding about others' material needs
(Matt. 6:11) and spiritual struggles (6:13), we can by praying

---

[50]Calvin 1960: 851-53 (3.20.3); which see for further answers to the
question, 'Is prayer not superfluous?' An earthly father too (cf. 7:9-11), while
he knows his children's needs better than they, and can usually provide
them without their asking, is pleased when they depend on him (instead of
vaunting their self-sufficiency), and appreciate his gifts (instead of taking
them for granted, or viewing them as rights). Davis (2002: 240), commenting
on 1 Kings 18, warns against 'Christian busyness' that emulates the prophets
of Baal (who sought by their frantic actions to impel their god to action, vv.
25-29) rather than Elijah (whose trust in Yahweh, the true and living God,
explains the simplicity of his prayer, vv. 36-37).

[51]These figures do not include (i) the closing ascription found in some
MSS. of Matthew, words later composed to adapt the prayer for liturgical
use in the church, or (ii) words added to the prayer of Luke 11:2-4 to
conform it to Matthew 6. (See comments in *TC*, 13-14, 131-32.) In the NKJV,
which contains these additions, the Matthean prayer still has only sixty-six
words, the Lukan version fifty-nine. Betz 1995: 375 calls the Lord's Prayer
'intentionally concise in the extreme.'

[52]Who speaks thus to an earthly friend? Such repetitions might indicate
misplaced trust (as though ten instances of God's names show more faith
than five), or misguided hope (as though the Father, hearing a host of his
names, will more likely grant our requests).

succinctly include a larger number of individuals.[53] We may also discover that praying aloud (whether alone or with someone else) and writing some of our prayers (since 'writing makes an exact man') helps to clarify and to articulate our thought.

The Lord's Prayer (6:9-13)

We have already begun to consider the prayer, given its connection with Matthew 6:7-8. What follows builds on the above comments.

1. Structure and language

The 'Lord's Prayer in Greek is a literary masterpiece.'[54] It manifests a sevenfold structure: an address followed by two sets of three petitions each. The second set rests on the first, and both are theocentric: the holy, sovereign God (Matt. 6:9b-10) may be trusted to meet his people's needs (6:11-13). The conjunction 'and' (*kai*) at the opening of verses 12 and 13 join together petitions four through six.[55] The first three are not so joined, and may be considered one threefold petition. The three parts of this opening petition are structurally parallel, as is especially clear in the Greek:

hagiasthētō to onoma sou ('let your name be hallowed'; 6:9b)
elthetō hē basileia sou ('let your kingdom come'; 6:10a)
genēthētō to thelēma sou ('let your will be done'; 6:10b)

In each line an opening aorist imperative in the third person singular is followed by a singular noun in the nominative case, joined to the definite article and followed by a singular pronoun in the second person and the genitive case. So carefully balanced are these three clauses, that 6:10c ('on earth as it is in heaven') is probably to be joined to all three, not just to the third.[56] The lines are conceptually connected in the

---

[53]Paul appears to have prayed intelligently for hundreds of people (Chamblin 1993: 232-37). Prayers 'ought to be brief, frequent, and intense' (Martin Luther, in Bruner 2004a: 291).

[54]Betz 1995: 375.

[55]See, e.g., esv and nasb. Unfortunately, niv leaves the *kai* of Matthew 6:12a untranslated.

[56]France 1985: 135.

closest way: when God's will is done on earth as in heaven, his kingdom will have fully come; and when that happens, his name will be universally hallowed.[57]

While the petitions of 6:11-13 do not exhibit structural parallels comparable to those of 6:9b-10, there are several matters of note: (i) The Greek text of verses 11-13 contains thirty-three words, compared to eighteen in verses 9b-10, itself indication that making specific requests of the Father (6:8b) is to be a cardinal feature of disciples' prayers. (ii) Whereas each part of verses 9b-10 uses an aorist imperative in the third person singular, each of these petitions contains an aorist imperative in the second person singular: *dos* ('give,' 6:11), *aphes* ('forgive,' 6:12) and *rhysai* ('deliver,' 6:13b). The *mē eisenegkēs* of 6:13a, an aorist subjunctive of prohibition, second person singular ('do not lead us'), serves the same purpose. All these imperatives express dependence on God, and make entreaty of him. At the same time, each one implies or presupposes that God mobilizes his people's wills when answering their prayers.[58] (iii) In contrast to the singular pronouns of Matthew 6:9b-10, and in keeping with the address, '*our* Father,' all eight pronouns in verses 11-13 are plural.

The prayer of Luke 11:2-4 is much shorter (as noted above), but its structure is the same. All nine words of 11:2b appear in Matthew 6:9b-10a, and in the same order. Luke 11:3-4 and Matthew 6:11-13 address the same needs in the same order; the

---

[57]Cf. Keener 1999: 220. The content of 6:9b-10 is akin to the *Qaddish* (from *qdš*, 'holy'), an ancient Aramaic prayer to conclude the synagogue service: 'Exalted and hallowed be his great name in the world which he created according to his will. May he let his kingdom rule in your lifetime and in your days and in the lifetime of the whole house of Israel, speedily and soon. Praised be his great name from eternity to eternity. And to this, say: Amen' (quoted by Jeremias 1971: 198, who states that this prayer would have been familiar to Jesus from childhood).

[58]Every imperative in the prayer voices entreaty or request (*GGBB*, 487-8). Gerhardsson 1984: 213 says of Matthew 6:9b-10: 'With the circumlocutory third person imperatives it is easier to combine the fact that God's mighty works...demand a suitable human response.' Perhaps so: but as we shall see, neither the requests of 6:9b-10 nor those of verses 11-13 can be offered with integrity apart from a resolve to live responsibly and obediently in the world.

opening words of the matching petitions are identical.[59] Rather than inquiring which version is 'the original' with respect to length or wording, we can say that Jesus is responsible for both forms; that on various occasions he presented the prayer in varied forms to underscore and amplify its lessons; and that the variety in wording discouraged a magical use of the prayer (which might more easily develop if there were only one authorized set of words).[60]

The prayer of Matthew is prefaced by the words 'pray this way [houtōs]' (6:9a); that of Luke by 'when [hotan] you pray, say' (11:2a). Jesus obviously does not mean that prayer must be confined to these words (cf. e.g., the prayers in Paul's letters). Nor does he require that one invariably use the same precise prayer (as noted, Luke's wording differs from that of Matthew; and after a time relatively few would know Aramaic or Greek). But these introductory words, taken together, teach us that one or both versions of the Lord's Prayer should be offered frequently; that this prayer should be kept in view whenever we pray;[61] and that all of its components must be taken seriously for prayer to be sufficiently comprehensive. The prayer itself indicates not just frequent but daily use: 'give us today' (Matt. 6:11); 'give us each day' (Luke 11:3).

2. 'Our Father in heaven' (6:9b)
Behind 'Father' is *pater*, the vocative singular of *patēr*. In Mark 14:36, Jesus addresses God as *Abba ho patēr*. In Galatians 4:6, the Spirit of God's Son cries *Abba ho patēr*. And in Romans 8:15 believers themselves, by the Spirit's agency, cry *Abba ho patēr*. We may therefore conclude that *abba* underlies the *pater* of Matthew 6:9 and Luke 11:2; that Jesus thus draws his disciples

---

[59]See the first five Greek words of Matthew 6:11 (= Luke 11:3a); the first three of 6:12 (= 11:4a); and the first six of 6:13 (= 11:4c). On varieties of wording in these petitions, see below.

[60]For support, see Morris 1992: 143; France 1985: 133; Tasker 1961: 72. For various scholarly views, see Jeremias 1971: 193-96; Betz 1995: 370-73. The Lord's Prayer as quoted in *Didache* 8:2 (a Christian manual from the first or second century) is virtually identical to Matthew 6:9b-13.

[61]The conjunction *hotan* (applied to praying in Luke 11:2; Matthew 6:5, 6) can mean *whenever* as well as *when* (BAGD s.v.). As Stott says (1978: 145),

into an intimacy with God akin to his own; and that the rest of the prayer presupposes this deeply personal bond between the Father and his children.[62] Yet, that relationship, while real and permanent, is only akin, not identical, to the union between the Father and the divine Son (cf. 11:25-27). Jesus says in 6:9a, 'Therefore you [*hymeis*] pray this way.' Never does he join with the disciples in addressing God as 'our Father.' Significantly, he says to Mary: 'I am ascending to my Father and your Father, to my God and your God' (John 20:17; cf. comments on p. 140).

God is 'our [*hēmōn*] Father.' This plural pronoun, anticipating those of Matthew 6:11-13, reminds disciples that they pray – even when in solitude (6:6) – as members of a *community*. The prayer's address calls us away from self-absorption (wherein all the plural pronouns are changed to singulars) and invites us to use each line of this prayer, as well as those based upon it, as an occasion for intercession. There is no room for individualism or isolationism in the church of Christ the King.

God is 'our Father in heaven [*en tois ouranois*].' Not only does this phrase distinguish the heavenly Father from earthly ones (as in 7:11). It 'points to divine majesty as a complement to divine fatherhood.'[63] Given the intimacy reflected in their utterance of *Abba*, let disciples remember that they are also addressing the Lord of heaven and earth (11:25). They may well be securely at home in his presence, and able freely to

---

'we can both use the prayer as it stands and also model our own praying upon it.' For examples of the latter, see Matthew Henry, *A Method for Prayer* (Ross-shire: Christian Focus, 1994), chapter 8.

[62]See Jeremias 1971: 197. As Hendriksen says (1973: 326), 'this model prayer is for believers in the Lord Jesus Christ, for them alone.' 'This is a relationship that denotes both respectful dependence and affectionate intimacy as well as obedience.... In first-century Jewish Palestine children were powerless social dependents and fathers were viewed as strong providers and examples on whom their children could depend' (Keener 1999: 216). Yet adult Jews continued to use *abba* in addressing their fathers (Gundry 1994: 105). Correspondingly, Jesus' adult disciples remain children of the heavenly Father who are expected to behave accordingly (Matt. 11:25; 18:2-4).

[63]Gundry 1994: 106; cf. Psalm 8:1, 9. The address reminds us that God is 'exalted beyond the entire universe' (Calvin 1994: 206); cf. 11:25; Psalm 113:4-6.

speak from their hearts' depths; but they cannot be chatty and frivolous as they might choose to be in the company of an earthly father. 'For nothing is more contrary to reverence for God than the levity that marks an excess of frivolity utterly devoid of awe.'[64] Perhaps one reason for the brevity of this prayer is suggested in Ecclesiastes 5:2, 'Be not rash with your mouth, nor let your heart be hasty to utter a word before God, for God is in heaven and you are on earth. Therefore let your words be few' (ESV).

3. 'Let your name be hallowed' (6:9c)

The name (*onoma*) of God signals his 'invocable presence' and his 'accessible power.'[65] The whole prayer calls upon the 'Father in heaven' to disclose his presence and to display his power, on earth as in heaven. As an inevitable consequence of his doing so, his name shall be hallowed, and the Father in heaven revered as the only true and living God. Cf. Yahweh's earlier question to Israel: 'If then I am a father, where is my honor [*kābôd*]?' (Mal. 1:6a, ESV; in 1:6b the priests are charged with showing contempt for Yahweh's name, *šēm*).

The ultimate hallowing of the divine name awaits the kingdom's consummation, 10a, when all three members of the Godhead (see *onoma* in Matt. 28:19) will receive universal acclaim. Disciples' sadness and madness over the widespread, perennial and flagrant defilements of God's holy name causes them to pray the more fervently for the imminent arrival of that day.[66] By uttering these words disciples also ask the Father to empower them for present obedience, that their words and deeds will so honor his name that non-believers, including

---

[64]Calvin 1960: 854 (3.20.5). We recall how disclosures of God affected Moses (Exod. 3:6), Job (Job 42:1-6), Isaiah (Isa. 6:5) and the twenty-four elders (Rev. 4:10-11). Davis 2002: 86-87 notes how Solomon's prayer in 1 Kings 8:27-30 joins 'immensity and intimacy.' In C. S. Lewis' *Chronicles of Narnia*, children bury their heads in Aslan's mane, but also tremble before his roar.

[65]See page 208 above, including n. 35.

[66]See Exodus 20:7; Leviticus 24:16; Psalms 74:10, 18; 79:6; 102:15; 113:2-3; Daniel 2:20; Malachi 1:6, 11; Romans 2:24; 1 Timothy 6:1; James 2:7; Revelation 13:6; 16:9.

those who formerly reviled him, will learn to revere his name and to invoke him as their own 'Father in heaven.'[67]

4. 'Let your kingdom come' (6:10a)

In 2 Samuel 7:12-16, Yahweh pledges to establish David's kingship forever. David's answering prayer (7:25-29) pleads those very promises. The prayer of Matthew 6:10 is likewise offered in the confidence that God's eschatological rule (*basileia*) will one day be consummated (Matt. 24:14). But this prayer also rests upon the incontrovertible fact that this rule was inaugurated with the coming of Messiah, the one destined to reign from David's throne forever.[68] Since the promises of 2 Samuel 7:12-16 have already found a mighty 'Yes' in Jesus, Christians can pray 'let your kingdom come' with greater assurance and expectation than could David.[69]

At the consummation, as at the inaugural, God will indeed let his kingdom *come* (*elthetō*): his rule will be fully and finally established 'on earth as in heaven' (Matt. 6:10c). The Father will 'bring all things together in [Christ], things in heaven and things on earth' (Eph. 1:10); at the end Christ will restore harmony to a fragmented cosmos, and bring heaven's glory to earth.[70] The paradise in store for his people will be just as earthy as the first one; and its material blessings will far exceed those they now receive (Matt. 6:25-34).[71]

God's rule is already being established on earth. Disciples who rightly offer this prayer will seek to advance God's rule in the various sectors of their society, and will personally submit to his authority in their places of responsibility *today* (6:33-34). This entails fidelity to the way of life Jesus describes

---

[67]See Matthew 5:16; 1 Corinthians 10:31-33. The name 'Father,' signaling disciples' relation to God through Messiah, is the one especially (though not exclusively) to be hallowed. Cf. Gundry 1994: 106.

[68]See Matthew 4:17, 23; 12:28, as well as comments on Matthew 1–2.

[69]See 2 Corinthians 1:20; Hebrews 11:39-12:2; and Davis 1999: 88-89, on the links between 2 Samuel 7:25-29 and Matthew 6:9-10.

[70]Lincoln 1990: 32-35 (on Eph. 1:10); Revelation 21:1 ('a new heaven and a new earth') *et seq.*

[71]See the statement about future reward on pages 395-96, in connection with Matthew 6:4b.

and prescribes elsewhere in the Sermon, beginning with the Beatitudes.[72]

5. 'Let your will be done, on earth as it is in heaven' (6:10b)

All six instances of the noun *thelēma* ('will') in Matthew, starting with this one, refer to God's will.[73] The subject here is not his *secret* (or decretive) will, by which all things are determined and governed; but his will as *revealed* in Holy Scripture, to which his human creatures and his redeemed people are obediently to submit, but against which they repeatedly and willfully rebel.[74] As observed earlier, this line is closely joined to the preceding two. It also prepares for the petitions of Matthew 6:11-13, each of which is to be offered in awareness of, and in submission to, the Father's will (cf. James 4:15).

As this prayer recognizes, God's will is already done in heaven: the angels' singular and perpetual task is to praise and serve him (Ps. 103:19-20; Isa. 6:2-3). By culminating his rule, God will cause the same to be done on earth. Conversely, when God's will is done on earth as in heaven, then and there his rule is complete and his kingdom established.[75]

This line, like the preceding two, summons me to active obedience in a fallen world. As Jesus was utterly committed to doing his Father's will on earth, so are his disciples to be. 'The petition, then, is not merely that I may patiently suffer God's will but also that I may vigorously do it. I must be an agent as well as a patient. I am asking that I may be enabled to do it [cf. Phil. 2:13].... For there isn't always...some great affliction looming in the near future, but there are always duties to be done; usually,

---

[72]*Basileia* occurs five times in the sermon before 6:10, all in the phrase 'the kingdom of heaven,' and all at critical junctures: 5:3, 10 (beatitudes 1 and 8); and 5:19, 20 (verses prefacing the exposition of law in 5:21-48). On the kingdom in Matthew, see pages 141-45, 287-92.

[73]His will is directly in view in 6:10; 7:21; 12:50; 18:14; 26:42; indirectly in 21:31.

[74]See Deuteronomy 29:29. Calvin 1960: 906 (3.20.43) notes this distinction when discussing Matthew 6:10. See also *WSC*, nos. 7, 39.

[75]As Augustine recognized, all three – the hallowing of God's name, his sovereign rule, and the doing of his will on earth as in heaven – 'will continue for all eternity' (in *ACC* 1a: 138).

for me, neglected duties to be caught up with. "Thy will be *done* – by me – now" brings one back to brass tacks.'[76]

6. 'Our bread for the coming day, give us today' (6:11)
This translation follows the Greek word order. The first words, *ton arton hēmōn ton epiousion* ('our bread for the coming day'), are the accusative direct object of the aorist imperative *dos* ('give'), which is followed by the dative indirect object *hēmin* ('us') and the adverb of time *sēmeron* ('today'). The opening construction stresses both the noun *arton* and the adjective *epiousion*.[77] As the closing word of the sentence, *sēmeron* is also emphasized.

Scholars have long debated *epiousios*. The term is very rare – in the NT it occurs only here and in the parallel text of Luke 11:3 – which makes its meaning harder to decide.[78] Three views have merit: (i) *epiousios* is from *epi tēn ousian* and means *necessary for existence*. (ii) *ep.* is from *epi tēn ousan* (*hēmeran* understood) and means *for the current (day)*. (iii) *ep.* is from *hē epiousa* (*hēmera* understood) and means *for the following (day)*.[79] We shall take account of all three.

---

[76]Lewis 1964: 40. 'God's will is done where men carry it out' (Schweizer 1975: 152); cf. 7:21; 12:50. Watson 1993: 151 says that we thus pray both for *active* obedience ('that we may do God's will actively in what he commands') and for *passive* obedience ('that we may submit to God's will patiently in what he inflicts'); see his discussion on 251-93. Jesus obeys the Father in both ways: see e.g. 26:39-42; John 4:34; 5:30; 6:38; Philippians 2:6-8; Hebrews 10:7.

[77]In this order – article (*ton*), noun (*arton*), article (*ton*), adjective (*ep.*) – 'both substantive and adjective receive emphasis and the adjective is added as a sort of climax in apposition with a separate article' (*GGNT*, 776). Were the prayer using the more common order – article, adjective, noun (*ton epiousion arton*) – the adjective would be stressed more than the noun (ibid.).

[78]The Lord's Prayer, as quoted in *Didache* 8:2, also contains *epiousios*. The term 'occurs nowhere else except perhaps in a fragment of an Egyptian account book, published in the last century but since lost!' (France 1985: 135).

[79]As stated in BAGD s.v. *epiousios*, 1.-3. For these and other views, see W. Foerster, *TDNT* 2: 590-99; Davies and Allison 1988: 607-9. In (i) the substantive *ousia* (from *eimi*) means 'what one has' (i.e., 'property, possessions, estate'; GT s.v.). In (ii) the participle *ousan* (from *eimi*) means 'the one that is.' In (iii) the participle *epiousa* (from *epeimi*) means 'the next one.'

Some early writers, thinking that Matthew 6:11 must match 6:9b-10 in grandeur and gravity, understood 'bread' (*artos*) to be spiritual in character – the word of God or the bread of the Lord's Supper. On the contrary, the bread is literal and material, like the manna of Exodus 16 (termed *lechem*, 'bread,' in 16:4, etc.), and like the bread from which Jesus distinguished the word of God (Matt. 4:4). The 'high and lofty One' is not aloof from his lowly people (Isa. 57:15); providing food for them is a sign of his covenant-keeping fidelity (Ps. 111:5). It is clear from Matthew 6:19-34 that disciples' most commonplace needs are the heavenly Father's concern, and that the 'bread' of verse 11 represents not only food in general (as does *lechem* in, e.g., Judg. 13:16; 1 Sam. 14:24; and Ps. 136:25), but everything needed for maintaining life in the physical realm.[80]

Whatever the meaning of *epiousios*, the petition focuses on present and immediate needs, both ours and others': 'give us today [*dos hēmin sēmeron*].' Luke 11:3 ('give us each day [*didou hēmin to kath' hēmeran*])' likewise speaks of daily provision.[81] Thus was manna given in the wilderness. Moreover, in keeping with Yahweh's instructions at that time, this prayer discourages avarice.[82] It also reflects the condition of many disciples past and present who, utterly devoid of economic security, must daily depend on God to meet their physical

---

[80]Stott 1978: 148-49. Augustine joins the literal to the spiritual, but favors the latter: 'We are to ask for all at once as daily bread, both the bread necessary for the body, and the visible hallowed bread (*sc.* Holy Communion) and the invisible bread of the word of God' (in ibid., 148). The rendering of *epiousios* in the Vulgate – *superstantialem* ('supersubstantial,' i.e., beyond what is needed to support life) – Calvin calls 'quite absurd' (1994: 209). For Martin Luther, 'bread' stands for 'everything necessary for the preservation of this life, like food, a healthy body, good weather, house, home, wife, children, good government and peace' (in Stott 1978: 149). Watson 1993: 203 calls 'bread' in Matthew 6:11 'a synecdoche...for all temporal blessings of this life.'

[81]Matthew uses the aorist imperative *dos*; the form in Luke 11:3 – *didou*, a present iterative (or distributive) imperative – accords better with 'each day.' Cf. 1 Kings 8:59; 17:15-16; Davis 2002: 93, 'Yahweh is Lord of the last day [Matt. 6:10] but also of every day [6:11].'

[82]See Exodus 16:4 ('gather a day's portion every day'), 16-20; Matthew 6:19-24.

and material needs.[83] The prayer 'give *us* today' encourages affluent Christians to serve the economically disadvantaged.[84] As a service to the poor and an antidote to greed, almsgiving (Matt. 6:2-4) well attends this prayer. So does personal industry: depending on God for bread does not exempt one from laboring six days a week or from attending to his and his family's material needs; now, as in Eden, God governs and provides for his creatures by employing their skills and energies.[85]

The heading of this section shows my preference for the third reading of *epiousios*. The other two are also conceptually compatible with the verse's accent on 'today.' Disciples are asking God to supply what is 'necessary for [today's] existence' (i). 'Our bread for the current day, give us today' (ii) seems redundant; yet it sharpens the focus on present needs, and voices impoverished disciples' pleas more urgently. Still, 'our bread for the coming day' (iii) is preferable on linguistic grounds.[86] Offered in the early morning, the prayer for 'the coming day' is for 'the current day' and expresses the same urgency. Used in the evening, the prayer asks God to provide *tomorrow's* food *today* as a safeguard against anxiety (Matt. 6:34).[87]

Viewing this petition for 'the coming day' in light of the rest of the prayer, and of Jesus' ministry as a whole, Joachim Jeremias argues that in God's kingdom (6:10) all earthly things, including bread, are hallowed; that 'earthly bread,' such as Jesus blessed at his table fellowship and at the Last Supper, is 'at the same time the bread of life'; that every meal, not just the Last Supper, anticipates the feasting at the kingdom's

---

[83]Contrast the workers of Matthew 20:1-16 with the rich man of Luke 12:15-21. See also Carson 1984: 171; Keener 1999: 221-22. Agur asks God to give him *neither* poverty *nor* riches, but instead 'the food that is needful' for him (Prov. 30:8-9).

[84]See Sider 1997 *passim*; and the comments on Matthew 25:31-46; 26:6-13.

[85]Gen. 1:26-30; 2:15; Exodus 20:9; 1 Corinthians 3:5-9; Ephesians 4:28; 2 Thessalonians 3:10; 1 Timothy 5:3-8.

[86]This appears to be the dominant view among scholars. For linguistic evidence, see Black 1967: 203-4; Jeremias 1971: 199-200; Colin Hemer, 'Epiousios,' *JSNT* 22 (1984): 81-94; Davies and Allison 1988: 608-9.

[87]The prohibition against anxiety in Matthew 6:34 (as in vv. 25 and 31) presupposes 6:11. Cf. Philippians 4:6 (which uses the same verb, *merimnaō*, 'be anxious about'); Psalm 4:5-8.

consummation; and that, accordingly, this petition implores God to grant tomorrow's bread – the bread of life, the life of the kingdom – already today, 'in the midst of our sorry existence.'[88] A fourfold response may be offered: (i) Ordinary bread can be a metaphor for the bread of life, but is never equated with it. Moreover, in John 6 the bread of life is not an abstract entity but Jesus himself. (ii) Food for common meals is indeed to be received with thanksgiving as God's gift, and to be consecrated by his word and by prayer (1 Tim. 4:4-5, including the verb *hagiazō*); but by virtue of Jesus' words at the Last Supper, the bread of the Eucharist is uniquely hallowed, or set apart. But even this bread does not become the bread of life. Instead, as one receives the earthly bread, one also by faith feeds upon Jesus the Bread of Life (see comments on Matt. 26:26). (iii) The Last Supper, as a Passover meal, was *distinguishable* from, but also *inseparable* from, Jesus' regular table fellowship. Likewise, the celebration of the Lord's Supper in Corinth was joined to, but distinguished from, an ordinary meal.[89] The Lord's Supper anticipates the kingdom's consummation as ordinary meals do not (cf. 26:29; 1 Cor. 11:26); yet the latter, joined as they are to the former, are fitting occasions to express longings for fullness of fellowship with Jesus, and to remember that God's provisions at the end will be fully as material as those he gives us now (cf. Luke 14:15). (iv) Longing for the coming of God's rule (both now and hereafter) is indeed expressed in the Lord's Prayer – but *alongside* verse Matthew 6:11 (especially in vv. 10 and 13), not *within* verse 11.

7. *'And forgive us our debts, as we also have forgiven our debtors'* (6:12)
This petition, unlike the preceding, consists of two clauses. The word order of Matthew 6:12a differs from that of 6:11. Here the aorist imperative *aphes* ('forgive') comes first (after the *kai* linking this petition to the preceding), then the indirect object *hēmin* ('us') and the direct object *ta opheilēmata hēmōn* ('our debtors'). Verse 12b, whose language and structure are

---

[88]Jeremias 1971: 199-201. Cf. Davies and Allison 1988: 609-10.

[89]Fee 1987: 541 judges that 'the Lord's Supper is eaten in conjunction with a communal meal.' See the comments on Matthew 26:26-30.

very similar to 12a, is the only clause in the prayer which lacks an imperative, and which refers directly to human activity: the conjunctions *hōs* and *kai* ['as also'] are followed by the personal pronoun *hēmeis* and the aorist indicative *aphēkamen* ['we have forgiven'], and they by the indirect object *tois opheiletais hēmōn* ['our debtors'].[90] The right to offer this petition, together with the rest of the prayer, is reserved for Jesus' followers.[91] But what is their true condition? Are they genuinely Jesus' disciples, or just apparently so? And if the former, how do matters stand between them and the Father in heaven? between them and other disciples? These are questions we are bound to ask in light of verses 14-15. As Jesus there resumes the present subject, further comments on this petition are reserved for then.

8. 'And lead us not into temptation, but rescue us from the evil one' (6:13)
Having asked God to forgive their past sins (6:12), disciples now ask his protection from future sins. This petition, like that one, consists of two clauses. Here the linguistic parallels are weaker, but the structural parallels stronger, than there. Verse 13, like 12, opens with the conjunction *kai*; 13b begins with the strong adversative conjunction *alla* ('but'). Next come the aorist subjunctive of prohibition *mē eisenegkēs* ('lead... not') and the accusative object *hēmas* ('us'; 6:13a); and the matching aorist imperative *rhysai* ('rescue') and the *hēmas* of 6:13b. Concluding each line is a prepositional phrase: *eis peirasmon* ('into temptation'; 6:13a); and *apo tou ponērou* ('from the evil one'; Matthew 6:13b). Translating this phrase this way (so, e.g., NIV), rather than 'from evil' (so, e.g., ESV) makes it a reference to the devil. This rendering is preferable for several reasons: (i) this phrase contains the definite article, whereas the matching phrase of 6:13a lacks it; (ii) some of the other instances of *ho ponēros* in Matthew denote the devil; the rest denote personal beings as opposed to abstract evil; (iii) in the

---

[90]The implied direct object would be *ta opheilēmata autōn* ('their debts'). Matthew 6:9a (the address) and 6:10c ('as in heaven also on earth') lack verbs and so do not qualify as clauses. The structure of the two clauses in Luke 11:4 is very similar.

[91]See the comments on the prayer's address, pages 406-08.

wilderness, Jesus was delivered not just 'from evil' but 'from the evil one'; and (iv) the OT uses the terms 'good' and 'evil' to distinguish Yahweh from false gods.[92]

Jesus speaks here, as earlier in the sermon (starting with Matthew 5:3-12), of trials and evils besetting his people both now and as the end approaches. Believers living in every generation between the advents of Jesus require this prayer. All must 'watch and pray,' lest they 'enter into temptation [*peirasmos*]' (26:41). All will assuredly be confronted by subtle appeals and fierce assaults from the evil one. Present trials anticipate the 'great tribulation' at the end; present 'evil days' foreshadow the intensified evil preceding and precipitating Christ's victorious return.[93]

Some take this petition to mean: 'Do not bring us into a test or a trial; but if you choose to do so, then – weak and vulnerable creatures that we are – let us not be ensnared and enslaved by the evil one: instead, rescue us from his clutches.'[94] Matthew 4:1-11 might be invoked to support this view: Jesus is not said to have entered the desert on his own initiative, but by the leading (or compulsion, Mark 1:13) of the Spirit (cf. Matt. 6:13a); and the Father indeed rescues him from the evil one (6:13b).

On that reading of the petition, the second clause follows logically from the first. A second view reverses that order. We pray, 'deliver us from the evil one' (6:13b) in order that hidden

---

[92]*Ho ponēros* denotes the devil in Matthew 5:37; 13:19, 38 (with 39a); other persons in 5:39; 12:35; 13:49. On Jesus' rescue from the evil one, see *GGBB*, 233; cf. Jesus' prayer in John 17:15. For 'evil' and 'good' to distinguish false gods from Yahweh, see Hosea 7:15; 8:3; Amos 5:14-15; Micah 3:2; Isaiah 5:20, texts that 'are using the language of religious allegiance as much as that of ethical evaluation' (Andersen and Freedman 1980: 476-77). 'The Lord's Prayer stretches from the Father at the beginning to the devil at the end, from heaven to hell...' (Bruner 2004a: 315).

[93]Cf. the teachings of Matthew 10:17-39; 13:19, 38-39; 24:4-14; also Ephesians 5:16; 6:10-18; 2 Thessalonians 2:1-12; 1 Peter 5:8-11; Revelation 12:1-17 *et passim*. In view of such passages, Jeremias' restriction of *peirasmos* to 'the last great trial' (1971: 202) is unjustified. The absence of the definite article before *peirasmos* is noteworthy in this regard. Keener 1999: 223-25 well stresses that Matthew 6:13 embraces both present and future trials.

[94]For this view, see, e.g., France 1985: 136.

sins may be purged from our hearts, so that the Father will not be forced 'to put us to the test' (6:13a) to reveal our true condition.[95] This reading, unlike the first, finds no support from Matthew 4:1-11.

Neither of those views takes sufficient account of the strong parallelism between the two clauses of Matthew 6:13 and of the strong adversative *alla* ('but on the contrary') at the beginning of 6:13b. These features indicate that the two clauses are voicing the same request – the first positively, the second negatively, the two together for emphasis. We may paraphrase: 'Father, let us not fall victim to the temptations of the evil one; on the contrary, rescue us from his mighty power.' Jesus' experience in the desert is illustrative. As noted in comments on Matthew 4, Jesus is *tested* by the Father and the Spirit for a good purpose, but the devil tests him *by tempting him*. He is *confronted with* temptations, but he does not *succumb* to them, he does not *enter into* them (cf. 26:41), he is not brought under their power. His trust in the Father is sorely tested, but it does not fail. He is rescued from, and victorious over, the evil one. Thus encouraged by their Champion's example, and empowered by the same Spirit, disciples will continue to offer this prayer – both for themselves and for fellow believers – until the kingdom has come, tribulation has ceased, Satan has been crushed, and final victory is won.[96]

9. The closing doxology

'For Yours is the kingdom and the power and the glory forever. Amen.' Thus does the Lord's Prayer conclude in the NKJV. As noted earlier, these words are absent from the original text of

---

[95]Foster 1992: 189: 'We want to be progressing in the realms of transformation with no hidden sins so that God will not be forced to put us to the test.'

[96]For support of this reading of Matthew 6:13, see James 1:13-15; Calvin 1994: 212 (the two lines of 13 are 'one and the same'); Jeremias 1971: 202 (citing a Jewish morning and evening prayer: 'Bring me not into the power of sin, And not into the power of guilt, And not into the power of temptation, And not into the power of anything shameful'); Gundry 1994: 109; Keener 1999: 223-25. 'We cannot of ourselves stand against temptation; if we could, [this] prayer were needless' (Watson 1993: 282, on 6:13). See also the comments on Matthew 4:1-11.

Matthew. Yet, given their abiding presence in our actual use of
the prayer, some further comments are in order: *a.* The opening
'for' (*hoti*) links the doxology to the preceding verses, and its
content is suggested by the prayer itself, especially verses 9-10
and 13. *b.* Jewish prayers, some of which are similar to the
Lord's Prayer, typically ended with doxologies, some of which
are quite close to this one. *c.* The version of the Lord's Prayer
recorded in the *Didache* concludes very similarly: 'for thine is
the power and the glory forever' (8:2; cf. 9:4; 10:5). *d.* For such
reasons as those, its later addition to the text of Matthew is not in
the least surprising. *e.* We will continue to use it, of course; and
we may do so with a clear conscience, if we remind ourselves
and our people of the matters raised in this paragraph.[97]

Prayer and Forgiveness (6:12, 14-15)
Concluding his teaching on prayer (Matt. 6:5-15), Jesus returns
to the subject of 6:12, evidence of its immense importance.

1. The language
All three verses speak of sin. Verse 12 uses the terms *opheilēmata*
('debts') and *opheiletai* ('debtors'), whereas verses 14-15
speak of *paraptōmata* ('transgressions'). Luke 11:4a asks God
to forgive *tas hamartias hēmōn* ('our sins'), but 11:4b uses the
language of Matthew, *panti* *opheilonti* *hēmin* ('everyone *indebted*
to us').[98]

The connection between 'debt' and 'sin' is already clear
from these parallel clauses in Luke. Behind both *opheilēma*
and *hamartia* is the Aramaic noun *hôbā,'* 'which had the literal
meaning of monetary debt and the figurative meaning of sin as
a moral debt.'[99] 'Sin is likened to a "debt" because it deserves
to be punished.'[100] Similarly, the proximity of *paraptōmata* to
opheilēmata in the Matthean text, and the *gar* ('for') linking
Matthew 6:14-15 to the preceding prayer, show that these two

---

[97]See above, n. 51; Jeremias 1964: 31-32; Keener 1999: 225-26.

[98]The verb is *opheilō*, a cognate of the nouns used in Matthew 6:12.

[99]Gundry 1994: 108. Cf. Black 1967: 140. Note how the *hamartōloi* of
Luke 13:2 parallels the *opheiletai* of 13:4.

[100]Stott 1978: 149.

terms denote the same reality. All three verses speak also of forgiveness, and apply the verb *aphiēmi*, 'forgive,' to acts both human and divine.[101] Both are crucial. Persons who refuse to forgive are denied God's forgiveness; yet without this there is no hope (Ps. 130:3-4).

2. *The point of departure: the gospel of the kingdom*

Jesus presents the prayer of Matthew 6:12, and judges the actions of 6:14-15, in light of his entire sermon and his whole mission. Accordingly, Matthew wants these verses to be read together with the rest of the sermon and the rest of his book. Both the petition of 6:12 and the teaching of 6:14-15 *presuppose* the gospel of the kingdom (4:23). These verses, like the Beatitudes, are addressed to persons who, acutely aware of their sin and misery, have embraced the grace of God's rule, experienced its powers and submitted to its commands. Central to that *euangelion* is the work of Messiah: Jesus has come to save his people from their sins; he possesses authority on earth to forgive sins; he gives his life as a ransom for many; and he sheds his own blood 'for many for the forgiveness of sins.' Sin (*hamartia*) is indeed a debt (*opheilēma*) deserving punishment – punishment which Jesus willingly bears on his people's behalf and in their stead.[102]

3. *The disciples' request*

'Forgive us our debts,' they ask the Father (Matt. 6:12a). Joachim Jeremias interprets 6:12 as he does verse 11. Disciples here view their sins in light of the Last Judgment; they acknowledge that God alone can save them from the wrath to come; and they implore him to grant them forgiveness, 'this one great gift of the Messiah's time, already in this day and

---

[101]If *ta paraptōmata autōn* originally appeared only in 6:14a, the structure of 6:14-15 is chiastic: 'forgive their transgressions' (a); 'forgive you' (b); 'forgive men' (b'); 'forgive your transgressions' (a'); cf., e.g., NASB. If the phrase originally appeared also in 6:15a (cf., e.g., ESV, 'if you do not forgive others their trespasses...'), the chiasm is disturbed. See *TC*, 14.

[102]See Matthew 4:17, 23; 1:21; 9:2, 6; 20:28; 26:28, 39, 42; 27:46; and pages 146-48 above.

in this place.'[103] Certainly verse 10 compels us to keep that consummation in mind throughout the prayer; but verse 12 focuses primarily on disciples' *present* and *recurrent* relational conflicts, which are faced moreover in light of Jesus' teaching about divine forgiveness as a *present provision* as well as a future hope.[104]

Forgiveness is one of the Father's choicest gifts to his children, one he delights to bestow, but one for which they must nonetheless ask (7:11). Having taken account of the holiness of God and the gospel of the kingdom (6:9-10) and Jesus' prior teaching, they perceive their debts with far greater clarity: they have broken the law's commands, including its prohibitions against murder, adultery and divorce; they have sworn falsely, returned evil for evil, and hated their enemies (5:17-48); they too have been controlled by pride and have behaved like hypocrites (6:1-18). They also recognize that the basis of their forgiveness lies not in this petition (however earnest and trusting it may be) but in Messiah's redemptive sacrifice. This is also a prayer of intercession: 'forgive *us our* debts.' We ask that others – including 'our debtors' – may heed Jesus' exposition of the law, and may therefore recognize the enormity of their sins, confess them to God, and implore his forgiveness for the sake of his Son.

4. The disciples' prior actions

Verse 14 speaks of disciples who do, and verse 15 of those who do not, forgive the transgressions of other people. Those who offer the petition of verse 12 represent the first group, or at least claim to do so: 'as we also have forgiven [the aorist *aphēkamen*] our debtors.' The same holds true for the words of Luke 11:4: 'for we ourselves also forgive [the present *aphiomen*] everyone who is indebted to us.' The Aramaic perfect tense, which probably underlies Matthew's aorist verb, could bear a present sense, 'so

---

[103]Jeremias 1964: 27.

[104]On forgiveness as a present reality in Jesus' teaching, see Matthew 9:2, 6; Luke 7:47-48. Similarly, Paul addresses the churches' myriad relational difficulties within the context of God's saving righteousness already received (Rom. 3:21–5:21) and eagerly awaited (Gal. 5:5).

that Luke's present is more idiomatically correct, Matthew's aorist more "Semitic."'[105] As noted, this is the only clause of the prayer which lacks an imperative, and refers directly to human activity. 'It looks almost like an alien body; that makes clear that a very heavy emphasis is placed on it.'[106]

Jesus has already identified some of the sins that will be committed against his disciples: injustice, oppression and persecution; slander, insult and false accusation; broken vows, infidelity and divorce.[107] Their debtors (Matt. 6:12) may include powerful people who have stolen or withheld things needed to sustain life (6:11) or who have otherwise mediated assaults from the evil one (6:13). A disciple's willingness to forgive such transgressions is impressive. That a disciple prays for (not just about) an enemy (5:44) shows that he has already forgiven the other, or that he offers this prayer as a means to doing so.

Showing mercy to one's debtors by forgiving them (5:7; 6:12) is the very response expected from persons whose own enormous debts the merciful God has cancelled by virtue of Messiah's work. Jesus drives the point home in a later parable: see 18:24-27 with verses 28-30. Paul also instructs Christians to forgive each other as God forgave them (Col. 3:13; Eph. 4:32-5:2). Yet their acts, however notable and noble, cannot compare to God's. The *paraptōmata* they forgive are primarily transgressions against God's holy law. Moreover, while a given disciple is assailed by a limited number of wrongs, *all* sins violate God's law. Only some are debtors to us; *all* are debtors to God – we as surely as others. The transgressions we

---

[105]France 1985: 136. Matthew's *aphēkamen* could stand for the Aramaic *šᵉbaqnan*, a *perfectum praesens*, and thus be rendered 'as we forgive.' Cf. Hagner 1993: 150; Jeremias 1971: 201.

[106]Jeremias 1971: 201. The 'Eighteen Benedictions' (on which see p. 163 above) contain a prayer for forgiveness without an attached condition. But the apocryphal Ecclesiasticus states in 28:2, 'Pardon your neighbour any wrongs done to you, and when you pray, your sins will be forgiven' (NJB). For other citations from Jewish literature, see Davies and Allison 1988: 610. Said Chrysostom: 'Nothing makes us so like God as our readiness to forgive the wicked and wrongdoer' (in *ACC* 1a: 139).

[107]See especially Matthew 5:6, 11-12, 22, 27-28, 31-32, 33, 39-41, 44.

forgive are as nothing compared to the enormous debts God cancels. What disciples do (6:12b) is truly an image but only an image of what God does (6:12a). The 'as' (*hōs*) of 12b 'does not imply a comparison; how could Jesus' disciples compare their poor forgiving with God's mercy?'[108] Having received such mercy, should I not willingly forgive a fellow Christian 77 or even 490 times (18:22), and just as readily recognize that such compassion pales by comparison to God's (18:27)?

What about the disciple who fails to forgive (Matt. 6:15) or who falsely claims to have done so (6:12)? If he is a true disciple, he urgently needs to examine himself (has the utterance of his lips [6:12b] belied the state of his heart [15:8]?); to restudy the *euangelion* in Matthew and elsewhere; to recognize anew what happened at the cross; to confess to the Father *this very debt* ('I have *not* forgiven my debtors') and ask for his forgiving mercy. It is yet more urgent that the spurious disciple do those things; that he perceive the appalling consequences for spurning the divine grace; and that he ask God to forgive him, precisely because he has not forgiven others, and will not and cannot do so until he himself is redeemed. Perhaps, for both kinds of people, one spur toward forgiving others will be the realization that mounting bitterness resulting from their refusal to forgive is destroying their own souls.[109] Moreover, while understanding the cross will move both of them to acts of forgiveness, such acts will also help them better to understand the cross. Forgiveness is always costly: such love 'keeps no score of wrongs' (1 Cor. 13:5, REB); it refrains from getting even; it absorbs the wrong committed against oneself and allows it no new lease on life. Having genuinely forgiven another person, I will be newly gripped by the fact that the Father forgave my sins by laying them upon his Son (Isa. 53:4-6), and that the Son voluntarily bore them without flinging them back in my face – leaving me an example to follow (2 Cor. 5:14-15; 1 Pet. 2:18-25).

---

[108]Jeremias 1964: 27.

[109]For the consequences of apostasy, see, e.g., Hebrews 6:4-6; 10:26-30; 2 Peter 2:20-22. On bitterness and rage as effects of an unforgiving spirit, see Eph 4:31-32.

5. *The Father's responses*

'If you forgive...,' says Jesus, 'your heavenly Father will also forgive [*aphēsei*] you' (6:14). 'But if you do not forgive..., neither will your Father forgive [*oude...aphēsei*] your transgressions' (6:15). As is now clear, the sole *basis* for the Father's response in 6:14 is the saving work of his Son, just as the ultimate reason for his response in 6:15 is the person's rejection of that gospel. It is just as clear that the disciple's action – whether that of verse 14 or of verse 15 – is an essential *condition* for the Father's response. To be interpreted accordingly is the language of the matching petition – in both 6:12b ('as we also have forgiven') and Luke 11:4b ('for we ourselves also forgive').[110]

The verb used here – *aphēsei*, a future indicative of *aphiēmi* – denotes the Father's responses both now and hereafter. He readily forgives the sins of disciples (6:12a, 14b) whose profession (6:12b) accords with reality (Matt. 6:14a). Those sins may well include an unforgiving heart – of which the disciple has repented, as evidenced by subsequent acts of forgiveness. The confession of 6:12a, like the prayer of 6:6, the Father hears and rewards: he remits the debts on the basis of Christ's work; the disciple's conscience is cleansed; his communion with the Father is restored and deepened. By such means the Father reassures his child of vindication at the Last Judgment.[111] This manifold reward is not dependent on the response of the disciple's debtor (6:12b) – it may be that the offender will not or cannot receive the offer of forgiveness – but when the two

---

[110]C .F. D. Moule, in Carson 1984: 172, rejects *desert* ('earning or meriting forgiveness') in favor of *capacity* ('adopting an attitude which makes forgiveness possible'). Reflected in Matthew 6:12b, say Davies and Allison (1988: 610-11), is the desire to receive God's forgiveness, not a claim to deserve it. Calvin 1994: 212 says 6:12b expresses a 'condition,' not a 'cause,' of God's forgiveness. Gundry 1994: 108 calls 6:12b 'a paradigm of forgiveness rather than a reason for forgiveness.' The 'for' (*gar*) of Luke 11:4b means not that divine forgiveness is based on human activity (cf. Luke 23:34), but that the disciples' *request* for forgiveness takes account of their own practice (Green 1997: 443-44). The same holds true for Matthew 6:12b if we translate *hōs kai* 'since also' (so BDF, par. 453; *GGNT*, 963). Cf. above, page 328, n. 46.

[111]See Acts 10:42-43; Romans 5:9-11; Colossians 1:12-14; Hebrews 9:11-28; 10:12-23; James 4:7-10; 1 John 1:6–2:2; 4:7-21.

parties are reconciled to each other, the disciple's reward is yet greater.[112]

But the Father will 'not forgive' (*oude...aphēsei*) disciples (Matt. 6:15b) who do not forgive their debtors (6:15a) or who falsely claim to have done so (6:12b). If the disciple is a Christian, he cannot lose his salvation, but an unforgiving spirit will seriously impede his fellowship with God; that is, the verb applies to present life, not to the final verdict. Even true members of the covenant community who willfully sin or refuse obedience or harbor guilt cannot expect a hearing from God.[113] As Jesus has already made clear, this includes not only persons needing to *offer* forgiveness to another (6:14-15) but those needing to *seek* forgiveness from another (5:23-24).[114] Moreover, such acts and attitudes always hinder and sometimes destroy fellowship among true believers.[115] On the other hand, a recurrent or habitual failure to forgive one's debtors may indicate that the disciple is no true believer at all, in which case the Father's present judgment (Matt. 6:15b) anticipates the verdict at the end.[116] The terrifying prospects for the unforgiving disciple are vividly depicted at the close of the parable in Matthew 18:23-35. Yet such a

---

[112]Cf. Romans 12:18. The other may refuse to acknowledge his sin and therefore his need of forgiveness; or he may have died. Lewis B. Smedes, 'Keys to Forgiving,' *Christianity Today*, Dec 3, 2001, page 73, rightly says: 'There can be no reunion without forgiving, but there *can be* forgiving without reunion.'

[113]See Matthew 6:15; Joshua 7:10-15; Psalm 66:18; James 4:17; 1 Peter 3:7. Since we cannot pray without the Spirit's help (Gal. 4:6; Rom. 8:15, 26-28), we may infer that grieving the Spirit by refusing to forgive others (Eph. 4:30-32), or quenching the Spirit by rejecting preaching on the subject (1 Thess. 5:19-22 with Matt. 6:14-15), will adversely affect our prayer life.

[114]Offering prayer (6:9-13) is comparable to offering a gift at the altar (5:23-24). Cf. the comments on these two verses.

[115]This is abundantly clear from Paul's letters: see, e.g., Galatians 5:13-15; 1 Corinthians 1:10-13; 3:16-17; Philippians 2:1-4. Once we honestly assess our own relationships, we may not so quickly identify unforgiving Christians as non-Christians, and we may more readily agree with Paul that true Christians sometimes find it extraordinarily hard to get along with each other.

[116]The spurious disciple's condition is that of the weeds in the parable of Matthew 13:24-30, and of the bad fish in the parable of 13:47-50. See those comments.

person's conversion could begin just here: his horror over the condemnation awaiting him for his transgressions of the law, including its command to forgive others, may jolt him into taking the actions described above.[117]

D. Fasting (6:16-18)

Jesus again recognizes and endorses an established practice: 'When you fast [nēsteuēte]...' (Matt. 6:16a). His purpose here, as when teaching about almsgiving and prayer, and as already made plain in verse 1, is to challenge listeners to consider from what motives and to what ends they practice their piety. The verb nēsteuō ('fast') appears four times in these three verses. The nēsteuēte of 6:16a, like its counterparts in 6:2a and 5a, is a present subjunctive.[118] Matthew first applies the term to Jesus' forty-day fast in the desert (4:2); the only other instances in Matthew are in 9:14-15, where Jesus again addresses this subject. As these and kindred texts make plain, true fasting is voluntary, deliberate and purposeful.[119]

Reasons for Fasting

'Throughout Scripture fasting refers to abstaining from food for spiritual purposes.'[120] The singular purpose in each case

---

[117]See the last paragraph under 4. Disciples who refuse to seek forgiveness are given similar warnings (5:21-26); see those comments.

[118]See page 387, n. 3.

[119]The people in Matthew 15:32 are hungry (nēsteis), but not fasting. R. K. Harrison, *ISBE* 2: 284, calls fasting a 'deliberate and sustained abstinence from all food for a specific period of time.' Pratt 1987: 173 calls it 'the voluntary self-denial of food or drink for the purpose of expressing to God our intense concern and preoccupation with something.' All 20 NT instances of nēsteuō have this sense. Three of the five instances of the noun nēsteia are so used: Luke 2:37; Acts 14:23; 27:9. The other two denote forced deprivations and not true fasts: 2 Corinthians 6:5 ('hunger,' NIV, rather than 'fastings,' NKJV); 11:27 ('often without food,' ESV, rather than 'in fastings often,' NKJV). For this distinction, see BAGD s.v., 1. and 2.

[120]Foster 1988: 48. A fast is thus distinct from a hunger strike, whose purpose is political or social; and from dieting, whose purpose is physical (though fasting may benefit the body). Cf. ibid. The objectives of fasting, according to Calvin 1960: 1242 (4.12.15), are to subdue the flesh, to prepare for prayer and meditation, and to abase oneself as a sinner before God.

is to seek the face of God and to commune with him. In OT
accounts of individual and corporate fasts, people (i) *plead*
with God to act in face of human need and impotence; (ii)
mourn before God in face of sin or loss; and (iii) *wait* upon
God to reveal himself and to fulfill his promises.[121] Fasts
in Jesus' day served the same three purposes. Jews fasted
on the Day of Atonement (ii and iii), at the New Year, and
at four times during the year to commemorate Jerusalem's
fall in 586 B.C. (ii).[122] The Pharisees observed fasts beyond
those: see Matthew 9:14; Luke 18:12. So did disciples of
John the Baptist, which was fitting in view of John's call to
repentance (ii) and his promise of Messiah (iii), as well as his
imprisonment (i).[123] Anna fasted in the temple in expectation
of Jerusalem's redemption (Luke 2:37-28) (iii). It may well be
that Jesus fasted in the desert for all three reasons: that he
pled with the Father to empower him for service (i); that he
grieved over Israel's sins (ii); and that he eagerly awaited
the Father's answers (iii). Similarly, it is probable that during
his three-day fast in Damascus (Acts 9:9) Paul besought
God to cure his blindness (i), mourned over his sins (ii), and
awaited Jesus' further instructions (iii). Jesus foretells the
day when his disciples will fast (Matt. 9:15), both in sorrow
for his absence (ii) and in longing for his return (iii). As the

---

[121]For (i) see Judges 20:26; 2 Samuel 12:16-17; 2 Chronicles 20:3-4; Ezra 8:21;
Esther 4:3, 16; Psalm 35:13-14; for (ii) 1 Samuel 7:6; 31:13; 2 Samuel 1:11-12;
3:35; 1 Kings 21:27; Ezra 10:6; Nehemiah 1:4; 9:1-2; Daniel 9:3-6; Joel 1:13-14;
2:12-15; Jonah 3:5; for (iii) Exodus 34:28; Deuteronomy 9:9. 'Afflicting, or
denying, oneself' (*'ānâ nepeš*) for the Day of Atonement (Lev. 16:29, 31; 23:27,
32; Num. 29:7) included fasting: cf. Leviticus 16:29 in ESV (text, 'you shall
afflict yourselves'; mg., 'you shall fast') and NJB ('you will fast'); Psalm 35:13
('I afflicted myself with fasting,' ESV); J. Behm, *TDNT* 4: 927). Fasting in this
case was related to confessing sins (ii) and awaiting atonement (iii). For
other references to the OT and Judaism, see Behm, 927-31; Keener 1999:
226. Fasts might last one day or night (1 Sam. 14:24; 2 Sam. 3:35; Dan. 6:18),
three days (Est. 4:16), seven days (1 Sam. 31:13; 2 Sam. 12:16-18), or 40 days
(Exod. 34:28; Deut. 9:9; 1 Kings 19:8).

[122]These four fasts were observed in the fourth, fifth, seventh and tenth
months: see Zechariah 7:3, 5; 8:19; Marshall 1978a: 221; Scott 1995: 157. See
also Behm, 929-30; R. Banks, 'Fasting,' *DJG*, 233.

[123]See Matthew 3:2; 9:14; 11:2-3, 18; Behm, 930.

Christians of Antioch are worshiping and fasting – that is, waiting on God (iii) – the Holy Spirit directs them to set apart Paul and Barnabas for service (Acts 13:2). The fasting that accompanies the commissioning of these men (13:3), and those of 14:23, expresses the church's dependence on God to equip, empower and protect them (i), in faithfulness to his promises (iii).

Fasting and Prayer
Linguistically and structurally, Matthew 6:16-18 is especially close to 6:5-6. Verse 16, like verse 5, begins with the practice ('when you fast,' a plural verb as in 5); warns against behaving 'like the hypocrites' (the very phrase of 6:5); reveals their desire for human acclaim; and recognizes their reception of reward (the last eleven words of 6:5 recur in 6:16, with one addition: the participle *nēsteuontes*). Verse 17, like verse 6, turns from the company of disciples to the individual and begins with the emphatic singular pronoun *sy* ('you'); and the last eighteen words of 6:18 are virtually identical to the last eighteen of 6:6.[124]

Those affinities and the placement of teaching about fasting immediately after teaching on prayer, accord with the fact that prayer and fasting are often closely associated in practice. This connection is expressly stated in several of the OT texts cited above, and seems implicit in all the rest.[125] The same holds true for the NT. Anna worships 'with fasts and prayers' (Luke 2:37). Matthew 9:14 relates that John's disciples fasted; Luke 11:1, that he taught them to pray. Luke 5:33 indicates that disciples both of John and of the Pharisees fast and pray. Paul both fasts and prays in Damascus (Acts 9:9, 11). The church at Antioch commissions Paul and Barnabas with fasting and prayer (13:3). These two do the same when appointing elders in the churches (14:23). In view of such passages and the practices there reflected, we can understand

---

[124]The only difference is that Matthew 6:6 uses *kryptō* and 6:18 *kryphaiō* for the 'secret' place.

[125]See the texts on page 426, n. 121, especially 2 Samuel 12:16; 2 Chronicles 20:3-12; Ezra 8:21-23; Nehemiah 1:4; 9:1-2; Psalm 35:13; Daniel 9:3; Joel 1:13-14.

why references to fasting were added to texts which originally spoke of prayer alone.[126]

While it is hard to imagine a fast without prayer, Jesus nowhere teaches that prayer must be accompanied by fasting to be effective. Matthew 9:14-15 indicates that during his ministry his followers did not regularly fast, but nowhere is this said about prayer. (The gospels often speak of Jesus' prayers, but they never expressly affirm nor deny that he fasted beyond the forty days in the desert.) Yet the fundamental reason for fasting is the same as for praying: to center upon God and to seek deeper fellowship with him.[127] To encourage both practices, Jesus promises the nearness of the Father: he who is there 'in the secret place' (*tō en tō kryptō*) of prayer (6:6a) is also there (*tō en tō kryphaiō*) for the one who fasts (6:18a). Moreover, the very needs which evoke the petitions of 11-13 can prompt fasts as well. Indeed, so acute may be our longing for God to forgive our sins and to rescue us from the devil's attacks, that we will willingly abstain from daily bread for a time. Andrew Murray 'says that prayer and fasting are like two hands. Whenever we pray, it is as though we are reaching out and putting one hand on the mercy seat, the place that symbolized God's forgiving presence on the Ark of the covenant. But when we fast, we take our other hand off the legitimate things of this world (such as the comforts of food) and cast all earthly supports aside in order to put both hands on that mercy seat.'[128] In other words, fasting can serve to rivet our attention upon God, and to strengthen our trust in him, in a way that prayer alone does not; and it can also serve – by that very means – to deepen our communion with God in prayer.[129]

---

[126]The NIV of Mark 9:29, Acts 10:30 and 1 Corinthians 7:5 speak only of prayer, the NKJV of fasting as well. See *TC*, 85, 331, 488.

[127]The *negative* act of abstaining from food serves the *positive* act of communing with God. So it was for Jesus in the wilderness: see page 274, including n. 17. Contrast Zechariah 7:5.

[128]Douglas F. Kelly, *If God Already Knows, Why Pray?* (Brentwood: Wolgemuth & Hyatt, 1989), 177.

[129]'If we want to communicate with God in ways that reveal deep need and yearning for Him, we must make fasting a part of our lives' (Pratt 1987:

The Fasting of Hypocrites

'Do not look gloomy [skythrōpoi] as the hypocrites do,' says Jesus, 'for [gar] they make their faces unsightly [aphanizousin], that they may be seen [phanōsin] by men to be fasting' (Matt. 6:16a). The adjective skythrōpos appears nowhere else in Matthew. In the only other NT instance, in Luke 24:17, the Emmaus disciples are 'looking sad' over events of recent days. Their sadness is quite genuine, but that of the hypocrites is deliberate and pretentious. Because their faces are *not seen*, their fasting *is seen*; they make their fasting visible by making their true visage invisible.[130]

'Truly, I tell you, they receive in full their reward' (6:16b). Jesus used these very words when speaking of the hypocrites' almsgiving (6:2b) and prayer (6:5b). This accords with the fact that in all three practices such persons' singular purpose – and assured reward – is being seen, lauded and magnified by other people. On this subject, comments under A. (pp. 386-90) will suffice.

The Fasting of Disciples

'But you [sy], when you are fasting, anoint [aleipsai] your head and wash [nipsai] your face, that your fasting may be seen not by men but [alla] by your Father who is in the secret place' (6:17-18a). As in 6, the shift to the singular sy is noteworthy. The opening exhortation, 1, already applied to almsgiving (Matt. 6:2-4, and to prayer (6:5-6), is reinforced. A private fast – particularly one of mourning – may be so serious that one neglects to bathe, uses no oil, stays unkempt or anoints himself

---

175). As Paul was for three days without sight, food and drink (Acts 9:9), he could more readily commune with God (9:11) and also ponder anew the Scriptures' teachings about God, his Messiah and his plan of salvation.

[130]The verb aphanizō can mean to 'render [one's face] invisible or unrecognizable,' or to 'disfigure' it (BAGD s.v.). It recurs in Matthew 6:19, 20 (the only other instances in Matthew) with the meaning 'destroy, ruin,' of pests' effects on earthly goods (ibid.). The contrasting phanōsin, an aorist passive subjunctive from phainō (as in 6:5), means 'appear, show oneself' (ibid.). The contrary command of 6:17 implies that the persons of 6:16 have failed to clean and groom themselves. Recalling the use of hypokritēs in the theater (pp. 388-89 above), we may say that the *natural* face is hidden by the *actor's* face (in this case [6:16], one that feigns gloom).

with sackcloth and ashes.[131] But if he ventures into public with his visage thus marred – and further distorted by a gloomy or sullen expression – he may even be unrecognizable. No, says Jesus: if during a fast you must encounter other people, do what is normal and expected – first clean and groom yourself with the aid of olive oil and water.[132] Unlike David's action in 2 Samuel 12:20, the intent here is not to end the fast but to refrain from calling attention to it (which is different from denying that one is fasting). Let your fasting be reserved, says Jesus, for the gaze of your heavenly Father.

There is, I believe, a further motivation for Jesus' dual command in Matthew 6:17. When in public, disciples 'are to appear as they normally do, or even as if prepared for a feast.'[133] The point is not that fasts are replaced by feasts, as in Zechariah 8:19 or in Matthew 9:14-15 (John's disciples fast as those who await Messiah; Jesus' disciples feast because Messiah has come); but that fasts *themselves* are henceforth to bear the marks of celebration, given all the blessings attending the dawn of God's rule (starting with those announced in 1:21 and 5:3-12). Nor does joy eclipse sorrow; rather, the two are joined, as is often true in prayer. 'Repentance [4:17] is a head anointed with oil [6:17], not as a new form of hypocrisy, but as an expression of joy at the salvation that has been given.'[134] Because the kingdom has really come, even fasts of mourning can include rejoicing; but because the kingdom has not fully come, even joyous times contain an element of

---

[131]See, e.g., Matthew 11:21; 2 Samuel 13:19; Esther 4:3; Job 2:8; 42:6; Jeremiah 6:26. Cf. 2 Samuel 14:2.

[132]Before appearing in public ancient Jews normally did some or all of the following: trimmed their beards; changed clothes; washed their faces; and used olive oil 'to clean and anoint their skin, especially on their heads... probably to lubricate dry scalps' (Keener 1999: 227-28). Both *aleipsai* and *nipsai* (Matt. 6:17) are aorist middle imperatives of command. The Greek *elaion*, 'oil' (25:3, 4, 8), comes from *elaia*, 'olive tree' (cf. 21:1, *to Oros tōn Elaiōn*, 'the Mount of Olives').

[133]Manson 1957: 172.

[134]Jeremias 1971: 157-58. Cf. Jesus' sitting at table with repentant sinners (Matt. 9:10-13) in anticipation of festive meals in the kingdom of heaven (8:11).

sadness.[135] Or, in the terms of 9:14-17, sorrowful fasts will commence when the bridegroom is snatched away, and they will continue until his return; but because he has come, and is sure to return, and is assuredly with us in the interim (28:20), those very fasts are invested with joy and hope.

'And,' concludes Jesus, 'your Father who sees what is done in secret will reward you' (6:18b). The Father's highest reward corresponds to the fast's principal purpose: he discloses himself to those who have sought him through fasting, and grants to them – amid the fast – fellowship with himself. There is no greater reward beyond this, only the promise of its own renewal and increase through ongoing fasting and prayer.[136] Yet with that reward the Father gives others. In keeping with the three purposes for fasting noted above, he (i) grants his power and protection to weak and vulnerable human beings; (ii) forgives his people's sins; and (iii) keeps his promises and proves himself to be his people's faithful, covenant-keeping God. Three further rewards may be mentioned. (iv) An antidote to pride. This is what fellowship with the holy God becomes for the disciple who, having fasted secretly, wishes to compare himself favorably to the ostentatious hypocrite. (v) Food and drink. Fasting both combats gluttony and deepens appreciation for those gifts of God from which one has abstained.[137] (vi) Rewards associated with almsgiving (6:2-4). Abstention

---

[135]Disciples are blessed as they mourn (5:4) and they rejoice when persecuted (5:11-12). Paul experienced victories *in* trials (Rom. 8:35-37); God's servants are 'sorrowful, yet always rejoicing' (2 Cor. 6:10). Edwards 1959: 339 says that Christians' joy, even though inexpressible and glorious, is 'a brokenhearted joy.' Sadness over sin and suffering in ourselves and others, and joy over God's salvation, are mingled in our hearts; and we long for the day when the promises of Revelation 21:3-4 come true.

[136]Communion with God is the highest reward for both fasting and prayer: see the comments on 6:6.

[137]Says Ben Patterson, 'Adventures in Fasting,' *Christianity Today*, March 2, 1998, page 48: 'The fast focused my mind on the simple goodness of God's creation.... I rediscovered how good a mere carrot can be. Or a bare slice of bread, or a crisp apple.' Cf. 1 Timothy 4:3-5. Freedom from gluttony increases rather than diminishes one's enjoyment of food (cf. comments on Matthew 6:25-34). For fasting as an antidote to gluttony, see Kreeft 1992: 179-80.

from food and drink may bring to light my slavery to money and material things; but it may also help to free me from that bondage, so that I can begin to use 'unrighteous mammon' to aid the needy, and thus to advance God's rule in the world.[138]

---

[138]With the joining of fasts to almsgiving in Matthew 6:1-18, cf. the Pharisees' practice of both fasting and tithing (9:14; 23:23; Luke 18:12). On rewards for almsgiving, see pages 394-96. On using money for God's rule, see 6:24-34 (and comments); Luke 16:1-13. In Isaiah 58:1-12, in face of Israel's grievous personal and social sins, Yahweh spurns the usual fasts and calls instead for fasts which free the oppressed, aid the afflicted and feed the poor.

VI.
'CHILDREN OF THE HEAVENLY FATHER'[1]
(6:19-34)

The sermon's middle section, 'The Righteousness of the Kingdom' (5:17–7:12), continues. The recurrence of this term 'righteousness' (*dikaiosynē*) in 6:33 recalls the instances of 6:1 and 5:20. As 6:1-18 has made clear, the 'surpassing righteousness' required for entering the kingdom of heaven (5:20) is devoted not to advancing oneself but to pleasing, obeying and honoring the heavenly Father. With 5:20 still in view, Jesus now commands his followers to 'seek first the kingdom and his [i.e., God's] righteousness [*tēn dikaiosynēn autou*]' – in this context, not God's own righteousness but the righteousness, the holiness of life, that he requires of his people.[2] Matthew 6:19-34 explore some implications of the sermon's prior teachings, as well as further expounding the character of a God-centered heart and life. This section may be divided into two parts, 6:19-24 and 6:25-34, the second being founded on the first (6:25 opens with *dia touto*, 'therefore').

A. Two Ways of Living in the World (6:19-24)

Besides providing a basis for Matthew 6:25-34, these verses commend a mentality – a view of the world and life, a metaphysics – which is essential for obeying all of Jesus' teachings.[3] The passage naturally divides into three paragraphs: 6:19-21, 6:22-23 and 6:24.

---

[1]The opening words of a hymn by Caroline V. Sandell Berg (ca. 1855), translated by Ernst W. Olson (1925).

[2] The *autou* is therefore an objective, not a subjective genitive. See Davies and Allison 1988: 661; and comments on Matthew 6:33 below. According to 6:1-18, bondage to others' approval hampers growth in holiness; according to 6:19-34, bondage to wealth (cf. Willard 1998: 188).

[3]Similarly, says Romans 12:2, being transformed by the renewing of one's mind is essential for discerning and doing the will of God.

Two Kinds of Treasure (6:19-21)
The theme of these verses complements the preceding contrast
between rewards from men and from God.[4] The verb *thēsaurizō*
('store up') appears twice here and nowhere else in Matthew;
the noun *thēsauros* ('treasure') occurs three times here and
nowhere else in the sermon.[5] The language of 6:20 is very close
to that of 6:19 (thirteen of the eighteen words in the Greek text
of 6:19 recur in 6:20, in the same order); and the command of
6:20 is antithetical to that of 6:19 (every clause of 6:19 becomes
its opposite in 6:20). In those verses, Jesus addresses disciples
generally (the plural verb *thēsaurizete* and the plural pronoun
hymin). But the concluding declaration (6:21; joined to 6:19-20
by *gar*, 'for'), is addressed to the individual: *ho thēsauros sou*
('*your* treasure'), *hē kardia sou* ('*your* heart').[6]

1. Earthly treasures (6:19)
'Do not store up [*Mē thēsaurizete*] for yourselves [*hymin*]
treasures [*thēsaurous*] on earth,' says Jesus. The verse opens
with a present imperative of prohibition. The tense here
denotes customary or habitual practice, which is accentuated
by the cognate accusative *thēsaurous*. Jesus commands
disciples to avoid or to discontinue the practice. The dative
plural pronoun *hymin* here has a reflexive force.[7] Jesus is
obviously not denigrating the earth itself or its produce,
nor telling his disciples to stop providing for their and their
families' material needs: see the comments on Matthew 6:11.

Beyond verses 19-20, *thēsaurizō* occurs only once in the
gospels (Luke 12:21), a text that is doubly instructive. In the first
place, not only is this rich man in the habit of storing up goods
on earth. As they increase, his desire to hoard them intensifies
(Matt. 6:16-19); that is, the greater one's earthly treasures,

---

[4]Noted by France 1985: 138.

[5]Two of the six other instances in Matthew denote a 'treasure' (Matt.
13:44; 19:21); and four a 'treasury' of some sort (2:11; 12:35 *bis*; 13:52).

[6]This recalls Jesus' address to the individual disciple in 6:2-4, 6, 17-18.

[7]See *GGBB*, 487 (imperative of prohibition); 521-22 (customary or
habitual present); 189-90 (cognate accusative); 325 (the instances of *hymin*
in Matthew 6:19-20 may be the only places in the NT where a personal
pronoun in the *second* person is used reflexively).

the graver the danger of being enslaved and consumed by them.[8] Secondly, this is a man 'who lays up treasures [*ho thēsaurizōn*] for himself [*heautō*] and is not rich toward God [*eis theon*]' (6:21). As in Matthew 6:19, the pronoun is reflexive: 'for himself.' Jesus indicts the man, not because he farms (and works with the soil, i.e. 'the earth') or because he is wealthy but because he is selfish. Had he acknowledged his plenty to be a gift from God and therefore employed it in the service of God – for example, by helping the needy – he would have been 'rich toward God,' that is, a person who stored up treasures in heaven, and who received rewards from God (one of which may have been a longer life).[9] Storing up treasures 'on earth' (*epi tēs gēs*; Matt. 6:19) is incompatible with doing God's will 'on earth' (*epi gēs*; 6:10).

God called the rich man of that parable a 'fool' because he failed to take account of his own mortality.[10] It is the vulnerability of the treasures themselves that Jesus highlights here in Matthew. Earth is a place 'where moth [*sēs*] and corrosion [*brōsis*] destroy, and where thieves [*kleptai*] dig through [*dioryssousin*] and steal [*kleptousin*]' (6:19b). (These cognate forms, the noun *kleptai* and the verb *kleptousin*, mirror those of 6:19a, the verb *thēsaurizete* and the noun *thēsaurous*.) The term *brōsis* basically means 'eating,' and here probably includes assaults of rust on metals and of pests besides moths (such as worms and rats) on garments, food and other goods; the translation 'corrosion' seeks to capture this dual sense.[11]

---

[8] See Psalm 62:10b; Matthew 19:23-24; 1 Timothy 6:17.

[9] See Luke 12:33-34 (vv. close to that parable, and parallel to Matt. 6:19-21); 16:19-21; Matthew 6:2-4; 19:21; 22:37-39; Ephesians 4:28; 1 Timothy 6:18-19; James 5:5; 1 John 3:17.

[10] Luke 12:20. Cf. Ecclesiastes 5:15; Job 1:21; 1 Timothy 6:7.

[11] According to *Webster's Dictionary* 'corrode' means both 'to eat away by gnawing' (cf. Latin *corrodere*, from *rodere*, 'to gnaw,' whence 'rodent') and 'to wear away gradually [usually] by chemical action.' Cf. James 5:2-3a: 'Your riches have rotted and your garments are moth-eaten [*sētobrōta*, from *sēs* + *bibrōskō*, a cognate of *brōsis*]. Your gold and silver have corroded [*katiōtai*], and their corrosion [*ios*] will be evidence against you...' (ESV). See also BAGD s.v. *brōsis*, 1. and 2.; Carson 1984: 177; Davies and Allison 1988: 629-30, who cite Gospel of Thomas 76: 'the treasure...which endures, there where no moth comes near to devour and no worm destroys.'

As a moth chews through a coat, or a rat through a bag, so a thief might literally dig through the sun-dried brick wall of a Palestinian dwelling.[12] As one's earthly treasures increase in quality and quantity, there is ever graver threat from corrosive forces and from thieves, and thus ever greater cause for owners' fear and anxiety.

2. Heavenly treasures (6:20)

'But store up for yourselves treasures in heaven, where neither moth nor corrosion destroys, and where thieves do not dig through and steal.' Were life 'on earth' one's only existence, what incentive could there be for heeding the command of Matthew 6:19? Knowing that I am mortal, believing that death marks my end, and realizing that I will lose all earthly belongings (whether by ruin or theft or death), the logical response is to seek enjoyment in those things for as long as I can. For a materialist or a naturalist, the thinking of Luke 12:17-19 is perfectly sensible (cf. 1 Cor. 15:32). It is the reality and the nature of heaven (*ouranos*) that expose the rich man's folly, and that offer the strongest incentive for obeying the commands of Matthew 6:19 and 20. Cf. Hebrews 10:34; 12:28.

Heaven is the habitation of the sovereign God (Matt. 6:9), the place where his rule is fully realized and his will perfectly done (6:10).[13] Heaven is therefore preeminently *real* – a place that C. S. Lewis describes as *heavier, more solid* than earth.[14] God's dwelling, unaffected by the fall, is invulnerable to pests and corrosion, to thieves and predators; treasures stored up there are perfectly safe (cf. 1 Pet. 1:4). As this sermon makes plain, disciples 'store up' such treasures by obeying Jesus' teachings, doing his Father's will and thus advancing his rule in the world. The treasures are indeed for the disciples' benefit:

---

[12]BAGD s.v. *dioryssō*. In Mark 2:4, the related verb *exoryssō* ('dig out') probably means that the men made a hole by digging through the clay of which the roof was made (BAGD s.v.).

[13]Note too, among prior instances of *ouranos*, the phrases 'the kingdom of heaven' (Matt. 3:2; 4:17; 5:3, 10, 19, 20); 'your Father in heaven' (5:16, 45: 6:1); and heaven as 'the throne of God' (5:34). For *ouranos* applied to the creation that will pass away, see comments on 5:18.

[14]See Lewis 1946. Cf. Willard 1998, especially chapters 1, 3 and 10.

this *hymin* too is reflexive, 'for yourselves.' Likewise Jesus spoke of 'your reward' in heaven (Matt. 5:12), *misthos* being another name for the heavenly *thēsauros*. But it is the heavenly Father who grants this treasure, this reward; and the primary reason for his doing so is not the disciple's achievement but his own magnanimity. So it is his name, not the disciple's, which is hallowed in the process (cf. comments on pp. 394-96).

3. *The treasure and the heart (6:21)*

'For [*gar*] where [*hopou*] your treasure [*ho thēsauros sou*] is, there will your heart [*hē kardia sou*] be also.' The conjunction *gar* joins 6:21 to 6:19-20. So does the adverb *hopou*, which occurs four times in verses 19-20. The noun *thēsauros* and the personal pronoun *sou* also provide connections; but the shift from the plurals of 6:19-20 (*thēsaurous* and *hymin*) to the singulars of 6:21 is noteworthy.[15] But it is especially the closing phrase – *hē kardia sou* – that captures our attention. The whole verse is addressed to the individual; but whereas 'your treasure' denotes what the disciple *has*, 'your heart' denotes who he *is*. Moreover, with this latter phrase the paragraph reaches its climax; and whereas other terms in 6:21 have antecedents in 6:19-20, *kardia* appears here for the first time since 5:28, and for only the third (and last) time in the sermon (see also 5:8).

For storing up treasures in heaven, the condition of the heart is crucial. Heaven is heaven because God dwells there; it is he who explains the durability and security of the heavenly treasure. Obedience to the commands of Matthew 6:19-20 depends on fidelity to that 'great and first commandment,' which is to love God with all one's heart (*kardia*; 22:37-38). For such a person heaven's greatest treasure is God himself (5:8); disciples long for heaven because Jesus, their 'priceless treasure,' is there (Phil. 1:21-23).[16] Otherwise the promise of heavenly treasures can pose a graver danger than the lure of earthly ones. If, like the rich man of Luke 12, I am centered

---

[15]The *sou*, twice in 6:21, is genitive singular; the *hymin*, twice in 6:19-20, dative plural.

[16]See also Psalm 73:25-26; John 14:1-3; 2 Corinthians 5:8; Colossians 3:1-4; 1 John 3:1-3; and Johann Franck's hymn 'Jesus, Priceless Treasure' (1655).

on myself and my future welfare, I can employ the command of Matthew 6:20 selfishly: 'I desire to accumulate riches for myself [cf. 6:20, 'for yourselves'].

Earthly riches are perishable, and heavenly riches are durable; so it is eminently sensible for me to invest in the latter. Who would not choose a stock that both pays a high rate of interest and is risk-free?' The only sure antidote to preoccupation with *things*, whether earthly or heavenly, is a heart that loves God, and that longs above all else to obey him and to be fully united with him. Thus, 1 Timothy 6:17-19 exhorts the rich 'not to fix their hopes on the uncertainty of riches but instead upon God [*all' epi Theō*],' by serving whom they will be 'storing up for treasures for themselves [*apothēsaurizontas heautois*] as a good foundation' for the life to come. This accords with the earlier conclusion that disciples 'store up treasures' by obeying Jesus' teachings and doing his Father's will.

'Where your heart is, there will your treasure be also': thus says the above paragraph. Love of God and therefore of neighbor is the chief motive for obeying Jesus' commands in this sermon and elsewhere. But here in Matthew 6:21 Jesus puts the matter the other way around: 'where your treasure is, there will your heart be also.' That is, the disciple discovers – perhaps to his surprise – that his fidelity to those commands causes his love for God and for his neighbor to increase.

Two Kinds of Eyes (6:22-23)

This contrast is as strong as that of the preceding verses; and the literary parallels between 6:22b and 6:23a recall those between 6:19 and 6:20. By means of one kind of eye, identified as *haplous*, the whole body is flooded with light (6:22b) the other kind of eye, called *ponēros*, leaves the whole body full of darkness (6:23a). These two adjectives are obviously crucial for understanding the text. In my judgment each bears two senses: one accords with the physiological image, the other with Jesus' theological purpose. As in 21, he addresses the individual disciple: the genitive singular pronoun *sou* (used twice in 6:21) appears here four times; note too the dative singular *soi* (6:23b).

1. The picture

'The lamp [*Ho lychnos*] of the body [*tou sōmatos*] is the eye [*ho ophthalmos*]. If therefore your eye is sound [*haplous*], your whole body [*holon to sōma sou*] will be full of light [*phōteinon*]. But if your eye is bad [*ponēros*], your whole body [*holon to sōma sou*] will be full of darkness [*skoteinon*]. If therefore the light [*to phōs*] which is in you is darkness [*skotos*], how great is that darkness [*to skotos*].'

For physical sight, one organ is essential: 'the eye *alone* is the light of the body' (6:22a).[17] To fulfill this function, it must be *haplous*: sound and healthy (6:22b). But if the eye is *ponēros* – sick and unhealthy – the person is left blinded and groping in the dark (6:23a).[18] If the very organ of light (*phōs*) is *itself* darkness (*skotos*), the person's condition is hopeless (6:23b). The pleas of the blind in 9:27 and 20:30-31 are perfectly understandable.

2. The purpose

Jesus employs this language figuratively. In Hebrew thought, the eye 'represents the direction in which one is looking and therefore stands for the aims and interests of life.' Cf. Matthew 13:15-16, where *ophthalmos* marks a shift from 'sense perception' to 'mental and spiritual understanding.'[19] To have a sound eye, or healthy outlook, in this sense is to interpret the whole of reality, and the entirety of one's life, *in the light of the sovereign God and his coming rule* – in other words, to adopt the very view that Jesus expounds in the Lord's Prayer

---

[17]*GNTG*, 3: 183. Matthew 6:22a contains both a subject and a predicate nominative. In the usual Greek construction, the subject has the definite article (as here: *ho lychnos*) and the predicate nominative does not. But the article may be used (as here: <u>*ho*</u> *ophthalmos*) 'if the predicate noun is supposed to be a unique or notable instance' (ibid.). In such a case both subject and predicate 'are definite, treated as identical, one and the same, and interchangeable' (*GGNT*, 768).

[18]For this sense of *haplous*, cf. BAGD s.v. ('clear, sound, healthy'); esv and nrsv ('healthy'); nasb ('clear'); reb ('sound'). For this sense of *ponēros*, cf. BAGD s.v. ('in poor condition, sick'); nrsv ('unhealthy'); niv, nasb and reb ('bad').

[19]The quotations are from Motyer 1999: 53; and BAGD s.v. *ophthalmos*, 2., respectively.

and the rest of this sermon. Perceiving and embracing these central verities is the key to understanding everything else.[20] Conversely, the person whose eyes are bad, who remains blind to these verities or who willfully suppresses them, will understand nothing else. If that condition continues – if one persists in rejecting the truth that Jesus has placarded before his very eyes – there will come a time when he *cannot* understand that truth, when his blindness to it becomes incurable, and then a time when he is banished from God and Messiah and the kingdom forever: note the threat implicit in 6:23b.

The adjectives *haplous* and *ponēros* highlight one respect in which those outlooks are diametrically opposed to each other. Elsewhere in the NT, cognates of the first term can denote generosity or liberality. In James 1:5, God is said to give 'generously' (the adverb *haplōs*); and in Romans 12:8, Christians are exhorted to give with 'liberality' (the noun *haplotēs*).[21] Conversely, there are texts where *ponēros*, joined to *ophthalmos*, signals stinginess, greed or envy: cf. Matthew 20:15b: 'is your eye [*ho ophthalmos sou*] envious [*ponēros*] because I am good?' (cf. 20:9-14); and Mark 7:22b: 'deceit, sensuality, envy [*ophthalmos ponēros*].'[22] That generosity and envy are featured in Matthew 6:22-23 is strongly supported by the immediate context: Jesus has just called for storing up treasures in heaven rather than on earth (6:19-21), and he is about to warn against slavery to money (6:24).[23] Given this context, and the sermon as a whole, we may conclude that the metaphor *haplous* has a dual sense; that it denotes not only a *generous* eye (intent on

---

[20]You may in the early morning see the rising sun, and discover that, in its light, all else becomes clear. Just so, when the Holy Spirit enlightens 'the eyes of your heart' to understand Scripture (Eph. 1:13-18) you find that its truth illuminates the rest of reality. Cf. Psalm 19:1-14.

[21]So most translations. See BAGD s.v. *haplōs*, 2. (though in some texts outside the NT the term can mean 'simply, sincerely,' s.v. 1.); and ibid. s.v. *haplotēs*, 2., citing Romans 12:8; 2 Corinthians 8:2; 9:11, 13 (though some take all these instances to denote 'simplicity, sincerity,' s.v., 1.).

[22]So most translations. See BAGD s.v. *ophthalmos*, 1.; Hagner 1993: 158; Keener 1999: 232 (and the sources they cite).

[23]This strong contextual support is peculiar to Matthew. Whereas 6:22-23 has a parallel in Luke 11:34-35, the parallels to Matthew 6:19-21 and 24 come in Luke 12:33-34 and 16:13 respectively.

loving neighbors) but also a *single* eye (intent on loving God); and that this singleness of focus – this undivided loyalty to God – explains one's generosity.[24]

Two Kinds of Slavery (6:24)

Jesus begins by stating a general principle: 'No one can [*Oudeis dynatai*] be a slave [*douleuein*] to two masters [*dysi kyriois*].' The parallel statement at the close of the verse applies the principle to two particular masters: 'you cannot [*ou dynasthe*] be a slave [*douleuein*] to both God [*theō*] and wealth [*mamōna*].' The middle clauses explain why that is so: 'For [*gar*] either he will hate the one and love the other, or he will be devoted to the one and despise the other.' The four verbs form a chiasm: hate, *miseō* [a]; love, *agapaō* [b]; be devoted to, *antechomai* [b']; despise, *kataphroneō* [a'].

1. The nature of slavery

In the ancient world, a slave might work for more than one master; so the middle portion of the verse is not purely theoretical, but could be proven from many a slave's actual experience.[25] The point of the saying 'is that a man cannot render the exclusive loyalty and service which is inherent in the concept of [*douleia*] to more than one master.'[26] Especially is this true for God and wealth. Not only does each demand the slave's total commitment: so different are their ways of

---

[24]France 1985: 138-39 well affirms this dual sense. For *haplous* as 'single' see BAGD s.v. (where other meanings are also given); and KJV of 6:22. See also n. 21 above. Cf. *diplous*, 'double, two-fold' (BAGD s.v.).

[25]See examples in K. H. Rengstorf, *TDNT* 2: 270-71; cf. Acts 16:16.

[26]Marshall 1978a: 624, on Luke 16:13 (whose Greek is identical to Matthew 6:24, except that Luke contains *oiketēs*, 'house slave, slave,' which accounts for its presence in some mss. of Matthew). Gundry 1994: 115 thinks the verbs 'hate' and 'love' are meant comparatively: the slave loves one master more than the other. But this sense, found elsewhere (see 10:37, compared to Luke 14:26), is not so likely here, given the exclusivity inherent in *douleia*. Every *doulos* ('slave') is a *diakonos* ('servant'): note Jesus' use of the two terms in Matthew 20:26-27. But not every *diakonos* is a *doulos*: a *diakonos* might agreeably work for two employers, but not so a *doulos* for more than one owner (cf. France 1985: 139). For the outworking of this principle in Paul's teaching about slavery to sin and Christ respectively, see Chamblin 1993: 131-54.

teaching, using and rewarding their slaves – in short, so antithetical are their ways of ruling – that one could not possibly serve them *both*: a person who imagines that he can, has been duped by wealth's propaganda. But one can commit himself unreservedly to *either*. As before, Jesus calls for undivided loyalty to God. It is now plainer than before that storing up treasures on earth (Matt. 6:20) and behaving greedily or enviously (6:23a) are ways of serving the rival master. It could perhaps be said of Matthew, that when he rises to follow Jesus (9:9) an erstwhile slave of wealth is on his way to becoming a slave of God.[27]

2. Slavery to wealth

Jesus calls the rival master *mamōna* – an Aramaic term denoting *wealth* – both money and things money can buy, such as property, valuable possessions and slaves.[28] Beyond this text and its parallel in Luke 16:13, *mamōna* occurs only twice in the NT, both on Jesus' lips and both in the phrase 'unrighteous wealth' (Luke 16:9 [*mamōna tēs adikias*], 11 [*adikō mamōna*], a term that denotes possessions acquired dishonestly).[29] *Mamōna* is not inherently unrighteous; but it acquires this character when it is enthroned as a god, and receives monotheistic worship from those who possess it, who crave it (1 Tim. 6:9) and who steal it. Jesus later warns that 'the deceitfulness of wealth [*ploutou*] will choke the word' of the kingdom (Matt. 13:22) by convincing people that they will prosper more under wealth's rule than under God's. While love for God results in many a good (22:37-40), 'the love of money [*hē philargyria*] is a root of all kinds of evil' (1 Tim. 6:10;

---

[27]In 2 Chronicles 25:6-10, Amaziah first depends on wealth (he pays 100 talents of silver for mercenaries from Israel), then on God (he sends the soldiers home with their money). For trust in wealth instead of God, see also Psalm 52:7.

[28]The Greek *mamōna* (the dative singular of *mamōnas*) transliterates the Aramaic *māmôna*, the emphatic state for *māmôn*. See BAGD s.v.; and F. Hauck, *TDNT* 4: 388-89.

[29]See Matthew 16:8, 'unrighteous manager' (*oikonomon tēs adikias*). The Greek phrase of 16:9, with its noun *adikias* (a 'Hebrew Genitive': *GGBB*, 86-88), is equivalent to that of 16:11, with its dative adjective *adikō*. The corresponding Aramaic is *māmôn dišqar* (Hauck, ibid., 390).

cf. 2 Tim. 3:2-4: [*philargyroi*, 'lovers of money,' versus *philotheoi*, 'lovers of God'] and 1 Tim. 3:3 and Hebrews 13:5 [*aphilargyros*, 'not loving money']. (In Luke 16:14, immediately after the parallel to Matthew 6:24, Jesus calls the Pharisees *philargyroi*, 'lovers of money': which suggests that one important respect in which disciples' righteousness must surpass that of the Pharisees [Matt. 5:20] is their attitude toward wealth. That Luke places the saying about divorce nearby [16:18] indicates that slavery to wealth can destroy personal relationships.) By the same token, says 1 John 2:15-16, love for the world – two marks of which are 'the desire of the eyes [*hē epithymia tōn ophthalmōn*; cf. Matthew 6:23]' and 'pride in one's possessions [*hē alazoneia tou biou*]'[30] – is incompatible with love for God. Yet wealth deceives its devotees (Matt. 13:22). *Mamōna* is sure to fail (Luke 16:9). 'He who loves money will not be satisfied with money, nor he who loves wealth with his income' (Eccl. 5:10 [ESV]). Such satisfaction is reserved for slaves of God.

3. Slavery to God

All who rebel against God's rule and refuse Jesus' call to repentance (Matt. 4:17) reveal both that they hate God and that they love wealth (whether what they have or what they lack or both). But when they heed Jesus' call and submit to God's rule, they turn in disgust from a deified wealth and begin to love and serve God instead – all in response to his love and service to them through his Son and Messiah. Whereas their devotion to wealth was founded on love for self, their service to God is based entirely on love for the Master. Having set their hope on God rather than on uncertain riches, they discover that he richly provides all things for their enjoyment – *including the very wealth they have ceased to adore* (1 Tim. 6:17, with 4:3-5). They find pleasure in using money and possessions to help the needy (1 Tim. 6:18). Now that they love God instead of the world, those visible and tangible things on which they had once set their affections are dedicated to doing his will (1 John 2:15-17; cf. Jer. 9:23-24). Even 'unrighteous *mamōna*' is redeemed for advancing the kingdom of God (Matt. 6:33).

---

[30]So BAGD s.v. *alazoneia*, for the phrase in 1 John 2:16.

Compare Luke 16:8-13; and the Targums of Proverbs 3:9 ('Honor God with your mammon') and Deuteronomy 6:5 ('You shall love Yahweh your God with...all your mammon').[31]

Those two ways of living in the world (Matt. 6:19-24) dominate the next section as well.

B. Ways of Combating Anxiety (6:25-34)

In Matthew 6:19-24, *avarice* was the reason for slavery to wealth; here it is *anxiety*. Six of the seven instances of the verb *merimnaō* in Matthew occur in this passage (the other is in 10:19). Three of these appear in commands: 'Therefore [*Dia touto*] I tell you, do not be anxious [*mē merimnate*] about your life' (6:25); 'therefore [*oun*] do not be anxious [*mē merimnēsēte*]' about food and drink and clothing (6:31); 'therefore [*oun*] do not be anxious [*mē merimnēsēte*] about tomorrow' (6:34).[32] It is significant that the passage begins and ends on this note; that each command is based on nearby teachings (*dia touto...oun... oun*); and that the accent throughout is upon life's necessities. The other three instances of the verb appear in statements buttressing those commands: 'who of you by being anxious [*merimnōn*] can add one cubit...?' (6:27); 'why are you anxious [*merimnate*] about clothing?' (6:28(; 'for [*gar*] tomorrow will be anxious [*merimnēsei*] about itself' (6:34).[33]

The Effects of Slavery
How does the mentality condemned in 6:19-24 encourage and promote worry? And how does the mentality there commended discourage and demote it?

---

[31]These quotations from the Targums (Aramaic paraphrases) come from France 1985: 139. As Barzillai used his riches to help King David (2 Sam. 19:32), so we can devote our wealth to King Jesus. Cf. Foster 1985: 19-70 (chs. on 'the dark side of money, 'the light side of money,' and 'kingdom use of unrighteous mammon').

[32]Matthew 6:25 uses a present imperative of prohibition; verses 31 and 34, an aorist subjunctive of prohibition.

[33]Matthew 6:27 uses a present active participle of means; verse 28, a present active indicative (whose form is identical to the imperative in 25); verse 34, a future active indicative. For *merimnaō* in this sense ('have anxiety, be anxious'), see BAGD s.v., 1.; 1 Corinthians 7:33, 34b; Philippians 4:6.

1. Bondage to anxiety

Wealth dooms its slaves to debilitating anxiety. The master promises to supply them with life's necessities; but it cannot deliver what it promises. Faced with conditions in which wealth – in this case food and clothing – is urgently needed, they implore wealth to come to their aid but discover to their dismay that it is incapable of doing so, that it is not self-supplying.

Wealth also dupes its slaves into thinking that, however much they possess, it is less than they need; that what others call luxuries are really necessities; and that one can never have too many of these, given life's vicissitudes and uncertainties, including threats of sickness and starvation. Having accumulated wealth to assure their future, the slaves now worry that their belongings will be taken from them (by pests or blight or thieves or marauding armies), or that they will die and be bereft of them.

Infected as they all are by pride, one slave frets when another slave's wealth exceeds his own; therefore strives to surpass the other in riches; and, having succeeded in doing so, fears that somehow he will lose his wealth and thus his lofty standing.

2. Freedom from anxiety

It is knowing oneself to be a slave of God ('Therefore' [Matt. 6:25], pointing to 6:24) and a child of the heavenly Father (*ho patēr hymōn ho ouranios*, [6:26, 32]), and living accordingly, that offers 'the ultimate antidote to anxiety.'[34] The Father knows his children's material needs [6:32]. How could they ever doubt that he will supply them?

'Look at the birds of the air,' says Jesus (6:26). They do not harvest and store huge quantities of food: they are both carefree and unproductive. Yet when they search for food they find it, because your Father cares for them (cf. Pss. 50:11; 147:9). *How much more* can he be trusted to feed *you*, creatures made in his image and therefore worth far more than the birds.[35] If

---

For the more positive sense 'care for, be concerned about,' see ibid., s.v. 2.; 1 Corinthians 7:32, 34a; Philippians 2:20.

[34]France 1985: 140.

birds are carefree, should not humans be? And whereas the
birds gather no harvests, a man's doing so can both dispel his
anxiety and provide the Father a means of feeding him.

There is also much theology to be learned from 'the flowers
of the field' (*ta krina tou agrou*; Matt. 6:28) and 'the grass of the
field' (*ho chortos tou agrou*; 6:30), both of which are doubtless
visible on the mountainside.[36] Their garments – surpassing
those of Solomon in splendor (cf. 1 Kings 3:13) – owe nothing
to their wearers ('they neither toil nor spin'; Matt. 6: 28) and
everything to the master Artist. If God lavishes such beauty
upon creatures so ephemeral as clusters of flowers and clumps
of grass, creatures whose beauty a fire consumes in a moment,
how much more can he be trusted to array his human creatures
in garments both useful and beautiful, in part by employing
the services of skilled seamstresses (who *do* toil and spin).[37]
A slave who remains anxious in the face of such evidence
barely trusts the Father (6:30b: *oligopistoi*).

Jesus asks: 'Is not the life [*psychē*] more than food, and the
body [*sōma*] more than clothing?' (6:25b) – to which the expected
reply is 'Yes.' The Master furnishes food and clothing *for the sake
of* the life and the body. If the Father cares about the matters

---

[35]Here, as throughout Matthew 6:25-30, Jesus argues (as rabbis often
did: Keener 1999: 247, n. 231) from the lesser to the greater (Hebrew: *qal
wachomer*, 'light and heavy'). The parallel to 6:26a in Luke 12:24 speaks
specifically of ravens (*korakes*). Concluding a similar argument, Jesus says
in Matthew 10:31b, 'you are worth more [*diapherete*, as in 6:26b] than many
sparrows [*strouthiōn*].'

[36]The *krinon* may be 'the autumn crocus, Turk's cap lily, anemone, or
gladiolus' (BAGD s.v.); but the plural *krina* suggests that Jesus had no
particular species in mind 'but was thinking of all the wonderful blooms
that adorn the fields of Galilee' (ibid.). For 'lilies,' see ESV; for 'flowers,'
NJB. This *chortos* is 'wild grass in contrast to cultivated plants' (BAGD s.v.).
Many a grassy plant bore flowers: cf. Isaiah 40:6, LXX, 'as the blossom
of grass' (*hōs anthos chortou*). How wonderful – and how embarrassing –
that little sparrows and finches (that can neither speak nor read) and little
flowers (that cattle trample on and eat) should become theologians and
teachers to creatures made in God's image: so preached Martin Luther on
Matthew 6:25-34 (in Foster and Griffin 2000: 120-123).

[37]Cf. Exodus 35:25-26. Psalm 103:15-16 and Isaiah 40:6-8 (and
1 Pet. 1:24-25) join 'grass' (LXX, *chortos*) and 'flower' (LXX, *anthos*) for a
different purpose – to show how frail and fleeting is human life.

of lesser value (his children's food and clothing), *how much more* will he care about those matters of far greater value (their *psychē* and *sōma*).[38] Moreover, the One who creates and sustains life, determines its length. 'Who of you,' asks Jesus, 'is able, by being anxious, to add one hour to his span of life?' (6:27).[39] The obvious answer – 'None of us' – is intended to banish anxiety which, left to fester, might well shorten one's life. Let the slave trust the Master to grant him a life long enough to complete his allotted work (cf. Eph. 2:10; Ps. 90:9-17).

Focusing on those greater values (the life, the body) and especially on God himself, deters disciples from being anxious about what they eat and drink and wear (Matt. 6:25, 31). Preoccupation with the latter – both the *quantity* of one's holdings (do I really have enough?) and their *quality* (does their value equal or surpass my fellow slaves' possessions?) – arouses anxiety and serves the cause of the rival god.

The sole purpose of the slave of God, his one reason for living, is to do his Master's bidding. The Master's will for his slaves – the Father's will for his children – is concisely stated toward the close of the passage: 'Seek first [*prōton*] the kingdom of God and his righteousness [*tēn dikaiosynē autou*]' (Matt. 6:33a).[40]

---

[38]In Matthew 6:25a, *psychē* denotes 'earthly life,' which requires food to sustain it. For other such instances, see, e.g., 2:20 (Herod and others 'seek the life' of Jesus) and 20:28 (Jesus 'gives his life as a ransom'). But in 10:28-31, in an argument akin to that of 6:25-30, *psychē* denotes the 'soul' as distinct from the 'body' (*sōma*): men can kill the body but not the soul (6:28a); God can destroy both in Gehenna (6:28b). For other such instances, see, e.g., 22:37 (love God 'with all your soul') and 26:38 ('my soul is very sorrowful'). For these meanings, see BAGD s.v., 1.a.-c.

[39]'One hour' translates *pēchyn hena*, literally 'one cubit'; 'his span of life,' *tēn hēlikian autou*. While *hēlikia* can be used both spatially (Luke 19:3, of Zacchaeus' small stature) and temporally (Hebrews 11:11, of Sarah's being past the age for conceiving), here in Matthew 6:27 the latter is almost certainly in view. A very slight increase is called for: one hour is much smaller in relation to one's whole life than is a cubit (eighteen inches) in relation to one's full stature (see Luke 12:25-26). While most would choose to add even one hour to their life, few would wish to grow eighteen inches. See Psalm 39:5; BAGD s.v. *hēlikia* and *pēchys*; Davies and Allison 1988: 652; France 1985: 140; Hagner 1993: 164.

[40]For support of this reading (instead of NIV's 'his kingdom and his righteousness'), see *TC*, 15-16.

This latter phrase refers primarily if not exclusively to the righteousness that God requires – the life of holiness to which he and his Messiah summon members of the new community.[41] If you are thus submissive to God's rule, continues Jesus, 'all these things will be added [*prostethēsetai*] to you' (6:33b): that is, God will supply all these necessities of life – your food, your clothing and the rest. Correspondingly, in the Lord's Prayer the plea for the kingdom's coming (6:10) precedes the request for daily bread (6:11). In the case of some disciples the Master may also choose – in view of their fidelity and in expression of his love – to 'add to' them what they could not 'add to' themselves: hours or even years of life.[42]

The Effects of Prayer

One reason Jesus repeatedly commands his followers not to be anxious (6:25, 31, 34) is that anxiety is the natural and predictable human response when one is threatened with the loss of life's necessities and therefore of life itself. A farmer and his children face starvation because a crop has failed; villagers lose everything to foreign invaders; a peasant family huddles together in sub-freezing temperatures. From such people the questions 'What shall we eat, or drink, or wear?' are not requests for information but cries of desperation.

Jesus teaches that such cries should be directed to God: 'Our bread for the coming day, give us today' (Matt. 6:11). Desperate disciples should not suppress their anxiety, or strive to overcome it before they pray, but instead make prayer an avenue for their anxiety: see the Psalms, *passim*; Philippians 4:6-7 (which begins *mē merimnate*, the very language of Matthew 6:25a), 19 (which, like Matthew 6:8, uses

---

[41]The noun *dikaiosynē* thus has the same meaning in Matthew 6:33 as in 5:20 and 6:1 (see those comments), and the personal pronoun *autou* is an *objective* genitive. See Calvin 1994: 224; Davies and Allison 1988: 661; France 1985: 141-42; Hagner 1993: 166. While the accent is on present obedience, the exercise of God's own saving *dikaiosynē* at the kingdom's consummation may also be in view, as in 5:6 (see those comments), in which case the *autou* is also a *subjective* genitive (cf. *GGBB*, 119-21, on the 'plenary genitive'). See Psalm 15:1-2 with Psalm 24:3-5.

[42]This verb *prostithēmi* ('add to, provide'; 6:27, 33) occurs nowhere else in Matthew.

chreia, 'need,' a cognate of the verb *chrēzō,* 'to have need' [6:32]); and 1 Peter 5:7 (where the cognate noun *merimna* occurs).[43] Knowing that the prayer of Matthew 6:11 has come from God through the Son, let disciples offer it not in 'little faith' but in full confidence that the Father is both able (because he is sovereign) and willing (because he is loving) to provide his children's needs. When they truly believe that the Father will supply their 'bread for the coming day' (6:11, 33b), they will be less anxious about the morrow (6:34a). Less anxious but not more naive: 'for tomorrow will have its own share of anxiety [*merimnēsei heautēs*]' (6:34b). But if *today's* sources of anxiety are augmented by *tomorrow's,* the anxiety itself will surely be compounded. So beware, says Jesus: 'For each day has its own quite sufficient supply of evil [*hē kakia autēs*]' (6:34c).[44] And when disciples are beset by threats to the very life of the body (whether theirs or someone else's), they can join prayers of desperation (that life be prolonged, despite all signs to the contrary) to prayers of submission (that the Father's will be done on earth [6:10]).[45]

The Effects of Purity of Heart

This whole sermon calls upon disciples to be 'pure in heart' – to love God with their whole being and to serve him with undivided loyalty (see comments on 5:8). We found this to be the dominant note in 6:19-24. Within the present passage its strongest expression comes in 6:33a: 'Seek first the kingdom of God and his righteousness.'[46]

The tragic irony about slavery to wealth is that persons who *possess* it do not really *enjoy* it; for if they did, why would they constantly be craving more of the same (Matt. 6:32, with

---

[43]On 'the prayer of anxiety' in Philippians 4, see Chamblin 1993: 237-39.

[44]The translation of Matthew 6:34bc comes from Hagner 1993: 161. The counsel of 6:34 is underscored in James 4:13-15. Allied to the recognition that 'each day has its own...supply of evil,' is the need to offer the petitions of Matthew 6:12-13 (like that of 6:11) every day.

[45]Cf. 26:36-46 (Jesus); 2 Kings 20:1-6 (Hezekiah); Psalm 71 (an aged believer).

[46]Isaiah 51:1 describes persons who *both* pursue righteousness (a life of holiness) *and* seek Yahweh's presence. A central theme in the writings of the Danish philosopher Søren Kierkegaard is that of *willing one thing,* which for him was seeking first the kingdom of God (see Foster and Smith 1993: 108-9, 111).

the verb *epizēteō*, 'eagerly seek')? The expected satisfaction proves to be an ever elusive goal. Moreover, in their frantic efforts to assure material and earthly security, they cannot stop long enough to behold the birds of the air, or to consider the flowers of the field; and, in any case, such leisurely pursuits would be considered a waste of valuable time. Did the rich man in the parable of Luke 12:16-21 (whose sequel, 12:22-31, parallels Matthew 6:25-34) ever stand in *wonder* before the productivity of his land, and before the produce itself, or were they both in his eyes (cf. 6:23) only means to an end? In short, to be enslaved to wealth is to lose both God and wealth.

The delightful irony about slavery to God is that the master entrusts to his slaves the very wealth from whose bondage he delivered them (6:24, 33b; cf. 25:14-30); that persons preoccupied with God are able to enjoy earthly wealth; that those who 'store up treasures in heaven' can find pleasure in things others are hoarding on earth. God's slaves – the Father's children – now perceive wealth for what it really is, the handiwork and gift of God. They view life's necessities with new eyes (6:22): besides being nourishing, meals are found to be tasty, one reason being food's exquisite colors; a woolen coat is appreciated for both its warmth and its beauty; which helps to explain believers' contentment with food and clothing (1 Tim. 6:8). Now, perhaps for the first time since childhood, they 'behold the birds' and 'consider the flowers,' and stand in wonder before the Creator's endless wisdom and artistry.[47]

---

[47]In the language of Psalm 24, it is the 'pure in heart' (24:4) who perceive most clearly that 'the earth and all that it contains belong to Yahweh' (24:1). Wrote Isaac Watts: 'Lord, how your wonders are displayed where'er I turn my eye.' See also Ecclesiastes 2:24-26; C. S. Lewis, 'First and Second Things,' in *God in the Dock*, ed. Walter Hooper (Grand Rapids: Eerdmans, 1970), 278-81 ('You can't get second things by putting them first; you can get second things only by putting first things first,' 280); Lewis 1952: 104 ('Aim at Heaven and you will get earth "thrown in": aim at earth and you will get neither'); John Eldredge, *The Journey of Desire* (Nashville: Nelson, 2000), 163-95; Philip Yancey, *Rumors of Another World* (Grand Rapids: Zondervan, 2003), *passim*.

VII.
'ALL I DESIGN OR DO OR SAY'[1]
(7:1-12)

The long middle section of the Sermon on the Mount (5:17–7:12) now concludes; 7:12 forms an inclusion with 5:17. The present passage opens with a prohibition ('do not judge'), as did the earlier ones in this section: 'do not suppose' (5:17); 'be careful not to practice' (6:1); 'do not store up' (6:19). Jesus' address to the 'hypocrite' in 7:5 recalls his use of this term (*hypokritēs*) in 6:1-18. Echoes of 6:19-34 in 7:1-12 are especially noteworthy. As 6:22-23 featured the eye, so does 7:3-5; as 6:19-24 spoke of wealth, so does 7:6 ('pearls'); as 6:25-34 stressed the heavenly Father's care for his children and argued from the lesser to the greater, so does 7:7-11.[2]

A. Making Judgments (7:1-6)
Jesus first tells disciples not to judge other people's sins, both because of the risks involved and because of their own sins (7:1-5a). When the would-be judge has heeded that counsel, he will be in a better condition to make judgments about other sinners (7:5b-6).

From Judging Others to Judging Oneself (7:1-5a)
'Do not judge [*Mē krinete*], so that you may not be judged [*mē krithēte*]. For [*gar*] with the judgment whereby [*en hō...krimati*] you judge [*krinete*] you shall be judged [*krithēsesthe*], and with the measure whereby [*en hō metrō*] you measure [*metreite*], it shall be measured [*metrēthēsetai*] to you' (Matt. 7:1-2). Jesus addresses the disciples collectively: every 'you' is plural.[3]

---

[1]Words from the hymn 'Awake, My Soul, and with the Sun,' by Thomas Ken (1695).

[2]Davies and Allison call Matthew 7:1-12 'the structural twin' of 6:19-34; see their analysis (1988: 626).

[3]There are five such verbs (four forms of *krinō*, 'to judge,' one of *metreō*, 'to measure'), and one pronoun (*hymin*, 'to you').

He commands them not to judge – or to cease from judging – lest they themselves be judged.[4] It is not retaliatory human judgments they are to fear, but the judgment of God himself: the verbs *krithēte*, *krithēsesthe* and *metrēthēsetai* are all instances of the 'divine passive.'[5] The very judgment (*krima*) by which they have judged others, and the very standard (*metros*) by which they have measured others' guilt, God will employ when judging them. Jesus' words (i) show that the human judges employ the right standard, namely the law of God (cf. Rom. 2:12b); (ii) suggest that the judges' own besetting sins are the ones they most readily condemn in others (cf. Rom. 2:1, 21-22; and see further below); and (iii) speak of God's judgments both now and at the End.[6]

Then, as often in Matthew 5–6, Jesus moves from addressing the whole company of disciples to confronting the individual (6:3): 'Why do you look at [*blepeis*] the speck of sawdust [*karphos*] in the eye [*ophthalmō*] of your [*sou*] brother [*adelphou*], but do not notice [*ou katanoeis*] the log [*dokon*] in your own eye [*ophthalmō*]?' All the terms in Matthew 7:4-5 are likewise singular. All three verses concern relationships between Christians: as in 5:22-24, the 'brother' (*adelphos* appears three times in 7:3-5) is a fellow member of the new community.[7] The prominence of the word 'eye' in these verses (*ophthalmos* occurs six times in 7:3-5) recalls its use in 5:29 and 6:22-23, statements also addressed to the individual disciple. The attitude which Jesus condemns in 7:3-5a is integral to the outlook he described as 'evil' (*ponēros*) in 6:23.

---

[4]According to *GGNT*, 890, the present imperative of prohibition in Matthew 7:1a – *Mē krinete* – is used 'to forbid what one is already doing.' Cf. Gundry 1994: 120.

[5]The first is an aorist passive subjunctive; the other two are future passive indicatives.

[6]God's present judgments anticipate his Final Judgment: for one or both aspects, see 6:14-15 (and comments); Romans 2:1-5; 14:10-12; 1 Corinthians 11:30-32; James 2:8-13; 4:11-12.

[7]James 4:11-12 warns against judging a brother (the verb *krinō*, the noun *adelphos*) with slanderous speech (the verb *katalaleō*) and (like Matthew 7:1-5) shifts from plural to singular. This text argues that such judgments (i) transgress the law (in this case, Leviticus 19:18) and thus sit in judgment on the law; and (ii) usurp the prerogative of God, the one Lawgiver and Judge.

By the same token, the course of action commended in 7:5b-6 accords with the outlook described as 'sound' (*haplous*) in 6:22.

Jesus draws a verbal cartoon: the picture of someone trying to remove a 'speck of sawdust' from another's eye while oblivious to the 'log' in his own, is as amusing as that of a person straining out a gnat but swallowing a camel (Matt. 23:24).[8] Not only is the judge oblivious to the obvious (as was the emperor to his 'new clothes'): the presence of the log makes it quite impossible to see and to remove the speck in the other person's eye; similarly, 23:24 speaks of '*blind* guides.' The point of the metaphor is not that the quantity of the judge's sins far exceeds that of the brother (though it may: cf. 18:24, 28); that brother may be judging him in the same way (the judgment of the one may well have provoked the judgment of the other) and thus have his own log to deal with. Rather, Jesus wants each disciple to face the enormity of his own sin. None of them will do so easily: we perceive others' sins more clearly than our own, and others detect our sins more readily than we do.[9] Jesus' hyperbole is an attention-getting device: Can you not *see* the obvious? Are you scrutinizing your brother's sins to escape notice of your own? Are not those sins in him that most upset you, the very ones that most sorely afflict you? Does not your preoccupation with his lust or jealousy reveal this to be one of your besetting sins (i.e., do not the sawdust and the log come from the same tree)? Is your apparent virtue concealing sins far worse than the ones you are judging? Do you not realize that you proudly taking a position above

---

[8]*Karphos*, related to the verb *karphō* ('make dry or withered'), denoted a small, dry particle, e.g. of straw, chaff, wood or wool (BAGD and LSJ s.v.). A *dokos* was a beam, or log, of wood (BAGD s.v.). I translate *karphos* 'speck of sawdust' to express its parallel with *dokos*.

[9]Says Screwtape to Wormwood: 'Aggravate that most useful human characteristic, the horror and neglect of the obvious. You must bring him to a condition in which he can practise self-examination for an hour without discovering any of those facts about himself which are perfectly clear to anyone who has ever lived in the same house with him or worked in the same office' (Lewis 1953: 20-21, in Letter 3). Cf. C. S. Lewis, 'The Trouble with "X"...,' in *God in the Dock*, ed. Walter Hooper (Grand Rapids: Eerdmans, 1970), 151-55.

your brother because you think yourself holier than he is the worst sin – the biggest plank – of all?[10]

That exposé is meant to be devastating, and to lead to decisive action: 'Hypocrite [*hypokrita*], first remove the log from your own eye' (6:5a). This vocative of address is just as arresting, and just as devastating, as the preceding metaphor: elsewhere in the sermon *hypokritēs* appears only in 6:2, 5, 16, references to persons outside the disciples' circle; 7:5 is the only place in Matthew where Jesus applies the term to the disciples themselves. The response required of each disciple is plain: let him lament his grievous sin, and fling it away in horror and disgust.[11]

From Judging Oneself to Judging Others (7:5b-6)

If every disciple sought to obey Matthew 7:1-5a, the peace of the church would be advanced immeasurably. But Jesus seeks the purity of the church too, so there remains a place for discerning and dealing with the sins of other Christians.[12] To the same end, judgments are required to determine when a disciple's profession is genuine; whether a person should be allowed to enter, or to remain in, the church; and when the church should curtail its witness to certain people.

Deal decisively with your own sin, says Jesus, 'and then you will see clearly [*diablepseis*] to remove the speck of sawdust from the eye of your brother' (Matt. 7:5b). When the log blocked your view, you could barely *see* the speck (7:2, the verb *blepō*); now, without the log, you can see it *clearly* (7:5, <u>diablepō</u>).[13] Considering how scant knowledge of the brother affected you,

---

[10]One sin condemned in Matthew 7:3-4 is 'judging a fellow disciple out of self-righteousness, i.e., in a way that shows failure to surpass the ostentatious righteousness of the scribes and Pharisees' (Gundry 1994: 121). See 5:20; 6:1-18 (and comments); Luke 16:15 (where Jesus says to the Pharisees, 'You are those who justify yourselves before men'); 18:9-14; Philippians 3:2-11.

[11]The hypocrite's motive for removing the log is closely akin to the lustful person's motive for removing his eye and his hand: the verb of 7:5, *ekballō* ('take out'), is a compound of the verb used in Matthew 5:29-30, *ballō* ('throw'). Cf. James 4:8-10; Isaiah 64:6; Philippians 3:8.

[12]In Baxter 1974, an appeal for the unity (peace) of the church, 156-63, is immediately followed by a call for church discipline (purity), 163-72.

[13]The added *dia* intensifies the meaning of the verb (Davies and Allison 1988: 673).

it might be expected that deeper insight into his sin would further heighten your sense of spiritual superiority. But no: that insight has come from insight into your own sin, and from your own chastened and repentant condition, so that you now desire to place yourself not above the brother but beside him, to bear and to relieve his burden. Having become 'poor in spirit' from seeing the enormity of your own sin, will you not deal compassionately with a brother guilty of the same?[14]

For light on what happens henceforth, we turn to 18:15-20, teaching that presupposes 7:1-6. Having removed the log from his own eye, the disciple (perhaps emulating a Christian who once confronted him) goes to the brother (*adelphos* again) in order to reveal his sin and lead him to repentance. If the brother heeds the admonition, his drift into sin is arrested and he is restored to fellowship with this disciple and the rest (18:15). If he refuses to listen, judgment from the individual disciple is followed by communal judgment – first from two or three disciples, then (if need be) from the whole church (18:16-17a). If the sinful brother remains adamant in his refusal, he is to be treated as a non-believer (18:17b); whether he is so in fact, the sequel will clarify (13:24-30, 36-43, 47-50; cf. 1 Cor. 5:5, 13). The basis for this ruling to excommunicate – and for the corresponding ruling to admit or restore a person to the church's fellowship – is the truth which Christ revealed and entrusted to his apostles (Matthew 18:18, with 16:19 and comments on these two texts).

The private encounter described in 7:5b matches that of 18:15. So too, in accord with the communal judgments of 18:16-17, Jesus in 7:6 (as in 7:1-2) addresses the disciples collectively: 'Do not give [*Mē dēte*] what is holy to the dogs, and do not throw [*mēde balēte*] your pearls in front of the pigs, lest they trample them with their feet and turn to slash you with their teeth' (Matt. 7:6).[15]

---

[14]Cf. Matthew 18:21-35, with 18:15-20 (and comments); Philippians 2:3-4; Galatians 6:1-5 (and comments in Chamblin 1993: 115-16, 121-23); Hebrews 5:2 (the high priest 'can deal gently with the ignorant and wayward, since he himself is beset with weakness,' ESV).

[15]The verbs in the prohibitions are aorist subjunctives, second person plural (from *didōmi* and *ballō*). The pronouns in the second person are also plural (*hymōn* and *hymas*). 'With their feet' translates *en tois posin autōn*;

The 'dogs' (*kynes*) of the metaphor are not domesticated pets (as in Matthew 15:26-27, where the diminutive *kynaria* is used) but those packs of wild and vicious scavengers that roamed the streets and rubbish heaps. 'Pigs' (*choiroi*) were, according to the law, unclean animals, and could be as wild and fierce as dogs. The proverb of 2 Peter 2:22 joins the two as creatures equally repulsive.[16] The structure of Matthew 6:6 is probably chiastic: giving dogs what is holy [a]; throwing pearls before pigs [b]; pigs' trampling pearls [b']; dogs' attacking their benefactors [a'].[17] How are these commands to be applied?

In my judgment, 'what is holy' (*to hagion*) and 'your pearls' (*tous margaritas hymōn*) both denote Jesus' gospel (*euangelion*) of the kingdom (4:17, 23). Declaring as it does the coming of God's rule, and salvation from sin through God's Messiah, this gospel has no peer: it is uniquely holy, uniquely set apart. For the same reasons, the message is a pearl of incomparable value: see 13:45-46, which contain the only other instances of *margaritēs* in Matthew.[18]

Verse 6 directs that the gospel be withheld from certain persons. Jesus is clearly not using 'dogs' and 'pigs' as epithets for Gentiles as such (though some Jews might do so): his gospel is for both Jews and Gentiles; and this command, accordingly, applies to persons – whether Jew or Gentile – who in some way have rejected the gospel.[19] On the one hand, there are those whose commitment to the gospel was once

---

'slash...with their teeth' paraphrases the verb *rhēgnymi*, 'tear (in pieces),' since animals tear with their teeth (BAGD s.v., 1.).

[16]For dogs and/or pigs as vicious, despised or unclean animals with disgusting or destructive habits, see Exodus 22:31; 1 Samuel 24:14; 2 Samuel 3:8; 16:9; 1 Kings 14:11; 16:4; 21:19, 23-24; 2 Kings 8:13; Job 30:1; Psalm 22:16, 20; 59:6, 14; 80:13; Proverbs 11:22; 26:11; Ecclesiastes 9:4; Isaiah 65:4; 66:3, 17; Luke 16:21; Philippians 3:2; Revelation 22:15. Keener 1999: 243, cites other Jewish texts. On reasons for pigs' legal uncleanness (Lev. 11:7; Deut. 14:8), see comments on Matthew 15:10-20.

[17]Within the metaphor, 'what is holy' may be meat for temple sacrifice. For the view that the structure is chiastic, see Carson 1984: 185; Davies and Allison 1988: 677; Gundry 1994: 123. I say 'probably' so, not 'certainly,' for dogs could trample pearls and pigs could attack people.

[18]For this understanding of 'holy' and 'pearls' in 7:6, cf., e.g., Carson 1984: 185; Davies and Allison 1988: 676; Hagner 1993: 171.

[19]This point is not contradicted by 10:5 and 15:24 (see those comments).

judged authentic, and who were thus received into the church (18:18b, 'whatever you loose,' cf. 16:19b); who later stubbornly refused to repent of sin, and were therefore banned from the fellowship (18:16-17; and 18a, 'whatever you bind,' cf. 16:19a); and who thereafter (and perhaps therefore) repudiated the message and its adherents. Those whose sin consisted of false teaching began to subvert the truth of the message while still in the church: see 7:15-23, and the indictment of false teachings in 2 Peter 2:1-21 prefacing the proverb of 2:22.

It is not a further declaration of the gospel that such people need, but sober reflection upon the gospel previously received, together with its demand for repentance (Matt. 4:17). Did they really understand the message they heard, or know the one who imparted it to them? Did they actually submit to God's rule, and count the cost of doing so? Were they ever gripped by the grace of forgiveness? Did they at the outset truly repent of a host of sins? If so, how can they now stubbornly refuse to repent of one or two? In this regard, see Matthew 13:10-17 and comments.

The dual command of 7:6 applies, on the other hand, to persons who have never joined the church; who have repeatedly spurned and scorned the gospel; who have termed its truth a lie and have sought to suppress it (i.e., to 'trample it underfoot'); who have repeatedly attacked and endangered its heralds (i.e., 'slashed them with their teeth');[20] and whose fury is only increased by fresh disclosures of the truth. Those who opposed the Master in those ways would not spare his servants – as is plain both from Jesus' warnings and from the apostles' experience. As Jesus makes equally clear, there comes a point when disciples are to stop witnessing to such persons, and to leave them (like those removed from the church) to ponder the truth already received.[21]

Three concluding observations are in order.

---

[20]Cf. the use of 'dogs' (*kynes*) in Philippians 3:2; Revelation 22:15.

[21]For the gospel's enemies (potential and actual), and judgments against them (sometimes shown by shaking dust from one's feet), see Matthew 5:11; 10:14-25; 12:31-32; 13:12-15; 22:1-14; 23:34-35; 24:9-14; John 15:18-25; Acts 13:44-51; 18:5-6; 28:17-28; 2 Timothy 3:8-13; Titus 3:10-11.

1. The character of the gospel itself explains the sternness of those actions against the apostates and the church's foes: to reject God's rule and Messiah's salvation – together the most splendid offer of grace ever – is to deserve the severest judgment. To partake of the means of grace within the new community, and then to renounce them, places one in the most perilous position.[22]

2. These judgments on the unbelieving are not irrevocable sentences to damnation; on the contrary, they can express love the intent of which is to save these enemies (5:43-48) from that final verdict. (Each true believer might well consider how *he* would want to be treated, if the situations were reversed; cf. 7:12.) Let it be hoped that the unbeliever will be sobered, even shattered, by the judgment and will in its light accurately assess his condition; and that, having recognized his sinful folly, he will flee – or return – in repentance and faith to the shelter and *shalom* of the covenant community.[23] 'Do not reprove a scoffer, or he will hate you; reprove a wise man, and he will love you.'[24] An excommunicated individual, or an erstwhile unbeliever, now made wise by the church's severe mercy, will love those who showed their love by judging him. Furthermore, the hatred of at least some scoffers is a desperate attempt to keep the Hound of Heaven at bay: perhaps their mounting hostility is a sign that they are about to capitulate to his claims upon them. Other scoffers, of course, will become yet more vehement and violent in the wake of such judgments: the sun that melts butter also hardens clay (cf. 2 Cor. 2:14-16).

3. The disciples' preeminent task is not to search zealously for ways to apply Matthew 7:6, but to obey the commission of 28:19-20, and patiently to persevere in imparting Jesus' teaching to persons both within and beyond the church.[25] It is not the case for maintaining this witness which must be proven, but the case

---

[22]See Matthew 11:20-24; 12:31-32; Hebrews 6:1-8; 10:26-31; 2 Peter 2:20-22.

[23]See 1 Corinthians 5:5; 1 Timothy 1:18-20; 2 Timothy 2:24-26.

[24]Proverbs 9:8, esv. I owe this reference to Carson 1984: 185.

[25]In so doing, they will be treating others as God and Jesus have treated them (Stott 1978: 183). Baxter 1974: 227 says that 'the worse [such persons] are, the sadder is their case, and the more to be pitied, and the more diligent should we be for their recovery.' Again he says, 237: 'Before we

for discontinuing it. Opting for the latter entails recognizing both how crucial are the issues concerned, and how perilous a hasty decision would be (cf. 1 Tim. 5:19). As it will often be extraordinarily and excruciatingly difficult to know when the time has come for excommunicating a person, or for curtailing a witness to outsiders, it is vital that judgments be *communal* – i.e., based on the careful deliberations of the gathered church and on the total deposit of apostolic teaching.[26]

B. Seeking Gifts (7:7-11)

The subject is again prayer, making requests of God: the verb *aiteō* ('ask'), which last appeared in Matthew 6:8 (just before the Lord's Prayer), is used five times in these five verses; the corresponding verbs *didōmi* ('give') and *epididōmi* ('give to') together occur five times as well (note also the noun *domata*, 'gifts,' 11). In Jesus' later teaching on prayer (during his journey to Jerusalem), material similar to 7:7-11 (see Luke 11:9-13) is closely joined to a shorter version of the Lord's Prayer (Luke 11:2-4). Why, we may ask, does Jesus choose to separate the teaching of Matthew 7:7-11 from that of 6:5-15? The present context suggests several reasons: *1.* Reserving this teaching

---

give them over, let us try the utmost, that we may have the experience of their obstinate contempt, to warrant our forsaking them. Charity beareth and waiteth long.'

[26]Cf. Matthew 18:17-18 (and the plural terms in 7:6 itself); 1 Corinthians 2:16 ('*we* have the mind of Christ'); 5:3-5 (with 4:5); 12:10 (on 'discerning spirits'); as well as assaults on false teachings in the letters of Paul, Peter, John and Jude. Bruner 2004a: 340-41 appraises three views of Matthew 7:6. (i) This verse underscores verses 1-5. 'When your Christian life is consumed with criticism you are using the gifts God gave you in a perversely wasteful way – you are throwing your pearls (your gift of the Christian life) before swine (by your excessively critical life).' (ii) Jesus urges disciples not to be fanatical in their mission. 'Aggressive evangelism often proves harmful – not only to the obdurate whose heart is hardened by the undifferentiating evangelist but also to the force-fed gospel.' (iii) This verse is a corrective to a one-sided application of verses 1-5. 'If all attempts at help must first of all be self-critical [vv. 1-5], this should not mean that we are to use no discernment at all with others. Some people have harmless specks in their eyes; others have harmful clubs in their hands. This Sum [v. 6] counsels disciples not to be stupid. We are not only to be "harmless as doves" but also "wise as serpents" (10:16).' He opts, as I have done, for the third. Willard 1998: 228-31, opting for the second view, also invokes 10:16.

for the close of the sermon's long middle section, underscores prayer's crucial importance in the life of holiness. 2. The kinship between Matthew 6:25-34 and 7:7-11 was noted above (p. 451). The promises of the second passage are stronger for being undergirded by those of the first. 3. The focus on personal relationships in both 7:1-6 and 7:12 indicates that the entreaties enjoined in verses 7-11 serve the same purpose, that the needs reflected in these surrounding verses supply much material for the disciples' prayers.

The Straightforward Appeal (7:7-8)
'Ask [*Aiteite*], and it will be given [*dothēsetai*] to you [*hymin*]; seek [*zēteite*], and you will find [*heurēsete*]; knock [*krouete*], and it will be opened [*anoigēsetai*] to you [*hymin*]. For [*gar*] everyone who asks [*pas...ho aitōn*] receives [*lambanei*], and the one who seeks [*ho zētōn*] finds [*heuriskei*], and to the one who knocks [*tō krouonti*] it will be opened [*anoigēsetai*].'

In 7:7, as in verse 6, Jesus addresses the disciples collectively: the verbs *aiteite, zēteite* and *krouete,* and the pronoun *hymin* (used twice) are second person plural. The verbs are conditional imperatives: 'if you ask [and you should], it will be given,' etc. They are also iterative presents: 'ask repeatedly...seek over and over again,' etc.[27] The acts here commanded are not successive: in that case the more natural order would be to seek, to knock and to ask. The three imperatives are joined for emphasis, to urge disciples to bring requests boldly and persistently to God; the verb most clearly expressive of prayer, 'ask,' comes first (note its further use in 7:8-11). That Jesus has already given disciples a pattern for such prayers (6:9-13) bolsters their confidence still more.[28] The presence in 7:7 of the imperative *zēteite* recalls its use in 6:33 (the only prior instance of the verb *zēteō* in the sermon): 'Seek first the kingdom of God and his righteousness.'[29] This suggests that the disciples' most

---

[27]*GGBB* uses Matthew 7:7 as an example of both the conditional imperative (pp. 489-90) and the iterative present (pp. 521-22).

[28]In Jesus' later teaching, the parable of Luke 11:5-8 (between the Lord's Prayer and teaching parallel to Matthew 7:7-11) encourages *audacity* in prayer, 8 (cf. ESV, 'impudence').

[29]The verb *krouō* ('to knock'; 7:7, 8) occurs nowhere else in Matthew.

ardent, most persistent request should be that the Father's name be hallowed, his kingdom come, and his will be done on earth (the threefold petition of Matthew 6:9b-10). Given the identity and the authority of the one who taught them this prayer, how could disciples doubt the Father's willingness and readiness to answer it (see Luke 12:32), together with requests based upon it (Matt. 6:11-13)? The other verbs in 7:7 should dispel all lingering doubt: *dothēsetai, heurēsete* and *anoigēsetai*. These are all future indicatives. The second (from *heuriskō*) is in the active voice: disciples will find. The first and the third (from *didōmi* and *anoigō*) are instances of the 'divine passive': God will give, and God will open. As noted, verbs for 'give' are prominent throughout the passage, as is the matching verb 'ask.'

That appeal, already strong, is reinforced in 7:8, whose opening *gar* ('for') joins it to verse 7. Having there addressed the whole company of disciples, Jesus now speaks of the individual, though in the third person and not (as often earlier) in the second. Yet his promise is as comprehensive as before: '*everyone* who asks....' The verbs used as present imperatives in 7:7 appear here as present participles: *aitōn, zētōn* and *krouonti*. Correspondingly, the *lambanō* of 8 matches the *didōmi* of 7:7; the verb *heuriskō* of 7:7 recurs in verse 8; and both verses use the same form of *anoigō*. Thus in these two verses Jesus states his appeal in the strongest terms; but his case for trusting the Father is not yet complete.

The Supportive Argument (7:9-11)

'Or what man [*tis...anthrōpos*] is there among you who, when his son asks for bread [*arton*], will give him a stone [*lithon*]? Or if he asks for a fish [*ichthyn*], he will not give him a snake [*ophin*], will he? If then [*oun*] you [*hymeis*], although evil [*ponēroi ontes*], know to give good gifts [*domata agatha*] to your [*hymōn*] children, how much more [*posō mallon*] will your [*hymōn*] Father who is in heaven give good things [*agatha*] to those who ask him?' Here, as in 7:7-8, Jesus addresses the whole company of disciples (7:11, with its plural terms noted above), but also challenges the individual listener (7:9-10, 'what man...among you?').

The questions of verses 9 and 10 are put to parents.[30] Bread and fish were the commonest of foods for Galileans.[31] Some loaves of bread were shaped like a round stone; and some fish, 'particularly the eel-like catfish of Galilee, *Clarias lazera*,' resembled a snake.[32] What father, whose hungry son has requested bread, would serve a stone instead – making him the butt of a cruel joke or demanding that he eat the inedible? Or what Jewish mother, whose daughter is awaiting broiled fish, would serve a snake instead – at best (if dead) an unclean animal, at worst (if alive) a dangerous one?[33] No explicit answers to Jesus' questions are needed: both naturally and grammatically, negative replies are assumed.[34]

That is confirmed in Matthew 7:11: parents know how to give, and do give, *good* gifts to their children. Yet these donors are described not merely as human but as *evil*, as *ponēros* – the only place in the sermon where this term is directly applied to the disciples collectively.[35] The word is meant to be shocking, and to point up the stark contrast between the best of earthly fathers (and mothers) and the heavenly Father. As elsewhere, Jesus argues from the lesser to the greater: 'If then *you*, although evil,[36] are in the habit of responding to your children's entreaties with good gifts, *how much more* will

---

[30]The noun *anthrōpos* includes women as well as men: cf. 7:9a in NLT, 'You parents....' Verse 9 speaks of a 'son' (*huios*), but verse 10 of 'children' (*tekna*, embracing sons and daughters).

[31]As noted on page 299, Jesus probably preaches this sermon on a mountainside overlooking the Sea of Galilee, which supplied fish in abundance. Near the same lake, he feeds a multitude on bread and fish (14:17; the same Greek terms as in 7:9-10); according to John 6:9, these loaves (of barley) and fish are supplied by a small boy, i.e., someone's son (cf. Matt. 7:9).

[32]France 1985: 144.

[33]The snake was legally unclean because it lacked fins for swimming and feet for walking: cf. Leviticus 11:9-12, 41-42; and Wenham 1979: 174, 178.

[34]The construction in both 7:9 and 10 is *mē epidōsei*, 'he will not give... will he?' The Greek *ou epidōsei* would be translated, 'will he not give...?' See BDF, par. 427.

[35]The closest approach to this usage, 6:23, 'if your eye is evil [*ponēros*],' is addressed to the individual. For the other instances, see 5:11, 37, 39, 45; 6:13; 7:17, 18.

[36]The pronoun *hymeis* ('you') is emphatic. In the phrase *ponēroi ontes* the present participle (from *eimi*, 'to be') is concessive (*GGNT*, 1129).

the heavenly Father – the God who is utterly free from evil and who alone is good [agathos, 19:17, with Mark 10:18] – give good things [agatha] to those who ask him?'[37]

'Thus the center of gravity lies in the heavenly Father's giving, not in the disciples' asking.'[38] That he is the great Giver is already clear from the passive verbs of Matthew 7:7-8, but his full name is reserved for the climax of the passage: 'your Father who is in heaven' (7:11b). This very name for God appeared most recently in 6:9a, which suggests that Jesus wants his listeners (and Matthew, his readers) to recall that prayer and its petitions.[39] As noted in comments on 7:7-8, God's *kingdom* (6:10) is one of the choicest of the 'good things' he gives. So also is the *Son* whom the Father sends to rule in that kingdom, through whose redemptive work the Father forgives his people's sins (6:12).[40] So too is the *Holy Spirit* through whose power God's will is done, and his rule established, on earth: whereas 7:11 promises *agatha* from God, the parallel in Luke 11:13 focuses on his gift of the *pneuma hagion*.

If the Father has bestowed those – the finest gifts of all – upon his people, can he not be trusted to meet their lesser needs as well (6:11; cf. Rom. 8:32)? Has not that truth been elegantly expounded in 6:25-34? Can he not also be trusted to equip disciples for dealing with the relational problems reflected in 7:1-12? Will he not supply the wisdom (*sophia*)

---

[37]For the same kind of argument (Hebrew *qal wachomer*, 'light and heavy'), see 6:25-30 (and p. 446, n. 35). The phrase used in 7:11, *posō mallon* ('how much more'), recurs in the kindred teaching of Luke 11:13; note again the parable in 11:5-8 (if an irate father, wakened from sleep, will supply a neighbor all the bread he needs, how much more can a loving Father, who never sleeps and cannot be irritated, be trusted to provide his people's daily bread?).

[38]Gundry 1994: 123.

[39]The phrases of Matthew 6:9 and 7:11 are identical except that the latter has the nominative for 'Father' (*patēr*, instead of the vocative *pater*) and the pronoun 'your' (*hymōn*, instead of *hēmōn*, 'our'). For earlier instances in the sermon, see 5:16, 45; 6:1. Slightly different language – 'your heavenly Father' – appears in 5:48; 6:14, 26, 32.

[40]Cf. 1:21; 20:28; 26:28. David, an evil father, was willing to give a good gift to his evil son Absalom (cf. 7:11a) by dying for him (2 Sam. 18:33). Yet *how much greater* the heavenly Father's love for his people in sacrificing his beloved Son for their sins; and *how much greater* the Son's own love for them in bearing their sins, something David could not do for Absalom.

needed for discerning the true condition of persons both within and beyond the church, and the love (*agapē*) needed for relating to persons whom they have both wrongfully and rightfully judged?[41] When disciples stop wrongly judging others, forgive those who have wronged them (perhaps by the same kind of judgments), and treat others as they themselves would want to be treated (7:12), will they not discover that the good gifts the Father grants them in return far exceed the ones they have given (Luke 6:37-38)?

Yet asking is vital: on this note the passage begins (Matt. 7:7a) and ends (7:11b). The point is not that the Father will supply *only* what his children request (see Eph. 3:20); nor that he will surely give them *everything* they ask for (see Matthew 21:22, and comments); but that all too often, we do not *have* because we do not *ask God* (see James 4:2).[42]

C. Doing Righteousness (7:12)

'Therefore [*oun*], all things – however many – which you want [*thelēte*] men to do for you [*hymin*], you yourselves are to do [*hymeis poieite*] for them [*autois*]; for this is the law and the prophets.' Jesus continues to address the whole company of disciples. He speaks of their relationships both to each other and to persons outside the church: 'men' (*anthrōpoi*) is all-inclusive, whereas 'brother' (*adelphos*; Matt. 7:3-5) specifically denotes fellow believers. We first consider the 'golden rule' itself, then its context (whose importance is indicated by the opening and the close of the verse).

The Content of the Rule

Jesus speaks both of *willing* (*thelēte*) and of *doing* (*poieite*). The acts contemplated are to be done for the sake of, for the benefit of, others; so the dative pronouns *hymin* and *autois* are translated 'for you' and 'for them.'[43] Also to be noted is the inexact parallel:

---

[41]The Holy Spirit promised in Luke 11:13 grants both *agapē* (Gal. 5:22; Rom. 5:5) and *sophia* (1 Cor. 2:6-16; Eph. 1:17).

[42]The verb *aiteō* ('ask') occurs in all three of these verses.

[43]Both verbs are second person plurals in the present tense, the first a subjunctive from *thelō*, the second an imperative from *poieō*. On the 'dative

'which you *want* men to do for you...*do* for them,' not 'what others *do* for you, *do* for them.' Nothing is said about responding to another's deed. Every disciple is challenged to initiate action: 'you yourselves' (*hymeis*) are to act – not in answer to another person's kindness (or advance 'reward') but in obedience to the Father's command (22:39) and in faith that he himself will reward you.[44]

This 'golden rule' appears often in ancient sources. Both here and in Luke 6:31 Jesus formulates the command positively: 'what you want others to do, do also.'[45] The negative form occurs, for example, in Tobit 4:15, 'Do to no one what you would not want done to you' (NJB).[46] The latter is of course a legitimate formulation. Scripture itself often commands love of neighbor in negative terms: see Leviticus 19:18 ('You shall not take vengeance... you shall love your neighbor'); Exodus 20:13-17 (five commands all beginning, 'You shall not...'); Romans 13:8-10 (which quotes four of those commands to show that loving one's neighbor means doing him no wrong); and Jesus' own negative formulations earlier in the sermon, for example in his teaching about murder and adultery (Matt. 5:21-30). Yet the positive formulation of 7:12 is closer than the negative to the heart of the love command: '*love* your neighbor...*do* for him.' The positive form embraces the negative, whereas adhering exclusively to the latter might justify negligence: a disciple might *both* resolve not to harm a neighbor *and* refuse to help him. Cf. Psalm 34:14, 'Turn away from evil *and do good; seek peace and pursue it*' (quoted in 1 Peter 3:11); 37:27a; James 4:17; and places earlier in this

---

of interest' (including advantage and disadvantage), see *GGBB*, 142-44. To render *hymin* and *autois* 'to you' and 'to them' (so ESV) suggests that they are merely indirect objects, and does not adequately express the element of personal interest.

[44]The *hymeis* is emphatic. On the rewards, see comments on Matthew 6:1-18.

[45]According to Keener 1999: 248, the positive form appears as early as Homer, and recurs in Herodotus, Isocrates and Seneca. One explanation for the term 'golden rule' is that a later Roman emperor, Alexander Severus, reputedly had it written in gold on his wall (France 1985: 145).

[46]For an example from an early Christian document, see *Didache* 1:2. For other instances of the negative form in Greek and Jewish sources, see Keener 1999: 248, 249.

sermon where Jesus enjoins disciples to give to others, and to overcome evil with good (e.g., Matt. 5:38-42, 43-48; 6:3; 7:5).[47]

The Context of the Rule

Matthew 7:11 made it plain that men's giving cannot compare to God's. At the same time, the heavenly Father's habit of giving good things to his children offers a pattern for their own behavior: thus the opening 'therefore' (*oun*) of verse 12 indicates, and so Jesus stated in 5:48.[48] Believers have freely received from the Father, so let them freely give to others (10:8). As noted above (p. 464), the *agapē* they require for heeding the instruction of 7:1-6, is itself one of the Father's *agatha*.

There is a larger context beyond 7:1-12. The first word in the Greek text of 7:12 – *panta*, 'all things' – shows that the rule's application is all-encompassing. The point is underscored at the close of the verse: 'for this is the law and the prophets.' These, the final words of the sermon's long middle section, form an inclusion with its opening verse (5:17), which also speaks of 'the law' and 'the prophets.' Jesus here declares that the OT's teaching about love for neighbor is captured in the golden rule, and thus that fidelity to this command is vital for

---

[47]See those comments. Implicit in the negative commands of Exodus 20:13-17 are calls for positive acts – e.g., saving human life and cherishing one's wife. Anticipating Jesus' language in 7:12 are a pair of earlier Jewish texts: Ecclesiasticus 31:15 ('Judge your fellow-guest's needs by your own, be thoughtful in every way,' NJB) and Letter of Aristeas 207 ('Just as you do not wish evils to befall you, but to participate in all that is good, so you should deal with those subject to you and with offenders': in Keener 1999: 248). France 1985: 145, having cited those texts, says that 'Jesus was apparently the first to formulate [the rule] explicitly, and he elevates it to a place of new importance' by saying that 'this is the law and the prophets' (Matt. 7:12b).

[48]Gundry 1994: 125 also stresses the link between 7:12 and 11.

[49]France 1985: 145 says that 7:12 presents the 'greater righteousness' of 5:20 'in a nutshell.' As noted, 7:12 (with its 'men') does not confine neighbors to fellow Christians; cf. Luke 10:27-37, where a Samaritan loves a Jewish neighbor as himself; and Romans 13:8-10, where among the neighbors to be loved are civil magistrates (13:1-7). Matthew 22:40, embracing as it does both love commands (22:37-39), speaks of 'the whole [*holos*] law and the prophets'; as 7:12 focuses on love for neighbor, the word 'whole' is lacking (noted by Gundry 1994: 125). Galatians 5:14 declares that 'the whole law' (*ho*...

attaining the greater righteousness of 5:20.[49] Disciples remain 'evil' (7:11), but they must nonetheless seek that righteousness – that holiness – required of persons under God's rule (6:33). So, 7:12 relates to everything Jesus has said about human relationships in 5:17-7:11; to ponder each of those texts in turn, with 7:12 always in mind, would be a helpful exercise. Let us also recall, from 6:1-24, that unless we love God supremely, we will not properly love our neighbors (note the verb *agapaō* in 6:24); and that love for God finds expression in love for other people. See comments on 22:34-40.

That middle section provides a bridge to 5:3-16, which is foundational for the whole sermon. On the one hand, these opening verses offer avenues for obeying 7:12 – for example, the good works (5:16) of showing mercy (5:7) and making peace (5:9). On the other hand, depicted here are persons who have failed to obey 7:12 (and all those other commands), who grieve over their sins and who recognize anew their acute need of divine grace and power (5:3-6).

---

pas nomos) is fulfilled in the command of Leviticus 19:18b; i.e., everything the Torah teaches about human relationships is thus summarized. Cf. Rabbi Hillel's comment on the golden rule's negative form: 'Do not do to your fellow what you hate to have done to you. This is the whole Law, entire; the rest is explanation. Go, learn!' (in Keener 1999: 249).

VIII.
'Confirm our Will to do the Right'[1]
(7:13-29)

Jesus has proclaimed 'the blessings of the kingdom' (5:3-16) and expounded 'the righteousness of the kingdom' (5:17–7:12). He now sets before all his listeners 'the two alternatives' (7:13-27). There are only these two. Nor is there neutral ground: every person chooses the one or the other. The sharp division Jesus makes here at the sermon's close is not between *disciples* and the *crowd* (though, as noted earlier, this is an important distinction): some present disciples will become apostates, and some members of the crowd will become true disciples. Nor does Jesus here divide those who have *heard* him from those who have *not*: both groups in 7:24-27 have heard his words.[2] Instead, Jesus divides those who *do* his words, and *do* his Father's will, from those who do *not* (7:21, 24, 26).[3] Those who obey will be richly rewarded; disaster awaits the lawless. At the chapter's close (7:28-29), Matthew describes the crowds' response to Jesus' teaching.

A. Ways Wide and Narrow (7:13-14)
'Enter [*Eiselthate*] through the narrow gate [*tēs stenēs pylēs*]. For [*hoti*] wide is the gate [*hē pylē*] and broad is the road [*hē hodos*] that leads [*hē apagousa*] to destruction, and there are many [*polloi*] who enter [*hoi eiserchomenoi*] through it. How [*ti*] narrow [*stenē*] is the gate [*hē pylē*] and confined is the road [*hē*

---

[1]Words from the hymn 'O Splendor of God's Glory Bright,' by Ambrose of Milan (340–97), translation compiled by Louis F. Benson (1910).

[2]Note the verb *akouō* ('to hear') in Matthew 7:24 and 26, its only occurrences in the sermon apart from the opening words of 5:21, 27, 33, 38 and 43.

[3]The verb is *poieō*: 'to do' the Father's will (7:21), 'to keep' Jesus' words (7:24, 26). This verb occurs nine times in 7:13-27, nearly as often as in the rest of the sermon (13).

hodos] that leads [*hē apagousa*] to life, and there are few [*oligoi*] who find it.' This translation is based on the text of *GNT*. One variant lacks the second 'gate' in Matthew 7:13 and reads 'the road is wide and easy' (RSV mg.). In another, 7:14 begins not with 'How' (*ti*) but – like 7:13b – with 'For' (*hoti*); so, e.g., ESV.[4] Literary features of the adopted text will be considered as we proceed.

It is already clear (i) that, in teaching about the two ways, Jesus again expounds an OT motif;[5] (ii) that here, as in Psalm 1, both ways represent responses to truth (or *torah*) from God, in this instance truth as imparted by the divine Messiah (5:3–7:12); (iii) that in some respects the two ways are alike (in each case a gate opens onto a road with a destination); (iv) that in other respects the two are polar opposites (one is wide, leading to destruction; the other is narrow, leading to life);[6] and (v) that making the right choice is urgent (the imperative in 7:13a, and the 'How' of 14a).

The Opening Imperative (7:13a)
The first word of 7:13 – *eiselthate*, from *eiserchomai* – is in the second person plural: Jesus addresses all his listeners. The mood of the verb is imperative – not one of entreaty but of command, given the urgency of the matter. As the lone imperative in the two verses, it stands out all the more. The aorist tense in this instance signals a single, decisive action.[7]

The reference in this command to a gate but not to a road, and the order 'gate...road' in both 7:13b and 14a, indicate that the gate stands at the entrance to the road, not at its end. We may envisage a man passing through the gate of his city to

---

[4]For support of the readings in *GNT*, see *TC*, 16-17; Hagner 1993: 177-78.

[5]Gundry 1994: 127 cites Deuteronomy 11:26-28; 30:15-20; Psalm 1:6; 119:29-30; 139:24; Jeremiah 21:8; and extra-biblical Jewish and Christian sources. Keener 1999: 250 cites Greek and Roman writers as well.

[6]In John Bunyan's *Pilgrim's Progress*, Christian travels *from* the City of Destruction to the Celestial City.

[7]The imperative of command (*GGBB*, 485-86) is distinct from the imperative of request, or entreaty (ibid., 487-88). Given the nature of the action in 13a (entering through a gate), and its urgency, it hardly matters whether the aorist *eiselthate* is termed ingressive or constative (the two kinds of aorist imperative discussed in ibid., 719-21).

embark on a journey to another.[8] This point of entry is again stressed in Matthew 7:13b: the many 'enter through' (the very verb and preposition of 7:13a) the wide gate onto the broad road.[9] At some future date, people will enter the kingdom of heaven (7:21; *eiserchomai* again). But the present hour is critical. The command of 7:13a calls for swift and resolute action, lest by deferring a decision, or deciding for the wrong path, one be denied the life of the kingdom. Exercise your will now, says Jesus; submit to God's rule and to Messiah's *torah*. For in the end it is their will, and theirs alone, which determines a person's destiny (7:21-23).[10]

To show how wise it is to obey that command, Jesus presents two supportive arguments, both of them statements of fact.

The Wide Way (7:13b)

This first argument is directly joined to the command by the opening 'For' (*hoti*). Jesus employs the imagery of a *wide gate*, such as one would pass through on entering or leaving a large city, and of a *broad road*, along which one would travel on relatively flat country.[11] In both constructions the adjective appears in the predicate position: 'wide [*plateia*] is the gate [*hē pylē*], and broad [*eurychōros*] is the road [*hē hodos*].' Moreover, this order (adjective, article, noun) rather than the other (article, noun, adjective) suggests that the adjective

---

[8]On the contrary view ('the intended picture is that of a roadway leading to a gate,' *TC*, 16), the order 'gate...road' is an instance of *hysteron proteron*, 'latter [then] former.'

[9]The phrase in Matthew 7:13a is *dia tēs...pylēs* ('through the...gate'); in 7:13b, *dia autēs* ('through it'). As both *pylē* and *hodos* are feminine nouns, the feminine pronoun *autēs* agrees with both. It is the common *dia* that links 'it' to 'gate' rather than to 'road.' Whereas the imperative of 7:13a, *eiselthate*, is aorist (see n. 7), the participle of 7:13b, *eiserchomenoi*, is present, signaling repeated or regular occurrences (*iterative* and *customary* presents respectively: *GGBB*, 520-22).

[10]Cf., e.g., the parables of Matthew 25. The end 'will not be the time for choosing: it will be the time when we discover which side we really have chosen, whether we realised it before or not. Now, today, this moment, is our chance to choose the right side' (Lewis 1952: 51).

[11]Gundry 1994: 127.

is slightly more emphatic than the noun.[12] What does this imagery depict?

Passing through the wide gate onto the broad road illustrates negative responses to the exposition of law in Matthew 5:17–7:12. Listeners might reason: we are already severely restricted by Moses' commands; Jesus would narrow our path yet further. Or: walking our present path is unbearably difficult owing to strictures imposed by the laws of Moses and 'the tradition of the elders';[13] adding Jesus' commands to those would immobilize us altogether. Or: we resolved to keep the law according to Jesus; but so radical are its demands that we failed at every turn to meet them, and are now more deeply mired in guilt than ever before. So it is not surprising that the promise of a broader way – one less confining and more liberating – appeals to many (*polloi*, 6:13b). Luring them onto that path are their own arguments or those of antinomian false prophets or both.[14] Moreover, such people's rejection of Jesus' law exposes their failure to embrace his *euangelion*, that other dimension of his *torah* (5:3-16, with 4:23-25). Indeed the main reason they find his laws frightening or repellant, is that they have ignored or spurned the gospel that undergirds them – and have failed to grasp that the gospel's promises are just as radical as the law's demands.

Commencing the journey on that broad way can be exciting and exhilarating: one is at last freed from slavery to law, and free for self-advancement and self-actualization. Yet this freedom promised by the propagandists (oneself and others) proves to be illusory. To replace God's law with one's own (for it is impossible to live without adherence to some law) is to be ensnared by a new slavery whose ultimate reward is destruction (*apōleia*; Matthew 7:13b; the LXX of Psalm 1:6 uses the matching verb *apollymi*).

---

[12]So *GGBB*, 307–8. When the adjective is in the 'second predicate position' (i.e., after the article and noun), as, e.g., in Matthew 5:12, noun and adjective appear to receive equal stress, or the noun slightly more (ibid., 308).

[13]See 15:1-9; 23:1-32, especially 4 and 13.

[14]On antinomian false prophets, see Gundry 1994: 127, and below on 7:15-23.

The Narrow Way (7:14)

The conjunction 'for' joins the argument of 7:13b to the opening command; this second argument makes the connection by using the very language of the command: 'How narrow [*stenē*] is the gate [*hē pylē*]' (7:14a) (cf. 'the narrow gate [*tēs stenēs pylēs*]' [7:13a]). As in 7:13b, Jesus' imagery is drawn from real life. This *narrow gate* was apparently 'a small, doorlike gate set within or beside the large city gate in order that known citizens might be allowed into the closed city at night and in times of danger.' And on mountainous terrain, as opposed to flat country, *confined* is the *road* one must travel.[15] Both the adjective *stenē* and the adjectival participle *tethlimmenē* ('confined,' from the verb *thlibō*, 'press') appear in the predicate position, like their counterparts in 7:13b and for the same purpose. Indeed, the whole structure of 7:14 very closely parallels that of 13b.[16]

Entering through the narrow gate onto the constricted path illustrates the positive response to the exposition of 5:17–7:12. Persons embark on this journey knowing how demanding these laws are, and how radical is the obedience Jesus requires of his followers – knowing, in other words, how narrow are the spaces they occupy. As with the 'many' of Matthew 7:13b, the response of the 'few' to Jesus' law reveals their attitude to his *euangelion*. The gospel too requires entry through a narrow gate: trusting (despite all appearances to the contrary) that God's kingdom has drawn near; submitting to his rule (rather than to my own); and repenting of sin. But the gospel *itself* is pure promise and pure grace: believing that promise, experiencing that grace, and loving the Messiah who announces and embodies them both, motivates persons to obey his commands. Having chosen this narrow path of fidelity to the law, one discovers precisely here, within the law's strictures, his true liberty and his surest protection from manifold evil.[17] Moreover, the Lawgiver

---

[15]Gundry 1994: 127. Entrances to colleges of Cambridge University similarly feature small doors within larger ones.

[16]On the adjectives of Matthew 7:13b, see page 470. Every term in 7:13b has its counterpart in verse 14; the matching terms all appear in the same order, and 12 of them are identical.

[17]Cf. Psalms 1:2-3 (the prosperity of the one who meditates on the *Torah*); 119:45 ('I shall walk in a wide place, for I have sought your precepts,' ESV).

himself accompanies those who travel this road, offering them his own example of fidelity to his teaching, and enabling them to keep his commands.[18]

While the broad road leads to destruction, this confined (*tethlimmenē*) road beset with difficulty (*thlipsis*) leads 'to life' (*eis tēn zōēn*).[19] This is the joyous discovery for those who persevere: *hoi heuriskontes* ('who find') *autēn* ('it,' namely 'life'). The Father promises (i) that he will give the kingdom to those who ask him for it (Matt. 7:7a) and who obey his will (6:10); (ii) that those who seek the kingdom, together with the holiness essential for it (6:33) will surely find it (7:7b; *heuriskō*, the verb of 7:14); and (iii) that he will open the door of his house to faithful believers who knock and ask for entry (7:7c) both now (at the kingdom's inaugural) and then (at its consummation).[20]

While many (*polloi*) take the broad path to destruction, there are few (*oligoi*) who find life. So a question arises, the very one later put to Jesus: 'Lord, will those who are saved be few [*oligoi*]?' (Luke 13:23, ESV). Very reminiscent of Matthew 7:13 is his reply (7:24): 'Strive to enter [*eiselthein*] through the narrow door [*dia tēs stenēs thyras*]; for [*hoti*] many [*polloi*], I tell you, will seek to enter [*eiselthein*] but will not be able.'[21] Although Jesus speaks of the 'many,' he does not directly answer the question: theoretically, there could be as many to enter through that door as not. Here, as in 7:13, the burden of the text lies in the opening command: let every listener

---

[18]See Matthew 11:28-30; 28:19-20. Jesus 'lived out the narrow standards of the Sermon on the Mount, and...demonstrated how different such narrowness is from a dry and loveless narrow-mindedness' (Wenham 1989: 195-96).

[19]Cf. Romans 6:15-23. *Thlibō* ('press, oppress, afflict') and *thlipsis* ('oppression, affliction, tribulation'), are cognates. Cf. Matthew 5:10-12; and the instances of *thlipsis* in 13:21; 24:9; Acts 14:22.

[20]Cf. Mark 10:15, 'Truly, I say to you, whoever does not *receive* the kingdom of God [as now proclaimed], will never *enter* into it [at the last day].' With the latter, cf. Matthew 7:21 ('shall enter into the kingdom...'), 22 ('on that day'). See also Keener 1999: 250.

[21]The aorist infinitive *eiselthein* corresponds to the aorist imperative *eiselthate* (Matt. 7:13). Luke 13:24 likewise uses a plural imperative (the present *agōnizesthe*), for Jesus is addressing a company of people even though an individual posed the question (13:23).

squarely face the most crucial question of all – the *way* of his salvation – and allow nothing, including curiosity about the relative *number* of the saved, to divert his attention from it.[22] Still, the straightforward declarations of 7:13b-14 remain; and they are most naturally interpreted to embrace the entire history of mankind (not just Jesus' generation), and to mean that the persons who perish will outnumber those who enter into life. Yet the fact also remains that during that history a huge number of people will enter through that narrow gate, so that in the end the redeemed will prove to be a 'great multitude [*ochlos polys*] that no one could number' (Rev. 7:9).[23]

B. Professions False and True (7:15-23)

The passage speaks of persons who appear to represent Christ (Matt. 7:15-20) and who profess to know him (7:21-23). The focus is especially on spurious disciples, and on tests for determining them to be so – tests which also identify reliable witnesses and true believers. From the opening warning to the terrifying close, these words are intended (as were those in 7:13-14) for both disciples and crowd.

Warnings about False Prophets (7:15-20)
Here, as in 7:13-14, an opening command is supported by the rest of the paragraph – which in this case offers listeners essential help for obeying the command.

---

[22]It might also be asked: Does the *polloi* of Matthew 7:13b include persons who have never heard of Jesus and his message? Though the question is worth pondering, one might use it to deflect the command of 13a. Nor does this text address this question. 'The whole picture seems to relate only to those who have had the opportunity of decision for or against Christ [see 5:1-2; 7:28-29]; it simply leaves out of view those who have never heard' (Stott 1978: 196).

[23]B. B. Warfield, 'Are They Few That Be Saved?' in *Biblical and Theological Studies* (Philadelphia: Presbyterian & Reformed, 1968), 334-50, commenting on Matthew 7:13-14 and Luke 13:23-24 (and Matthew 22:14), rightly stresses the cruciality of personal decision (338, 340). He further concludes, in light of the parables of 13:31-35, (i) that the 'few' in 7:14 refers only to 'the initial stages of the kingdom' (348), and (ii) that 'the number of the saved shall in the end be not small but large, and not merely absolutely but comparatively

1. The command

'Beware of [*Prosechete apo*] false prophets [*tōn pseudoprophētōn*], who come to you in sheep's clothes but inwardly are ravenous wolves' (7:15).[24] Dressed like sheep (*probata*), they appear to be true disciples. But in reality they are predatory wolves (*lykoi*) who imperil persons both within and beyond the church – or sheep both actual and potential.[25] Their disguise makes their prey more vulnerable to their assaults.

Who are these 'false prophets'? To judge from the immediate context, they pose various dangers. Verses 16-20 warn of disciples who behave like the hypocrites censured in Matthew 6:1-18; who honor God with their lips but do not love him 'inwardly' (*esōthen*), i.e., in their hearts; who do not practice what they preach; whose teaching therefore lacks authority, or leads people astray, or brings them under the prophets' power.[26] That this warning is immediately preceded by the figure of the two ways, indicates that some false prophets are luring people onto the broad road of antinomianism: besides 7:13-14 (and those comments), see 7:23, where Jesus banishes workers of 'lawlessness' (*anomia*), and 24:11-12, where *many* false prophets lead *many* astray (*polloi*, as in 7:13b), so that lawlessness (*anomia* again) increases.[27] The most insidious form of such propaganda

---

large; that...it shall embrace the immensely greater part of the human race' (349). In my judgment, 7:14 itself does not justify that restriction (i); and 13:31-35 illustrates the steady growth of the kingdom and the number of the redeemed, but not the reversal of which Warfield speaks (ii). Motyer (1999: 88) notes that Isaiah, like the NT, 'holds in tension the forecast of a (mere) remnant and the multitude of the redeemed.'

[24]The verb *prosechō* appears only once more in the sermon (and in Matthew) – in Matthew 6:1, where it is again a present imperative in the second person plural.

[25]'Sheep' (*probata*, pl. of *probaton*) serves as a picture of true disciples (10:16; 25:33) and of the lost who need saving (9:36; 10:6; 15:24). For wolves (*lykoi*, pl. of *lykos*) as a dire threat to sheep, i.e., to God's people, see 10:16; John 10:12; Acts 20:29.

[26]See Matthew 7:29; 15:7-9; 23:2-3 *et seq.* (including the use of *esōthen* in vv. 25, 27, 28); 24:11.

[27]The *anti*nomian is *against* law; *a*nomia (with *alpha-privative*) signals life *without* law.

comes from persons who, in the language of 23:28, appear to be law-keepers (*dikaioi*) but whose hearts (*esōthen* again) are full of hypocrisy (*hypokrisis*) and lawlessness (*anomia*). The present passage's immediate sequel (7:21-23) reveals moreover that certain false prophets will use extraordinary *visible* phenomena ('did we not cast out demons...and do many mighty works?') to strengthen the effect of their *verbal* witness ('did we not prophesy?'); cf. 24:24, where false prophets' 'great signs and wonders' threaten to lead even the elect astray.[28]

2. The test

The rest of the paragraph tells how such persons can be identified: 'From their fruits [*apo tōn karpōn*] you will recognize them. Men do not gather grapes from thorn-bushes, or figs from thistles, do they? So every good tree [*dendron agathon*] produces good fruits [*karpous kalous*], but the decayed tree [*sapron dendron*] produces bad fruits [*karpous ponērous*]. A good tree is not able [*ou dynatai*] to produce bad fruit, nor a decayed tree to produce good fruits. Every tree not producing good fruit is cut down and thrown into the fire. So then, from their fruits you will recognize them' (Matt. 7:16-20).

The opening of 7:16 is exactly repeated in verse 20. By means of this inclusion, the test for recognizing false prophets is stated in the clearest and the strongest terms.[29] The noun *karpos* ('fruit') occurs seven times in these five verses (and nowhere else in the sermon), further evidence that fruit-bearing is crucial. The NT speaks far more often of

---

[28]Cf. 2 Thessalonians 2:9-10; Revelation 13:13-14. As Hagner notes (1993: 182), the 'false prophets' of Matthew 7:15-20 need not be limited to one group, such as the 'charismatic enthusiasts' of 7:22. Still, false prophets of various persuasions might use 'signs and wonders' to enhance their credibility.

[29]'Recognize' translates *epiginōskō*. Adding the preposition *epi* to *ginōskō* ('know') sometimes intensifies the meaning: see the instances of *epiginōskō* in Luke 1:4; 1 Corinthians 13:12; Colossians 1:6; cf. BAGD s.v., 1. ('to know exactly, completely, through and through'). That is probably not the intent of *epiginōskō* here in 7:16, 20 (BAGD s.v., 2.); the very similar sayings of 12:33 and Luke 6:44 use *ginōskō*.

'fruit' (the collective singular *karpos*) than of 'fruits': the use of the plural in 7:16, 20, and in four of the five instances of *karpos* in 7:17-19, reflects the fact that *deeds* good and bad are in view.[30]

Those enclosing statements are supported by illustrations from botany (7:16b-19): note the 'so then' in 7:20a.[31] The questions of 7:16b obviously expect negative answers: grapes (*staphylai*) are gathered, not from a thorn bush (*akantha*) but from a grape vine (*ampelos*); and figs (*syka*), not from a thistle (*tribolos*) but from a fig tree (*sykē*). Grapes and figs are staples in the Palestinian diet; thorns and thistles are quite inedible.[32] Yet, the quality of the fruit depends on the condition of the plant (Matt. 7:17-18). A healthy fig tree, for example, will produce good figs, but a decayed or rotting tree will produce bad figs; neither tree is able to function like the other. What can be done with a diseased or decaying tree, except to cut it down and consign it to the flames (7:19)?

According to those metaphors, what a false prophet *does* clearly reveals who he *is*, and who he *is* inevitably governs what he *does*. As the fruits of a decayed tree are *ponērous*, so his works are *ponēra* – not just 'spoiled and worthless' like bad figs, but 'evil and wicked.'[33] These acts, with the accompanying prophecies, are inspired by the evil one himself, and they are positively dangerous and potentially fatal to the prophet's

---

[30]See the remaining instances of *karpos* in Matthew – eight of them singular (3:8, 10; 12:33; 13:8, 26; 21:19) and four plural (21:34, 41, 43).

[31]Greek *ara ge*. Adding the particle *ge* to the inferential particle *ara* strengthens the expression (BAGD s.v. *ara*).

[32]The particle that opens Matthew 7:16b, *mēti*, expects a negative answer. All the terms in 7:16b – *staphylas, akanthōn, syka* and *tribolōn* – are plural, in keeping with 'the fruits' (*tōn karpōn*) of verse 16a. For *ampelos*, see 26:29; for *sykē*, e.g., 24:32; cf. the instances of *akantha* in 13:7, 22. Note the parts played by the fig tree, the grapevine and the thornbush in the fable of Judges 9:8-15.

[33]See, respectively, BAGD s.v. *ponēros*, 1. a. ('bad, spoiled, worthless') and b. ('wicked, evil, bad'). The words *karpous ponērous* in Matthew 7:17-18 are the more notable, since the parallel sayings of 12:33 and Luke 6:43 have *karpon sapron* (in agreement with *dendron sapron*). But note also how both Matthew 12:34-35 and Luke 6:45 speak of men who are *ponēroi*.

followers.[34] The prophet's *nature* determines his actions: he is *incapable* of producing good fruits, because he himself does not belong to God. He is instead one of the 'sons of the evil one,' and very likely a slave of wealth too.[35] Like worthless trees, such persons are threatened with destruction: the language of Matthew 7:19 anticipates 7:23.[36]

While this paragraph is chiefly devoted to warnings about false prophets, the test for identifying them applies to true prophets as well. In their case, the sheep's clothing (7:15) accords with their real identity. As the fruits of a healthy tree are *kalous* (7:17), so their works are *kala* (5:16; the only prior instance of this adjective in the sermon). These acts, with the accompanying prophecies, are enjoined by Jesus; they bring blessing to others and glory to God. Here too the prophet's *nature* determines his actions: he is *incapable* of habitual evil because he belongs to God and obeys Messiah. By the same token, just as good fruits signal that a tree is healthy (*agathon*; 7:17), so the true prophet's 'good works' identify him as a 'good man' (*agathos anthrōpos*), as one of 'the sons of the kingdom,' as a faithful follower of Jesus.[37] This means that his *teaching* may be trusted as well – and recognized both as a *weapon* for identifying false prophets and combating wolves, and as *food* for enlightening the mind and nourishing the soul, or (we might say) as 'grapes and

[34]Cf. especially the instances of *poneros* in Matthew 5:37; 6:13; 13:19, 38 (and those of 12:34, 35, which come directly after judgment upon blasphemy against the Holy Spirit, 32). See also 2 Corinthians 11:13-15; 2 Thessalonians 2:9-12; 1 Timothy 4:1; and again the reference to wolves in Matthew 7:15, etc.

[35]The *ou dynatai* ('is not able') of 7:18 invites comparison with the language of 5:14, 36; 6:27; and especially 6:24. Cf. 12:33-35; and 13:38-39, which identifies the weeds among the wheat as 'the sons of the evil one,' planted by the devil (imagery which could depict the presence of false prophets and their followers in the church). See 1 John 2:18-19 (where false teachers' *departure* betrays their true *identity*; contrast 2:17, 'he who does the will of God'); 3:12 (where Cain, who *was* of the evil one, *did* evil works).

[36]As Jesus' proclamation of the kingdom (4:17) is identical to that of John (3:2), so is his warning of judgment: except for the conjunction *oun*, the Greek of 3:10b is exactly reproduced in 7:19. Moreover, 7:15-23 are an implicit call to 'bear fruit worthy of repentance' (3:8).

[37]See 12:33-35; 13:37-38; 16:24-27.

figs' in place of the 'thorns and thistles' offered by the false prophets.[38]

Warnings about the Day of Judgment (7:21-23)

'Not everyone who says to me, "Lord, Lord," will enter into the kingdom of heaven, but only the one who does the will of my Father who is in heaven. Many will say to me on that day, "Lord, Lord, did we not prophesy by your name, and by your name cast out demons, and by your name do many mighty works?" And then I will say to them plainly, "I never knew you. Depart from me, you workers of lawlessness."'

1. The Judge

Those words will be exchanged 'on that day' (*en ekeinē tē hēmera*; Matthew 7:22), namely 'on the day of judgment' (*en hēmera kriseōs*), a phrase Jesus uses on later occasions.[39] It is the very one now speaking from the mountain who will preside as Judge on that final day, and whose judgment will determine who enters the kingdom (7:21). It is therefore he whom every person will address; and they will call out to him, 'Lord, Lord' (*Kyrie, Kyrie*; 7:21, 22). All who utter those words – including those about to be condemned – will do so in the full awareness that Jesus Christ *is Yahweh* (cf. Phil. 2:9-11), God himself come to judge. He is also the Father's beloved Son (7:21), who knows and discloses the Father as does no other.[40] Accordingly, doing the will of the Father (7:21; cf. 6:10) and

---

[38]This very sermon serves both those purposes, as does Matthew as a whole. Cf. Jesus' charges to the twelve in 10:5-42 and 28:19-20; and to Peter in John 21:15-17; also Paul's charge to the Ephesian elders in Acts 20:28-32. For feeding on God's word, see also Jeremiah 15:16.

[39]See Matthew 10:15; 11:22, 24; 12:36. Jesus also speaks of the 'day' (*hēmera*) of his return (24:36, 42, 50; 25:13), and of the 'day' of the Messianic banquet (26:29).

[40]See 11:25-27. Here in 7:21-22, Jesus for the first time in Matthew applies *Kyrios* to himself (but see comments on 3:3). It is notable that in the very text where he tacitly claims the name Yahweh for himself, he also distinguishes himself from his 'Father in heaven' (thus witnessing to a distinction of persons within the Godhead); cf. John 1:1. For more on these matters, see pages 134-37 ('Son of Man'); 137-39 ('Jesus is Lord'); 139-41 ('Jesus is God the Son').

obeying Jesus' own teachings (7:24) are two descriptions of one habit.[41] It is therefore fitting that Jesus' forthright address to the lawless (Matt. 7:23) is spoken (as are his words to the righteous) in the presence of his Father (10:32-33).[42]

2. The judged

Jesus will judge all mankind (25:31-46); but 7:21-23 focuses on persons who claim to know him. They call him 'Lord'; they profess to have acted *by his name*, i.e., to have done their deeds by virtue of his presence and power; and their questions (7:22) expect affirmative replies.[43] Did not Judas cast out demons in Jesus' name (cf. 10:1-8)? In keeping with the accent in 7:15-20 on false prophets rather than true, 7:21-23 speak particularly of persons who are in the church but will be excluded from the kingdom, persons here identified as 'workers of lawlessness' (*anomia*; 7:23).

The 'many' (*polloi*) of Matthew 7:22 are principally if not exclusively the false prophets (*pseudoprophētai*) of 7:15-20. 'Did we not prophesy [*eprophēteusamen*]...?' is the first question posed in 7:22. The third question – 'Did we not do [*epoiēsamen*] many mighty works?' – recalls the five instances of *poieō* in 7:17-19. Jesus later warns that 'many false prophets [*polloi pseudoprophētai*] will arise' (24:11). In that same passage, he speaks of many (*polloi*) who will usurp his name for themselves: 'I am the Messiah' (24:5). The persons of 7:22 do not appear to have done that: 'Did *we* not prophesy in *your* name?' they say. The false prophets disguised themselves

---

[41]Cf. 12:50 ('whoever does the will of my Father') and its parallel in Luke 8:21 ('those who hear the word of God and do it'); also the parallel to Matthew 7:21 in Luke 6:46 ('Why do you call me "Lord, Lord," and not do the things I say?').

[42]The verb *homologeō* ('I will say...plainly': BAGD s.v., 4.), used negatively in Matthew 7:23, is matched by the *arneomai* ('deny') of 10:33. In 10:32, *homologeō* is used positively. The setting for 10:32-33 is most likely the same as for 7:21-23; cf. Mark 8:38.

[43]The *ou* that opens the threefold question in 7:22 expects the answer 'Yes.' The phrase 'by your name' (*tō sō onomati*) at the opening of all three clauses is an instrumental dative, indicating by what means the actions were accomplished (*GGBB*, 162); *sō* is the dative of the possessive adjective *sos*. On the significance of the name (*onoma*), see comments on 1:21, 23.

as sheep (7:15), not as the shepherd.[44] Nor does this passage suggest that they denied Jesus' deity, or that their prophecies were all untrue, or that their alleged exorcisms and miracles never happened. It is for other reasons that they are called 'workers of lawlessness.'

But also in view are persons who fell prey to those teachings and deceptions, in part from being dazzled by those extraordinary phenomena. As Jesus says in that later text, those many false prophets 'will lead many astray [*planēsousin pollous*]' (24:11); the messianic pretenders will do the same (24:5). Through the acts both of the false prophets and of their followers, lawlessness will increase (24:12; *anomia*, as in 7:23). Moreover, the language of 7:22 (*polloi*) and 7:21 (the verb *eiserchomai*) recalls the use of those terms in 7:13-14, where Jesus says that many (*polloi* here being not just false prophets but all unbelievers) will enter upon the road leading not to the life of the kingdom but to destruction.

Also present among the judged, by implication, are those 'few' who found the path leading to life (7:14). 'Not everyone who says...will enter' (7:21a) indicates that some will. The close of 7:21 reveals who they are: 'but only [for the strong adversative *alla*] the one who does the will of my Father,' and thereby shows that his allegiance to Jesus ('Lord, Lord') is genuine.

3. The judgment

To the persons who reminded Jesus of their words and works in his name, he declares, 'I never knew you [*oudepote egnōn hymas*]. Depart [*apochōreite*] from me, you workers of lawlessness [*hoi ergazomenoi tēn anomian*]' (7:23).

The focus of Jesus' judgment is not upon the exorcisms and miracles allegedly done by the false prophets and their devotees; nor is it upon the prophecies as such. Rather it is upon such persons' *anomia* – the lawlessness which resulted from that false teaching – and from preoccupation with those

---

[44]If they *did* once claim messianic status, they would and could not do so in the presence of the Messiah-Judge. The phrase of Matthew 24:5 ('in my name,' *epi tō onomati mou*) differs from that of 7:22 (see n. 43). On the relation between 7:22 and 24:5, see Davies and Allison 1988: 715-16.

extraordinary works. *Anomia* violates the *nomos* ('law'); cf. the use of *anomos* (*alpha-privative* + *nomos*), 'the lawless one,' in 2 Thessalonians 2:8.

This is the single instance of *anomia* in the sermon; placed at this juncture (Matt. 7:23), it takes account of the whole preceding exposition. The term embraces both failures to obey the law as taught by Jesus (sins of omission), and willful acts of disobedience (sins of commission). The expression '*workers* of lawlessness' shows that such persons do not really live without law: their sin is to do their own will rather than the Father's (7:21) and to replace his rules with their own.[45] At its heart, *anomia* violates the foundational command to love God and one's neighbor (22:37-40). As the figure of the elder brother shows (Luke 15:25-30), one may be a scrupulous law-keeper and still miss the point of the law.[46]

By the same token, it is possible to affirm that Jesus is God, to speak truth about him, to do mighty works in his name, and to tell others of his commands (as Judas apparently did in response to the commission of Matthew 10:5-42), yet fail to love him and to keep his commands as an expression of that love (cf. John 14:15). 'You shall love [*agapēseis*] the Lord [*Kyrion*],' says 'the great and first commandment' (Matt. 22:37). Spoken by the persons of 7:22, the cry *Kyrie* is itself one of the 'careless words' for which they will be condemned (12:36); for they do not love Jesus the Lord, and they call him Lord without keeping his commands (Luke 6:46), starting with the greatest command of all.[47]

---

[45]*Anomia* occurs about 200 times in the LXX (most notably in Psalms and Ezekiel), as a translation for some twenty-four Hebrew terms. Matthew 7:23b alludes to Psalm 6:8a (LXX 9a), 'Depart from me [*apostēte ap' emou*], all you workers of lawlessness [*pantes hoi ergazomenoi tēn anomian*].'

[46]Cf. Matthew 5:20; 23:23-24, 28. In Matthew's view, says Gundry 1994: 133, 'Jewish legalism in the church amounts to antinomianism.' Have not the proud ostensible law-keepers of 6:1-18 believed a false prophecy, and swallowed the devil's lie (cf. 1 Tim. 4:1) that they are spiritually superior beings? Thus convinced, they adore themselves; the God they seem to worship is 'imaginary,' says Lewis 1952: 96, who suggests that Matthew 7:22 speaks of such persons.

[47]Shortly after the command to love the Lord (*Kyrios*) is quoted in Luke 10:27, Jesus himself is four times called *Kyrios* (10:39, 40, 41; 11:1).

The heartbreaking words, 'I never knew you,' are addressed to persons who steadfastly refused to receive the Lord's *agapē* and to love him in return.[48] Inevitably, the increase of lawlessness (*anomia*) causes the love (*agapē*) of many (*polloi*) to grow cold (24:12), love not just for God but for neighbors as well (Matt. 24:9-10). It is shocking to learn that persons who testify – correctly – to stunning spiritual achievements, can nonetheless be condemned as 'workers of lawlessness.' (Does that not suggest that marvelous feats may serve to conceal, or to divert attention from, one's lawbreaking?) Paul is likewise shocking when (perhaps building on Jesus' present teaching) he condemns a fixation on spiritual gifts (*charismata*) that neglects or disdains the 'more excellent way' of love (*agapē*; 1 Cor. 12–14).[49]

'Depart [*apochōreite*] from me,' says Jesus to them. As the sole instance of the verb *apochōreō* in Matthew, this terrifying command stands out all the more starkly. In 13:41, Jesus similarly prophesies that his angels will gather from his kingdom 'the ones who do lawlessness [*tous poiountas tēn anomian*].' If heaven promises unbroken fellowship with Christ in the house of his Father (John 14:2-3), the essence of hell is to be banished forever from the presence of the Son, and therefore from fellowship with him, the Father and the Spirit (cf. Matt. 28:19).

Jesus later reveals what he will say to those who have done the Father's will: 'Come, you who are blessed by my Father, inherit the kingdom prepared for you...' (Matt. 25:34), which employs some of the language of 7:21. This latter verse implies that these people too will address Jesus as 'Lord, Lord' on the Day of Judgment: only on their lips the words express worship, love, trust and gratitude to the one who saved them

---

[48]Nowhere else in Matthew is the verb *ginōskō* used in this sense; but cf. 25:12, 'I do not know [*ouk oida*] you.' Cf. John, where two verbs expressive of the deeply intimate bond between Jesus and his people are *ginōskō* (10:14, 27; 17:3) and *agapaō* (11:5; 13:1, 23, 34; 14:21; 15:9).

[49]Having the gift of *prophēteia* but lacking *agapē*, 'I am nothing' (1 Cor. 13:2). In view of the accent on 'fruits' in Matthew 7:16-20, note that for Paul the foremost 'fruit' (*karpos*) of the Spirit is *agapē* (Gal. 5:22). On the relation of the gifts of the Spirit to the fruit of the Spirit in Paul, see Chamblin 1993: 208-20. The burden of Matthew 7:21-23, according to Hagner 1993: 184-89, is 'the insufficiency of the charismata.'

from their sins (1:21; cf. the use of the vocative *Kyrie* in 25:20, 22, 37). Moreover, many of them will have prophesied in Jesus' name, and in his name expelled demons and worked miracles. Paul did all three, and in every case his controlling motivation was 'the love of Christ.'[50]

C. Builders Wise and Foolish (7:24-27)

Linguistic artistry and poetic symmetry mark these closing words of the sermon. These are not, however, ends in themselves: Jesus uses both to make a last urgent appeal to his audience.

The Similes

Jesus likens one kind of listener to a wise or sensible man: *homoiōthēsetai andri phronimō* (Matt. 7:24b). The other kind is like a foolish or stupid man: *homoiōthēsetai andri mōrō* (7:26b). The first one built his house upon the rock: *hostis ōkodomēsen autou tēn oikian epi tēn petran* (7:24c); the second built his upon the sand: *hostis ōkodomēsen autou tēn oikian epi tēn ammon* (7:26c).[51] These adjectives – *phronimos* (7:24) and *mōros* (7:26) – are the very ones used in the parable of 25:1-13. As both men are occupied with building, so all ten virgins are provided with lamps. The man who builds on rock is like the girls who take oil for their lamps; the man who builds on sand is like those who fail to do so.[52]

Both houses are subjected to the same weather conditions: 'and the rain came down and the floods came

---

[50]In 2 Corinthians 5:14, *hē agapē tou Christou* probably embraces both Christ's love for Paul (*Christou* a subjective genitive) and Paul's love for Christ (objective genitive). Cf. *GGBB*, 120. For Paul's exorcisms and miracles, see, e.g., 2 Corinthians 12:12; Acts 14:3; 16:18; 19:11-12; 28:8.

[51]In the similar similes of Luke 6:48-49, the first man builds the foundation of his house (*oikia* again) 'upon the rock' (*epi tēn petran* again), and the second builds his house without a foundation 'upon the ground' (*epi tēn gēn*). To mark the simile Luke uses the adjective *homoios* ('like'; 6:47-49); Matthew uses the future passive indicative of the verb *homoioō* ('will be like'; 7:24, 26) On the variant reading *homoiōsō*, 'I will liken him,' see *TC*, 17.

[52]Apart from their use in Matthew 7:24-27 and 25:1-13, *phronimos* and *mōros* are very rare in Matthew (the first only in 10:16 and 24:45; the second only in 5:22 and 23:17).

and the winds blew and beat upon that house': *kai katebē hē brochē kai ēlthon hoi potamoi kai epneusan hoi anemoi kai prosepesan tē oikia ekeinē* (7:25a); 7:27a is identical, except that *prosekopsan*, 'beat against,' takes the place of *prosepesan*.[53] What were the effects? The first house 'did not fall, because it had been founded upon the rock': *kai ouk epesen, tethemeliōto gar epi tēn petran* (7:25b). But the second house 'fell, and its fall was great': *kai epesen, kai ēn hē ptōsis autēs megalē* (7:27b).

The identical features of the two descriptions are strikingly evident in the Greek text. For that very reason, the differences in the two pictures stand out the more vividly: *andri phronimō, andri mōrō; epi tēn petran, epi tēn ammon; kai ouk epesen, kai epesen*. The closings of the two descriptions are very dissimilar – the second says 'and its fall was great,' not 'for it had been founded on the sand' – a literary contrast that mirrors the actual contrast between the standing house and the heap of rubble.[54]

The Appeal

The words that introduce the similes (Matt. 7:24a and 7:26a) display that same symmetry. The first picture, says Jesus, represents 'everyone who hears these my words and does them': *pas...hostis akouei mou tous logous toutous kai poiei autous*. The second reference is very similar, though the finite verbs in the present tense are replaced by present participles, *akouōn* and *poiōn*. The only conceptual difference is that the second participle is joined by the negative particle – *mē poiōn*, '*not* doing.' Verses 24-27 contain no imperatives; yet Jesus is here imploring his listeners to heed his words, and these words about his words, before it is too late.

---

[53]'A cloud bursts, flash floods race down the usually dry ravines...and winds blow fiercely during the storm' (Gundry 1994: 135). Luke 6:48-49 speaks not of rain or winds, only of one river (*potamos*) overflowing its banks near the house.

[54]Cf. the contrast between Luke 6:48b (the river 'could not shake it, because it had been well built'; some later MSS. substitute the wording of Matthew 7:25b) and 6:49b ('and it fell immediately, and the ruin of that house was great').

1. Lessons from the context

The conjunction *oun* ('therefore') at the opening of 7:24 draws attention to the words about the judgment (7:21-23) and also to the warning against false prophets (7:15-20) and the picture of the two ways (7:13-14). The contrast in 7:24-27 matches that of 7:21-23; doing Jesus' words (7:24, with *poiei*) and doing the Father's will (7:21, with *poiōn*) are two expressions for one practice. Persons whose work is depicted in 7:24-25 will survive the judgment; the fall of the house in 7:27 illustrates the catastrophe awaiting the workers of lawlessness (7:23). The foolish virgins are likewise excluded: 'I do not know you,' says the bridegroom (25:12). Cf. Ezekiel 13:11-13, where, in an indictment of false prophets, Yahweh's coming wrath is likened to torrential rains and violent winds; and Ezekiel 33:30-34, where people who love to hear the prophet's words fail to do them.

As the beginning of the sermon (Matt. 5:3) recalls the opening of Psalm 1 ('Blessed is the man'), so the sermon's close recalls the rest of that psalm. The person Jesus commends does not walk 'in the counsel of the wicked' (Ps. 1:1), i.e. of the 'false prophets' (Matt. 7:15). His delight, instead, 'is in 'the *torah* of Yahweh' (Ps. 1:2), now expounded by Yahweh (*Kyrios*) himself (Matt. 7:21, 24). The stability of the 'tree' (Ps. 1:3) is matched by that of his 'house' built upon a rock (Matt. 7:24-25). As that tree perennially bears fruit (Ps. 1:3), so does his life (Matt. 7:16-20); the wicked, by contrast, are 'like chaff' (Ps. 1:4), whose lives (in the case of the false prophets) produce thorns and thistles (Matt. 7:16). 'Therefore the wicked will not stand in the judgment,' and their way will 'perish' (Ps. 1:5-6; Matt. 7:23, 27); but the righteous *will* stand in the judgment, and Yahweh will grant them entry into the heavenly kingdom's 'congregation of the righteous' (Ps. 1:5-6; Matt. 7:21, 25; cf. 13:43; 25:46).

2. Lessons from the similes

As both the men choose to build houses, so all of Jesus' listeners have chosen to hear his words. Building a house requires the choice of a foundation: the two options here depicted are rock and sand. The first illustrates those words of Jesus; the second, the vacuous teachings of Jesus' opponents, such as false prophets in the church (7:15) or scribes among the Jews (7:29). The floods and winds symbolize the trials and pressures which all the listeners will experience both in this life and at the Last Judgment.[55] Indeed, a time will soon come when literal waves and winds will test the disciples' faith (Matt. 8:24-27; cf. 14:24-33).

As the first man, aware of the rock, decides to build on it, so there are disciples who – knowing Jesus' teaching – wisely choose to build on it by doing it. In the language of James 1:22-25, they perceive what that 'perfect law of liberty' reveals about themselves and their needs, and determine to obey it. The higher the edifice rises – the more habitual and consistent their law keeping becomes – the more reliable the foundation proves to be.[56] It also stands firm amid threats from without: in the imagery of a later parable, the person rooted in that teaching does not fall away when troubles and persecution assail him, but instead bears much fruit (Matt. 13:21, 23; cf. 5:11-12).

As the second builder also represents people who hear Jesus' words, his choice of foundation is unbelievably stupid: knowing of the rock, he nonetheless opts for the sand. Like the first person in James 1:22-25, he listened to the word – he looked into that mirror – but soon forgot what it revealed and became self-deceived – a state of mind fostered by false prophets of various kinds. The more he builds upon their foundation of sand, the less trustworthy it becomes.[57] External threats undermine it altogether: or, to return to the parable in

---

[55]Cf. France 1985: 149. While Matthew 25:1-13 focuses more directly on the return of the Bridegroom, the appeal of the present passage is underscored there (see those comments).

[56]The point of Luke 6:48 (where the foundation is *laid on* the rock) is yet stronger in Matthew 7:24-25 (where the foundation *is* the rock). Cf. Gundry 1994: 135.

[57]Antinomianism *has* no foundation: again note the difference between 7:25b and 27b. 'But never, never pin your whole faith on any human being: not if he is the best and wisest in the whole world. There are lots of nice things you can do with sand; but do not try building a house on it' (Lewis 1952: 149).

Matthew 13, because this person is not rooted in Jesus' word, he falls away in time of testing (13:21).

D. Two Kinds of Teachers (7:28-29)

'And it happened when Jesus had finished [*etelesen*] these words [*tous logous toutous*], that the crowds [*hoi ochloi*] were astounded [*exeplēssonto*] at his teaching [*epi tē didachē autou*]; for [*gar*] he was teaching [*ēn...didaskōn*] them [*autous*] as one having authority [*exousian*], and not as their scribes [*hoi grammateis autōn*].' As we noted when considering the gospel's design, Matthew marks the end of all five discourses with such a formula as 7:28a (see p. 27). The whole sermon is in view, as the verb *teleō* ('finish') makes plain; yet the evangelist's reference to 'these words' underscores Jesus' closing appeal, where *tous logous toutous* occurs twice (Matt. 7:24 and 26), the only instances of this expression in the sermon itself.[58]

The preface to the sermon reported that Jesus' disciples (*mathētai*) came to him and that he began to teach them (*edidasken autous*; Matt. 5:1-2); nothing was said there of the crowds, though 4:25 reported that 'many crowds' (*ochloi polloi*) followed Jesus. This closing summary focuses on the crowds as recipients of Jesus' teaching (see the Greek above); the disciples are not mentioned.[59] This suggests that the appeals and warnings of 7:13-27, while addressed to both disciples and crowds, are chiefly intended for the latter; the former have shown at least an initial willingness to obey Jesus' words by *becoming* disciples.

The crowds' present response offers hope that they too will become disciples. They are *astounded* at Jesus' teaching: the verb is *ekplēssomai*.[60] The explanation for their astonishment (note the *gar*, 29a) is Jesus' authority – *exousia*, which here appears for the first time in Matthew. There are at least five reasons for this authority: (i) Jesus teaches this way by virtue

---

[58]There are only two other instances of *logos* in the sermon, both singular (Matthew 5:32, 37).

[59]On this distinction, and its bearing on the sermon's purposes, see pages 302–3.

[60]In the NT, *ekplēssō* occurs only in the passive voice.

of who he *is* – God incarnate (*exousia* means literally 'out of being'; 'authority' contains the word 'author') – so that all he says and does discloses God;[61] (ii) as the Son of God, he has been anointed by the Spirit of truth and power: see, e.g., 3:16; Luke 4:18-19 (and the instance of *exousia* in 4:32); (iii) his teaching accords with *reality*: e.g., the kingdom he *says* is coming, *is* coming; there will surely be a final judgment, and a heavenly reward; (iv) it is the Word of God revealed in the scriptures that he expounds, rather than merely human traditions: see, e.g., Matthew 5:17-48; 15:1-9; and (v) what he teaches others, he himself *does*: e.g., the gentleness of which he speaks (5:5; *praeis*) marks his own behavior (11:29; 21:5; *praus*); he himself loves the God he commands his followers to love (11:27, *epiginōskō*, 22:37, *agapaō*); and he commands his followers to love one another in light of his love for them (John 13:34, *agapaō*).

As scholars of the law, the Jewish scribes were also supposed to teach with authority. One reason they lacked the authority Jesus possessed (as the crowds perceived), is that they were mere men; but in this respect no scribe – Matthew included – could compare with Jesus. There are additional reasons, as Jesus reveals: (i) some of their teachings were based on human tradition rather than divine revelation (15:1-9); (ii) those teachings that *were* based on Scripture, they failed to obey (23:2-4, 25-28); and (iii) their practices, including their teaching, were motivated by love for self rather than love for God, by a desire that self be magnified rather than God (6:1-18; 23:5-7, 23; cf. Luke 11:42). If they knew and loved God, and therefore his *torah* (as did the writer of Psalm 119), would

---

[61]Lewis 1952: 41 observes that people often express their readiness to accept Jesus 'as a great moral teacher' – in part because of the present sermon – while rejecting his 'claim to be God.' But, Lewis continues, a 'man who was merely a man and said the sort of things Jesus said [including texts in this sermon: see, e.g., Matthew 5:21-22; 7:21-23] would not be a great moral teacher. He would either be a lunatic [cf. Mark 3:21]...or else he would be the Devil of Hell [cf. Matt. 12:24]. You must make your choice. Either this man was, and is, the Son of God: or else a madman or something worse.... But let us not come with any patronising nonsense about His being a great human teacher.'

they not recognize and love Jesus the Son of God, and desire to keep the *torah* he expounded?[62]

Both before and after the sermon, Matthew reports that 'huge crowds' followed Jesus (Matt. 4:25; 8:1), their predictable response to his authoritative teaching, as well as to his mighty works (of which we are about to learn more). But while the crowds' amazement (7:28) is encouraging, it is not enough.[63] What does it matter that they recognize the teacher's *exousia*, unless they obey his teachings? Indeed, those who hear Jesus' words and perceive his authority, yet fail to obey him, are in a more perilous position than those who never hear. Matthew may want those enclosing references to 'huge crowds' (*ochloi polloi*), to remind readers of Jesus' warnings that many (*polloi*) will take the path to destruction (7:13) and that many (*polloi*) will in the end be rejected as workers of lawlessness (7:22).[64] In any case, the evangelist sounds warnings from his Master: 'Beware lest you embrace scribal teachings which lack divine authority and are therefore like a foundation of sand. Instead, build your life on solid rock, on God's own *torah* as now expounded by God incarnate and safeguarded and imparted by his appointed scribes, including the author of this book.'[65]

---

[62]Cf. John 5:37-47; 7:45-52 (the Pharisees' response to the report, 'No man ever spoke like this!' v. 46); 8:42. As Matthew will show, the scribes do not merely refrain from loving Jesus but actively oppose and seek to destroy him: see 9:3; 16:21; 20:18, etc.

[63]Two other instances of *ekplēssomai* in Matthew are instructive in this regard: 13:54, about the people of Nazareth (cf. verses 57-58, on their unbelief); and 22:33, about the crowds again.

[64]This idea is the more attractive, because these are the only two instances of *polloi* in the sermon. All other forms of *polys* are singular (5:12, 20; 6:25, 30).

[65]See 13:52; 23:34 (in light of 23:2-33); 28:19-20; and pages 43-45 (on Matthew and other Christian scribes in relation to Jewish scribes).

Section 7

'All Authority and Power'[1]
(Matt. 8:1–9:38)

The authority of the foregoing discourse is further manifested
in these chapters, both in Jesus' teachings and especially in
his mighty works.[2] As the *exousia* of his teaching amazed the
crowds (7:29), so his twin work of forgiving sins and healing
paralysis causes the crowds to praise God for giving such
authority to men (9:8; with *oi ochloi* and *exousian toiautēn*). The
preface to the sermon (4:23-25) and the close of this narrative
section (9:35-38) together form an inclusion. Both 4:23 and
9:35 speak (in very similar terms) of Jesus' teaching, preaching
and healing. Chapters 5–7 are devoted to the first two; healing
miracles are the main focus of chapters 8–9, though these
accounts also contain potent words of Jesus, as we shall see.[3]

---

[1]The title of a hymn by Christopher Idle (1973).

[2]*Exousia* occurs three times in these chapters (Matt. 8:9; 9:6, 8); but the
reality is all-pervasive.

[3]Matthew typically excludes many narrative details provided by Mark,
'so as to concentrate attention on the miracle itself, and particularly on the
words of Jesus' (France 1985: 151). Stott 1972: 125 says that each of Jesus'
miracles was 'an acted parable.'

I.
'O CHRIST, THE HEALER'[1]
(8:1-17)

Seeing the huge crowds that followed him, Jesus had earlier ascended the mountain (Matt. 4:25–5:1). Now that he has descended, huge crowds again follow (8:1), many (perhaps most) of whom heard the sermon (7:28).[2] Matthew begins his present narrative by recording three healing miracles. It is not just affliction that unites the persons for whom Jesus acts: all three are in some way 'despised and rejected by men' (the language of Isaiah 53:3) – a leper, a Gentile and a woman.[3] (Are these first three miracles meant to recall the first three beatitudes [Matt. 5:3-5] about the poor in spirit, the mourning and the meek?) These accounts (8:2-15) are followed by a summary of Jesus' extensive healing ministry (8:16-17), including a quotation from Isaiah 53:4.

A. Jesus and the Leper (8:1-4)

Matthew 8:2 opens with the words *kai idou lepros*: 'and behold a leper.' As often, *kai idou* prepares readers for matters marvelous and momentous: cf. its use in 8:24, 32; 9:2, 20.[4] The presence of the 'huge crowds' (8:1) accentuates the lone figure of the leper. Both Matthew and Luke (5:12-16) employ Mark (1:40-45).

---

[1]The title of a hymn by Fred Pratt Green (1969).

[2]Matthew 4:25 and 8:1 have in common the nominative *ochloi polloi* and the aorist verb *ēkolouthēsan* (from *akoloutheō*, 'follow'). The aorist verb *anebē* (from *anabainō*, 'go up'; 5:1) is matched by the aorist participle *katabantos* (from *katabainō*, 'go down'; 8:1); and *eis to oros* ('into the mountain'; 5:1) by *apo tou orous* ('from the mountain'; 8:1).

[3]Cf. France 1985: 153, 157; also above, page 59, n. 38, on perceived triads in chapters 8–9.

[4]See also Matthew 8:29, 34; 9:3, 10; and page 263, with n. 23, on *kai idou* in 3:17 and elsewhere.

Desperation (8:2)

A *lepros* (Matt. 8:2) was afflicted with *lepra* (8:3), one of several infectious skin diseases. Leviticus 13 describes such maladies and prescribes their treatment.[5] A person so afflicted 'shall remain unclean as long as he has the disease. He is unclean. He shall live alone. His dwelling shall be outside the camp' (13:46, ESV). Moreover, the law 'provided no means of curing "skin diseases." The sufferer had to wait in hope of a cure from God, without human aid.'[6]

At the opening of the sermon the disciples came to (*prosēlthan*) Jesus (Matt. 5:1); here at the threshold of the narrative this *lepros* does the same (8:2; *proselthōn*), apparently in the presence of the 'huge crowds.'[7] His prostrating himself before (*prosekynei*) Jesus also expresses that desperation and the urgency of his appeal. Then he says: 'Lord [*Kyrie*], if you are willing [*ean thelēs*], you are able [*dynasai*] to cleanse [*katharisai*] me' (8:2b). The man's request clearly voices his confidence that Jesus mediates God's power ('you are able to cleanse me'), and that Jesus' own will is decisive in the matter ('if you are willing'). This assurance doubtless rests upon what he has heard, and perhaps personally witnessed, of Jesus' miraculous powers: see 4:23-25.

Precisely what sense he attaches to the word *Kyrie*, we cannot say (though 'sir' is clearly too weak). But the evangelist probably intends for this instance of the vocative to be read in light of those in 7:21, 22; and likewise for this instance of the verb *proskyneō* to be read in light of those in 2:2, 11, where it describes the magi's homage to Jesus. That is, Matthew wants readers to recognize that the One whom the *lepros* addresses is not only a man to whom God has granted stupendous

---

[5]The Hebrew term in Leviticus 13:2, etc., is *tsāra'at*, translated *lepra* in LXX. Whether one such infection was clinical leprosy – 'Hansen's disease' – is disputed: R. K. Harrison (*DNNT*, 2: 465) thinks it was 'undoubtedly included'; Wenham (1979: 195) thinks not ('Modern medical opinion is agreed...that leprosy is not one of the diseases being described' in Leviticus 13). Cf. BAGD s.v. *lepra*.

[6]Wenham 1979: 213.

[7]Both the verb of Matthew 5:1 and the participle of 8:2 are aorist forms of *proserchomai*. Davies and Allison 1991: 11 cite evidence that lepers were not totally isolated from the rest of society.

authority and power, but is himself God and therefore worthy of worship.[8]

Restoration (8:3)
'And stretching forth his hand, he touched him' (8:3a). Yahweh and Moses likewise 'stretched forth the hand' for a saving purpose: see, e.g., Exodus 7:5;14:16. The touch would make Jesus ritually unclean according to Mosaic law: see Leviticus 10:10; 13:45-46. But here the power is exerted in the opposite direction. For 'at Jesus' touch nothing remains defiled. Far from becoming unclean, Jesus makes the unclean clean.'[9] The touch does not signal that a healing is about to occur, or that Mosaic law is being abrogated (see below on Matthew 8:4), but is itself integral to the healing. Compare 8:15, which mentions Jesus' touch alone (though in the parallel of Luke 4:39 he also rebukes the fever); and Matthew 9:29, where his touch and words together heal the blind men.

The man is also healed by Jesus' mighty word (8:3b): 'I am willing: be cleansed [*Thelō, katharisthēti*].' This reply is notable for its conciseness (two Greek words) and its language (the same verbs the man used, *thelō* and *katharizō*).[10] The command *katharisthēti* (the aorist passive imperative of *katharizō*) *itself* achieves the healing: 'and immediately [*eutheōs*] his leprosy [*lepra*] was cleansed [*ekatharisthē*, the aorist passive indicative of the same verb]' (Matt. 8:3c).[11] In the language of Mark 1:42 and

---

[8]On *Kyrie* in 7:21, 22, see page 479; on *proskyneō* in 2:2, 11, pages 226-27 (cf. Jesus' use of this verb in 4:10). Matthew's *prosekynei* (8:2) is the more notable, since the parallel texts use different terms: Mark 1:40 has *gonypetōn* ('kneeling down'); Luke 5:12, *pesōn epi prosōpon* ('falling on his face'). Like Matthew 8:2, Luke includes the vocative *Kyrie*; Mark lacks it.

[9]Carson 1984: 198. Jesus' touch is a tangible sign of his pity and compassion, as expressly stated in Mark 1:41 (the verb *splanchnizomai*).

[10]Both instances of *thelō* are present (subjunctive in Matt. 8:2, indicative in 8:3); the two of *katharizō* are aorist (active infinitive in 8:2, passive imperative in 8:3).

[11]In Matthew, the cure of leprosy is always called a cleansing: see the forms of *katharizō* in 8:2-3; 10:8; 11:5. For another use of this verb, see 23:25-26. In the language of *GGBB*, 492, *katharisthēti* is a 'pronouncement imperative' – i.e., not a command which the leper himself can obey, but one which fulfills itself at the moment of speaking.

Luke 5:13, the *lepra* 'immediately left him': the disease is almost like a demon that has no choice but to flee at Jesus' word.

Confirmation (8:4)

The healing testifies that the kingdom of God has dawned, and that Jesus is the promised Messiah: see his reply to John in Matthew 11:4-6. Yet there is grave danger that such miracles as this will – precisely because they are *mighty works* – foster false notions of Messiahship among the people, who will then assail Jesus with the very temptations he repelled in the desert (4:1-11). Accordingly, he first charges the man: 'See that you tell no one' (8:4a).[12] To judge from the parallel accounts, however, he was unable to keep the good news to himself.[13]

Jesus commands positive action instead: 'but [the strong adversative *alla*] go, show yourself to the priest, and offer the gift which Moses prescribed, for a witness to them' (8:4b). Jesus, God's anointed Servant, has *made* the leper clean. It is now the task of the priest to *confirm* that the healing has occurred. The journey in view, from the vicinity of Capernaum (8:5) to Jerusalem, would cover over eighty miles (as the crow flies) and take three to four days.[14] Upon the man's arrival at the temple, a priest (*hiereus*) would examine him in accord with the detailed instructions of Leviticus 14:1-32. As Jesus' act of healing (Matt. 8:3) exemplified the marvelous grace attending God's dawning rule (cf. 5:3-16),

---

[12]See comments on Matthew 4:1-11. On Jesus' commands to silence respecting his Messiahship, see pages 133-34. Cf. France 1985: 153. That Jesus – acutely aware of such dangers – nonetheless does these mighty works, testifies to his great compassion: see, e.g., 9:36. Jesus' words in 8:4a may suggest that the healing itself took place in private, or that the physical effects of the healing were not immediately apparent to onlookers.

[13]See Mark 1:44-45 (the unnamed subject of 1:45a is possibly Jesus, but more likely to be the cured leper: see arguments in Gundry 1993: 97-98); Luke 5:14-15. Others of these miracles have the same effect: see Matthew 8:33-34; 9:26, 31.

[14]The directive for the journey is *hypage* (from *hypagō*, 'go'), a progressive present imperative of command (*GGBB*, 518). The directives for the acts in Jerusalem are *deixon* (from *deiknymi*, 'to show') and *prosenegkon* (from *prospherō*, 'offer'), constative (or punctiliar) aorist imperatives of command (*GGBB*, 557).

so this command (8:4) confirms his intent to honor God's ancient law (cf. 5:17-20 *et seq.*). To be sure, the prescriptions of Leviticus 14 will become obsolete by virtue of Jesus' atoning sacrifice; but until then, they remain valid – and themselves testify to the saving benefits of his death.[15]

Matthew 8:4 closes with the words *eis martyrion autois,* 'for a witness to them.' In accord with the prohibition of 8:4a, this testimony is not verbal but visible. Perhaps the witness consists in the man's showing himself to the priest as cured (proof that Jesus is the Messiah), and his presenting the sacrifice (proof that Jesus honors the Mosaic law); but the shift from the singular 'priest' to the plural 'them' tells against this view. Most likely the man and the priest will be testifying together to the people of Israel that this formerly alienated *lepros* has been cleansed and is now to be restored to the fellowship of the community – in other words, that the stigma of Leviticus 13:46 has been removed.[16] Given that prospect, it is highly probable that the man obeyed Jesus.[17]

B. Jesus and the Centurion (8:5-13)

His meeting with the leper having occurred (as would be expected) outside the town, Jesus re-enters Capernaum (Matt. 8:5), his chosen residence (4:13), near which he delivered the preceding sermon.[18] See also Luke 7:1-10, and compare John 4:46-54.

---

[15]See Matthew 5:17-20; and the comments on page 342, including n. 8. According to Leviticus 14, the priest shall by various means – including the guilt offering, the sin offering and the burnt offering – 'make atonement before Yahweh for him who is being cleansed' (14:31; cf. 18-20).

[16]Hagner 1993: 199-200 argues well for this view. Perhaps one reason Jesus commands silence (8:4a), is that he wants nothing to delay the man's return to society (and what better place than Jerusalem for that to happen?). The preface to the command in Mark (1:44a) supports this idea: 'And Jesus sternly charged him and sent him away at once' (1:43, ESV).

[17]He could obey Jesus' positive command as he disobeyed the negative, by spreading abroad the news of his healing (Mark 1:45a) on his way to Jerusalem.

[18]See the comments on Matthew 4:13 and 5:1.

The Opening Exchange (8:5-7)

Like the leper, this man 'comes to' Jesus (Matthew 8:5; an aorist of *proserchomai*, as in 8:2), and addresses him as 'Lord' (*Kyrie*; 8:6, as in 8:2).[19] Matthew identifies him as a centurion, a *hekatontarchos*, a military term for a 'ruler of a hundred,' one of sixty such men in a Roman legion.[20] Such forces were stationed in Judea and Samaria at the time, but not in Galilee; so apparently this officer is currently serving under Herod Antipas, tetrarch of the region.[21] The name *hekatontarchos* identifies him as a Gentile,[22] as do Jesus' words in verses 8:10-12. From the parallel account in Luke 7:1-10, we learn that the centurion addresses Jesus through chosen representatives, first through certain 'elders of the Jews' (8:3), then through his 'friends' (8:6).[23] His association with these Jewish elders, and their testimony – 'he loves our nation and built our synagogue' (8:5) – strongly suggest that he is a Gentile 'God-fearer,' like that other centurion, Cornelius (Acts 10:1-2).

The centurion appeals to Jesus on behalf of his *pais* (8:6). The term can denote a male or a female, depending on the definite

---

[19]*Prosēlthen* ('he came to'; 8:5) is an aorist indicative, and *proselthōn* ('coming to'; 8:2) an aorist participle, of *proserchomai*. The visible appeal of 8:2, *prosekynei* ('he prostrated himself'), is matched by the verbal one of 8:5, *parakalōn* ('imploring,' a participle of *parakaleō*).

[20]'The nominal strength of a legion was 6,000 men, about 5,300 infantry and 700 cavalry and technical specialists.... A legion was divided into ten cohorts of six centuries (one hundred men) each. It was commanded by a legate (normally of senatorial rank), with six tribunes serving as staff officers. The most important tactical officers in the legion were the sixty centurions (six in each of the cohorts), each of whom commanded a century. These were the professionals in the army, commonly promoted from the ranks' (Ferguson 1987: 38). The sole instance of *legiōn* in Matthew comes at 26:53 ('twelve legions of angels'); cf. its use in Mark 5:9, 15; Luke 8:30 (in accounts parallel to Matthew 8:28-34). The one instance of *hekatontarchos* in Matthew beyond 8:5-13 comes in 27:54; the parallel in Mark 15:39 has the Latin loan word *kentyriōn*.

[21]I. H. Marshall, 'Military,' *DJG*, 548; Gundry 1994: 141.

[22]'Jews were exempted from Roman military service' (Marshall, ibid.).

[23]Luke 7:6-8 quotes the centurion directly. 'Matthew quite reasonably attributes to him what was done at his request and in his name' (Calvin 1994: 247); note how the Syrian captain represents his king in 2 Kings 6:32-7:2, 17-20. At work here, as elsewhere in chapters 8–9, is Matthew's 'tendency to condense' (Carson 1984: 200; cf. France 1985: 151; Morris 1992: 191).

article; and one's own child or a servant, depending on the context. This *pais* is male: the article is *ho*. In the similar, but distinct, episode of John 4:46-54, the sick *huios* ('son') is also called *pais* ('child' or 'son'); and in Luke 8:51, 54, Jairus' daughter is called *pais*. But here in Matthew 8:5-13, *pais* denotes not a son (*huios* is lacking) but a servant: in Luke 7, he is called both *doulos* ('slave'; 7:2, 3, 10) and *pais* (7:7).[24] 'My servant,' says the centurion, 'is lying paralyzed [*paralytikos*] at home, suffering dreadfully [*deinōs basanizomenos*]' (Matt. 8:6). Demonic activity is not expressly indicated; the paralysis itself tortures and torments the man.[25] The centurion prizes him (Luke 7:6) not merely as a financial asset but as a companion: in present circumstances the soldier may have had no family but this servant.[26]

Jesus' reply – *Egō elthōn therapeusō auton* (Matt. 8:7 – may be rendered as a promise, 'I will come and heal him' (ESV), or as a question, 'Shall I come and heal him?' (TNIV). On the first reading, Jesus expresses his willingness to disregard or to surmount the cultic and social barriers separating Jews from Gentiles. But the latter reading accords better with the present focus of Jesus' mission (see his charge to the twelve in 10:5-6), and with his initial response to the Canaanite woman (see 15:23, 24, 26). Jesus is presently testing this Gentile master as he will test that Gentile mother.[27]

---

[24]See Morris 1995: 254-55, for arguments that the event of John 4 is different from that of Matthew 8 and Luke 7; and *TC*, 178, for arguments favoring *pais* over *huios* at John 4:51. For *pais* as 'servant' rather than 'son' in Matthew 8:6, 8, 13, see Davies and Allison 1991: 21; BAGD s.v., 1.

[25]Gundry 1994: 142 rightly calls the paralysis 'a malevolent force.' The gospels never apply the verb *basanizō* ('torture, torment') to demonic activity; on the contrary, demons themselves use the term to describe the punishment they expect from Jesus (8:29; Mark 5:7; Luke 8:28). Nor is the verb *ballō* ('throw') applied to demonic abuse (but see Mark 9:18, where a different verb is used); the perfect passive *beblētai* in Matthew 8:6 means that the man 'has been thrown,' i.e., forced to lie, on a sickbed.

[26]Keener 1999: 266 thinks the slave 'was probably the centurion's entire "family".... Roman soldiers were not permitted to have legal families during their two decades of military service.'

[27]Taking Matthew 8:7 as a question also makes better sense of Jesus' opening *Egō* and of the centurion's answer in verse 8. Also favoring this option are Carson 1984: 201; Jeremias 1958: 30; and Martin 1978: 15. As Jesus tests both these Gentiles, he also favors the one as he favors the other: compare 8:13 with 15:28.

The Centurion's Response (8:8-9)

'Lord [*Kyrie*], I am not worthy [*hikanos*], that you should come under my roof; but [*alla*] only say a word [*monon eipe logō*], and my servant will be healed' (Matt. 8:8). To judge from the rest of his reply, this man uses the vocative *Kyrie* (here and in 8:6) much as the leper did (8:2). That is, he honors Jesus as a man to whom the God of Israel has granted stupendous authority and power.[28] He expresses his unworthiness in response to Jesus' question, not (or not so much) because he fears Jesus the Jew will become ceremonially defiled by entering a Gentile's home, but because he recognizes Jesus to be a mightier and a holier man than he. John the Baptist expressed himself similarly, for much the same reason, in 3:11 (where the adjective *hikanos* recurs).[29] In that recognition, the centurion entreats Jesus to act without coming to his home, and to heal his servant now by merely speaking a word.[30] The absence of healings at a distance thus far in Matthew makes this request the more remarkable.[31] In grieving for his servant and desiring mercy for him, in humbling himself before Jesus and invoking divine power in face of human helplessness, the centurion exemplifies the character celebrated in the Beatitudes.

He then says: 'For [*gar*] I too [*kai...egō*] am a man under authority [*hypo exousian*], having soldiers under myself [*hyp' emauton*]. And I say to this one, "Go [*Poreuthēti*]," and he goes; and to another, "Come [*Erchou*]," and he comes; and to my slave, "Do this [*Poiēson touto*]," and he does it' (8:9). This verse provides the basis for the entreaty of 8:8b: note the opening

---

[28]As a rule, 'Roman soldiers participated in pagan religious oaths to the divine emperor' (Keener 1999: 264). But as noted, Luke 7:3-5 strongly suggests that this soldier was a 'God-fearer.'

[29]Cf. Carson 1984: 201; France 1985: 155; Gundry 1994: 143; K. H. Rengstorf, *TDNT* 3: 294, s.v. *hikanos* (he thinks the centurion, like John, confesses Jesus to be the Messiah). Cf. Acts 10:25, where Cornelius' behavior towards Peter recalls that of the leper in Matthew 8:2.

[30]The aorist *eipe*, from the verb *legō*, is an imperative of entreaty which here states the condition ('speak a word') on which the servant's healing depends ('shall be healed,' *iathēsetai*, a future passive indicative of *iaomai*). See *GGBB*, 489-90, on the 'conditional imperative.'

[31]But see John 4:46-54 for an earlier such example. Later in Matthew Jesus again heals at a distance with a word (15:28).

gar. 'I too' mediate authority, he says. On the one hand, I am 'under authority' – that of the legate who commands my legion, that of Herod Antipas whom I presently serve, and ultimately that of the emperor. On the other hand, as a centurion I have a hundred or so soldiers 'under myself.'[32] Significantly, he stresses not his superiors' authority over him but the authority he exercises over those under his command. By this means, he tacitly argues from the lesser to the greater: if a mere word or two (as in his examples) suffices to elicit action from one of his soldiers, how much greater the effect of a single word from Jesus. What choice would the servant's paralysis have but to obey, and instantly to depart?

Jesus' Words to the Crowd (8:10-12)

Hearing those words, 'Jesus marveled [ethaumasen] and said to those who were following [namely, the 'huge crowds,' 1], "Truly I tell you, with no one in Israel have I found such faith [tosautēn pistin]"' (Matt. 8:10).[33] As the adjective 'such' (tosautēs) makes clear, Jesus is not saying that Jews lack faith, only that theirs compares unfavorably to that of the centurion. Jesus elsewhere commends the faith of certain Jews: see 9:22, 29. On other occasions he acts in response to Jews' faith while not expressly praising it: see 9:2. The faith of the leper whom Jesus healed was obvious: placed opposite that story, Jesus' statement in 8:10 is the more remarkable. Significantly, the only place in Matthew where Jesus says 'Great [megalē] is your faith,' is when addressing another Gentile (15:28). Furthermore, nowhere is Jesus said to 'marvel' at an Israelite's faith. On the contrary: in the only place beyond 8:10 and its parallel in Luke 7:9 where the verb thaumazō is used of Jesus, he marvels at his townspeople's unbelief (Mark 6:6, apistia).

While there are doubtless reasons for Jesus' astonishment that escape us, we may suggest two. 1. The centurion's theological understanding. Joining what he has learned of the Hebrew Scriptures (from attending the local synagogue)

---

[32]See page 497, including n. 20.

[33]In place of 'with no one [par' oudeni] in Israel,' the parallel in Luke 7:9 has 'not even [oude] in Israel,' which explains the presence of the latter in some MSS. of Matthew 8:10 (TC, 17).

to what he has seen and heard of Jesus' ministry (which may include the healing of the leper, the earlier healing of John 4:46-54,[34] and the cure of other paralytics [Matt. 4:24]), he perceives that the God of Israel has endowed this man with great – perhaps unique – authority. On the other hand, many Jews – whose knowledge of the OT far exceeds his – either lack this insight or believe Jesus to be the enemy of God.[35] 2. His *practical obedience*. His knowledge of the truth impels him to action in face of a specific and serious need. Recognizing Jesus' great authority, how (we may ask) could he have behaved otherwise? Moreover, his appeal expresses both appreciative love for Jesus and love for a close, perhaps his closest, neighbor.

Jesus then declares 'that many [*polloi*] will come from the east and the west and recline at table [*anaklithēsontai*] with Abraham and Isaac and Jacob in the kingdom of heaven' (8:11). This meeting, together with the servant's healing, foreshadows the proclamation of the gospel to the nations, and the Gentiles' believing response: see 24:14; 26:13; 28:19. When those Gentiles come streaming into the kingdom, then both Jesus' prophecy in 8:11 and God's promises to the patriarchs themselves will be fulfilled.[36] That great event – the Messianic banquet at the kingdom's consummation – is adumbrated in Peter's table fellowship with Cornelius, and anticipated every time the Lord's Supper is celebrated.[37]

Prior to Jesus, 'such a banquet was thought to be a strictly Jewish affair..., with the Gentiles at best receiving the overflow from the blessing to the Jews. The Gentiles would indeed make their pilgrimage to Jerusalem at the end (Isa. 2:2-3), but mainly as witnesses of God's blessing of Israel, not as direct

---

[34]Carson 1984: 201 thinks this earlier healing may have strengthened the centurion's faith.

[35]If the centurion lacked synagogue teaching, his faith is yet more astonishing. On the divine Son's willing submission to the Father's authority, see John 5:17-47; Bruner 2004a: 381.

[36]To Abraham (Gen.12:3; 18:18; 22:18); to Isaac (Gen. 26:4); and to Jacob (Gen. 28:14); cf. Galatians 3:7-29. Matthew 8:11 presupposes bodily resurrection (Guthrie 1981: 819); cf. 22:23-33.

[37]See Acts 10:9-48; and the comments on Matthew 26:28-29.

participants in it. The references [to] the coming of many from east and west [e.g., Ps. 107:3; Isa. 43:5] were understood as referring to the return of diaspora Jews to Israel.'[38] Jesus says nothing of Jewish pilgrims: on the contrary, he says that Jews – 'the sons of the kingdom' – 'will be cast out [*ekblēthēsontai*] into the outer darkness,' where there will be 'weeping and grinding of teeth' (8:12).[39] Not all Israelites are to be excluded from the kingdom, of course: the Jewish patriarchs will welcome these Gentiles; the apostles whom Jesus commissions to evangelize the nations are all Jews; and one of those nations is Israel, many of whose people will be saved.[40] Nonetheless to hear simultaneously that many (*polloi*) Gentiles will enter God's kingdom, and that the same God will consign many Israelites to eternal destruction (*ekblēthēsontai* is a divine passive) – that is, that Gentiles will *replace* Jews as his favored people – would have been indescribably shocking to this crowd of Jews, and probably infuriating to most of them.[41] Jesus *meant* for his words to have that effect. He wanted Jewish listeners to be jolted out of their ignorance, hostility and unbelief; to acknowledge him as the promised Messiah, to embrace his gospel and submit to his law; to escape final destruction and to be welcomed instead into the bliss of the kingdom, there to recline at table with the patriarchs and those believing Gentiles. It is to the same end that the evangelist Matthew addresses non-believing Jews.[42]

---

[38]Hagner 1993: 205. The Greek *diaspora*, 'dispersion,' denotes Jews scattered among the nations, exiled from the homeland. Note its usage in John 7:35; James 1:1; 1 Peter 1:1. Davies and Allison 1991: 28 think that Jesus contrasts privileged and unprivileged *Jews* in Matthew 8:11-12.

[39]All these terms recur in Matthew 22:13 and 25:30, again to denote final punishment. There are further references to 'weeping and grinding of teeth' in 13:42, 50; 24:51. Present terror and anguish cannot compare to those eternal ones. Cf. comments on 18:8 ('the eternal fire').

[40]See 10:23; 28:19; also Acts (with its many references to evangelizing Jews); Romans 9–11 (with its promise of Israel's salvation, 11:26); James 1:1 (addressed to Jewish Christians).

[41]No doubt some were already angered by Jesus' praise for a *Roman* who was also a *soldier* (cf. Keener 1999: 265).

[42]See pages 173-77, 'Addressing Non-Believers.'

The Healing of the Servant (8:13)
'And Jesus said to the centurion, "Go, let it be to you as you
have believed." And the servant was healed in that hour.'
In response to the centurion's faith and in keeping with his
entreaty – 'only say a word' (8:8) – Jesus' utterance is the very
means by which the healing occurs. The servant was healed
'in that hour' (*en tē hōra ekeinē*), i.e., at the very time Jesus
spoke those words.[43] In obedience to the aorist imperative
genēthētō soi – 'let it happen for you' – the paralysis vanishes.
It is Yahweh incarnate who acts: *iathē* (from *iaomai*), 'was
healed,' is a 'divine passive.' That his word effects a cure *at
a distance* shows its incomparable power.[44] This method also
accords with Jesus' present focus on Israel: contrast Matthew
9:2-8, where a Jewish *paralytikos* is healed in Jesus' presence.
The servant in the present story is (apparently) a Gentile. We
know that he is his master's inferior socially and economically
– and also physically, for he is afflicted with paralysis, and
according to Luke 7:2 close to death. We know nothing of his
spiritual condition; whether he shared his master's faith, or
asked him to appeal to Jesus on his behalf, we are not told.
Yet, Jesus heals him without hesitation and without further
inquiry – bringing the grace of the kingdom to poignant
expression here at the story's climax.

Matthew 8:2-13 recalls the story about Naaman, a high-
ranking Gentile soldier and a leper, in 2 Kings 5. But that passage
has more in common with Luke 7:1-10 than with Matthew 8.[45]

C. Jesus and Peter's Mother-in-Law (8:14-15)
See also Mark 1:29-31 and Luke 4:38-39. Having entered
'into Capernaum [*eis Kaph.*]' (8:5), Jesus now comes 'into the
home [*eis tēn oikian*] of Peter' (8:14a). *Petros* appears here for
the first time since 4:18, where Jesus met him and the other

---

[43]ESV translates this phrase 'at that very moment.'

[44]The earlier miracle of John 4:46-54 is yet more astounding. Here too
Jesus' very word ('Your son lives'; 4:50) effects the cure (see 4:51-53). But,
whereas in Matthew 8, Jesus and the servant are both in Capernaum, in
John 4 the son lies ill in Capernaum and Jesus is in Cana, some fifteen miles
away. The *basilikos*, 'royal official' (John 4:46), may or may not be a Gentile.

[45]For the affinities between 2 Kings 5 and Luke 7, see Green 1997: 284.

three fishermen on the seashore nearby.[46] Peter's mother-in-law 'lay sick' (*beblēmenēn*) at home, as did the centurion's servant (*beblētai en tē oikia*; 8:6). She is 'suffering with a fever' (*pyressousan*, a participle of *pyressō*; cf. the noun *pyr*, 'fire,' 8:14b); in the language of Luke 4:38, 'with a high fever [*pyretō megalō*].' It 'may have been malarial; fever itself was considered a disease, not a symptom, at that time.'[47]

From the parallel accounts we learn that others speak to Jesus about the woman (Mark 1:30), and appeal to him on her behalf (Luke 4:38) as had the centurion for his servant. Matthew stresses Jesus' own initiative: he 'saw' (*eiden*) her (8:14), which Matthew alone states; 'and he touched her hand' (8:15a), as his hand had touched the leper (8:3), an act forbidden in rabbinic tradition.[48] The first effect is that 'the fever [*ho pyretos*] left her [*aphēken autēn*]' (8:15b). The previous stories showed the healing power of Jesus' words (8:3, 13). Here he is not said to speak: so mighty is his touch that the fever *departs*, which proves it to be a malady and not just a symptom. (Given the similarities between the previous story and that of John 4:46-54, it is interesting to observe that *ho pyretos* likewise 'left' [*aphēken*] the royal official's son [4:52].) Luke 4:39 reports that Jesus first stood over the woman and 'rebuked [*epitimēsen*] the fever,' which identifies it as a malevolent force and perhaps the effect of demonic activity.[49]

The fever having left, Peter's mother-in-law 'arose and began to serve him [*diēkonei autō*]' (Matt. 8:15c). By doing so ('immediately' according to Luke 4:39), she provides onlookers what the cure of Matthew 8:13 could not, and the cleansing

---

[46]The parallel to Matthew 8:14 in Mark 1:29 relates that all four are with Jesus in the house. Both Mark (1:29-30) and Luke (4:38) here use the name *Simōn* instead of *Petros*. In Matthew, he is called *Petros* far more than *Simōn* (23 times as opposed to 5), on account of Jesus' words in 16:18.

[47]Carson 1984: 204. Publius' father 'lay sick with fever and dysentery,' says Acts 28:8.

[48]'Touching a person with a fever was forbidden in rabbinic tradition' (Hagner 1993: 209).

[49]See page 498, n. 25. The verb *epitimaō* is used of Jesus' rebuke of demons in, e.g., Matthew 17:18; Mark 1:25; 9:25; Luke 4:35 with 4:41, instances flanking that of 4:39.

of 8:3 probably did not – visible proof of the healing.[50] How fitting that she should first be intent on serving the One who banished her fever![51]

D. Jesus and the Servant of Yahweh (8:16-17)

Verse 16 underscores and amplifies the witness of 8:2-15 and also of 4:23-24 to Jesus' authority as a healer. That evening 'they brought to him many who were demon-possessed; and he cast out the spirits with a word, and he healed [*etherapeusen*] all those who had illnesses.' This verb *therapeuō* appears in the question of 8:7, twice in 4:23-24 and again in the summary of 9:35. Behind 'they brought to him' is *prosēnegkan autō*, the very same terms used in 4:24.[52] Both verses likewise refer to the 'demon-possessed' (*daimonizomenous*) and to 'those having illnesses' (*tous kakōs echontas*). Both stress the comprehensiveness of Jesus' compassion and power: in 4:24 it was 'all' (*pantas*) who had these and other maladies whom he healed; here it is 'many' (*pollous*) demon-possessed, and 'all' (*pantas*) the ill. These healings of the demon-possessed anticipate those of 8:28-34 and 9:32-34; the verbs used here – *daimonizomai* and *ekballō* ('to cast out') – recur in both those passages. That Jesus cast out the spirits (*pneumata*) 'with a word' (*logō*), recalls the centurion's entreaty in 8:8 (including *logō*), together with Jesus' response to it.

Matthew 8:17 illuminates those healings: 'in order that [*hopōs*] what was spoken through Isaiah the prophet might be fulfilled [*plērōthē*], saying, "He himself took up [*elaben*] our sicknesses [*tas astheneias hēmōn*], and he carried [*ebastasen*] our diseases [*tas nosous*]."' Matthew quotes Isaiah 53:4a. The LXX

---

[50]The servant was not present when healed. Matthew 8:4 suggests that the leper's cleansing was not visible to the crowd (cf. page 495, n. 12).

[51]Whereas Matthew says *diēkonei autō* ('him'), Mark and Luke (both of whom have noted the presence of other people) have *diēkonei autois* ('them'). This verb is an ingressive (or inceptive) imperfect of *diakoneō* (so, 'she began to serve'); it may imply that the service continued for some time (cf. *GGBB*, 544). 'It is very fit that they whom Christ hath healed should minister unto him, as his humble servants, all their days' (Henry 1961: 1241, on v. 15).

[52]The term is an aorist plural of *prospherō*, 'bring to,' 'bear to'). Cf. its use in 8:4.

reads: 'This one carries [*pherei*] our sins [*tas hamartias hēmōn*], and he suffers pain [*odynatai*] for us [*peri hēmōn*].' Matthew is closer to the MT, which reads: 'Surely he lifted up [*nāśā'*] our sicknesses [*choʰlāyēnû*], and he carried [*seʰbālām*] our pains [*mak'ōbēynû*].'[53] As elsewhere in Matthew, the words of the quotation come *from* God *through* (*dia*) the prophet.[54] On Jesus as the fulfillment of the OT in Matthew, and the evangelist's use of the verb *plēroō*, see pages 97, 120-22.

This text from Isaiah did not prophesy that the Servant would himself experience sickness (*astheneia*) or disease (*nosos*), but rather that he would *take up* (the verb *lambanō*) other people's maladies and *bear* or *carry* (the verb *bastazō*) them.[55] Is he not the *Servant* of Yahweh, and does he not serve Yahweh by serving other people? And is it not precisely in *service* that he exercises his great *authority*?

In accord with this quotation of Isaiah 53:4a, Matthew's every other usage of *nosos* (4:23-24; 9:35; 10:1) likewise refers to literal disease; and while *astheneia* occurs nowhere else in Matthew, every instance of the matching verb *astheneō* (10:8; 25:36, 39) denotes bodily sickness. Yet, it is equally clear that these miracles are inextricably joined to Jesus' gospel about the dawn of God's rule: see the summaries of 4:23-24; 9:35; and 11:5. Moreover, integral to this gospel is the promise of sins' forgiveness through Jesus' redemptive sacrifice, the main work he came to accomplish: see 20:28; 26:28; also 9:1-8, where healing and forgiving are two dimensions of one saving action. By the same token, Isaiah 53:4a, the text quoted in Matthew 8:17, points to its own context, especially to *the bearing of sins* by this same Servant, these being a much heavier burden for him than diseases: see Isaiah 53:5-12.[56] Thus on the one hand, salvation is genuinely but not exclusively physical:

---

[53]These Hebrew terms are translated as in BDB. Matthew, MT and LXX all have the same word order for each clause: object, then verb.

[54]See page 96 and comments on Matthew 1:22.

[55]Cf. the two other instances of *bastazō* in Matthew: 3:11 (of John's not carrying Messiah's sandals) and 20:12 (of workers' bearing the burden of the day). The gospels never report that Jesus experienced illness or disease.

[56]Cf. the question of Matthew 9:5. Having learned how Jesus applied the OT to his person and work (see pp. 101-2), Matthew and other early

the forgiveness of sins is of far greater moment than the cure of paralysis (Matt. 9:1-8); all such healings offer images and illustrations of that greater cure – liberation from sin and its destructive powers. But neither is salvation purely spiritual: all these miracles – restoring sight, healing paralysis, cleansing lepers, curing deafness, raising the dead (11:5) – offer foretastes and glimpses of that wholeness to be experienced when, at history's consummation, the bodies of those whose sins are forgiven are raised whole, immortal and imperishable.[57]

Christians drew upon 'certain large sections' of the OT. 'These sections were understood as *wholes*, and particular verses or sentences [in this case Isaiah 53:4a] were quoted from them...as pointers to the whole context [in this case the rest of Isaiah 53]' (Dodd 1952: 126). Note how 1 Peter 2:22-25 (i) both quotes and alludes to Isaiah 53; (ii) draws from 53:4 as well as from verses 5-12; (iii) speaks of Christ's bearing our sins (1 Pet. 2:24a), in keeping with the LXX of 53:4a (see the above quotation); and (iv) alludes to 53:5 in 2:24b, 'by whose wound you were healed.' In Matthew 12:15-21, another passage about the Servant (Isa. 42:1-4) is related to Jesus' healings; but this quotation stresses Jesus' character and also his mission to the Gentiles – which his saving death precipitates.

[57]Cf. 1 Corinthians 15:3, 17-20, 51-57; Carson 1984: 205-6. After commenting on Matthew 8:1-17 and referring to James 5:14-15, Bruner 2004a: 391 notes that fear of the spectacular 'should not keep [today's] congregations from having quiet, simple meetings and visits for healings.'

II.
'OUR GOD IS SOVEREIGN'[1]
(8:18-34)

Jesus is God incarnate (Matt. 1:23). The reality and character of his sovereignty, already evident from his cure of various diseases (8:1-17), are now revealed in his encounters with disciples, in his mastery of the storm, and in his conquest of demons.

A. Jesus' Authority over Disciples (8:18-22)

As huge crowds followed Jesus upon his descent from the mountain (8:1), so now there is a crowd around him (8:18) – its numbers perhaps bolstered in the wake of those healing miracles (8:16).[2] Seeing the crowd, Jesus 'gave orders' – *ekeleusen*, a sign of his authority – that he and his disciples travel by boat (8:23) from Capernaum (8:5) 'to the other side' (*eis to peran*) of the Sea of Galilee (8:18). They disembarked in the land of the Gadarenes (8:28, where *eis to peran* recurs), evidence that they journeyed several miles in a southeasterly direction.

The First Disciple (8:19-20)

'And a scribe [*heis grammateus*] came up and said to him, "Teacher [*Didaskale*], I will follow you [*akoloutheso soi*] wherever you go"' (Matt. 8:19). The language of 8:21 – *heteros...ton matheton* [*autou*], 'another of the [or his] disciples' – indicates that the scribe is a disciple of Jesus.[3] At this stage of the Galilean ministry, *mathetes* denotes a person who follows

---

[1] Words from the hymn 'Our God Is Mighty,' by Margaret Clarkson (1976).

[2] The Greek MSS. use various terms for the crowd of Matthew 8:18. The most likely reading is *ochlon*, 'crowd' (see *TC*, 17). Among the alternatives are *ochlous*, 'crowds' (as in 7:28), and *pollous ochlous*, 'huge crowds' (as in 8:1).

[3] Thus, e.g., Carson 1984: 208. In this instance, the sense of *heteros* is no different from *allos*: note their use together in Matthew 16:14; cf. BAGD s.v.

Jesus about and attends to his teaching: see 5:1-2, which
contains the only prior instance of *mathētēs*. This man is not a
Christian *grammateus*: only later would the term be so applied,
even to Matthew (13:52; 23:34). Rather he is a Jewish scholar
of the law, a representative of the 'scribes and Pharisees'
(5:20).[4] To judge from his vow, the address – *Didaskale* – is
an expression of genuine respect (unlike that of 22:16). This
term, together with the nearness of the preceding sermon
(geographically, temporally and textually), suggests that he is
one of the disciples whom Jesus there addressed. Moreover,
the placement of this encounter suggests that Jesus' mighty
works have influenced the man as well.[5]

Verse 19 calls him 'one [*heis*] scribe.' While this could be
equivalent to 'a certain [*tis*] scribe,' here the numeral may be
emphatic: i.e., there is at least *one* scribe whose initial response
to Jesus has been affirmative.[6] Nor does anything in the text call
his sincerity into question. At the same time, this disciple stands
at a critical juncture. What will he do with what he has seen
and heard? How will he relate it to what he already knows?
How will it affect his beliefs and behavior henceforth? Does he
really understand what following Jesus entails? 'I will follow
you wherever you go [*hopou ean aperchē*],' he says. This may
refer only to the journey across the lake (the *apelthein* of 8:18,
'to depart,' comes from the same verb), but is probably more
comprehensive ('*wherever* you go').[7] Yet a desire to study under
rabbi Jesus for an extended period without an underlying and

---

heteros, 1. b. Even though *autou* ('his') is textually doubtful (*TC*, 17-18), these
are manifestly Jesus' (not someone else's) disciples.

[4]To say 'scribe' itself marks the man as a disciple (so Gundry 1994: 151)
is premature.

[5]Assuming these influences, we may wonder how he was affected
by Jesus' words in 5:20, and whether he recognized in Jesus' teaching an
authority lacking in his own (cf. 7:29); and also how he was affected by
Jesus' attitude towards the leper and the centurion (8:2-13).

[6]As *IB* notes, 125, *heis* is sometimes equivalent to *tis*. But at least in
Matthew, according to Gundry 1994: 152, the numeral 'carries an emphasis
lacking in the indefinite pronoun.'

[7]France (1985: 159) favors the first alternative; Hagner (1993: 216), the
second. The aorist infinitive *apelthein* (8:18) and the present subjunctive
aperchē (8:19) both come from *aperchomai*, 'go away.'

undying commitment to his person fails to comprehend what it means to follow him.[8] As Jesus' teaching powerfully attests, in the end the only true disciples are those who actually commit themselves to the rule of God and to the Lordship of Jesus; who personally embrace the grace of the gospel and repent accordingly; and who show their gratitude for grace and their love for Jesus by obeying the law he expounds. Jesus often challenges those who are disciples in *name* to become disciples in *fact*. He does so repeatedly in the preceding sermon – in part by means of that terrifying prophecy (Matt. 7:21-23) that at the Last Judgment some who think themselves to be his disciples will be banished from his presence.

Jesus replies (8:20): 'Foxes have dens and birds of the air have nests, but the Son of Man has nowhere to lay his head.' For the first time in Matthew Jesus refers to himself as 'the Son of Man,' *ho huios tou anthrōpou*. On his lips, this term signals his *divine sonship, majesty and authority* and also his *humanity, deprivations and sufferings*.[9] Matthew 8–9 speaks strongly of that kingly authority. But here Jesus focuses on his earthly privations – unthinkable experiences for a king in power, appalling experiences for a *man* in face of God's provisions for the *animals* (cf. 6:26). His having 'nowhere to lay his head' indicates not so much lack of lodging as rejection by people who should have welcomed him as their Messiah-King. Both as Son of Man and as Servant of Yahweh, he is 'despised and rejected by men.'[10] Some interpreters detect political overtones in Jesus' reply. T. W. Manson, for example, thinks that the 'foxes' symbolize Ammonites and Edomites, two of Israel's ancient enemies; that the 'birds of the air' stand for the Gentile

---

[8]See the comments on 4:20-22. France 1985: 160 calls this man 'an academic dilettante disciple.'

[9]See pages 135-36.

[10]Isaiah 53:3 (v. 4 is quoted in Matthew 8:17; cf. p. 135, n. 54, on the Son of Man, (Dan. 7), as a re-presentation of Isaiah's Servant of Yahweh). 'Homelessness stands for rejection by people rather than lack of lodging as such' (Gundry 1994: 152). Cf. Matthew 8:34 (Gadarenes beg Jesus to leave); 10:14 (disciples may be refused hospitality); Luke 9:52-53 (Samaritans deny hospitality to Jesus and his disciples; 9:58 parallels Matthew 8:19); but also texts that imply an offer of lodging to Jesus (Matt. 8:14; 9:10, 28; 13:1, 36; 17:25; 21:17; 26:6; Mark 10:10; Luke 10:38) and to disciples (Matt. 10:11). Does 8:19 help to explain why 8:24 mentions no 'cushion,' though Mark 4:38 does?

nations; and that their current representatives, the Idumean (Edomite) Herod Antipas and the Romans, have so imposed their power that the true Israel – the Son of Man, together with those joined to him – has been disinherited. Even if Jesus intends no such symbolism, he says in effect to this disciple: 'if you cast your lot with me and mine you join the ranks of the dispossessed, and you must be prepared to serve God under those conditions.'[11] Whether the scribe responded as the fishermen did (Matt. 4:20, 22), or instead as the rich man would (19:22), we are not told.

The Second Disciple (8:21-22)
This man says, in response to an implied summons ('Follow me,' explicit in the parallel of Luke 9:59): 'Lord [*Kyrie*], permit me first to go and bury my father' (Matt. 8:21). This address (the same as the leper's (8:2) and the centurion's (8:4) bespeaks a firmer commitment to Jesus than the scribe's 'Teacher' (8:19). Within a Jewish context, the request seems quite legitimate. It accords with the practice of the patriarchs (Gen. 25:9; 35:29; 50:5, 13); and with the fifth commandment (Exod. 20:12; Deut. 5:16; 27:16), which Jesus himself champions (Matt. 15:3-6). 'Palestinian piety, basing itself on the fifth commandment..., expected sons to attend to the burial of their parents.'[12] In all probability the father is still alive: had he just died, the son would be expected to stay at home in mourning, not to appear thus in public.[13] And were his father dying, the son might be expected to ask Jesus to come and heal him, as he had Peter's mother-in-law. With others, I conclude that the disciple is asking to postpone his duty to Jesus until his father dies – whenever that happens – so that he may fulfill his ultimate filial duty before leaving home.[14]

---

[11]See Manson 1957: 72-73, who is followed by Bailey 1980: 24-25. Jesus calls Herod a fox in Luke 13:32. To Hagner 1993: 216, finding symbolism in the foxes and birds 'seems unjustified and unnecessary.'

[12]Carson 1984: 208. Cf. Tobit 4:3; 6:14; 14:10-11; further references in Keener 1999: 276. Elisha's request (1 Kings 19:20) is closer to Luke 9:61, which has no parallel in Matthew.

[13]Bailey 1980: 26, *apud* Ibrahim Sa'id. Cf. Davies and Allison 1991: 57.

[14]Keener 1999: 276, following Bailey, ibid. See Keener, ibid., for the suggestion that the son has in view his father's *reburial* a year after his death.

Jesus replies (Matt. 8:22): 'Follow me, and leave the dead [*tous nekrous*] to bury their own dead [*tous heautōn nekrous*].' Some take this to mean, 'Let the (spiritually) dead bury the (physically) dead.'[15] Others think that the Aramaic underlying 'to bury' (*thapsai*) referred not to the act of burial but to the one who buries, the undertaker: 'Leave the dead to the burier of their dead.'[16] Jesus more likely means, 'Let that matter [*tous nekrous*] look after itself [*tous heautōn nekrous*].'[17]

However Jesus' words are understood, they are shocking – and are intended to be. What makes them so is not their alleged or perceived insensitivity to law-keeping (cf. 5:17-48!), or to death and grief (which would affect Jesus far more deeply than others: cf. 9:18-26; John 11). Rather, Jesus' unqualified and unyielding language is consistent with his Lordship, and with his insistence that loyalty to him take precedence over the most binding earthly obligations. Did not James and John leave their father to follow him (4:22)? And do not the demands of one's own family pose one of the most serious obstacles to true discipleship (10:34-39)? Says Jesus in effect to this disciple: 'Leave [*aphes*] that matter: yet more – far more – urgent matters require your attention.[18] Submit yourself unreservedly to God's rule, and do his will. Prove the genuineness of that address [*Kyrie*; 8:21] by giving me your highest and lasting allegiance, and doing what I say.[19] Instead of going away from me [*apelthein*, 21] to await your father's death and burial, go away with me [*apelthein*; 8:18; *aperchē*; 8:19], so that in time you may go away [*apelthōn*, Luke 9:60] to proclaim the kingdom of God.[20] Understand this: what makes sense of the *cost* of discipleship, is the *value* of God's kingdom

---

[15]So Carson 1984: 208.

[16]Noted (but not defended) in Manson 1957: 73; and in Hagner 1993: 218, who notes that the Aramaic *lᵉmiqbar* means 'to bury'; and *limqabber*, 'to the burier.'

[17]Thus Manson 1957: 73; cf. Hagner 1993: 218; Gundry 1994: 153.

[18]*Aphes*, from *aphiēmi*, is an aorist imperative of command: 'leave, abandon.' Cf. the use of the matching participle *aphentes* in Matthew 4:20, 22 (see those comments).

[19]Cf. 7:21-27, including the futile *Kyrie, kyrie*, of 7:21 and 22.

[20]All these terms come from *aperchomai*. Luke 9:60 (where 'go proclaim the kingdom of God' augments Luke's parallel to Matthew 8:22) comes from

and God's Messiah [Matt. 13:44-46].' As with the first disciple, we wonder what happened next. Whether in response to the command 'Follow [*Akolouthei*] me' (8:22), he joined those disciples who followed (*ēkolouthēsan*) Jesus across the lake (8:23), we cannot say.

Jesus' encounters with these two disciples occur within a passage dominated by his mighty works. One intent of the text may, therefore, be to warn readers that being dazzled by Jesus' miracles and marveling at their power are not alone an adequate basis for serious discipleship. Nor, for that matter, is being mesmerized by the wisdom and authority of his teaching (Matt. 7:28-29).

B. Jesus' Authority over Storm and Sea (8:23-27)

Jesus 'having gotten into the boat [*embanti autō eis to ploion*], his disciples followed him [*ēkolouthēsan autō*]' (8:23) – some in the same boat, some in others.[21] They are thus doing what that first disciple promised to do (8:19) and what Jesus commanded the second one to do (8:22). As noted, we cannot tell whether these two joined the others.

The Crisis

'And behold [*kai idou*], there arose [*egeneto*] a great storm [*seismos megas*] on the sea, so that the boat was being covered with the waves; but he himself remained asleep [*autos*

---

a later stage of Jesus' ministry and presupposes a longer period of teaching than does Matthew 8:22. Jesus demands more from a follower (Luke 9:61-62) than did Elijah from Elisha (1 Kings 19:20); for Jesus is far greater than Elijah (Matt. 16:14, 16; 17:1-13). (His greatness exceeds Elisha's too: see 14:13-21 and comments.)

[21]See Mark 4:36 (and Gundry 1993: 238). A *ploion* 'was a vessel of almost any size and description.... Here it is doubtless a fishing boat, big enough for a dozen or more men and a good catch of fish, but not large, and without sails' (Carson 1984: 214). It is likely that the twelve, already chosen (see above, p. 303), were in the boat with Jesus. Instead of *to ploion*, some MSS. of Matthew 8:23 read *ploion*, 'a boat,' perhaps under the influence of Mark 4:36 and Luke 8:22 (which also has *ploion*). *Embanti autō*, which joins an aorist dative participle (from *embainō*) to a dative singular pronoun, appears to be a rare instance of the dative absolute (see Matt. 14:6a for another). The aorist participle here signals action prior to that of the main verb *akoloutheō* (cf. *GGBB*, 624).

de ekatheuden]. And they came and aroused him, saying: "Lord [*Kyrie*], save [*sōson*], we are perishing [*apollymetha*]!'" (Matt. 8:24-25).

As in 8:2, *kai idou* braces readers for the startling and momentous (see p. 492). The noun *seismos* literally means 'a shaking,' and usually denotes an earthquake, as, e.g., in 28:2 (where *seismos megas* recurs); here a sudden and severe storm is in view.[22] The threat is real ('they were in danger,' *ekindyneuon*; Luke 8:23), as especially fishermen in the party would realize. Although the storm has struck, Jesus remains asleep in the stern (*prymna*; Mark 4:38), a picture of tranquility in contrast to the howling wind, the engulfing waves and the terrified disciples, and also evidence of Jesus' weariness from his many labors (e.g., as summarized in 8:16).[23]

Panic-stricken, the disciples awaken Jesus and cry: *Kyrie*, *sōson*, *apollymetha* (8:25b). The words' content, pointedness and brevity (three words, ten syllables) all reflect the disciples' alarm. The vocative *Kyrie* appears for the fifth time in the chapter; those who use it here are in graver immediate danger than were the leper (8:2) and the centurion (8:6). The aorist *sōson*, from *sōzō*, is an urgent imperative of entreaty. Apart from the mocking words of Matthew 27:40, *sōson* occurs elsewhere in Matthew only on Peter's lips in very similar circumstances (14:30, where *Kyrie* also recurs). The verb *apollymetha*, a progressive present indicative from *apollymi*, expresses their fear that they have already begun to perish.

---

[22]Hagner 1993: 219 translates Matthew 8:24a: 'And look, there was a great earthquake under the sea'; but the parallel references to 'a fierce gale of wind' (*lailaps megalē anemou*; Mark 4:37) and 'gale of wind' (*lailaps anemou*; Luke 8:23), and Jesus' rebuke of the winds (*anemois*; Matthew 8:26), favor taking *seismos* here as 'storm' (thus BAGD s.v.). 'It is well known that violent squalls ...develop quickly on Lake Galilee.... The surface is more than six hundred feet below sea level, and the rapidly rising hot air draws from the southeastern tablelands violent winds whose cold air churns up the water' (Carson 1984: 215).

[23]Behind 'remained asleep' is the verb *ekatheuden*, a progressive imperfect (cf. *GGBB*, 543). The preceding *autos* is emphatic: though the disciples were very much awake, 'he himself continued sleeping' (Hagner 1993: 219).

The Christil
'And he says to them, "Why are you afraid [*Ti deiloi este*], you of little faith [*oligopistoi*]?" Then he rose and rebuked [*epetimēsen*] the winds and the sea, and there came [*egeneto*] a great calm [*galēnē megalē*]' (8:26).

Jesus replies: *Ti deiloi este, oligopistoi;* He too is brief: there are four words and (again) ten syllables. And like the disciples' cry, Jesus' question is pointed – the more so since this is his only utterance in the passage. Why does he ask this question, and why does he identify his disciples as people of little faith? Have they not appealed to him as Lord? And have they not just voiced their confidence that he is able and willing to save them from death? They have indeed: they are not *apistoi* – people *without* faith. But, says Jesus, they are *oligopistoi* – people of *little* faith. For they apparently concluded from Jesus' being asleep that the situation was presently beyond his control: but how could the One who has been manifesting such authority and power (chs. 4–8) *ever* lack control? Moreover, their apparent fear that Jesus himself is threatened with death betrays an inadequate understanding of his mission: how could the Father's appointed Servant perish before accomplishing his principal work (cf., e.g., 16:21; 20:28) and before fully equipping these his chosen emissaries (28:18-20)?[24]

Jesus, who just said that he lacks even the natural provisions granted to animals (8:20), now shows himself to be Master of nature. The authority he has been demonstrating over human afflictions, he now exerts over the raging Sea of Galilee. Not only is Jesus fearless before the fury of the storm (why should he fear what he controls?); he takes the offensive, and *rebukes* the winds and the sea, this being the verb (*epitimaō*) used in

---

[24]Cf. Carson 1984: 216. All five NT instances of the adjective *oligopistos* appear on Jesus' lips. Four of these occur in Matthew: in the other three the term expresses the disciples' failure to trust the Father (6:30; the par., Luke 12:28, contains the fifth instance); Peter's failure to trust Jesus in face of his fear (Matt. 14:30); and the disciples' imperceptiveness (16:8, with vv. 5-12). The noun *oligopistia*, 'little faith,' appears only once in the NT, again on Jesus' lips and in Matthew, where it explains the disciples' inability to exorcise a demon (17:20).

17:18 and elsewhere of his assaults on demons.[25] In obedience
to this reproof (see 8:27b), the winds and the sea cease their
ragings and ravings. The resultant tranquility equals the
former tumult: where before *seismos megas egeneto* ('a great
storm came') upon the sea (8:24), there now *egeneto galēnē
megalē* ('came a great calm' 8:26).

The Catechesis
Always and everywhere, Jesus is teaching by word and work,
by truth verbal and visible. Since his public ministry began
(Matt. 4:17), he has chosen classrooms not only in synagogues
(4:23), but also on seaside and mountainside, on the road and
in the town, in private home and on the sea. Let us focus on
three lessons for Matthew's readers from the present episode.

1. Christ
When Jesus calmed the sea, 'the men [*hoi anthrōpoi*] marveled
[*ethaumasan*, the verb used of Jesus in 8:10], saying: "What sort
of person [*Potapos*] is this [*estin houtos*], that even the winds
and the sea obey him?' (8:27). The ESV's translation of the
question – 'What sort of man is this...?' – is most regrettable.
There is no *anthrōpos* to justify 'man' (found also, e.g., in NASB
and NIV). Matthew here calls the disciples not *hoi mathētai*
but *hoi anthrōpoi* – the only place where he thus identifies
them – which accentuates the absence of the noun from the
question. The disciples are not trying to determine what kind
of *man* Jesus is. Rather, reeling under the impact of what they
have just witnessed (not to mention all that Jesus has done
heretofore), they are beginning seriously to question whether
'man' (*anthrōpos*) is adequate for identifying him. In both
senses of the word, they *wonder*: 'Who *is* this?'

Certainly the evangelist Matthew wants readers, having
learned this story and pondered that question, to conclude that
Jesus is both man and God. Precisely what the disciples meant
by the address *Kyrie* (8:25), at this stage of their theological

---

[25]See page 504, n. 49. In Mark 4:39, Jesus says to the sea: 'Be silent, shut
up!'; he used the latter verb, *phimoō*, in 1:25 to silence a demon. In Luke 8:25,
Jesus commands (*epitassō*) winds and water; this verb was used in 4:36 of
his giving orders to evil spirits.

understanding, we do not know. But Matthew's meaning is not in doubt: here, as elsewhere, he presents Jesus as Yahweh incarnate. Do not the Scriptures teach that Yahweh, and he alone, rules storm and sea?[26]

2. Salvation

The disciples cry out, 'Lord, save [*sōson*], we are perishing [*apollymetha*]!' (Matt. 8:25). It is clear from Jesus' own use of this verb *apollymi* that the death which the disciples fear is as nothing compared to another kind: 'And do not fear those who kill the body but are not able to kill the soul. Instead, fear the one who is able to destroy [*apolesai*] both soul and body in Gehenna [*en geennē*]' (10:28).[27] By the same token, better for a bodily member to perish (*apolētai*) than for God to cast one's whole body into Gehenna (5:29-30).

Jesus came to rescue persons from death – not the death of the body (8:25; 10:28a), which would come to all, and which for many would become a graver threat once they became Christians, but the death of 10:28b, the *apōleia* of 7:13, which threatens the 'lost' (*apolōlota*) sheep of Israel (10:6; 15:24). 'He will save [*sōsei*] his people from their sins,' said the angel (1:21), the only instance of *sōzō* prior to 8:25. The salvation the disciples

---

[26]See Job 38:8-11; Psalms 29:3-4, 10-11; 65:5-7; 89:9; 107:23-30; Isaiah 51:9 (and Motyer 1993: 408); Jonah 1:15-16 (when the sea stopped raging, the sailors 'greatly feared Yahweh'). In light of the disclosure of Yahweh on this occasion, note that in Mark the disciples *ephobēthēsan phobon megan* ('feared a great fear') *after* Jesus stilled the storm (4:41); and that in Luke 8:25 the words *ethaumasan* etc. (par. to the question of Matthew 8:27) are prefaced by the participle *phobēthentes* ('having become fearful'). It is hard for us (convinced *Trinitarians* illuminated by the whole NT and those early ecumenical councils) to realize how these early disciples (all of them convinced *monotheists*) must have struggled to grasp the full truth of Jesus' identity. With the above quotation from Jonah in mind, note (i) that Jonah, like Matthew, features a storm at sea which terrifies people, and during which the main figure sleeps (1:4-6); and (ii) that, whereas in Jonah, Yahweh sends the storm to judge the main figure, in Matthew the main figure – Yahweh himself – stills the storm to save his people.

[27]In the active voice, as in the aorist infinitive *apolesai* (Matt. 10:28), *apollymi* means 'destroy'; in the middle voice, as in *apollymetha* (8:25), it means 'perish.' The active can also mean 'lose' (as in 10:42); and the middle, 'be lost' (as in 10:6). See BAGD s.v.

experience on the sea is truly an image but only an image of that greater work. Without the forgiveness of sins through Messiah's sacrifice (26:28), all are doomed to destruction; yet those many who are purchased by his blood (20:28) will *never* perish (see the instances of *apollymi* in 18:14; John 3:16; 10:28).

3. Discipleship

This passage underscores the lessons of Matthew 8:18-22. On the one hand, the great storm illustrates those hazards to which Jesus alludes in answering the first disciple – 'the dangers against which Jesus warns anyone who over-thoughtlessly presses to become a disciple.'[28] On the other hand, by stilling the storm and rescuing his disciples Jesus gives assurance that he is well able 'to reward the sacrifice of abandoning earthly ties such as stand in the way of the second follower.' That is, the story depicts both the *danger* and the *glory* of discipleship.[29]

C. Jesus' Authority over Demons (8:28-34)

Having traveled for several miles in a southeasterly direction, Jesus comes 'to the other side' (*eis to peran*; 8:28a) His command has been obeyed (see 8:18, with *eis to peran*), and his victory over the storm is complete. He now enters 'the country of the Gadarenes [*tōn Gadarēnōn*]' (8:28b). Matthew identifies the region by Gadara, a city in the Decapolis (see 4:25 and comments), some six miles southeast of the Sea of Galilee. According to the other Synoptists, Jesus came into 'the country of the Gerasenes [*tōn Gerasēnōn*]' (Mark 5:1; Luke 8:26), just as fitting a description, since Gerasa, though more than thirty miles southeast of the Sea of Galilee, was another city of the Decapolis and the capital of the region.[30] Jesus thus enters

---

[28]Bornkamm 1963: 57.

[29]Ibid. These lessons, he says, are for persons in 'the little ship of the Church,' (55).

[30]These two names, together with *Gergesēnōn* ('Gergesenes,' for Gergesa), occur in MSS. for all three texts: see, e.g., ESV text and mg. at Matthew 8:28; Mark 5:1; Luke 8:26. For reasons favoring 'Gadarenes' in Matthew and 'Gerasenes' in Mark and Luke, see *TC*, 18-19. France 1985: 162 thinks this 'Gerasa' may be the modern *Kursi* (on the eastern shore of the lake) rather than the Roman city of Gerasa (over thirty miles away). The reading 'Gergesenes' was introduced, apparently by Origen, one reason being that

territory mainly populated by Gentiles – as the presence of
'many pigs' (Matt. 8:30) attests.[31]

Demonic Power

Jesus having disembarked, 'two demon-possessed men, coming
forth from the tombs, confronted him [*hypēntēsan autō*]; they
were very dangerous [*chalepoi lian*], so that no one was able to
pass along that road' (Matt. 8:28c). The demonic tyranny that
explains the men's danger to themselves and others has also
decreed their destruction. It is as though the tombs among which
they roam are waiting to receive them once their servitude is
over. The verb *hypēntēsan* suggests a hostile intent towards one
who dares to take a road others avoid.[32]

Whereas Mark 5:1 speaks of 'a man [*anthrōpos*] with an
unclean spirit [*en pneumati akathartō*],' and Luke 8:27 of 'a
certain man [*anēr tis*] possessed by demons [*echōn daimonia*],'
Matthew speaks of two demoniacs (*dyo daimonizomenoi*).
Some conclude that there was in fact only one such man;
and that the presence of two in Matthew (i) accords with
9:27-31 and 20:29-34, each of which reports the healing of
two blind men, although in each account of such a miracle in
Mark (which Matthew employs) there is only one blind man
(8:22-26; 10:46-52); (ii) heightens the effects of both demonic
and Messianic power; and (iii) compensates for Matthew's
omission of the exorcism of Mark 1:21-28.[33] Others, myself
included, believe (i) that there were in fact two demoniacs;
(ii) that whereas literary features of this gospel may favor the
first view, historical considerations favor this one; (iii) that

---

Gergesa was thought to be on the lake, unlike Gadara and Roman Gerasa
(*TC*, 19, with n. 1; France 1985: 162, n. 1; BAGD s.v. *Gergesēnos*).

[31]The Decapolis was 'a primarily Gentile area with a large Jewish
population' (Keener 1999: 282). Pigs were unclean animals according to
Jewish law: see Leviticus 11:7; Deuteronomy 14:8.

[32]The verb *hypantaō* usually means 'meet': thus in Matthew 28:9 (the only
other instance in Matthew) and perhaps here too (so BAGD s.v.). But in
Luke 14:31, the verb signals aggressive hostility; that this is also the sense
here in Matthew is suggested by the demons' initiative ('they encountered
him') and their subsequent questions (on which see below).

[33]Gundry 1994: 158 holds this view. On Matthew's fondness for pairs,
see page 58 above.

Matthew, who probably witnessed the miracle, gives us in this respect a fuller account than do Mark and Luke (neither of whom was present at the time); and (iv) that two demoniacs offer fiercer opposition than does one, so that Jesus' power over them is all the more impressive.[34]

'And behold, they cried out, saying: "What is there between us and you [*Ti hymin kai soi*], Son of God? Did you come here to torment us before the time?"' (Matt. 8:29). This idiom, *Ti hymin kai soi*, means 'What do we and you have in common?' or 'What business do we have with each other?' (NASB), or 'Our concern is not yours' – in other words, 'Leave us alone!'[35] This question, including the address 'Son of God,' makes it clear that 'they' who cried out (*ekraxan*) are not the men, but demons using men's voices.[36] They recognize Jesus' authority to torment – i.e., to destroy – them when God's kingdom is consummated and final judgment executed.[37] In their vexation – perhaps thinking that the end is closer than they supposed – they say to Jesus in effect: it is too early for you to meddle in our affairs.[38] In trying to defend their territory, they also take the offensive: the address 'Son of God,' besides revealing their

---

[34]Carson 1984: 217 defends this view; cf. Hendriksen 1973: 413-14. Calvin 1994: 283-84 follows Augustine in affirming that there were two demoniacs, and suggests that the other evangelists mention the one 'on the ground that this was the more notorious, and, because of the savagery of his affliction, was the subject of a more striking miracle.' In this regard, note how Mark 5:3-5 and Luke 8:27 describe the demon's effects on the man. 'That tombs...were unclean...and considered haunts of demons and magic... increases the audience's suspicion that these demons were inordinately powerful' (Keener 1999: 281).

[35]The expression, originally Semitic (see, e.g., David's question to the sons of Zeruiah in 2 Sam. 16:10), found its way into Greek speech. Jesus' question *Ti emoi kai soi* (John 2:4) refuses Mary's request, at least momentarily. See BAGD s.v. *egō* (p. 217b); *GGBB*, 150-51.

[36]In the parallel accounts, the one who speaks (Mark 5:7, 9a; Luke 8:28, 30a) proves to be a host of demons (5:9b; 8:30b).

[37]'To torment' translates *basanisai*, an aorist infinitive of *basanizō*, the verb used in Matthew 8:6 (see p. 498, n. 25). For torment as a mark of ultimate punishment, see *basanizō* in Revelation 14:10; 20:10; *basanismos* (noun) in Revelation 14:11; 18:7, 10, 15; and *basanos* (noun) in Luke 16:23, 28.

[38]We learn from Mark that the demonic cry (5:7; par. to Matt. 8:29), is an impudent retort to Jesus' command (5:8, 'for he was saying, "Come out!"'). Contrast Mark 1:23-25.

knowledge of Jesus' true identity, is a subtle attempt at using his holy name to influence or manipulate him.[39]

Messianic Power

'A herd of many pigs' (*agelē choirōn pollōn*) was feeding some distance away (*makran*; 8:30), but close enough to be seen (8:33).[40] Verse 28 spoke of the 'demon-possessed' (*daimonizomenoi*); verse 31a now refers directly to 'the demons' (*hoi daimones*). Knowing that Jesus is their superior, and that he is about to exert his authority over them, the demons 'began to entreat [*parekaloun*] him, saying: "If you cast us out [*Ei ekballeis hēmas*], please send [*aposteilon*] us into the herd of pigs"' (8:31b). The expulsion is not in doubt, only the destination.[41]

'And Jesus said to them, "Go [*Hypagete*]!"' (8:32a). Of all the testimonies in this chapter to the stupendous authority of Jesus' utterances, this concluding one is the most powerful. With two words (in Greek) leprosy was cleansed (8:3); with five the centurion's servant was pronounced well (8:13). Having reported Jesus' rebuke of the winds and the sea indirectly (8:26), Matthew here returns to direct speech. Here the single word *Hypagete* – which, as Jesus' only utterance in the passage

---

[39]Cf. Satan's use of 'Son of God' in Matthew 4:3, 6. 'To know the name of someone – i.e., to know his character as revealed in the name - was to gain influence over or through him' (Gundry 1994: 159); or (8:29) to try doing so. On *name* as sign of presence and power, see comments on 1:21, 23, 25, and on 6:7-8. In Mark 5:7b, in an attempt 'to exorcise Jesus out of exorcising it,' the demon 'uses the most potent name possible,' namely *God's* (Gundry 1993: 250). According to Mark 5:9 and Luke 8:30 (texts without parallel in Matthew), one way Jesus gained power over the demon was to ask for its name, a request which Legion was powerless to refuse. In Genesis 32:27-29, the Opponent learns Jacob's name but refuses Jacob's request for his.

[40]*Makran* is an adverbial accusative (*GGBB*, 201).

[41]This is the sole instance of the masculine *daimōn* in the NT; the usual term is the neuter *daimonion* (in, e.g., Matt. 7:22). With Hagner 1993: 224 (and NASB) I take *parekaloun* (from *parakaleō*) to be an inceptive imperfect (*GGBB*, 544-45). The demons' utterance takes the form of a first class conditional sentence. The *Ei* of the protasis (or 'if-clause') is rightly translated 'if' rather than 'since' (*GGBB*, 690-94); but the demons are in no doubt that Jesus is going to expel them (ibid., 692-93, including the reference to 12:27-28; and Hagner 1993: 227). As *aposteilon* is an aorist imperative of entreaty from *apostellō* (*GGBB*, 487-88), I have added the 'please.'

stands out all the more strongly – is sufficient. In obedience, the demons come out of the man (the verb *exerchomai*) and go away into the pigs (*aperchomai*; 8:32b).[42] Facts from the other accounts about the number of demons and the size of the herd make the potency of this 'one little word' yet plainer.[43] 'And behold [*kai idou*], the whole herd rushed down the steep bank into the sea and died in the waters' (8:32c). As often elsewhere, *kai idou* prepares readers for the marvelous and the momentous.[44] The shift from the singular verb 'rushed' (*hōrmēsen*, an aorist of *hormaō*) to the plural 'died' (*apethanon*, an aorist of *apothnēskō*) does not mean that the second verb denotes the demons as well as, or instead of, the herd. The text speaks not of the demons' destruction, only of their effect on the pigs: the whole herd (viewed collectively) plunged down the hill and all of them (however many) drowned in the sea – spectacular evidence of the demons' destructive power, of their potential effects on the men, and of Jesus' superior might.[45]

What happened to the demons the text does not disclose. Perhaps they wandered about in search of new or former victims (cf. Matt. 12:43-46). Nor does any account explain why Jesus allows the destruction of about 2,000 pigs, no less God's creatures for being unclean. Yet, Matthew's accent on Jesus'

---

[42]The verb *hypagete* is a present imperative from *hypagō*. With the one word, Jesus both commands the demons to leave, and grants their request. GGBB, 488-89, calls this a 'permissive imperative (imperative of toleration).'

[43]In Mark 5:9 and Luke 8:30, the name given to the demons possessing the *one* man is *Legiōn*, a military term denoting a force of about 6,000, not counting auxiliary troops (cf. p. 497, n. 20; and BAGD s.v.). Mark 5:13 numbers the herd at about 2,000.

[44]*Kai idou* also occurs in Matthew 8:29, 34, but not with quite the same dramatic effect.

[45]Gundry 1994: 160 argues that *apethanon* (Matt. 8:32) refers to the demons' 'going to the torments of hell [cf. *basanizō*; 8:29] when the herd plunged [*hōrmēsen*] in the sea.' The parallels in Mark 5:13 and Luke 8:33 indicate otherwise. Like Matthew, both begin with *hōrmēsen*. Mark's second verb is plural (*epnigonto*, an imperfect of *pnigō*): 'they [namely 'about two thousand' pigs, 13] were drowned.' Luke's second verb is singular (*apepnigē*, an aorist of *apopnigō*): 'it [namely 'the herd,' 33] was drowned.' See the arguments in Carson 1984: 219; and Hagner 1993: 228, who notes that the 'switch from a singular verb with a collective subject ("herd") to a plural verb without a change of subject is not at all unusual.'

authority supplies at least a partial answer: he who commands the winds and sea (8:23-27) also governs the animal kingdom. If 'the cattle on a thousand hills' belong to him (Ps. 50:10), so do 2,000 pigs on a single hill, and he may do with them what he pleases.[46]

Thereupon 'those who tended the pigs fled [*ephygon*]; and going into the town [*eis tēn polin*] they reported everything, including what happened to the demon-possessed men' (8:33). Not only could Jesus and the others see the herd; these herdsmen were close enough to witness the cure of the two men. Fleeing the scene, they go into the town (which may or may not be Gadara[47]) and there spread the news. 'And behold, the whole town went out to meet Jesus [*eis hypantēsin tō Iēsou*]; and when they saw him, they begged him to leave their territory' (8:34). Matthew says nothing of the astounding change in the two men's condition (contrast Mark 5:15 and Luke 8:35). Although the herdsmen had told them about the demoniacs, the townspeople went out to meet *Jesus*.[48] We are not expressly told why they implored him to leave their country. One reason – in the wake of the irretrievable loss of 2,000 pigs – may well be dread of socio-economic catastrophe.[49] But to judge from Matthew 8:34b, the main reason for the plea is the unbearable magnitude of Jesus himself. The response of these Gentiles is akin to that of the disciples in the boat: 'Who *is* this, that even demons by the thousands obey him?' (to paraphrase the question of 8:27).[50]

---

[46]Cf. Carson 1984: 219; Calvin 1994: 287 ('we should accept God's hidden judgment with reverence').

[47]If Gadara is meant (Hagner 1993: 228), the men traveled some five miles. But the *polis* may be 'a local settlement near the lake within Gadarene territory' (France 1985: 163).

[48]The noun *hypantēsis* (Matt. 8:34) matches the verb *hypantaō* (8:28).

[49]'They cared for nothing but the fact that their pigs were drowned and "their hope of making money was gone" (Acts 16:19)' (Ryle 1993: 62).

[50]Cf. Blomberg 1992: 152-53. In the same regard, according to Mark 5:15 and Luke 8:35 the people became *afraid* when they saw the man *restored* – just as the disciples became afraid *after* Jesus calmed the storm (Mark 4:41; Luke 8:25); cf. Luke 5:8, 10. This liberated man responds to Jesus in a very different way from the townspeople: see Mark 5:18-20; Luke 8:38-39.

III.
'JESUS! WHAT A FRIEND FOR SINNERS!'[1]
(9:1-17)

Matthew continues to proclaim Jesus as Savior from physical affliction (9:2-8). Moreover, here and in 9:9-13, in accord with the angel's promise to Joseph (1:21), Jesus exercises his authority to save people – including the evangelist himself – from their sins. Fasting (9:14-17) must henceforth be governed *both* by the witness of the OT to this Savior, *and* by the fact that he has now come.

A. Jesus' Return to Capernaum (9:1)

'And entering the boat [*embas eis ploion*], he crossed over [*dieperasen*] and came to his own city.' Reversing the previous journey (Matt. 8:23, 28) and complying with the Gadarenes' request (8:34), Jesus now travels in a northwesterly direction and returns to Capernaum (8:5), his chosen home (4:13).[2]

All three Synoptists present Jesus' words and works both chronologically and topically; and no two of them do either in precisely the same way (see pp. 110-16). Consider, for example, the miracles reported in Matthew 8–9 and also in both Mark and Luke; and how Matthew's arrangement differs from theirs. He records (in this order) the cures of a leper and of Peter's mother-in-law; the stilling of the storm and the healing of the Gadarene demoniacs; the cures of a paralytic and of a woman with internal bleeding, and the raising of Jairus' daughter.

---

[1]The title of a hymn by J. Wilbur Chapman (1910).

[2]*Embainō* ('enter,' or 'embark' in this case) and *ploion* ('boat') also occur in Matthew 8:23. With *dieperasen* ('he crossed over'), cf. *eis to peran* ('to the other side'; 8:28). In 9:1a (as in 8:23a), it is *Jesus* who embarks, and in 9:1b (as in 8:28), *he* who reaches his destination; yet the presence of disciples (see 8:23b) is implied throughout. That Jesus comes to 'his own [*idian*] city' underscores the importance of Capernaum for his mission (see comments on 4:12-17).

The order in Mark and Luke is as follows: the cures of Peter's mother-in-law, of a leper and of a paralytic (Mark 1:29-31, 40-45; 2:1-12; Luke 4:38-39; 5:12-14, 17-26); the stilling of the storm, the healings of the Gerasene demoniac and of the woman with bleeding, and the raising of Jairus' daughter (Mark 4:35-5:43; Luke 8:22-56).[3] All three place the call of Matthew (Levi) and his dinner party *after* the healing of the paralytic (Matt. 9:2-13; Mark 2:1-17; Luke 5:17-32); but the stilling of the storm and the cure of the Gadarenes (Gerasene) come *before* this healing in Matthew, and *afterwards* in Mark and Luke. Yet no account requires dating the dinner immediately after Matthew's call; nor need Matthew 9:1-2 mean that the paralytic was healed upon Jesus' return from the land of the Gadarenes.

I conclude (i) that Peter's mother-in-law, the leper and the paralytic were cured *before* Matthew's call, as all Synoptists report; (ii) that some time elapsed between that call and the dinner party, and that Jesus calmed the storm and exorcised the demons in the land of Gadara (Gerasa) *after* that call and *before* the dinner party; (iii) that all the Synoptists keep Matthew's call and dinner party together, given their logical connection; (iv) that the bleeding woman was healed, and Jairus' daughter raised, after the dinner, as all Synoptists report; and (v) that Matthew, both in joining these seven miracles together more closely than do Mark and Luke, and in departing from strict chronology (in 8:23-9:1), shows the same fondness for *topical* arrangement as when fashioning the five discourses and the book as a whole.[4]

B. Good News for a Paralytic (9:2-8)

'And behold [*kai idou*], they brought to him a paralytic [*paralytikon*] lying [*beblēmenon*] on a bed' (9:2a). This meeting occurs in Jesus' 'own city' (9:1), i.e., Capernaum (as Mark 2:1 expressly states). It was here that Jesus healed the other

---

[3]The healing of the centurion's servant is reported only in Matthew 8:5-13 and Luke 7:1-10. The miracles of Matthew 9:27-34 (the healings of the blind men and of the mute and demon-possessed man) are not reported in Mark and Luke.

[4]See pages 492, 51-53; and Carson 1984: 221, on matters addressed in this paragraph.

paralytikos (Matt. 8:5-13); but that one, presumably a Gentile like his master, 'lay [the verb *ballō* again] at home' and was healed at a distance. But here a Jewish paralytic is brought into Jesus' presence.[5]

Forgiveness

'And Jesus, seeing their faith [*idōn...tēn pistin autōn*], said to the paralytic, "Take heart, child [*tharsei, teknon*]; your sins are forgiven [*aphientai sou hai hamartiai*]"' (Matt. 9:2b). As Jesus responded to the centurion's faith on behalf of his paralyzed servant (*pistis*, 8:10; *pisteuō*, 8:13), here he acts in response to the perceived faith of the paralytic's friends – though '*their* faith' probably includes the paralytic's own.[6] The vocative *teknon* voices both Jesus' authority over the man, and his tenderness towards him.[7] By the same token, *tharsei*, a present imperative of *tharseō*, is both an authoritative command (not just a polite entreaty) and also – given its basis in the words about forgiveness – an expression of compassion. The verb in this pronouncement – *aphientai* (from *aphiēmi*) – is a *present* indicative in the *passive* voice, signaling that the sins are forgiven as the words are uttered (an 'instantaneous present'), and that God is the one who forgives (a 'divine passive'). Moreover, the construction places the weight upon the verb.[8] *Aphiēmi*, in the sense 'forgive,' appears here for the first time since 6:12, 14-15, texts about the Father's forgiving disciples, and their forgiving other people. Jesus now, for the first time in Matthew, expressly and directly ('*your* sins') declares a person

---

[5]Mark 2:3-4 relates that the paralytic was carried by four men, then lowered through a hole which his friends had dug in the roof. Matthew typically excludes narrative details found in Mark's miracle stories (p. 491, n. 3); see especially Mark 5:1-20 vis-a-vis Matthew 8:28-34.

[6]So Calvin 1994: 258; Keener 1999: 288; and Hagner 1993: 232, who cites Acts 14:9.

[7]Mark 2:5 also uses the vocative *teknon*. Luke 5:20 has *anthrōpe* ('man') instead.

[8]Mark 2:5 also has *apheōntai* (Luke 5:20 uses the perfect passive *aphe-ntai*, 'have been forgiven'); placed before the subject in all three accounts, the verb is emphatic (cf. *IB*, 166). *GGBB*, 517 cites this (Mark 2:5) as an 'instantaneous present': the 'act itself is completed at the moment of speaking.' So too Gundry 1994: 163. On the 'divine passive,' see *GGBB*, 437-38.

forgiven.[9] This is also the first time *hamartia* ('sin') appears on Jesus' lips: significantly, he first uses the term in the plural (*hamartiai*) and in a declaration of forgiveness, both of which accord with the foundational promise of 1:21.[10]

'And behold [*kai idou*], some of the scribes said to themselves [*en heautois*], "This man is blaspheming [*Houtos blasphēmei*]"' (9:3). This *kai idou*, like that of 9:2a, prepares for the dramatic. These scribes (*grammateis*) accuse Jesus of blaspheming God, of reviling his holy name, because he – in their eyes a mere man (cf. 8b) – usurps the divine prerogative. 'Who can forgive sins but God alone?' they ask themselves (as we learn from Mark 2:7 and Luke 5:21). 'The Jews of Jesus' day expected forgiveness in the messianic age..., but did not expect the Messiah himself to forgive sins or to be divine.'[11] This mention of *grammateis* recalls Matthew 5:20 and 7:29 (texts in light of which the scribes' present behavior is not altogether surprising), and also 8:19 (a scribal response that now seems yet more commendable).

'And Jesus, seeing their thoughts [*idōn...tas enthymēseis*], said, "Why are you thinking evil things [*ponēra*] in your hearts [*en tais kardiais hymōn*]?"' (9:4). As Jesus perceived (*idōn*) the men's faith (9:2), he now perceives (*idōn*) the scribes' thoughts.[12] On the heart's rational dimension, see comments on 3:2; in Revelation 2:23 Jesus says that he searches minds (*nephrous*) and hearts (*kardias*). Furthermore, says Jesus, the thoughts of these scribes are evil (*ponēra*). As he later says, 'For from the heart [*ek...tēs kardias*] come evil deliberations [*dialogismoi ponēroi*]...slanders [*blasphēmiai*]' (Matt. 15:19). Just so, in the present passage the scribes are guilty of these sins. Having

---

[9]Jesus previously used *aphiēmi* in the senses of 'leave' (Matt. 5:24) and of 'let' (5:40; 7:4).

[10]Matthew 6:12 has *opheilēmata* ('debts'); 6:14-15 contains *paraptōmata* ('trespasses'). The only other prior instance of *hamartia* comes in 3:6 (in response to John people confess their sins).

[11]Gundry 1994: 163; cf. 26:65, with both the verb *blasphēmeō* and the noun *blasphēmia*. On the Jews' concept of blasphemy, cf. Hagner 1993: 233. Jesus is said to blaspheme in 9:3, because he ascribes to himself one of 'the incommunicable attributes of God' (Bengel 1873: 222).

[12]Some MSS. read *eidōs* ('knowing') instead of *idōn* ('seeing'). For arguments favoring the latter, see *TC*, 19-20.

correctly understood the pronouncement of 9:2, they deny
rather than affirm Jesus' right so to act; more than that, they
accuse him of blasphemy in making such a pronouncement.
Jesus' charge against them is the converse of theirs against
him: they demand that he – the divine Son of God and himself
God incarnate – behave as though he were a mere man; and
by that demand they revile his holy name (see 1:23).[13]

Wholeness
'For [*gar*] which is easier, to say "Your sins are forgiven," or to
say "Rise and walk"?' (Matt. 9:5). Jesus' question acknowledges
the close connection between the guilt of sin and the afflictions
of the body (cf. Ps. 103:3). According to the Scriptures a
physical ailment is sometimes judgment for personal sin: see
Numbers 12:8-10 (Miriam); John 5:14 (another paralyzed man);
1 Corinthians 11:29-32 (participants in the Lord's Supper).

But the Bible also warns against universalizing that
principle: see the story of Job; John 9:2-3 (which denies, not
that the man and his parents sinned, but that his or their sin
caused his blindness); 2 Corinthians 12:7 (the thorn in the flesh
to *discourage* sin). At the deepest level, of course, Scripture
traces *all* suffering to the Fall, and to the entry of sin and
death into the world in consequence of Adam's disobedience
(Rom. 5:12).[14] This is precisely why Jesus begins as he does: his
words in Matthew 9:2b (exactly repeated in 9:5) address the
man's severest malady and deepest need.[15] The scribes may
well misjudge the motive for that declaration: Jesus' question
in 9:5, coming as it does immediately after his question in
9:4 (note the connecting *gar*), suggests that the scribes' evil is
compounded (*ponēra* [9:4] is plural) by the suspicion that Jesus
deliberately speaks of sins rather than of paralysis to avoid
exposure as a fraud. For from a human perspective it *is* easier
to say 'Your sins are forgiven' than to say 'Rise and walk': if
the first *were* done, who could tell? if the latter were *not* done,

---

[13]See also the comments on Matthew 12:31 (with *blasphēmia*); 26:65 (with
blasphēmia and *blasphēmeō*); and 27:39 (with *blasphēmeō*).

[14]Cf. Chamblin 1993: 49-50.

[15]In this regard, see the comments on Matthew 8:16-17.

who could miss it? Not so from the perspective of God and Messiah: just as sin is a far graver problem than paralysis, so it is far easier for Jesus to say 'Rise and walk' than to say 'Your sins are forgiven,' as the sequel in Matthew will show.[16]

'"But in order that you may know [*eidēte*] that the Son of Man has authority on earth to forgive sins [*hoti exousian echei ho huios tou anthrōpou epi tēs gēs aphienai hamartias*]" – then he says to the paralytic, "Rise, take your bed and go to your house." And he rose and went to his house' (Matt. 9:6-7). In 9:6, Jesus first addresses the scribes (*eidēte*, from the verb *oida*, is plural), then the paralytic; Matthew's parenthesis marks the transition.[17] In Jesus' address to the scribes (9:6a), *exousian* ('authority') occurs first in its clause (after the conjunction *hoti*, 'that') for emphasis.[18] Moreover, the word order here, *epi tēs gēs aphienai hamartias* ('upon earth to forgive sins'), differs from that of Mark 2:10b, *aphienai hamartias epi tēs gēs*. Both are to be translated the same way (see, e.g., the ESV of both verses); but the Matthean order makes plainer the point of the saying – which is not that sins are committed and forgiven on earth (as all persons present would agree), but that the Father has granted the Son of Man *authority on earth* to effect forgiveness.[19]

To drive home this truth, Jesus orders the paralytic to rise and depart, a command he forthwith obeys.[20] If Jesus' words

---

[16]See 20:28; 26:28; and pages 147-48 on 'The Cost of Forgiveness.'

[17]Jesus' words to the scribes are an instance of *anacoluthon*: i.e., the purpose clause ('that you may know') is *not followed* by a main clause: on this grammatical feature, see *GGNT*, 435-40. On the parenthesis in NT Greek, see ibid., 433-35.

[18]The same applies to the word order in Matthew 9:2b (see p. 526). The word order of 9:6a agrees with Mark 2:10a. Luke 5:24 places *exousian* after 'the Son of Man.'

[19]Cf. 28:18; Gundry 1994: 164; Davies and Allison 1991: 93. The order of Luke 5:24 agrees with Matthew 9:6a. Jesus' Father is 'the Ancient of Days' of Daniel 7. On Jesus as 'the Son of Man,' see above, pages 134-36, also comments on Matthew 8:20.

[20]Forms of the verb *egeirō* occur here three times. *Egeire* (9:5) is a present imperative. *Egertheis* (9:6, 7) is an aorist participle of attendant circumstance (*GGBB*, 640-45), is translated 'rise' in 9:6 (in accord with the imperatives *aron*, 'take,' and *hypage*, 'go'; cf. Mark 2:11, *egeire aron... kai hypage*), and 'he rose' in Matthew 9:7 (in accord with the indicative *apēlthen*, 'he went'). Jesus

about healing can achieve what they command (9:6b), can
not his words about forgiveness achieve what they declare
(9:2b)? And if this man's sins did account for his paralysis,
does not his healing certify that those sins have been
forgiven?[21]

Here, as in Jesus' ministry as a whole, the lesser work (in
this case liberation from paralysis) witnesses to the greater one
(salvation from sins). Conversely, by doing the lesser work as
well as the greater one on this occasion, Jesus witnesses to the
wholeness in store for his forgiven people when their bodies
are raised from the dead.[22]

Fearfulness

'And having seen [*idontes*], the crowds became frightened
[*ephobēthēsan*], and they glorified God who had given such
authority [*exousian toiautēn*] to men [*tois anthrōpois*]' (Matt. 9:8).
Matthew now reveals that 'the crowds' (*hoi ochloi*) are present
on this occasion.[23] The opening participle *idontes* (from *horaō*),
which has no object, appears to embrace everything reported
in 9:2-7. It is yet plainer that the *exousia* for which they praise
God was manifested both in Jesus' healing act and in his
pronouncement of forgiveness. Indeed, to judge from Jesus'
own use of the term *exousia* in the passage (9:6) and from
the whole thrust of his argument, the people are thinking
especially of his authority to forgive sins. Having witnessed
such *exousia*, the crowds are filled with *both* fear *and* praise;
and it is chiefly Jesus' act of forgiveness which accounts for
both: see respectively Psalms 130:3-4 and 103:1-3. Is not their
response to Jesus on this occasion much like that of the disciples

---

said, 'go to your house [*eis ton oikon sou*]' (9:6c); so the man 'went to his
house [*eis ton oikon autou*]' (9:7). His obedience to the command 'take your
bed' (9:6b) is made explicit in Mark 2:12 and Luke 5:25.

[21]'In the opinion of the onlookers, only a cure could confirm the
pronouncement of forgiveness. Continuance of the illness would mean
persistence of guilt' (Gundry 1994: 163). 'Hence there is a bodily sign in
order to demonstrate a spiritual sign' (Jerome in *ACC* 1a: 175).

[22]See again the comments on 8:16-17.

[23]The 'crowds' (*ochloi*) were last mentioned in Matthew 8:1; the 'crowd'
(*ochlos*) in 8:18.

in the boat (Matt. 8:27) and for much the same reason?[24] Is there not, from Matthew's perspective, a certain irony in the closing word *anthrōpois* – both in the term itself and in the plural? Does not the crowds' fear – like the disciples' wonder – suggest that the word *man* is inadequate to identify the one who has just exercised *such* authority (*exousian toiautēn*)? Is it conceivable that God would grant *such* authority to men *other than* Jesus?[25]

Matthew does not say how the *grammateis* (9:3) responded; but we may observe how the other accounts close: 'they were all [*pantas*] amazed and glorified God' (Mark 2:12); 'and amazement seized them all [*hapantas*], and they glorified God and were filled with fear' (Luke 5:26). These texts may suggest that at this stage of Jesus' ministry a number of scribes joined the crowds (Matt. 9:8a; cf. 7:28-29) in responding favorably to Jesus' exercise of authority, and that the *grammateus* of 8:19 is not so isolated a figure as he first appears.[26]

C. Good News for Matthew and His Friends (9:9-13)

These verses well match 9:2-8. There the major theme was Jesus' authority to forgive *sins*: the noun *hamartia* occurred three times (9:2, 5, 6). The present passage speaks mainly of Jesus' close association with *sinners*: the noun *hamartōlos* appears three times (9:10, 11, 13), the first instances in Matthew. We first meet an individual sinner, then a company of people like him.

---

[24]I render *ephobēthēsan* (9:8a) as an ingressive aorist, 'they became frightened' (cf. *GGBB*, 558-59). Some MSS. substitute *ethaumasan* ('they marveled'), the verb used of the disciples' response in 8:27 (see those comments). According to *TC*, 20, this change was made by 'superficial readers and copyists [who failed] to see the deep meaning of "were afraid" (i.e., people felt a profound sense of awe and alarm in the presence of One who had the right to forgive sins).' Cf. BAGD s.v. *phobeō*, 1. '*be afraid*, the aor. oft. in the sense *become frightened*' (where 9:8 is cited). Thus I prefer esv('they were afraid') to nasb ('they were awestruck').

[25]We may compare David's conduct toward Mephibosheth. The king lacked authority to heal his lameness or to forgive his sins; but his 'steadfast love' (Hebrew *chesed*) to Jonathan's son (2 Sam. 9) provides an image (or type) of Jesus' mercy to this paralytic.

[26]Cf. Matthew 9:3, 'some [*tines*] of the scribes...'; also comments on chronology, pages 524-25.

The Calling of Matthew (9:9)

'As Jesus was passing on from there, he saw a man called Matthew [*Matthaion legomenon*] sitting at the tax office; and he said [*legei*] to him, "Follow me [*Akolouthei moi*]." And he got up and followed him [*ēkolouthēsen autō*].' *Matthaios* appears here for the first time in Matthew. The parallels in Mark 2:14 and Luke 5:27 speak instead of *Leui*. It was earlier concluded that both names belong to the same person; that *Leui* is his tribal name, and *Matthaios* (which means 'gift of Yahweh') his personal name; that his father's name is *Alphaios* (Mark 2:14); and that the use of the personal name is natural if the author is referring to himself, as here.[27]

1. The tax collector

When Jesus sees him, Matthew is sitting 'at the tax office,' *epi to telēnion*. He is identified by the matching term *telōnēs*, 'tax collector,' in 10:3. The Jews of Jesus' day paid fewer taxes to their own leaders (see 17:24-27 on the temple tax) than to the occupying Romans. Roman taxes were mainly of three kinds: 1. The *land tax*, on produce, accounted for most of the revenue. The assessments cannot be precisely determined; but probably 'most of those in the agricultural sector lived close enough to minimal subsistence to feel almost any amount of tribute as a threatened or real burden.' 2. The *head tax*, or poll tax, was probably one denarius a year (cf. 22:17-21) and paid by most Jewish males aged fourteen to sixty-five. Its collection was aided by a periodic census (cf. Luke 2:1-5; Acts 5:37). 3. *Tolls and duties.* These were collected, at ports and at tax offices near city gates, from persons engaged in commerce. 'Rates varied from two to five per cent of value, but goods were subject to multiple taxation on long journeys.'[28]

Those first two were *direct* taxes; the third was *indirect*. 'Tax collectors' (Aramaic *gabbāyā*) were Jewish officials, usually from aristocratic families, who were responsible for taking in

---

[27]See the comments on Matthew 9:9 on page 41. On Matthew as the author of this gospel, see pages 25-48, especially the summary on pages 46-48.

[28]These three points and the quotations come from T.E. Schmidt, 'Taxes,' *DJG*, 804-5.

the *direct* taxes – the land tax and the head tax. '*Toll* collectors' (Aramaic *mōkᵉsā*) worked for 'toll farmers,' wealthy persons to whom Rome 'farmed out' the responsibility for collecting the *indirect* tax of tolls and duties in a given district – because they had outbid others in paying for the right to do so – and who then 'farmed' the district for taxes.[29] Toll *farmers* might be Jewish or Gentile; their correct Latin name would be *publicani*. For their subordinates the toll *collectors*, who were Jewish as a rule, the right term is *portitores*.[30]

Given the toll farmers' practice of paying for the position, it is interesting to note that *telōnēs* – the term used of Matthew in 10:3, and of his guests in 9:10-11 – is formed from *telos* ('tax, customs duties') and *ōneomai* ('to buy').[31] Does this mean that Matthew and these guests are all toll collectors? Not necessarily: 'tax collectors' and 'toll collectors' are both represented by *telōnēs* and are generally joined together in Jewish writings.[32] I think it probable that both are numbered among the *telōnai* with whom Jesus often associates, and that on this occasion the <u>*polloi*</u> *telōnai kai hamartōloi* (9:10) more likely represent both groups than just one (since it is doubtful that Capernaum would need large numbers of either kind).[33] But Matthew himself may well have been a toll collector: his *telōnion* (9:9) is in Capernaum (9:1), a town ideally located for collecting revenues on merchandise leaving the tetrarchy of Herod

---

[29]Jeremias 1971: 110; Schmidt, 805. On 'state tax-farming and tax-farmers in antiquity,' including Rome and Palestine, see O. Michel, *TDNT* 8: 89-103.

[30]On one view (BAGD s.v. *telōnēs*; Carson 1984: 159), the 'toll farmers' (*publicani*, 'farmers of state revenues') were usually foreigners, while their 'tax collectors' (*portitores*, 'custom-house officers') were usually Jews. On another view (Schmidt, 805), these 'tax farmers' were also Jews, but not *publicani*, a term which was inapplicable after 30 B.C. The Greek *dēmosiōnēs*, which normally renders the Latin *publicanus*, never appears in the NT.

[31]For *telos* in this sense, see Matthew 17:25; Romans 13:7. For *ōneomai*, see Acts 7:16.

[32]France 1985: 167. *Telos* ('tax, custom duties') is joined to *kēnsos* ('tax, poll tax') in 17:25; and to *phoros* ('tribute, tax') in Romans 13:7 (cf. 6 for *phoros* with the verb *teleō*).

[33]Cf. the par. in Luke 5:29, *ochlos polys* [large crowd] *telōnōn kai allōn* [and others].

Philip and entering that of Herod Antipas.[34] Whether in this capacity or the other ('tax collector'), Matthew may have had dealings with the four fishermen of 4:18-22.[35]

2. The sinner
In either capacity, Matthew would have been despised by his fellow Jews. Both kinds of *telōnai* (i) associated and collaborated with Gentiles, in this case the Roman oppressors; (ii) routinely handled currency with pagan inscriptions and iconography; (iii) took money from other Jews (offensive enough in itself) and entrusted it to the foreign power, thus aiding continued oppression; and (iv) were often greedy and corrupt, persons who stole from others by taxing excessively, and who gained wealth by exploiting others, notably the poor.[36] We can therefore better understand why the people call Zacchaeus *hamartōlos* ('sinner'; Luke 19:7); why the *telōnēs* in the temple uses this term in his prayer of confession (Luke 18:13); and why *telōnai* and *hamartōloi* are joined together in Matthew 9:10-11; 11:19, and elsewhere.[37]

That the author himself is a *hamartōlos* in that sense is clear from 9:9 (where he is said to occupy the *telōnion*) and especially from 9:10-13. Moreover, by placing this passage immediately after Jesus' encounter with the paralytic (as Mark and Luke also do), Matthew implies that he too is a man whose sins need to be forgiven.

---

[34]'Not only ports, but boundaries of cities and tetrarchies, charged customs duties, raising the price of imported goods' (Keener 1999: 293). By the same token, the Jewish *architelōnēs* Zacchaeus, living as he does in Jericho, is probably a toll farmer governing the collection of tolls and duties for goods entering Judea (thus Green 1997: 668).

[35]In light of inscriptions from Asian cities about 'those who are concerned with the toll on fish,' it is 'possible that a toll on incoming fish was collected in Capernaum as well' (Lane 1974: 102). Gundry 1994: 166 thinks it probable that Matthew collected the direct taxes from fishermen.

[36]For these points, see Luke 3:12-13; 19:2, 8; Gundry 1994: 167; Jeremias 1971: 110-11; Keener 1999: 292-93; Michel, *TDNT* 8: 101-3; Schmidt, *DJG*, 805-6. Note that both Matthew 5:46-47 and 18:17 associate *telōnai* with *ethnikoi* ('Gentiles').

[37]Besides the texts parallel to 9:10-11 (Mark 2:15-16; Luke 5:30), see Luke 7:34; 15:1. Matthew 21:31-32 join *hoi telōnai* to *hai pornai* ('prostitutes'). For more on Jewish judgments against *telōnai*, see the sources cited in the preceding note.

3. The summons

The text's offer of hope to Matthew begins before his call (9:9b). For Jesus comes into his presence, and looks upon him (9:9a) directly after declaring a man's sins forgiven (9:2-8). In light of all that the Galilean ministry thus far (4:12-9:8) has disclosed about Jesus' *authority*, and therefore about his *being*, can there be any doubt that he is both able and willing to forgive even a man like Matthew, whose sins by all indications far exceed those of the paralytic? By his words '*Jesus* saw *a man* [*ho Iēsous...eiden anthrōpon*],' Matthew may imply a contrast between his own humanity and Jesus' divinity, in which case a contrast between his sinfulness and Jesus' holiness is implicit as well. Such an intent would fully accord with the evangelist's presentation of Jesus thus far.[38]

As in 4:18-22, Jesus takes the initiative. His command, *Akolouthei moi* ('Follow me'), appears for the second time in Matthew (for the first, see 8:22), though the *Deute opisō mou* of 4:19 required the same response. Those calls were as surely based on grace as this one; but there Jesus spoke to *fishermen*. Some would consider that choice surprising (why fishermen and not scholars?); far more would be shocked to learn that Jesus had deliberately asked – indeed commanded – a despised *telōnēs* to become his disciple. This call attests with special poignancy that Jesus has come to save his people *from their sins* (Matt. 1:21), a purpose confirmed in the pronouncement of 9:13.

As in 4:18-22, Jesus here calls for a commitment not just to his teaching but to his *person*. And like the fishermen, Matthew responds obediently and decisively: 'he got up and followed him [*ēkolouthēsen autō*]' (9:9b), the very language of 4:20, 22 (*ēkolouthēsan autō*). Moreover, his decision, like theirs, entailed sacrifice: they abandoned their nets (4:20), their boat and their father (4:22); he rose and followed after 'abandoning everything' (Luke 5:28, par. to Matthew 9:9).[39] Whether Matthew was previously

---

[38]Cf. Gundry 1994: 166.

[39]Matthew 4:20, 22 use the verb *aphiēmi*; Luke 5:28, *kataleipō*. See further the comments on 4:18-22.

acquainted with Jesus, we cannot say.[40] But we do know that his present decision translated into a lasting commitment. Whether that earlier *grammateus* maintained his resolve once Jesus warned him of coming deprivations (8:19-20) is not stated. But Matthew, once a despised *telōnēs*, and a secular *grammateus*, was to become a respected *apostolos*, in which capacity he would again do service as a *grammateus* (13:52) by writing the gospel we are studying. As argued earlier, it is probable that the name *Matthaios* ('gift of Yahweh') was conferred by Jesus upon Levi (as was *Petros* upon Simon). In any case, both Jesus and salvation were such gifts to Matthew – who in turn became Yahweh's gift to the church.[41]

Jesus' Dinner with Tax Collectors and Sinners (9:10-13)
'And it happened that as he was reclining at table [*autou anakeimenou*] in the house [*en tē oikia*], behold [*kai idou*], many tax collectors and sinners came and reclined at table [*elthontes synanekeinto*] with Jesus and his disciples' (Matt. 9:10). The scene has shifted from Matthew's *telōnion* (9:9) to his *oikia*, and to a dinner in progress.[42]

1. The guests
Jesus is the guest of honor, and thus the first person to be mentioned;[43] Luke 5:29 reports that 'Levi prepared a great banquet for him.' The *kai idou* again prepares for the startling – the announcement that *polloi telōnai kai hamartōloi* are also present. That Matthew is able to serve *many* such guests, indicates that he has prospered in his occupation; again note

---

[40]It was argued earlier that Jesus called Matthew, and also chose him as one of the twelve, before the sermon of chapters 5–7 (see p. 303). We recall that Matthew presents his material both chronologically and topically (see pp. 110-16, 524-25).

[41]Cf. *Matthaion legomenon* (9:9) to *legomenos Petros* (10:2); and see comments on pages 42-43. On the *grammateus* of 13:52, and its application to Matthew, see pages 43-45.

[42]The house belongs to Matthew (see p. 41), not to Jesus (as Gundry thinks, 1994: 167). Here, as always in the NT, *anakeimai* means 'recline at table,' i.e., 'dine' (cf. Matt. 22:10, 11; 26:7, 20; BAGD s.v.); and *synanakeimai*, 'recline at table with, eat with' (cf. 14:9; BAGD s.v.).

[43]Jesus is the 'he' in *autou anakeimenou*, a genitive absolute construction.

Luke 5:29. As already intimated in comments on Matthew 9:9, *hamartōloi* in this couplet is a technical term to mark certain Jews as exceptionally sinful: it 'partly means those who live a flagrantly immoral life (murderers, robbers, deceivers etc.) and partly those who follow a dishonourable vocation or one which inclines them strongly to dishonesty.'[44] As persons of the second sort, and in some cases of the first as well, the *telōnai* of the couplet are not distinguished from the *hamartōloi* but are expressly mentioned as notable representatives of the latter (in v. 11b the two terms appear under one definite article). Yet *hamartōloi* in this expression *is* to be distinguished from *am ha-aretz*, 'the people of the land.' The latter term is much broader: it denotes the vast majority of Israel's population, from whom members of an elite minority distinguished themselves (for reasons religious, intellectual, political, social or economic), but among whom were pious persons devoted to the law, and persons who (in some cases because of poverty) would share others' loathing of a person like Matthew.[45]

Matthew's motives are plain: 1. As noted, he desires to honor Jesus, whom he has now followed for some time (see pp. 524-25). Matthew hereby expresses gratitude for Jesus' impact upon his life. 2. The size of the dinner party reflects his eagerness that other people – as many of them as possible – be affected by Jesus as he himself has been. 3. He invites persons of the same occupation; persons who in other respects are like himself (perhaps including some previously unknown to him); and persons who – again like himself – desperately need the gospel that Jesus proclaims and the law that he expounds. 4. Matthew's fellow disciples have also been invited – which indicates that they, and the host himself, can be expected to testify to the *telōnai kai hamartōloi* about that gospel and that law (as they are soon to do on a broader scale [ch. 10]). In all four respects, Matthew provides a model for doing personal evangelism.

---

[44]K. H. Rengstorf, *TDNT* 1: 327, with sources he cites.

[45]The point is not that the *am ha-aretz* escaped censure from the scrupulously law-abiding (cf. John 7:47-49); but that *hamartōloi* in Matthew 9:10-11 denotes 'blatant violators of the law' (Keener 1999: 295), which certainly does not apply to all the 'people of the land.' See Keener's balanced discussion, 294-96 (with many references to Jewish sources); also Scott 1995: 234-35.

2. The offense

'And when they saw this, the Pharisees said to his disciples, "Why does your teacher eat with the tax [or toll] collectors and sinners?"' (9:11). This objection arises from the same quarter as that of 9:3; according to the parallel accounts, Pharisees as well as scribes were present there, and scribes as well as Pharisees are present here.[46] But whereas those scribes (and Pharisees) witnessed Jesus' encounter with the paralytic, these Pharisees (and scribes) did not dine with Jesus and the others. Had they been invited (itself highly improbable), they would surely have declined – one reason being their refusal to socialize intimately with *telōnai kai hamartōloi*, another being their fear of ritual defilement.[47] Yet, increasingly attentive as they are to Jesus' behavior, they see what has happened in Matthew's home, and afterwards they accost Jesus' disciples.

'Why does your teacher [*ho didaskalos hymōn*] eat with...?' they ask. The questioners do not identify Jesus himself as *hamartōlos* in the above sense: their term for him, *didaskalos*, is respectful (though it may mask disrespect). Yet the question is more a tacit accusation than a request for information. The phrase 'with tax [or toll] collectors and sinners' stands near the beginning of its clause for emphasis: 'Why does he eat *with such people*?'[48] Jesus' intimate association with them raises serious doubts about his right to be recognized as a reliable rabbi – doubts exacerbated by reports from the episode of 9:2-8.[49] If Jesus continues *both* to attach supreme importance to his teaching *and* to court ritually defiled and grossly immoral people, will he not himself be exposed as the worst kind of sinner?

---

[46]See Luke 5:21 (par. to Matthew 9:3); and Mark 2:16 and Luke 5:30 (par. to 9:11).

[47]Says Bornkamm 1960: 80, 'Eating with others is for the Jew the closest form of intimacy.' States a rabbinic regulation (cited in Morris 1992: 221, n. 26): 'If tax gatherers entered a house (all that is within it) becomes unclean.'

[48]On the nature of the question, see Carson 1984: 225. On placing words at the beginning of a sentence for emphasis, see *IB*, 166.

[49]Says a rabbinic dictum (cited in Morris 1992: 221, n. 27): 'Keep thee far from an evil neighbour and consort not with the wicked.' Does the questioners' phrase '*your* teacher' reflect a desire to distance themselves from Jesus and his circle? Does their approaching the *disciples* reflect doubts about their ability to withstand Jesus' own authority?

3. The grace

'But when he heard this, he said, "It is not the healthy people who need a physician, but [*alla*] those who are sick. Go and learn what this means: 'I desire mercy and not sacrifice.' For I did not come to call the righteous but sinners"' (Matt. 9:12-13).

It is precisely *because* of such people's condition that Jesus calls them. Is not the doctor's singular duty to help the *sick* (note the strong adversative *alla*)? The imagery of 9:12 confirms that the chief purpose of this Physician is to cure the malady of sin (9:2, 13), and that his healing of the literally sick is integral to this mission (9:6-8).[50] So Jesus does not insist that sinners repent before he receives them (how could one be called a doctor who withheld his services until his patients were cured?). On the contrary, as he later declared in the presence of another *telōnēs*, Jesus came *to seek and to save the lost* (Luke 19:10). So he deliberately joins such people in order to affect his own cure, and to woo them to repentance.[51]

Then, in 9:13a, Jesus admonishes these Pharisees – especially the scholars (*grammateis*) among them – to re-study an OT text (Hosea 6:6a): 'I desire mercy [*eleos*] and not sacrifice [*thysian*],' the very wording of the LXX. *Eleos* translates the Hebrew *chesed*, a term denoting covenant-keeping love and loyalty; behind *thysia* is *zebach*, a general term for levitical sacrifice. The text declares the primacy of *chesed* without denigrating or dismissing the cult. Hosea has in mind 1 Samuel 15:22: 'Does Yahweh delight in offerings and sacrifices/ As much as in obedience to the voice of Yahweh?'[52] Moreover, the parallel in Hosea 6:6b – 'and the knowledge of God rather

---

[50]See comments on Matthew 9:2-8. The term for 'those who are sick' in 9:12 (*hoi kakōs echontes*), is the very one used of the physically afflicted in 4:24 and 8:16. In the language of Zephaniah 3:19, Jesus comes both to 'save the lame' (Matt. 9:2-8) and to 'gather the outcast' (9:9-13).

[51]Cf. 4:17; and the parallel to 9:13 in Luke 5:32, 'to call sinners to repentance.' 'The Pharisees would have received repentant sinners, but they would not seek them out. Jesus did. He actively sought sinners to bring them to repentance. This was a new thing in Judaism' (Morris 1992: 221, n. 27). Did these sinners come at *Jesus'* invitation as well as Matthew's?

[52]Thus do Andersen and Freedman (1980: 430-31) interpret Hosea 6:6a and translate 1 Samuel 15:22a. Cf. Psalm 51:18-19 in relation to verses 1-17. On Amos 5:25, see Smith 1998: 253-54.

than burnt offerings' – makes it clear that human expressions of *chesed* begin with love and loyalty to Israel's God (cf. Hos. 4:1), without which the sacrifices are useless, hypocritical and offensive. By citing Hosea 6:6 in Matthew 9:13, Jesus implies that the Pharisees' concern for ritual purity and their consequent objection to his behavior, betray ignorance of God himself. For does not God himself show *chesed* to the sinful and erring? And is not one sign of a person's answering *chesed* to God, a willingness to show such *chesed* to other people? Does not one show love for God by thus loving his neediest neighbors (22:37-40)? As Immanuel, Jesus embodies both God's inaugurating *chesed* and man's answering *chesed*. These questioners are both ignorant of God and oblivious to Jesus' true identity. Furthermore, Jesus' own life makes it clear that showing mercy (*eleos, chesed*) does not exclude offering sacrifice. On the contrary: his foremost act of mercy is his redemptive sacrifice (20:28; 26:28) – by virtue of which Matthew and these other sinners are forgiven.[53]

'For [*gar*] I did not come to call the righteous [*dikaious*] but sinners [*alla hamartōlous*],"' concludes Jesus (Matt. 9:13b). The linking *gar* certifies that Jesus shows *eleos* by dining with sinners and calling them to repentance and discipleship. This contrast between the *dikaioi* and the *hamartōloi* calls for several comments. 1. Frequently in Scripture the adjective *dikaios* or its equivalent denotes genuinely righteous behavior: see, e.g., Job 1:1; Psalm 15:2-5; Luke 1:6 (Zechariah and Elizabeth); Mark 6:20 (John the Baptist is called *dikaios*); 1 Thessalonians 2:10 (Paul recalls how *dikaiōs* he had lived among his people); and Matthew 5:20 (where *dikaiosynē* denotes holiness of life: see those comments). 2. That righteousness is always based on, and responsive to, God's saving grace. This finds fullest expression in Paul: the righteousness (*dikaiosynē*) of God in the work of Christ is the sole basis of salvation (Rom. 3:21-26; Phil. 3:9, etc.); in grateful response Christians

---

[53]Cf. the prayer of the *telōnēs* in Luke 18:13: 'God, be merciful [*hilasthēti*] to me, the sinner,' the ultimate answer to which comes in the cross. Note the use of this verb, *hilaskomai*, in Hebrews 2:17; and of the cognate *hilasmos* in 1 John 2:2; 4:10.

become, by the Holy Spirit's power, righteous and holy in their conduct (Rom. 8:1-4; Eph. 4:23-24).[54] 3. In both OT and NT, the truly *righteous* are acutely aware of their *unrighteousness* and of their ongoing need of God's mercy and forgiveness: see, e.g., Luke 1:6 (Zechariah and Elizabeth are righteous and blameless as those who keep God's commands – one of which is to offer sacrifice for sins, as especially a *priest* would recognize); and the comments on *teleioi* in Matthew 5:48. Such persons 'have no need of repentance' (the language of Luke 15:7) because they have *already repented*. 4. Both in Luke 15:7 and here in Matthew 9:13, *dikaioi* – as applied to some – is ironic. Do not these Pharisees supplant the first part of that quotation, 'I desire mercy' (which Jesus here shows by receiving sinners *as sinners*), with the second, 'I desire sacrifice' (on which basis sinners may be received *as repentant and forgiven*)? By opposing Jesus' *eleos* to the *hamartōloi*, do they not show themselves to be *hamartōloi*? Does their denial of mercy mean they have forgotten how God forgave their own huge indebtedness (cf. 18:23-35)? Is not the spiritual pride which the Pharisee exhibits in the presence of the *telōnēs*, (Luke 18:9-14), the worst sin of all? Are not the Pharisees of Matthew 9:11 like the elder brother of Luke 15:25-32 (cf. 15:1-2)? Do they not need to offer the prayer of Luke 18:13?

D. The Place of Fasting (9:14-17)
In response to an inquiry, Jesus again takes up the subject of 6:16-18. Present comments presuppose those on the earlier passage.

A Practice Suspended and Restored
Some disciples of John the Baptist come and ask Jesus, 'Why do we and the Pharisees fast [often], but your disciples do not fast [*ou nēsteuousin*]?' (Matt. 9:14).[55] By their fasting, both

---

[54]Join Genesis 15:6 (Abraham's trust in God's promise) to 26:5 (his consequent obedience to God's law); and Psalm 24:5 to Psalm 15:2. See also (i) Psalm 18:20-24 with 18:30-34; (ii) Habakkuk 2:4b, and Robertson 1990: 175-83 (he translates 'but the justified – by his steadfast trust he shall live'); and (iii) 2 Samuel 22:21-31, and Davis 1999: 238-40, on 'the importance of our righteousness.'

groups maintain a long-standing tradition. Reasons for fasts in
the OT and among the Jews of Jesus' day were summarized on
pages 425-27, where were also noted the supererogatory fasts
of the Pharisees (cf. Luke 18:12) and the particular reasons for
the fasts of John's disciples. Significantly, the question is raised
(both here and in the other Synoptics) immediately after the
account of Matthew's dinner party. There are no indications
that John's disciples are offended (as were the Pharisees) by
Jesus' choice of company. Rather, the question appears to be
prompted by the meal itself. John's own asceticism (3:4; 11:18)
helps to explain his followers' fasts. Does Jesus' contrary habit
(9:10-11; 11:19) help to explain why his disciples do *not* fast?
Given all that unites the two men, how are those differences
to be explained?[56]

Jesus answers: 'The attendants of the bridegroom are not
able to mourn, are they, as long as the bridegroom is with them?
But the days will come when the bridegroom is taken away
from them, and then they will fast' (9:15). Jesus uses metaphor,
not simile: he is not like a bridegroom; he is 'the bridegroom'
(*ho nymphios*), and his disciples are his 'attendants' (*hoi huioi
tou nymphōnos*, literally 'the sons of the bridal chamber').[57]
A wedding reception calls for celebration, not for mourning; for
feasting, not for fasting; for wine, not for water (John 2:1-11). Just
so, the dawn of God's final rule, and the arrival of his Messiah,
is *euangelion* (Matt. 4:23), tidings meant to evoke shouts of
praise and songs of joy. How can one *not* so respond to the
wonders recorded thus far in Matthew 8–9, such as the healing
of leprosy, the expelling of demons and the forgiving of sins –
all of them testimony to Messiah's authority and grace? Recent
behavior of the scribes and Pharisees (9:2-13) suggests that they
cannot so respond owing to their spiritual blindness. But have
not John's own preaching (Matt. 3:2, with 4:17), and his own

---

[55]Whether *polla* ('often') is original is uncertain; so with *TC*, 20, the term
is bracketed. In the parallel of Luke 5:33, the adverb *pykna* ('often') is not
textually doubtful.

[56]Jesus' words in Matthew 11:4-19 acknowledge the differences between
himself and John, but lay greater stress on their common mission.

[57]Otherwise in Matthew *nymphios* appears only in the parable of 25:1-13;
and *nymphōn* only as a variant reading in 22:10, where it means 'wedding hall.'

joy over Messiah the Bridegroom (John 3:27-30), prepared his people for such merrymaking?

But a time is coming, says Jesus, when the bridegroom will be 'taken away' (*aparthē*) – 'snatched away' – from them, an allusion to Jesus' arrest, trial and execution: see the prophecy of 16:21.[58] Imagine the bridegroom's enemies forcing their way into the wedding reception, seizing him, stealing him away from his bride and friends and brutally murdering him – or worse still, doing so in the wedding hall itself to the horror of the onlookers. (In this regard, we recall that Christ the bridegroom shows his love for his bride the church by sacrificing himself for her [Eph. 5:25-33]; and that the sign he provides at the wedding reception in Cana points to his death [John 2:1-11].) Upon the death of the bridegroom, a fast of mourning will indeed be appropriate.[59] To be sure, disciples' grief will be turned into joy once he rises from the dead (John 16:20-24). Yet between his ascension and his glorious return, he is both with them and absent from them. Because Jesus is absent, and has not finally subjugated the powers of sin and death, his people will mourn (*pentheō*, Matt. 5:4; cf. 5:6; 6:10) and have fasts of mourning (9:15, *pentheō* again) until his return. 'The days' (*hēmerai*) during which his followers 'shall fast' (*nēsteusousin*; 9:15) span the whole history of the church.[60] But because Jesus is present (28:20), and has already achieved victories which assure the final outcome, even fasts of mourning are not bereft of joy. As Richard Pratt says, 'Christians who are gloomy all the time have forgotten what Christ has already done; and those who are happy all the time have forgotten what he has yet to do.'[61]

A Practice Defended and Deepened

Jesus then offers a twofold illustration (9:16-17; or *parabolē*, Luke 5:36). 'No one sews a piece of unshrunk cloth onto an

---

[58]The verb is an aorist passive of *apairō* (*apo* + *airō* = 'take from, take away').

[59]For fasts of mourning in OT Israel, see page 426, including n. 121.

[60]Gundry 1994: 169. In Matthew, *pentheō* ('mourn') appears only in 5:4 and 9:15.

[61]See, e.g., 5:3-12; 6:9-13; and comments on 6:16-18 (especially on disciples' fasting).

old garment, for the patch pulls away from the garment and a worse tear results. Nor do people pour new wine into old wineskins; otherwise, the skins burst and the wine is spilled and the skins are destroyed. On the contrary [*alla*], they pour new wine into new wineskins, and both are preserved.' These pictures relate fasts since the kingdom's inaugural to those of former times.

One reason for avoiding those two actions is that the *old* is endangered. The stitching may have been so skillfully done that the patch is indistinguishable from the rest of the garment; but at the first washing the patch will shrink, pull away from the garment and make its tear even worse (*cheiron schisma ginetai*). Fresh animal hides were well chosen for bottling wine, for as the wine expanded upon fermentation, so did the hides; but wine newly fermenting inside old skins, now dried out and inflexible, will surely cause them to burst and be destroyed (*kai hoi askoi apollyntai*).[62] Thus, in keeping with his teaching in Matthew 5:17-20, Jesus makes it clear that he has not come to abolish fasting (cf. *katalysai*, 5:17) or to denigrate the OT's witness to the practice.

Those acts are also foolish because they threaten the *new*. The patch of cloth (Matt. 9:16) is not damaged (now shrunk after a soaking, it is apparently ready for use on another garment); but in a closely related saying of Jesus (Luke 5:36) the act is doubly foolish, for the patch is obtained by tearing a new garment but fails to match the fabric of the old. And when the wineskins burst (Matt. 9:17a), the new wine is spilled and lost; Mark 2:22 says that the wine is destroyed (*apollytai*) as well as the skins. Thus Jesus, again in keeping with Matthew 5:17-20 *et seq.*, teaches that the practice of fasting must henceforth accord with the facts that God's kingdom has dawned, that Israel's Messiah has come, and that the Law and the Prophets have reached their appointed goal.[63] Just as new

---

[62]Cf. Wenham 1989: 32.

[63]See page 542. Luke 5:39 (which lacks pars. in Matthew and Mark) speaks of persons who prefer old wine to new. While that normally shows good taste, here it shows bad: these are persons so intoxicated with the past that they refuse the new. In this case the *new* wine – the dawn of God's kingdom – is the better! So it was at the wedding reception in Cana (John 2:10).

wine requires a new wineskin for both to be preserved (9:17b), so present realities require present history for the truth of both to be safeguarded. Trying to fit the realities belonging to the time of fulfillment into the framework proper for the time of preparation, would betray one's blindness to the progress of history, distort the teaching both of Moses and of Jesus, and threaten one with the loss of both. The 'wine' of the kingdom's dawning is far too potent to be contained by the 'wineskin' of former times. At the same time, choosing new wineskins for new wine means that those old wineskins and their old wine can be preserved as well – and that the Law and the Prophets can continue bearing their witness to the truth, both as revealed for God's people during the time of preparation, and as now expounded and enlarged by Jesus the Messiah.

IV.
'WHERE PEOPLE SUFFER, HOPELESS IN DISTRESS'[1]
(9:18-38)

This closing section of chapters 8–9, like the preceding, accentuates Jesus' authority as a miracle worker: here he heals another four individuals, and he also raises a person from the dead – an act unprecedented in Matthew. The summary of 9:35 echoes 4:23; embraces the teachings of chapters 5–7 and the words and works of chapters 8–9; and prepares for Jesus' commissioning of the twelve to extend his manifold ministry (9:36–10:1).

A. A Grieving Father, an Afflicted Woman and a Dead Child (9:18-26)

The father and the woman suffer for very different reasons; moreover, anguish has just struck him, while hers is protracted. Both appear to be 'hopeless in distress,' but the conduct of both indicates otherwise. The girl no longer suffers, yet by all indications her condition is the most hopeless of all. What we know about these persons, we learn from this account and its parallels. Matthew reveals none of their names (though Mark and Luke do in one case): what defines them, and what most unites them, is that all three meet Jesus and experience his grace and power.[2]

The Grieving Father (9:18-19)

While Jesus was answering John's disciples, 'behold [*idou*] a ruler came and knelt before him, saying, "My daughter has just

---

[1]Words from the hymn 'The Sending, Lord, Springs,' by William J. Danker (1966).

[2]Even the father and his daughter are united more firmly by Jesus' actions than by their family bond. Peterson 1997a: 95 observes that those who gathered to David in the cave of Adullam (1 Sam. 22:1-4) were defined

died...'" (Matt. 9:18a). Matthew calls the man a 'ruler' (*archōn*).
Mark 5:22 and Luke 8:41 further identify him as Jairus, 'one
of the synagogue rulers' (*heis tōn archisynagōgōn*, Mark), 'a
ruler of the synagogue' (*archōn tēs synagōgēs*, Luke). Such a
person would have been esteemed in Capernaum. Probably
chosen from among the elders of the congregation, he was
responsible for maintaining the building, for ordering public
worship and for fostering the congregation's fidelity to Torah.[3]
He tells Jesus that his daughter has just died (*arti eteleutēsen*).
As elsewhere in these two chapters (most notably in 8:28–9:8),
Matthew condenses Mark's account; so, as in the story of the
centurion (8:5-13), there is no reference to intermediaries.[4]
That the father interrupts Jesus and kneels before him (the
verb *proskyneō*) reflects the urgency of the situation. This
president of a synagogue neither stands on his dignity nor
evidences the opposition to Jesus which readers of Matthew
are coming to expect from Israel's religious leaders (cf. Matt.
9:3, 11): has his extremity served to dispel his suspicions?[5]

---

not by their needs (such as debt, distress and discontent), nor 'by where
they came from or what they did but by what God did in and for them.'

[3]See BAGD s.v. *archisynagōgos*; W. Schrage, *TDNT* 7: 844-47; E. Yamauchi,
'Synagogue,' *DJG*, 782, who quotes from the Talmud: 'Our rabbis taught:
Let a man always sell all he has and marry the daughter of a scholar. If he
does not find the daughter of a scholar, let him marry the daughter of [one
of] the great men of the generation. If he does not find the daughter of [one
of] the great men of the generation, let him marry the daughter of a head
of a synagogue....' Sometimes there was more than one *archisynagōgos*: see
Acts 13:15; cf. Mark 5:22. While *archisynagōgos* and *archōn* were sometimes
distinguished, in the gospels the terms are synonymous (Schrage, ibid.,
847). See also Luke 13:14; Acts 18:8, 17; Appendix A.

[4]In the other accounts, it is first related (by Jairus) that the girl is dying,
then reported (by friends from home) that she has died (Mark 5:23, 35;
Luke 8:42, 49). Calvin 1994: 270 says 'this is nothing strange, if Matthew
aiming at brevity mentions in one breath what the others space out more
accurately, as it took place.' Cf. the comments on 8:5-13.

[5]This man is called *archōn heis*, 'one ruler,' which recalls the *heis
grammateus*, 'one scribe,' of 8:19. We again have the two options noted there
(p. 509). The *heis* may be equivalent to *tis*: 'a certain ruler.' Or it may be
emphatic: i.e., here is at least *one* ruler in Israel who expresses trust in Jesus.
On the question whether the original read *heis elthōn* ('one having come') or
eiselthōn ('having entered'), see Carson 1984: 231.

'But come,' he continues, 'lay your hand upon her, and she will live [*zēsetai*]' (Matt. 9:18b). The father is in distress but not in despair (cf. 2 Cor. 4:8). He has lost his only daughter (Luke 8:42) but has not lost hope for her recovery. Not only is his request strikingly audacious: touching a corpse made a person ceremonially unclean (Num. 19:11-12). He also voices remarkable trust. It may be that his faith falls short of the centurion's (who asked that Jesus not come to his home, but simply speak a word from a distance, to heal his servant; Matthew 8:8), thus illustrating the distinction Jesus makes in 8:10.[6] At the same time, this father believes that Jesus' *mere touch* will *raise the dead to life* (note *zēsetai*, a future indicative of *zaō*) – even though, to judge from Matthew, he lacks evidence that Jesus has previously done so.[7] So perhaps *this* Israelite is the exception who proves the rule of 8:10. In any case 'Jesus rose [*egertheis*: perhaps from table fellowship] and followed him, with his disciples' (9:19).[8] Even if this man's faith was not as great as the centurion's, Jesus' response shows that he is less concerned about the *size* of faith (cf. 17:20) than about its *presence* and its *object*.

The Afflicted Woman (9:20-22)
'And behold [*Kai idou*] a woman who had suffered from a hemorrhage for twelve years came up behind him and touched the edge of his garment' (9:20). Like the father, she comes to Jesus in her extremity. But whereas he sought help overtly, she does so covertly; he had no reason to feel shame, she does. By all indications, her malady is menorrhagia, abnormal and chronic bleeding from the womb.[9] Thus she is ritually defiled

---

[6]For this view, see Carson 1984: 230.

[7]Matthew 4–9 speaks nowhere else (not even in the summaries of 4:23-24; 8:16; 9:35) of Jesus' raising the dead. But in 10:8, Jesus commands the twelve to do so.

[8]Jesus' sitting at table with disciples is stated in 9:10 and implied in 9:14-15.

[9]The terms of the three accounts are all used in the LXX, invariably of bleeding from the uterus and the vagina (Keener 1999: 302, n. 102). For *haimorroeō*, 'suffer with hemorrhage' (9:20), see Leviticus 15:33. For *rhysei haimatos*, 'flow of blood' (Mark 5:25; Luke 8:43-44), see Leviticus 15:19, 25; 20:18. For *pēgē tou haimatos*, 'spring of blood' (Mark 5:29), see Leviticus 12:7;

(Lev. 15:19-33), and socially deprived: 'anyone she touched or whose cloak she touched became unclean.... Her ailment probably had kept her from marriage if it started at puberty, and almost surely would have led to her divorce if it began after she was married.'[10] Her pressing need overrides any fear of defiling Jesus or members of the crowd (*ochlos*, Mark 5:24; Luke 8:42). Approaching from the rear, she touches the *kraspedon* of Jesus' outer garment. This term may denote the garment's 'border,' or (as in Matthew 23:5) the 'tassel' attached thereto as a mark of Jesus' fidelity to Numbers 15:37-41 and Deuteronomy 22:12, in particular, and to God's commands, in general.[11]

'For she was saying to herself, "If only I touch his garment, I will be healed [*sōthēsomai*]." Jesus, turning and seeing her, said, "Take heart, daughter; your faith has saved [*sesōken*] you." And the woman was healed [*esōthē*] from that hour' (Matt. 9:21-22). The brevity of Matthew compared to Mark and Luke is especially evident here; the effect is to emphasize two elements of the story:

1. *The authority of Jesus.* So great is his healing power, the woman reflects, that its being unleashed in her womb requires only that she *touch* (not cling to) his *clothing* (not his person). Yet here, as often in Matthew 8-9, the authority of Jesus' *words* is crucial. The imperative 'take heart' (*tharsei*) has power to achieve what it commands. The address, 'daughter' (*thygater*), expresses both Jesus' tenderness towards the woman and his rule over her.[12] Most importantly, it is only when Jesus *declares* her healed, that she *is* healed: see the two instances of *sōzō* in 9:22.[13] Jesus is not defiled by the woman's touch;

20:18. Luke adds that no one could heal her (8:47); Mark, that the care of many physicians had consumed her money, increased her suffering and worsened her condition (5:26) – details Doctor Luke omits!

[10]Keener 1999: 303.

[11]See BAGD s.v. *kraspedon*, 1. and 2. The LXX uses *kraspedon* at Numbers 15:38-39 for the Hebrew *tsîtsit* ('tassel'); at Deuteronomy 22:12 for the Hebrew *kānāp* ('corner').

[12]Jesus addressed the paralytic the same way: 'Take heart, child' (*Tharsei, teknon*; 9:2); see comments on page 526. Neither Mark nor Luke uses the verb *tharseō* in either passage.

[13]The same holds true for Mark (see 5:34), even though the woman stopped bleeding the very instant she touched Jesus' clothes (5:29).

nor does he merely withstand such defilement; rather, by his great authority he heals the defiled person and conquers the defilement.[14]

2. *The faith of the woman.* Her confidence in Jesus' power to heal (9:21) is astonishing. Then he says to her, 'Your faith [*pistis*] has saved you' (9:22). Twice before in these chapters Jesus healed in response to faith (note *pistis* in 8:10 and 9:2, and *pisteuō* in 8:13), and he will do so again (9:28-29, where *pistis* and *pisteuō* recur). But nowhere else in Matthew does Jesus say, *hē pistis sou sesōken se*.[15] That the sole *cause* of her cure was Jesus' healing power, the woman would fully realize: the suggestion that she trust in (and then praise) her trust would strike her as absurd. By the same token, Jesus' pronouncement about faith (9:22) is effectual in a way that faith itself cannot be. Here, as elsewhere, faith is *instrumental* in the healing. It is essential but not meritorious. In the language of Paul, she is saved 'through faith' (*dia pisteōs*), not 'because of faith' (*dia pistin*).[16] Martin Luther called faith the empty, outstretched hand of a beggar – which essentially describes this woman's act. Furthermore, the prominence of the verb *sōzō* – 'save, heal' – in this passage (three instances in 9:21-22) reminds us that forgiving sins and healing diseases are inseparable aspects of Jesus' ministry, and that the saving work at the center of his mission (1:21, where *sōzō* first occurs in Matthew) is of far greater moment than his healing a physical malady.[17]

The Dead Child (9:23-26)
On entering the ruler's house, Jesus sees 'the flute players [*tous aulētas*] and the boisterous crowd [*ton ochlon thoryboumenon*]' (Matt. 9:23). According to the *Mishnah* (a compilation of teachings from about A.D. 200), 'Even the poorest in Israel

---

[14]See the comments on 8:3.

[15]For the same statement, see the pars. in Mark 5:34 and Luke 8:48. It recurs in Mark 10:52; and in Luke 7:50; 17:19; 18:42.

[16]For *dia pisteōs*, see, e.g., Ephesians 2:8. The phrase *dia pistin* never occurs in the NT. 'The *Gratis* [by grace] *propter Christum* [for Christ's sake] *per Fidem* [through faith] Teaching of Salvation in Reformation Theology' is discussed in Bruner 2004a: 442-44.

[17]See pages 505–7 (on 8:16-17); 517 (on 8:25); 529-30 (on 9:6-7); BAGD s.v. *sōzō*, 1-3.

should hire not less than two flutes and one wailing woman' for a funeral.[18] As indication of the ruler's wealth and status, a crowd of mourners is present on this occasion, some of them 'hired to display grief as ostentatiously as possible.'[19]

'And he said, "Go away, for the little girl [*to korasion*] has not died [*ou...apethanen*]; she is only sleeping [*alla katheudei*]." And they laughed at him' (9:24). We can now better understand the laments: death has taken a twelve-year-old child, her parents' only daughter, who now is denied marriage and children of her own.[20] As Jesus is distinguishing death from sleep, the verb here is *katheudō*, used elsewhere in Matthew of actual sleep, not *koimaomai*, the verb typically used for the 'sleep' of death.[21] The latter is a fitting image for an experience which will be interrupted at the last trumpet, when all the dead are aroused to face the final judgment. So too, Jesus' language here, far from denying the reality of the girl's death (cf. 9:18), expresses confidence in his power to save her from the protracted sleep of death.[22] The answering laughter (the verb *kategelaō*) is evidence both that the child has died and that the crowd is utterly unprepared for what Jesus is about to do.

---

[18]*Ketuboth* ('Marriage Deeds') 4:4, in Danby 1964: 250.

[19]Keener 1999: 304. This noisy crowd 'was made up of friends mourning, not in the hushed whispers characteristic of our Western funerals, but in loud outbursts of grief and wailing augmented by cries of hired mourners' (Carson 1984: 231).

[20]Cf. Keener 1999: 302, n. 98. *Korasion* is the diminutive of *korē*, 'girl.' We learn of the child's age, and of her mother, from the other accounts (Mark 5:40, 42; Luke 8:42, 51). Luke 8:42 also calls her the father's only (*monogenēs*) daughter.

[21]For *katheudō* in the first sense, see, e.g., Matthew 8:24; 13:25; 25:5; 26:40. For *koimaomai* in the second sense, see, e.g., 27:52; Acts 13:36 (and the LXX of 1 Kings 2:10); 1 Thessalonians 4:13-15. But the latter is also used of actual sleep (e.g., 28:13; Luke 22:45); and the former, of the sleep of death (e.g., 1 Thess. 5:10; and the LXX of Daniel 12:2).

[22]Jesus restores this girl to life more quickly than he does Lazarus (Matt. 9:18; John 11:39). In John 11:11-15, Jesus affirms the reality of Lazarus' death, and uses both *koimaomai* and *apothnēskō* (whose aorist form is *apethanon*) to do so; and he also makes it plain that he will surely awaken him from the sleep of death. Peter Chrysologus (ca. 380–450) said that 'God can bring a dead person back to life sooner than a sleeping person can be wakened from sleep by humans' (in *ACC* 1a: 184); cf. 1 Corinthians 15:51-52.

Having removed the crowd, Jesus 'went in and took her hand, and the little girl arose' (Matt. 9:25.)[23] According to the law, contact with a corpse made a person unclean for seven days (Num. 19:11). But here, as before, the influence is exerted in the opposite direction: by grasping the girl's hand, Jesus simultaneously removes her defilement and raises her back to life.[24] Thus does Matthew record, with surprising brevity, Jesus' most marvelous miracle so far. Of course, 'news of this spread through that whole region' (Matt. 9:26), its first bearers being those members of the crowd whose laughter was turned to wonder (see Mark 5:42).[25] How, we may wonder, did this amazing grace affect this ruler from the synagogue in Capernaum? Did he become a disciple of Jesus, as one and perhaps two *archisynagōgoi* were later to do in Corinth (Acts 18:1-17; 1 Cor. 1:1, 14)? That his name – Jairus – is preserved (Mark 5:22; Luke 8:41) suggests that he may well have done so.

It is most unlikely that we will ever witness such a raising of the dead. Yet, we are promised a twin reality that is better by far. Persons who were 'dead in trespasses and sins' are already being 'raised' and 'made alive' by God's mighty 'word of truth' (Eph. 1–2; cf. Rom. 6). And whereas this little girl would one day die again, Jesus' personal and permanent victory over death assures that all his people will 'be raised imperishable' on that final day (1 Cor. 15:52).[26]

---

[23]The crowd 'was driven out' (*exeblēthē*, an aorist passive of *ekballō*; Matthew 9:25a). It is Jesus who removes them (as made explicit in Mark 5:40, where *ekballō* recurs), which suggests that the crowd did not readily heed his command 'go away' (*anachōreite*; Matthew 9:24). Cf. 2 Kings 4:33.

[24]Matthew 9:25 describes Jesus' actions with a participle of 'attendant circumstance' (the aorist *eiselthōn*, 'going in,' from *eiserchomai*), followed by a finite verb (the aorist indicative *ekratēsen*, 'he took hold,' from *krateō*). As usual in such a construction, the finite verb receives the greater stress: Jesus' crucial act is taking the girl's hand; in order to do so, he enters the room. Cf. *GGBB*, 642-43. As we learn from Mark 5:41-42 and Luke 8:54-55, the girl also rises in response to Jesus' authoritative command.

[25]Now that Jesus has raised the dead, there is graver danger that people will become obsessed with his miraculous powers, and ignore or reject his understanding of Messiahship: thus his orders in Mark 5:43. See also Matthew 8:4; 9:30.

[26]See again the comments on 8:17.

B. Two Blind Men and a Mute Demoniac (9:27-34)

The collection of miracle stories begun in Matthew 8:1-4 now concludes. The earlier ones all had Synoptic parallels; the present healings are reported in Matthew alone.[27] While 4:23-24 and 8:16 provide comprehensive summaries of Jesus' healing ministry, here for the first time we meet the adjectives *typhlos* ('blind'; 9:27-28) and *kōphos* ('mute' or 'deaf'; 9:32-33). The verb *daimonizomai* ('to be possessed by a demon') appeared earlier (4:24; 8:16, 28, 33); but now for the first time one person is said to suffer from this affliction together with another (9:32).

Jesus and the Two Blind Men (9:27-31)

Jesus, having gone 'into the house' (*eis tēn oikian*) of the ruler (9:23), now departs from there (9:27a) and comes 'into the house' (*eis tēn oikian*; 9:28a), probably that of Peter's family (cf. 8:14, *eis tēn oikian Petrou*), elsewhere in Capernaum.[28] As he walked from the one place to the other, 'two blind men followed him, crying out and saying, "Have mercy on us, Son of David!"' (9:27b). Here, as in 8:28-34 (the two demoniacs), Matthew is historically accurate; the surrounding stories about individuals whom Jesus heals, show that the evangelist is not obsessed with 'doublings.'[29] These two men are following Jesus, not (or not yet) as disciples but as members of the crowd, whence they emerge – like the ruler and the woman in the previous passage – to implore Jesus' help.[30] They are the first persons in Matthew to call Jesus 'Son of David [*Huios Dauid*],' i.e., the royal Messiah; and they are the first to entreat

---

[27]Mark 8:22-26 (which also lacks pars.) comes from a later time. Matthew 20:29-34 is par. to Mark 10:46-52. The closest par. to Mark 3:20-30 and Luke 11:14-23 is Matthew 12:22-32.

[28]Cf. 9:1 (and comments); Hagner 1993: 253-54.

[29]On Matthew's two demoniacs, see pages 519-20. Healings of individuals dominate both Matthew 8 (leper; centurion's servant; Peter's mother-in-law) and chapter 9 (paralytic; bleeding woman; ruler's daughter; mute demoniac).

[30]For explicit or implicit references to the 'following' (the verb *akoloutheō*) of the 'crowd[s],' *ochlos* (*-loi*), see 4:25; 8:1, 10. Adding the instances of *ochlos* in 8:18; 9:8, 33, 36, we get the impression that the crowds witness most of the events of chapters 8–9. The *ēkolouthēsan* of 9:27 may be an ingressive aorist, they 'began to follow' (thus GGBB, 559).

him with the words 'Have mercy on us [*Eleēson hēmas*].'[31] In
light of all that the context reveals about events in and around
Capernaum, there can be no doubt that the men's use of this
title and their cry for mercy are based on reports of Jesus'
stupendous healing powers. They already possess insight
that some sighted people lack.[32]

The men having come into the house, 'Jesus says to
them, "Do you believe [*Pisteuete*] that I am able to do this?"
They say to him, "Yes, Lord [*Nai, Kyrie*]"' (Matt. 9:28). Jesus'
question reiterates a cardinal teaching of these two chapters,
namely that faith is a vital response to the words and works
of Messiah, and a vital condition for further manifestations of
his authority and power.[33] The men's *Nai* avows that their cry
(9:27) arises from the confidence that Jesus can indeed cure
their blindness: the 'this' (*touto*) of Jesus' question can mean
nothing else.[34] The address, *Kyrie*, does not acknowledge
Jesus' divinity but voices the respect due the Davidic Messiah:
cf. the blind men's entreaty in 20:31, identical to that of 9:27,
except for the addition of *Kyrie*.[35]

'Then he touched their eyes, saying, "According to your
faith let it be done for you." And their eyes were opened'
(9:29-30a). This sequel confirms that the men's words (*Nai,
Kyrie*) match rather than mask their true convictions (cf.
15:8). And we learn yet again that while Jesus responds
to faith, the sole *cause* of healing is his own willingness
and ability to do so (cf. 8:2-3). The men's cry for help and
confession of faith do not produce the cure: only by the
dual authority of Jesus' touch and utterance are the men's

---

[31]The only prior instances of *huios Dauid* come in 1:1 and in the angel's
address to Joseph, 1:20. On Jesus as the kingly Messiah, see pages 132-33.
Eleēson (from *eleeō*) is an aorist imperative of entreaty (*GGBB*, 487-88). For this
or a similar entreaty, see 15:22; and 20:30-31 (on the lips of two other blind men).

[32]'They saw the truth which teachers of the law and Pharisees could not
see; they saw that Jesus of Nazareth was the Messiah' (Ryle 1993: 68). Cf.
John 9:39-41; Ephesians 1:18.

[33]See Matthew 8:10, 13, 26; 9:2, 22, and comments on those texts.

[34]But cf. 20:31-32, where, in response to a very similar entreaty from two
other blind men, Jesus asks, 'What do you want me to do for you?'

[35]Matthew, of course, uses *Kyrios* to declare Jesus' deity: see comments
on 8:25.

eyes opened.[36] Moreover, joining this healing to earlier ones reveals that Jesus exercises his authority with sovereign freedom: sometimes he heals by touch alone (Matt. 8:15; 9:6, 25); sometimes by word alone (8:13, 32; 9:22); sometimes by both together (8:3; 9:29).[37]

'And Jesus sternly warned [*enebrimēthē*] them, saying, "See that no one knows about this." But they went out and spread news of him through that whole region' (8:30b-31). Jesus' charge recalls his words to the leper, 'See that you speak to no one' (8:4), the parallel to which in Mark 1:43-44 uses this verb, *embrimaomai*. The purpose here, as there, is to discourage the spread and growth of false Messianic hopes.[38] Yet the men cannot keep the joyful news to themselves: taking advantage of their newly granted sight, they travel far and wide to declare the fame of the one who healed them – just as witnesses to the previous miracle had done (Matt. 8:26).[39]

Jesus and the Mute Demoniac (9:32-34)
'As they [the two blind men] were going away, behold [*idou*] they brought to him a mute, demon-possessed man [*anthrōpon kōphon daimonizomenon*]. And when the demon had been cast out [*ekblēthentos tou daimoniou*], the mute man spoke [*elalēsen*]' (Matt. 9:32-33a). As the verb in 9:33a shows, *kōphos* in this instance means 'mute' or 'dumb': it is otherwise in 11:5, 'the deaf hear [*kōphoi akouousin*].'[40] We also learn from 9:33a that the

---

[36]Cf. comments on Matthew 9:22.

[37]As noted more than once, Mark and Luke sometimes augment Matthew in these respects.

[38]See comments on 8:4.

[39]The language of Matthew 9:31 is very close to that of verse 26: (i) both *exēlthen* (9:26) and *exelthontes* (9:31) come from *exerchomai*; (ii) *phēmē* (9:26) and *diephēmisan* (9:31) are cognates; and (iii) *eis holēn tēn gēn ekeinēn* (9:26) is close to *en holē tē gē ekeinē* (9:31). Mark 1:45 reveals that the leper too 'spread the news' (*diaphēmizein*) about Jesus; and Mark 5:43, that Jesus charged people not to make known his raising of Jairus' daughter.

[40]The man in Mark 7:32 is both deaf (*kōphos*) and impaired in speech (*mogilalos*). An unclean spirit has made the boy of Mark 9:25 both dumb (*alalos*) and deaf (*kōphos*). Gundry 1994: 179-80 thinks *kōphos* in Matthew 9:32-33 includes deafness. 'Dumbness receives the emphasis in this story because its reversal in the gift of speech is more quickly obvious than the reversal of deafness.'

two afflictions are really one: the *daimonion* enslaves the man by robbing him of speech. Saying that such a symptom *never* signals demonic activity would be just as wrong as saying it *always* does. (The same applies to blindness and deafness: cf. 12:22; Mark 9:25.) With the greatest economy of words, Matthew declares that Jesus rescues the man from his dual bondage. This action is expressed by the aorist passive participle *ekblēthentos* (from *ekballō*), 'having been cast out,' Jesus by implication being the one who expels the demon.[41] Unless Matthew is implying that the mere presence of Jesus achieves this result, we are probably to infer that this demon, like those of 8:32, is banished by Jesus' mighty word. Perhaps we are also to infer that those who brought this man to Jesus, acted in faith as did those of 9:2. On the other hand, Jesus may on this occasion be expending healing grace for the purpose of *evoking* faith.

'And the crowds marveled [*ethaumasan*], saying, "Never was anything like this seen in Israel"' (9:33b). Thus had the miracle at sea affected the disciples (8:27, where this same form of *thaumazō* occurs). The immediate cause of the crowds' response is Jesus' healing of the mute demoniac.[42] But there is a larger explanation for their exclamation. These words recall the close of Matthew 5–7. As 'the crowds [*hoi ochloi*] were astonished [*exeplēssonto*]' at the authority of that sermon (7:28-29), so now the crowds (*hoi ochloi* again) marvel at the authority evidenced in the works of these two chapters. The cumulative effect of Jesus' miracles, as of his teachings, is quite overwhelming.[43] These deeds are indeed unprecedented in Israel: for God's kingdom has dawned and God's Messiah has come (cf. 11:2-6; 12:28).

'But the Pharisees were saying, "By the prince of demons [*En tō archonti tōn daimoniōn*] he casts out demons [*ekballei ta daimonia*]"' (Matt. 9:34).[44] Here too the immediately preceding

---

[41]The words *ekblēthentos tou daimoniou* form a genitive absolute.

[42]If the man's cure occurred indoors (9:28), the crowds learned of it afterwards; if it happened outside, they (or some of them) probably witnessed it.

[43]Cf. France 1985: 173.

[44]For arguments favoring the inclusion of Matthew 9:34, see *TC*, 20-21. The *en* of the prepositional phrase is instrumental: 'by the power of' (Hagner 1993: 255); 'with the help of' (BAGD s.v., III. 1. b.).

miracle precipitates the response: these terms, *ekballō* and *daimonion*, both occur in 9:33. But like the crowds, the Pharisees are feeling the total impact of Jesus' deeds in chapters 8–9. It is not the present miracle that explains this reaction, but their and their scribes' previous encounters with Jesus: see 9:2-8, 9-13, also 14-17. Already the seeds are being sown for the full-grown conflict of 12:22-32; and already the Pharisees' charge – that a ruler of *demons* would aid the expulsion of *demons* – betrays its own absurdity (cf. 12:26).

It is sobering and saddening to reflect that the Pharisees and the crowds are responding to the same phenomena, and that the glories and graces of Jesus can affect people in such radically different ways. The same sun that melts butter hardens clay (cf. 2 Cor. 2:14-16).

C. Laborers for the Harvest (9:35-38)
This passage forms a bridge. It both reviews Jesus' manifold ministry and prepares for its extension through his disciples.

The Labors of Jesus
The summary of 9:35 replicates that of 4:23. The earlier text has twenty-seven Greek words, this one twenty-eight; the two have twenty words in common, all in the same order. These texts enclose the accounts of Jesus' words and works in Matthew 5–9. Moreover, in accord with 4:24-25 (not echoed here), chapters 8–9 report that Jesus healed diseases and expelled demons, and that he served both Jews and Gentiles.[45] Thus does Matthew underscore the depth, breadth and impact of Jesus' ministry.

'And seeing the crowds [*tous ochlous*], he was moved with compassion [*esplanchnisthē*] for them, because they were harassed and helpless like sheep not having a shepherd' (9:36). This text reveals one of Jesus' chief motives for serving the crowds through this whole period (cf. the reference to *ochloi polloi* in 4:25).[46] His love for the crowds is captured in the verb

---

[45]For more on Matthew 4:23-25 and the terms of 9:35, see pages 295-98.

[46]Between Matthew 4:25 and 9:36, there are eight other instances of *ochlos* (-*oi*).

splanchnizomai, which appears for the first time in Matthew. Each time the term is used of Jesus, this deep emotion finds expression in action. In three later instances, he shows his compassion by healing and feeding people in the crowd (14:14; 15:32), and by giving sight to the blind (20:34).[47] Here the crowds are described as 'harassed' (*eskylmenoi*, a perfect passive participle of *skyllō*) and as 'helpless' (*errimmenoi*, a perfect passive participle of *rhiptō*); and they are likened to sheep without a shepherd. These Israelites lack the guidance and protection their appointed leaders were meant to give them. These shepherds – like negligent parents – have neither taught the people well nor set before them a godly example, so that the sheep are confused, and vulnerable to assaults. More tragically still, the shepherds themselves have become predators whose false piety and intolerable demands threaten to destroy the sheep.[48] As Yahweh appointed Joshua to succeed Moses so Israel would not lack a shepherd (Num. 27:17), the Father has appointed his Son – the latter-day Joshua (Matt. 1:21) – to shepherd his people (2:6); to supplant the negligent and tyrannical shepherds; to teach the sheep anew about God's truth, grace and power; and to rescue and protect them from enemies both human and demonic.[49] As we shall learn before this book ends, this shepherd's compassion comes to supreme expression when he 'lays down his life for his sheep' to save them from their

---

[47]The only other instance of the verb comes in a parable (18:27). The matching plural noun *splanchna* ('bowels' as seat of 'mercy' and 'affection') does not occur in Matthew.

[48]It is especially, but not exclusively, the scribes and Pharisees who are guilty of these sins of omission and commission. See 5:20; 6:1-18; 15:1-9; 16:1-12; 21:12-16; 23:1-32.

[49]See Jeremiah 23:1-6, where Yahweh, in face of shepherds who destroy and scatter his sheep, promises 'to raise up for David a righteous Branch' who will reign wisely and justly (23:6); Ezekiel 34, where he promises to remove the shepherds who abandon, tyrannize and scatter his sheep (34:1-10) and to grant them his own guidance, nurture and protection (34:10-31) through the 'one shepherd, my servant David' (34:23); Micah 5:1-5, where he promises that his appointed shepherd will come from Bethlehem; and Zechariah 10:2-3 (with 9:9; 12:10; 13:7). All these prophecies are fulfilled in Jesus 'the good shepherd': see John 10:1-30, also comments on Matthew 2:6, 23.

sins.[50] By opposing and attacking Jesus – the shepherd come to seek and to save the lost – the false shepherds endanger the sheep as never before, and place themselves under the direst judgment.

The Need for Laborers

That very compassion prompts Jesus' ensuing words to his disciples: 'The harvest is plentiful [*therismos polys*], but the workers are few [*hoi ergatai oligoi*]. Therefore, ask the Lord of the harvest [*tou kyriou tou therismou*] to send out workers [*ergatas*] into his harvest [*eis ton therismon autou*]' (Matt. 9:37-38). The imagery has changed, but the mission has not: these laborers are to be sent forth as representatives of Jesus the good shepherd, as agents of his compassion to the harassed and helpless crowds (9:36).

The dominant theme of this text is the *harvest*: the noun *therismos* occurs three times. A bountiful harvest is already *there*, ripe for reaping (cf. John 4:35). Despite all obstacles, the kingdom of God is advancing mightily, and many people are already submitting, or are ready to submit, to his rule. Jesus' command (9:38a; *deēthēte*, 'ask') presupposes that of 6:9a (*Houtōs... proseuchesthe*, 'thus pray').[51] The Lord (*Kyrios*) of the harvest is the 'Father in heaven' (6:9b). The harvest belongs to him (9:38b); it is he who will send forth the harvesters, and he who will govern their actions.[52] In offering the entreaty of 9:38, disciples voice the threefold petition of 6:9c-10. Those

---

[50]See 1:21; 26:31 (the quotation of Zechariah 13:7); John 10:11-18. 'What causes Jesus' deep compassion at this point [Matt. 9:36] is not the abundance of sickness he has seen but rather the great spiritual need of the people...' (Hagner 1993: 260).

[51]The deponent verb *deomai*, 'ask' (of which *deēthēte* is an aorist passive imperative plural) often denotes a prayer: see also, e.g., Luke 22:32; Acts 4:31; Romans 1:10.

[52]*Autou* (Matt. 9:38b) is a possessive genitive (*GGBB*, 81-83). 'Lord of the harvest' probably represents the Aramaic *rab chetsādā* ('chief harvester'), 'the person responsible for hiring and dismissing harvest workers' (Albright and Mann 1971: 114). Gundry 1994: 181 thinks Jesus himself is 'Lord of the harvest' (so too Chrysostom, *ACC* 1a: 190). It is better, in my judgment, to say Jesus sends forth the apostles (10:5) in accord with the Father's will (6:10; cf. John 17:1-26).

workers go forth to do God's will on earth, in anticipation of the day when God's rule will be all-encompassing and his name universally revered.[53]

Given the readiness of the crop, a host of harvesters is needed. Whereas at the end of history, the Son of Man will send forth his angels to reap a harvest of persons destined for destruction (13:39-42; note *therismos* in 9:39, also 9:30), here he seeks workers to rescue people from the wrath to come. The disciples' prayer to that end, far from compromising the sovereignty of God, becomes his instrument. Does not this command to pray come from Yahweh incarnate? Did he not also command the prayer of 6:9-13? Do not the persons to be 'harvested' by these workers already belong to that vast company of Christ's elect (*eklektoi*) whom his angels will gather at the end (24:31)? Did not Jesus encourage his disciples to pray in the confidence that the heavenly Father delights to give good gifts to his children? And what better gift could these workers receive than a harvest of the redeemed? God may, of course, choose to raise up laborers where no prayer has been offered; yet the prayer of faith remains a vital means which he ordains for fulfilling his saving purpose. 'Keep hold of both points, then: our prayers are anticipated by Him in His freedom, yet, what we ask we gain by prayer.'[54] To judge from the following passage, some of these disciples may actually have gained more from their prayers than they asked.

---

[53]Cf. the parables of the kingdom (*basileia*) in Matthew 13, especially those about the sower, the mustard seed and the leaven. See also the comments on 7:13-14.

[54]Calvin 1994: 204, on Matthew 6:8. Likewise, in 1 Kings 18, 'Yahweh wills to send rain [v.1] – and he wills that his will come to pass through Elijah's prayer [v. 42]' (Davis 2002: 249).

Section 8

'Publish Glad Tidings'[1]
(Matt. 10:1-42)

This is the second of Matthew's five great discourses. The first is preceded by the summary of 4:23; this one, by the matching words of 9:35. Matthew 5:1-2 prefaces the first (5:3–7:27); 10:1-4, the second (10:5-42). The uniting theme of Matthew 10 is Jesus' charge to his missionaries. Verses 5-15 focus on the immediate mission of the twelve. But the scope of Jesus' charge is considerably broader in 16-42, a passage that anticipates his Great Commission in 28:18-20.[2] So, while the whole discourse is for the twelve (cf. 11:1, 'When Jesus had finished giving instructions to his twelve disciples...'), its greater part is for their successors as well.

---

[1]Words from the hymn 'O Zion, Haste,' by Mary A. Thomson (1968).

[2]While Matthew 10:5-15 has pars. in Mark 6:8-13 and Luke 9:2-6, pars. to 10:16-42 occur at various later places in the other gospels (especially in Mark 13 and Luke 12 and 21), evidence both of Matthew's thematic arrangement and of the broader scope of 10:16-42. On 'progress in narrative and teaching' as it applies to chapter 10, see pages 51-55.

I.
'So Send I You'[1]
(10:1-15)

This passage records an answer to the prayer of 9:38. Some of the very disciples Jesus told to pray that way, he now commissions to gather that harvest: note the echo of *ergatai*, 'workers' (9:37-38) in *ergatēs*, 'worker' (10:10). (Whether any of the twelve were shocked or dismayed by this answer to their prayer, the text does not reveal.) God the Father remains 'the Lord' who sends out workers (9:38; the verb *ekballō*); yet it is Jesus who sends forth the twelve (10:5; the verb *apostellō*). There is no room for competition between the Father and the Son: the Trinity is not a dysfunctional family.

As the authorized representative of God the Father, God the Son becomes a 'Lord of the harvest' in his own right (cf. Matt. 13:39-41; 24:30-31). The name Yahweh (*Kyrios*) belongs both to him and to the Father (cf. p. 139).

A. The Commissioned (10:1-4)
'And having summoned his twelve disciples, he gave them authority over unclean spirits, to cast them out, and to heal every kind of disease and every kind of sickness. The names of the twelve apostles are these' (10:1-2a).

The Twelve
Here for the first time Matthew speaks of Jesus' *twelve* disciples (*dōdeka mathētas*). They are not chosen on this occasion, but commissioned. As noted earlier (p. 303), they were selected from a larger number of *mathētai* before the sermon of chapters 5–7. An essential period of learning has transpired; only now are they equipped for a mission of their own.[2] Jesus,

---

[1]The title of a hymn by Margaret Clarkson (1954, 1963).

again exercising his authority, now grants authority (*exousia*) to the twelve. As stated more fully in verses 7-8, this is manifold authority to speak and to act *as he himself has done* (chs. 4-9). Verse 1 says nothing about preaching but focuses on working miracles, probably because this is the main way Jesus exercised his *exousia* in the preceding two chapters. The twelve are given authority 'to cast out' (*ekballein*) 'unclean spirits' (*pneumata akatharta*). This term appears for the first time in Matthew (and recurs only in 12:43, in the singular); but chapters 8–9 report that Jesus himself took such action more than once.[3] The last seven Greek words of 10:1, *kai* through *malakian*, are virtually identical to the last seven used in 9:35 to describe Jesus' own activity.[4]

Only in 10:2 does Matthew speak of twelve *apostles*; indeed *apostolos* occurs nowhere else in Matthew. Here it is fitting, for Jesus is about to send these men forth (10:5, the verb *apostellō*), to enlarge his ministry. His choice of *twelve* apostles recalls the twelve tribes of Israel (cf. 19:28), and signals that he has come to reconstitute the people of God around his own person (16:18) and under his own rule (23:8-10); see pages 151-52. The twelve are listed as six pairs (note the instances of the conjunction *kai* in 10:2-4), which reflects the fact that Jesus sent them forth 'two by two' (Mark 6:7) but need not mean they were invariably paired as here.[5] When the twelve are divided into three groups of four each,

---

[2]See Mark 3:14. Says Chrysostom: 'Note the careful timing of their mission. They were not sent out at the beginning of their walk with him. They were not sent out until they had sufficiently benefited by following him daily' (in *ACC* 1a: 192).

[3]Note the instances of this verb, *ekballō*, in Matthew 8:16, 31; 9:33, 34. Matching his use of *daimonizomai* to describe the demon-possessed (8:16, 28, 33; 9:32; also 4:24), Matthew's usual term for 'unclean spirits' is *daimonia* (9:33, 34; 10:8, etc.).

[4]The same words and word order also occur in 4:23b. The one difference is that 4:23 and 9:35 use the participle *therapeuōn*, and 10:1 the infinitive *therapeuein*.

[5]E.g., in Matthew 10:3 (and in the Synoptic pars.) Philip is paired with Bartholomew, and Thomas with Matthew; but in Acts 1:13, Philip is paired with Thomas, and Bartholomew with Matthew. The pairings are more easily discerned in Matthew 10:2-4, given its use of *kai*, than in the parallels of Mark 3:16-19 and Luke 6:14-16, given *their* use of *kai*. Cf. Jeremias 1971: 235, who notes that the pairings protected the messengers (cf. Eccl. 4:9-12) and honored the principle of Deuteronomy 17:6; 19:15.

the same name appears first in each group in all three Synoptics. The same is true in Acts 1:13, but then there are eleven; only when Matthias replaces Judas are there again twelve (1:25-26). Even in the interim, *twelve* remains important (1 Cor. 15:5).

Their Names

'First, Simon [*Simōn*], who is called Peter [*Petros*], and Andrew [*Andreas*] his brother; and James [*Iakōbos*] the son of Zebedee, and John [*Iōannēs*] his brother' (Matt. 10:2b). The prominence given to the call of these four men (4:18-22) helps to explain their preeminence in the list. Conversely, the fact that Peter, James and John came to enjoy a special closeness to Jesus (17:1; 26:37; Mark 5:37) helps to explain the record of their call and their position here. It is natural that the name of Andrew, Peter's brother, should be joined to theirs.[6] Matthew alone prefaces *Simōn* with *prōtos*, whose significance is traceable not to 4:18-22 (where Simon is the first, or one of the first, to be called into discipleship) but to 16:13-20 (where see comments), a text that also explains the *ho legomenos Petros* of 10:2, language without parallel in the list of twelve. The presence of James and John in the circle of the twelve, and in its inner circle, helps to explain their mother's request on their behalf in 20:20-21.[7] Interestingly, Andrew's name never appears hereafter in Matthew.

'Philip [*Philippos*] and Bartholomew [*Bartholomaios*], Thomas [*Thōmas*] and Matthew [*Matthaios*] the tax collector' (10:3a). Neither Philip nor Bartholomew is mentioned elsewhere in Matthew. Philip met Jesus early in Judea, at which time a man named Nathanael received Philip's witness about Jesus and himself became a disciple (John 1:43-51). As Philip's name is joined to Bartholomew's here (and in the Synoptic pars.), and to Nathanael's in John; as Bartholomew never appears in John,

---

[6]In Mark 13:3, Andrew joins Peter, James and John in privately questioning Jesus about the future. Before the call of Matthew 4:18-22, Jesus became acquainted with Peter, Andrew and John in Judea (John 1:35-42). On this see page 294, n. 25.

[7]Matthew does not record these disciples' surname 'sons of thunder' (Mark 3:17), nor the incident where the brothers want to call down fire on a Samaritan village (Luke 9:51-56).

and Nathanael never in the Synoptics; as Nathanael is closely identified with other members of the twelve in John 21:2; and as 'Bartholomew' means *bar Talmai*, 'son of Talmai,' there is good reason to think that these two disciples are one and the same – Nathanael bar Talmai.[8] Thomas' name occurs nowhere else in Matthew. Matthew, significantly, is the only member of the twelve identified by trade, *ho telōnēs* (though referring to the four men in Matthew 10:2 as fishermen would have occasioned no surprise) – a fingerprint of the author, not to distinguish himself from another *Matthaios* but to indicate the kind of life out of which Jesus called him.[9]

'James [*Iakōbos*] the son of Alphaeus, and Thaddaeus [*Thaddaios*]; Simon the Cananaean [*Simōn ho Kananaios*], and Judas the Iscariot [*Ioudas ho Iskariōtēs*], who also betrayed him' (Matt. 10: 3b-4). This James is thus identified to distinguish him from James the son of Zebedee (10:2b). Mark 2:14 calls Levi 'the son of Alphaeus.' But this is almost certainly a different *Alphaios*; for if Levi (Matthew) and this James were brothers, we would expect them to be joined here as are Simon and Andrew, and James and John.[10] Thaddaeus is also named in Mark 3:18; but Luke 6:15-16 and Acts 1:13 lack this name and include 'Judas son of James [*Ioudas Iakōbou*].' I believe that both names belong to the same person, Thaddaeus being his personal name, and Judas his tribal name (this Jacob fathered a Judah, as did the patriarch [Matt.1:2]), on the analogy of Matthew Levi.[11] Thaddaeus is mentioned nowhere else

---

[8]Cf. *Simōn Bariōna*, 'Simon Bar-Jonah' (Matt. 16:17). For the Hebrew name *Talmāy*, see, e.g., Judges 1:10, where LXX has *Tholmi*. Cf. M. J. Wilkins, 'Disciples,' *DJG*, 180.

[9]On *Matthaios* and *telōnēs*, see pages 42-43 (on Matt. 10:2-4), and 532-36 (on 9:9). The parallels in Mark 3:18 and Luke 6:15 do not identify Matthew as 'the tax collector.'

[10]Nor are Levi (Matthew) and this James so connected anywhere else in the NT. Cf. pages 41 (n. 47) and 42 (n. 51).

[11]'The uniformity of the rest of the names from list to list assures us that these names [Thaddaeus and James] refer to the same person' (Wilkins, ibid., 181). As in 1:2, so in the LXX of Genesis 35:23 (e.g.), the father is *Iakōb* and the son *Ioudas*. *Iakōbos* is a Hellenized form of *Iakōb*. In place of *Thaddaios*, some MSS. at 10:3 read 'Lebbaeus [*Lebbaios*],' or 'Thaddaeus who was called Lebbaeus,' or 'Lebbaeus who was called Thaddaeus.' See *TC*, 21.

in Matthew. James the son of Alphaeus may be the *Iakōbos* identified in 27:56 as son of Mary and brother of Joseph: see those comments.

This Simon's surname, *ho Kananaios*, distinguishes him from Simon Peter. It identifies him not as a man from Cana (cf. John 21:2) nor as a Canaanite, but as an 'enthusiast' or 'zealot' (the meaning of the Aramaic *qan'ān*), as the translation of Luke 6:15 and Acts 1:13, *Zēlōtēs*, makes clear. In all probability, it is the *Torah* for which Simon is zealous: thus does Paul apply *zēlōtēs* to himself (Acts 22:3; Gal. 1:14). Such zeal moved Phinehas to violence in the days of Moses (Num. 25:6-13); likewise Mattathias in the time of the Maccabees (1 Macc. 2:15-28) and Saul in the early days of the church (Gal. 1:13-14; Phil. 3:6, with *zēlos*). For the same reason, Simon may well have displayed the kind of 'revolutionary patriotism' which would in time give rise to the party of the Zealots (formed in the late 60s A.D.).[12]

That both Simon and Matthew are among the twelve testifies both to the inclusiveness of Jesus and to the breadth of his appeal. Such diversity also accords with his mission to reach all 'the lost sheep of the house of Israel' (Matt. 10:6).

Judas' surname, *ho Iskariōtēs*, distinguishes him from 'Judas son of James' (on whom see above), and probably refers to his town of Kerioth in Judea.[13] His name always appears last in the lists, for the reason given here, 'who also betrayed [*paradous*] him.'[14] All remaining references to Judas come, significantly, in chapters 26–27. This Simon appears nowhere else in Matthew.

---

[12]Cf. Keener 1999: 311, whence the quoted phrase; France 1985: 177. The epithet *zēlōtēs* 'may well refer to [Simon's] intense nationalism and hatred of Rome' (Hagner 1993: 266). According to W. J. Heard, 'Revolutionary Movements,' *DJG*, 696, the origins of the Zealot party are traceable to the clash between the Jerusalem citizenry and the Roman procurator Florus (A.D. 64–66), and the party itself was formed in the winter of A.D. 67–68.

[13]Mark 3:19 and Luke 6:16 use the indeclinable *Iskariōth*. Judas' father Simon is also called *Iskariōtēs*, John 6:71; 13:26. The Hebrew *'îš qᵉrîyyôt* means 'man of Kerioth.' Kerioth was in southern Judea, twelve miles south of Hebron (see Josh. 15:21, 25). A variant at Matthew 10:4 and 26:14, *Skariōtēs*, has prompted various suggestions, including 'a leathern girdle or apron, a bandit or assassin, a liar or traitor, and a man of ruddy complexion' (*TC*, 21). Cf. ibid.; BAGD s.v. *Iskariōtēs*; Hagner 1993: 266.

[14]Mark 3:19 likewise says that Judas 'betrayed [*paredōken*] him'; and Luke 6:16, that he 'became a traitor [*prodotēs*].' This verb, *paradidōmi*, appears

B. The Commission (10:5-15)

'These twelve Jesus sent out [*apesteilen*], having instructed them as follows...' (10:5a). The immediate mission of the twelve is in view. The rest of the discourse is also addressed to them (cf. 10:16, where 'you' means the twelve, and 11:1); but, as we shall see, it is much broader in scope.[15] Jesus grants authority (Matt. 10:1) by wielding authority: the present passage contains no fewer than sixteen of his commands.[16]

Apostles and Audience

These twelve *apostoloi* whom Jesus chose (10:2) he now sends out (10:5; the verb *apostellō*), to represent him, and to speak and act in his name. As he is under the Father's authority, so are they under his: 'The one who receives you, receives me; and the one who receives me, receives the one who sent me' (10:40). Just as Yahweh appointed the OT prophets, so has Jesus – Yahweh incarnate – commissioned these apostles to speak his very words and to display his very power (10:7-8). In 10:41, he applies the name *prophētēs* to these men and others.[17]

'Do not go into the way of the Gentiles, and do not enter a city of the Samaritans; go instead to the lost sheep [*ta probata ta apolōlota*] of the house of Israel [*oikou Israēl*]' (Matt. 10:5b-6). The disciples are to confine their mission to Galilee, and to avoid Gentile territories to the east, north and west, and Samaritan territory to the south. Within Galilee they are to devote their

---

several times later in Matthew to denote Judas' act. For more on this, and on Judas' motives, see comments on Matthew 26:14-16.

[15] See also the comments on page 561.

[16] Of these, thirteen are expressed by the imperative mood (one in 6, one in 7, five in 8, two in 11, one in 12, two in 13, one in 14), and three by the subjunctive (two in 5, one in 9).

[17] Cf. 23:34; and Keener 1999: 314-15. For arguments that the Christian concept of apostleship originates with Jesus; that his understanding is similar to that reflected in the OT use of the Hebrew verb *šālach* ('send'; LXX, *apostellō*); and that the functions of his *apostolos* were akin to those of the *šālîach* in Judaism, see C. G. Kruse, 'Apostle,' *DJG*, 27-33, and sources he cites. The authority of the *apostolos*, like that of the *šālîach*, 'was entirely limited to the extent of his commission and the fidelity with which he carried it out. That Jesus authorizes disciples to perform acts of compassion (9:36) in his name does not authorize them to use his power to get whatever they want (4:3)' (Keener 1999: 314).

attention to fellow Jews, as Jesus himself does (15:24, whose wording is very close to 10:6). They are to show no respect of persons, for the whole nation urgently needs their witness.

The point of Jesus' imagery is not that some sheep have strayed from the fold, but that the whole flock has gone astray: the lost sheep *are* the house of Israel.[18] That Jesus commissions *twelve* apostles, recalls ancient Israel's twelve tribes, and reflects his longing to address the whole nation, and to draw them into the new Israel of God.[19] This mission is mainly for the crowds, those harried and helpless sheep for whom Jesus showed compassion (Matt. 9:36). But it is not for them exclusively: the shepherds who abandoned and exploited the sheep are themselves lost sheep wandering toward destruction. Nor, of course, do these instructions exclude Gentiles and Samaritans from the blessings of the kingdom. Matthew has already testified more than once to Yahweh's and Messiah's saving grace for Gentiles; and later in this discourse Jesus speaks of an evangelistic witness to Gentiles (10:18). More than once he has already healed Gentiles – two of them in Gentile territory! – and he will do so again. And while these miracles are the exceptions that prove the present rule, they are also foretastes of the gospel's global outreach. Indeed, a primary purpose for the present mission to Jews is that they in turn may become a light to the nations (28:18-20). The latter-day Joshua here authorizes apostles to conquer the *land*; he will later commission them to conquer the *world*.[20]

Mission and Motive
'And as you go, proclaim, "The kingdom of heaven has drawn near." Heal the sick, raise the dead, cleanse the lepers, cast

---

[18]Thus *oikou* (Matt. 10:6b) is not a partitive (or 'wholative') genitive, 'lost sheep *within the house*' (cf. *GGBB*, 84-86), but a genitive of apposition, 'lost sheep, *namely the house*' (ibid., 95-100).

[19]Cf. page 563 (on 10:2); Jeremias 1971: 235; and Paul's language in Galatians 3:29; 6:16.

[20]For Jesus' healing of Gentiles, see 8:5-13, 28-34; 15:21-28, and comments on those passages. See also pages 149-51 ('Israel and the Nations' within the people of God), and 173-75 ('Good News for Jews and for Gentiles' among Matthew's non-Christian readers).

out demons. Freely you received, freely give' (Matt. 10:7-8). This text makes it exceptionally clear that Jesus commissions the twelve for the precise purpose of extending his own ministry. The participle *poreuomenoi* ('as you go') echoes the imperative *poreuesthe* ('go') in 10:6. Here in verse 7, by means of the imperative *kēryssete* ('proclaim'), Jesus accentuates the disciples' preaching – whose content is identical to his (4:17; cf. the use of *kēryssō* in 24:14 and 26:13). In 28:19-20, the risen Jesus will again command eleven of these disciples both to go (the participle *poreuthentes*) and to make disciples (the imperative *mathēteusate*) – by means of his teaching, not theirs.[21]

All the miracles Jesus commands the twelve to accomplish have their precedents in his own ministry: six of the eight Greek terms used here, and the cognate of a seventh, were earlier applied to his mighty works.[22] As Jesus actually did all four kinds of miracles, so will his apostles: none of their works – including the raising of the dead – is to be reduced to the purely spiritual.[23] Although Matthew does not report directly on this mission of the twelve, it is probable that their works and words are included with those of Jesus in the summary of 11:5, which reports the cleansing of lepers, the raising of the dead, the healing of three kinds of *astheneia* (blindness, lameness and deafness), and the evangelizing of the poor, tantamount to proclaiming the gospel of the kingdom. Then, says Jesus, 'Freely you received [*dōrean elabete*], freely give [*dōrean dote*].' The closing imperative is preceded by a statement of fact. The *dōrean* is emphatic: the twelve have received the manifold blessing of the kingdom *free*

---

[21]Matthew 28:19a will be translated 'Go [*poreuthentes*] therefore and make disciples [*mathēteusate*] of all the nations'; see those comments. This matches the imperatives *poreuesthe* and *kēryssete* in 10:6-7. See also the comments on 9:25.

[22]All four verbs were thus used: *therapeuō* ('heal') in (e.g.) 4:23; 9:35; *egeirō* ('raise') in 9:25; *katharizō* ('cleanse') in 8:2-3; *ekballō* ('cast out') in (e.g.) 8:16; 9:33. So were two of the nouns: *lepros*, 8:2; *daimonion*, 9:33-34 (cf. the verb *daimonizomai*, e.g., 4:24; 8:16). The participle *asthenountas* ('the sick'), from *astheneō* (here for the first time in Matthew), is a cognate of *astheneia* (8:17). The adjective *nekros* ('dead') was used in 8:22 but not of a miracle.

[23]Well stressed by France 1985: 179. Jesus gave apostles power to raise the literally dead (Acts 9:36-43; 20:7-12). The proposal of Fenton 1977: 157-8 (and in an earlier article cited by France) that the commands of Matthew 10:8 be taken metaphorically, is to be rejected.

of charge, so let them impart it to others the same way.[24] Here
again, the prime motivation for obeying Messiah's commands
comes not from the commands themselves but from the great
indicatives of grace that undergird them – namely, his and the
Father's saving actions.[25]

Journey and Provisions

'Do not acquire [*Mē ktēsēsthe*] gold or silver or copper coins
[*chalkon*] for your money belts [*zōnas*], nor a knapsack [*pēran*] for
the road, nor two shirts [*dyo chitōnas*], nor sandals [*hypodēmata*],
nor a staff [*rhabdon*]. For the worker is worthy of support'
(Matt. 10:9-10).[26] According to the parallel in Mark 6:8-9: 'he
instructed them that they take [*airōsin*] nothing for the road
except a staff [*rhabdon*] – no bread [*arton*], no knapsack [*pēran*],
no copper coin [*chalkon*] for the money belt [*zōnēn*] – but to wear
sandals [*hypodedemenous sandalia*], and not to wear two shirts
[*dyo chitōnas*].' Both texts teach that each traveler is to refrain
from taking money or a knapsack or a second shirt (tunic) on
the journey.[27] Nor is anyone to take a second pair of sandals,
as is clear from reading Matthew 10:10 in light of Mark 6:9.
Likewise the statement about others' 'support' – *trophē*, 'food,
nourishment' – in Matthew 10:10b (without parallel in Mark),
and the prohibition of 'bread' in Mark 6:8 (without parallel in
Matthew) complement each other.[28]

But what of the difference between Matthew 10:10 and
Mark 6:8 concerning the *rhabdos*? Three explanations may be

---

[24]*Dōrean*, the accusative singular of *dōrea*, 'gift,' is here used as an adverbial
accusative (*GGBB*, 200-201). It stands first in each clause, for emphasis.

[25]See comments on 'Gospel and Law,' pages 171-72. Gundry 1994: 185
thinks 'Freely you received' refers to Jesus' gift of authority to the disciples.
But they do not 'freely give' authority: instead, *with* authority they impart
the blessings of the kingdom described in Matthew 10:7-8.

[26]As translated by Hagner 1993: 267.

[27]So too the parallel in Luke 9:3. The *chitōn*, or 'tunic,' was worn next to
the skin beneath the *himation*, 'cloak, robe.' These are the terms in 5:40 (see
comments on page 372, n. 94). For descriptions of the *zōnē* ('belt, girdle'), see
Hendriksen 1973: 457.

[28]In Luke, Jesus' charges to the twelve (9:3-5) and to the seventy-two
(10:2-7 *et seq.*) complement each other in the same way: i.e. the former
prohibits taking bread on the journey (9:3) but says nothing of workers'
wages, whereas the latter mentions wages (10:7) but not bread.

suggested: 1. The 'staff permitted in Mark is the walking stick or shepherd's crook which became the symbol of office, while the rod prohibited by Matthew and Luke was the shepherd's club designed for protection.'[29] 2. Each disciple is to *take* the staff he already owns (Mark, the verb *airō*), not to *acquire* a new one (Matthew, the verb *ktaomai*).[30] 3. The number *dyo*, attached to *chitōnas* (Matt. 10:10a) applies by implication to the next two nouns as well – not only to *hypodēmata* (as noted above) but also to *rhabdon*: i. e., two staffs are no more needed than two shirts or two pairs of sandals.[31] Whatever solution one chooses, the main reason for this and the other instructions of Matthew 10:9-10a is clear from verse 10b: 'For [*gar*, joining this statement to the preceding commands] the worker [*ho ergatēs*] is worthy [*axios*] of support [*tēs trophēs autou*].' Jesus' servants are to depend on others to supply their needs. These provisions are not payments for the verbal and visible blessings of the kingdom: the twelve are not to take empty money bags with a view to filling them during the journey; in any case who could calculate the value of these blessings (cf. Acts 8:20)? Rather, the providers are expressing gratitude for the benefits described in Matthew 10:7-8: having themselves freely received, they now freely give. In doing so, they become instruments by whom the heavenly Father faithfully meets his children's needs: the *trophē* ('food') of 10:10, like the *artos* ('bread') of 6:11, represents all of one's material and physical necessities.[32] Those who seek

---

[29]E. Power, as cited in Lane 1974: 207, n. 31. Cf. Calvin (1994: 293): 'Matthew and Luke mean the heavy sticks, which would be a burden to carry, but Mark means the light stick that gives travellers support and comfort,' including a reference to Jacob's words in Genesis 32:10, 'for with only my staff I crossed this Jordan' (ESV).

[30]'The acquisition of a new staff to replace the old will also not be necessary and here is not even allowed' (Hendriksen 1973: 458).

[31]This view, unlike the second, need not rely heavily on the difference between *ktaomai*, 'acquire' (Matthew), and *airō*, 'take' (Mark) – an argument weakened by Luke 9:3, which says not to take (*airō*) a *rhabdos*. On the question of the staff(s), see further Blomberg 1992: 172; Carson 1984: 247; Lane 1974: 207-8, and sources they cite.

[32]So *trophē* was earlier translated 'support'; see comments on Matthew 6:11. Underlying 10:10b is Numbers 18:31, which contains the noun *śākār*, 'wages, reward'; the LXX's *misthos* has the same meanings. The parallel to 10:10b in Luke 10:7b uses this very language, 'worthy of his wage/reward [*tou misthou*

first God's kingdom – as the twelve are to do on this mission – surely need not fret about what they will eat and drink and wear (6:25-34). Furthermore, the lighter load will expedite their journey.[33]

Reception and Response

The word 'worthy,' *axios*, applied to the twelve in 10:10 now becomes the criterion for making judgments about the people they encounter (10:11, 13). Who the *axioi* are, we learn from 10:14a: 'whoever does not receive [*mē dexētai*] you or listen to [*mēde akousē*] your words....' Jesus here implies that some *will* receive the twelve; and that those who do, will receive them *as his disciples*: 'the one who receives [*dechomenos*] you, receives [*dechetai*] me,' he says in 10:41. Verse 14 also implies that some *will* listen to the message of the twelve – i.e., heed the gospel of the kingdom, obey its call to repentance, and become Jesus' disciples: so too the Hebrew verb *šāma'* (usually 'hear') can mean 'heed' or 'obey,' e.g., in Exodus 24:7 (LXX, *akouō*).

Such people's personal merits, however genuine, are not in view. Jesus counts them worthy for the same reason he commends others for their faith: they perceive the truth of Jesus' manifold message and respond aright. The center of attention is not believers' worth, or value, but the intrinsic worth of Messiah and his gospel.[34] How are the twelve to search for the *axioi* (Matt. 10:11), except by obeying the commands of verses 7-8? And where people show acceptance of that initial witness by offering hospitality, how are they to be judged truly *axioi* except by the twelve's bearing further such

---

autou],' as does the quotation of this text in 1 Timothy 5:18. Joining 10:10b to Luke 10:7b shows that Jesus understands 'wage' or 'reward' to be 'not opulence, but simply sustenance' (H. Preisker, *TDNT* 4: 698, n. 6). In 1 Corinthians 9:3-18 Paul affirms both his right to be recompensed for preaching the gospel, and his right to relinquish that right – his highest reward (*misthos*) being to offer the *euangelion* free of charge (9:18) as a witness to its free grace.

[33]For this reason the seventy-two will be told to 'greet no one on the road' (Luke 10:4).

[34]'A man is worthy...as and because he receives [the Gospel]; all thought of merit is excluded by the nature of the Gospel' (W. Foerster, *TDNT* 1: 379). On the place of faith, see comments on Matthew 9:22. Note how 10:14 accentuates the twelve's *verbal* witness (cf. v. 7) as distinct from their *visible* witness (cf. v. 8).

witness in the home? When you enter the home (*oikia*), says Jesus, 'greet it' (10:12) – with words such as those expressly stated in Jesus' charge to the seventy-two: 'Peace [*Eirēnē*] be to this house' (Luke 10:5), this being a way to announce the good news of the kingdom (10:9). Upon that household (*oikia*) whose members are confirmed to be genuinely *axioi*, Messiah's benediction shall remain: 'let your peace [*eirēnē*] come upon it' (Matt. 10:13b).[35]

Yet others' initial acceptance of the gospel will be exposed as spurious – perhaps when the twelve begin to clarify what Jesus demands of his followers. From such a household, that *shalom* is to be withdrawn (Matt. 10:13c). Speaking to the twelve about those who reject their witness at one stage or another, Jesus says: 'When you leave that house or town, shake off the dust from your feet' (10:14) – i.e., treat such a place as though it were inhabited by Gentiles, and deliver it to God's judgment.[36] Indeed, such Jews are *worse* than Gentiles: 'Truly I tell you, it will be more bearable for the land of Sodom and Gomorrah on the day of judgment than for that town' (10:15). The phrase 'day of judgment' (*hēmera kriseōs*) appears for the first time in Matthew: this is the 'day' (*hēmera*) of 7:22, on which the present speaker will execute the judgment he here envisages.[37] Those OT cities will not be punished so severely as these; for those wicked and immoral places never received such grace as this, and their contemporary counterparts have yet to receive it (10:5; 28:19). But what hope can there be for *Jews* who, already blessed beyond measure, reject this, the ultimate expression of their God's favor?[38] Such people do

[35]In light of 10:12b (and Luke 10:5b), the sense of 10:13b may be 'let your peace *remain* upon' the household (cf. Hagner 1993: 272).

[36]The par. to Matthew 10:14 in Luke 9:5 adds the phrase 'for testimony against them [*ep' autous*].' Jews returning to the holy land might shake the dust of unclean Gentile lands from their feet (and might also, on entering the holy temple, shake off the profane dust of the land of Israel): Keener 1999: 320; Hagner 1993: 273; and texts they cite. Such an act 'signifies a separation that results in deliverance to divine judgment' (Gundry 1994: 190). Paul and Barnabas so act in Acts 13:51.

[37]Cf. the comments on 7:21-23.

[38]Sodom and Gomorrah were places of gross iniquity (Gen. 13:13; 18:20-21; 19:4-5, cf. *sodomy*) which experienced God's fiercest judgment (Gen. 19:24-29),

not thwart his purpose: the coming of his kingdom is not contingent upon their acceptance, it is an announced fact (10:7). But, by trampling upon these Messianic graces (10:7-8), they rob themselves of the kingdom's blessings and imperil their own future.[39]

---

as will nations like them (Isa. 13:19; Jer. 49:18; 50:40; Zeph. 2:9; 2 Peter 2:6; Jude 7). Sinful Israel is also compared to them, and threatened with similar judgment (Deut. 29:23; 32:32; Isa. 1:9-10; 3:9; Jer. 23:14; Lam. 4:6; Ezek. 16:44-58; Amos 4:11; Rom. 9:29; Rev. 11:8). But Sodom's rejection of angels (Gen. 19) was not so serious as Israel's rejection of Messiah (cf. Keener 1999: 321). Matthew 10:15 anticipates Jesus' words in 11:20-24; see those comments.

[39]Cf. Luke 10:9 ('The kingdom of God has come near *to you*'), 11 ('*Nevertheless*...the kingdom of God has come near').

II.
'AND SHALL I FEAR TO OWN HIS CAUSE?'[1]
(10:16-42)

Jesus is still instructing the twelve (cf. 11:1). But, as he now shows, their journey is to be the first stage of a larger mission – one for Gentiles (Matt. 10:18), as well as Jews (10:17, 23), in other words, one for 'all the nations' (28:19-20). Matthew records these instructions so that missionaries of later generations may keep them, in fidelity to that same commission.

A. Jesus' Charge to Vulnerable Missionaries (10:16-25)

'Behold [*idou*], I am sending [*egō apostellō*] you as sheep into the midst of wolves. Therefore [*oun*] be shrewd [*phronimoi*] as serpents and innocent [*akeraioi*] as doves' (10:16). Again, *idou* prefaces an astonishing statement. What prospect is there for these sheep but to be ravaged and devoured? Could there be a more vivid picture of disciples' vulnerability? Yet Jesus, fully knowing these perils, deliberately *sends* his servants into their midst, even stressing that he himself does so (*egō*, 'I,' makes the subject emphatic). But with that same authority, he teaches them how to face such conditions: precisely because of the grave dangers (note the *oun*) they must be *both* shrewd (without being sinful) *and* innocent (without being naive).[2]

---

[1]Words from the hymn 'Am I a Soldier of the Cross?,' by Isaac Watts (1724).

[2]The adjective *phronimos* can mean 'sensible, thoughtful, prudent, wise,' also 'shrewd' (for all these see BAGD s.v.). Given the comparison with serpents (*opheis*), 'shrewd' is the best choice here. This term is used of the serpent in the LXX of Genesis 3:1 (for the Hebrew *'ārûm*: BDB, 'crafty, shrewd, sensible'). The disciples' shrewdness is not sinful, for (unlike Satan's) it is commanded by Jesus. Moreover, it is combined with innocence. The adjective *akeraios*, literally 'unmixed (*a* privative + *kerannymi*, 'to mix'), means 'pure, innocent' (BAGD s.v.). It occurs only twice more in the NT, in Paul: Romans 16:19 expresses his wish that readers be wise (*sophoi*) about the good and innocent (*aker.*) about the evil; Philippians 2:15, his hope that they be blameless (*amemptoi*) and innocent (*aker.*; NIV, 'pure') in a crooked and depraved generation.

The Warnings of Persecution
These 'wolves' (*lykoi*; Matthew 10:16) will 'pursue' and 'persecute' the disciples (10:23a; the verb *diōkō*, which bears both meanings), an experience of which Jesus spoke earlier (see *diōkō* in 5:10-12, 44). Three times the verb *paradidōmi* – 'hand over, betray' – describes oppressors' actions (10:17, 19, 21). 'They will hand you over to courts [*synedria*], and in their synagogues [*synagōgais*] they will scourge [*mastigōsousin*] you' (10:17b). Each local Jewish community had its own court (Hebrew *bet din*, 'house of justice'); it is these *synedria* which are mainly in view, though some of Jesus' followers – notably Stephen – would be tried before the 'high council,' the Sanhedrin in Jerusalem (Acts 6:12).[3] The language – '*their* synagogues' – foretells a rift between Jews and Christians: cf. the divisions described in Matthew 10:21, 34-36. The act denoted by the verb *mastigoō* ('whip, flog, scourge') would often apply the ruling of Deuteronomy 25:3.[4] Moreover, says Jesus, 'on account of me you will be brought before governors [*hēgemonas*] and kings [*basileis*] for a witness to them and to the Gentiles [*ethnesin*]' (Matt. 10:18). These are, in the first instance, governors from Rome and kings over the Jews. But some such trials would occur beyond Palestine – as a testimony to the *ethnē* ('nations'), the noun used in 24:14 and 28:19. And Paul for one would appear before the Roman *basileus*, the emperor.[5] These apostles

---

[3]*Synedrion* earlier occurred in Matthew 5:22; see those comments. 'In Palestinian communities there were local councils or sanhedrins distinct from the synagogal ruling body...but it is probable that in the Diaspora local Jewish courts were generally closely identified with the synagogal structure' (Hare 1967: 102). Cf. BAGD s.v. *synedrion*, 3. ('local council').

[4]For the penalty of 39 stripes, to avoid exceeding the limit of forty, see 2 Corinthians 11:24. For this punishment, according to the Mishnah, 'a strap of calf leather with interwoven thongs [was] brought against the condemned person's back 26 times and breast 13 times' (Keener 1999: 323, with further details). This is probably the punishment the unsaved Saul (Paul) sought for Christians (Acts 26:11). On the Jews' 'judicial floggings,' see also Hare 1967: 43-46.

[5]Cf. the use of *hēgemōn* ('governor, procurator') for Felix (e.g., Acts 23:24) and Festus (Acts 26:30) as well as Pilate (e.g., Matt. 27:2); and of *basileus* for Herod Agrippa I (Acts 12:1) and Herod Agrippa II (e.g., Acts 26:2) as well as their forebear Herod the Great (e.g., Matt. 2:1). For Caesar as *basileus*, see John 19:15; Acts 17:7; 1 Peter 2:13, 17; Revelation 17:9; for Paul's appeal

and other missionaries to Jews will be pursued, or persecuted, from one town to the next, (10:23a). Even members of their own families will betray them to death (10:21; with the noun *thanatos*, 'death,' and the verb *thanatoō*, 'put to death'). Indeed, because they bear Jesus' name they will be objects of universal hatred (10:22a; cf. 24:9).[6] Cf. Jesus' summary of such ordeals in 23:34, where deaths by crucifixion are expressly mentioned.

Beset with such persecution and perfidy, the twelve and other missionaries are to maintain their innocence. Like the dove's mission after the Flood, theirs is to remain one of *shalom* (10:12-13; see comments on 3:16). They are not to return evil for evil (5:39) or hatred for hatred (5:43) by persecuting their persecutors (5:44), or mounting a *jihad* of their own. At the same time, it is vital that they be prudent, wise and shrewd: 'Beware of men [*prosechete...apo tōn anthrōpōn*],' 'be on your guard' against them. Don't be 'gullible simpletons.'[7] Some of the people you trust – among your friends or even within your family – appear to be sheep, but they are really wolves in sheep's clothing (cf. 7:15, where the verb *prosechō* is again used). Nor must your wish to think well of everyone blind you to the reality of evil persons bent on your destruction: those are *wolves*, not sheep in wolves' clothing. Prudence may well counsel you to *flee* from one place to another (10:23a; the verb *pheugō*, whence 'fugitive'), rather than to tarry in the ideal but vain hope of making peace with an implacable enemy. Compare John Knox's flight from 'Bloody Mary.'[8]

---

to Caesar and his appearance in the imperial court, see Acts 25:11-12; 2 Timothy 4:16-17.

[6] In our day, to insist that Jesus is the only way to God (John 14:6) and that salvation lies in his name alone (Acts 4:12) assures a response of hatred from many: cf. Bruner 2004a: 478.

[7] This term, from France 1985: 182, is also used in comments on Matthew 5:42 (which see).

[8] On the variant readings at 10:23a, see *TC*, 23. As noted above(p. 328, n. 45), Clement of Alexandria invoked 10:23 when opposing zeal for martyrdom. Persecution sometimes prompted Paul's expulsion, flight or departure from a city, (Acts 13:50-51; 14:5-6, 19-20; 17:8-10, 13-14).

The Opportunities for Witness
The twelve and other missionaries are being sent out (*apostellō*,
10:16) for the singular purpose of testifying about the kingdom
of God and his Messiah (10:7-8). Those persecutions, far from
impeding their mission, will aid it. By both perseverance and
flight (10:23a) the gospel is spread.[9] What are those *synedria*
and *synagōgai* (10:17), if not forums for the same witness that
caused the Christians' arrest? Why does Jesus permit his
people to be dragged before *hēgemonai* and *basileis*, if not 'for
a witness [*eis martyrion*] to them [*autois*] and to the Gentiles'
(10:18)? As he says in the parallel statement of Luke 21:13: 'This
will be your opportunity [*apobēsetai hymin*] to bear witness [*eis
martyrion*]' (ESV). As is especially clear from Paul's conduct
in such circumstances, this is a witness *for*, not *against* the
audience: the apostle's words to Herod Agrippa II (Acts 26)
are not so much a legal defense as an evangelistic appeal.[10]

   'But whenever they hand you over,' says Jesus, 'do not be
anxious about how or what you should speak [*lalēsēte*]; for
[*gar*] it will be given [*dothēsetai*] to you in that hour what you
should speak [*lalēsēte*]. For [*gar*] you are not the ones speaking
[*hoi lalountes*]; rather [*alla*] it is the Spirit of your Father who
speaks [*to laloun*] through you' (Matt. 10:19-20). As in the
mission generally (10:7, 14), *verbal* witness is paramount:
forms of *laleō* ('speak') occur four times in these two verses. In
the hour of trial, let apostles and their successors rely upon the
Holy Trinity: upon Jesus, who has instructed them by word
and work (chs. 4–9); upon the Father, who is the subject of
dothēsetai (10:19, a 'divine passive'); and upon the Holy Spirit,
whom the Father sent to equip his Son (3:16) and who may
likewise be trusted to enlighten and empower his servants in
their distress (*thlipsis*, 24:9).

   This promise, however, is no excuse for laziness. Does it not
presuppose efforts to love God with all one's understanding
(*dianoia*, 22:37) and therefore to grasp what Messiah has said

---

[9]Cf. Acts 8:1-5; Gundry 1994: 194; Plummer 1911: 152.

[10]The *autois* of Matthew 10:18b is a dative of advantage ('for them,' 'for
their benefit'), not of disadvantage ('against them, 'to their detriment');
cf. *GGBB*, 142-44; Gundry 1994: 193. Yet, it would be to listeners' great
disadvantage to reject this witness.

and done? During those courtroom proceedings, is not the disciples' main task to bear witness to him; and the Spirit's, to bring those words and works to mind (cf. John 14:26; 15:26)? Using this promise to justify not studying for an examination, or not preparing a sermon, would convert a text into a pretext. Jesus is pledging help for an extraordinarily critical time – 'in that hour.' As I once heard Leon Morris say, the promise of Matthew 10:19-20 is 'an emergency ration, not a staple diet.'

When bearing this witness, disciples must be both *akeraioi* as doves and *phronimoi* as serpents (Matt. 10:16b). Let them indeed be innocent of charges leveled against them; let them not be guilty of wrongs deserving punishment.[11] Let their testimony be free of dishonesty, pretense and guile; and let them not return evil for evil by mounting false charges against their accusers. But let them also be shrewd, and constantly 'on their guard' in the presence of their adversaries (10:17a). Let them weigh their words carefully, in the awareness that acquittal will free them for further ministry (cf. Acts 14:5-7). Let them not be ashamed to identify themselves with Messiah's offenses; but let them beware giving needless offense. Let their defense, with the help of their divine advocate, be as persuasive as possible; and let them be prudent, lest by rash or foolish speech they jeopardize their and other disciples' witness. Paul again provides a model: in all these respects he sought to be *phronimos*.[12]

The Promise of Salvation

'But the one who endures to the end – this one will be saved. Whenever they persecute you in this city, flee to another; for truly I say to you, you will by no means have gone through all the cities of Israel before the Son of Man comes' (Matt. 10:22b-23). Verse 23 is said to be 'among the most difficult in the NT canon.'[13] I shall argue that the text refers primarily to Christ's return at the close of present history, and secondarily to an anticipatory coming before the close of his

---

[11]Cf. the counsel from one of the twelve: 1 Peter 2:15-17, 20; 3:13-17; 4:15-16.
[12]See Acts 22:1-21; 23:6-8; 24:10-21; 25:8-11; 26:2-29; 1 Corinthians 10:32-3; 2 Corinthians 4:2; 6:3-10; 1 Thessalonians 2:3-6.
[13]Carson 1984: 250.

own generation; and that, correspondingly, two stages of the mission to Israel are in view.

1. The Son of Man's glorious return and the church's mission

At the heart of this text is the assurance that Jesus, the Son of Man, will at some future date (known only to the Father) appear with power and great glory to establish his (and the Father's) final rule, to execute final judgment, and to accomplish his people's final salvation. *a.* We find here the very language used of that culminating event: 'before the Son of Man comes [*elthē ho huios tou anthrōpou*]' (Matt. 10:23b); 'the Son of Man coming [*ton huion tou anthrōpou erchomenon*] upon the clouds of heaven' (24:30); 'when the Son of Man comes [*elthē ho huios tou anthrōpou*] in his glory,' (25:31); 'the Son of Man...coming [*ton huion tou anthrōpou...erchomenon*] upon the clouds of heaven' (26:64).[14] *b.* The attendant promise is likewise the same: 'the one who endures [*ho hypomeinas*] to the end [*eis telos*] shall be saved [*houtos sōthēsetai*]' (10:22b), the very words Jesus uses in 24:13, just before declaring that the end (*telos* again) awaits the universal proclamation of the gospel (10:14).[15] In both instances, *sōthēsetai* (from *sōzō*) is a 'divine passive,' describing the joint work of God and Messiah. In the same regard, when the Son of Man comes (24:30), he will send forth his angels to gather his elect from the four winds (10:31), thus bringing his saving work (1:21) to its appointed goal. *c.* As noted earlier, the church's larger mission is in view in 10:16-23. Like the other nations (*ethnē*), Israel is to be evangelized until 'the close [*synteleia*] of the age' (28:18-20) i.e., until the Son of Man's *parousia* (24:3, 27). *d.* The reason for Jesus' special focus on Israel in 10:23, is that in his own generation the main opposition to the church's mission would come from Jews (cf. 23:33-36; Acts, *passim*). So he assures the apostles and their immediate successors (including Matthew's original readers)

---

[14]Both *elthē* (an aorist subjunctive) and *erchomenon* (a present participle) are forms of the verb *erchomai* ('come').

[15]In Matthew, the verb *hypomenō* ('endure') occurs only in 10:22 and 24:13; and the noun *telos* means 'end' only in 10:22 and 24:6, 13, 14 (elsewhere 'tax,' 17:25, and 'outcome,' 26:58). On the distinction between *telos* (10:22; 24:13) and *to telos* (24:6, 14), see comments in chapter 24.

that the mission to Israel will continue, not only through the present generation but until the very end. Indeed the Son of Man will return *before* that mission has run its course, and *before* missionaries have exhausted their cities of refuge.[16] Here, as in the witness to other nations, the gates of hell cannot halt the church's mighty advance (16:18), owing to the presence and authority of the church's Lord (28:18-20), a great consolation to Christian sheep going into the midst of Jewish wolves (10:16).[17]

2. The Son of Man's imminent judgment and the church's mission
While his own glorious return at history's *telos* occupies the center of this text, Jesus also foretells his 'coming' before the close of his own generation to execute judgment upon the Jewish nation: *a*. Despite all the evidence of the Father's goodness, the kingdom's dawning and Messiah's presence, the Jews of Jesus' generation (*genea*) have remained childish and demanding, wicked and adulterous, faithless and perverse.[18] They are about to commit the supreme sacrilege by putting God's own Messiah and Son to death (Matt. 16:13-21); and afterwards they will pursue and persecute his followers with equal vehemence (23:34). For these acts, and those of their forebears too, they will suffer divine retribution: 'Truly I say to you, all these things will come upon this generation [*epi tēn genean tautēn*]' (23:35-36). See also the parables of 21:33-41; 22:1-14; and the further reference to 'this generation' (*hē genea hautē*) in 24:34, harking back to 24:15-25. *b*. As shown in that

---

[16]Jesus also makes it clear that some such missionaries will lose their lives (Matt. 10:21, 28). As the verb *teleō* states that Jesus 'finished' or 'completed' a discourse (7:28; 11:1, etc.), so in 10:23b, *ou mē telesēte* (an aorist subjunctive of strong negation) means that missionaries will by no means 'finish' going through such cities, or 'complete' their mission to them, before the end.

[17]For arguments that 10:23 speaks of Jesus' second advent, see also Gundry 1994: 194-95; Keener 1999: 324-25. While Paul in Romans 9–11 (i) acknowledges Israel's rejection of the gospel, and God's consequent judgment (e.g., 10:16-21; 11:7-10), he also (ii) perceives that God has not finally rejected his people (11:1-24); (iii) advocates an ongoing mission to Jews (10:1-21; cf. 1:16-17); and (iv) foresees the salvation of 'all Israel' (i.e., elect Israel within ethnic Israel), at Christ's return (11:25-32, with 9:6). Cf. Ridderbos 1975: 354-61.

[18]See the use of *genea* in Matthew 11:16-19; 12:39, 45; 16:4; 17:17.

passage (24:15-21, with 23:38; 24:1-2), the most catastrophic effects of that judgment will be the destruction of Jerusalem and the temple at the climax of the Jewish war with Rome (i.e., in A.D. 66–70).[19] With these events the 'age of the kingdom comes into its own, precisely because so many of the structured foreshadowings of the OT, bound up with the cultus and nation, now disappear.... The Son of Man comes.'[20] *c.* Jesus has those same events in view (perhaps together with earlier ones) in 16:28: 'Truly I say to you that there are some standing here who will by no means taste death until they see the Son of Man coming [*erchomenon*] in his kingdom [*basileia*].'[21] Significantly, this coming is associated in the closest way with the Son of Man's final coming (16:27, (where the verb *erchomai* recurs). For the Son of Man's judgment of Israel in A.D. 70 foreshadows his judgment of Israel and the other nations at the End (19:28; 25:31); the earlier event is not a *different* judgment but an *anticipatory* one.[22] So it is with the *basileia* itself: the rule of God now dawning (12:28) will in time be fully established (6:10), just as the mustard seed and the full-grown plant are successive expressions of one reality (13:32). *d.* Jesus thus encourages these apostles and their immediate successors (notably Paul) to persevere in their mission to Israel (10:6), despite ongoing persecution. For divine judgment will surely fall on the church's Jewish oppressors; and when it does, there will still be cities of Israel where the missionaries can both bear witness and find refuge. Here too there is promise of rescue for those who endure 'to the end' or 'to the last' (*eis telos*; Matt. 10:22b).[23]

---

[19]On these matters, see the comments on 24:15-21.

[20]Carson 1984: 252.

[21]See comments on 16:28.

[22]So too in Matthew 24, by 'prophetic foreshortening' (Hendriksen 1973: 468) the judgment on Israel (vv. 15-21) is closely joined to the later coming of the Son of Man (vv. 29-31). In the language of 1 Thessalonians, God's present wrath against the Jews for their opposition to Messiah and his people 2:14-16 (wrath unleashed in the events of A.D. 70, in my judgment), manifests and foreshadows the final outpouring of 'the coming wrath' (1:10).

[23]The *eis telos* of 1 Thessalonians 2:16 also applies to A.D. 70, but has the sense 'at last' (ESV), or 'completely' (ESV mg.). For arguments that these

The Example of Jesus

'A disciple [*mathētēs*] is not above the teacher [*didaskalon*], nor a slave [*doulos*] above the master [*kyrion*]. It is enough that the disciple be like his teacher, and the slave like his master' (Matt. 10:24-25a). The missionaries' effective exercise of authority (10:1) depends on their recognizing that it belongs to Jesus, and that they are under his authority (23:8-12). Yet, the danger addressed in 10:24 is not so much that disciples will try to teach or rule Jesus (though cf. 16:22; 26:14-16), but that they will refuse a duty beset with dangers (10:17-23) and thus fail to emulate their master.[24]

For all that Jesus commissions the twelve and their successors to do, he himself does. He models the instructions of verses 5-15: he too conducts a manifold ministry to Israel, depends on others' hospitality and judges people's responses. The same holds true for verses 16-23. Jesus too is like a sheep thrust into the midst of wolves (10:16a): as he himself is also the shepherd, who is to protect him (cf. 26:31)? He is utterly innocent and guileless (1 Pet. 2:22); yet amid all the debates and trials of Passion Week, he is superlatively shrewd (Matt. 21–27 and parallels, *passim*; 10:16b). He too is handed over to death by a member of his own family (10:21; cf. 10:4, again the verb *paradidōmi*; and see 12:46-50); he too is delivered over (10:17a) to a Jewish court (26:57-68) and to appearances before a king (Luke 23:6-12) and a governor (Matt. 27:11-26). He too is flogged (10:17b; 27:26; John 19:1). He too, with the aid of the Spirit, bears a faithful witness in both Jewish and Gentile courts (Matt. 10:20; 27:64; 27:11; John 18:20-23, 36-37). And as the one who endures to the end, he too is saved (10:22 – by being raised from the dead; 28:6-7). So let disciples persevere as did their teacher and master; and in the hour of extreme peril (10:21, also 10:28), let them be heartened by their Lord's victory over death itself. In case others ascribe their exorcisms (10:8)

---

events fulfill Matthew 10:23, see Carson 1984: 252-53; France 1971: 140; Hagner 1993: 279-80, and sources they cite.

[24]Cf. Jesus' similar words in Luke 6:40; John 13:16; 15:20.

to Satanic power, let them be dismayed but not surprised. For if people are blind enough and blasphemous enough to attach the name *Beelzeboul* to the *Master* of the house (the *oikodespotēs*) when *he* casts out demons (Matt. 9:34; 12:24), will they not be yet more reckless and contemptuous when his household's *lowly members* (the *oikiakoi*) do the same (10:25b)?[25]

B. Jesus' Encouragement to Fearful Missionaries (10:26-33)

There are four instances of the verb *phobeomai* in this passage, all of them in commands. The first is a solemn and urgent prohibition: 'Therefore, do not fear [*Mē...phobēthēte*] them' (Matt. 10:26a), 'them' being the various enemies of verses 10:16-25.[26] The next two appear in 10:28: 'do not fear [*mē phobeisthe*],' i.e., stop fearing those who kill the body; and 'fear [*phobeisthe*],' i.e., start fearing, and keep fearing, the one who can destroy both soul and body.[27] The fourth comes in 10:31: 'therefore do not fear [*mē...phobeisthe*],' both reiterating the command of 10:28a and (with its *oun*, 'therefore') forming an inclusion with 10:26a.[28] There is also, as we shall see, a close connection between 10:26-31 and 10:32-33 (as indicated by the *oun* of 10:32a). Jesus fully understands the disciples' fears (was it not he who spoke the words of vv. 16-25?), and he now addresses them.

---

[25]Again, note John 15:20. The same kind of argument, again with *posō mallon* ('how much more'), occurs in Matthew 7:11; see those comments. For this charge against Jesus, see comments on 12:22-32 (where the name *Beelzeboul* occurs twice).

[26]The construction consists of the negative particle *mē* and the aorist passive subjunctive, second person plural. In the NT all such prohibitions (aorists in the second person) use the subjunctive mood rather than the imperative (*GGBB*, 723). The form in Matthew 10:26 is a 'constative' aorist: stress lies on the solemnity and urgency of the action (ibid., 720).

[27]The verb in these instances is a present middle (deponent) imperative, second person plural. The first, a prohibition (with *mē*), acknowledges, and seeks to dispel, existing fear (cf. *GGBB*, 724). The second seeks to implant another kind of fear: i.e., 'begin to fear God, and continue doing so' (the usage *GGBB*, 721, calls 'ingressive-progressive').

[28]Very common in the OT is the command 'do not fear.' For the singular (MT, *'al-tîrā'*; LXX, *mē phobou*), see, e.g., Genesis 15:1; for the plural (MT, *'alōtîrā'û*; LXX, *mē phobeisthe*), e.g., Genesis 43:23.

Two Kinds of Disclosure (10:26-27)
'For [*gar*] there is nothing hidden [*kekalymmenon*] which will not be revealed [*apokalyphthēsetai*], nor secret [*krypton*] which will not be made known [*gnōsthēsetai*]' (Matt. 10:26b). This statement, with its opening *gar*, provides the basis for 10:26a. That command's link with 10:16-25 ('do not fear *them*') shows that the matters presently hidden from view are the sins of the church's enemies. But not one of those evils has escaped the notice of God and his Messiah, and they will surely bring them all to light: both future indicatives (from *apokalyptō* and *gnōrizō* respectively) are 'divine passives.' Such disclosures as occur in the events of A.D. 70 anticipate the day when the Son of Man will expose and judge the secrets of all mankind.[29] On that final day, the twelve apostles (10:2) will join him in judging their fellow Israelites (19:28), including those guilty of persecuting Jesus and his servants. (Of course, Judas will have been replaced by another apostle; he himself will be judged.)

The motif of Matthew 10:26 continues in verse 27, but attention shifts from the oppressors' wickedness to the missionaries' words (as in 10:7, 14, Jesus stresses the verbal witness as distinct from the visible). 'What I say [*legō*] to you in the dark, say [*eipate*] in the light; and what you hear whispered [*eis to ous*, lit. 'into the ear'], proclaim [*kēryxate*] on the housetops.' Jesus speaks to them in the darkness (*skotia*), and whispers truth in their ears – i.e., he teaches them privately. The present discourse is a case in point: whereas in chapters 5–7 Jesus taught the disciples in the hearing of the crowd, here he addresses disciples exclusively.[30] But these are not esoteric teachings reserved for a secret society. On the contrary, the very words Jesus says in the dark are to be brought into the light (*phōs*; 10:27a); truth once whispered, missionaries are to preach on the housetops for the widest possible hearing.[31]

---

[29]Cf. comments on Matthew 10:23. On disclosures at the Last Judgment, see also Romans 2:16; 1 Corinthians 3:13; 4:5; Chamblin 1993: 247-49.

[30]Cf. Matthew 13:10-17; also the use of the phrase *kat' idian* ('privately') in 17:19; 20:17; 24:3; Mark 4:34; Luke 10:23.

[31]*Eipate* (10:27a) is an aorist imperative of *legō*, the verb used earlier in the verse. The flat 'housetops' or 'rooftops' (*dōmata*; 10:27b) provided natural platforms; proclamations made here were more easily heard than those delivered in the streets below (France 1985: 186; Keener 1999: 326).

The whole of Jesus' teaching is to be made public (cf. 28:19, 'all things, as many as I have commanded you'), as the writing of the Gospel according to Matthew testifies. So the preaching will include warnings of the judgment that is sure to fall on Messiah's enemies. But judging from the use of the verb *kēryssō* elsewhere in Matthew, the cardinal theme of that proclamation will be the gospel of the kingdom, by heeding which the listeners can escape the wrath to come.[32] The hope is that many of the church's persecutors will be horrified by disclosures of their deeds; will repent of their wickedness; and will – like Paul – receive grace from the very One they sought to destroy (cf. 1 Pet. 2:12). What an antidote to fear, to witness the redemption of a former persecutor. One imagines that Paul's conversion brought incalculable encouragement to hundreds if not thousands of Christians.

Two Kinds of Death (10:28)

'And do not fear those who kill [*apoktennontōn*] the body [*sōma*] but are not able to kill [*apokteinai*] the soul [*psychēn*]. Instead, fear the one who is able to destroy [*apolesai*] both soul [*psychēn*] and body [*sōma*] in Gehenna [*geennē*].' In Matthew 10:21 Jesus warned disciples that members of their own families would hand them over to death. Now he assures them that such an experience, however terrifying and excruciating, has only limited effects. Those who carry out this sentence indeed kill the body, but they are quite incapable of killing the soul: note the repetition of *apokteinō*.[33] The *sōma* without the *psychē* is dead; the *psychē* without the *sōma* lives on.

Even the effects of those executions on the body are limited. For at the end God will raise the *sōma* of every

---

[32]Besides 10:27, there are eight instances of *kēryssō* in Matthew. Three expressly refer to the *euangelion* of the kingdom (4:23; 9:35; 24:14); the other five imply that the same message stands at the heart of the preaching (3:1; 4:17; 10:7; 11:1; 26:13).

[33]This verb occurs here for the first time in Matthew, first as a present participle (behind which is the variant spelling *apoktennō*), then as an aorist infinitive.

[34]For the resurrection of both just and unjust, see Daniel 12:2-3; John 5:28-29; Acts 24:15; Revelation 20:11-15. For this distinction between

human being from the dead, and rejoin it to its disembodied *psychē*.[34] Some of the persons thus reintegrated, he will usher into eternal life. By the same token the sovereign God alone has authority and power to destroy (the verb *apollymi*) **both** soul **and** body – i.e., the whole person – in Gehenna (10:28).[35] Destruction here means not extinction or annihilation, but loss of true humanity and eternal separation from the divine presence.[36] It is this God, therefore, whom missionaries must fear: in 10:28b the verb *phobeomai* signals both adoring reverence for the 'Father in heaven' (6:9) and healthy dread of the penalty he will inflict on his foes – whether the church's enemies or apostate disciples (10:33; 13:21). Such fear is thus a spur for disciples to worship God, to evangelize their persecutors and to stay faithful to Christ when on trial.

Two Kinds of Creatures (10:29-31)

Is not a young sparrow – a *strouthion* – almost worthless? If needed for food, cannot two of them be purchased for a mere *assarion*, a coin worth one-sixteenth of a *dēnarion* (Matt. 10:29a)?[37] 'Yet not one of them falls to the ground without the knowledge and consent of your Father [*aneu*

---

sōma and *psychē*, and their separation from each other between death and resurrection (in contrast to belief in their indissoluble unity), see page 447, n. 38 (where other senses of *psychē* are also considered); Blomberg 1992: 177-78; Keener 1999: 326-27 ('Contrary to most commentators, most extant early Jewish writers also distinguished body and soul,' n. 40); Cooper 1989 *passim*; Chamblin 1993: 42-46, 54-55; *WSC* no. 37.

[35]God is not named in Matthew 10:28b; but it is clearly his, not Satan's, powers that are meant (cf. James 4:12; Blomberg 1992: 178; Marshall 1978a: 513-14). On Gehenna as the place of final punishment, see comments on 5:22 and on 5:29-30 (where *sōma* twice occurs). This punishment is called 'the second death' in Revelation 2:11; 20:6, 14; 21:8.

[36]Note the use of *aiōnios* ('eternal') in Matthew 18:8; 19:16, 29; 25:41, 46. Comparing 25:34 and 41 shows that hell is not humanity's proper home; on hell's dehumanizing effects, see Lewis 1943: chapter 8; and 1946. On hell as separation from God, see, e.g., 7:23; 25:10-12, 30, 41, 46.

[37]*Strouthion* is a diminutive of *strouthos*, 'sparrow' (or other small birds: LSJ). 'The sparrow was used for food by very poor people' (Carson 1984: 255). On the copper *assarion* (or *as*) and the silver *dēnarion* (a workman's average daily wage), see the entries in BAGD.

tou patros hymōn]' (10:29b).[38] Not *its* Father, says Jesus, but *yours*. The sparrow is indeed governed by God's providence, as this saying shows; but *you*, as creatures made in God's image, are able to *understand* his providence as a sparrow cannot. Moreover, says Jesus, he is your *Father* – not just because you are human but because you belong to his Son.[39] Since he is *your* Father, will not his care for *you* surpass his care for *them*? If not a single one of them escapes his notice, how could you? If he is fully aware of all of them, and each of them, is it any surprise that 'even the hairs of your head are all numbered' (10:30)? Is not this thorough knowledge also a sign of the Father's protecting care?[40] As the one who governs the sparrow's fall, is it not also 'your heavenly Father' who sustains its life (6:26a, with the name *ho patēr hymōn ho ouranios*)? Can he not therefore be trusted to provide food on your journey (10:10)?[41] Are you not worth far more to him than many sparrows (10:31b) – indeed, more than all the birds of the air (6:26b)?[42]

When on trial, your anxiety to add even hours to your life (6:27) is sure to be acute. In that case, remember who your true Sovereign and Judge is. Trust him who will not let your life 'fall to the ground' until your work is done (cf. Acts 23:11); and when sentenced to death (10:28a), be assured that your heavenly Father will raise you to life eternal.[43] 'Therefore [*oun*: for all these reasons] do not fear [*mē... phobeisthe*],' says Jesus (Matt. 10:31a). Fear God (10:28) – a fear of which you need not be afraid – and you need not fear your adversaries (10:26a).

---

[38]This translation of *aneu* ('without') is based on BAGD s.v., 1. Cf. Psalm 50:11.

[39]See especially Matthew 6:9. *Patēr* is 'a term of intimacy and endearment' (Hagner 1993: 286).

[40]A person whose life is spared can be said to lose 'not one hair': see 1 Samuel 14:45; 2 Samuel 14:11; 1 Kings 1:52; Acts 27:34; and below on Luke 21:18.

[41]The noun *trophē* ('food', Matt. 10:10) is a cognate of the verb *trephō* ('feed', 6:26).

[42]Each text contains the verb *diapherō* and a genitive of comparison (*GGBB*, 110-11).

[43]'But not one hair of your head will perish [*ou mē apolētai*],' says Luke 21:18 (which lacks a parallel in Matthew). Jesus promises his disciples,

Two Kinds of Testimony (10:32-33)
'Therefore [*oun*] whoever confesses [*homologēsei en*] me before men, him too will I confess [*homologēsō...en*] before my Father who is in heaven.[44] But whoever denies [*arnēsētai*] me before men, him too will I deny [*arnēsomai*] before my Father who is in heaven.' (Cf. Luke 12:8-9, 'before the angels of God.') The opening *oun* links these verses to Matthew 10:26-31 and so to 10:16-25 (and vv. 5-15 as well). These words embrace the entirety of the missionaries' public witness: preaching the kingdom (10:7) calls for acknowledging and confessing the truth about Jesus the Messiah; one denies this truth by refusing to declare it or by supplanting it with falsehood. But while including proclamations from the housetops (10:27), Jesus especially has in view the conduct of disciples when on trial before men who have power to afflict, imprison and kill them (10:16-25, 28).[45]

Confessing Jesus at such a time means remaining true to his commission, and to the totality of his verbal and visible witness (Matt. 10:7-8) – including its implicit claims about Jesus himself. So scandalous will be these claims, especially when related to certain of Jesus' words and works that thus acknowledging him will often entail grave risk, even threat to life.[46] A strong impetus to speaking truth amid those perils is the sure promise (10:32b) that Jesus will make a confession of

---

not that they will all escape death at the hands of their persecutors (on the contrary: see 21:16 and its parallel in Matt. 10:21), but that they will be spared final destruction (note the verb *apollymi*, the same used in Matt 10:28b). The resurrected body will include a full head of hair!

[44]The *en* after the verb reflects Aramaic usage and is not to be translated (BDF, par. 220).

[45]The repeated 'whoever' (*hostis*) suggests that Jesus also refers, though indirectly, to those who hear the disciples' witness (whether on the streets, in the homes or in the courts). Those who acknowledge Jesus will be saved (Rom. 10:9-10, with two instances of *homologeō*); those who reject him stand under judgment (Acts 3:13-14, with two instances of *arneomai*).

[46]See Matthew 10:16-23; John 9:22 (with *homologeō*: confessing Jesus to be the Christ means expulsion from the synagogue; cf. 12:42; Matthew 10:17); Acts 7:58 (Stephen, having witnessed to Jesus [7:52] is executed by the Sanhedrin); and 24:14 (with *homologeō*: Paul, threatened with death [25:11] and testifying before Felix and Agrippa, acknowledges his Christian faith).

his own in the highest court of all; that there, before his Father, the supreme Judge, he will speak on his faithful servants' behalf; and that he will thus acknowledge them, not only at the Last Judgment but (as the story of Stephen shows) in the very hour of their earthly trial.[47] Thus the Father's beleaguered children are aided by both the Son of the Father and the Spirit of the Father (10:20).

One can deny Jesus in such a crisis (as at other times) by refusing to acknowledge association with him or by expressly denying the association (as in Matt. 26:69-75); by withholding the truth about him, or by declaring falsehood about him (how often have persecutions given rise to heresies?).[48] His faithful witnesses, on the other hand, will deny room to denial: they will refuse to refuse Jesus, whatever the consequences.[49] Yet those who deny Jesus are threatened with far worse – Jesus' denial of them before the Father at the final judgment.[50] It is clear that persons whom he thus judges have committed final apostasy. What then of Peter's denials of Jesus (26:69-75, which contains the two other instances of *arneomai* in Matthew)?

At this point, the 'trustworthy saying' of 2 Timothy 2:11-13 is illuminating. It concludes, 'If we deny [*arnēsometha*] him [this object is implicit], he also will deny [*arnēsetai*] us; if we are faithless, he remains faithful, for he is not able to deny [*arnēsasthai*] himself' (2:12b-13). Verse 12b, like Matthew 10:33,

---

[47]For Jesus' acknowledgment of his people at the End, see Matthew 25:31, 34 ('blessed by my Father,' because the Son claims them for his own); Revelation 3:5 (with *homologeō*). In Acts 7:56, the Son of Man *stands* to testify to God on Stephen's behalf (cf. Dan. 7:13-14). Paul exhorts Timothy to persevere (1 Tim. 6:11-16) by recalling his 'good confession' in public (6:12, *homologeō* and the noun *homologia*), and also Jesus' 'good confession' before Pilate (6:13, *homologia*).

[48]One feature of Israel's coming tribulation (Matt. 24:13-28) is the rise of false christs and false prophets (24:24). For links between persecutions and heresies, see Frend 1967. For instances of *arneomai* in references to false teachings about Jesus, see 2 Peter 2:1; 1 John 2:22-23; Jude 4.

[49]See the instances of *arneomai* in Revelation 2:13; 3:8; and John 1:20 (John *confesses*, and does *not* deny, but *confesses*, 'I am *not* the Messiah'); and of *epaischynomai* ('be ashamed') in Romans 1:16; 2 Timothy 1:8, 12.

[50]For Jesus' rejection of people at the End, see Matthew 7:21-23; 25:12, 41; Mark 8:38; Luke 9:26.

alerts disciples – including Peter – to the real danger of apostasy. But verse 13 offers hope to him and to us. Because Jesus is faithful (*pistos*) to pray for Peter, he is protected from final apostasy (Luke 22:31-32; John 21:15-19). When Peter proved unfaithful to Jesus (*apistos*) by contradicting the confession of Matthew 16:16, Jesus remained faithful to himself, to his promise and to his apostle. Yet, Peter's experience stands as a sobering reminder to all of us – especially to those responsible for nurturing Christ's flock (John 21:15-17) – that denials short of apostasy are still serious. Does not Jesus say that, on the Day of Judgment, we will have to account for every careless word (Matt. 12:36)?

C. Jesus' Warning to Double-Minded Missionaries (10:34-39)

Jesus here confronts his disciples with what are probably the two most serious obstacles to their becoming the kind of missionaries he requires – or, in the language of 5:8, to their becoming pure in heart. The first is being more deeply committed to one's family than to Jesus (10:34-37). The second and graver danger is being more intent upon safeguarding one's life at all costs, than upon obeying Jesus at whatever cost (10:38-39).[51] A person of either mentality, says Jesus, 'is not worthy [*axios*] of me' (10:37b, 38b).

The Sword of Division (10:34-37)

'Do not suppose that I came [*Mē nomisēte hoti ēlthon*] to bring peace to the earth. I came not [*ouk ēlthon*] to bring peace, but [*alla*] a sword' (Matt. 10:34). This verse's language and structure are very close to 5:17; all the Greek words noted here, also occur there and in the same order.[52] This text, like that one, reflects Jesus' awareness of responses to his work. As some of his contemporaries did indeed believe he had

---

[51]Similarly, in 6:25-34 Jesus tells disciples not to be consumed with anxieties about their life (*psychē*) and body (*sōma*, v. 25), but rather to seek first God's kingdom, v. 33.

[52]Each verse also features a repeated aorist infinitive: here it is *balein* (from *ballō*, 'throw'; of peace, 'bring'); there it is *katalysai* (from *katalyō*, 'destroy'; of the law, 'abolish').

come to abolish the Scriptures (see p. 340), so some supposed he had come to establish peace. They had good reason for thinking so. Did not Jesus bless the peacemakers (5:9)? Has he not just told his missionaries to bestow peace (*eirēnē*) upon worthy households (10:13)? Is he not the Son of David (1:1), the promised Prince of Peace (Isa. 9:6)?[53] Yes indeed, to all those questions.

But Messiah, like David, establishes peace by conquest: in order to *end* war, he *declares* war. The fiercest assaults ever on Satanic strongholds begin with Jesus' arrival (Matt. 12:28).[54] With the same force he confronts those spheres where human beings exercise and recognize authority. His purpose in each case is to test whether the authority in question has exceeded its assigned limits and claimed for itself an ultimacy which is rightfully God's alone. Jesus elsewhere speaks of those who wield, and who submit to, authorities *political* and *religious*.[55] Here he focuses on the *domestic* sphere.

'For [*gar*] I came [*ēlthon*] to turn [*dichasai*] a man "against his father, and a daughter against her mother, and a daughter-in-law against her mother-in-law." And "a man's enemies will be persons of his own household"' (10:35-36). That third conflict was more likely than one between father-in-law and son-in-law, since young couples usually lived with the husband's family.[56]

Jesus quotes from Micah 7:6.[57] *1. The text in Micah's day.* In Micah 7:1-6, the prophet laments the sins of Judah. Godly and

---

[53]Cf. Luke 1:79; 2:14. *Eirēnē* occurs four times in Matthew, only in 10:13, 34. One might think the words of 10:34 explain the scarcity. But in Mark, which lacks this saying, the noun occurs only once; and in Luke, which contains the saying, the noun occurs fourteen times.

[54]Likewise, in Luke 2:13-14, a multitude of the heavenly *army* announces peace on earth.

[55]For Jesus' teaching about exerting and acknowledging power in the political sphere, see, e.g., Matthew 20:25-26 (Gentile rulers and their subjects); 22:15-22 (claims of God and Caesar). For the same in the religious sphere, see, e.g., 15:1-9 (the word of God vs. human traditions); 23:1-39 (warnings to scribes and Pharisees, and their adherents).

[56]Davies and Allison 1991: 219; Keener 1999: 330.

[57]The quotation in Matthew 10:35-36 uses the very four expressions of Micah 7:6. By contrast, in the parallel of Luke 12:53, the fourth of these is

upright persons are not to be found; wickedness pervades the whole society; relationships within the family are marked by mistrust, hostilities and flagrant violations of the fifth commandment. Micah, knowing that God's judgment is about to fall (7:4) places his hope in God's salvation (7:7). According to some later Jewish texts, the social disintegration described by Micah would recur during the great tribulation presaging the dawn of God's kingdom.[58] *2. The text in Jesus' day.* As Jesus uses 7:6, the depicted strife does not presage the kingdom; rather, the dawn of the kingdom and the advent of Messiah *arouse* the strife. Jesus knows that when God's rule confronts the family's rules, conflicts are in many cases inevitable – namely, where the authority that *is in fact* supreme challenges domestic authority that *thinks itself to be* supreme (cf. Matt. 10:21). But Jesus not only predicts divisions; he precipitates them. He wields his sword (*machaira*; 10:34b) in order to divide one member of the family from another.[59]

Yet here, no less than in 15:1-9 and 19:19, Jesus shows himself to be for the family. Whereas the sins deplored in Micah 7:6 threatened to destroy the family, Jesus acts to save the family from itself. For parents and children who are more devoted to each other than to God and Messiah (10:38) – i.e., who honor the fifth commandment above the first – are seriously endangering themselves. So, the sooner these misplaced loyalties are brought to light and directly challenged, the greater the hope for the parties concerned. So deep-seated are these loyalties, and so powerful are their attendant demands, that drastic action is required. Yet like a

---

lacking, and each of the first three is joined to a matching statement absent from Micah (e.g., *'father against son, and* son against father'). While the quotation in Matthew well conveys the sense of the original, its wording differs in some respects from the MT and the LXX of Micah 7:6 (e.g., it contains no verbs; uses 'man' instead of 'son' in Matthew 10:35a; and uses 'household members' instead of 'males' in 10:36).

[58] Among sources cited by Davies and Allison 1991: 21-20, and Hagner 1993: 292, are Jubilees 23:16, 19-20; 1 Enoch 56:7; 100:2; 4 Ezra 5:9; 6:24; Mark 13:12. See also 2 Timothy 3:1-2. On corruption in Micah's day, see also pages 221-23 above.

[59] The *gar* (10:35a) joins verse 34b to verses 35-36. The language of 10:34b, *balein...machairan* (literally, 'to hurl a sword'), indicates aggressive action.

surgeon using a scalpel to remove a cancer, Jesus severs ties for people's good. He says in effect: 'I've come to...cut through these cozy domestic arrangements and free you for God.'[60] Better to endure the pain of these divisions, and learn their intended lesson, than to be judged as in Matthew 24:51 (where a person is 'cut in pieces').

Jesus now explains why the sword of division must be used. 'The one who loves [philōn] father or mother more than me is not worthy of me; and the one who loves [philōn] son or daughter more than me is not worthy of me' (Matt. 10:37). The verb phileō, like agapaō, includes the affections but comes to fullest expression in actions – in this instance, deeds of friendship and loyalty towards God and the members of one's family.[61] According to the parallel in Luke 14:26, one must hate (the verb miseō) his father and mother and children (and others) in order to be Jesus' disciple. This demand appears to be greater than the other, but it is in fact the same demand stated in starker terms: the disciple is to love Jesus above all others; to whatever extent another person seeks to usurp the place reserved for him, that person must be denied. Who but God himself has the right to claim such devotion? Who, indeed?[62] Nevertheless, some persons thus denied

---

The aorist infinitive dichasia (10:35a) from dichazō ('to cleave asunder, divide in two, separate'), here denotes purpose (GGBB, 590-92). On Jesus' lips in Matthew, 'I came [ēlthon]' and 'the Son of Man came [ēlthen]' (two aorist indicatives of erchomai) concern matters central to his mission: besides 10:34-35 and 5:17, see 9:13; 11:19; 20:28.

[60]Matthew 10:35, as rendered by Peterson 1993.

[61]LSJ s.v. phileō ('love,' 'treat affectionately or kindly, welcome, befriend'); Hagner 1993: 292, on Matthew 10:37 ('loyalty and commitment').

[62]Cf. comments on Matthew 22:37-38. For other instances of phileō to denote love for Jesus, see John 16:27; 21:15-17; 1 Corinthians 16:22. For the Hebrew verb śānē' ('hate') in the sense 'love less,' see Genesis 29:31; Deuteronomy 21:15; Malachi 1:2-3; and Jewish sources cited in Keener 1999: 330; Manson 1957: 131. 'Many viewed honoring one's parents...as the highest social obligation...; even if some spoke of honoring one's teacher more..., no teacher would speak of "hating" one's parents by comparison. God alone was worthy of that role...' (Keener 1999: 330). Green 1997: 565 notes that 'hate' in Luke 14:26 primarily denotes 'a disavowal of primary allegiance to one's kin.' Yahweh demands exclusive worship: Exodus 20:3-6; 1 Kings 14:7-11 (and Davis 2002: 162-64).

will become yet more virulent in their opposition to Jesus' claims. What of a son, for example, whose deepest love was once reserved for his father (Matt. 10:37), but is now given to Jesus instead? If the father then seeks to have his son put to death (10:21), the son will surely be appalled but let him not be altogether surprised.[63] But what if both father and son acknowledge Jesus' supremacy, and both pledge to him their highest loyalty? Then they shall find themselves joined to one another in a new family (12:46-50); and let them not be surprised to discover that their love for each other is deeper than before. One can imagine such a father saying, 'I would not love you, son, so much, loved I not Jesus more.' Was it not precisely by preaching the Rule of God (3:2) that John the Baptist would 'turn the hearts of the fathers to the children' (Luke 1:17)?[64]

The Cross of Surrender (10:38-39)
'And whoever does not take his cross and follow me, is not worthy of me. Whoever finds his life will lose it, and whoever loses his life for my sake will find it.' 'Follow' (*akoloutheō*) has been used of discipleship several times already; but no prior text states so strongly the cost of following Jesus.[65] Even the preceding prophecies of persecution and execution are not quite so jarring. For in those cases, missionaries fall prey to the willfulness of wicked men; but here the disciple is asked to take up an instrument of execution *voluntarily* – i.e., in some sense *to will his own death.* The twelve, Jesus' original listeners, would, of course, be acquainted with crucifixion; but at this stage they would not know what lay ahead for Jesus personally (he first expressly speaks of his crucifixion

---

[63]One can easily imagine a father's violent reaction to news of the conversation in Matthew 8:21-22 and of his son's obedience to that summons of Jesus. See comments on that passage.

[64]Cf. Matthew 19:29 and its par. in Mark 10:29-30; also C. S. Lewis on 'first and second things' (above, p. 450, n. 47). On the competition between *storgē* (family affection) and *agapē* (love in the Christian sense), see Lewis 1960: chapters 3 and 6.

[65]See the instances of *akoloutheō* in Matthew 4:20, 22; 8:19, 22, 23; 9:9. The noun 'cross' (*stauros*) occurs here for the first time in Matthew.

in Matthew 20:19; but see already 16:21, 24). Yet, Matthew's readers would know that Jesus had been crucified; and that he had foretold such a death for some of his followers (23:34). Indeed, a very member of the twelve would be 'like his teacher' (10:24) in the manner of his death. One day, Simon Peter would lose his 'life' – his *psychē*, not just his 'soul' but his 'earthly life' – in the very way Jesus had done (20:28, where *psychē* recurs).[66]

But Jesus has more than martyrdom in view. Returning to the subject of 10:38-39 at Caesarea Philippi (16:24-25), he exhorts a would-be follower to deny himself and to take up his cross *daily* (*kath' hēmeran*; Luke 9:23, par. to Matt. 16:24). Doing so is yet more demanding than going to a martyr's death; the one thing harder than dying for Jesus is living for him in the way here prescribed – namely, willingly denying *oneself* (as distinct from denying oneself *things*), and surrendering oneself utterly to Christ, at whatever cost, every single day. It may be agonizing to die to a relationship that obstructs one's service to Christ; but genuinely and voluntarily dying to oneself – in Pauline terms, crucifying the flesh (Gal. 5:24) – will almost certainly be excruciating. For is not each of us by nature a fallen, egocentric human being bent upon self-rule and self-determination? In the language of Luke 14:26, is not 'hating' one's own life (*psychē*) much harder than 'hating' the members of one's family? Is not the relinquishing of a proud ego to the Lordship of Jesus a stupendous miracle of sovereign grace?

The disciple who thus 'loses his life' finds it for the first time (Matt. 10:39b). His is a *living* sacrifice in the service of God (Rom. 12:1); his life is one of perpetual crucifixion for the sake of other people (2 Cor. 4:10-11). Such a person can now become – 'like his master' (Matt. 10:25) – a humble servant (20:26-28). What room is there for pride and selfish ambition (20:20-25) in someone bearing a cross to a place of execution? What does he have to lose by serving others, and being real with them?[67] By the same token, if a disciple has already willed

---

[66]*Psychē* can mean 'soul' (see comments on 10:28) or one's 'earthly life' (see p. 447, n. 38). Peter's crucifixion under Nero, ca. A.D. 67, is recorded in *HE* 2.25.5.

to *lose* his life for Jesus' sake (10:39b), how can an enemy *take* that life from him (10:16-33)? On the other hand, what does a person intent on 'finding his life' (10:39a) have to gain? Will not his self-absorption and self-protectiveness be the very means of his destruction?

D. Jesus' Promise to Recipients of the Missionaries' Witness (10:40-42)

Here at the close, as throughout the discourse, Jesus addresses the missionaries ('you,' 10:40), whom he identifies in four ways (10:41-42). But he focuses especially on persons who respond favorably to his emissaries: there are six instances of the verb *dechomai* ('receive'), four in 10:40 and two in 10:41. Jesus offers these recipients 'precious and very great promises' (2 Pet. 1:4). Let missionaries too be encouraged by these words: amid all the hostility that awaits them, let them expect such responses as these.

The Promise of God (10:40)

'The one who receives you, receives me; and the one who receives me, receives the one who sent me' (10:40). Jesus endows his emissaries – the twelve and their successors – with his own authority (10:1-8; 28:18-20). Their being received as though they were Jesus depends on their faithfully exercising that very authority. Not that the missionary is confused with Jesus, but that he effectively represents the one who has sent him.[68] Proof that the witness has been effective, comes when a person *receives* Jesus – i.e., embraces the gospel of the kingdom and becomes Messiah's disciple (cf. comments on 10:14, which contains the one prior instance of *dechomai* in the discourse). Moreover, to receive Jesus is to receive God: for Jesus himself is 'God with us' (1:23); and he perfectly reveals the character of the Father who sent him on his mission (10:40b).[69] What could

---

[67]On the cost of discipleship, see also page 310, n. 24; and comments on 16:24-26. On the outworking of 10:38-39 in Paul's life, see Chamblin 1993: chapter 8, 'Power in Weakness.'

[68]Cf. Galatians 4:14, 'You received me as [*hōs*] an angel [or messenger: *angelos*] of God, as [*hōs*] Christ Jesus'; and the rabbinic saying, 'A man's emissary or agent is like the man himself' (quoted in Hagner 1993: 295).

ever compare to receiving the Father and the Son? Will not the recipients' final and highest reward (10:41-42) be unbroken fellowship with both the Father and the Son, together with the Holy Spirit (28:19)? Cf. comments on 6:19-21.

The Promise of Reward (10:41-42)

'The one who receives a prophet because he is a prophet [*eis onoma prophētou*] will receive the reward of a prophet [*misthon prophētou*]; and the one who receives a righteous person because he is a righteous person [*eis onoma dikaiou*] will receive the reward of a righteous person [*misthon dikaiou*]. And whoever gives one of these little ones [*tōn mikrōn toutōn*] merely a cup of cold water because he is a disciple [*eis onoma mathētou*], truly I say to you, he will by no means lose his reward.' All four terms – 'prophet' (*prophētēs*), 'righteous person' (*dikaios*), these 'little ones' (*mikroi*) and 'disciple' (*mathētēs*) – apply potentially both to the twelve and to all their successors. Are not all of Jesus' missionaries to be 'prophets,' i.e., people who faithfully impart all his teachings (Matt. 28:20a), beginning with the gospel of the kingdom?[70] Are they not all to be 'righteous,' and to do those 'good works' expected of Messiah's followers (see comments on 5:16, 20)? Are they not all his 'little ones,' his vulnerable little flock (10:16; Luke 12:32), the poor and needy children of the heavenly Father (Matt. 5:3-10; 11:25-27)? Is not every true 'disciple' meant, in some way or another, to bear witness to Jesus (5:13-16)? Yes indeed, to all those questions. Some missionaries, of course, are more gifted and more faithful than others: cf. the parables of 25:1-30, as well as Judas' distinction from the other eleven apostles in 10:4. Who would presume to compare his prophetic powers to those of

---

[69]See also Matthew 3:16-17 (with Isa. 61:1-2); 8:9 (and comments); 11:25-30; John 1:18; 13:20; 14:6, 9; 1 Timothy 2:5.

[70]Here (Matt. 10:41), *prophētēs* denotes a follower of Jesus for the first time in Matthew (all prior instances—and most later ones—denote OT prophets); for this usage, see also 23:34. Jesus applies the term to himself in 13:57. For the vital distinction between prophecy as a vehicle for divine revelation, and prophecy as proclamation and application of existing revelation, see Chamblin 1993: 208-13. Only the latter sense applies in our day; but it does in fact apply.

Peter, or his holiness to that of Paul? But by the same token, who could speak so genuinely of being 'the least of Christ's little ones' as those two (cf. 26:75; Eph. 3:8)?[71]

These missionaries are received because they are recognized to be prophets, righteous ones and disciples (Matt. 10:41-42).[72] That is, they are known to be Jesus' emissaries (10:40) and are welcomed for this very reason: '*because* [*hoti*] you belong to Christ,' says Mark 9:41, which parallels Matthew 10:42. Jesus here mentions only this one sign of a missionary's favorable reception: a cup of cold water. Is not this – *merely* (*monon*) a cup of water – the very least to be expected from a friendly host? But is not this – a cup of *cold* (*psychros*) water – also a most refreshing gift to a person traveling in a hot and dry climate, and a further mark of the host's kindness?[73] Moreover, given the environment of hostility amid which this mission is conducted (vv. 16-23), many of these hosts will put themselves at risk by showing hospitality to Jesus' servants.[74]

Whoever thus welcomes a prophet, a righteous person or a disciple is promised a reward: note how the three instances of *misthos* are distributed in Matthew 10:41-42. Even the donor of that smallest gift (10:42a) will not go unrecompensed: Jesus declares emphatically, 'Truly [*amēn*] I say to you, he will by no means lose [*ou mē apolesē*] his reward' (10:42b).[75] How and when are such people rewarded? In keeping with the 'already' and the

---

[71]Verse 40 refers primarily to the twelve (cf. 11:1), but not exclusively. It is possible that each successive term in 10:41-42 denotes a larger company of Christians: i.e., that 'prophets' is restricted to certain leaders; that 'the righteous' denotes 'a broader category of relatively mature believers'; and that 'little ones' 'would include all the ordinary, unobtrusive, and even marginalized members of the community of faith' (Blomberg 1992: 182). But cf. Carson (1984: 258): 'The order "descends" only according to prominence. But the classes mentioned are not mutually exclusive, since "these little ones" surely includes the apostles, prophets, and righteous men; they are all "little ones" because they are all targets of the world's enmity.'

[72]The repeated *eis onoma* ('in the name...') is a Semitism meaning 'because he is' (Davies and Allison 1991: 226).

[73]*Psychros*, absent from the parallel in Mark 9:41, occurs nowhere else in the gospels.

[74]Other evidences of hospitality are reflected in Matthew 10:9-14. Risks to the hosts are noted, e.g., by Blomberg 1992: 182; and Gundry 1994: 201-2.

'not yet' of the kingdom's coming, there are rewards both now at the kingdom's dawning and hereafter at its consummation. By welcoming the missionaries, these people show that they have come under God's benevolent rule (10:7); have themselves become Jesus' disciples; and have thus come to be numbered among those Jesus pronounces *makarioi* (5:3-12). Some will also have been blessed by his healing powers (10:8). They now receive from Christ, through his apostle or prophet or righteous person or disciple, the very rewards the missionaries themselves received earlier. By the same token, the future rewards awaiting the missionaries will be theirs as well – salvation at the Last Judgment, and eternal life in the heavenly kingdom.[76]

Thus Jesus' mighty discourse, while principally a charge to missionaries, closes with words of encouragement for recipients of the message. They first help to fulfill the great commission (24:14; 28:19-20) by themselves becoming believers. By thereafter supporting the messengers of the gospel, they participate in the mission itself. 'Some might be tempted to pass over 10:1-42 on the grounds that it is addressed to missionaries only. But 10:42 is an invitation for all the faithful to involve themselves in whatever way they can with the apostolic mission. And if the invitation is accepted, then chapter 10 cannot but become meaningful even to those who stay at home.'[77] Furthermore, as already noted, Jesus summons all his disciples – wherever they live – to bear witness to the non-believing world around them (5:13-16).

---

[75]The particle *amēn* is asseverative (BAGD s.v., 2.). Cf. its use elsewhere to introduce sayings about rewards and punishments, e.g., Matthew 10:15; 5:26; 6:2, 5, 16; 19:28; 23:36. The double negative (*ou mē*) and the aorist subjunctive *apolesē* (from *apollymi*) form an 'emphatic negation subjunctive' (*GGBB*, 468).

[76]The closing words of 10:42, *ton misthon autou* ('his reward'), clearly denote a reward this person receives and possesses: the *autou* is a 'possessive genitive' (*GGBB*, 81-83). This strongly suggests that the comparable phrases of 10:41 – *misthon prophētou* and *misthon dikaiou* – likewise denote rewards the prophet and the righteous person receive and possess, rather than rewards they impart. In the latter case, *prophētou* and *dikaiou* would be genitives of origin (a usage suggested by Davies and Allison 1991: 227); but Jesus is the true origin of the rewards, even when – as with the gifts of 10:7-8 – they are mediated by his servants.

[77]Davies and Allison 1991: 229-30.

Section 9
'Who is on the Lord's Side?'[1]
(Matt. 11:1–12:50)

Matthew has presented splendid summaries of Jesus' own ministry thus far (Matt. 5–9), together with his plan for extending that ministry to Israel and beyond through his chosen emissaries (ch. 10). How then are people in Israel, the present mission field, responding to Jesus? We already know from preceding chapters that he has a circle of disciples; that immense and fervent crowds clamor for his authoritative words and healing powers; that he is encountering opposition from Israel's religious leaders; and that perilous times, and responses both positive and negative, await his followers.[2] In the present two chapters varying responses to Jesus, mostly negative in character, become the dominant subject. Chapter 11 records the inquiry from John; the response of 'this generation' to John and Jesus; woes on the unrepentant cities; and Jesus' distinction between the 'wise' and the 'little children.' In chapter 12, the Pharisees oppose Jesus' conduct on the Sabbath; accuse him of employing demonic powers; and, together with the scribes, request from him an authenticating sign from heaven – this despite all the evidence he has already given.

---

[1]The opening words of a hymn by Frances R. Havergal (1877).
   [2]See, e.g., Matthew 4:23-25; 5:1-2; 7:28–8:1; 8:16; 9:3, 10-11, 33-38; 10:11-25.

I.
'Hail to the Lord's Anointed'[1]
(11:1-15)

Verse 2 speaks of 'the works of the Messiah' (*ta erga tou Christou*) – an arresting phrase, both because the name *Christos* has not appeared since chapters 1–2, and because the very next verse records John's question about Jesus' identity. Here at the beginning of the chapter, as at the beginning of his whole book (1:1), Matthew leaves readers in no doubt what *he* believes about Jesus, and what he wants them to believe as well. This, the evangelist's confession of faith, anticipates that of his fellow apostle in 16:16.[2]

A. Jesus Continues His Work (11:1)
Matthew 11:1 marks the close of the foregoing discourse: the first six Greek words are identical to those of 7:28a (on this feature of Matthean style, see p. 51). Matthew states that Jesus finished instructing (the verbs *teleō* and *diatassō*) the twelve disciples (11:1a), but says nothing about their departure or the course of their mission (contrast Mark 6:12-13; Luke 9:6). It is on Jesus that he concentrates: 'he went from there in order to teach [*tou didaskein*] and to preach [*kēryssein*] in their cities' (Matt. 11:1b).[3] These same verbs appear in the summaries of 4:23 and 9:35; but whereas those texts, and Jesus' instructions to the twelve in 10:7-8, speak also of miraculous healings, this one does not. I believe Matthew, anticipating 11:2-6, is implying that Messiah's foremost work is not *visible* but *verbal*

---

[1] The opening words of a hymn by James Montgomery (1821, 1828).

[2] As well as that of another member of the twelve in John 20:31 (with *ho Christos*). Some MSS. of Matthew 11:2 read instead 'the works of Jesus [*Iēsou*],' probably to make verse 2 more compatible with the uncertainty reflected in the question of verse 3 (Hagner 1993: 299).

[3] The two present infinitives denote purpose (cf. *GGBB*, 590-92).

– proclaiming the gospel of the kingdom to the poor (11:5; cf. 4:23; 9:35).[4]

Jesus taught and preached 'in their cities' (*en tais polesin autōn*; 11:1b). 'Their' (*autōn*) no doubt refers primarily to the Israelites – as in 'their [*autōn*] synagogues' (4:23 and 9:35). There may be a secondary sense as well – namely, that the 'their' of 11:1b applies to 'the twelve disciples' of 11:1a, and that these cities are theirs – i.e., places they themselves had visited. Have the twelve been Messiah's forerunners?[5]

B. Jesus Answers John (11:2-6)

It is fitting that the first recorded response to Jesus comes from the one who heralded his arrival. In 9:14, disciples of John made inquiry of their own (though the question about fasting may have come ultimately from their master). Here John himself speaks for the first time since chapter 3.

John's Inquiry (11:2-3)

Herod Antipas had arrested John and imprisoned him in the fortress of Machaerus.[6] Having heard from his disciples about Jesus' ministry, he now sends two of them (Luke 7:18) to him (Matt. 11:2).[7] The question itself comes from John: 'he said [*eipen*] to him, "Are you the one who is to come [*Sy ei ho erchomenos*], or must we await another [*ēheteron prosdokōmen*]?"' (11:3). Or, to bring out the force of the Greek more clearly: 'You – are *you* the one who is to come, or it is another on whom we must rest our hopes?'[8] On John's lips, *ho erchomenos* is unmistakably a name

---

[4]The preeminence of the verbal is clear in prior chapters. Jesus' public ministry starts with proclamation (Matt. 4:17); the summaries of 4:23; 9:35; and 10:7-8 speak of teaching and preaching before healing; the sermon of chapters 5–7 precedes the miracles of chapters 8–9. Cf. below on 11:4-5.

[5]Cf. the use of *polis*, 'city,' in 10:5, 11, 14, 15, 23. Keener 1999: 333 says Matthew moves 'almost directly from the instructions to Jesus' ministry in the cities where disciples had prepared the way.'

[6]Cf. Matthew 4:12; 14:3; Josephus, *Antiquities of the Jews*, 18.5.2; Scott 1995: 97.

[7]We also learn from Luke 7:18 that John's disciples reported to him 'about all these things,' especially the teachings of 6:20-49 and the miracles of 7:1-17.

[8]The subject is already present in the verb *ei* (present tense, second person singular, of *eimi*, 'to be'), so the addition of the personal pronoun *Sy*

for Messiah, the one whose advent the Baptist foretold: cf. his words in 3:11: 'but the one who is coming after me [*ho de opisō mou erchomenos*] is mightier than I.'[9] His testimony in John 3:28 is yet more direct: 'I myself [*eimi egō*] am not the Messiah [*ho Christos*]; but I have been sent before him.'

Why does John ask this question? We might have expected his disciples' account of Jesus' activity to underscore the lessons he learned at Jesus' baptism (Matt. 3:13-17) and to confirm him in the belief that Jesus is indeed the promised Messiah. Yet despite that report, John still harbors doubts. To judge from his preaching as recorded in 3:10-12, John is not troubled by what Jesus *is* doing so much as by what he is *not* doing. He appears to be asking: If you are the Coming One, where is the imminent and decisive judgment that I prophesied? Is not the whole nation to be refined at your hands, and the unrighteous consumed in fire? If you are the promised Servant of Yahweh, are you not expected to announce the day of his vengeance, and to liberate prisoners from their dungeons, (Isa. 61:1-2 ,with 42:7)? Why then am I still being held captive by a petty tyrant?[10]

Jesus' Reply (11:4-6)

'Go and tell John the things you hear and see. The blind receive their sight [*anablepousin*] and the lame walk [*peripatousin*]; lepers are cleansed [*katharizontai*] and the deaf hear [*akouousin*]; and the dead are raised [*egeirontai*], and the poor are being evangelized [*euangelizontai*]' (Matt. 11:4b-5). All six Greek verbs in 11:5, here noted, appear in the present

---

('You') makes the subject emphatic. *Sy* and *heteron* ('another') also receive some stress as the first terms in their clauses (*IB*, 166). In Luke 7:19-20, John's disciples repeat his question verbatim.

[9]See also the use of *ho erchomenos* in Matthew 21:9; 23:39; John 6:14; 11:27; Acts 19:4; Hebrews 10:37; Revelation 1:4, 8. Even if 'the coming one' was 'not a recognized Messianic title in Judaism' (France 1985: 192), there are OT antecedents: see Psalm 118:26; Daniel 7:13; Malachi 3:1 (and the LXX's use of *erchomai* in all three texts). Cf. Hagner 1993: 300.

[10]For this understanding of John's question, see Keener 1999: 335, and sources he cites. Perhaps John also wondered whether the conduct of Messiah and his followers could differ so markedly from that of the forerunner and his disciples: see Matthew 9:11, 14; 11:18-19; France 1985: 192 (but tax collectors

tense; and all are *customary* or *habitual* presents.[11] Some miracles may occur more often than others (e.g., there may be more blind people cured than dead people raised), and Jesus probably evangelizes the poor more regularly than he does any one kind of healing; but all six matters are essential and recurrent features of his Messianic mission. Five are expressly mentioned in preceding chapters. Two blind men (*typhloi*) receive their sight in 9:27-31. The term *chōlos*, 'lame,' first occurs in 11:5; but the 'paralytic' (*paralytikos*) of 9:2-8 is lame, and Jesus enables him to walk.[12] (Note how the blind and the lame are also joined in the eschatological promises of Isaiah 35:5-6 and Jeremiah 31:8.) A *lepros* is cleansed in 8:2-4; and a dead person (*nekros*) is raised in 9:23-25.[13] Among the 'poor' (*ptōchoi*) who receive good news are the 'blessed' of 5:3-10 (which contains the only prior occurrence of *ptōchoi* [11:3]), and the sick and afflicted whom Jesus heals; the verb of 11:5, *euangelizomai*, occurs nowhere else in Matthew, but note the use of the cognate noun *euangelion* in 4:23 and 9:35.

While there is no clear precedent for the remaining member of Matthew 11:5 – 'the deaf [*kōphoi*] hear' – this language recalls the cure of the mute (*kōphos*) demoniac in 9:32-34.[14] Furthermore, the placement of this summary indicates that it includes the mission of the twelve: cf. 10:7-8, where Jesus tells

and prostitutes responded favorably to John's preaching [21:32]). Did John, confined as he was in prison, know more about the *works* of Jesus (cf. 11:2) than about his *words*, and thus lack a vital means for interpreting the works?

[11]On this kind of present, see *GGBB*, 521-22.

[12]The verb of Matthew 11:5, *peripateō*, occurs in 9:5. Never in the NT do *paralytikos* and *chōlos* occur together. In Matthew, the first appears only in the early chapters (4:24; 8:6; 9:2, 6); the second occurs for the first time in the summary of 11:5, which strongly suggests that those 'paralytics' are numbered among these 'lame.' Both *paralytikos* and *chōlos* are translated 'lame' in BAGD s.v. In two NT passages the matching verb *paralyō* and *chōlos* occur together: in Acts 8:7, there is some distinction between them; in Hebrews 12:12-13, they appear to be synonymous.

[13]*Katharizō* ('cleanse'; Matthew11:5) occurs in 8:2-3; *egeirō* ('raise'; 11:5) occurs in 9:25.

[14]On one view, the *kōphos* of Matthew 9:32-33 includes deafness (see p. 555, n. 40). The verb of 11:5, *akouō* ('hear'), is nowhere used earlier of a healing miracle. Isaiah 35:5-6 (noted above) promises that the ears of the deaf will be unstopped and the tongues of the mute will sing for joy.

them (in the very terms of 11:5) to raise the dead and cleanse the lepers.

Matthew 11:4b speaks of 'the things you hear [*akouete*] and see[*blepete*].' These verbs are *progressive* or *descriptive* presents, related to what John's messengers are currently witnessing.[15] The parallel in Luke 7:21 is instructive: 'In that hour he cured many people of diseases and afflictions and evil spirits, and he gave sight to many who were blind.' John's disciples not only hear a summary of Jesus' earlier ministry: they personally hear his gospel of the kingdom and see his mighty works.[16] As Luke relates, exorcisms were among these; and while such works are not expressly included in the summary of Matthew 11:5, they are well attested in the earlier chapters.[17]

'And blessed [*makarios*] is the person who does not fall into sin [*mē skandalisthē*] on account of me,' concludes Jesus (11:6). This *makarios*, joined directly to the evangelizing of the poor (*ptōchoi*; 11:5b) strengthens the tie with 5:3-12, where the plural *makarioi* occurs nine times (these being the only prior instances of the term in Matthew). That is, the Beatitudes describe the kind of persons who do not take offense at Jesus, and who do not fall into sin on his account.[18] Those who recognize him to be sent from God, and who pledge their loyalty to him at whatever cost, will be blessed (*makarioi*): great will be their reward in heaven (10:40-42; 5:11-12). But those who do find him offensive, and who therefore reject him, are in danger of committing the worst sin of all, and of falling under the severest judgment –

---

[15]This kind of present describes 'a scene in progress, especially in narrative literature' (*GGBB*, 518).

[16]Related to what John's disciples personally witness, the words of Matthew 11:4b-5 form a chiasm: 'you hear' [a]; 'you see' [b]; 'blind see... dead are raised' [b']; 'poor are evangelized' [a'].

[17]See 4:24; 8:16, 28-34; 9:32-34; also Jesus' charge to the twelve (10:1, 8). I say 'not expressly included,' since some of the afflictions mentioned in 11:5 are on occasion attributed to demonic influence: cf., e.g., 12:22, 'a demoniac who was blind [*typhlos*] and mute [*kōphos*]'; and Mark 9:25, 'you mute [*alalon*] and deaf [*kōphon*] spirit.'

[18]The verb *skandalizō* was used in 5:29-30, in the active voice. In 11:6, the voice is passive: '*be led into sin, be repelled by someone, take offense at someone*' (BAGD s.v., 1. b.).

as later texts in these two chapters will confirm (see 11:20-24; 12:22-32, 38-45). This issue confronts not only those Israelites whom God has addressed through John and Jesus, but now also John himself.

Jesus provides John's messengers the very sort of evidence – both visible and verbal – that prompted John's question in the first place (11:5 and 2). Jesus says nothing about the Day of Judgment, although he earlier affirmed its certainty (see 7:33; 10:15). That Day is not eliminated but postponed, *so that* the gospel of the kingdom may be universally proclaimed (24:14) and people from Israel and the other nations rescued from 'the wrath to come.' Moreover, as Jesus is about to show (11:20-24), the very actions described in 11:5 have themselves precipitated a process of judgment (see also John 3:16-21) – and woe to those who reject or actively oppose these marvelous and unprecedented manifestations of God's saving grace and power.

In other words, the refining and purifying of Israel which John foretold (Matt. 3:11) is already underway, and the truth of Israelites' spiritual condition (3:12) is already coming to light (see comments on p. 256). Indeed, judgments about true and false children of Abraham were already being made during John's own ministry (3:7-10).

We are not told how John responded to Jesus' response. But all later evidence in Matthew, beginning with 11:7-19, strongly suggests that John was confirmed in his earlier beliefs and that he answered his own question affirmatively.[19]

C. Jesus Addresses the Crowd (11:7-15)
Matthew 11:1-3 imply that John's disciples posed his question as Jesus was preaching and teaching in one of the cities. Verse 7 implies that the crowds (*ochloi*) heard Jesus' reply to John and that Jesus now addresses them in that light.

---

[19]See comments on Matthew 11:7-19; 14:1-12; 17:10-13; 21:23-27, 31-32. For this view, see Chamblin 1964: 15, against Maurice Goguel, who thinks John answered his question negatively.

John the Baptist in Israel (11:7-9)
At the messengers' departure, 'Jesus began to speak to the crowds about John: "What did you go out [*Ti exēlthate*] into the wilderness to see [*theasasthai*]? A reed being shaken by the wind? What then did you go out [*alla ti exēlthate*] to see [*idein*]? A man clothed in soft garments? Behold [*idou*], those who wear soft garments are in kings' houses. What then did you go out [*alla ti exēlthate*] to see [*idein*]? A prophet? Yes, I tell you, and more than a prophet."' Jesus puts the same question to the crowds three times: note the repeated interrogative pronoun (*ti*), indicative verb (*exēlthate*) and infinitive (*theasasthai*, then *idein*).[20] Three answers are proposed (these too in the form of questions): a fragile reed (*kalamon*), a finely attired man (*anthrōpon*) and a prophet (*prophētēn*).[21]

The multitudes who went out to the wilderness of Judea to see and hear John would have seen plenty of reeds blowing in the wind along the Jordan River.[22] But no one acquainted with the boldness of John's preaching to Israel, or with the courage of his witness to Pharisees and Sadducees on the one hand (Matt. 3:7) and to Herod Antipas on the other (14:4), would ever choose such a metaphor to describe him. A solid and immovable marble pillar, yes; a weak and shaky papyrus reed, no. Such vacillation is not to be found in John but in Herod Antipas (cf. 14:3-11) and in the crowds themselves (cf. 21:8-11; 27:20-23). The question of 11:7b so obviously expects a negative answer that none is recorded. With this question, Jesus also appears to be cautioning the crowd not to conclude from the previous conversation (Matt. 11:3-6) that John is theologically unstable or indecisive.[23]

---

[20]The verb is an aorist of *exerchomai*. The infinitives are also aorist, the first from *theaomai*, the second from *eidon*, which serves as the aorist of *horaō*.

[21]As the object of the 'seeing,' each noun is in the accusative case.

[22]For *erēmos* ('wilderness,' Matthew 11:7), see also 3:1, 3. The Jordan River is mentioned in 3:5, 6, 13. Weak, tall papyrus reeds were easily tossed by the wind. 'The banks of the Jordan... hosted reeds growing as high as five meters' (Keener 1999: 337). Cf. Gundry 1994: 207.

[23]'Jesus is denying that his warning against apostasy [Matt. 11:6] implies instability in John, whose courageous condemnation of the illicit marriage between Herod Antipas and Herodias caused him to be imprisoned [cf. 11:2a; 14:1-12]' (Gundry 1994: 207). John is currently *undecided* about

Nor was John clad 'in soft garments' (*en malakois*; Matt. 11:8): on the contrary, his clothing was made 'from camel's hair' (*apo trichōn kamēlou*; 3:4). Nor would the crowds have expected John to be wearing fine apparel. The fastidious people who can afford, and insist on, such attire live 'in the palaces of kings' (*en tois oikois tōn basileōn*); their choosing to dwell in the Judean wilderness would have been inconceivable. The allusion to Herod Antipas is plainer here than in verse 7: see 14:1-12, where he is called both 'tetrarch' (*tetraarchēs*; [14:1], and 'king' (*basileus*) [14:9].[24]

A positive answer to the question about the prophet (11:9) is just as obvious as are negative answers to the questions of 11:7-8. Jesus makes the answer explicit – 'Yes [*nai*], I tell you' – thus stressing the importance of John's prophetic function. Indeed, it is precisely in fulfillment of his prophetic calling that John behaves as he does (standing firmly for truth and not being swayed by contrary opinions), and dresses as he does (like Elijah rather than Ahab). But no sooner is John called a *prophētēs* (and this for the first time in Matthew) than Jesus declares him to be 'more than a prophet' (11:9b). What he means by this, he explains in the following verses.

John the Baptist in History (11:10-15)
Jesus says of John: 'This is the one concerning whom it stands written [*gegraptai*], "Behold [*Idou*], I am sending [*egō apostellō*] my messenger [*ton angelon mou*] before your face [*pro prosōpou sou*]; he will prepare [*kataskeuasei*] your way [*tēn hodon sou*] before you [*emprosthen sou*]"' (Matt. 11:10.) *1. Two OT texts.* The first is Exodus 23:20a, where Yahweh says to Israel in the wilderness, 'Behold, I am sending an angel [*mal'āk*] before your face'; the LXX uses the very Greek words of Matthew 11:10a, noted above. The second text is Malachi 3:1a, where Yahweh again says to Israel, 'Behold, I am sending my messenger [*mal'ākî*], and he will prepare [*pinâ*] the way before

---

Jesus; whether he will prove to be *indecisive* depends on what he does with Jesus' reply (see comments on vv. 2-6).

[24]*Tetraarchēs* (lit., 'ruler of the fourth part of a realm') is politically correct; see comments on Matthew 14:1. The father of Herod Antipas, Herod the Great, is called *basileus* in 2:1, 3, 9.

my face'; the LXX translates the first part *idou egō exapostellō ton angelon mou*, and the second part *kai epiblepsetai hodon pro prosōpou mou*.[25] 2. *The text of Matthew 11:10.* Both those OT texts are incorporated, but Jesus is referring primarily to Malachi 3:1. *a.* His preface to the quotation makes it clear that John – a human (not an angelic) messenger – is in view; and 'my messenger' is the language of Malachi, not Exodus.[26] *b.* The verb in the second half of the quotation, *kataskeuasei*, well translates the Hebrew verb *pinâ*, which is used in Malachi 3:1 but not in Exodus 23:20.[27] *c.* In keeping with its application to John the Baptist, the quotation also refers to Jesus himself, not (as in Exodus 23:20) to the nation of Israel. 3. *The theology of Matthew 11:10.* We now learn what makes John 'more than a prophet' (11:9b). Not only does he, like OT prophets, foretell Messiah's coming: he is Messiah's immediate forerunner, and so occupies a unique position. Nor is this Messiah merely a man in whom Yahweh is uniquely active: he is himself Yahweh incarnate. Both as the 'messenger' of Malachi 3:1 and as the 'voice' of Isaiah 40:3, John still prepares for the coming of Yahweh (note that these two Hebrew texts have in common the Piel of *pānâ*: see n. 27). Only now in the quotation of Matthew 11:10, in distinction from the wording of Malachi 3:1, God the *Father* (who is Yahweh) addresses God the *Son* (who is also Yahweh) about his forerunner. Furthermore, the exact words of Exodus 23:20 are retained (see above): only now they refer not to Israel but to Jesus – or, more accurately, to that Son whose advent was foreshadowed when Yahweh called Israel his son out of Egypt (Matt. 2:15).[28]

---

[25]In Jewish synagogue worship, Malachi 3:1 was the prophetic text chosen to accompany the Torah reading of Exodus 23 (Hagner 1993: 305).

[26]Both Hebrew *mal'āk* and Greek *angelos* can mean both 'angel' and 'messenger.'

[27]*Kataskeuasei* ('he will prepare, make ready'; Matthew 11:10) is a better translation than LXX's *epiblepsetai* ('he will look upon, have regard for') for MT's *pinâ*, a Piel form of *pānâ* that means '*make clear*, free from obstacles' (BDB s.v.).

[28]See the comments on Matthew 2:15, as well as those on 3:11-12 (both Malachi 3:2-3 and Matthew 3:11 depict Messiah's *refining* work). Jesus' application of Malachi 3:1 to John 'implies that his own (Jesus') coming...is the coming of God himself, an implication which is the more staggering for being so calmly assumed' (France 1985: 194). Cf. France 1971: 91-92, 155.

'Truly I say to you, among those born of women there has arisen no one greater than John the Baptist. Yet the one who is least in the kingdom of heaven is greater than he' (Matt. 11:11, ESV). In this solemn declaration (with its opening *amēn*), Jesus contrasts two realms: the one, inhabited by 'those born of women,' we may call 'the kingdom of men'; the other is 'the kingdom of heaven.' According to the best criteria for judging human character, says Jesus, there has never been a greater person than John. Yet, as earlier chapters have repeatedly shown, all that matters ultimately is whether one submits to God's rule and embraces his Messiah. Reception into the kingdom of heaven rests not on what one *possesses* but on what he *lacks*; it depends not on *human endeavor* but on *divine achievement*.[29]

Verse 11 does not exclude John from the kingdom. All its citizens were once 'born of woman.' A favorable response to Jesus' message (11:4-6) will assure John's entry into the kingdom whose coming he foretold (3:2). Yet it is equally certain that his greatness does not entitle him to special treatment. He needs the grace of God and the gospel for the poor (11:5) as much as anyone; his sins too must be forgiven.[30] He who is among the greatest must be numbered among the lowliest. Jesus' language in 11:11b – 'the least [*ho mikroteros*] in the kingdom' – implies distinctions among its subjects.[31] Yet all of them are 'little ones' (*mikroi*), all of them children of the heavenly Father; and there is a sense in which the very least in the kingdom receive its greatest

---

[29]'And the meanest citizen of [this] kingdom is greater than the greatest of the former – not because of superior merit (merit he may lack completely), but simply because he is a citizen of the Kingdom of *God*' (Chamblin 1964: 16).

[30]Each member of God's kingdom 'experiences an elevation in grace through God...that cannot be achieved by even the mightiest human endeavour' (Schnackenburg 1963: 134).

[31]The comparative adjective *mikroteros* is to be translated as a superlative, both here (in contrast to 'the greatest' of Matthew 11:11a) and in the one other instance in Matthew (13:32, the mustard is 'the smallest of all seeds'). The superlative form *mikrotatos* does not occur in the NT. For distinctions within the kingdom, see the instances of *elachistos* (which serves as a superlative of *mikros*: BAGD s.v. *elachistos*) in 5:19; 25:40, 45.

blessings.[32] Is not this a lesson of the beatitudes, and does not Matthew portray John as the sort of person 'to whom the kingdom of heaven belongs' (5:3-10)? He is humble in spirit (3:11; cf. John 3:27-30).[33] He mourns over the people's sins, calls them to repentance, and longs for God to establish righteousness in the land (Matt. 3:2-10). In baptizing the repentant (3:6), he mediates God's mercy. As the latter-day Elijah, he is a peacemaker (11:14; 17:11; cf. Luke 1:17, 76-79; Sirach 48:10). He is 'persecuted on account of righteousness' (Matt. 14:1-12; 17:12). John both heralds Messiah's coming and embodies his teachings. God's wisdom is vindicated by its deeds – as accomplished both in Messiah and in his forerunner (11:2-6, 16-19).

'From [*apo*] the days of John the Baptist until now the kingdom of heaven has been forcefully advancing [*biazetai*], and violent men [*biastai*] are plundering it. For all the Prophets and the Law prophesied until John' (11:12-13). *1. John and the Old Testament.* The phrase 'the Prophets [*prophētai*] and the Law [*nomos*]' denotes the OT. In every other instance of this couplet in the NT the terms are reversed, in accord with the canonical order: e.g., 5:17; 7:12; 22:40; and the par. to 11:13 in Luke 16:16. Here, the placement of *prophētai* before *nomos*, and the choice of the verb *eprophēteusan* (from *prophēteuō*, lacking in Luke 16:16), accentuate the OT's prophetic function, in keeping with John's own calling (*prophētēn*; Matt. 11:9). John stands not *within* the time of 'the Prophets and the Law' but *beyond* it: in him, OT prophecies – notably those of Isaiah (Matt. 3:3) and Malachi (Matt. 11:10, 14) – come to fulfillment.[34] *2. John and the kingdom of*

---

[32]See the instances of *mikros* in 10:42; 18:6, 10, 14; earlier references to the disciples' heavenly Father, e.g., 6:9, 26, 32; 7:11; 10:20, 29; and Jesus' promises to the lowliest of his servants in such passages as 19:30; 20:16, 26-27; 23:11-12.

[33]One reason for the restricted diet of John and his disciples (3:4; 9:14) may have been to express their repentance and humility before God (Chamblin 1964: 14; Scobie 1964: 139-40).

[34]Note that it is the last of the OT writing prophets (i.e., Malachi) who promises the one in whom the prophetic gift will be revived over 400 years later and through whom God first announces publicly the dawn of the kingdom and the presence of Messiah.

heaven. The opening *apo* is inclusive. That is, it is with John, not with Jesus, that the mighty advance of the kingdom (*biazetai*) commences: Jesus' opening proclamation (4:17) repeats that of John (3:2); John witnesses to tax collectors and sinners (21:32), as does Jesus (9:10); Jesus' prophecies of Messianic judgment (e.g., 25:31-46) underscore those of John (3:11-12). Moreover, the first to suffer violence at the hands of the kingdom's enemies (*biastai*) is the Messianic herald (4:12) – persecution that presages what is in store for Messiah himself (17:12).[35]

Matthew 11:12 thus understood sheds further light on the matters that prompted John's question (11:3). The kingdom is indeed forcefully advancing; and despite the most virulent opposition, it will surely be consummated (6:10). Yet, despite John's prophecies, Messiah has not swiftly and decisively conquered the kingdom's enemies. On the contrary, the more the kingdom advances, the stronger the opposition becomes; indeed, the fiercest assaults on Messiah are still to come. But so too is Messiah's greatest triumph (Matt. 28). Wicked

---

[35]Ridderbos 1962: 54 says of Matthew 12:12a: 'We shall have to understand the word "since" [*apo*] in an exclusive and not in an inclusive sense. John is on the threshold, he leads on from the old to the new dispensation; he himself still belongs to the old period. With Jesus, the new era has come, that of the kingdom of heaven pushing its way with force into the world.' For *apo* as inclusive instead, see Chamblin 1964: 10-11; Gundry 1994: 209; Wink 1968: 20-22. The above translation of *biazetai* (so NIV; Carson 1984: 267) accords with its dominant usage: 'nearly always a middle deponent, *apply force*' (BAGD s.v.). On another view, *biazetai* means 'suffer violence' (so ESV; Gundry 1994: 209-10; Hagner 1993: 307), in which case 12:12a and 12:12b are synonymous. On the above translation, *biastai* denotes persons hostile to the kingdom; this accords with the term's usual sense (see BAGD s.v.). We may with Carson (1984: 267) view 12 as 'a form of antanclasis (a figure of speech in which the same word is repeated in a different or even contradictory sense), based in this instance not on exactly the same word but on a cognate [*biazetai* and *biastai*].' Gundry (1994: 204-13) thinks the passage is dominated by the theme of persecution, a chief means by which opponents seek to 'plunder the kingdom.' On another view, both clauses of verse 12 are understood in a favorable sense, in keeping with the closest Lukan parallel (16:16). But this reading of Matthew 12:12b does not fit the Matthean context as well as the other. In my judgment, Jesus' saying in Luke 16:16 comes from a later period of his ministry (his journey to Jerusalem) and supplements, rather than duplicates, his earlier saying in Matthew 11:12.

and violent men are presently 'plundering' (*harpazousin*) the kingdom (11:12b), but their efforts will ultimately fail.[36]

'And if you are willing to accept it, he is Elijah, the one to come. He who has ears, let him hear' (11:14-15). Verse 14 confirms that John stands within the time of the end: for 'the Prophets and the Law prophesied' that a latter-day Elijah would appear to herald 'the great and awesome day of Yahweh' (Mal. 4:5; MT, 3:23), with 4:6; Matthew 17:10-13; Luke 1:17. Will the crowds willingly believe John to be this figure? It is vital that they do so, says verse 15. This solemn appeal, *ho echōn ōta akouetō*, appears twice more in Matthew, both at critical junctures (13:9, 43). The right response is crucial, says Jesus, in face of judgments both present (13:10-17) and future (13:37-43). And that response entails recognizing both Messiah and his forerunner. *If indeed* John is the Elijah who is 'about to come,' is not 'the great and awesome day of Yahweh' about to come, or perhaps already here? *If indeed* John is the messenger of Malachi 3:1, is not Yahweh himself soon to appear to execute judgment (3:1-5)? In this case, what is one to believe about Jesus himself?

---

[36]The verb *harpazousin* (from *harpazō*, 'snatch, seize, plunder': see BAGD s.v., 2. b.) is here a *conative* present: an act is attempted but fails to succeed (Carson 1984: 267; *GGBB*, 534). Jesus will succeed, however, in plundering the kingdom of Satan (Matthew 12:29, where *harpazō* recurs).

II.

'And None the Longed-For Christ Would Know'[1]
(11:16-24)

Matthew 11:12b spoke of assertive opposition to the advance of God's rule in John and Jesus (11:4-15). The present text also has negative responses in view; but now Jesus focuses on Israel's childish demands (11:16-19) and damnable inaction (11:20-24. The crowds (*ochloi*) of 11:7 are probably still present; in any case these are words that all listeners – and readers – should soberly reflect upon.

A. The Dissatisfied Generation (11:16-19)

'But to what shall I liken [*homoiōsō*] this generation [*genean*]?' Jesus asks (11:16a). In accord with the question, he first employs an extended simile (i.e., a parable; 11:16b-17).[2] Then, in 11:18-19 (joined to the preceding by 'for,' *gar*, 11:18a), he explains the parable.

The Parable (11:16b-17)
Jesus says this generation is 'like children [*paidiois*] sitting in the marketplaces [*agorais*] and calling to others' (11:16b). The adjective 'like' (*homoia*) agrees with the verb 'liken' (*homoioō* in the future tense (11:16a).

The children first call out: 'We played the flute [*ēulēsamen*] for you, and you did not dance [*ouk ōrchēsasthe*]' (11:17a). The first verb is from *auleō*. A flutist (*aulētēs*) might play a flute (*aulos*) for joyful and for sorrowful occasions, for weddings and for funerals (cf. 9:23, the one instance of *aulētēs* in Matthew). The second verb, from *orcheomai*, shows that these

---

[1]From the hymn 'My Song Is Love Unknown,' by Samuel Crossman (ca. 1624-1683).

[2]Cf. the similes of Matthew 7:24-27, where the verb *homoioō* last occurred in Matthew.

flutists are providing music for merrymaking.[3] Who could resist dancing at a wedding reception, especially when flutists strike up a tune for that purpose? Yet when these children (*paidia*) decide to conduct a 'pretend wedding,' and begin to play their imaginary flutes (perhaps 'reed' instruments), the others (*heteroi*) refuse to dance. In face of such a response, one can easily imagine the first group flying into a tantrum, thus bringing the 'ceremony' abruptly to an end before its end.

The children also call out: 'We sang a dirge [*ethrēnēsamen*], and you did not mourn [*ouk ekopsasthe*]' (Matt. 11:17b). This usage of the verb *thrēneō* recalls several texts in the LXX, notably 2 Samuel (LXX 2 Kings) 1:17: 'And David lamented [*ethrēnēsen*] with this lament [*thrēnon*] over Saul and over his son Jonathan.'[4] The song of 1:19-27 expresses David's own grief, and is to be preserved (1:18) so that others may grieve with him. So too the dirge in the parable both expresses the singers' sorrow and elicits that of others – here denoted by the verb *koptomai*, which can mean to '*beat one's breast as an act of mourning*.'[5] If, in Matthew 11:17a, the 'girls complain that the boys have not responded to their flute playing with a round dance (danced by men) in a game of mock-wedding,' here in verse 17b 'the boys complain that the girls have not responded to their singing a dirge with mourning (done professionally by women) in a game of mock-funeral.'[6] 'And so their noisy quarrels put an end to play.'[7]

---

[3]In the one other instance of *orcheomai* in Matthew, the daughter of Herodias is dancing at Herod's birthday party (14:6).

[4]The noun *thrēnos*, 'dirge,' absent from *GNT*, occurs in the LXX of Jeremiah 31 (LXX 38):15, and in some MSS. of this text as quoted in Matthew 2:18.

[5]BAGD s.v. *koptō*, 2. These two verbs appear together in one other NT text (Luke 23:27), where women 'were mourning [*ekoptonto*] and lamenting [*ethrēnoun*]' for Jesus.

[6]Gundry 1994: 212; cf. Luke 7:32, 'calling to one another [*allēlois*].' Jeremias 1963: 161 notes that 'the round dance at a wedding is the men's dance,' and that 'the mourners' dirge is the women's business' (on this, see again Luke 23:27).

[7]Jeremias 1963: 161.

The Lesson (11:18-19)
'For John came neither eating nor drinking, and they say, "He has a demon." The Son of Man came eating and drinking, and they say, "Behold, a glutton and a drunkard, a friend of tax collectors and sinners." Yet wisdom is vindicated by her deeds.'

According to one view, the children who speak represent Jesus and John, the messengers of God, while 'the others' stand for contemporary Israelites. When Jesus the bridegroom proclaims the good news of the kingdom (Matt. 4:23) and calls upon the people to make merry (9:15), they refuse (like the elder brother in Luke 15:25-32). When John commands the people to repent (Matt. 3:2), to prepare for Messiah's advent (3:7-12) and to fast accordingly (9:14), they also refuse (like Herod Antipas in 14:1-12). On this reading, the answer to the opening question – 'To what shall I liken this generation?' – is not 'the children sitting in the marketplaces,' but the entirety of 11:16b-17 (i.e., here is a picture of what happens when the kingdom of heaven encounters a generation of people).[8]

For several reasons, it is preferable to interpret the parable in the opposite way. *1.* The language of Matthew 11:16 – the verb *homoiōsō* followed closely by the adjective *homoia* – suggests that the children who sit and speak are themselves illustrative of 'this generation.' NB the parallel in Luke 7:31-32. *2.* On this showing, Matthew 11:17 expresses the people's displeasure, first over John's way of life (when they wanted to celebrate, he chose to fast), then over that of Jesus (when they wanted to mourn, he chose to make merry); which agrees with the order of 11:18-19 (first John, then Jesus). *3.* The three instances of *legousin* are hereby used consistently: to denote complaints from

---

[8]This is grammatically permissible. It would compare to Matthew 13:24, where Jesus means not that 'the kingdom of heaven is like a man...,' but that the following parable (13:24-30) depicts what happens when the kingdom comes. For this reading of 11:16-19, see, e.g., Manson 1957: 70; France 1985: 196-97; Gundry 1994: 212.

the children (v. 17); and grievances against John (v. 18) and Jesus (v. 19).[9]

To judge from the rest of Matthew, the 'children' who most severely censure both John and Jesus are Israel's religious leaders. More than once this gospel records the crowds' favorable estimate of John (11:9; 21:26, 32). 'The chief priests and the elders of the people,' on the contrary, did not believe John (21:25, 32). They, together with 'the Pharisees and Sadducees' whom John accused of being a 'viper's brood' in danger of 'the wrath to come' (3:7-10), are the persons most likely to say he 'has a demon' (*daimonion echei*, 11:18).[10] The crowds' enthusiasm for Jesus is yet greater, given his powers as teacher and miracle worker (4:25; 7:28; 9:8, etc.); and it is in fact Jesus' association with their more disreputable members that evokes the censure of 11:19. It is the Pharisees who condemn Jesus for making merry with tax collectors and sinners, and also (by implication) for neglecting the appointed fasts (9:11, 14). By the same token, on the lips of these scrupulous law-keepers the charge that Jesus is 'a glutton and a drunkard' is probably an allusion to the son of Deuteronomy 21:18-21, who rebels against his parents and thus against the law, and who is also called 'a glutton and a drunkard' (Matt. 11:20, ESV).[11]

While 11:16-19 features differences between Jesus and John, they are utterly united in their mission. This is already clear from verse 12 (and texts to which it alludes); and it is underscored in the last sentence of verse 19. The wisdom (*sophia*) of God is vindicated (*edikaiōthē*) by her deeds: that

---

[9]For this reading of Matthew 11:16-19, see e.g. Jeremias 1963: 160-62; Davies and Allison 1991: 262; Green 1997: 302-3; Keener 1999: 341. This passage discredits the view that 'Jesus never uses a child to illustrate foolishness or ignorance' (Davies and Allison 1991: 229, n. 81).

[10]This charge 'could suggest "prophetic" madness or an association between recluses and possession..., but it may suggest a familiar spirit, such as those that belonged to magicians...' (Keener 1999: 342).

[11]Cf. Keener 1999: 342, who suggests that Jesus may have been considered a rebellious son because he, though the eldest of the children, left home to engage in ministry (cf. 8:21-22; 10:34-39; 12:46-50; 13:53-58; Luke 2:41-52). The rendering of this phrase in the LXX of Deuteronomy 21:20 differs from the Greek of Matthew 11:19.

is, deeds (*erga*) accomplished in accord with God's revealed wisdom, and in obedience to his will, reveal that wisdom to be precisely what it claims to be – the truest and the highest *wisdom*.[12] Such are the works done both by Messiah (11:2, where *erga* also occurs) and by his forerunner. Both of them are submissive to God's rule; both of them preach and practice 'the way of righteousness' (3:15; 21:32); and both are faithful to their calling, even unto death. Their differences of behavior point not to contradictory views of wisdom, but to their different identities: John awaits Messiah, Jesus is Messiah (see comments on 9:14-17).[13] Considering the sorts of people who oppose them, and the ferocity of the opposition, it might be thought that Jesus and John represent 'the way of the wicked' rather than 'the way of the righteous' (see Ps. 1). But viewed in the light of OT revelation, the accomplishments of John and Jesus are clearly seen to be 'good works' (cf. Eph. 2:10); and the divine wisdom is thereby exonerated. The soundness and splendor of that wisdom is yet plainer when reading Matthew as a whole, than it would have been when witnessing the deeds of John and Jesus originally.[14]

---

[12]That Matthew 11:19b uses the passive voice of the verb *dikaioō*, 'justify, vindicate' (BAGD s.v., 2), shows that wisdom's works (*erga*) are the subject of the action. 'But wisdom is proved right by her actions' (NIV), namely those to which verses 16-19 allude. The par. in Luke 7:35 speaks instead of wisdom's 'children' (*tekna*), a reference to followers of Jesus and John (Stein 1992: 233).

[13]The unity of their mission is also reflected in the fact that both John and Jesus are accused of working in demonic power: see Matthew 9:34; 11:18; 12:24; also John 8:39-59, where Jesus is twice accused (as is John in Matthew 11:18) of 'having a demon' (vv. 48, 52).

[14]Matthew as a whole fully sets forth God's 'wisdom-vindicating works' (Bruner 2004a: 520). Some think that 'the works of Messiah' (11:2) and 'the works of wisdom' (11:19) are one and the same; i.e. that Christ himself is identified as Wisdom (so Gundry 1994, 213; Davies and Allison 1991: 264-65). Yet, the proverbial nature of the saying and the subject of the immediately preceding verses favor viewing *sophia* (11:19) as the wisdom of God earlier revealed in the OT and now in the works of both Jesus and John (so Carson 1984: 271). In Matthew, Jesus possesses and imparts the greatest *sophia* (cf. 12:42; 13:54), but is not expressly equated with it (as, e.g., in 1 Cor. 1:24). On the relation between Luke 11:49 and Matthew 23:34, see comments on the latter.

B. The Unrepentant Cities (11:20-24)

'Then Jesus began to reproach the cities in which most of his mighty works had been done, because they did not repent' (Matt. 11:20). The opening 'then' (*tote*) joins these verses both logically and chronologically to 11:7-19. This passage, like that one, describes the largely negative response of 'this generation' (11:16) to Jesus. It is likely that he himself took the action prescribed for his apostles when leaving unrepentant cities (10:14). He also issued the present warnings more than once: note that 10:15 anticipates 11:24; and that the words of Luke 10:13-15 (which are parallel to Matthew 11:21-24) are placed within the context of his later journey to Jerusalem.

The Witness to Jewish Cities

Jesus accentuates his *dynameis* ('mighty works'), a term used three times in the passage (Matt. 11:20, 21, 23). Here is an echo of verse 5, which featured a variety of such miracles; and here too is evidence that Jesus' witness is greater than John's, for the latter did no miracle.[15] Nor do Jesus' *dynameis* stand alone; they are allied to, and elucidated by, his preaching and teaching, as is plain from the summaries of 4:23; 9:35; 11:5; and accounts of certain miracles in chapters 8–9 (e.g., 9:2-8).[16]

Jesus has done these works 'throughout Galilee' (4:23), in many a *polis* ('city') and *kōmē* ('village'; 9:35); the first term is broad enough to include 'small lakeside towns.'[17] The present text, in keeping with 11:1, focuses on the cities (note *polis*, without *kōmē*, in vv. 1 and 20). In the NT, the name Chorazin occurs only here (11:21) and in the parallel of Luke 10:13; it is evidently to be located about two miles north of Capernaum.[18] The name Bethsaida (Matt. 11:21) appears nowhere else in

---

[15]See John 10:41. As noted in comments on Matthew 3, John resembled Elijah as an anointed preacher but not as a miracle worker.

[16]Calvin 1995a: 16 says that the 'mighty works' of 11:21 include teaching, 'for Christ was not dumb while He was showing them the power of the Father. In fact the miracles were joined to the Gospel so as to draw attention to the voice of Christ.' Cf. 1 Kings 17:23-24.

[17]The quoted phrase is from France 1985: 197. The twelve would likewise visit both cities and villages (Matthew 10:11: *polin...kōmēn*).

[18]W. Harold Mare, 'Korazin,' *DBA*, 282.

Matthew. The town lay just north of the Sea of Galilee and some five miles east of Capernaum; also east of the Jordan River, it was still associated with Galilee.[19] Mark 8:22 reports that Jesus heals a blind man at Bethsaida; and Luke 9:10 (with Mark 6:45), that Jesus feeds the 5,000 in this vicinity. Capernaum stands alone (Matt. 11:23) as a place of special importance (see 4:13-17) and, in all probability, witnessed more of Jesus' miracles than any other city. Not that these are the only places facing judgment; rather, they represent all the other cities (11:1). The geographical proximity of Chorazin and Bethsaida to Capernaum may help to explain why they are expressly mentioned.

Despite those mighty and merciful works, none of those cities repented (Matt. 11:20). Though one greater than Jonah was in their midst, they did not emulate the Ninevites (12:41). Yet, that unbelief was not universal; in those very cities God disclosed truth about his Son to 'little children' (11:25-27). Did not three of the twelve – Philip, Andrew and Peter – come from Bethsaida? And did not five of them – Peter, Andrew, James, John and Matthew – answer Jesus' call in Capernaum?[20]

The Witness of Gentile Cities

Chorazin and Bethsaida compare unfavorably to Tyre and Sidon (11:21). These Phoenician towns lay on the Mediterranean coast, Sidon about twenty-five miles north of Tyre, and were places of great commercial import.

---

[19]Archeological 'remains in the locality suggest that there was a double site of considerable size some [295 feet] above lake level, one part standing [about two miles] from the shore, and the other, a fishing village, situated by the lake' (E.M. Blaiklock, 'Bethsaida,' DBA, 100). Bethsaida is Aramaic, meaning 'house of fishing' or 'fisherman's house' (D.F. Payne, 'Beth-Saida,' IBD 1: 190). I believe this 'Bethsaida' and 'Bethsaida in Galilee' (John 12:21) are the same place; see arguments in Morris 1995: 142-43. Hendriksen 1973: 494 thinks they are different.

[20]John 1:44 identifies Bethsaida as the hometown of Philip, Andrew and Peter. The latter two moved to Capernaum before the beginning of Jesus' ministry (Matt. 4:13, 18; 8:5, 14). For the calls of the four fishermen and of Matthew, see 4:18-22; 9:9 (and for evidence of how a 'mighty work' of Jesus affected Peter, see Luke 5:1-11). Cf. also comments on Matthew 7:13-14.

Exemplars of pagan pride and power, they both fell under God's judgment.[21] But, says Jesus, had they beheld his mighty works, Tyrians and Sidonians would long ago have repented 'in sackcloth and ashes' – as had the king of Nineveh (cf. Jon. 3:6).[22] The implication is that Yahweh would therefore have withheld judgment from Tyre and Sidon, as he had from Nineveh. The *an...metenoēsan* ('they would have repented') at the close of Matthew 11:21 stands in contrast to the *ou metanoēsan* ('they did not repent') at the close of verse 20.

Capernaum is also compared to two OT cities (Matt. 11:23). The language in 11:23a alludes to the taunt against Babylon's king in Isaiah 14:13, 15. His vaulting ambition makes the pride of Tyre and Sidon seem as nothing.[23] But that monarch was destined for Sheol and that whole empire for destruction.[24] Jesus does not mention Babylon by name, or say how it would have responded to his miracles. Does he imply that the city was *too proud* to humble itself as the other three would have done? In any case, having likened Capernaum to Babylon, Jesus declares it to be unlike Sodom (Matt. 11:23b). Had Sodom witnessed the miracles done in Capernaum, 'it would have remained to this day,' which implies its prior repentance. Thus responding to Jesus' mighty works of salvation (11:5) would have spared it those mighty works of destruction (Gen. 19:23-29).[25]

---

[21]For history and archeology, see E.M. Blaiklock, 'Sidon,' *DBA*, 414; 'Tyre,' ibid., 459; and D.J. Wiseman, 'Sidon,' *IBD*, 1449-50; 'Tyre,' ibid., 1603-5. For judgments against Tyre and Sidon, see Isaiah 23; Ezekiel 26-28; Amos 1:9-10; Jeremiah 25:15, 22; Zechariah 9:2-4.

[22]*Sakkos* ('sackcloth') and *spodos* ('ashes', Matthew 11:21b) are used in the LXX of Jon. 3:6.

[23]On the king's 'soaring self-esteem' and 'envisaged...deification,' see Motyer 1999: 120. Cf. Gen. 11:4 (the *hybris* at the tower of Babel); Jeremiah 51:53. The verb in Matthew 11:23a is *hypsoō*, 'exalt' (on textual variants, see *TC*, 24-25); cf. its use in 23:12.

[24]For history and archeology, see D. J. Wiseman, 'Babel,' *IBD*, 154-57; 'Babylon,' ibid., 157-62; 'Babylonia,' ibid., 162-70. For judgments against Babylon, see, e.g., Isaiah 21:1-10; 46:1-47:15; Jeremiah 50:1–51:64; Daniel 5.

[25]For more on Sodom (and Gomorrah) in the OT, see page 573, n. 38.

The Judgment of Jesus

Jesus knows that the inhabitants of those Jewish cities are unrepentant, and that the people of those Gentile cities would have repented, in face of his mighty works. In that light, he speaks of the coming Day of Judgment in Matthew 11:22 and (with the same language) in verse 24.[26] The earlier judgments against Tyre, Sidon and Sodom (also Babylon) anticipate the most critical judgment of all. Moreover, on that last day, it will be 'more tolerable' (*anektoteron*) for those three cities than for the present three – for the reason given in 11:21 and 23. Capernaum is expressly said to be destined for Hades (11:23). Like *geenna* in 5:22, *hadēs* here denotes the place of final punishment. Jesus' intent is not to assure listeners that the whole populations of those OT cities will escape *hadēs*, but rather to impress on them the appalling wickedness of these NT cities and others like them. The penalty awaiting Tyre, Sidon and Sodom (as foreshadowed in their earlier destruction) will be less severe than that in store for Chorazin, Bethsaida and Capernaum. For, whereas those Gentile cities sinned in great ignorance, these Jewish cities have sinned *both* against God's prior revelations (as recorded in their Scriptures) *and* in face of these ultimate disclosures of his glory and grace in Israel's Messiah.[27] The joint witness of John

---

[26]Nine of the thirteen words in the Greek text of Matthew 11:22 recur in verse 24, in the same order.

[27]Cf. 23:29-39; Hebrews 10:26-31. *Hadēs*, literally 'not seen' (*a*-privative + *idein*, 'to see'), recurs in Matthew 16:18. The LXX almost always uses *hadēs* to translate Sheol (*šeʾôl*); by Jesus' day both *hadēs* and *geenna* denoted the place of final punishment (and *paradeisos* the abode of the blessed); see comments on 5:22. For degrees of punishment, see Luke 12:47-48; Dante's *Inferno*. In Calvin's judgment (1995a: 16), Christ's words in Matthew 11:21 'mean that in malice and insane contempt of God, Tyre and Sidon were only surpassed by Chorazin and Bethsaida.' Yet God 'justly appoints to destruction' all four cities (ibid.). Ryle comments (1993: 85) that the people of Chorazin, Bethsaida and Capernaum 'are to be in the lowest hell because they had heard the Gospel [cf. 11:5b] and yet did not repent....' 'The vengeance of the Gospel is heavier than the vengeance of the Law' (Rutherford 1984: 441). See comments on 12:22-32. Yet, just as the truth about the Father and the Son was revealed to 'little children' in places like Capernaum, so could it happen in places like Tyre and Sidon: cf. Yahweh's grace to the widow of Zarephath (located between Sidon and Tyre; 1 Kings 17:8-24); and see comments on Matthew 15:21-28.

and Jesus is indeed to be taken seriously (11:7-19). But given what Jesus *says* (he speaks with authority surpassing John's), what he *does* (he works miracles, John does not) and who he *is* (he is Messiah, John was his forerunner), those who reject his witness are in greater peril than those who reject John's alone.

It was in view of the coming Day of Wrath that Jesus did those mighty works: they themselves were means for demolishing barriers to the rule of God, for placarding the grace of the kingdom, for awakening people out of their theological slumbers, and for summoning them into Messiah's service. (Yahweh's stupendous miracle on Mount Carmel [1 Kings 18] served a similar manifold purpose.) For the same reason, Jesus speaks the words of Matthew 11:21-24, an alarm anticipated in 10:15 and underscored in Luke 10:13-15. Here, for the first time in Matthew, Jesus uses the word *Ouai* ('Woe!'; Matthew 11:21 – all remaining instances are on his lips as well). It joins dismay to disapproval, sorrow to censure (REB translates 'Alas...!').

But its utterance proceeds from grace. 'Woe to you!' is not the same as 'Damn you!' Rather it is a warning intended to shock listeners into an awareness of their true condition, and of the condemnation that awaits them unless they take swift and decisive action (cf. Prov. 29:1).[28] So, you inhabitants of these Jewish cities, consider how you *really* compare to those Gentile cities: be appalled by the magnitude and depth of your wickedness; be terrified of the impending punishment. You (especially you, Capernaum) who pride yourself on your imagined national and spiritual superiority, repent of your folly and humble yourself before God. Beware lest in face of your indifference to these mighty works of grace, God and Messiah withdraw their blessings from you and give them to Gentiles instead.[29] And having heeded all these warnings,

---

[28]John's preaching (Matt. 3:2-12) was so motivated (see pp. 242-57). So was Matthew's address to the church's Jewish opponents (see pp. 175-77). So were Yahweh's words of judgment to Ahab through Elijah (1 Kings 21:17-24); note how Ahab was affected (21:27-29; see Davis 2002: 313-15). Cf. BAGD s.v. *ouai*. In LXX *ouai* translates both *'ôy* ('woe!') and *hôy* ('alas!').

[29]Elijah's journey to Zarephath (between Tyre and Sidon; 1 Kings 17:7-12) signals *both* that Yahweh is showing his favor to Gentiles (the widow and

will you not be ready, at last, to embrace the gospel for the poor, designed as it is for the wretched and the despairing (Matt. 11:5; 5:3-10; 9:12-13)? And will you not therefore come to me, learn of me and find rest for your souls (11:28-30)?

---

her son) *and* that he is removing his favor from Israel (Davis 2002: 214). Cf. Matthew 8:11-12; 15:21-28 (where Jesus goes to the region of Tyre and Sidon and imparts grace to a Canaanite woman and her daughter); Luke 4:16-30. There arose Christian communities in Tyre and Sidon, as we learn from Acts 21:3-6; 27:3.

III.
'JOIN ALL THE GLORIOUS NAMES'[1]
(11:25–12:21)

This passage celebrates the glorious splendor of Jesus' majesty (cf. Ps. 145:5). He is here declared to be the only Son of God the Father (Matt. 11:25-30); the Son of Man who is Lord of the Sabbath (12:1-14); and the Servant of Yahweh (12:15-21). The character of Messiah (11:2-6 *et seq.*) is now further disclosed. The more this manifold Christology grips us, the more we will be appalled by the plot of 12:14, and outraged by the blasphemy of 12:24; and the better we will understand the judgment of 12:32.

A. Jesus the Son of God (11:25-30)

By all indications, 11:2-24 reports events of a single period. These closing verses are closely joined chronologically to the rest of the chapter: 'At that time Jesus answered and said...' (11:25a). The present passage is also connected theologically to the preceding, especially to verses 16-24.[2] The picture of verses 16-17 does not apply to every Israelite of 'this generation': some of them are not *childish* in that way, but rather *childlike* in their response to the Father. Nor have *all* the inhabitants of those cities (11:20-24) remained unrepentant: as already observed, some have heeded the message of the kingdom (4:17) and have submitted as little

---

[1] The opening words of a hymn by Isaac Watts (1707).

[2] *Apokritheis...eipen* ('answering, said') sometimes occurs when no 'answer' is called for, as, e.g., in Matthew 28:5 (see *GGBB*, 650). But every prior instance of this participle (from *apokrinomai*) in Matthew denotes a response to someone (3:15; 4:4; 8:8; 11:4); and in 11:25 Jesus replies to what he himself said in the preceding verses. Hagner 1993: 315 translates, 'Jesus, responding to this unbelief, said....' The partial parallel to 11:25-30 in Luke (10:21-22) follows woes on the cities (vv. 13-15) and the return of the seventy-two missionaries (vv. 17-20).

children to the Father's benevolent rule. Moreover, among those to whom the Son now offers rest (11:28-30) are people who heretofore have spurned his grace and refused to repent.

The Father and His Children (11:25-26)

Jesus said: 'I praise you, Father, Lord of heaven and earth, because you have hidden these things from the wise and intelligent and have revealed them to the childlike. Yes, Father, because this was your good pleasure.'[3]

1. The Father's disclosure

Jesus' repeated address, 'Father' (*pater*, then *patēr*),[4] anticipates his words in 11:27 about the relationship between Son and Father. This address also recalls the prayer in 6:9-13, which likewise begins with *pater*. It was noted there that the Son's relationship to the Father is unique, but also that disciples are granted an inexpressibly deep communion with the Father because they belong to his Son.[5] Matthew 11:27 will witness to both those realities.

'These things' (*tauta*) which the Father has hidden from some and revealed to others (11:25) are the 'mighty works' of which Jesus has just spoken (11:20-24). In one sense, of course, Jesus' works were on display before all: those cities are judged *because* they witnessed these miracles but still refused to repent. Yet in another sense they *saw* these mighty works but did not *perceive* their meaning (note the use of these verbs in 13:14), despite Jesus' accompanying verbal explanations (e.g., 9:6; 12:28). As this prayer makes plain, the external evidence from the Son must be augmented by internal light from the Father. A human being cannot understand truth about God the Son unless God the Father *reveals* it (11:25b: the verb *apokalyptō*). One such 'little child' was Simon Peter: he confessed Jesus to be the Messiah, *the Son of the living God*

---

[3]As translated by Hagner 1993: 315-16.
[4]The *pater* of 11:25 is vocative; 11:26 uses the nominative *patēr* as a vocative.
[5]See further the comments on Matthew 6:9.

(16:16), because Jesus' Father had graciously disclosed this very truth to him (16:17, where *apokalyptō* recurs).[6]

2. The Father's good pleasure

In 11:26a, Jesus acclaims the action just described: 'Yes, Father [*nai ho patēr*].' He then explains why the Father conceals that truth from some, and reveals it to others: 'because [*hoti*] this [or thus: for the adverb *houtōs*] was your good pleasure [*eudokia*]' (11:26b). This *eudokia* may be considered in two ways, both based on the fact that the One who shows such favor is 'Lord of heaven and earth' (11:25a).

a. God's sovereign *initiative*. It is the Father's 'good pleasure' to reveal saving truth about his Son to those he has chosen for salvation, namely to his elect ones, and to withhold it from others. It is these *eklektoi* whom the angels will gather from the four winds at Jesus' second advent (Matt. 24:31).[7] Correspondingly, at his Son's first advent God commissioned a multitude of angels to proclaim 'peace among those with whom he is pleased' (Luke 2:14, ESV) – or, 'peace to men of [his] good pleasure [*eudokias*].'[8] In the language of Paul, God 'has predestined us for adoption as his own sons through Jesus Christ in accordance with his good pleasure [*kata tēn eudokian*] and will.... He has made known to us the mystery of his will, in accordance with his good pleasure [*kata tēn eudokian autou*] which he purposed in Christ' (Eph. 1:5, 9 [as translated by Lincoln 1990: 9]). The *ground* of salvation lies nowhere but in the Father's good pleasure and saving purpose. It is because the Father has granted them light and insight that the disciples respond favorably to Jesus' mighty works. The

---

[6]Given the rarity of *apokalyptō* in Matthew, the instances of 11:25 and 16:17 stand out all the more sharply (the verb appears only twice more, in 10:26 and 11:27). For the Father's witness to the Son, see also John 5:32, 36-37; 6:44-45; 8:18; 1 John 5:9-11. Davis (2002: 271-72) reflects on Jezebel's failure to be moved by Yahweh's 'mighty work' in 1 Kings 18: 'There was a blaze of light on Mt. Carmel, but unless Yahweh grants internal light to see his external light the darkness remains.' Cf. 1 Corinthians 2:6-16; and *WCF* 1.6, on the necessity of 'the inward illumination of the Spirit of God.'

[7]See also Matthew 24:22, 24; and 22:14 (with comments).

[8]For a defense of this reading of Luke 2:14b, see *TC*, 111, which adds that 'God's peace rests on those whom he has chosen in accord with his good pleasure.'

Son's praise for the Father's sovereign work (*Exomologoumai soi*, 'I thank you' [Matt. 11:25a]) anticipates the doxological theology of Eph. 1:3-14.

b. God's sovereign *response*. The Father also acts in accord with what he perceives in the human heart (cf. 1 Sam. 16:7; 1 Chron. 28:9; Ps. 138:6; Prov. 3:34). So on the one hand it is his *eudokia* to hide (the verb *kryptō*) truth about Jesus 'from the wise [*sophōn*] and intelligent [*synetōn*]' (Matt. 11:25b). It is not wisdom and intelligence as such that God opposes (how could we think so after reading Proverbs or 1 Corinthians?), but rather intellectual pride. Competitive as it is by nature, pride suppresses truth about God (he being the most serious threat to the proud) and instead makes human reason the final arbiter of truth.[9] Is not a prime explanation for certain Jews' opposition to Jesus, their reason's inability to fathom – and therefore its unwillingness to accept – that Jesus is both God and man?[10] Such thinking is not only a *cause* of God's judgment but also a *consequence*. God resists these proud persons (cf. James 4:6) by hiding from them the truth about his Son. Does not their indifference to his mighty works (Matt. 11:20-24) show how foolish they are? Does not the charge of 12:24 betray the speakers' stupidity? Yet on the other hand it is God's *eudokia* to give grace to the humble (James 4:6 again): he reveals (the verb *apokalyptō*) truth about Jesus to 'the childlike' (*nēpioi*, Matt. 11:25c). Jesus here speaks figuratively (hence this translation for *nēpioi* rather than 'little children'), as in 18:3, where he says listeners must 'become like little children [*paidia*]' to enter the kingdom of heaven.[11] This is not a call to become *innocent* (even *paidia* become selfish without the least instruction), but to be *trusting* and *teachable*, *helpless* and

[9]Pride likewise explains the hypocrisy of Matthew 6:1-18 (see p. 389). Cf. Romans 1:18-32.

[10]Cf., e.g., John 5:18. The truth about Jesus the God-man is not *irrational*; but neither can human reason fully *comprehend* it. The incarnate Christ both *dispels* and *deepens* the mystery of God; cf. Colossians 1:26-27; 2:2; 4:3 (and Chamblin 1993: 260-61).

[11]In Matthew 21:16, the one other instance of *nēpios* in Matthew, real little children are in view; cf. *pais* ('child') in Matthew 21:15. Little children may be childlike! See also the comments on 19:13-15.

dependent, in the presence of truth from God – or, in the language of Matthew 11:29, 'meek and humble in heart' (cf. 5:3, 5). The only hope for 'the wise and intelligent' is that they become 'childlike' in this sense. Let them acknowledge their sinful folly (1 Cor. 3:18) and humbly entreat God to grant them the true wisdom.[12]

With both those paragraphs in view, we may observe (i) that both the judgment against 'the wise and intelligent' and the salvation of 'the childlike' are foreordained by God; (ii) that the *cause* for the election of the latter and not the former lies not in human behavior (whether pride or faith), but solely in the *eudokia* of God's sovereign will; (iii) that the pride of 'the wise and intelligent' is to blame for God's hiding truth from them; (iv) that the faith of 'the childlike' is God's appointed means for the salvation of his elect; and (v) that 'the Lord of heaven and earth' is hereby praised, both for his justice (in the condemnation of the wicked) and for his mercy (in the salvation of his elect).[13]

3. Praying to the Father

How might the prayer of Jesus in Matthew 11:25-26, viewed together with that of 6:9-13, affect our own prayers? *a.* At the very moment Jesus uttered the words of verses 25-26, there were perhaps thousands of other prayers being offered to God. One of 'the childlike' might well ask: 'How can God hear all those prayers at one time?' But this Father is different from earthly fathers who may have difficulty listening to two children at once. He is 'the Father *in heaven*' (6:9), 'Lord *of heaven and earth*' (11:25). He is not imprisoned within time but reigns above time. He is not in fact listening to 'all those prayers *at one time*'; on the contrary, he 'has infinite attention to spare for each one of us.'[14] *b.* Since perceiving

---

[12]Such acknowledgment is itself a sign of wisdom. Paul's account in 1 Corinthians 1–4 of the conflict between 'the wisdom of God' and 'the wisdom of this age' (cf. Chamblin 1993: 116-21) illuminates the present text. Matthew 11:25, viewed together with 11:20-24 and 7:13-14, is a sober reminder how firm is pride's grip on fallen human beings.

[13]For support of these points, see John 6:35-65; Acts 13:48; Romans 8:29-30; 9:6–10:21; 11:33-36; Ephesians 1:3-14; Calvin 1960: 920-87 (3.21.1 through 3.24.17); WCF chapters 3, 9, 10, 14.

[14]Lewis 1952: 131. See the whole chapter, 'Time and Beyond Time,' 130-3. The same applies to space: see Psalm 113:4-6. When some years ago a Soviet cosmonaut returned to earth and announced that he had not found God in

the truth about Jesus depends on revelation from the Father, let us boldly and persistently ask him thus to illuminate our unbelieving friends.[15] Will not their salvation achieve the Father's will on earth, cause his name to be hallowed, and advance his rule (Matt. 6:9b-10)? Who knows how many of those scornful skeptics and proud professors are among God's elect? *c.* Having witnessed the salvation of 'the childlike' (including some from the ranks of 'the wise and intelligent'), let us too give thanks to the Father (11:25) for his goodness and grace.

The Father and the Son (11:27)

The linguistic simplicity of this text is matched by its theological profundity. 'All things [*Panta*] have been entrusted [*paredothē*] to me by [*hypo*] my Father,' begins Jesus. The neuter plural *panta* signals a manifold endowment: the Father so loves the Son that he gives all things into his hand.[16] The Father bestows the Spirit of wisdom and might (Matt. 3:16; 12:18 [cf. Isa. 11:2; Luke 4:18]). The Son is thus empowered to work miracles (chs. 8–9; 11:20-24 [the *panta* of v. 27 recalls the *tauta* of v. 25]; 12:28). He is also equipped to teach (chs. 5–7, 10). The verb in 11:27a, *paradidōmi*, was used to denote the transmission of sacred tradition (so, e.g., in 1 Cor. 15:3); but whereas 'the tradition [*paradosis*] of the elders' (15:2) was traced from one authorized rabbi back through another, through the men of the great synagogue (in the post-exilic time) to Moses, Jesus receives instruction directly from his Father (note the preposition *hypo*) – the One who imparted the Torah to Moses in the first place.[17]

---

outer space, C. S. Lewis replied that the really surprising thing would have been his *finding* God in outer space. Cf. comments on 6:9.

[15]For calls to such prayer, see, e.g., Matthew 7:7-11 (and comments); Luke 11:5-13 (where the promise of the Holy Spirit [v. 13] includes his own enlightening work); 18:1-8.

[16]Cf. Matthew 3:17, 'my Son [*ho huios mou*], the beloved [*ho agapētos*]'; John 3:35, 'the Father loves [*agapa*] the Son [*ton huion*], and has given [*dedōken*] all things [*panta*] into his hand' (see also John 13:3). The verb *paradidōmi* (Matt. 11:27) is a compound of *didōmi*, used in John 3:35. The form in Matthew 11:27 – *paredothē*, an aorist passive indicative – is a 'divine passive' (like the *edothē* of 28:18); in this instance the subject is explicit ('by my Father').

This is one reason Jesus' teaching possesses an authority lacking in that of the scribes (Matt. 7:28-29), which is to say that among the *panta* which the Father grants the Son is the universal authority (*pasa exousia*) of 28:18.[18] Yet foremost among those *panta* are people – as is clear from the prayer of 11:25 (with its reference to 'the childlike'), the remainder of 11:27 and the appeal of 11:28-30 (with its masculine *pantes* [11:28a]).

Jesus continues: 'and no one knows [*epiginōskei*] the Son except the Father; nor does anyone know [*epiginōskei*] the Father except the Son' (Matt. 11:27b). Jesus affords a glimpse into the incomparable and incomprehensible communion between Father and Son. In the verb used here, *ginōskō* ('know') is prefaced by the preposition *epi*. In some such compounds the preposition intensifies the meaning, so that *epiginōskō* might be rendered 'fully know.'[19] But a simple 'know' (as in the above translation) suffices: sometimes the adding of a preposition does not affect the meaning of the verb; the parallel in Luke 10:22 uses *ginōskō*; and the rest of Matthew 11:27 shows this to be the fullest and deepest knowledge imaginable.[20] Moreover, it is plain from other texts (i) that the language of 'knowing' expresses not just intellectual recognition but the love that Father and Son have for one another; (ii) that the Holy Spirit participates in this holy communion; and (iii) that the knowledge of 11:27c-30 is *based on* and *akin to*, but not *equivalent to*, the knowledge of verse 27b; i.e., that believers will truly know God, but not in

---

[17]For *paradidōmi* to denote transmission of tradition, see BAGD s.v., 3. As the Son is taught by (*hypo*) by the Father, there is no room for an intermediary: contrast Matthew 1:22, 'spoken *by* [*hypo*] the Lord *through* [*dia*] the prophet.' See comments on Matthew 15:1-9; cf. John 5:19-20; 7:16-18.

[18]Such *exousia* includes the right to judge (Matt. 19:28; 25:31; John 5:22). Were the *paredothē* of Matthew 11:27 equivalent in meaning to the *edothē* of 28:18, it could be considered a 'proleptic (or futuristic) aorist' (*GGBB*, 563-64). But the verb in 11:27 has a broader meaning (as we saw above), so it is to be considered a 'constative (or comprehensive) aorist' (*GGBB*, 557-58).

[19]Thus, e.g., Hagner 1993: 316, 320.

[20]For this understanding of *epiginōskō*, see BAGD s.v., 2. (contrast 1.). Compounding a preposition with a verb may intensify the meaning, change the meaning or have 'no effect at all' (*GGNT*, 562-63).

the very way the Father, the Son and the Holy Spirit know each other.[21]

The sentence concludes: 'and anyone to whom the Son wills [*boulētai*] to reveal [*apokalypsai*] him' (11:27c). Knowledge between the Father and the Son is incomparable, but it is not exclusive. Each reveals to human beings truth about the other: this aorist infinitive of *apokalyptō* recalls the aorist indicative of this verb in 11:25; in each case persons receive instruction from the One who best knows the other. The Son's 'willing' (the verb *boulomai*) corresponds to the Father's 'good pleasure' (*eudokia*, 11:26); and it is implied that the Son reveals the Father to the very kind of people the Father chooses, namely 'the childlike' (*nēpioi*, 11:25).[22] Nor do 11:25 and 27 represent different curricula: as Matthew 11:27b itself reveals, it is vital not only to know the first and second persons in the Godhead, but to know them as *Father and Son*, i.e., to know *the relationship between them*.[23]

---

[21]For (i) see John 3:35; 5:20; 10:15, 17; 15:9; 1 John 4:7-8; cf. 1 Corinthians 8:3; Philippians 1:9; Ephesians 3:19; for (ii), Matthew 3:16-17 (and p. 267, including n. 34); 28:19; 1 Corinthians 2:11; 2 Corinthians 13:13; for (iii), comments on pages 140, 406-7 about the uniqueness of Jesus' sonship.

[22]Cf. the closing paragraph in the commentary on Matthew 3. For the Son's disclosure of the Father, see also John 1:18; 3:31-34; 10:32; 12:44-45; 14:9-11; 17:6, 25-26. The remarks about the Father's sovereign *initiative* and *response* (pp. 628-30) apply also to the Son; note how Paul joins *eudokia* to *boulē* ('purpose, plan') and *thelēma* ('will, wish') in Ephesians 1:5-11. As all these disclosures are for 'the childlike,' loving God with all one's being (Matt. 22:37) counts for far more than one's intellectual capacity. 'The width of our knowledge about [God] is no gauge of the depth of our knowledge of him. John Owen and John Calvin knew more theology than John Bunyan or Billy Bray, but who would deny that the latter pair knew their God every bit as well as the former? (All four, of course, were beavers for the Bible, which counts for far more anyway than a formal theological training)' (Packer 1973: 34).

[23]Following Theodor Zahn, Stonehouse 1958: 212 comments that 'the knowledge of the Father and the knowledge of the Son are two sides of the same mystery, which is now revealed, and so the Father and the Son in fellowship with one another are both subject and object of revelation.' This disclosure serves in turn as a spur to Christian unity (John 17:11, 21-23).

The Son and His People (11:28-30)

Jesus' words in 11:25-26 are a prayer to the Father; those of verse 27 are a declaration in the hearing of the crowds (cf. 11:7). Jesus now appeals directly to his listeners: 'I will give *you* rest...*you* will find rest' (11:28-29). Verses 28-30 are clearly to be interpreted in the light of (and, by all indications, were spoken at the time as) verses 25-27; and as noted on page 626, these closing six verses are joined both chronologically and theologically to the rest of the chapter, especially to verses 16-24.

'Come to me, all who are weary and burdened [*pantes hoi kopiōntes kai pephortismenoi*], and I will give you rest [*kagō anapausō hymas*]' (Matt. 11:28). Jesus addresses persons who toil under burdens others have imposed on them. Scribes and Pharisees 'tie up heavy burdens [*phortia*], hard to carry, and place them on men's shoulders' (23:4); lawyers ' burden [*phortizete*] men with burdens [*phortia*] hard to carry' (Luke 11:46).[24]

While human commands are doubtless included (cf. Matt. 15:1-9), the principal 'burdens' are God's own laws. Do not the scribes and Pharisees 'sit on Moses' seat,' and does not Jesus command his followers to practice what they teach (23:2-3a [words spoken just before the censure quoted above])? Are not God's laws far *weightier* than man's (Acts 15:10)? Does not the law Jesus condemns in Matthew 15:5 *relieve* people of the burden of honoring their parents (15:4, 6)? In light of all that, Jesus makes his present appeal; most significantly, he first calls burdened people to himself ('Come to me,' 11:28a), and only thereafter to his law ('Take my yoke,' 11:29a). 'And *I* [*kagō*] will give you rest,' he promises (11:28c).[25] Otherwise, trying to keep the law – even God's law – will bring you toil and misery.

---

[24]Matthew 11:28 and Luke 11:46 account for the only two instances of the verb *phortizō* in the NT: the first text uses a perfect passive participle ('having been burdened'), the second a present active indicative ('you burden'). Matthew 11:30; 23:4; and Luke 11:46 contain the only instances of the noun *phortion* in the gospels. The parallel terms *grammateis* ('scribes') and *nomikoi* identify experts in Jewish law (*nomos*).

[25]The subject of this clause is contained in the verb *anapausō*: 'I will give rest.' The presence of *kagō* – the conjunction *kai* + the personal pronoun *egō* – makes the 'I' emphatic.

Without me, you can do nothing (John 15:5); in my power, you can do all I require (Phil. 4:13). The help other teachers refuse (Matt. 23:4b), I will provide (11:28-30). Those teachers' hearts are far from God (15:4); I know and love the Father as does no other (11:25-27). As Jesus also exemplifies love of neighbor, he issues this invitation to faithful law-keepers who, loving God and desiring to obey him, feel the weight of his commands most acutely; to transgressors of the law who will not or cannot bear its burdens; to scholars and teachers of the law whose own disobedience (23:3) reveals law-keeping to be a greater burden for them than might appear; and to persons (including some of the above) who heretofore have spurned or opposed his witness (11:16-25).[26]

'Take my yoke upon you, and learn from me, because I am meek and humble in heart, and you will find rest for yourselves' (11:29). 1. *The yoke.* A yoke (Greek *zygos*, Hebrew *'ōl*) on one's neck and shoulders was a means for bearing a load.[27] Used figuratively, the term could denote both servitude to an oppressive master and service to Yahweh – who is also praised as the One who frees his people from the yoke of slavery.[28] Jewish sources from Jesus' time and afterwards speak of serving Yahweh as accepting 'the yoke of the law' or 'the yoke of the kingdom.' Accordingly, verse 11:29a – 'Take my yoke [*arate ton zygon mou*] upon you' – is a command to submit to God's rule as Jesus proclaims it, and to God's law as

---

[26]The Beatitudes (Matt. 5:3-12) were likewise an overture of grace to non-disciples (see pp. 326-30). That God incarnate appeals in 11:28 to persons heretofore hostile to him and his teachings should not surprise us: ponder Yahweh's grace to Ahab in 1 Kings 20:1-22 (Davis 2002: 287-91).

[27]A 'man who carries a load places the yoke upon his neck and shoulders, so that the load may be taken by the chains or cords at each end of the yoke' (Jeremias 1963: 194). Oxen might be joined together under one yoke to pull a plow or cart (note the use of *zeugos* in Luke 14:19).

[28]'Yoke' denotes oppressive servitude, or Yahweh's rescue from it, in Leviticus 26:13; Deuteronomy 28:48; 1 Kings 12:4; Isaiah 9:4; 10:27; Jeremiah 28:4; 30:8; Ezekiel 34:27. It denotes service to Yahweh, or people's efforts to be freed from it, in Jeremiah 2:20; 5:5; Lamentations 3:27; Hosea 10:11a ('I placed upon her neck a fine yoke' – 'enabling good work, not burdensome...': so Andersen and Freedman 1980: 560, 567); Zephaniah 3:9 (LXX, 'to serve [Yahweh] under one yoke').

Jesus expounds it. The expression '*my* yoke' (*mou* is a genitive of possession) reflects Jesus' unique authority as Yahweh incarnate to establish that rule and to interpret that law.[29] 2. *The teacher.* In commanding listeners to wear his yoke, Jesus appears to be increasing rather than lightening their load; for God's laws as expounded by the New Moses (e.g., 5:17-48) are the *weightiest* of all. For this very reason, Jesus directs attention on the character of the teacher himself: 'and learn from me [*mathete ap' emou*],[30] because I am meek and humble in heart [*hoti praus eimi kai tapeinos tē kardia*]' (11:29b). This is the sort of language Jesus used in the beatitudes: the plural of *praus* occurs in 5:5, and *tapeinos tē kardia* is very close to *ptōchoi tō pneumati*, 5:3 (and the Son who knows the Father,11:27, is utterly *katharos tē kardia*, 5:8).[31] That is, Jesus identifies himself as a person who needs, trusts and obeys God (see pp. 313-20). Unlike the teachers of Matthew 23:3, he submits to God's rule and keeps his commands. He chiefly instructs his students by *embodying* the truth he expounds (see p. 322-24); he himself is his most potent lesson. He, the lowly Servant, deals gently and mercifully with the weary and the erring (12:17-21; 9:13; cf. the Servant's words in Isaiah 50:4). Himself 'meek and humble

---

[29]For Jewish sources, see Keener 1999: 348, n. 36. K. H. Rengstorf, *TDNT* 2: 900, recognizes the correspondence between 'my yoke' (Matt. 11:29) and 'the yoke of the law.' Jesus' words in 11:28-30 recall the invitation of Joshua ben Sira at the close of the apocryphal book Ecclesiasticus: 'Draw near to me, you who are uneducated.... Place your neck under the yoke, and let your soul accept training – she is near if you wish to find her. Witness with your own eyes that I have labored little, yet have found much rest for myself' (from 51:23-27; translation in Keener 1999: 349). 'No doubt Jesus and his hearers knew and valued this book, but Jesus' invitation reveals a higher authority: it is his own yoke that he offers, and he himself gives the rest which Ben Sira had to win by his "little labours"' (France 1985: 200). On the relation between these two passages, see further Gundry 1994: 220; Keener, ibid.

[30]All three instances of the verb *manthanō* in Matthew take the form *mathete*, a second aorist imperative of command; see also 9:13; 24:32. As a constative (or comprehensive) aorist, *mathete* envisages the learning as a whole (cf. *GGBB*, 557-58). The preceding *arate* ('take') is a constative (or punctiliar) aorist (ibid.).

[31]See pages 314 (with n. 8), 317 (with n. 17). Numbers 12:3 describes the first Moses as 'very meek' [LXX *praus sphodra*].'

in heart,' he is not too proud to bear the burdens of the frail and the fallen (Matt. 8:17; 20:25-28; contrast 23:4b). Moreover, in his *meekness* (*prautēs*) he *conquers* the powers of darkness.[32] And since the Son discloses his Father (11:27b), those who study Jesus learn that the Father too is 'meek and humble in heart.'[33] 3. *The rest.* Once you obey those commands – 'take' (*arate*) and 'learn' (*mathete*) – 'you will find rest for yourselves [*tais psychais hymōn*]' (11:29c). Disciples find rest (the noun *anapausis*) because Jesus gives rest (the verb *anapauō*; 11:28); and paradoxically, they find rest by 'taking up Jesus' yoke' – by obeying his commands.

What better example than the fourth commandment, which dominates 12:1-14? One experiences the sabbath *rest* precisely by keeping the sabbath *command*; and it is rest not just for the 'soul' (so most translations of 11:29c), but for the body as well.[34] Yet, this only happens for persons intimately related to 'the Lord of the Sabbath' (12:8). In Jesus' hands, the law is an instrument of grace, a guide for loving God and neighbor. Wielded by alien powers (demonic or human), the law becomes enslaving and destructive.[35]

'For [*gar*] my yoke [*ho...zygos mou*] is easy to wear [*chrēstos*], and my burden [*to phortion mou*] is easy to bear [*elaphron*]' (Matt. 11:30). Joined to the preceding by the opening *gar*,

---

[32]The meek figure of Matthew 11:29 is the warrior of 12:28-29. The lowly king of 21:5 (where *praus* recurs) establishes peace by conquering the malevolent powers. Paul appeals to Christ's meekness (*prautēs*; 2 Cor. 10:1) in a context of battle (10:2-6). The Spirit grants meekness (*prautēs*; Gal. 5:23), so that Christians may conquer the works of the flesh (5:16-26).

[33]The same holds true in Philippians 2:6-8 (cf. Chamblin 1993: 66-7, 121-2). On the other hand, if Jesus 'were merely a man, humility and meekness are the very last characteristics we could attribute to some of His sayings' (Lewis 1952: 40); cf. above, page 489, n. 61.

[34]In Matthew 11:29, *psychē* denotes one's whole earthly life (so too in 2:20; 6:25); in 10:28-31, the 'soul' as distinct from the 'body.' See page 447, n. 38.

[35]In Pauline terms, sin uses the law destructively (Rom. 7:7-14); so do the demons (Gal. 4:3-11). Law keeping without Christ becomes 'a yoke [*zygos*] of slavery' (Gal. 5:1); those bound to 'the law of Christ' love their neighbors and bear their loads (5:14; 6:2). To honor the Sabbath command, one must hold fast to Christ the Head (Col. 2:16-19). Cf. Chamblin 1988: 188-95; ibid., 1993: 49-50, 53, 149-51. So too in the OT, those who loved the Lawgiver found liberty and rest in keeping his law (cf. Ps. 119 *passim*; Jer. 6:16).

this verse further explains the rest promised in 11:29c. The yoke and the burden are distinguishable but inseparable: 'the function of a yoke (the sort worn by humans) is to make a burden easier to carry.'[36] In verse 30, the 'yoke' stands for Jesus' commands, and the 'burden' for the law keeping he requires. Both remain *his*: each instance of *mou* here, as in verse 29 (*ton zygon mou*), is a genitive of possession. This means both that Jesus himself keeps his commands, and that he helps his people to do so (see again John 15:5; Phil. 4:13). To the latter end, he imparts to them his empowering Spirit (see, e.g., Gal. 5:16–6:5; Rom. 8:1-17). Therefore, his commands are 'not burdensome' (1 John 5:3).[37]

Jesus' overture of grace (Matt. 11:28-30) is sounded in the presence of persons already threatened with condemnation (cf. 11:6, 16-24). If they refuse *this* invitation, what hope can remain for them?

B. Jesus the Lord of the Sabbath (12:1-14)

This passage is joined to the preceding both chronologically (the opening of 12:1, 'At that time,' *En ekeinō tō kairō*, is identical to that of 11:25) and theologically (the promise of rest; 11:28-30) introduces teaching about the Sabbath (forms of *sabbaton* occur eight times in 12:1-14). These verses record two episodes from a single Sabbath day, probably in Capernaum.[38]

---

[36]France 1985: 201; cf. above, n. 27. My younger daughter uses the 'yoke' of a strap to carry the 'burden' of a guitar. Cf. Isaiah 58:6: 'the cords of the yoke.'

[37]A Jewish writer, Haym Solevetchik, says 'the perception of God as a daily, natural force is no longer present to a significant degree in any sector of modern Jewry, even the most religious .... Zealous to continue traditional Judaism unimpaired, religious Jews seek to ground their new emerging spirituality less on a now unattainable intimacy with Him, than on an intimacy with His Will, avidly eliciting Its intricate demands and saturating their daily lives with Its exactions. Having lost the touch of His presence, they now seek solace in the pressure of His yoke': quoted by Lauren F. Winner, *Books & Culture*, Nov/Dec 2000, 14. Winner (a Jewish Christian) responds: 'Indeed, there is something about a God-made-flesh that facilitates relationship. That was the first thing that attracted me to Jesus.... Christianity is made for intimacy.... The dichotomy between law and God's will on the one hand, and intimacy and relationship on the other, is ultimately a false one: one achieves intimacy with God by doing His will.'

In both, the Pharisees oppose Jesus' conduct. At the heart of the passage, both literally and thematically, stands the great declaration of verse 12:8: it both climaxes the first episode and introduces the second.

Plucking Grain on the Sabbath (12:1-8)

The Pharisees, having witnessed the disciples' behavior, charge them with law breaking (Matt. 12:1-2). Verses 3-8 are devoted exclusively to the answering words of Jesus. He confronts the accusers, and refutes their accusation, by appealing in turn to all three divisions of the Hebrew Bible – Torah (12:5-6), the Prophets (both Former, 12:3-4, and Latter, 12:7) and the Writings (12:8).[39] The whole paragraph attests to the truth of verse 8.

1. Disciples and Pharisees (12:1-2)

'At that time Jesus went through the grain fields on the Sabbath. His disciples were hungry, and they began to pluck heads of grain and to eat' (12:1). This is the first reference to the Sabbath day in Matthew: here the form is plural (*tois sabbasin*), as also in 12:5a and 12:10-12; the singular occurs (with no change of meaning) in 12:2, 5b and 8.[40] All three Synoptists report that the disciples plucked the heads of grain, which was probably wheat.[41] Both Matthew and Luke report that the men ate what

---

[38]Parallel to Matthew 12:1-14 is Mark 2:23-3:6. Cf. Mark 1:21 ('they went into Capernaum...he entered the synagogue'); 1:29 ('he left the synagogue'); 2:1 ('when he returned to Capernaum'); 2:23 ('One Sabbath'); 3:1 ('And again he entered the synagogue', par. to Matthew 12:9).

[39]First was *Torah* (Genesis through Deuteronomy); then *Prophets*, Former (Joshua through Kings) and Latter (Isaiah through Malachi); then *Writings* (Psalms through Chronicles: Ruth, Esther, Lamentations and Daniel were included here). Cf. Matthew 23:35 (and comments); Luke 24:44 (where the Writings are represented by Psalms, the first and longest book in this division).

[40]See BAGD s.v. *sabbaton*, 1. Sabbath, a. (singular) and b. (plural). Beyond 12:1-14, *sabbaton* occurs only three times in Matthew: the singular of 24:20 refers to the day; the plurals of 28:1 denote respectively the day and the week (BAGD s.v., 2.). Davies and Allison 1991: 320 (and Jeremias 1971: 6) think the plural stands for the 'emphatic singular' of the Aramaic *šabbᵉtā'*. Hagner 1993: 328 (with BDF, par. 141.3) explains *tois sabbasin* as 'the plural used of festivals.'

they picked.[42] But Matthew alone expressly states that they 'were hungry' (*epeinasan*): on the significance of this, see below. No Synoptist says that Jesus himself plucked or ate grain; but his silence implies approval of the disciples' action.

'Having seen this, the Pharisees said to him, "Look, your disciples are doing what is not lawful to do on the Sabbath"' (Matt. 12:2). They address Jesus, as a teacher responsible for his disciples' conduct. In the other gospels their words take the form of a question – put to Jesus in Mark 6:24, and to the disciples in Luke 6:2. In Matthew, the response is heightened into an accusation.[43] The act itself is permissible: 'If you go into your neighbor's standing grain, you may pluck the ears [LXX *stachys*] with your hand, but you shall not put a sickle to your neighbor's standing grain' (Deut. 23:25, ESV). What is 'not lawful' (*ouk exestin*), they contend, is doing such reaping on the Sabbath. Says Exodus 34:21: 'Six days you shall work, but on the seventh day you shall rest. In plowing time and in harvest you shall rest' (ESV).[44] Adding weight to the charge are (i) the opening 'Look' (*idou*); (ii) the repeated verb *poieō* (they '*are doing* [*poiousin*] what is not lawful *to do* [*poiein*]'); and (iii) the placement of the phrase *en sabbatō* at the close of the statement.[45]

---

[41]Forms of *tillō* ('pluck, pick') occur in 12:1; Mark 2:23 (which adds that they were 'making their way'); Luke 6:1. *Sitos*, Matthew 3:12; 13:25, 29, 30, meant 'wheat' (so ESV in all these instances), then 'grain' generally (BAGD s.v.). Cf. Mark 4:28 (NASB): '...first the blade, then the head [*stachyn*], then the mature grain [*siton*] in the head.' Wheat and barley were the main crops in Palestine (cf. Ruth 2:23; Joel 1:11), wheat being the more valuable (F. N. Hepper, 'Agriculture,' *IBD*, 20). A better translation than 'corn' for the Hebrew *dāgān* is 'grain' (see Gen. 27:28 in KJV and NKJV respectively). Still, the REB of Matthew 12:1 says that 'Jesus was going through the cornfields,' and that his disciples 'began to pluck some ears of corn....'

[42]Forms of the verb *esthiō* ('eat') occur in 12:1 and Luke 6:1 (which adds that they were 'rubbing [the heads] with their hands').

[43]See Gundry 1994: 222. The Pharisees' actual response may well have included both declarative and interrogative sentences.

[44]Reaping was 'one of the 39 areas of work explicitly forbidden on the Sabbath according to Mishnah *Shabbath* 7:2' (France 1985: 202). See Keener 1999: 353, for other such references.

[45]The word order in Mark 2:24 ('why are *they doing on the Sabbath* what is not lawful?') focuses more on the disciples' act. The order in Matthew

2. Jesus and the Former Prophets (12:3-4)

Jesus asks: 'Have you not read what David did when he was hungry, and those with him – how he went into the house of God, and they ate the loaves of the presence, which it was not lawful for him to eat nor for those with him, but for the priests alone?' Jesus' rejoinder to the accusing statement is an accusing question. 'Have you not read [*Ouk anegnōte*]...?' expects a positive reply (i.e., Surely you Bible scholars are well acquainted with the story of 1 Samuel 21:1-6?).[46] But the question implies that these 'wise and intelligent' people have not yet perceived the true import of the passage (cf. Matt. 11:25).

David went into 'the house of God' – into the tabernacle, at that time located at Nob.[47] There in the holy place, opposite the lampstand, stood a wooden table, overlaid with gold, concerning which Yahweh had commanded: 'And you shall set upon the table the bread of the Presence [*lechem pānîm*] before me [*lᵉpānay*] continually' (Exod. 25:30), Hebrew terms to which the Greek of Matthew 12:4a (*tous artous tēs protheseōs*) exactly corresponds. These twelve loaves served as a reminder that Yahweh had been unceasingly faithful to the twelve tribes (not least in providing their daily bread [Exod. 16]), and that the Israelites lived perpetually in his holy presence; pure incense was sprinkled on the loaves and offered by fire as a memorial to Yahweh (Lev. 24:5-7). Each Sabbath, the high priest was to provide new loaves in place of the old, which were then to be eaten inside the holy place by the priest and his sons, by them and no others, since the bread is 'a most holy portion out of Yahweh's food offerings' (Lev. 24:8-9; 1 Sam. 21:6; Matt. 12:4b). According to this regulation, David and his men did indeed eat what was 'not lawful' (*ho exon* [12:4], echoing *ouk exestin* [12:2]) for them to eat.[48]

12:2 (they 'are doing what is not lawful to do *on the Sabbath*') focuses more directly on the Sabbath law itself. See Gundry 1994: 222; Hagner 1993: 327 (*en sabbatō* stands 'in the emphatic final position').

[46]On this use of *ouk*, see BDF par. 427. Cf. Jesus' question to a Pharisee in John 3:10.

[47]Nob (1 Sam. 21:1) was one or two miles north of Jerusalem (cf. Isaiah 32:10; and R. A. H. Gunner, 'Nob,' *IBD*, 1093).

[48]See also Exodus 25:23-30; 26:35; 37:10-16; D. Freeman, 'Showbread,' *IBD*, 1447.

Neither 1 Samuel 21 nor Matthew 12 indicates that David entered the house of God on a Sabbath, although there is a link between 1 Samuel 21:6 and Matthew 12:5 (see below).[49] Nor does Jesus reflect upon the ethics of David's behavior toward Ahimelech.[50] Instead, Jesus tacitly argues from the lesser to the greater (Hebrew *qal wachomer*, 'light and heavy'): 1. David is Yahweh's anointed (though not yet reigning) king (1 Sam. 16). He and his men are hungry (Matt. 12:3, *epeinasen*), perhaps acutely so, since they are fugitives from Saul; and to satisfy that hunger, they eat (12:4, *ephagon*).[51] Yahweh uses the holy bread from the tabernacle to supply their daily bread;[52] and he hereby honors the *sixth* commandment (Exod. 6:13), one purpose of which is to sustain human life. Jesus thus respects and upholds the OT, in this case a passage from the prophets (cf. Matt. 5:17). 2. Jesus' disciples are also hungry (12:1, *epeinasan*), and they too satisfy their hunger by eating (12:1, *esthiein*) food of the same nature as that supplied to David.[53] Is not '*daily* bread' (6:11) promised for the Sabbath, as well as for other days? Is not Yahweh here feeding Jesus' disciples as surely as he fed David and his men?[54] And if God thus favored David, his chosen king, *how much more fitting* that he honor the followers of his beloved Son, the King appointed to reign from David's throne forever? Moreover, if David was

---

[49]According to a Jewish tradition, this episode occurred on a Sabbath (Gundry 1994: 223).

[50]Nor does the writer of 1 Samuel (despite 21:2): 'the text neither condemns nor justifies' David; his conduct is not recommended, only reported (Davis 2000: 175).

[51]The parallels in Mark 2:26 and Luke 6:4 read *ephagen* ('he ate'). So, at Matthew 12:4, the plural *ephagon* ('they ate') is more likely to have been changed to *ephagen* than vice versa (*TC*, 26). David brought out the bread of the Presence to share with his companions (ibid.).

[52]This is well affirmed by Davis 2000: 176. David 'had need [*chreian*]' (Mark 2:25).

[53]*Esthiein* is a present infinitive, and *ephagon* (Matt. 12:4) an aorist indicative, of *esthiō*, 'eat.' The 'heads' of Matthew 12:1 may have been wheat (n. 41); the loaves of the Presence may have been made from 'wheaten flour' (NJB at Leviticus 24:5).

[54]'Whereas the law forbade *preparing* food on the Sabbath [Exod. 16:22-30; 35:3]...it certainly did not forbid *eating* it..., and Jewish people kept the Sabbath with joyous feasting' (Keener 1999: 353).

allowed to suspend a stipulation of the law, *how much greater* the right of the Lord of the Sabbath to do so. A far greater one than David has appeared on the scene; and he has come, not to correct the law but to transcend it.[55]

3. Jesus and the Torah (12:5-6)

'Or have you not read in the law [*en tō nomō*], that on the Sabbath the priests in the temple profane the Sabbath yet are guiltless?' (Matt. 12:5). This question is formulated like that of verse 3 (it too begins *ouk anegnōte*), and with the same intent: you scholars will surely know these passages from the *Torah* (is it not your foundational authority?); yet your accusation betrays your blindness to their true meaning. Having argued from an historical episode, Jesus now alludes to legal texts, namely those that instruct the priests to change the bread of the Presence on the Sabbath (Lev. 24:8; 1 Sam. 21:6), and to double the burnt offerings (Num. 28:9-10).[56]

The Sabbath is thus profaned (the verb *bebēloō*); yet the priests are guiltless (*anaitioi*), because their actions are stipulated by the law itself and thus by God himself.[57] This means that, in some sense, the temple is more important than the Sabbath, the holy *place* more sacred than the holy *day*. And what could that sense be, except (i) that the main reason the covenant people exist is to love, worship and serve Yahweh; (ii) that Yahweh chose the tabernacle (the 'house,' *oikos*, of Matthew 12:4), then the temple (*hieron*; Matthew 12:5) to be

---

[55]For this line of argument, see also France 1971: 46-47; 1985: 202-03. Cf. my earlier remarks on typology in Matthew (pp. 123-29, especially 126-27, on persons as types and antitypes); also the comments on 5:17-20.

[56]Jesus appeals to the *nomos* (legal texts) within the *nomos* (Torah); *nomos* in Matthew 12:5 appears to embrace both senses (cf. *nomos* in 5:17-18; 7:12; 11:13; 22:36, 40). The argument of 12:5 is *halachic* (from the Hebrew verb *hālak*, 'to go, walk'); it invokes tenets of law prescribing how one is to 'walk,' i.e., to live. This augments the argument of 12:3-4, which is *haggadic* (from the verb *nāgad*, 'to report, tell'); it infers a lesson from an OT story. Thus Gundry 1994: 223.

[57]'When He says that the Sabbath was profaned by the priests, it was imprecise language; Christ was adapting Himself to his hearers. For when the Law commands men to abstain from their works, it does not forbid holy work' (Calvin 1995a: 29). Cf. Carson 1984: 281.

his special dwelling place, and tells his people to show their
love for him by worshiping and serving him there; and (iii)
that the Sabbath day serves that manifold purpose?[58]

'But I tell you, that something greater [*meizon*] than the
temple is here' (Matt. 12:6). Jesus' use of *meizon*, a neuter
comparative adjective, might suggest a non-personal reality
akin to the temple of God – namely the eschatological
rule of God. But the 'something greater' is primarily if not
exclusively Jesus himself: the neuter 'stresses the quality of
superior greatness rather than Jesus' personal identity'; and
see 12:41-42, where another neuter adjective (*pleion*) appears
in comparisons with OT *persons*.[59] The *qal wachomer* argument
is now enlarged: if Jesus is greater than the temple, and the
temple is greater than the Sabbath, then he is greater than the
Sabbath as well; and if those temple priests who profane the
Sabbath are innocent, then *how much plainer* the innocence of
disciples whose master is both Lord of the temple and Lord
of the Sabbath?

4. Jesus and the Latter Prophets (12:7)
'But if you had known what this means – "I desire mercy and
not sacrifice" – you would not have condemned the guiltless.'
Augmenting his references to the Former Prophets (12:3-4)
and the Torah (12:5-6), Jesus invokes the Latter Prophets
by quoting Hosea 6:6a. He now censures the scholars more
explicitly than before: 'if you had known [*ei...egnōkeite*]...

---

[58]For (i) see Exodus 20:2-7; Deuteronomy 5:2-11; 6:1-5; for (ii), Exodus
25-31, 35-40; Leviticus *passim*; Deuteronomy 12:1-28; 1 Kings 8:22-53;
for (iii), Exodus 16:22-30 (23, 'a holy Sabbath to Yahweh'); 20:8-11 (10, 'a
Sabbath to Yahweh your God'); 31:12-17 (14-15, 'the Sabbath...holy for
you...holy to Yahweh'); Leviticus 23:3 ('a holy convocation' on the Sabbath);
Deuteronomy 5:12-15; Isaiah 56:1-8; 58:13-14. Thus the idea that the temple
is more important because it was made for God and the Sabbath for man
(Mark 2:27) is simplistic (cf. Gundry 1994: 224): both temple and Sabbath are
for man, but each primarily exists for the glory of God. Cf. *WSC* nos. 57-62.

[59]The quotation is from Gundry 1994: 223. Cf. Davies and Allison 1991:
314; *GNTG* 3: 21 ('the neuter gender may refer to a person...provided that
the emphasis is less on the individual than on some outstanding general
quality'); NIV's 'one greater' (Matt. 12:6, 41, 42). Of course, Jesus reveals his
'superior greatness' by ushering in God's final rule; cf. 12:28.

you would not have condemned [*ouk an katedikasate*]....'[60] In Matthew 9:13, Jesus quoted these very words to explain his table fellowship with sinners; those comments apply to the present passage too. Here, as there, Hosea's words are crucial. Does not Yahweh himself show mercy (*eleos*; Hebrew *chesed*) to the priests who serve him in the temple (Matt. 12:5-6) to David and his men (12:3-4) and to Jesus' disciples (12:1)? Has he not in mercy granted his people a day of rest every week? Does not the fourth commandment – which contains no directions for offering sacrifices – show that Yahweh chiefly desires mercy from his people? Will not 'obedience to the voice of Yahweh' as recorded in Exodus 20:8-11 find expression in deeds of mercy rather than in 'offerings and sacrifices' (cf. 1 Sam. 15:22)?[61] Are not such deeds evidence that the merciful (Matt. 5:7) know the merciful God (cf. Hos. 6:6b, 'and the knowledge of God rather than burnt offerings')? As the OT priests were 'guiltless' (*anaitioi*, 12:5) in Yahweh's eyes, so does Yahweh incarnate consider his disciples to be (*tous anaitious*, 12:7). Do not the Pharisees, on the contrary, value the *ceremonial* dimension of the Sabbath law above the *ethical*? Do they not, in the terms of Hosea 6:6, desire sacrifice and not mercy? The fact that the action of Matt. 12:1 evokes their condemnation rather than their mercy (which might have found expression in silence!), betrays their ignorance not only of the Scriptures but of God himself.

5. Jesus and the Writings (12:8)

'For [*gar*] the Son of Man [*ho huios tou anthrōpou*] is Lord [*kyrios*] of the Sabbath.' Jesus, invoking the third and final

---

[60]Verse 7 takes the form of a second-class (or contrary-to-fact) conditional sentence (on which see *GGBB*, 694-96). As is typical in such a construction, the protasis (or 'if clause') contains the conjunction *ei* ('if'); the apodosis contains the particle *an*; and both clauses contain an indicative verb in a secondary tense (a pluperfect of *ginōskō*, 'know,' in the protasis, and an aorist of *katadikazō*, 'condemn,' in the apodosis).

[61]The Decalogue 'does not include rules for the offering of sacrifice' (Andersen and Freedman 1980: 430). Yet, 'sacrifice is not denigrated; it is simply put in second place' (ibid.). Cf. comments on 9:13. For mercy over Levitical ritual, see Luke 10:25-37 (*eleos* occurs in v. 37); for judgment on ritual that replaces true worship, Amos 4:4-5 (and Smith 1998: 192-95).

division of the Hebrew Bible, speaks of the Son of Man in
Daniel 7. This reference is akin to those in the preceding
verses. Jesus' personal superiority to David is only implicit in
Matthew 12:3-4; he speaks of 'some*thing* [not some*one*] greater'
than the temple (12:5-6); and Hosea 6:6 is presented, not as his
own authoritative pronouncement (though it is that), but as a
citation from Scripture. So too 'the Son of Man' on Jesus' lips,
while clearly a reference to himself, is allusive in character;
it is in fact a concise parable which – like his language in
Matthew 12:3-7 – requires a response from listeners.[62]

The subject is 'the Son of Man'; but the first word in the
sentence is the predicate nominative, *kyrios*, which in this
position is emphatic.[63] Jesus is *Kyrios* in the absolute sense:
Yahweh incarnate. Moreover, this verse – with its opening *gar*
– undergirds all that Jesus has said in 12:3-7. His disciples are
'guiltless' (12:7) because he – the Lord of the Sabbath – declares
them to be. For the same reason, he and his people are entitled
to privileges exceeding those granted to David and his men
(12:3-4) and to the high priest and his sons (12:5-6). On Jesus'
lips, the words of Hosea 6:6 are an authoritative guide for
Sabbath observance (12:7) and a sovereign indictment of his
accusers (11:2).

How does the presence of the Lord of the Sabbath
affect his people's view of the Sabbath day and the fourth
commandment? The present passage, together with the rest
of Matthew, answers this question in two main ways: 1. Jesus
safeguards the day and upholds the command. In declaring
himself to be 'Lord of the Sabbath,' he affirms the ongoing
reality and validity of the day; and he earlier made it plain
(Matt. 5:17) that he has not come to destroy this command.
Now, as before, the Sabbath is God's good gift, an expression
of his *eleos* and *chesed* to his people. Now, as before, this is
an exceptionally favorable day for God's people to praise his
name, to rejoice in his goodness, and to respond with love

---

[62] For 'the Son of Man' as a parable, see page 137, with the whole
discussion on pages 134-37.

[63] Cf. *IB*, 166; Davies and Allison 1991: 316. As the subject, 'Son of Man'
has the definite article (*ho*); as the predicate nominative, 'Lord' lacks it.

for him and for their neighbors. Indeed, given the events associated with the dawn of God's rule, there is now greater cause than ever before for Sabbath praise and joy.[64] 2. Jesus abrogates or alters certain Sabbath practices. His death will make temple sacrifices obsolete (27:51; Hebrews *passim*); the temple itself is soon to be destroyed (24:2), making acts like those of 12:4, 5 impossible. Such was the impact of Jesus' resurrection on the church, that the appointed day was changed from the seventh to the first day of the week.[65] Jesus' tacit approval of the disciples' action (12:1, 7) reflects the fact that the OT rule about 'harvesting' on the Sabbath must be viewed in light of God's dawning rule: to judge from 12:1-14, if it is a work of *necessity* or of *mercy*, it is both permitted and encouraged.[66]

Healing on the Sabbath (12:9-14)

This passage is joined to the preceding in the closest way. A further event from that same Sabbath, probably in Capernaum, is here recorded. The scene now shifts from the grain fields to the synagogue, where the debate begun in 12:1-8 intensifies.[67]

1. Prelude to the healing (12:9-12)

Jesus 'went into *their* synagogue [*tēn synagōgēn autōn*]' (12:9). In this instance, the personal pronoun reflects the growing rift between Jesus and the nation's leadership, represented here by the Pharisees – whose forthcoming action (12:14) is

---

[64]See below on Matthew 12:9-14. On the purpose of the Sabbath under Moses, see pages 643-44, with n. 58. On law-keeping under Christ the Lord, see page 637, with n. 35.

[65]Cf. *WCF* 21.7; *WSC* no. 59; also Chamblin 1993: 150-51.

[66]Cf. *WCF* 21.8; *WSC* no. 60. See also page 342, with n. 8 (and comments on the whole of 5:17-20, pp. 339-47); and comments on 15:1-20.

[67]See opening comments on 12:1-14, where its connection with the close of chapter 11 was also noted. The events of 12:1-14 are also joined in Mark 2:23-3:6 and Luke 6:1-11.

[68]Matthew 4:23 and 9:35 contain the phrase 'in their [*autōn*] synagogues.' Hagner 1993: 80 thinks these texts 'may reflect the distancing of Matthew's community from the synagogues.' In my judgment the pronoun is not so loaded in these two summaries.

a chilling reminder of 10:17: 'in their [*autōn*] synagogues they will scourge you.'[68]

'And behold [*kai idou*], a man with a withered [*xēran*] hand' (Matt. 12:10a). As often, this opening arrests readers' attention, and prepares them for matters striking and dramatic; cf. *kai idou* (or *idou*) as a preface to miracles in 8:2, 24; 9:2, 20, 32. The adjective *xēros* basically means 'dry, dried (up)'; it describes land in 23:15, wood in Luke 23:31. The cognate verb *xērainō*, in the passive voice, means 'become dry, dry up, wither'; in the three instances in Matthew, this happens to plants (13:6; 21:19-20). This man's hand is motionless, useless, lifeless.[69] That his *right* hand is thus affected (Luke 6:6) makes his condition yet more lamentable.

The question of Matthew 12:10b – 'Is it lawful to heal on the Sabbath?' – matches the charge of 12:2. The terms *exestin* ('lawful') and *Sabbaton* occur there as well. The Pharisees' purpose is to 'accuse him' (the verb *katēgoreō*; 12:10c – to provoke him into words or actions that can later be used against him in court).[70] 'Rabbinic law allowed medical help on the Sabbath where life was immediately endangered.... Obviously, the healing of a withered hand could wait a day.'[71] This is the very argument of the synagogue ruler in Luke 13:14, after another Sabbath healing.

Responding to the question of Matthew 12:10 with one of his own, Jesus directly challenges his accusers (12:11): 'What man [*Tis...anthrōpos*] is there among *you* [*ex hymōn*] who has one sheep [*probaton hen*]...?'[72] The OT does not expressly sanction the

---

[69]Like Matthew 12:10, Luke 6:6 uses the adjective; Mark 3:1 uses the verb. The adjective could also be translated 'paralyzed' (BAGD s.v. *xēros*, 2.): ESV translates 'withered' in Matthew 12:10, but 'paralyzed' at John 5:3 (compare 5:8-9 to Matt. 9:6-7).

[70]*Katēgoreō* was used as a legal technical term: '*bring charges* (in court)' (BAGD s.v., 1.).

[71]Gundry 1994: 226. Keener 1999: 357 notes (with references) that teachers 'found ways to circumvent some of their regulations,' and that 'many teachers probably permitted medicine if it had been prepared before the Sabbath...or the act was medically urgent.'

[72]Rabbis often answered questions with questions. For other instances of Jesus' doing so, see, e.g., Matthew 9:14-15; 15:2-3; 19:16-17; 21:23-25.

specific act of lifting a sheep from a pit (*bothynos*) on the Sabbath. Yet, in contrast to the stricter Essenes, 'the Pharisees and most Jewish people accepted the necessity of rescuing an animal on the Sabbath.'[73] Especially would the need be felt in the case of a man threatened with the loss of his *one* sheep (*probaton hen*).

Jesus' question clearly expects a positive reply, on which basis he concludes: 'By how much, then [*oun*], does the worth of a man surpass that of a sheep! Therefore it is lawful to do good on the Sabbath' (12:12). This *qal wachomer* argument is as strong as that of verse 6; and given the truth of the Torah, starting with Genesis 1–2, Jesus' interrogators would readily agree that a human being is worth far more than a sheep.[74] The *anthrōpos* ('man') of Matthew 12:12a recalls the use of this term in verse 11 (a *man* who cares for a sheep will care much more for a fellow *man*), and especially in verse 10 (here is a *man* with a withered hand). So *Yes*, says Jesus to the question of v. 10: it *is* lawful (*exestin* again) 'to do good' (*kalōs poiein*) on the Sabbath (12:12b), especially to a man (12:12a) – which in this case means 'to heal' (*therapeusai*) *this* man (12:10).

Why should his healing be delayed another day? Did not God praise his handiwork on the first Sabbath (Gen. 1:31–2:3)? Does not Israel await a great Sabbath, the establishing of God's final rule (Heb. 3:7–4:11)? Is not the weekly Sabbath, standing as it does between those great events, an *especially appropriate* day for celebration and joyous expectation? Since the kingdom is now dawning, *what better day* than the Sabbath to declare the fact, and to display the grace of God's rule? Given the joy and praise sure to come from a healing miracle, *what better day* than the Sabbath for such an act? Consider Jesus' answer, in Luke 13:16, to the objection of 13:14 (noted above): 'Ought not [*ouk edei*] this woman, a daughter of Abraham whom Satan bound for eighteen years, to have been loosed from this bond on the

---

[73]Keener 1999: 358, with references; he also sheds light on how the accident of verse 11 might occur. Rabbinic sources called for giving 'indirect assistance that would enable an animal to extricate itself' (Gundry 1994: 227).

[74]The terms of 12:12a are, in this order, *posō* ('by much,' here exclamatory), *diapherei* ('is worth more') and *probatou* ('than a sheep,' a genitive of comparison).

Sabbath day?' What better day for a *liberation* (Luke 4:16-21, with Lev. 25)?

2. The healing and its aftermath (12:13-14)

Jesus now addresses the afflicted person: *tō anthrōpō* ('to the man'; 12:13a) recalls the instances of this noun in 12:10, 11 and 12 (see above comments). 'Stretch out your hand [*Ekteinon sou tēn cheira*],' says Jesus. 'And he stretched it out [*exeteinen*], and it was restored [*apekatestathē*], made healthy like the other' (Matt. 12:13bc). Jesus' words effect the cure; nothing more is needed. His command (the aorist imperative *ekteinon*) enables the man to obey by putting a motionless hand in motion (the aorist indicative *exeteinen*). The following aorist verb (from *apokathistēmi*) I take to be a 'divine passive': the man's hand 'was restored' – i.e., the Lord of the Sabbath, God incarnate, restored it. The healing is the climactic event of 12:1-14, and Jesus' crowning contribution to the present debate: this visible proof (12:13c) that Jesus spoke the words of 12:13b with stupendous authority, testifies also to the authority of his arguments in verses 3-8 and 11-12.[75] Jesus here enacts the mercy (*eleos*) of which he spoke in 12:7; and he meets a physical need far greater than that of David and his men (12:3-4). The Lord of the Sabbath does not stand grandly aloof from frail and fallen human beings. Instead, as the meek and humble Servant of Yahweh, he addresses their afflictions and bears their burdens (11:28-30; 12:18-21).

Jesus thus does more than defend the actions of others – disciples, David and priests – in face of the Pharisees' objections. He personally takes action which in their view violates the Sabbath, and it is this which precipitates the response of 12:14: 'But the Pharisees went out and took counsel [*symboulion elabon*] against him, how they might destroy [*apolesōsin*] him.' This is a terrifying text, for two reasons: *1.* It is horrifying to be

---

[75]Likewise, in Matthew 9:2-8, Jesus exercises his authority to heal paralysis, so that witnesses may know he has authority to forgive sins. See those comments.

[76]The verb is better rendered 'destroy' (ESV) than 'kill' (NIV), though Jesus will in the end 'be killed' (the verb *apokteinō*, e.g., 16:21). Note the contrast in 10:28 between men who kill (*apokteinō*) the body and God who can destroy (*apollymi*) both soul and body in Gehenna.

told of this plot against Jesus. The verb *apollymi* is very strong: it was earlier used of Herod's design against Jesus (2:13).[76] The Pharisees' plan is the more appalling because it stands in stark contrast to the miracle that has just occurred. Jesus restores a man's health on the Sabbath; they begin to plot a man's destruction. Jesus upholds the sixth commandment; they flagrantly violate it.[77] 2. It is horrifying to contemplate the judgment in store for these 'wise and intelligent' people (Matt. 11:25) who, having witnessed yet another miracle of grace (cf. 11:20-24), not only refuse to trust Jesus but actively seek to destroy him.

C. Jesus the Servant of God (12:15-21)

The portrait of Jesus, Son of the Father (11:25-30), Son of Man and Lord of the Sabbath (12:1-14) grows yet richer. Dominating the present passage is a lengthy quotation from Isaiah 42, in which Yahweh honors his chosen Servant.

Conduct

'Jesus, knowing [the Pharisees' intent, 12:14], withdrew [*anechōrēsen*] from there' (12:15a). This same verb (an aorist of *anachōreō*) was used in Matthew 2 of the magi's action, and of Joseph's, in face of grave danger; and in 4:12, of Jesus' departure to Galilee after John's arrest. Jesus' present action shows that the time has not yet come for him to be handed over to his enemies (and that will be a time of his own choosing); his mission to Israel is yet to be completed. So, in accord with his instructions to the apostles, he wisely and shrewdly moves from one place to another, and there freely continues his work.[78]

'And many [*polloi*] followed [*ēkolouthēsan*] him, and he healed [*etherapeusen*] them all' (12:15b). Despite the

---

[77]Cf. Mark 3:4, where Jesus asks: 'Is it lawful on the Sabbath...to save life or to kill?' See also John 5:1-18; 7:19-24.

[78]See Matthew 2:12-14, 22; 4:12; 10:16, 23; and the comments.

[79]While the *ochloi* of 12:15b is textually doubtful, the *polloi* doubtless denotes the crowds; 4:25; 8:1; 19:2 relate that 'many crowds [*ochloi polloi*] followed him.' Cf. *TC*, 26.

leadership's opposition to Jesus, the crowds remain his enthusiastic followers.[79] Nor have Jesus' enemies in the least inhibited his healing power. This instance of the verb *therapeuō* recalls that of verse 10, as well as those in the summaries of 4:23 and 9:35. Does Matthew suggest, from his placement of this report, that Jesus accomplished all these healings – like that of 12:13 – *on the Sabbath*? In this case Jesus' mercy (12:7) is yet more strongly evident, and the occasions for joy and praise are greatly multiplied.

Jesus warned (the verb *epitimaō*) those whom he healed, 'that they should not make him known' (Matt. 12:16; in the par. of Mark 3:18 the demons are so warned). He issues such commands elsewhere in Matthew, notably after Peter's confession (16:20); and the same motive is at work here.[80] Only now Jesus' purpose is more deeply explored: 'in order that [*hina*] what was spoken through Isaiah the prophet might be fulfilled' (12:17). Jesus himself does not publicly boast of his mighty works (12:19), nor does he want others to do so (12:16). Yet these works and this attitude are *themselves* a revelation. Jesus is hereby *being disclosed* as the meek and humble Son (11:28-30), as the Servant of Yahweh: '*Behold [Idou] my Servant*' (12:18). These texts are vital for understanding who Jesus really is. Some, perceiving that he is indeed such a figure, and that he requires such character in his followers (cf., e.g., 5:3-16), will remain loyal to him; others will dismiss or disown him.[81]

Commendation
Verses 18-21 are peculiar to this gospel, and contain its longest OT quotation, words from Isaiah 42:1-4. Matthew's

---

[80]The verb in Matthew 16:20 is *diastellomai* ('command'); but the parallels in Mark 8:30 and Luke 9:21 use *epitimaō*. See pages 133-34 on Jesus' commands for silence concerning his Messiahship.

[81]Cf. the quotation from T. W. Manson on page 134 above. Keener 1999: 360 observes both that 'Judaism in Jesus' day rarely applied the servant passages to the Messiah,' and that Matthew provides in 12:15-21 'a hermeneutical key for his entire Gospel.'

[82]Matthew is probably translating directly from the Hebrew, with the LXX in view. Cf. pages 98-99 above; Davies and Allison 1991: 323; France

language reflects his indebtedness to both the MT and the LXX, especially the former.[82] In the passage, Yahweh speaks through the prophet (12:17, quoted above) to his people about his Servant (12:18a).[83] As we now know from the context in Matthew, the Father speaks here about his beloved Son. As the Son reveals his Father's humility in 11:27-30, so in 12:18-21 the Father acclaims the humility of his Son.

'Behold, my servant [*pais*] whom I chose [*hēretisa*], my beloved [*agapētos*] in whom I [*hē psychē mou*] am well pleased [*eudokēsen*]. I will put my Spirit upon him [*ep' auton*]...' (Matt. 12:18ab). These words are strongly reminiscent of Jesus' experience at the Jordan (3:16-17). There the Spirit comes 'upon him' (*ep' auton*); there too Jesus is identified as the Father's 'beloved' (*agapētos*), in whom the Father is 'well pleased' (the verb *eudokeō*).[84] Matthew, like the LXX, renders the Hebrew '*ebed* – 'servant' – not *doulos* (the term used in 10:24-25) or *diakonos* (used in 20:26), but *pais*. The fact that *pais* can mean either *servant* or *son* 'makes the application to Jesus even more effective.'[85] It may be noted that both in the text here recalled (3:17) and in the text here anticipated (17:5), the Father expressly identifies Jesus as his Son (*Huios*).

'He will not quarrel [*ouk erisei*] or cry out [*oude kraugasei*], nor [*oude*] will anyone hear his voice in the streets [*en tais plateiais*]. A bruised reed [*kalamon syntetrimmenon*] he will not

---

1985: 206; Keener 1999: 361. Instances of Matthew's wording, as compared to MT and LXX, are considered below.

[83]On the language of the introductory formula in Matthew 12:17, see pages 96-97, 120-22. The quotation in 12:18-21 accords with the original intent of Isaiah 42:1-4; for there too Yahweh was addressing an individual, not the nation (see Motyer 1999: 26-27, 259, also 309 on Isaiah 49:3).

[84]In contrast to MT and Matthew, in the LXX of Isaiah 42:1 Yahweh addresses 'Jacob' and 'Israel' (cf. n. 83). Matthew's *hon hēretisa* (from *hairetizō*), 'whom I chose,' replaces LXX's *antilēmpsomai* ('I will help'), and matches LXX's *ho eklektos mou* ('my chosen one,' which literally renders the Hebrew *bᵉchîrî*). In place of this phrase, Matthew has *ho agapētos mou* ('my beloved'), which recalls the Father's praise of his Son in 3:17 (cf. Keener 1999: 361). *Psychē* (for Hebrew *nepeš*) here denotes not just the 'soul' but the whole being (as, e.g., in Gen. 2:7). See comments on page 266, with n. 30.

[85]Hagner 1993: 338. See BAGD s.v. *pais*, 1. a. and b.

break [*ou kateaxei*], and a smoldering wick [*linon typhomenon*]
he will not extinguish [*ou sbesei*]' (Matt. 12:19-20b). Each
verb is negated (*ouk...oude...oude...ou...ou*). 'It was in what
Jesus did *not* do that the distinctiveness of his mission was
most clearly seen in contrast with the aggressive Messiah
of popular expectation.'[86] The Father here ratifies the Son's
witness to himself in 11:28-30 (cf. John 5:31-37). Many rage
against Jesus (e.g., 12:14); but he is 'meek' (*praus*) and does
not respond in kind.[87] He is 'humble in heart,' and is not
intent on winning others' praise by publicly reciting his
prayers (6:5) and accomplishments (cf. 12:16).[88] Nor does
he use his power as an insecure tyrant might, to destroy
the weak and vulnerable (cf. Herod in chapter 2).[89]

Yet Jesus does more than refrain from such behavior.
He – the Servant King – stoops to his subjects' weaknesses,
bears their loads, shows them mercy (Matt. 11:28-30;
12:7). He cures, restores and forgives them, as Matthew
has repeatedly testified. Not only does he hold the reed
tenderly, lest it be broken; he heals its bruises and makes
it whole. Not only does he protect the flickering wick; he
reignites the candle. In 8:16-17, announcing the fulfillment
of Isaiah 53:4, Matthew focused on the Servant's mighty
works. Here, invoking Isaiah 42:1-4, he celebrates the
character of the Servant himself.[90]

---

[86]France 1985: 206.

[87]Cf. Matthew 5:5 (and comments); 1 Peter 2:23. The LXX renders the first
two Hebrew verbs of Isaiah 42:2 by forms of *krazō* ('cry out, scream') and
aniēmi ('loosen' the tongue?). Matthew instead has forms of *erizō* ('quarrel,'
wrangle') and *kraugazō* ('cry out, scream'); the first interprets the character
of the speech in question.

[88]Yet the One who sought praise from his Father rather than from men
(cf. John 12:43) had (at least for a time) an incomparably huge following
(Matt. 12:15b). The Hebrew behind Matthew's 'in the streets' is adequately
represented in the LXX's 'outside' (*exō*): does Matthew's *plateia* allude to 6:5,
the only other instance of this noun in the gospel?

[89]The MT of Isaiah 42:3ab is well represented in both LXX and Matthew
The Servant will not break (LXX *syntribō*; Matthew *katagnymi*) a reed that is
bruised (a passive participle of *thlaō* in LXX; of *syntribō* in Matthew). Nor
will he extinguish (*sbennymi* in LXX and Matthew) a wick that is smoldering
(a passive participle of *kapnizō* in LXX; of *typhō* in Matthew).

[90]So also France 1985: 206.

Conquest
'And he will proclaim [*apangelei*] justice [*krisin*] to the nations [*tois ethnesin*],' says Yahweh of the Servant, and the Father of the Son (Matt. 12:18c). Gentleness will mark Jesus' behavior (12:20ab) 'until he brings forth [*ekbalē*] justice [*tēn krisin*] to victory [*eis nikos*]' (12:20c). 'And,' concludes the quotation, 'in his name [*tō onomati autou*] the nations [*ethnē*] will hope [*elpiousin*]' (12:21).

The Servant-Son proclaims and achieves *krisis* (12:18, 20), which, in this context, means not 'judgment,' but 'justice.' Jesus is the promised Son of David (12:23), by whose reign righteousness (*dikaiosynē*; Hebrew *tsedeq*) and justice (*krisis*; Hebrew *mišpāt*) will be established forever.[91] Moreover, it is *as the Servant* that he exercises royal authority; it is *as the meek and humble one* that he conquers injustice (see p. 637, with n. 32); and it is *as this kind of person* that he is praised both by the Father (12:18-21) and by all creation (Phil. 2:6-11).

In establishing justice, the Servant liberates people from injustice. Amazingly, Isaiah 42:1-4 speaks not of Israel's deliverance from Gentile (specifically, Babylonian) oppression but of the Gentiles' own salvation.[92] They are among those whom Jesus calls in Matthew 11:28 (with *pantes*, 'all'): their only hope (the verb *elpizō*) is to call on his name (*onoma*).[93] What

---

[91]Cf. BAGD s.v. *krisis*, 3. '*right* in the sense of *justice, righteousness*'; instances of *tsedek* in Isaiah 11:4-5; and comments on Matthew 5:6. LXX's 'he will lead out' (the verb *ekpherō*) in Isaiah 42:1c is closer to MT (the verb *yātsā*') than is 'he will proclaim' (the verb *apangellō*) in Matthew 12:18; Matthew's language suggests that Jesus brings forth justice *by* proclaiming it. LXX's *eis alētheian* ('in truth' or 'in fidelity') in Isaiah 42:3 is closer to MT (*le'ₑmet*) than is *eis nikos* ('to victory'; Matt.12:18). As Ottley notes (1906: 2.307), the two phrases 'come near to touching one another at this point'; the Servant's fidelity is rewarded with victory. There is a third instance of *mišpāt* in Isaiah 42:4b, a clause not quoted by Matthew.

[92]As Motyer shows (1999: 256-59), the Servant is 'the great solution' (Isa. 42:1-9) to 'the plight of the Gentile world' (41:21-29).

[93]Cf. Isaiah 49:6; Jeremiah 1:5. Matthew's rendering of Isaiah 42:4c (he does not quote 4ab) – 'in his name the nations will hope' (Matt. 12:21) – agrees with LXX. MT of Isaiah 42:4c reads 'and the coastlands wait for his teaching [*tôrâ*]' (NRSV). In Matthew 28:18-20, the nations are promised both the name (i.e., the presence and the power) of the Trinity, and the teaching (or *torah*) of Jesus.

of Israelites themselves? Let them not resent Yahweh's grace to Gentiles (cf. Luke 4:16-30). Instead, let them recognize their own favored position (Matt. 10:5-6), and their own need of Messiah's salvation (1:21). And having thus been enlightened (11:25), let them become Jesus' followers, to join with him in fulfilling the mission Yahweh intended for Israel from the beginning.[94] In the event they are persecuted by fellow Jews (as Jesus has been), let that be an impetus for them to evangelize Gentiles.[95]

---

[94]See Genesis 12:1-3; Isaiah 49:6; Luke 2:29-32; also pages 149-51 ('Israel and the Nations'), 173-75 ('Good News for Jews and Gentiles').
[95]See comments on Matthew 10:5-15, 16-25; Gundry 1994: 230.

IV.
'AND HEED NOT HIS MERCIES?'[1]
(12:22-50)

The opening miracle (Matt. 12:22) shows the Servant of verses 18-21 mercifully and mightily at work. No further miracles are reported in the passage. Instead, attention is devoted (as in chapter 11) to the various responses Jesus evokes, and especially to his judgments about them (of the 28 verses in the passage, all but five contain his words).[2] Relatively few may be guilty of the blasphemy expressed in 12:24; but Jesus says his generation (*genea*) is evil and adulterous and threatened with condemnation (12:39, 41, 42, 45), language which indicates (as had 11:20-24) that most of his contemporaries have reacted sinfully to his manifold witness and are therefore in grave danger. The crowds' question in the wake of the miracle is a step in the right direction (12:23). But the single concrete response that Jesus approves – the fruit that is essential for identifying a tree as good (12:33) – is the one described in the closing two verses of the chapter.

A. Jesus and Beelzeboul (12:22-37)

Words matter greatly. This is the conclusion to which the whole passage leads (12:37). We also learn here, as in the rest of Matthew, that Jesus' own speech is exceptionally important: verses 25b-37 consist entirely of his words. One reason that words matter so much is that they reveal the condition of the speaker's heart (*kardia*; 12:34).[3] As Jesus knows the thoughts of the heart (9:4; 12:25) and speaks with unique authority (7:29;

---

[1]From the hymn 'Softly and Tenderly Jesus Is Calling,' by Will L. Thompson (1880).

[2]This reckoning excludes Matthew 12:47; see comments *in loc*.

[3]This is true for Jesus as for others. See his words in 11:29, with *kardia*.

9:6), what he says about others' speech – in this case, about the Pharisees' accusation (12:24) – is decisive.

Jesus is Accused (12:22-24)

A man who is demon-possessed (*daimonizomenos*), blind (*typhlos*) and mute (*kōphos*) is brought to Jesus – who heals him (the verb *therapeuō*), so that the man both speaks (the verb *laleō*) and sees (the verb *blepō*; 12:22). That Matthew records no words of Jesus – whether to the man or to the demon – is noteworthy, given the quotation in 12:19. In 9:27-34, Jesus successively heals two blind men (*typhloi*; 12:27) and a demon-possessed man who was mute (*kōphon daimonizomenon*; 12:32). That he now heals a man afflicted in all three ways witnesses to the Servant's extraordinary powers. The expulsion of the demon is not mentioned here – that is reserved for Matthew 12:28 – but the man's speech and sight show that he has been freed from demonic mastery.

'And all the crowds were amazed [*existanto*], and were saying, "Could this be [*Mēti houtos estin*] the Son of David [*ho huios Dauid*]?"' (12:23). The first verb, from *existēmi*, occurs nowhere else in Matthew: it expresses 'the feeling of astonishment mingled w[ith] fear, caused by events which are miraculous, extraordinary, or difficult to understand.'[4] Not surprisingly, then, the crowds' question reflects a quandary about Jesus himself. While the interrogative particle *mēti* appears in questions that expect a negative answer (e.g., 7:16b), here the questioners are 'in doubt concerning the answer.' Elsewhere in Matthew, all those who directly address Jesus as the Son of David are in desperate need.[5]

'But when the Pharisees heard this, they said, "This man casts out demons only by Beelzeboul [*en tō Beelzeboul*], the prince of

---

[4]BAGD s.v. *existēmi*, 2. b. *Thaumazō* ('wonder, marvel, be astonished') describes people's response to miracles in Matthew 8:27; 9:33; 15:31; 21:20. *Ekplēssō* (passive, 'be amazed, overwhelmed') is reserved for responses to Jesus' teaching (7:28; 13:54; 19:25; 22:33).

[5]The quotation is from BAGD s.v. *mēti*; cf. 26:22, 25; John 4:29; France 1985: 208. King David did no miracles, which helps explain the crowds' bewilderment (Matt. 12:23). This is even more understandable if the Jews 'did not expect the Davidic Messiah to perform healings or exorcisms' (Gundry 1994: 231). For cries to Jesus as Son of David, see 9:27; 15:22; 20:30-31.

demons"' (12:24). As in 9:34, they focus not on the exorcism itself but on the means (*en*) by which it was done. There they charged that Jesus was empowered 'by [*en*] the prince of demons'; they now further identify this figure as 'lord of the dwelling' – *Beelzeboul*, a Hebrew wordplay on *ba'al*, 'master, lord,' and *z^ebûl*, 'abode, dwelling.' Cf. 12:29 (which speaks of entering and plundering a strong man's house), and 10:25 (where *Beelzeboul* is called *oikodespotēs*, 'master of the house').[6] In this context, Beelzeboul is a name for Satan (*ho Satanas*, 12:26, who is elsewhere called a prince (*archōn*, e.g., in John 12:31; Eph. 2:2).

The explanation for the Pharisees' accusation lies not in the miracle itself (Matt. 12:22), but in Jesus' stance against them in verses 1-14 (as the reason for their charge in 9:34 was not the healing of 9:33 but Jesus' prior words and works). It is inconceivable, they reason, that God would grant healing power to a man who so flagrantly violates the Sabbath laws. The words of 12:24 are repulsive but, in light of 12:14, not altogether surprising. Moreover, the Pharisees' charge is for the crowds' instruction: they spoke upon 'hearing [*akousantes*] this' (i.e., the question of 12:23). 'Be not deceived,' they say in effect; 'this man is *not* the Son of David, but a messianic pretender of the worst kind.' Contrast a leading Pharisee's explanation of Jesus' powers in John 3:2.

Jesus Addresses the Accusation (12:25-29)

The Pharisees voice their accusation not to Jesus but to the crowds: 'This man [*Houtos*]...' (Matt. 12:24). But Jesus knows 'their thoughts [*enthymēseis*]'(12:25a). So too, in 9:4, he perceived the 'thoughts' of the scribes (the only other instance of *enthymēsis* in Matthew) – colleagues of the Pharisees who were saying to themselves (9:3): 'This man [*Houtos*, as in 12:24] blasphemes [*blasphēmei*, the verbal counterpart to the noun Jesus himself will use in 12:31].'

---

[6]The term may have been inspired by *ba'al z^ebûb* ('lord of the flies'), a Philistine deity (2 Kings 1:2). For further discussion, see Davies and Allison 1991: 195-96; Hagner 1993: 282, who support the view taken here. On the instrumental *en* in 9:34 and 12:24, see page 556, n. 44.

1. Refuting the charge (12:25b-27)
Divisions of the sort described in the proverbial sayings
of 12:25b can and do occur, with predictable results. A
kingdom (*basileia*) divided against itself will surely be laid
waste (*erēmoutai*), and its population decimated.[7] Of course,
no city (*polis*) or household (*oikia*) divided against itself will
stand (*stathēsetai*): a city's stabilizing structures collapse; 'a
family that's in a constant squabble disintegrates.'[8] 'And if
Satan casts out [*ekballei*] Satan, he is divided against himself
[*eph' heauton emeristhē*]. How then will his kingdom [*basileia*]
stand [*stathēsetai*]?' (12:26). The Pharisees used *ekballei* in their
accusation (12:24). The other Greek terms here indicated
appeared in the proverbs of 12:25b. Jesus uses these repetitions
to build his argument. Satan knows the truth of those proverbs
as well as anyone. Would not a ruler so cunning and crafty
as he recognize the catastrophic effects of a divided realm?
Would not so powerful and ruthless a dictator crush the least
hint of such division among his underlings?

'And,' Jesus continues, 'if I cast out demons by Beelzeboul,
by whom do your sons cast them out?' (Matt. 12:27a). Verse 26
already exposed the folly of the Pharisees' charge; but Jesus has
not completed his argument. Again building on the preceding,
he uses several terms from the accusation of 12:24 (*ekballō,
ta daimonia* and *en Beelzeboul*); and 12:27a, like verse 26a, is
a first class conditional sentence.[9] Other Jews – namely, the
Pharisees' own associates and disciples – are casting out
demons.[10] Since the Pharisees clearly approve of these acts, it
is also clear that they do not object to exorcisms as such and

---

[7]The verb is a present passive indicative of *erēmoō*, so 'be laid waste,
depopulated' (cf. BAGD s.v.). One thinks of the United States during the
Civil War (1861–65).

[8]As paraphrased by Peterson 1993: 40 (at 12:25). The verb is a future
passive indicative of *histēmi*, so 'stand firm, hold one's ground' (cf. BAGD
s.v., II. 1. d.).

[9]In each of these conditional sentences, the protasis (or 'if-clause') is
assumed to be true for the sake of argument. So we translate 'If Satan...' and 'If
I....' 'Since Satan...' and 'Since I...' are obviously erroneous. See *GGBB*, 690-93.

[10]Thus are 'your sons' (*hoi huioi hymōn*) to be identified. Cf. BAGD s.v.
huios, 1. c.; Hagner 1993: 343; Keener 1999: 363.

thus that they oppose Jesus on other grounds (noted above). 'Because of this [i.e., the charge of 12:24], they themselves [*autoi*] will be your judges [*kritai*]' (12:27b). Will the followers judge the masters for their hypocrisy and inconsistency? Or for their blindness to the fact (perceived by the judges) that Jesus expels demons by God's power? Or will some of these Jewish exorcists, having recognized that Jesus' powers far exceed theirs, actually become *his* disciples and judge their former masters for their opposition to him?

2. Replacing the charge (12:28-29)

'But if I [*egō*] by the Spirit of God cast out [*ekballō*] demons [*ta daimonia*], then the kingdom of God has come upon you' (12:28). Jesus keeps preceding statements in view by repeating their language: as in 12:26, 27, he uses a first class conditional sentence; the verb *ekballō* here occurs for the fifth time in the passage (cf. 12:24, 26, 27), and the noun *daimonion* for the fourth (cf. 12:24, 27).

In 12:28 the tightly knit argument reaches its climax. Having refuted the Pharisees' charge in 12:26-27, Jesus now supplants their explanation with its opposite. *a.* He works 'by the Spirit *of God* [*en pneumati theou*],' with his aid and by his power (*en* again); and by this means he conquers the 'unclean spirit' (*akatharton pneuma*; 12:43), the 'evil spirit' (*ponēron pneuma*; 12:45), and the 'demonic spirit' (*pneuma daimoniou*; Rev. 16:14).[11] *b.* The *egō* of Matthew 12:28a, besides strengthening the literary link with verse 27a (which also uses this pronoun), makes the reference to Jesus emphatic. It is *he* whom the Spirit thus empowers – evidence that *he* is God's

---

[11]Placed at the front of its clause, *en tō pneumati theou* is emphatic (the position of *en Beelzeboul* in Matthew 12:27 is comparable; contrast the placement of *en tō Beelzeboul* in 12:24). The par. in Luke 11:20 states that Jesus casts out demons 'by the finger [*en daktylō*] of God,' an allusion to Exodus 8:19; Yahweh's victory over the Egyptian gods through Moses and Aaron prefigures Jesus' conquest of Satan's kingdom (cf. pp. 123-29 on typology in Matthew). Whether the source Q (on which see pp. 78-86) spoke of 'finger' or 'Spirit,' or both, is hard to say (cf. Dunn 1975: 44-46); but, in any case, these are two expressions for one reality (Carson 1984: 289; Keener 1999: 364).

Messiah and Servant-King (Matt. 3:16-17; 12:18; cf. Acts 2:22, 36; 1 John 3:8). *c.* By virtue of Messiah's presence and the Spirit's power, 'the kingdom *of God* [*hē basileia tou theou*] has come [*ephthasen*]...,' his eschatological rule is inaugurated. Those other exorcisms (Matt. 12:27), even though authentic, cannot be so interpreted.[12] *d.* Satan seeks to enlist Jesus in his service, but Jesus steadfastly opposes him (4:1-11; 16:21-23). Jesus' enemies appear to oppose Satan but actually represent him. Does not the charge of 12:24 come from the father of lies? Does not this utterance show that Satan has mastered these people?

The parable of 12:29 concludes Jesus' argument and illuminates the pronouncement of 12:28. Satan, 12:26, is here represented as 'the strong man' (the adjective *ischyros*, 12:29a, b) who rules over a 'household' (*oikia*, 12:29a, b); as noted, *Beelzeboul* means 'lord of the dwelling.' There is no internal threat to this household (12:25b, with *oikia*), to this kingdom (12:26b, with *basileia*). But the devil is now being assailed from without as never before, by a far greater kingdom and a far mightier king. Jesus not only resists Satan's temptations; he takes the offensive and penetrates the enemy's stronghold (so will his church; 16:18). Once inside, he subjugates the servants of the *oikia* (i.e., he casts out demons). But he does more: possessing authority surpassing that of his predecessors and contemporaries, he binds (the verb *deō*) the master of the household; in a series of decisive encounters he subdues Satan

---

[12]The verb *phthanō* means 'arrive, come' (BAGD s.v., 2.). I take *ephthasen* to be a *constative* aorist denoting past action, as distinct from a *proleptic* aorist viewing future action as completed, as is true of *ephthasen* in 1 Thessalonians 2:16; see *GGBB*, 555, 557, 563-64. Matthew speaks of 'the kingdom of heaven' far more often than of 'the kingdom of God' (cf. pp. 141-42). The latter, in Matthew 12:28b, matches 'the Spirit of God' in 12:28a and opposes 'his [i.e. Satan's] kingdom' in 12:26 (Davies and Allison 1991: 339). 'Jesus accepts the miracles of others but holds his own to be of different import because of his identity. What is decisive is not the exorcisms but the exorcist' (ibid.). Other Jews cast out Satan's underlings (12:27); Jesus' exorcisms signal his assault on Satan himself (12:29). The presence of the Spirit signals the dawn of God's rule (see p. 262, n. 18). John the Baptist preached the coming kingdom (3:2) in the Spirit's power (Luke 1:15, 17). But the Spirit did not equip John, as he did Jesus, to cast out demons (cf. John 10:41).

himself.[13] Yet the defeat of the 'strong one' (*ischyros*) is but a means to an end. The 'stronger one' (*ischyroteros*; Luke 11:22) has come to 'seize' (the verb *harpazō*; 12:29a) the master's goods (*skeuē*), 'thoroughly to plunder' (the verb *diarpazō*; 12:29b) the master's household – i.e., to liberate victims of Satanic tyranny. Such was the man of 12:22 until Jesus healed him.[14]

Jesus Addresses His Accusers (12:30-37)
Jesus began addressing the Pharisees in 12:25a; and he directly challenged them in 12:27 ('by whom do your sons... they will be your judges') and 12:28 ('has come upon you'). But the main focus of 12:25-29 was the accusation of verse 24. In that light, Jesus now tells his accusers how grave is their sin and how perilous their condition. Yet, there is still hope for them. In 12:31-32 Jesus sounds the most urgent of warnings to persons on the brink of damnation (and he does so again in chapter 23). If they obey the first command of 12:33 instead of the second, they may yet be saved; the address of 12:34 has the same intent as in 3:7. Let the Pharisees loathe and repudiate their blasphemous words and with their mouths confess Jesus as Lord (12:30; cf. Rom. 10:9), before it is too late (Matt. 12:37).

1. The fundamental issue (12:30)
'The one who is not with me [*met' emou*] is against me [*kat' emou*], and the one who is not gathering with me [*met' emou*] is scattering.' Here, as in Matthew as a whole, the most critical matter is how one understands Jesus himself (note the

---

[13]See Matthew 4:1-11; Luke 10:17-19; John 12:31-32; 1 Corinthians 2:7-8; 1 John 3:8; Revelation 12:1-12. In Revelation 20:2, an angel 'binds' Satan (*deō* again) for a thousand years. For such references in Jewish apocalyptic literature, see Keener 1999: 365, n. 78.

[14]Matthew 11:29 may well allude to Isaiah 49:24-25 (Manson 1957: 86). Jesus 'binds' (*deō*, 29) the enemy who himself 'bound' his captives (Luke 13:16, with *deō*). In Luke 11:22 (par. to 12:29) Jesus seizes Satan's 'whole armor' (*panoplia*), which may represent the demonic host (Manson, ibid.; cf. Eph. 6:11-13 in this light); and he 'divides his spoil,' which may allude to Isaiah 53:12 (Jeremias 1963: 122, n. 34). With Matthew 12:28-29, compare Judges 3:9-11, where Othniel, endowed with the Spirit of Yahweh (3:10a), conquers a foreign king (3:10b), frees the Israelites (3:9b) and brings rest to the land for forty years (3:11).

repeated personal pronoun [the genitive *emou*] and compare
16:13-16). Having witnessed his words and works (whether
as his contemporary or as a reader of Matthew), one must
become his follower or his enemy; in the end, there is no
neutral ground (see below on 12:32a).

The accusation of 12:24 reveals the Pharisees to be against
Jesus and instruments of his most implacable enemy. On the one
hand, they fail to *gather* with Jesus (the verb *synagō*) – i.e., to join
him and his disciples in reaping the eschatological harvest.[15] At
the same time, they *scatter* (the verb *skorpizō*) – both by refusing
to join Jesus (when workers are urgently needed to gather his
harvest; 9:37) and by actively seeking to prevent others from
becoming his disciples (as, e.g., in 12:23-24), which is, of course,
the mission of the evil one himself (13:19; 2 Cor. 4:4).

2. Blasphemy against the Son of Man (12:31a, 32a)

'Because of this [*Dia touto*] I tell you, every sin and blasphemy
will be forgiven [*aphethēsetai*] men.... And whoever speaks a
word against [*kata*] the Son of Man will be forgiven [*aphethēsetai*].'
As the opening prepositional phrase shows, Jesus bases 12:31-32
(and vv. 33-37) on his preceding words, most immediately
on the declaration of 12:30. Both 12:31a and verse 32a speak
of God's forgiveness.[16] He will forgive many a sin (*hamartia*;
12:31a; but the particular one mentioned here 12:32a) is abusive
speech – *blasphēmia* – against the Son of Man.[17] Moreover, Jesus
here addresses these Pharisees ('I tell you') – persons who are
currently against him (cf. the use of *kata* in 12:30a) and who are
themselves guilty of blasphemy (12:24).

---

[15]Note the instances of *synagō* in Matthew 3:12; 13:30, 47; also in 22:10 (of
gathering people for the wedding feast). Cf. Hagner 1993: 344.

[16]The repeated verb, a future passive indicative from *aphiēmi*, is an
instance of the 'divine passive.'

[17]*Blasphēmia* denotes abusive and defamatory speech of various kinds
(BAGD s.v.). The instances of 12:31 are the first in Matthew; there are two more,
in Jesus' catalogue of sins in 15:19, and in the high priest's accusation against
Jesus in 26:65. The matching verb *blasphēmeō* occurs three times: in 9:3 and 26:65,
Jesus is accused of blasphemy (by scribes and high priest respectively); in 27:39,
people hurl derisive speech at Jesus on the cross. See those comments.

We already know from Matthew that Jesus came to save sinners (1:21), and that to this end he initiated fellowship with the worst of them (9:13). For that very reason, these sinners must respond to him. Let them not be impetuous, but weigh carefully the claims implicit and explicit in Jesus' words and works. But they cannot remain forever undecided; they must not only ask but answer such questions as those of 11:3 and 12:23. They must finally acknowledge Jesus or disown him (10:32-33), stand with him or against him (12:30). Those who persist in postponing faith and repentance will, in the end, be judged as unbelieving and unrepentant (cf. 11:20-24).

When once his disciples rebuked a non-disciple for casting out demons in his name, Jesus replied, 'Do not hinder him, for the one who is not against you [*kath' hymōn*] is for you' (Luke 9:49-50). That person is in a very different position from the Pharisees of Matthew 12:24. But even he cannot remain there, as is clear from Jesus' later saying in Luke 11:23 (par. to Matt. 12:30), 'The one who is not with me is against me [*kat' emou*].' See comments on Matthew 13:10-17.

Consider Paul, himself a former Pharisee. By his own testimony, he was once 'a blasphemer [*blasphēmon*], persecutor, and insolent opponent' of Jesus (1 Tim. 1:13, ESV), the very worst of sinners (1:15; cf. 1 Cor. 15:9). But as he also testifies, he received God's mercy, grace and forgiveness; the glory and grace of Jesus were disclosed to him on the Damascus Road. How did he respond? Not by suppressing that truth and intensifying his assaults on the church, nor merely by ceasing from his blasphemies and persecutions – but by becoming utterly committed to Christ the Lord, and to the task of gathering the Master's harvest.[18]

3. Blasphemy against the Holy Spirit (12:31b, 32b)
'But the blasphemy against the Spirit [*hē...tou pneumatos blasphēmia*] will not be forgiven [*ouk aphethēsetai*].... But whoever speaks against [*kata*] the Holy Spirit [*tou pneumatos tou hagiou*], it will not be forgiven [*ouk aphethēsetai*] him, either

---

[18]See Acts 9:1-22; 22:6-21; 26:12-20; 1 Corinthians 15:10; 2 Corinthians 4:6; 1 Timothy 1:12-16.

in this age or in the coming one.' Jesus stresses the gravity of this sin in several ways. *a.* This is the lone exception to his comprehensive promise of forgiveness in Matthew 12:31a. *b.* Twice in rapid succession he says that God will not forgive this sin.[19] *c.* Not only is the statement repeated, but 12:32b is more emphatic than verse 31b. Consider the horror of the sin, says Jesus: it is blasphemy against *the Spirit* (12:31b) – indeed, against *the Holy Spirit* (12:32b).[20] This sin will not be forgiven, say both 12:31b and 32b; but 12:32b expressly states that this holds true for both the present age (*aiōn*) and the age to come. This sin will *never* be forgiven. Such persons are both judged in this life and excluded from life in the coming kingdom of God.[21]

What then is the nature of this sin? *a.* This sin is committed when deeds achieved by the *Spirit's* power (Matt. 12:28) are ascribed to *Satanic* power, (12:24). *b.* Since it is Jesus who accomplishes the miracles in question, we might think that 'blasphemy against the Son of Man' and 'blasphemy against the Spirit' are the same sin. Yet, Jesus clearly distinguishes them from each other (12:31-32). By all indications, those who speak against Jesus (12:32a) do so in ignorance of his true identity. This was true for Paul (as noted), for most people in the crowds, and for some of their rulers.[22] The accusation of 12:24 comes from persons who have witnessed the same phenomena as

---

[19]Except for the negative particle *ouk*, the forms of *aphiēmi* in Matthew 12:31b and 32b match those of 12:31a and 32a: see n. 16. The 'blasphemy against the Spirit,' (12:24, where *pneumatos* is an objective genitive: *GGBB*, 116-8), and speech 'against the Holy Spirit' (12:32b) are the same sin: see n. 17.

[20]Note the position of *pneumatos* in Matthew 12:31b. In this construction of verse 32b, both noun (*pneumatos*) and adjective (*hagiou*) are emphasized (cf. *GGBB*, 306–7).

[21]The noun *aiōn* (here for the first time in Matthew) usually means 'time' or 'age,' only rarely 'world' (BAGD s.v., 1.-3.); nkjv rightly corrects kjv at 12:32. The par. in Mark 3:29 states that one who blasphemes against the Spirit 'never has forgiveness ['never' translates *ouk...eis ton aiōna*], but is guilty of an eternal [*aiōniou*] sin.' For the concept of the two ages in Judaism and Christianity, see BAGD ibid., 2. a. and b.; Ladd 1993: 42-46.

[22]See Matthew 16:13-14; John 12:42; and note the use of *agnoia* ('ignorance') in Acts 3:17, and of *agnoeō* ('to be ignorant') in Acts 13:27; 1 Timothy 1:13; and 2 Peter 2:12 (with *blasphēmeō*).

the crowds. The difference is that these Pharisees falsely interpret this evidence 'in full awareness' of what they are doing – 'thoughtfully, willfully, and self-consciously rejecting the work of the Spirit even though there can be no other explanation of Jesus' exorcisms than that.'[23] (Cf. the distinction between *unwitting* and *defiant* sins in Num. 15:22-29.) Satan opposes Jesus precisely *because* he knows who Jesus is[24] and his servants can be expected to do the same. Having identified the devil as 'the father of lies' and certain Jews as his dutiful children, Jesus says to them: 'But *because* [*hoti*] I tell the truth, you do not believe me' (John 8:44-45). Like their father, they hate the truth. Since Jesus is the very embodiment of truth (John 14:6), and the supreme revelation of God (John 1:18), he will be the special object of their fury. The more fully the glory of Jesus is disclosed, the more vehement their opposition to him will become (cf. John 8:58-59; 10:31-39). Does the very absurdity of the charge in Matthew 12:24 (as exposed by Jesus in 12:25-27) reflect the Pharisees' awareness that they are questioning the unquestionable?[25] *c.* How could God forgive such a sin? If the very one the Father authorizes to forgive sins (1:21; 9:6) is viewed as God's enemy rather than his servant, then, in the nature of the case, such persons' forgiveness is impossible. *d.* As noted earlier (p. 663), there is still hope for Jesus' accusers. He does not directly accuse them of having already committed this sin. The words of 12:25-32 are his overture of grace to persons on the brink of

---

[23]Carson 1984: 291-92.

[24]See, e.g., Mark 1:24; 3:11-12; John 8:42-59; 2 Corinthians 4:4.

[25]In Matthew 12:31b, 32b, Jesus warns 'against the conscious disputing of the indisputable *which is here made evident*' in his mighty works (Berkouwer 1971: 340). These Pharisees are 'deliberately and maliciously turning light into darkness' (Calvin 1995a: 46). 'The Son of Man was...present in veiled form and was thus not unmistakable.... But the blasphemy of the Spirit amounts to final rejection of God's plain salvific activity' (Hagner 1993: 347, following E. Lövestam). As Berkouwer argues (ibid., 339-45), once the 'veiled and humiliated' Christ (342) is raised from the dead, apostasy entails 'blatant and willful' rejection of truth (344) about both Jesus and the Spirit, as is clear, e.g., from Hebrews and 1 John. In this regard, see the comments on Hebrews 6:4-6 in Hughes 1977: 206-22; and on 1 John 5:16-17 in Marshall 1978b: 245-50.

damnation; his appeal that their understanding of his work be totally changed; his urgent plea that they repent of their sin and blasphemy before it is too late.

Four notes of pastoral counsel are in order: *a.* Lest they emulate the Pharisees of Matthew 12:24, let Christians be extraordinarily cautious in ascribing spiritual phenomena in the visible church to demonic influence.[26] *b.* Conversely, let them be very wary of charging others (within or beyond the church) with having committed this unforgivable sin. 'Ultimately only God can know when an individual's opposition to his work has reached this stage of irreversible rejection.'[27] *c.* Let Christians heed the marks of this sin according to this passage – together with the promises of 12:31a, 32a – lest awareness of the enormity of their sin cause them falsely to conclude they are beyond forgiveness.[28] *d.* Let non-Christians also take this passage seriously, lest they make that same error – or foolishly conclude that there is no such thing as an unforgivable sin, or that, if there is, there is no danger of their committing it.

4. The cruciality of words (12:33-37)
The words of the Pharisees – whom Jesus is still addressing (see p. 663) – reveal their character. Matthew 12:33 speaks of a tree (*dendron*) that is good (*kalos*), whose fruit (*karpos*) is therefore good; and of a bad (*sapros*) tree that produces bad fruit. This recalls 7:16-20, where all four of these Greek words occur. That passage addressed false teaching (7:15) and so does this one (12:24). As noted there (pp. 477-78), what a false

---

[26]Persons in the Calvinist and the Pentecostal traditions have been known to exchange such accusations (cf. Blomberg 1992: 205). There is indeed a need to 'distinguish between spirits,' but doing so requires both the Spirit's gift (1 Cor. 12:10-11; 1 Thess. 5:19-22) and his fruit (Gal. 5:22-23).

[27]France 1985: 211. Cf. Matthew 7:1-6 (and comments); 1 Corinthians 4:5.

[28]'These verses have been made the ground of much unnecessary fear for over-sensitive Christians whose supposed "unforgivable sin" bore no resemblance to the deliberate stance adopted by these Pharisees' (France 1985: 211). Blomberg 1992: 204 judges that 'professing believers who fear they have committed the unforgivable sin demonstrate a concern for their spiritual welfare which by definition proves they have not committed it.' Observe how believers dealt with loads of guilt in Psalms 32, 38 and 51. Cf. the discussion in Bruner 2004a: 568-70.

prophet *does* reveals who he *is*, and who he *is* governs what he *does*. So it is with these Pharisees. The 'fruit' of their 'tree' is speech. What the mouth *says* (the verb *laleō*), shows what fills the *heart* (*kardia*, 12:34b) i.e., discloses what a person *is*. Since Jesus' accusers *are* evil (*ponēroi ontes*), they cannot *say* (*laleō* again) good things (12:34a).[29] On the contrary, they can and do say evil things (12:24). The evil man (*ho ponēros anthrōpos*) of 12:35b represents the *ponēroi* of 12:34a. In stark contrast to the activity of 'the good man' (*ho agathos anthrōpos*; 12:35a), he 'brings forth from [*ek*] his evil [*ponērou*] treasury evil things [*ponēra*]' (12:35b). In this context, the 'treasury' (*thēsauros*) is the storehouse of the heart (as made explicit in the parallel of Luke 6:45). Drawing things out of (*ek*) this treasury (Matt. 12:35) is the same as speaking 'out of [*ek*] the abundance [*perisseumatos*] of the heart' (12:34b); and, in this instance, the owner draws from his evil horde – i.e., his mouth speaks – evil things, which show him to be an evil person who serves the evil one (*ho ponēros*).[30] As John addressed Pharisees (and Sadducees) as a 'brood of vipers' (*gennēmata echidnōn*; 3:7), so does Jesus (12:34a). His intent is the same as John's – that, having perceived their true condition, they may repent of their sin and escape the divine wrath that threatens to consume them. 'Either make [*poiēsate*] the tree good...or make [*poiēsate*] the tree bad...,' Jesus commands (12:33a).[31] These are the only two choices; neutrality is impossible (Matt. 12:30). Either be confirmed in your condition as a bad tree sure to produce bad fruit and to be destroyed (7:19); or else repent of your sins, invoke the power of the very Spirit you have blasphemed, and

---

[29]*Ontes* is a present participle of *eimi* ('to be'). On the heart as a person's 'integrating center,' see page 248 (and n. 20). Cf. Matthew 5:8; 15:18-19; 22:37; Proverbs 4:23; Isaiah 59:13; Romans 3:10-14.

[30]For the devil as *ho ponēros*, see comments on Matthew 6:13. In the metaphor of 12:35, the 'bad things' may be counterfeit coins (so Gundry 1994: 240). The Greek of 12:35b exactly parallels that of verse 35a. As noted on pages 63-64, Matthew himself illustrates 'the good man.'

[31]I take this repeated verb – an aorist imperative of *poieō* – to be a genuine command (cf. *GGBB*, 485-86). Yet there is a conditional element: *if* the tree becomes good (or bad), *then* the fruit will be good (or bad). Cf. Hagner 1993: 350; *GGBB*, 489-90 (which notes that even conditional imperatives are issuing orders). Cf. comments on Matthew 3:7.

be transformed into a good tree before judgment falls (cf. the command to the Pharisee in 23:26).

'I tell you,' concludes Jesus, 'that every careless word [*pan rhēma argon*] which men speak, they will give account [*logon*] for it on the day of judgment. For [*gar*] by your words [*ek...tōn logōn sou*] you will be justified [*dikaiōthēsē*], and by your words [*ek tōn logōn sou*] you will be condemned [*katadikasthēsē*]' (Matt. 12:36-37).[32] *a. The adjective. Argos* can mean 'useless': such is faith apart from works (James 2:20). Since a useless thought is better left unsaid, its utterance is 'careless.'[33] Moreover, *argos* (from *alpha*-privative + *ergon*, 'work') can denote a 'work-less' word – a confession of faith without matching deeds (James 2:20 again), a broken promise, an unpaid vow. The charge of Matthew 12:24 is unspeakably *argos*.[34] *b. The heart.* Since those words are worthless, they might be thought insignificant. On the contrary, says Jesus: words – including those that are *argoi* – reveal the true state of the heart (12:34). A word that is *argos* as defined above is bad (*sapros*) fruit signaling a bad tree worthy of destruction (12:33). Sometimes a person's real condition is more accurately reflected in an apparently careless or casual remark than in one that is cautious and calculating.[35] *c. The judgment.* On that day each person (note the singular pronoun *sou*; 12:37) must

---

[32]If 'every careless word' (the neuter *pan rhēma argon*) is nominative, and the subject of Matthew 12:36a, then 12:36b, where the subject is 'they' (the 'men' of 36a), does not follow grammatically from 12:36a – an instance of anacoluthon (*alpha*-privative + *akoloutheō*, 'follow' = 'not following'). Or *pan rh. ar.* may be accusative by attraction to the relative pronoun 'which' (*ho*). Cf. GGNT, 435-40; BDF, par. 466. Note the word play on *logos* in 12:36 ('account') and 12:37 ('word').

[33]BAGD s.v., 3. Thus, e.g., ESV, NASB and NIV at 12:36. REB has 'thoughtless.'

[34]Cf. comments on 5:33-37; France 1985: 212 (quoting G. B. Caird). Jeremias 1971: 220 thinks 12:36 speaks of a word 'that does not accord with the truth.' In light of the etymology, note that *argos* means 'unemployed, idle' in 20:3, 6; and 'idle, lazy' in 1 Timothy 5:13; Titus 1:12. Cf. BAGD s.v., 1. and 2.

[35]'Every man's heart is a store-house, and his words show what he keeps there. Even lightly spoken words do that, and what is said on the spur of the moment is sometimes better evidence of a man's disposition than what he says deliberately, for the latter may be calculated hypocrisy' (Plummer 1911: 181). Cf. Carson 1984: 293, following Krister Stendahl. On the cruciality of speech, see also James 3:1-12.

give an account of every 'careless' and every 'work-less' word (12:36b). Words dishonest and untrue will then be useless, for the heart's deepest secrets and innermost motives will be exposed.[36] On that day some will be justified (a passive of *dikaioō*) by their words, and others condemned (a passive of *katadikazō*; 12:37). Yet God's verdict (each verb is a 'divine passive') is not ultimately determined by the words themselves. In each case, the *basis* for the judgment is what the words reveal – what is on the *heart*, who this person *is*. The one who has been justified (a passive of *dikaioō*) by faith in Jesus, who has been incorporated into him, whose heart has been transformed by the power of the Holy Spirit, and who therefore speaks good things (*agatha*, 12:34, 35) about Jesus and the Spirit, need fear no condemnation at the Last Judgment.[37] But all the others – including some who have spoken and acted in Jesus' name – will be banished from his presence (7:21-23, which is joined to 7:15-20 as 12:36-37 is to 12:33-35).

B. Jesus in his generation (12:38-50)

Jesus here refers four times to the present 'generation' (*genea*, 12:39, 41, 42 and 45); in the enclosing instances he calls it 'evil' (*ponēra*). One explanation for its character is the willful blindness of its leaders (12:38-42), whom Jesus has just described as evil (*ponēroi*, 12:34, 35). Another is that unclean spirits are mightily at work (12:43-45; note the comparative adjective *ponērotera*, 'more evil,' in 12:45). Family ties themselves pose a danger; the only deliverance from rampant evil comes from trusting and obeying Jesus the Lord (12:46-50).

Revelation Old and New (12:38-42)

Some scribes and Pharisees now address Jesus: 'Teacher, we want to see a sign from you' (Matt. 12:38b). As is clear from 12:38a (the adverb *tote*, 'then,' and the verb *apokrinomai*, 'answer'), this request is their response to Jesus' words in 12:25-37. They ask from him a 'sign' – *sēmeion*, the first instance

---

[36]Romans 2:16; 1 Corinthians 3:13; 4:5.

[37]See, e.g., Romans 3:21-26; 5:1; 8:1; 1 Corinthians 1:30; 2 Corinthians 5:21; Philippians 3:9-11; and Chamblin 1993: 73-76. See also Hendriksen 1973: 531, on Matthew 12:37.

of this term in Matthew. What they seek, in the language of
16:1, is 'a sign [*sēmeion*] from heaven [*ek tou ouranou*],' i.e., one
which is unmistakably and indisputably from *God*, and which
therefore could not possibly be interpreted as that exorcism
had been (12:22-24).[38]

1. *Visible signs (12:39-40)*

Several of Jesus' miracles are recorded in Matthew 8–9 and
two more in the present chapter (see vv. 10-13 and 22). At least
one was witnessed by 'some of the scribes' (9:3, with vv. 4-8).
Pharisees apparently witnessed at least three of them (9:32-34;
12:9-14, 22-24).

Has not God the Father, by his Spirit, empowered his Son
to do all these miracles (3:16-17; 12:15-21, 28)? Has not many a
sign from God already been granted? Yet, were not the scribes'
and Pharisees' responses to those earlier miracles uniformly
negative (9:3, 34; 12:14, 24)? Have not these inquirers (or
others like them) already contested the incontestable? What
would another sign from God do but further validate his Son,
and evoke yet fiercer opposition from Jesus' enemies?

Responding to that request, Jesus says: 'An evil and adulterous
generation seeks for a sign [*sēmeion*]; but no sign [*sēmeion*] will
be given to it except the sign [*sēmeion*] of Jonah the prophet'
(12:39). Unlike the evangelist John, Matthew never directly
applies *sēmeion* to the miracles of Jesus (but see comments on
16:1-4). Jesus himself does 'mighty works' (*dynameis*; 11:20, 21,
23); it is *false* Messiahs and *false* prophets who will perform
'great signs [*sēmeia*] and wonders [*terata*]' (24:24).[39] Yet, says
Jesus, to this generation one sign 'will be given' (*dothēsetai*, a
future passive from *didōmi*). In accord with the request of 12:38,
God will give this sign (that verb is a 'divine passive'), and it
will be unmistakably and indisputably *his*. Was not the prophet
Jonah 'in the belly of the great fish three days and three nights'

---

[38]Cf. Gundry 1994: 242; Tasker 1961: 131 (Jesus himself 'would not
originate' the sign).

[39]In Matthew 13:54, 58; 14:2, others call Jesus' miracles *dynameis*; in 7:22,
he uses the term of mighty works done in his name. For the positive usage
of *sēmeion*, see, e.g., John 2:11; 20:30.

(12:40a)? And was it not Yahweh who commanded the fish to vomit Jonah onto dry land (Jon. 2:10)?[40] Will not the Son of Man likewise spend 'three days and three nights in the heart of the earth' (Matt. 12:40b)? And is it not God the Father who will raise him from the dead?[41]

Yet, even *that* sign requires a response of faith. While Jesus implies that he will reside in the realm of the dead *only* three days and nights, he does not expressly refer to his resurrection – as he will do when addressing his disciples in Matthew 16:21. Nor does any disciple – much less a scribe or Pharisee – witness the resurrection *itself*. The risen Christ indeed appears to his followers (Matthew 28 and parallels), and commissions them to declare the glad tidings of this event. Whether others of this generation, including these scribes and Pharisees, will *see* this sign (12:38) and be saved from their wickedness and infidelity (12:39) depends on their *hearing* and *believing* the apostolic proclamation.[42] It is by no means certain that they will do so (cf. Luke 16:31).

2. Verbal witness (12:41-42)
Words are crucial, not only in responses to divine revelation (Matt. 12:33-37), but in the revelation itself – as implied in 12:40 (see above), and made explicit in verses 41-42.

---

[40]The Greek of the quoted words in 12:40a is exactly that of the LXX in Jonah 2:1 (English 1:17).

[41]'Jesus stayed in the realm of the dead [here called 'the heart of the earth'] parts of three 24-hour periods, not three whole days and nights. But the reference to three days and three nights comes out of Jonah 2:1 rather than from the story of Jesus and causes no problem in view of the Jewish method of reckoning part of a 24-hour day for the whole' (Gundry 1994: 244, with references). Matthew elsewhere speaks of Jesus as rising 'on the third day' (Matt. 16:21) and 'after three days' (27:63). In Jewish usage, 'after three days' (in Mark 8:31, par. to Matthew 16:21) meant 'the day after tomorrow' (France 2002: 336-37). Cf. Morris 1992: 326, with n. 101. Passive forms of the verb *egeirō* indicate that Jesus 'is raised' by the Father – and thus 'rises' – from the dead: see 16:21; 17:9, 23; 20:19; 26:32; 28:6, 7; BAGD s.v., 2. c. Cf. instances of the active voice of *egeirō* in Romans 8:11; 10:9; 1 Corinthians 6:14; Galatians 1:1.

[42]*Moichalis* ('adulterous'; Matthew 12:39) means unfaithful to God (cf. Jer. 3; Hos. 1-3). Jesus' resurrection is central in the apostolic preaching of Acts, e.g., 1:22; 2:22-36; 3:12-26.

In response to Jonah's preaching (*kērygma*), the men of Nineveh repented (the verb *metanoeō*; 12:41b). 'And behold [*kai idou*], something more [*pleion*] than Jonah is here' (12:41c, a pronouncement like that of 12:6 [see those comments]). This neuter comparative adjective (*pleion*), like that of 12:6 (*meizon*), refers primarily to Jesus himself: this is especially clear here, where he is compared to OT persons (it was the temple in 12:6): Jonah and the queen of the south (12:42; where *pleion* recurs). Jonah was saved from the belly of the fish, but Jesus will be raised from the *dead*. Jonah said nothing to the Ninevites about his miraculous rescue; Jesus' followers will proclaim his resurrection clearly and openly. God consigned Jonah to the fish as judgment for disobedience; Jesus' burial followed his supreme act of obedience, wherein God judged him for others' sins.[43] Jonah preached with a derived authority and is not said to have done any miracles; Jesus speaks with inherent and unrivaled authority, underscores his preaching and teaching with his mighty works, and explains his deeds with his words (12:28). Jonah's sole message was a warning of judgment (Jon. 3:4), but Jesus preaches 'the gospel [*euangelion*] of the kingdom' (Matt. 4:23). In response to Jonah's preparatory and partial witness, the Ninevites believed God, called a fast and repented of their sins (Jon. 3:5-9). Most of Jesus' contemporaries, on the contrary, greet his full and final revelation of God with indifference, disobedience or open hostility.[44]

A Hebrew prophet, Jonah, took Yahweh's message to a distant Gentile city. By contrast, the Gentile 'queen of the south' took the initiative, and traveled a greater distance – indeed 'from the ends of the earth' – to gain wisdom (*sophia*) from Solomon, a Hebrew king (12:42b). Once in Jerusalem, she learned that his – and his God's – greatness far surpassed

---

[43]One anonymous ancient writer identified the 'sign of Jonah' as the 'stumbling block of the cross' (in *ACC* 1a: 256).

[44]Some such contrasts are noted by Chrysostom (*ACC* 1a: 257). On typology in Matthew, see above, pages 123-29, especially 127-28; France 1971: 43-46.

what she had been told.[45] 'And behold [*kai idou*], something more [*pleion*] than Solomon is here' (12:42c). Solomon's wisdom, for all its brilliance, cannot compare to that of Jesus, for the same reason Jonah's preaching cannot match his (see above). Solomon's wisdom was founded on the teachings of Moses; but Jesus' authority exceeds that of Moses (pp. 301-02). One reason for Jesus' superiority is that he both faithfully teaches and unfailingly obeys the will of God, whereas Solomon in later life turned from great wisdom to gross folly (1 Kings 11:1-8). Nonetheless, Solomon in wisdom recognized (i) that one far greater than he – Yahweh's Messiah – would one day reign wisely and justly over a universal realm, and (ii) that kings from the nations, including Sheba, would pay him homage, and present him gifts far more splendid than those he himself received from the queen of the south.[46] Will not the present generation's enthusiasm for Jesus' wisdom therefore surpass – or at least equal – that of the queen for Solomon's? To be sure, many of these people are impressed by Jesus' teaching (Matt. 7:28-29); yet in the end most refuse to obey it (7:13-14). The most appalling thing is that Israelites who study, teach and apply the received wisdom, and who should therefore be especially receptive to the wisdom Jesus imparts – namely the scribes and Pharisees, together with the priests – are the very ones who most fiercely oppose him.[47]

---

[45]The queen came from Sheba, or Saba (modern Yemen), at the southern tip of the Arabian Peninsula, east of the Red Sea and far southeast of Jerusalem. Her visit is recorded in 1 Kings 10:1-10, 13 (par. 2 Chron. 9:1-9, 12), her praise of Solomon and Yahweh in verses 6-9. Neither account suggests that the queen had heard of, or hoped to witness, a 'sign from heaven' like that of 2 Chronicles 7:1-3. See D. A. Hubbard, 'Sheba, Queen of,' *IBD* 1431.

[46]See Psalm 72:8-11, 15 (in a psalm 'Of Solomon'); cf. Isaiah 2:2-3; 11:1-10; 60:1-7; Davis 2002: 41, 107-9. Matthew 2:10-11 alludes to Psalm 72 and Isaiah 60 (pp. 225-26 above). Cf. Psalm 72:12-14 to Matthew 12:20 (Isa. 42:3). 1 Kings 10:9 better applies to Jesus than to Solomon.

[47]'But these men [Matt. 12:38] and priests [16:21], whose task it was to love wisdom, showed contempt for the wisdom placed on their lap before their very eyes' (*ACC* 1a: 258, quoting an anonymous figure). Should not scribes and Pharisees – occupants of Moses' seat (23:2) – have gladly welcomed wisdom from the New Moses? Contrast the teachers' response in Luke 2:46-47.

Both the men of Nineveh and the queen of the south 'will rise up in the judgment with this generation and will condemn it' (Matt. 12:41a, 42a). These Gentiles will be raised from the dead and appear at the Last Judgment as witnesses for the prosecution.[48] Will they not be appalled by the evidence they hear concerning the present generation of Israelites? The OT Gentile cities of 11:20-24 *would have* repented, had they witnessed Jesus' words and works; the citizens of Nineveh *did* repent at Jonah's preaching and will condemn those who did *not* repent at Jesus' preaching. The Gentile queen who lauded the wisdom of Solomon will condemn those who spurned the greater wisdom of Jesus. Then he – the Son of Man – will make the final judgment and pronounce the sentence. Let this evil generation and its leaders remember that sins and blasphemies against the Son of Man may yet be forgiven (12:31-32). Let them heed the example of those repentant Ninevites; let them also recall that Nineveh reverted to great evil and suffered the severest judgment (Nahum); and let them repent of their great wickedness before time runs out.[49]

The Peril of an Empty House (12:43-45)
Jesus tells a parable about demonic activity (12:43-45b, then applies it to 'this evil generation' (12:45c). Accordingly, he addresses not just scribes and Pharisees (12:38), but the crowds (12:46).

1. The parable
'When the unclean spirit [to akatharton pneuma, i.e. 'demon,' daimonion] comes out [exelthē, i.e., is cast out] of a person, it

---

[48]Some think anistēmi (Matt. 12:41a) and egeirō (12:42a) mean 'appear in court' to give evidence (so REB). But the use of egeirō instead of anistēmi in verse 42a (whose other terms exactly parallel 12:41a), and the theme of verse 40, favor taking the verbs as references to resurrection from the dead (n. 41 above; REB mg., 'will rise again'; Davies and Allison 1991: 357-58; Gundry 1994: 246). Now raised, the Ninevites and the queen provide the requisite two witnesses (Deut. 19:15) and more!

[49]And time *is* running out: cf. e.g., 13:10-17; the conflicts and judgment in chapters 21–22; and the woes of chapter 23. On Jesus as Judge, see, e.g., 7:21-23; 19:28; 25:31-33; John 5:19-30. On the grace in words of judgment, see pages 663, 669-70.

wanders through waterless places [*anydrōn topōn*, natural abodes of demons] seeking rest but does not find it ['since he can only be satisfied where he can wreak destruction']' (Matt. 12:43).[50] 'Then it says, "I will return to my house [*ton oikon mou*: cf. *oikia* in 12:25, 29 and *Beelzeboul* in 12:24, 27] whence I came out [i.e., the person from whom I was expelled]." And having arrived, it finds the house unoccupied, swept clean and put in order [*kekosmēmenon*, i.e., 'prepared for the ceremonious reception of a guest']' (12:44).[51] 'Then it goes and brings with it seven other spirits more evil than itself [as seven is the number of perfection, 'the seven evil spirits represent every form of demonic seduction and wickedness']; and they enter in and make their dwelling [*katoikei*] there. And the last state [*ta eschata*] of that man becomes worse than the first [*tōn prōtōn*]' (12:45ab).[52]

2. The warning

'Thus it will be for this evil generation' (12:45c). Empowered by the Spirit of God to advance the rule of God (12:28), Jesus has expelled a demon from a man (12:22, 43). Yet, it would be disastrous for this vacated 'house,' now restored to order (12:44), to be left uninhabited. Jesus' warning is intended, not just for liberated demoniacs but for all his contemporaries: there is evil in all of them which needs to be repelled and replaced by good (cf. Rom. 12:21). It is not enough that demons, and doctrines of demons, be expelled; nor that people acknowledge Jesus to be uniquely empowered to achieve both kinds of expulsions. The true Lord, Yahweh incarnate, must reign in place of Beelzeboul, 'lord of the dwelling'; the abode once tyrannized by an unclean spirit (*pneuma*) must be filled with the Holy Spirit (*Pneuma*). What demon – or even host of demons – would dare try to enter such a house (cf. Matt.12:45a)?

---

[50]The bracketed quotations are from Jeremias 1963: 197. For demons as unclean spirits, see Matthew 10:1, 8; for deserted places as their haunts, see 4:1; 8:28 (further texts in Keener 1999: 369).

[51]The passive participle, from *kosmeō*, might be rendered 'decorated' (BAGD s.v., 2.).

[52]The neuter plural *pneumata* ('spirits') takes a singular verb, *katoikei* (from *katoikeō*). These demons 'settle down' for a long stay – as did Joseph in Nazareth (2:23), and Jesus in Capernaum (4:13 [both verses use *katoikeō*]).

Moreover, false teachings must be supplanted by the truth Jesus imparts; otherwise the mind will be left vulnerable to the most devilish doctrine of all (12:24) – which, once embraced, leaves the pupil in the worst imaginable condition (12:45b, 32).[53]

The New Family (12:46-50)

While Jesus is addressing the crowds (*ochloi*), his mother (*mētēr*) and his brothers (*adelphoi*) arrive, asking to speak to him (Matt. 12:46). Cf. 13:55, where the names of the mother and the brothers are given; and Mark 3:21, which reveals that they have come to take Jesus into custody, believing him to be 'beside himself,' that is, 'out of his mind.'[54]

Having learned of their presence (Matt. 12:47-48a), Jesus says, 'Who is my mother [*mētēr*], and who are my brothers [*adelphoi*]? (12:48b). Answering his own question, he points to his disciples (*mathētai*) and says, 'Behold [*Idou*] my mother [*mētēr*] and my brothers [*adelphoi*]. For [*gar*] whoever does the will of my Father in heaven, this one is my brother [*adelphos*] and sister [*adelphē*] and mother [*mētēr*]' (12:49-50).[55] These words call for several comments. *1*. To become a disciple of

---

[53]'The house must not remain empty when the spirit hostile to God has been expelled. A new master must reign there, the word of Jesus must be its rule of life, and the joy of the Kingdom of God must pervade it' (Jeremias 1963: 198). 'The former house of the demon must become God's property, what Paul calls...the dwelling place of the Holy Spirit' (Manson 1957: 88; cf. 1 Cor. 3:16; Eph. 2:22). Augustine (*ACC* 1a: 260) contrasts the 'sevenfold evil' of 12:45a with the 'sevenfold operation of the Holy Spirit' in Isaiah 11:2. Even the liberated demoniac of Matthew 12:22 will have to decide for or against Jesus (12: 30). True repentance entails not just being sorry for past sins, but swearing allegiance to Jesus and bearing fruit accordingly (4:17; 11:21; 12:30, 33, 41; 13:3-9; Tasker 1961: 132). Later passages about apostasy warn (in effect) that a person who enters a house ruled by Jesus but then willfully departs will find himself in a far worse state than when he entered (see 2 Peter 2:20-22; and n. 25 above).

[54]Mark 3:21 records the judgment of Jesus' family, not of the crowd (3:20; see arguments in France 2002: 165-67). Mark does not say why the family views Jesus this way. While their interpretation of him differs greatly from that of the scribes (Mark 3:22, par. to Matt. 12:24), the two groups are united in the belief that Jesus' behavior departs from accepted norms.

[55]There is some doubt about the originality of 12:47: most versions (e.g., NASB, NIV) include it in the text; ESV places it in the margin (see comments in

Jesus is to enter a genuine family. Given the arrival of Jesus' *mētēr* and *adelphoi* (12:46), the accent on these terms in 12:47-50 is especially noteworthy. Conspicuous by its absence from these references to human beings is the term *patēr*: Joseph has apparently died; and within the family of Jesus' followers, the heavenly Father is the only one to whom this name is rightly applied (23:9). Jesus here speaks of '*my* Father [*tou patros mou*],' which makes it plain that the only others permitted to address God in this way are those who belong to Jesus (6:9).[56] 2. While Jesus teaches love for the neighbors within one's own family (15:4-9; 19:19), he also insists that commitment to him and his mission must exceed all others (see comments on 8:21-22; 10:34-39). 3. This passage, far from excluding Jesus' mother and brothers from the circle of his disciples, invites them to join it: '*whoever* does the will of my Father' (12:50). On this occasion, his mother and brothers show a lack of faith (Mark 3:21); and John 7:5 reports that 'his brothers did not believe in him.' But Mary is at the cross (John 19:25-27); and both she and Jesus' brothers gather with other believers in the upper room to await the coming of the Spirit (Acts 1:14).[57] 4. The mark of the true disciple, and the one escape from this generation's rampant evil, is doing the heavenly Father's will (Matt. 12:50) – which especially means loving him and loving one's neighbors (22:37-40), by which means good conquers evil (Rom. 12:21), the very point of verses 43-45.

TC, 26-27). In the parallel of Mark 3, Jesus speaks *to* the crowd sitting around him (3:32) about *others* sitting around him (3:34), namely his disciples (who are identified in 4:10 as 'those around him with the twelve').

[56]See also, e.g., 5:16, 45, 48; 11:25-27. Nowhere does Matthew call Joseph Jesus' *patēr* (see pp. 197-98, with n. 7). With *adelphē*, 12:50, cf. 13:56, where Jesus' sisters (*adelphai*) are mentioned but not named. In light of the language of 12:50, the statement of 23:8 – 'you are all [*pantes*] brothers [*adelphoi*]' – may be rightly translated to include *adelphai* (as in ESV mg.). Paul's favorite term for Christians is *adelphoi* (see, e.g., 1 Thess. 1:4, and ESV mg.).

[57]Augustine says that 'it is greater for Mary to have been a disciple of Christ than the mother of Christ' (*ACC* 1a: 261). On Jesus' brothers James and Judas, see comments on 13:55.

Section 10

'My People, Give Ear, Attend to my Word'[1] (Matt 13:1-58)

The first of Jesus' five major discourses (Matt. 5–7) presented his *torah* for the citizens of the kingdom; the second (ch. 10), his instructions to the heralds of the kingdom. This third one (i.e., ch. 13) consists of seven parables of the kingdom (13:3-50, with 53). While this teaching presupposes all that goes before, the link with chapters 11–12 is especially close. We learn from 13:1 that, 'on that day' (which commenced at some point in chapter 12), Jesus left 'the house' (where he was just addressing the crowd as his family stood outside; 12:46). Like those two chapters, these parables (and the accompanying explanations, including verse 10-17) depict the various responses to Jesus and the resultant twofold division to be brought fully to light at the Last Judgment.[2] This chapter's closing references to the disciples (12:51-52) and the people of Nazareth (12:54-58) illustrate two of those responses and prefigure that final division. We will discover that these parables likewise elucidate – for disciples and readers alike – matters to be reported in chapters 14–28.[3]

---

[1] The title of a hymn based on Psalm 78 (*The Psalter*, 1912).

[2] For these subjects, see especially Matthew 11:16-24; 12:22-42.

[3] For the relation of chapter 13 to its context and to the other discourses, see pages 51-57, especially 51, 55. Chilton 1996: 101 calls Jesus' total activity 'a parable of the kingdom.'

I.
'IN PARABLES NEW.'[1]

Jesus, having left the house, 'sat beside the sea' (Matt. 13:1b).[2] 'And great crowds gathered to him; so he got into a boat and sat there, and the whole crowd stood on the shore. And he told them many things in parables [*en parabolais*], saying...' (13:2-3a). The scene recalls that of the first discourse, delivered from a nearby mountainside. Here, as there, Jesus sits to speak. There he taught his disciples in the hearing of the crowds; here, at least initially, he addresses the crowds directly.[3]

A. The Term *Parabolē*

The instance of this noun in 13:3 is the first in Matthew; eleven of the remaining sixteen uses occur in this chapter.[4] The Greek *parabolē* has close affinities with the Hebrew *māšāl*; both are broader in scope than 'parable.' The noun *māšāl* is related to the verb *māšal*, whose original sense is 'to be similar, like.' *Parabolē* is likewise related to the verb *paraballō*, 'to throw [*ballō*] alongside [*para*],' i.e., 'to compare'[5] (cf. Luke 22:41, *lithou bolēn*, 'a stone's throw'). In the MT, *māšāl* can denote (i) a proverbial saying (many of which contain comparisons), or

---

[1]From a hymn (the title of which is given above) based on Psalm 78 (*The Psalter*, 1912).

[2]The 'house' (*oikia*) is in Capernaum, and may belong to Peter or Matthew; note *oikia* in Matthew 8:14 and 9:10. The town lay on the Sea (*thalassa*) of Galilee; note this term in 4:15, 18.

[3]See pages 299-300, 302-03 (from introductory comments on chapters 5–7). For *ochlos* ('crowd'), used twice in 13:2, see also 5:1 and 7:28 (three of the four instances are plural). The verb for 'sit' in 13:1, 2 (*kathēmai*) is different from that in 5:1 (*kathizō*). The verb *elalēsen* ('he told'; 13:3a) is a constative, or comprehensive, aorist (*GGBB*, 557-58).

[4]See 13:10, 13, 18, 24, 31, 33, 34 (*bis*), 35, 36, 53.

[5]F. Hauck, *TDNT* 5: 747, thus translates *māšal*; cf. BDB s.v. ('represent, be like'). For *paraballō*, see LSJ s.v., II. 2. ('*to set side by side*, so as *to compare* one with another').

a collection of proverbs; (ii) a riddle, or a solution thereto; (iii) a byword used in mockery, an adage used as a taunt; and (iv) a developed similitude, or parable.[6] Almost every instance of *parabolē* in the LXX (of the MT) translates the noun *māšāl* or the verb *māšal*. Matthew contains *parabolai* where this term does not occur, and instances of *parabolē* where 'parable' is not the best translation.[7] In Matthew 13, the sense 'parable' (iv. above) predominates. These parables both conceal and reveal truth (ii.; 13:10-17, 35); some of their words, if not taunting (iii.), are tantalizing (13:4-7, 25-30); and Jesus' concluding lesson (13:52) contains 'a comparative proverb' (cf. i.).[8]

B. The Design

Seven parables are here gathered together and the number is probably deliberate.[9] The parable of the soils, together with its explanation and the intervening words (Matt. 13:3-23) has parallels in both Mark (4:3-20) and Luke (8:5-15), as does the parable of the mustard seed (Matt. 13:31-32; see Mark 4:30-32; Luke 13:18-19). The parable of the yeast (Matt. 13:33) is paralleled in Luke alone (13:20-21); and the commentary of Matt. 13:34-35 in Mark alone (4:33-34). Peculiar to Matthew are the remaining four: the parables of the wheat and the weeds, together with its explanation (13:24-30, 36-43); the hidden treasure (13:44); the pearl (13:45-46); and the net (13:47-50).[10] Jesus doubtless taught and assembled such parables on many

---

[6]For *māšāl* in these senses, see, e.g., (i) Proverbs 1:1; 26:7; (ii) the parallel clauses of Psalms 49:4; 78:2 (quoted in Matt. 12:35); Proverbs 1:6; (iii) Isaiah 14:4; Jeremiah 24:9; Ezekiel 12:22; Habakkuk 2:6; (iv) Ezekiel 17:2; 24:3. These four are discussed by Hauck, ibid., 747-49.

[7]For parabolic (or proverbial) sayings without the term, see, e.g., 7:24-27; 9:16 (which the par. in Luke 5:36 calls a *parabolē*); 11:16-19; 12:25-26, 29 (the par. in Mark 3:24-27 is said to consist of *parabolai*; 3:23), 43-45. The *parabolē* in Matthew 15:15 ('parable' in ESV, REB, etc.) has 'the broad sense of proverb, riddle, or wisdom saying' and may be translated 'analogy' (Hagner 1995: 436, 434). The instance in 24:32 is well rendered 'lesson' in ESV, REB, etc.

[8]Davies and Allison 1991: 444. For NT instances of *parabolē* in the sense 'type, figure,' see BAGD s.v. 1.

[9]Keener 1999: 393 calls 13:52 'an eighth parable.' But see above (p. 58, including n. 35); and Hagner 1993: 363, 401.

[10]Here, as in the previous discourses, Matthew combines material from Mark (see pp. 71-77), 'Q' (pp. 78-86) and 'M' (pp. 86-90).

another occasion (comments on the collection of material in chs. 5–7 apply here too, *mutatis mutandis*; see pp. 303-05). Yet, there is no comparable collection anywhere else in the Synoptic Gospels. Later chapters of Matthew contain parables; but the closest approaches to this set of seven are the three of 21:28–22:14 and the three of 25:1-46. Luke records many parables, but the closest he comes to a special collection is the three parables of the 'lost' in 15:1-32.

Matthew 13:3a, 'he told [*elalēsen*] them [namely the crowds; v. 2] many things [*polla*] in parables [*en parabolais*],' and 13:53a, 'when Jesus finished these parables [*tas parabolas tautas*],' frame the collection. Matthew also provides a frame in 13:34a, whose language is very close to verse 3a: 'All these things [*tauta panta*] Jesus told [*elalēsen*] to the crowds [*tois ochlois*] in parables [*en parabolais*].' In this light, it is noteworthy (i) that Jesus hereafter leaves the crowds and returns to the house (13:36; cf. 1), where he addresses all the teachings of 13:37-50 to his disciples exclusively; and (ii) that each of the four parables in 13:3-33 (the seed and the soils, the wheat and the weeds, the mustard seed, and the yeast) is expressly identified as a *parabolē* and that none of the three in 13:44-50 (the treasure, the pearl, and the net) is so identified.[11]

The special import of the parable of the seed and the soil is reflected in the structure. *1.* This is the first parable recorded (13:3b-8) after the weighty introduction (13:1-3a; cf. the relation of 5:3-12 to 5:1-2). *2.* 'Behold' (*Idou*, 13:3b) does not recur in the chapter, which suggests that here it prefaces the momentous (as often elsewhere, e.g., 1:20, 23). *3.* The command of 13:9 – 'He who has ears, let him hear' – shows that people in the crowd must be especially attentive to this parable. In the one other instance of this statement in the discourse (13:43), Jesus addresses disciples.[12] *4.* This parable and its explanation (13:18-23) enclose the crucial words of 13:10-17. These points are underscored

---

[11]See the instances of *parabolē* in Matthew 13:3, 24, 31, 33; verse 36 harks back to the parable of the wheat and the weeds (13:24-30, which Jesus explains in 13:36-43). The aorist indicative *elalēsen* (from *laleō*, 'tell'; 13:3, 34, also occurs in verse 33).

[12]'Let him hear [*akouetō*]' (13:9, 43) does not merely grant permission; it requires action (cf. *GGBB*, 486, n. 97). Cf. 11:15, and *TC*, 24, on the textual variant in these three texts.

by Jesus' questions in Mark 4:13: 'Do you not understand this parable? How then will you understand all the parables?'[13]

The remaining six parables together exhibit some interesting structural features. *1*. Unlike the opening of the first parable ('A sower went out to sow,' Matt. 13:3), these six have in common the opening 'The kingdom of heaven [*hē basileia tōn ouranōn*] is like [the adjective *homoia*]' (13:31, 33, 44, 45, 47) or 'may be likened to [*hōmoiōthē*, from the verb *homoioō*]' (13:24). *2*. The first three of these parables (the wheat and the weeds, the mustard seed, and the yeast) are followed by the explanatory words of 13:34-35; the other three (the treasure, the pearl and the net), by the closing lesson of 13:51-52. *3*. The six may be viewed chiastically. The first and the sixth (i.e., the wheat and the weeds, and the net) both emphasize the separation that will occur at history's end (compare the explanatory words of 13:40-42 to those of verses 49-50).[14] Parables two and three (i.e., mustard seed and yeast) form a pair (13:31-33), as do parables four and five (i.e., treasure and pearl). Moreover, the hidden treasure corresponds to the hidden yeast; and the smallness of the pearl to that of the mustard seed.[15] These features might be represented as *a* [24-30], *b* [31-33], *b'* [44-46], *a'* [47-50]; or as *a* [24-30], *b* [31-32], *c* [33], *c'* [44], *b'* [45-46], *a'* [47-50].

C. Parable and Allegory

Through most of the church's history, Jesus' parables were commonly interpreted allegorically. Adolf Jülicher, in a work published in 1888–89, argued, on the contrary, that Jesus used no allegory and that such features (as found, e.g., in 13:19-23, 37-43) were to be ascribed to the evangelists. A hundred years later, the relation between these two terms was said to be 'among the most debated issues in NT studies.'[16]

---

[13]ESV; the questions have no parallel in Matthew. 'Mark uses the parable of the seeds as a parable about parables' (Gundry 1993: 191).

[14]Cf. Gundry 1994: 251.

[15]So Hagner 1993: 396, with 363. The yeast was *hidden in* the flour (Matt. 13:33; the verb *egkryptō*); the treasure was *hidden* in the field (13:44; the verb *kryptō*, twice).

[16]K.R. Snodgrass, 'Parable,' *DJG* (published in 1992), 594. See ibid., 591-3 for the 'history of interpretation' of parables.

Distinctions

A parable is an extended *simile*, a similitude, a 'like-saying.'
To shed light on a spiritual reality, Jesus 'throws alongside it'
a picture or a story (see A. above).[17] An allegory is an extended
metaphor. The Greek verb *allēgoreō* consists of *allos* ('other')
and a variant of *agoreuō* ('to speak'), and thus means, literally,
'to speak so as to imply other than what is said' (LSJ s.v.). In
the single NT instance of *allēgoreō* (Gal. 4:24), the language is
metaphorical: 'Hagar *is* [or *represents*] Mount Sinai' (4:25a; cf.
ESV). 'Hagar is *like* Mount Sinai,' of course, would be a simile.

Parables are typically true to life. There are no better
examples than those of Jesus. Matthew 13:4-8 describe actual
effects of sowing. We can picture a woman preparing bread
as in 13:33 and men sorting fish as in verse 48. 'In a parable
things are what they profess to be: loaves are loaves, stones
are stones, lamps are lamps.' An allegory, on the other hand,
'may stray off into some "never never" world where eagles
can plant vines and stars become bulls. The room which the
woman sweeps in the parable of the Lost Coin [Luke 15:8-10]
is a room in any Galilean [dwelling]; the room which the man
sweeps in *The Pilgrim's Progress* is not a room but "the Heart
of a Man that was never sanctified by the sweet Grace of the
Gospel."'[18] By the same token, in a full-blown allegory, most
features of the story have counterparts in the meaning: *The
Pilgrim's Progress* is again a good example. The details of a
parable sometimes *have* meaning, as we shall see; but more
often they *support* the meaning – and help to drive it home
– by making the parable realistic and vivid.[19] John Bunyan
wrote his book as an allegory; it is precisely as such that it has
such power. But Augustine's famous allegorical reading of the
parable of the good Samaritan (Luke 10:25-37) obscures the
story's purpose and reduces its power.[20]

---

[17]Snodgrass, ibid., 594, defines parables as 'stories with two levels of
meaning; the story level provides a mirror by which reality is perceived and
understood.' Ryken 1987: 61 says that in parables profound truth becomes
incarnate in stories.

[18]Both quotations are from Hunter 1964: 10.

[19]Hunter, ibid., says the details are 'like the feathers which wing the arrow.'

[20]For Augustine's reading of this parable, see Dodd 1961:1-2.

Yet in some parables, while all the figures remain real, events occur which would almost certainly *not* occur in real life. Would any actual landowner behave as does the one in Matthew 21:33-39? Would he really expect tenant farmers to respect his son after they have murdered so many of his servants? Yet, when interpreted allegorically, this story depicts how wondrous and how patient is the steadfast love of Israel's God.[21]

Combinations

The term Matthew consistently uses for these teachings is *parabolē*; the noun *allēgoria* never occurs here, nor anywhere else in the NT (as noted, the matching verb appears only in Gal. 4:24). Yet, within Matthew 13, the two longest parables (13:3-9, 24-30) are expressly interpreted allegorically (13:18-23, 36-43). Why should this be considered strange or foreign to Jesus? The very ingredients of the two parables lend themselves to such interpretation. (The same holds true for the parable of 21:33-39, which lacks the explanation supplied for the other two.)

On what basis is it decided in advance that Jesus' chosen method was *strictly parabolic*? Why should the early Christians be any more disposed to incorporating allegorical features than Jesus, especially when the OT contains allegory as well as parable, if not more allegory than parable? To *distinguish* 'parable' from 'allegory' is not to *separate* them. Is not a teacher in the Hebrew tradition – especially one so free, creative, subtle and wise as Jesus – perfectly free to interlace them in his teaching?

Jesus uses allegorical features as expressions of his pedagogical artistry and within the framework and under the control of his chosen parabolic medium. The parable of the weeds begins, 'The kingdom of heaven is like this: a man sowed good seed in his field' (Matt. 13:24); so we are ready for

---

[21]This may help to explain why Snodgrass (ibid., 594) calls parables 'imaginary gardens with real toads in them.' The debt of Matthew 18:24 far exceeds what a real servant would ever owe – which is just the point, given the parable's accent on the grace of God (see those comments). But this story, unlike that of 21:33-39, does not lend itself to allegorical interpretation.

an extended *simile*. But according to the following explanation,
'the one who sows...*is* [*estin*] the Son of Man, the field *is* [*estin*]
the world' (13:37-39); so we may speak of an extended *metaphor*,
or of an extended simile framing an extended metaphor, or of
'an allegorical parable' (as, e.g., in Ezek. 24:1-14) – though not
of 'a parabolic allegory.' In short, Jesus depicts reality in both
parabolic and allegorical terms, especially the former.[22]

[22]For support of these points, see Moule 1969: 107-11; Carson 1984:
301-03; France 1985: 217-18; Blomberg 1990; 1992: 211-12; Snodgrass, ibid.,
591-94; Keener 1999: 372-75, 381-84.

II.
'LIKE SEED INTO THE GROUND'[1]
(13:3-23)

In view of Jesus' own description (13:18), we will call this 'the parable of the sower.' Yet, in both the parable (13:3-9) and its explanation (13:18-23), Jesus focuses not on the sower (contrast 13:24, 37), but on the seed and the soil – i.e., not directly on himself, but on responses to his preaching. Forms of the verb *akouō* ('hear') occur fifteen times in the passage. Nothing is said of plowing, so it is unclear whether it preceded the sowing, or followed (there is evidence for both); nor is answering this question essential for understanding and applying the picture.[2] In the intervening verses (13:10-17), Jesus distinguishes two basic responses to his 'word of the kingdom' (13:19).

A. The Parable of the Sower (13:3-9)

'Behold [*Idou*], the sower [*ho speirōn*] went out to sow [*tou speirein*]' (Matt. 13:3b).[3] In the following description, seeds fall on four kinds of soil (note the repeated *epesen* ['fell'] in 13:4, 5, 7 and 8).[4]

Some (*ha*) of the seeds fell on hardened soil 'beside the path' (*para tēn hodon*) which ran around or across the field (13:4b). The seeds could therefore not penetrate the surface and were easily devoured by the birds (13:4c).[5]

---

[1]From the hymn 'Almighty God, Your Word Is Cast,' by John Cawood (1819).

[2]On this matter, see Gundry 1994: 253, and especially Payne 1978: 123-29.

[3]On the opening *Idou*, see page 684. The subject *ho speirōn* may be a typical sower; but the use of the definite article with the participle suggests a subtle reference to Jesus (note the language of 37). *Tou speirein* is an infinitive of purpose. Both terms are present forms of *speirō*.

[4]This is an aorist singular from *piptō*. The respective subjects are *ha* (Matt. 13:4) and *alla* (13:5, 7, 8), neuter plurals which agree with the implied *spermata* ('seeds'), and call for a singular verb.

[5]In the other three instances, the preposition is *epi* ('on' in 13:5, 8; 'among' in v. 7), which favors taking the *para* of 13:4 to mean 'beside' rather than 'on'

Other seeds (*alla*) fell on 'rocky ground' (*petrōdē*) covered by
a thin layer of topsoil; and 'because they had no depth of earth'
(*dia to mē echein bathos gēs*), they sprouted quickly (Matt. 13:5).
When the sun rose, they were scorched; and 'because they
had no root' (*dia to mē echein rhizan*), they withered (13:6).[6]

Others (*alla*) fell among thorn bushes (*akanthai*) – onto
ground not known to contain seeds of thorns, or accidentally
among dried up thorn bushes from the previous year (cf.
Jer. 4:3).[7] In either case (or both), the thorn bushes grew up
and choked the seeds (Matt. 13:7). So, as Mark 4:7 reports, this
seed 'produced no fruit' (*karpon ouk edōken*). Cf. the reference
to *akanthai* in Matthew 7:16.

'But others [*alla*] fell on good soil [*epi tēn gēn tēn kalēn*] and
kept producing fruit [*edidou karpon*], some a hundredfold,
some sixty, some thirty' (Matt. 13:8).[8] The prepositional
phrase *epi...kalēn* stresses the fine quality of this soil.[9] Given
the consequent productivity of these seeds, the choice of
the imperfect verb *edidou* (from *didōmi*, 'give') instead of the
aorist *edōken* (as in Mark 4:7) is noteworthy.[10] By not including
some words found in Mark 4:8 ('growing up and increasing

(for the latter, see BAGD s.v., III. 1. d.); cf. the use of *para* in 20:30. Hagner
1993: 366 translates 'along the edge of the path.' As the farmer sowed 'near
the path, some seed accidentally fell on the edge of the path' (Gundry 1994:
253). Luke 8:5 adds that this seed 'was trampled underfoot.'

[6]The present infinitive *echein* (from *echō*, 'have') here expresses cause
(*GGBB*, 596-97). 'Either the sower does not know that rock lies immediately
below the surface of certain parts of his field, or some seed falls accidentally on
those parts' (Gundry 1994: 253). For botanical explanations of Matthew 13:5-6,
see ibid.

[7]Not so likely is that seeds are deliberately sown among thorns with a
view to plowing; for seeds of old thorns would produce new ones to choke
out the grain (cf. Gundry 1994: 254).

[8]Each 'some' translates the neuter singular relative pronoun *ho*, for
an implied *sperma* (cf. n. 4). Here, the singular is 'to be understood as a
distributive plural' (Hagner 1993: 369).

[9]In this construction (article-noun-article-adjective) 'both substantive
and adjective receive emphasis' (*GGNT*, 776); cf. *GGBB*, 306-7.

[10]This is an iterative imperfect (*GGBB*, 546-47). The translation 'kept
producing' is Hagner's (1993: 369). Given the prevalence of the aorist tense
in Matthew 13:4-7 (eleven instances in all), the use of the imperfect in 13:8
is all the more striking. The expression 'to give fruit' is Semitic, and occurs
often in the LXX (Davies and Allison 1991: 384).

and yielding,' ESV), Matthew highlights the reference to fruit bearing.[11] Moreover, he begins with the most fruitful plants of all – 'some a hundredfold' – whereas Mark 4:8 begins with 'thirtyfold.' The figures are true to life: an increase of a hundredfold was 'excellent but not fantastic.'[12]

For Matthew 13:9, see the comments on page 684.

B. Truth Revealed and Hidden (13:10-17)

The disciples (*hoi mathētai*) now come and ask Jesus, 'Why do you speak [*laleis*] to them [*autois*] in parables [*en parabolais*]?' (13:10). 'Them' means 'the crowds' (cf. 13:3a: 'he spoke [*elalēsen*] to them [*autois*, namely the *ochloi* or *ochlos* of 13:2] many things in parables [*en parabolais*].' In the present passage, Jesus relates his ministry to both disciples and crowds, and also to the prophecy of Isaiah.

Jesus and the Disciples
Jesus first responds to his disciples by saying, 'Because [*Hoti*] to you it has been given [*dedotai*] to know the mysteries [*ta mystēria*] of the kingdom of heaven' (13:11a).[13] That statement is augmented in 13:12a: 'For [*gar*] whoever has, more will be given [*dothēsetai*] to him, and he will be granted great abundance [*perisseuthēsetai*].'

Jesus addresses persons who have already embraced 'the gospel [*to euangelion*] of the kingdom' (4:23; i.e., 'the word [*ho logos*] of the kingdom,' 13:19) and have become his followers. In

---

[11]Cf. Gundry 1994: 254. The additional words in Mark 4:8 accentuate the potency of the seed and the abundance of the crop (the verb *anabainō*, 'grow up,' used of thorn bushes in Matthew 13:7, here describes the good plants). Note also the plural *alla* (13:8a), in contrast to the singular terms *ho* (Matt. 13:4) and *allo* (13:5, 7). As we saw, all four of Matthew's terms are plural.

[12]Gundry, ibid.; cf. Genesis 26:12; Keener 1999: 378, with n. 18. Says Calvin (1995a: 73): 'Jerome foolishly applies these three grades to virgins, widows, and wives, as if the harvest the Lord demands of us related only to celibacy and the godliness of the married were not often more richly fruitful in virtue. It should also be understood...that Christ was not exaggerating when He spoke of a hundred-fold fruit, for many regions were then very fertile....'

[13]With Davies and Allison (1991: 389), I take the conjunction *hoti* to be causal (to respond to the 'Why' of 10) rather than recitative (to introduce direct discourse, in which case it is left untranslated). Cf. BAGD s.v., 2. and 3.; Carson 1984: 307.

that light and for that reason, he has begun to disclose to them 'the mysteries of the kingdom' (chs. 5–12). He will continue to do so through these parables of the kingdom. Explanations such as those of 13:18-23 and 13:36-43 offer insight into these *mystēria*. But so do parables that lack explanations: could not many a disciple readily identify with the man of 13:44 and the merchant of 13:45-46?

The Father and the Son who previously imparted truth concerning each other (11:25-30) will continue their enlightening work. The *dedotai* of 13:11a (perfect tense) and the *dothēsetai* of 13:12a (future tense) are both 'divine passives' (from the verb *didōmi*) which together comprehend that work, and encompass both God's sovereign *initiative* (in election) and his sovereign *response* (to the disciples' trust).[14] The accompanying verb in 13:12a, *perisseuthēsetai*, a form of *perisseuō* in the future tense, is another 'divine passive.'[15] By the end of Matthew, the triune God will indeed have given the disciples 'great abundance' of understanding, a treasure to be continuously replenished and enlarged as disciples obey and impart what they have learned.[16]

Jesus and the Crowds

In speaking to the disciples about themselves (Matt. 13:11a, 12a) Jesus exceeded their request; for they had inquired about the crowds (13:10). Jesus directly addresses their question in 13:11b, 12b and 13.

---

[14]*Dedotai* is an 'intensive' (or 'resultative') perfect, which stresses the effects of a past action (cf. *GGBB*, 574-76). The disciples' 'eyes are opened to the dawn of the Messianic time…, to the incursion of the divine rule in the word and work of Jesus. This perception is not the result of their own perspicacity or a reward for their own achievement. It is the gift of God's free and sovereign grace' (G. Bornkamm, *TDNT* 4: 818-19, s.v. *mystērion*). Cf. 2 Thessalonians 2:13-14. On God's 'good pleasure' (*eudokia*), see comments on Matthew 11:26; and Carson 1984: 309.

[15]The verb is transitive; the dative *autō* serves as object for both passive verbs in 12a (cf. BAGD s.v. *perisseuō*, 2.; 1 Thess. 3:12).

[16]Cf., e.g., Matthew 7:15-27; 10:1-42; 12:33-37; 13:51-52; 28:18-20; cf. Luke 6:38; Colossians 1:9-10.

1. Unbelief

The disciples asked, 'Why [*Dia ti*] do you speak [*laleis*] to them [*autois*] in parables [*en parabolais*]? (13:10). Jesus pointedly answers in 13:13: 'For this reason [*dia touto*] I speak [*lalō*] to them [*autois*] in parables [*en parabolais*], because [*hoti*] although seeing [*blepontes*] they do not see [*ou blepousin*], and although hearing [*akouontes*] they do not hear [*ou akouousin*], nor do they understand [*oude syniousin*].' In 13:13, the causal phrase *dia touto* points forward to the causal conjunction *hoti*; together they answer to the *Dia ti* of 13:10 (literally 'because of what?'). The rest of 13:13a uses the very language of the question in verse 10.

The people in the crowds have heard Jesus' preaching and teaching, and they have witnessed his mighty works (Matt. 4:23–12:23, *passim*). Yet, they have not believed his gospel of the kingdom, nor repented of their sins nor become his obedient followers. As the quotation from Isaiah in 13:14-15 will make plain, Jesus speaks not merely of the crowds' *inability* to see and hear, but of their *unwillingness* to do so.[17] Not only in light of that response, but because of it (*dia touto* and *hoti*), Jesus chooses to speak to the crowds 'in parables.'

2. Judgment

The question of Matthew 13:10, 'Why [*Dia ti*] do you...?,' receives a further answer in verse 11: 'Because [*Hoti*] ...to those [*ekeinois*, i.e., *autois*; 13:10b] it has not been given [*ou dedotai*].' The insights God grants to disciples (13:11a; *hymin dedotai*), he withholds from the crowds.[18] Disciples learn about 'the mysteries of the kingdom' from both the parables themselves and their explanations. But for the crowds the parables are puzzling riddles rather than enlightening images; they conceal rather than disclose those mysteries. And these

---

[17]*Blepontes* and *akouontes* are verbal participles of concession (*GGBB*, 634). The present indicatives (also from *blepō* and *akouō*), read in the light of Isaiah 6:9-10, reveal the people's 'willful closed mindedness' (Hagner 1993: 373). For the same attitude, see Ezekiel 3:7.

[18]*Hymin* and *autois* are personal pronouns, *ekeinois* is a demonstrative pronoun; all three are datives of indirect object (*GGBB*, 140-42). For *dedotai*, see n. 14.

people, who appear most urgently to need such explanations as those of 13:18-23 and 13:36-43 are denied them.[19] In short, Jesus' parables are acts of judgment upon the crowds. The reason for such action is stated in 13:13b: the crowds have responded to Jesus' words and works with willful unbelief. Cf. 2 Thessalonians 2:10-12.

Correspondingly antithetical to Matthew 13:12a is verse 12b: 'But whoever does not have, even what he has will be taken away [*arthēsetai*] from him.' The verb *arthēsetai* (a form of *airō* in the future tense), like *dothēsetai* (13:12a) and *dedotai* (13:11a), is a 'divine passive.' These words state in the most striking terms (for how can one *lose* what he never *had*?) the threat of utter loss. Jesus' use of the saying in 25:29b elucidates the present text. That servant (25:29) had received one talent from his master (25:15), but failed to invest it (25:18, 27a); in the end he had no interest to report (25:27) and he lost the original talent as well (25:28, which, like verse 29, uses the verb *airō*). To the persons in view in 13:12b – members of the crowd – Jesus has presented 'the gospel [or word] of the kingdom.' But since it remains unused and bears no fruit (13:8, 23; cf. 25:24, 26), it is as though it was never received; and there is danger that it will be taken away (*arthēsetai*; 13:12; 25:29) – i.e., that persons presently *unwilling* to embrace the gospel will one day be *unable* to do so.[20]

3. Mercy

Jesus addresses the crowds in parables *because* they are willfully deaf and blind to his words and works, not *in order to* inflict deafness and blindness upon them (on the conjunction *hina* in Mark 4:12, see below). The parables indeed enact judgment (see 2.); but it would be 'simplistic to say that the

[19]Jewish teachers used parables as sermon illustrations *to explain a point they were teaching....* To offer an illustration without stating the point, however, was *like presenting a riddle instead*' (Keener 1999: 378). Cf. Jesus' parables for disciples and crowds respectively.

[20]Cf. comments on Matthew 12:31-32. Some suggest that 'what...will be taken away' (13:12b) is Judaism or some other religion at variance with the kingdom of heaven (cf. France 1985: 222; Hagner 1993: 373). But the view stated above is, to my mind, much more likely (cf. Hendriksen 1973: 553-54, who also cites the parable of Matthew 25). The parallel to 13:12b in Luke 8:18 reads, 'even what he thinks [*dokei*] he has will be taken away.'

sole function of parables to outsiders was to condemn them.'[21] On the contrary, as often elsewhere, Jesus offers mercy even when pronouncing judgment.

The seed in the parable of Matthew 13:3-8, as verse 19 explains, is 'the word of the kingdom.' This *explanation* is withheld from the crowds, but this *word* is assuredly not. On the contrary, Jesus and his apostles continue to proclaim this 'gospel of the kingdom' to the crowds, and to press its claims upon them.[22] Were not the disciples themselves once members of the crowds, and are there not yet many of God's elect within the crowds (to whom the words of 13:11a will, in time, apply)? Is not the 'whoever' (*hostis*) of 13:12a broad enough to include people not yet converted? Will not persons in the crowds who embrace the gospel and submit to God's rule, be granted insight into these very parables of judgment, and find them to be means of grace?

By his words in 13:9, Jesus commands the crowds (13:2-3) to pay the closest attention to the crucial parable of 13:3-8, to ponder it with utmost seriousness. Is he not hereby challenging them to *solve this riddle* – to pick the lock on the door he has fastened – and to take action accordingly? Are not his parables meant to *disarm* them (as happened with David, 2 Sam. 12:1-15)? Does he not want them to perceive *themselves* in 13:4-7 and to aspire to become like the seeds of 13:8 instead? Is not one purpose of the imagery in 13:30 to awaken the crowds to the punishment awaiting *them*, so that they might flee to the gospel and repent of their sins before it is too late?[23]

---

[21]Carson 1984: 309.

[22]See 4:17, 23; 9:35; 10:7; cf. 24:14; 26:13.

[23]Cf. Mark 4:33: 'And with many such parables he was speaking the word [*ton logon*, namely the gospel of the kingdom, 4:14; 1:14-15] to them [*autois*, namely the crowd, 4:1-2, 34], as they were able to hear.' This indicates (as the par. in Matt. 13:34 does not) that the parables themselves were vehicles for the gospel, and that some in the crowd gave heed to it. Hooker 1991: 137-38 rightly says that 4:33 shows Mark's understanding of 4:10-12. Snodgrass (*DJG*, 593) calls *māšāl* (on which see pp. 682-83 above) 'any dark saying intended to stimulate thought.' Moule 1969: 96-103 argues that Jesus' parables are meant to stimulate, provoke and educate outsiders. Thiselton 1985: 112 perceives both judgment and mercy in Mark 4:11-12 and its parallels. On the one hand, 'a person who has neither the will nor the

Jesus and Isaiah

Still speaking of the crowd, Jesus says in Matthew 13:14a:
'With them indeed is being fulfilled [*anaplēroutai*] the prophecy
of Isaiah which says....' Then, in 13:14b-15, Jesus quotes from
Isaiah 6:9-10; Matthew's wording is almost exactly identical
to the LXX (some differences from the MT are noted below).[24]
The verb *anaplēroō* occurs nowhere else in Matthew. This
preface, like those with *plēroō*, signals both (i) that the content
of the ensuing quotation applies both to OT times (in this
case, Isaiah's day) and to Jesus' time, and (ii) that present
occurrences will in important respects surpass or intensify
those of the earlier period.[25]

1. Fulfillment in judgment on unbelief

In the preceding verses Jesus spoke of judgment (13:11b, 12b),
then of the unbelief that precipitated it (13:13b). That reflects
the order in the quotation from the LXX of Isaiah, which
also refers to judgment (6:9) before unbelief (6:10). Given the
progress from Isaiah to Jesus, present unbelief is the more
culpable, and present judgment the more severe.

---

capacity to understand suffers the inbuilt penalty which this failure carries
with it.' On the other hand, parables 'prevent a premature and superficial
rejection of the gospel. The crowd of opponents can indeed "see" *that* they
are challenged; but only when they are grasped by the parable at a more
than merely superficial conscious level is response precipitated in such
a way that they "see" its full *point*.' Cf. Carson 1984: 309-10. Art – in this
case the parable – is 'the ice axe to break the sea frozen inside us' (Franz
Kafka, quoted by Roy Anker, *Books & Culture*, Nov/Dec 1998, p. 8). In light
of Ezekiel 3:7 (noted above), observe Yahweh's commissions to Ezekiel in
3:18 and 33:18.

[24]France 1985: 222, arguing against the view that Matthew 13:14-15 are a
later addition, thinks it likely that these verses are 'Matthew's own addition,
along the lines of his formula-quotations..., to underline the allusion in
Jesus' words.' I believe that Jesus himself is responsible for the quotation:
in the Greek text, 13:14 continues the sentence begun in 13:13; quotations
from Isaiah 6:9-10 are found on his lips in Mark 4:12 and Luke 8:10 (John
12:40 is the evangelist's); and see above, pages 92-94, 101-02, for Matthew's
indebtedness to Jesus' OT quotations. As noted on page 98, when Matthew's
quotations are drawn from Mark or Q (as here), they typically agree with
the LXX.

[25]On Jesus as the fulfillment of the OT, see pages 120-22. If *plēroō* is
intensified in the compound *anaplēroō*, the meaning is 'completely fulfilled'

Speaking of the crowds' unbelief in Matthew 13:13b, Jesus already alludes to Isaiah; the verbs of 13:13b – *blepō* ('see'), *akouō* ('hear') and *syniēmi* ('understand') – all recur in 13:14b-15.[26] Isaiah 6:10, quoted in 13:15, vividly portrays that unbelief. The text is chiastic: 'For the *heart* [a] of this people has become dull, and with their *ears* [b] they have hardly heard, and their *eyes* [c] they have closed, lest they see with their *eyes* [c'], and hear with their *ears* [b'], and understand with their *heart* [a'], and they turn and I heal them.' To signal past actions, all three verbs in 13:15a are aorist indicatives.[27]

The judgment in store for the crowds (Matt. 13:11b, 12b) Jesus emphatically restates in 13:14 in the words of Isaiah 6:9. 'With hearing you will hear, but you will by no means understand; and with seeing you will see, but you will by no means perceive.' Stating the consequences of unbelief, this verse uses two *future* indicatives, together with two aorist subjunctives of strong negation.[28] The Hebrew of 6:9 voices this judgment by means of commands: 'Keep on hearing, but do not understand; keep on seeing, but do not perceive.'[29] Moreover, whereas the LXX of 6:10, and Matthew 13:15, describe the unbelief that evoked the judgment, the MT of Isaiah 6:10 commands Isaiah to impose judgment in face of Israel's unbelief (which is fully documented in Isaiah 1–5; see, e.g., 5:12b): 'Make the heart of this people dull, make their ears heavy, and blind their eyes; lest they see...and hear...and understand...and turn and be healed.'[30] Like the MT,

---

(Hagner 1993: 373). Cf. GT s.v. *anaplēroō: ana* 'to, up to, e.g. to fill a vessel up to the brim.'

[26]This helps to explain the textual variants at Matthew 13:13; see *TC*, 27. In 14-15 *blepō* occurs twice, *akouō* three times, and *syniēmi* twice.

[27]*Epachynthē* ('has become dull') is an aorist passive from *pachynō*; *ēkousan* ('they have ...heard') and *ekammysan* ('they have closed') are aorist actives, from *akouō* and *kammyō*.

[28]The indicatives are *akousete* ('you will hear'), from *akouō*; and *blepsete* ('you will see'), from *blepō*. The first is accompanied by the noun *akoē*, an instrumental dative of means ('with hearing'); the second by *blepontes*, an adverbial participle of means ('with seeing'). The first subjunctive of strong negation is *ou mē synēte* ('you will by no means understand'); the verb is *syniēmi*. The second is *ou mē idēte* ('you will by no means perceive'); the verb is *horaō*, so the translation differs from that for *blepō*. On this kind of subjunctive, see *GGBB*, 468-69.

[29]ESV, which well renders the Hebrew, each part of which contains a Qal imperative, infinitive absolute, and negatively formulated imperfect.

the quotations from Isaiah 6:9-10 in Mark 4:12, Luke 8:10 and John 12:40 concentrate on the theme of judgment – though, like the text in Isaiah, they all presuppose unbelief. The quotation from the LXX of Isaiah 6:9-10 in Matthew 13:14-15, speaking as it does of *both* judgment *and* unbelief, better represents the breadth of Jesus' teaching than do those quotations in the other gospels.[31]

2. Fulfillment in mercy to the unbelieving

Through Isaiah 1–12, precisely in face of imminent and irretrievable judgment, there resounds the promise of salvation. So grievous is the sin that the remedy must be radical; if the people are to be saved at all, their Judge must become their Savior (see further p. 201). Is not the terrifying word of judgment in the Hebrew text of Isaiah 6:9-10 itself a means of grace – to shock Israelites into awareness of their perilous condition, and to summon them out of their indifference and rebellion into repentance and faith? Does not the word of truth which Yahweh commissions Isaiah to proclaim, announce both judgment on sin and salvation from sin? Isaiah's structure is itself instructive in this regard. The second major division of the prophecy (chs. 6–12) opens with Isaiah's vision of Yahweh's splendor, and his commissioning (6:1-13), and it closes with songs of praise to Yahweh the Savior (12:1-6). Does this not mean that some of the people described in 6:10 were cured of their deafness and blindness and callousness of heart, and brought to repentance? Are not the praises of Isaiah 12 all the more joyful because of the apparently hopeless conditions amid which Isaiah's ministry began? Is not this salvation all the more glorious because of the King whose coming is prophesied in the enclosed texts (chs. 7–11)? By the same token, are not people who reject

---

[30]This translation is very close to ESV. The Hebrew of Matthew 13:10a contains three imperatives.

[31]Luke 8:10 quotes from Isaiah 6:9; Mark 4:12, from Isaiah 6:9 and 10b. It is fitting that the conjunction *hina* ('in order that') prefaces each of these quotations, since each depicts judgment as an *effect of* the parables (the parables of Mark 4:3-8 and Luke 8:5-8 depict the antecedent unbelief). The conjunction *hoti* ('because') is a fitting preface at Matthew 13:13b, since unbelief is here a *reason for* the parables. (Matthew's closest approach to

these overtures of grace in graver danger of destruction than before?[32]

In this respect, as in others, the prophecy of Isaiah 6:9-10 'is being fulfilled' in Jesus' day; this we saw when discussing Matthew 13:11-13. Now, as in Isaiah's day, the willful unbelief described in 13:15 will only be overcome by the mighty initiative of Israel's God. There may be a hint of this sovereign grace in 13:15b itself. This was earlier translated, 'lest they see with their eyes, and hear with their ears, and understand with their heart [etc.].' Behind 'lest' is the Greek *mēpote*, which serves both as a conjunction of purpose ('that...not,' 'lest') and as an interrogative particle ('whether perhaps'). Could it be that this text *both* expresses the crowds' determination to remain blind and deaf and hardened, *and* ponders the possibility of some such persons' being marvelously converted? Both nuances appear to be embraced in the REB: 'Otherwise, their eyes might see, their ears hear, and their mind understand, and then they might turn to me, and I would heal them' (cf. 2 Timothy 2:25, 'correcting his opponents with gentleness. God may perhaps [*mēpote*] grant them repentance leading to a knowledge of the truth', ESV).

3. Another kind of fulfillment

Then, in Matthew 13:16-17, Jesus says: 'But blessed [*makarioi*] are your eyes, because they see [*blepousin*]; and your ears,

the *hina* of Mark and Luke is not the *hoti* of 13:13b but 13:14b, the preface to the quotation itself.) Close to Matthew 13:13-15 is John 12:37-40; while Isaiah 6:10 serves in Matthew 12:40 as a pronouncement of judgment, 12:37-38 – quoting from Isaiah 53:1 – ascribes the judgment to Jewish unbelief. Also reminiscent of Matthew 13:13-15 is Acts 28:23-28; the quotation of Matthew 13:14b-15 is exactly duplicated in 28:26b-27. For the judgment of Isaiah 6 as God's response to Israel's unbelief, chapters 1–5 (etc.), see page 201, with n. 14. On the relation of Matthew 13:14b-15 to MT and LXX of Isaiah 6:9-10, see Hendriksen 1973: 555, n. 524.

[32]Motyer 1999: 73 says of Isaiah 6:9-10 that Isaiah 'was to bring God's word with fresh, even unparalleled clarity – for only the truth could win and change them; but in their negative response his hearers would pass the point of no return. The opportunity which could spell their salvation would spell their judgment.' See ibid., 74 (on 'the holy seed' of 6:13); 36, 108 (on the structure of Isaiah 6–12); and 289-93 (on 45:14-25). Ezekiel too was to be hopeful against all appearances (12:1-6; Eichrodt 1970: 150).

because they hear [*akouousin*]. For truly I tell you that many prophets [*prophētai*] and righteous persons [*dikaioi*] longed to see [*idein*] the things which you are seeing [*blepete*] but did not see [*eidan*] them, and to hear [*akousai*] the things which you are hearing [*akouete*] but did not hear [*ēkousan*] them.'

As the quotation of 13:14-15 applied to the crowds and amplified 13:11b, 12b-13, these two verses apply to the disciples and augment 13:11a and 12a. The positive usage of the verbs *blepō* and *akouō* in 13:16-17 stands in sharp contrast to the negative formulations in 13:13-15.[33] Reading 13:11a, 12a and 16-17 together makes it clear that disciples' seeing and hearing – past, present and future – are gifts from God, and that (conversely) his saving initiative always bears fruit in the human response. The adjective *makarioi* recalls the language of the beatitudes (5:3-12), a passage that also speaks of God's grace to the needy.[34]

Jesus' words of 13:17 follow naturally from his declaration about fulfilled prophecy in 13:14-15. Among those *prophētai* stand several of whom Jesus expressly speaks in Matthew, including Jonah (12:39) and Isaiah himself. And among those *dikaioi* stand several who figure prominently in Matthew, including the two introduced at the very beginning, Abraham and David (Matt. 1:1). One great difference between the days of preparation and the time of fulfillment is that those realities described and foretold by the OT prophets are now being realized in time and space. What Abraham and Isaiah could only envisage, the followers of Jesus can *see* and *hear*. He is the supremely righteous one (*dikaios*) and he comes to establish righteousness (*dikaiosynē*, 5:6). He is also merciful (*eleēmōn*,5:7); the same mercy Yahweh granted repentant

---

[33]In Matthew 13:14-15, a distinction between the two verbs for 'see' – *blepō* and *horaō* (aorist *eidon*) – was noted (I translated them 'see' and 'perceive' respectively). In 13:16-17, they are synonymous.

[34]The only instances of *makarios* in Matthew prior to 13:16 come in 5:3-11 and 11:6. Note that Luke 10:21-22 is parallel to Matthew 11:25-27; and Luke 10:23-24, to Matthew 13:16-17.

Ninevites in face of certain doom (Jon. 3:1-10), Yahweh
incarnate now offers stubborn Israelites (Matt. 13:10-17).[35]

C. The Parable of the Sower Explained (13:18-23)

The reason for the structure of Matthew 13:3-23 now becomes
plainer. Verses 18-23 both illuminate the parable of 13:3-9 and
illustrate the distinctions made in 13:10-17; and verses 10-17,
no less than 13:3-9, are foundational for the explanation to
follow.[36]

The Sower, the Seed and the Soils

'You [*Hymeis*], therefore [*oun*], hear [*akousate*] the parable
[*tēn parabolēn*] of the sower [*tou speirantos*]' (13:18). The *oun*
bases the ensuing explanation on verses 10-17; the emphatic
reference to disciples (*Hymeis*) recalls 13:11a; the imperative
akousate enjoins them to receive the deeper insight promised
in 13:12a; and the object *parabolēn* is elliptical for 'the meaning
of the parable' of 13:3-8.[37] In 13:18, as in verse 3, *speirō* is used
of the sower; the verb recurs in 13:19 (twice), 20, 22 and 23 to
describe what is sown.[38] There are corresponding references
to the seed – namely the *logos* ('word') – in 13:19 ('the word of
the kingdom'), 20, 21, 22 and 23. Given the nature of the seed,
there are matching instances of *akouō* ('hear') in 13:19, 20, 22
and 23. As seed becomes one with the soil on which it falls,
so here the recipients of the word are identified with both
the seed and the soil: in 13:20, for example, 'the one *sown* on
rocky ground *is* the one who *hears* the word.' The four kinds

---

[35]Cf. Hebrews 1:1-2; 11:13; 1 Peter 1:10-12. For the foresight of Abraham
and Isaiah, see John 8:56; 12:41 (Isa. 6:10 is quoted in 40). On Jesus and
Jonah, see comments on Matthew 12:38-42. On persons and events as 'types
and antitypes' in Matthew, see pages 126-28.

[36]Matthew 13:1-23 has the structure of Mark 4:1-20, as does Luke 8:4-15;
on Matthew's use of Mark, see pages 71-77. 'Jesus' parable of the sower
frames his explanation of the purpose for his parables precisely because it
explains the same concept in a different way' (Keener 1999: 381).

[37]Davies and Allison 1991: 399.

[38]The sower is denoted by the aorist active participle *speirantos*; (Matt.
13:18); the seed by the aorist passive participle *spareis* ('sown'; 13:19-23). Verse
19 also uses the perfect passive participle *esparmenon* ('what has been sown').

of soil, with the seed, represent four responses to Jesus' gospel of the kingdom.[39] In each case persons are said to hear (the verb *akouō*). The first three correspond to 13:13-15, the fourth to Matthew 13:16-17; note the use of *akouō* in all these verses.

The Hardened Soil (13:19)

The soil whose surface is too hard for the seed to penetrate (13:4) depicts the person who hears the word but *does not understand* it: *mē synientos* (13:19a). This is the very verb – *syniēmi* – used three times in verses 13-15. As those verses show, this person is not merely incapable of understanding the word but willfully resistant to it: see especially the comments on 13:13, page 693.

As in the parable the birds did not cause but took advantage of the soil's hardness (13:4), so too 'the evil one' (*ho ponēros*), the devil, is not said to harden the person but to exploit this condition by snatching away (the verb *harpazō*) the word that was sown in the heart (*kardia*). The individual might hereby experience some relief: one need no longer resist what has been taken away. In actual fact his condition is exceedingly perilous. For the devil is mediating God's judgment: in the language of 13:12b, the word which the person had (it was 'in his heart'; 13:19) yet never made his own, is now taken away from him. A further danger is that the heart bereft of 'the word of the kingdom' will succumb to Satanic propaganda instead: see comments on 12:22-37, 43-45. What hope is there for such people except to expropriate the believers' prayer, 'Rescue us from the evil one [*apo tou ponērou*]' (6:13)?

The Shallow Soil (13:20-21)

The next seed in the parable was sown on 'rocky ground' covered by a thin layer of topsoil (13:5). This is the person, says Jesus, who upon hearing the word 'immediately [*euthys*] receives it with joy [*meta charas*]' (13:20). The person who truly understands the *gospel* of the kingdom (13:23) can be expected to respond this way: see 13:44, where *chara* ('joy') recurs.

[39]Cf. Gundry 1993: 205.

But the description also applies to people in the crowds: as Matthew relates, they constantly follow Jesus about (see most recently 13:2, 'many crowds,' *ochloi polloi*), and enthusiastically respond to his words and works (see, e.g., 7:28; 9:8, 33; 12:23).[40]

The seeds that lacked depth of soil 'had no root' (*mē echein rhizan*) and withered under the blaze of the sun (Matt. 13:5-6). This person too 'has no root [*ouk echei...rhizan*] in himself but lasts only for a time [*proskairos*]; when tribulation [*thlipseōs*] or persecution [*diōgmou*] rises on account of the word, immediately [*euthys*] he falls away [*skandalizetai*]' (13:21). His commitment is as fleeting as it is fervent: note *proskairos,* 13:21, and *euthys,* both 13:20 and 13:21. By escaping trials that occur 'on account of the word [*ton logon*],' he betrays the very message – 'the word [*ton logon*] of the kingdom' (13:19) – that once excited him. His action may also imply a presumption that Jesus' miraculous powers leave no room for suffering.[41] On the contrary, says Jesus, tribulation and persecution assuredly await both him and his followers. The dawn of God's rule is unmistakably good news (4:23); but submission to God's rule on Messiah's terms is unavoidably costly.[42] The *ochloi* still favor Jesus during and after his entry into Jerusalem (21:8-11; 22:33). But in 26:47, a large *ochlos* comes to arrest him; and in 27:20-21, the *ochloi* vote to destroy him.

The Crowded Soil (13:22)

The seed that was choked by the thorn bushes (13:7) stands for a third person who hears the word (13:22a). In his case, 'the anxiety of the age and the deceitfulness of wealth choke [*sympnigei*] the word, and it becomes unfruitful' (13:22b).[43]

---

[40]See also the instances of *ochlos* in Matthew 4:25; 8:1, 18; 12:15, 46; 14:13-14; 15:30-31; 19:2; 20:29; 21:8-11, 46; 22:33.

[41]This passive of *skandalizō* (Matt. 13:21b) may be rendered '*let oneself be led into sin, fall away*' (BAGD s.v., 1. a.). Cf. the use of this verb in 11:6 (see p. 606, with n. 18); 13:57; 15:12; 24:10; 26:31, 33.

[42]See the other instances of *thlipsis* in 24:9, 21, 29. *Diōgmos,* 13:21, occurs nowhere else in Matthew; but see *diōkō* ('persecute') in 5:10-12, 44; 10:23 (with vv. 16-39); 23:34. Cf. the summons of 16:24-25.

[43]The Greek verb noted here, from *sympnigō,* '*(crowd together and) choke*' (BAGD s.v.), is a compound of *pnigō,* used in 7b. In Mark (though not in Matthew and Luke) the parable itself (4:7) stated that this seed 'produced no fruit.'

This hearer appears to take the word more seriously than did the first two. The picture of the birds devouring the seed (13:4) suggests that no growth occurred in the first case (cf. Mark 4:15, 'Satan immediately comes...'); and the rootless plants withering under the sun (Matt. 13:6) lasted 'only for a time' (13:21). Only here in 13:22 is the word said to be 'unfruitful' (*akarpos*), which suggests that the plant had progressed to a stage where fruit might be expected.

But it was not to be. Affairs of 'the age' (*aiōn*) – what Paul calls 'the present evil age' (*aiōnos... ponērou*, Gal. 1:4) – divert this person's attention from the gifts of 'the age to come.'[44] The anxiety (*merimna*) of this age saps energy that might have been devoted to advancing the kingdom of God (see Matt. 6:33, with 6:25-34, where the matching verb *merimnaō* ['be anxious, worry'] appears six times). Seduced by the deceitfulness (*apatē*) of wealth (*ploutos*), the person becomes a slave of *Mamōnas* (6:24); perhaps he does so more readily in view of the sacrifices required of Christ's followers.[45] Finding that wealth's promise of life abundant falls short of expectations, he becomes increasingly anxious (6:25-34; see those comments). Yet, by all those desires (cf. Mark 4:19; 1 John 2:15-16) the word (*logos*) is choked, so that it becomes extraordinarily difficult to reclaim the worldly and wealthy for the kingdom of God (Matt. 19:16-26). One person who fits the description of 13:22 is Judas Iscariot (see comments on 26:14-16; cf. John 6:66-71).

Reflecting on those first three responses to the word, one scholar thinks it 'possible that the path represents failure to hear by not loving God with the heart, the rocky soil failure to hear by not loving God with the soul (i.e., by not risking one's life for the word in times of persecution), and the thorny soil failure to hear by not loving God with might (i.e., with the

---

[44]For this distinction, see Matthew 12:32 (and p. 666, n. 21). Jesus promises his people *zōē aiōnios*, 'eternal life,' i.e., the life of the age (*aiōn*) to come (19:29, with its par. in Mark 10:30).

[45]Writes Rutherford 1984: 216, 'Now, Madam, I persuade you, that the greatest part but play with Christianity; they put it by-hand easily.' Cf. Matthew 7:13-14.

sacrifice of one's material wealth) – all of this after the pattern of Deuteronomy 6:4-5.'[46]

The Fruitful Soil (13:23)
Finally, what was sown on good soil (cf. Matt. 13:8) represents the person 'who hears [*akouōn*] and understands [*synieis*] the word [*logon*]' (13:23a). The other three also *hear* the word: both *akouō* and *logos* occur in 13:19, 20 and 22. This one alone is said to *understand* it: by contrast, the earlier instances of *syniēmi* in the passage (vv. 13, 14, 15 and 19) all appear in negative formulations.

There is proof of that understanding: 'who indeed [*dē*] bears fruit [*karpophorei*] and produces [*poiei*], one a hundredfold, one sixty, one thirty' (13:23b). Here, as in 13:8, Matthew emphasizes the bearing of fruit.[47] This *karpos* – which denotes what one does and how one lives – reveals who one *is*, as Jesus has already taught in 7:16-20 (with 7:21-27) and 12:33-37 (see those comments). Which is to say: within this parable (13:3-8) and its explanation (13:18-23), verses 8 and 23 alone describe Jesus' true disciples. Moreover, while Matthew (by reversing the Markan order) highlights the most abundant yield ('a hundredfold'), there is no suggestion that the lesser ones result from negligence. On the contrary, the whole of Matthew 13:23b is positive: the point of 'thirtyfold' is not that it should have been 'a hundredfold' or even 'sixtyfold,' but that from this *one* seed came *thirty*; so that this disciple is very different from the servant whose one talent earned no others.[48]

---

[46]Gundry 1994: 261, following Birger Gerhardsson. Cf. 22:37; Mark 12:30; Luke 10:27.

[47]See pages 690-91 for comments on Matthew 13:8. The particle *dē* contributes to the emphasis in 13:23 (its only occurrence in Matthew); cf. BAGD s.v. The verb *karpophoreō* ('bear fruit') is a more natural expression in Greek than *edidou karpon* (13:8; 'it gave fruit'); cf. page 690, n. 10. In the Greek text the last nine words of 13:23 are identical to those of 13:8. In Matthew, 'an understanding life under God's *Word* leads "of course" [*dē*] to a fruitbearing life in God's *world*' (Bruner 2004b: 25).

[48]'No blame is attached to the lesser harvest' (Filson 1960: 161). In the parable of Matthew 25:14-30, the descending order of the talents (five, two, one) matches 13:23b (100, 60, 30); but had the servant of 25:18 earned but one talent more, his master would have rewarded him.

The fruit bearing illustrates discipleship in the present world, not the harvest at the Last Judgment – a theme reserved for two of the later parables.[49] Yet let us remember that it is the word (*logos*), or gospel (*euangelion*), of the kingdom that causes this fruit to be borne. The abundance of the harvest, (Matt. 13:23) eclipses the failure of the other seeds[50] and presages that universal proclamation of the gospel by virtue of which the end will come (24:14; 26:13).[51]

---

[49]Cf. Matthew 13:30, 39-43, 38-50; Gundry 1994: 261.

[50]The sower's success is stated yet more strongly in Mark: see page 691, n. 11; Gundry 1993: 206.

[51]Believers bear fruit when Jesus' words remain in them (John 15:5-8). The gospel itself bears fruit and grows (Col. 1:6), one evidence of which is that believers bear fruit (1:10). See also Acts 6:7; 12:24; 19:20.

III.
'THE HEAV'NLY KINGDOM COMES'[1]
(13:24-58)

The kingdom (*basileia*) is the subject of all seven parables, the first as surely as the others (cf. the use of *basileia* in 13:11, 19). But these six are distinguished by their common preface, 'The kingdom of heaven [*hē basileia tōn ouranōn*] is like [*homoia*; in the first instance *hōmoiōthē*]...'; 'the point of comparison in all these cases is not strictly the noun which follows [e.g., 'man' in 13:24, 'mustard seed' in v. 31] but the parable as a whole.'[2] Two of the six describe the incomparable joy of those who presently discover the kingdom (13:44-46). Two others speak of the kingdom's growth from its inaugural to its consummation (13:31-33). The remaining two focus especially on the final judgment (13:24-30, with vv. 36-43 and 13:47-50). Given the separation that will then occur, it matters terribly how people respond to the message of the kingdom – and whether they believe Jesus (13:51-52) or not (13:53-58). Furthermore, this passage is illuminated by an OT text (13:34-35), as was the previous one (13:14-15).

A. The Parable of the Weeds (13:24-30)
Jesus now puts 'another parable' (*allēn parabolēn*) before 'them' (*autois*, 13:24a; i.e., the crowds, 13:2-3). Like the first parable (13:3-8), this one features the sowing of seed (the verb *speirō*, used in 13:3-4, recurs here [13:24, 27]); and in this case too Jesus reserves the parable's explanation for his disciples (13:36-43). Moreover, verses 34-35 prepare for this explanation as 13:10-17 had for the previous one.

---

[1]From the hymn 'Lead On, O King Eternal,' by Ernest W. Shurtleff (1888).

[2]France 1985: 225. For the prefaces, see Matthew 13:24, 31, 33, 44, 45, 47; *hōmoiōthē* (13:24) is an aorist passive from *homoioō* ('make like' or 'compare'). *Basileia* also occurs in 13:38, 41, 43, 52.

We first learn of a man (*anthrōpos*) who sows good seed (*kalon sperma*) in his field (*agros*, 13:24b). 'But while the men were sleeping, his enemy came and sowed [*epespeiren*] weeds [*zizania*] in the midst of the wheat [*sitos*] and went away' (13:25). The 'men' (*anthrōpoi*) are the master's slaves, perhaps together with the master himself (cf. 13:24, 27). *Zizanion* denotes the poisonous darnel, a weed that plagued grainfields; botanically it 'is closely related to bearded wheat, and in the early stages of growth is hard to distinguish from it.'[3] This 'enemy' (*echthros*) will be identified as the devil in 13:39; but the parable itself speaks simply of *an* enemy, not *the* enemy, of this man.[4]

'But when the stalks of wheat sprouted and produced grain [*karpon*], then the weeds [*zizania*] also appeared' (13:26). The slaves would not be surprised to find some *zizania* amid the produce of the *kalon sperma* (13:27a); their question – 'Where then did the weeds come from?' (13:27b) – 'therefore implies a large number due to deliberate sowing.'[5] The master confirms that this is indeed what happened (13:28a).

Verses 24-28a prepare for the main part of the parable. The servants' question (13:28b) is natural, since it was 'customary to weed out darnel, even repeatedly.'[6] But since the weeds' roots are now thoroughly intertwined with those of the wheat, the master defers action till the harvest (13:29-30a).[7] 'And at the time of the harvest I will tell the reapers, "First collect the weeds and bind them in bundles for burning, but gather the wheat into my barn"' (13:30b). These instructions anticipate the major emphasis in the explanation to follow (13:39b-43).[8]

---

[3]Jeremias 1963: 224, following Gustaf Dalman; cf. BAGD s.v. The neuter *zizanion* is uniformly plural (*zizania*) in Matthew 13, its only NT occurrences.

[4]Cf. Matthew 13:28a: 'An enemy did this.' The Greek of 13:25 (*autou ho echthros*) can be rendered 'an enemy of his'; see Jeremias 1963: 224, 11, n. 2.

[5]Gundry 1994: 264.

[6]Jeremias 1963: 225.

[7]Jeremias 1963: 225; Gundry 1994: 265. 'Premature action will damage the crop and curtail the growth' (Wenham 1989: 58).

[8]For the collecting of the weeds, Matthew 13:30 uses an aorist imperative of *syllegō*; for the gathering of the wheat, an aorist imperative of *synagō*. We are not to think that the darnel 'was rooted up immediately before the reaping of the grain, but that, as the reaper cut the grain with his sickle, he

B. The Parables of the Mustard Seed and the Leaven (13:31-33)

These are the last two parables addressed to the crowds (see Matt. 13:34). Like the first two, they depict growth; but here the accent is on the *potency* of the process – like that which transforms the smallest seed into the largest plant, or which causes fermentation to pervade a huge batch of dough. Even the verbs Matthew uses to preface these four parables form a small chiasm: 'he told [*elalēsen*] them' (13:3) [a]; 'he put before [*parethēken*] them' (13:24) [b]; 'he put before [*parethēken*] them' (13:31) [b']; 'he told [*elalēsen*] them' (13:33) [a'].[9]

The Pictures

A man takes a seed (*kokkos*) of mustard (*sinapi*) and sows it in his field (13:31), a verse whose language recalls the opening of the previous parable (13:24).[10] This, says Jesus, 'is the smallest of all the seeds; but when it has grown it is the largest of the garden plants [*meizon tōn lachanōn*] and becomes a tree [*dendron*], so that the birds of the air come and nest in its branches' (13:32). 'The mustard seed was the smallest of Palestinian seeds that could be seen with the naked eye and had become proverbial for smallness.'[11] (Cf. Jesus' use of the same imagery in Matt. 17:20.) Yet, this garden herb (*lachanon*) could reach a height of eight to twelve feet – more than enough for nesting birds.[12] Jesus uses hyperbole – 'the *smallest*

---

let the darnel fall, so that it was not gathered into the sheaves... The binding of the darnel into bundles is not an unnecessary process; it was evidently dried and used for fuel...' (Jeremias 1963: 225, following Gustaf Dalman). Some of the language of this parable appears in John's teaching (3:12) and in the parable of Mark 4:26-29 (but there the miraculous growth of the seed is stressed, and here the growing of wheat and weeds together: cf. Hagner 1993: 383).

[9]For other stylistic features of these and the other three parables, see pages 683-85.

[10]In addition to *anthrōpos* ('man'), *speirō* ('sow') and *en tō agrō autou* ('in his field'), the two verses have in common *hē basileia tōn ouranōn* ('the kingdom of heaven'). Besides, *kokkos* (Matt. 13:31) is a synonym of *sperma* ('seed'; 13:24), the plural of which occurs in verse 32; and the verb *homoioō* (13:24) is akin to the adjective *homoia*; 13:31).

[11]Gundry 1994: 267, with references to Jewish literature.

[12]Cf. Gundry, ibid.; BAGD s.v. *lachanon* ('*edible garden herb*'). In Luke 13:19 (par. to Matthew 13:31), the seed is planted in a 'garden' (*kēpos*). I have seen

of *all* the seeds...becomes a *tree'* – for the sake of the truth he is illustrating (see below).[13]

In the first parable, a man (*anthrōpos*) takes (the participle *labōn*) a mustard seed; in the second (Matthew 13:33, a woman (*gynē*) takes (the matching participle *labousa*) leaven (*zymē*).[14] This 'she hid in three measures of flour until the whole was leavened [*ezymōthē*].' 'The bread was leavened not with fresh yeast, but by keeping a piece of fermented dough from the previous baking and mixing it with the new batch. (The fermentation process could be begun from scratch in various ways, e.g., by letting barley and water ferment or by mixing bran and wine.)' Roman cities had bakeries, but Galilean women baked their own bread, 'so the mysteriously powerful process of leaven at work and dough bubbling and rising would be well known.'[15] In this instance the leaven is mixed 'into three measures [*sata tria*] of wheat flour [*aleurou*].' The Greek *saton* was equivalent to about thirteen liters, so three *sata* came to nearly forty liters. This is the largest amount a woman could knead at one time; and it would supply about fifty kilograms of bread, enough to feed between 100 and 150 people.[16]

This imagery is instructive in three ways: *a.* As that smallest of seeds is hidden in the soil (13:31), so this leaven is hidden

---

birds' nests in shrubs less than eight feet high. My translation of Matthew 13:32 treats the comparative adjectives *mikroteron* and *meizon* as superlatives: 'smallest' and 'greatest' respectively (so too, e.g., NIV; NRSV; Hagner 1993: 385).

[13]As noted on pages 686-87, the ingredients of parables are *real* but not always *true to life*. NIV's 'the smallest of all your seeds' at 13:32a is understandable in view of the Palestinian context; but it reduces the hyperbole – restored in TNIV, 'the smallest of all seeds.' Likewise, the NIV of the parallel in Mark 4:31b ('the smallest seed you plant in the ground') is changed in TNIV to 'the smallest of all seeds on earth.'

[14]These aorist participles – masculine and feminine respectively – are from *lambanō*.

[15]Wenham 1989: 55-56; cf. Keener 1999: 388; J. D. Douglas, 'Leaven,' *IBD*, 891. For the workings of yeasts (plants classed as *fungi*), and of the enzymes or ferments they produce, see a good encyclopedia – or cook book, e.g., *Joy of Cooking*, by Irma S. Rombauer and Marion Rombauer Becker (Indianapolis: Bobbs-Merrill, 1964), 502-4.

[16]France 1985: 227 estimates 100; Hagner 1993: 390 estimates 150. See also BAGD s.v. *saton* and *modios*.

in (the verb *egkryptō*) – engulfed by – a huge amount of flour. Yet that piece of leaven is powerful enough to affect the whole (the adjective *holos*) batch of dough. *b.* Here, as in 13:32, Jesus' language is hyperbolic. 'A housewife would not normally fix so much meal...; the unnatural magnitude of the illustration probably suggests that the kingdom far exceeds daily examples to which it may be compared.'[17] *c.* Yet in real life a woman might indeed prepare that much bread for a *festive* occasion. (Cf. Gen. 18:6, where Abraham instructs Sarah to prepare – from three measures (*sᵉ'îm*) of fine flour – cakes for Yahweh and two of his angels.)[18]

The Teachings

Each parable *as a whole* depicts the coming of God's rule: see the quotation on page 707.

Each one illustrates the kingdom's present *inaugural*. As the tiny seed is buried in the field, and the leaven is lost in three measures of flour, so the kingdom's beginnings are small and in some ways hidden from view (for the condition of the *heart* is crucial). It is precisely in their hidden state that the seed and the yeast exert their potency: so too the kingdom's stupendous powers are being released here and now, in the very place and time of its small beginnings (e.g., Matt. 11:4-6; 12:28; cf. John 12:24). Those powers are *already* influencing societies and transforming cultures. Moreover, as the mustard tree is potential in the seed, and as the leavening of the three measures of flour is latent in the fermented dough, so too the kingdom presently being manifested *is* the very kingdom that will one day be fully realized.[19]

Each parable also pictures the *consummation* toward which the kingdom is ineluctably progressing. The powers unleashed at the beginning do not abate until they have

---

[17]Keener 1999: 389. I would delete 'probably' from this quotation.

[18]This Hebrew term is the plural of *sᵉ'â* ('seah') which, by way of the Aramaic *sā'tā'*, accounts for the Greek *saton* (BAGD s.v.). Cf. Gundry 1994: 268.

[19]Cf. pages 144-45, 153-54. Like believers' praying 'Your kingdom come' (Matt. 6:10), Jeremiah's buying the field in Anathoth (Jer. 32) was 'a deliberate act of hope. All acts of hope expose themselves to ridicule because they seem impractical, failing to conform to visible reality. But in fact they are the reality that is being constructed but is not yet visible' (Peterson 1983: 176).

achieved their full effect. The smallest seed grows into a full-grown tree (so we could correctly speak of 'the parable of the mustard tree'). In the OT, the figure of a tree could represent a great empire; and birds, the nations brought under its protection. In that light, it is highly probable that the tree of Matthew 13:32 represents God's coming universal dominion – that the tree is planted, so to speak, in 'the field' which is 'the world' (13:24, 31, 38) – and that the nesting birds stand for the Gentiles who will become Jesus' disciples through the universal proclamation of the gospel.[20] As the leaven remains active until the whole batch of dough is permeated, so in the end God's rule will encompass the whole world and all its peoples. Moreover, as this woman may be preparing for a festive meal, so the parable may point to eschatological celebration.[21]

C. The Parables as Fulfillment (13:34-35)

With these two verses, together with 13:2-3a, Matthew frames the four parables Jesus addressed to the crowds.[22] In 13:34, Matthew forcefully underscores Jesus' reply to the disciples' question (13:10), especially his words in Matthew 13:13. Moreover, 13:35 elucidates verse 34 as 13:14-15 did verse 13. When Jesus tells parables to the crowds, both Isaiah 6:9-10 and Psalm 78:2 are *fulfilled*. The preface in 13:35a (with the verb *plēroō*), like that in verse 14a (with *anaplēroō*), signals both (i) that the content of the ensuing quotation applies both to OT times (in this case, Asaph's day) and to Jesus' time, and (ii) that present occurrences

---

[20]Cf. Matthew 24:14; 26:13; 28:18-20; Ezekiel 17:23 (and Ezekiel 31:1-18; Daniel 4:1-37, where trees thus described are rivals to God's rule and are therefore cut down); Manson 1935: 133, n. 1 (with references to Jewish literature); France 1985: 227; Gundry 1994: 267, 268.

[21]Cf. 8:11; 22:1-14; 25:1-13; 26:29. With Gundry 1994: 268, we may ask: 'Is Jesus hinting at the messianic banquet?' Foster 1998: 226 joins the metaphor of leaven to those of 5:13-16: 'Light exists to penetrate the darkness; salt exists to penetrate the meat; leaven exists to penetrate the dough. And we exist to penetrate the world!'

[22]As noted (p. 684), 13:34 has several terms in common with verses 2-3a.

[23]These same comments were made about Matthew 13:14-15 (p. 696).

will, in important respects, surpass or intensify those of the earlier period.[23]

Psalm 78:2 in the Time of Asaph

This psalm, together with several others, is ascribed to Asaph, a leading musician during David's reign. He states his purpose in 78:2: 'I will open my mouth in a parable [*māšāl*], I will declare riddles [*chîdôt*] from ancient times.' A *māšāl*, a term already considered (pp. 682-83), 'uses one realm of life to illuminate another'; a *chîdâh* is 'a lesson taught indirectly.'[24]

Asaph traces Israel's history from the Exodus (especially vv. 12-53) to the time of David (vv. 67-72), or from *Zoan* (v. 12, to *Zion* (v. 68).[25] The psalm recounts both Yahweh's wondrous and mighty deeds, and his people's recurrent ingratitude and obduracy. Asaph recites Israel's *past* for the sake of *present* and *future* generations (vv. 1-8).

But are not those facts well known? How can Asaph speak of parables and riddles? 1. For many listeners and readers, those events remain parabolic and enigmatic, because their underlying patterns and deepest meanings have not been understood. Asaph addresses that need and helps to solve those puzzles by his careful selection and combination of material and by the consistently theocentric character of his presentation.[26] 2. The indicatives Asaph recites – about both Yahweh's wonders and Israel's rebellions – are *veiled* imperatives, *indirect* exhortations (cf. above on *chîdâh*), calling Israelites to renewed praise, thanksgiving and obedience. As both points make clear, Asaph writes this psalm *in order that* these parables may be comprehended and these dark sayings illuminated (see again vv. 1-8).

---

[24]The respective quotations are from Kidner 1975: 281; and BDB s.v. *chîdâh* (on 78:2).

[25]Kidner 1975: 280. For Asaph, see, e.g., 1 Chronicles 15:19; 16:5; 29:30; 25:1-2 (with his sons); and the superscriptions of Psalms 50, 73-83.

[26]'The pattern of history is not self-evident; but the psalmist will show what it is really all about' (Carson 1984: 321). 'God' or 'Yahweh' (or 'he' or 'him') dominates the whole psalm.

Psalm 78:2 in the Time of Jesus
Jesus quoted from 'the prophecy [*prophēteia*] of Isaiah'
(Matt. 13:14a); Matthew speaks of what 'was spoken [by God]
through the prophet [*dia tou prophētou*]' (13:35a), but does
not include his name (cf. the language of 1:22). As noted, the
superscription of Psalm 78 identifies the author as Asaph,
who, in 1 Chronicles 25:2, is said to 'prophesy' (the verb *nābā'*),
and in 2 Chronicles 29:30 is called a 'seer' (*chōzeh*), a kind of
prophet.

In light of the quotation in Matthew 13:14-15, it is of interest
that some manuscripts ascribe the quotation in 13:35 to Isaiah;
but we may, with *GNT*, consider this name a later insertion.[27]
The quotation itself reads: 'I will open my mouth in parables;
I will declare things hidden from the foundation of the world'
(Matt. 13:35b). The quotation in 13:14-15, which is shared with
the other gospels, closely follows the LXX. This one, which is
peculiar to Matthew, departs from the LXX in its second line
and appears to depend directly on the Hebrew.[28] Like *māšāl*
and *chîdôt* in the Hebrew of Psalm 78:2, in Matthew 13:35
parabolais ('parables') and *kekrymmena* ('things hidden') stand in
synonymous parallelism; which illustrates the earlier point that
parables can take the form of riddles or dark sayings (see p. 683).

Like Asaph, Jesus and Matthew invoke the past in order to
instruct present and future generations: both of them select and
combine material from the OT to elucidate the work and words
and person of Messiah. But whereas Asaph stood *within* the OT

---

[27]NIV does not mention this variant; ESV includes it in the mg. The
inclusion of 'Isaiah' might be favored as the more difficult reading, 'for it
is easy to suppose that so obvious an error would have been corrected by
copyists' (cf. the textual variants at 27:9). 'On the other hand, if no prophet
were originally named, more than one scribe might have been prompted to
insert the name of the best known prophet.' The committee for *GNT* chose
to follow 'the preponderance of external evidence.' These quotations are
from *TC*, 27-28, which see for further comments.

[28]The distinctions noted here are true of Matthew's OT quotations generally
(see pp. 98-99). Matthew's *kekrymmena* ('things hidden') is closer to MT's *chîdôt*
('riddles, obscure sayings') than to LXX's *problēmata* ('problems' or 'barriers').
Cf. Davies and Allison 1991: 426. The genitive *kosmou* ('of the world') is in some
doubt textually; but not in Matthew 25:34, the only other instance of the phrase
'from the foundation of the world' in Matthew (cf. *TC*, 28).

period, Jesus stands *beyond* it as the one in whom all those OT promises and patterns reach their appointed goal (see p. 712, under C.). Thus the reign of David can now be seen in a far clearer light than when Asaph wrote Psalm 78. For not only do we possess the full record of David's history (i.e., 1 Sam. 16–1 Kings 2; 1 Chron. 11–29); 'the Son of David,' whose reign David prefigured, has appeared in time and space. Moreover, this regal figure is also the Suffering Servant of Yahweh; the Messianic King foreseen in Scripture is 'also the stricken Shepherd equally foreseen in Scripture.... Who clearly foresaw that both streams would merge in one person?'[29] In short, unless Jesus is understood and interpreted to be the central focus of the whole Bible, that history is sure to remain enigmatic.

Matthew relates the quotation from Psalm 78:2 to Jesus' teaching of the *crowds* (Matt. 13:34). These people too have witnessed the wondrous and mighty deeds of Yahweh, indeed of Yahweh incarnate (1:23; cf. Ps. 78:4). Yet they remain unbelieving, like their OT counterparts (Matt. 13:13; cf. Ps. 78:22, 32). Therefore they too stand under judgment – and a severer one than before, given the character and the time of the witness they have spurned (Matt. 11:5-6, 20-24). As Jesus taught in 13:10-17, his parables are acts of judgment upon the crowds; but as we also learned from that passage, these same parables express the divine favor – both to the believing disciples and to the unbelieving crowds (see pp. 691-701). It is this latter reality – God's overture of grace to the refractory crowd – which is accentuated in the quotation of 13:35. The judgment *stated* in 13:14 (the quotation from Isaiah 6:9) is here *presupposed*. It is clear from Matthew 13:35 that Jesus, no less than Asaph, wants to *disclose* secrets and to *clarify* riddles. The 'things hidden from the foundation of the world,' which are now being explained to the disciples, are potentially intelligible for people in the crowds as well. Some of them will in time understand those 'hidden things' (*kekrymmena*), whereupon they will rejoice like the man

---

[29]Carson 1984: 322. Jesus the Messiah 'unites in himself streams of revelation from the old covenant that had not been so clearly united before' (ibid.). Cf., e.g., Matthew 3:17; 12:17-21; 20:28; 21:4-11; 26:28, 31.

who found the treasure 'hidden' (*kekrymmenō*) in the field
(13:44).[30]

D. The Parable of the Weeds Explained (13:36-43)

Having deliberately 'left [*apheis*] the crowds,' Jesus went 'into
the house [*eis tēn oikian*]' (13:36a), whence he had come (13:1,
with *oikia*).[31] 'And his disciples came [*prosēlthon*] to him, saying,
"Explain [*Diasaphēson*] to us the parable of the weeds [*tōn
zizaniōn*] of the field"' (13:36b). Here, as in 5:1 and 13:10, the
disciples *come to* Jesus for instruction (the verb *proserchomai*).[32]
His response (in 13:11-23) to the inquiry of 13:10 prompts
their present request. Their name for the parable determines
the title used here, and in the exposition of verses 24-30. Jesus
first identifies seven elements in the parable (13:37-39), then
expounds its principal lesson (13:40-43).

Elements Identified (13:37-39)
'The one who sows the good seed is the Son of Man; the
field is the world; and the good seed stands for the sons of
the kingdom' (13:37-38a). Jesus the Son of Man (*ho huios tou
anthrōpou*) sows the seed ('the word of the kingdom', 13:19)
which produces good fruit in people's lives (13:8, 23); here
such people are themselves depicted as the good seed (*ton
kalon sperma*). While Jesus applies the name 'Son of Man' to his
saving work (e.g., Matt. 9:6; 20:28), here his authority to *judge*
is especially in view: note the recurrence of this name in 13:41
(cf. 16:27; 19:28; 25:31; p. 135, no. 3). In the parable, it was his
own field (*agros*) that the master sowed (13:24, 27). It is now

---

[30]According to Gundry 1994: 270, 'the hidden things, or parables, *are*
the hidden treasure of the kingdom. One finds and gains the kingdom by
understanding the parables.'

[31]*Aphiēmi* can mean 'send away': so BAGD for this instance (s.v., 1.); also
Hagner 1993: 391 ('he dismissed the crowds'). A better choice, in view of
Matthew 13:11-15, 34, is 'leave' (e.g. ESV, NIV; cf. BAGD s.v., 3.). But 'leave,'
in the sense of 'abandon,' would be too strong; cf. comments on *aphiēmi* in
4:20, 22. On *oikia* in 13:1, see page 682, n. 2.

[32]All three texts use aorist plural forms: the indicative *prosēlthan* (5:1) is a
variant spelling of *prosēlthon* (13:36); the *proselthontes* of 13:10 is a nominative
participle.

being identified as the world (*kosmos*), further witnesses to the Son of Man's universal dominion (cf. 28:18-20).[33]

'But the weeds are the sons of the evil one, and the enemy who sowed them is the devil; the harvest is the end of the age, and the harvesters are angels' (Matt. 13:38b-39). This is the first reference to 'the devil' (*ho diabolos*) since 4:1-11 (for the meaning of the name, see those comments). He, 'the evil one' (*ho ponēros*) who in the earlier parable snatched away the good seed from the heart (13:19), now sows seeds of his own – they being his 'sons' (*huioi*), people under his authority and bound to do his will. As surely as 'the sons of the kingdom' are enlisted to advance their Father's rule (13:43; 6:33), 'the sons of the evil one' seek – with their father – to thwart its progress and undo its achievements.[34] Yet, they cannot prevent the harvest (*therismos*) – the close of the age (*synteleia aiōnos*) – nor the disclosures and the separation which will then occur with the aid of the harvesters (*theristai*), the angels (*angeloi*).

Judgment Executed (13:40-43)

'Therefore [*oun*], just as the weeds are gathered and burned in fire, so will it be at the close of the age' (13:40). Having identified elements in the parable, Jesus now expounds its major lesson, namely what happens at the final judgment. Verse 40 (with its opening *oun*) connects most directly with 13:39b, which also speaks of 'the close of the age.'[35] Moreover, the aspect of judgment on which Jesus dwells at greatest length is the condemnation of the wicked. The single statement from the parable echoed in Matthew 13:40 is 13:38b: both texts speak of gathering (the verb *syllegō*) weeds (*zizania*) for burning (the verb *katakaiō*). The angels whom the Son of Man sends forth at

---

[33]In light of Matthew 13:37-38a, we can better understand why the parable says the seed is sown by 'the man' (i.e., 'the master') himself (13:24, 27), not by 'the men' or 'the servants' (13:25, 27).

[34]Cf. John 8:44; 1 John 3:10. The term 'the sons of the kingdom' occurs once more in Matthew (and in the NT) – 8:12, where the usage is closer to 13:38b ('the sons of the evil one') than to 13:38a ('the sons of the kingdom').

[35]Some MSS. read 'at the close of this [*toutou*] age' in 13:40. The adjective is a later addition, to conform this phrase to that of 12:32.

harvest time 'will gather [*syllexousin*, from *syllegō*] out of his kingdom all causes of offense [*panta ta skandala*] and those who practice lawlessness [*tous poiountas tēn anomian*]' (13:41). This first object (which is neuter), no less than the second, indicts personal behavior: Jesus later teaches that *skandala* – causes of stumbling, enticements to sin – come through people (18:7); it is they who cause others to stumble and to fall into sin (the verb *skandalizō*; 18:6).[36] As the weeds were burned 'with fire' (*pyri*; 13:40), so these persons will be cast 'into the furnace of fire' (*eis tēn kaminon tou pyros*). 'In that place there will be weeping and grinding of teeth' (13:42).[37]

That judgment will be global in scope and will embrace all peoples from every generation. Within that context, the Son of Man will judge the visible church. These two statements may be supported as follows: 1. The field is the *world* (*kosmos*, 13:38), not the *church* (*ekklēsia*), a term which does not appear until 16:18.[38] The Judge, the Son of Man, possesses universal authority (28:18); at the end there will be no rule (*basileia*) but his and the Father's (13:41, 43; Rev. 11:15). So the commissioned angels who gather all wickedness 'out of his kingdom' (*ek tēs basileias autou*, 13:41) are purging not just the church but the whole world. The same judgment is depicted in 25:32, where 'all the nations' are gathered before the Son of Man, and all their inhabitants divided into two companies.

---

[36]BAGD s.v. *skandalon*, 2.-3.; *skandalizō*, 1. a. Jesus calls Peter himself a *skandalon* in Matthew 16:23.

[37]This statement first occurred in 8:12 (see p. 502, n. 39); there it is 'the sons of the kingdom' who suffer this torment (cf. n. 34 above). In Daniel 3, 'sons of the kingdom' are cast 'into the burning fiery furnace' (*eis tēn kaminon tou pyros tēn kaiomenēn*, v. 6 LXX) but survive. Matthew 13:42 describes the place of punishment both final (see comments on 5:22, 'Gehenna of fire') and eternal (see comments on 18:8, 'eternal fire'). Jesus teaches that the same torment awaits 'the devil and his angels' (25:41).

[38]Calvin 1995a: 75 fails to convince: 'And it is a most apt comparison when the Lord calls the Church His field [but 13:24 speaks of *the kingdom*], for believers are His seed. Although Christ afterwards adds that the field is the world [13:38], there can be no doubt that He really wants to apply this name to the Church, about which, after all, he was speaking. But because His plough would be driven through all the world and He would break in fields everywhere and sow the seed of life, He transfers by synecdoche to the world what is more apt of a part of it.' Matthew 13:41b alludes to

2. That same judgment will separate members of the visible church, that realm where the rule of God is most fully realized before the end. While some of 'the sons of the evil one' oppose the church from without, others do so from within. Are not the weeds sown *among* the wheat (Matt. 13:25) and does not the darnel resemble the wheat (see p. 708)? Will not Jesus, at the Last Judgment, declare some disciples to be 'workers of lawlessness' and banish them from his presence (7:21-23)?[39] Will not some church people be exposed as spurious believers even before the end (13:20-22; 18:15-35; cf. 1 Cor. 5:1-13)?[40]

Not only are there weeds to be consumed; there is wheat to be gathered into the master's barn (Matt. 13:30). The Son of Man who appoints angels to remove the wicked (13:41-42) also sends them forth to gather his elect from all over the world (24:30-31). Not only are the wicked condemned; at the Last Judgment, the true people of God will be vindicated and granted entry into life (25:46). 'Then the righteous will shine as the sun in the kingdom of their Father' (13:43a). The righteous (*hoi dikaioi*) are those disciples who have produced good fruit (7:15-20), whose lives witness to the righteousness (*dikaiosynē*) essential for entering the kingdom (5:20; see those comments). They are now revealed as persons fully conformed to the

---

Zephaniah 1:3 ('I will sweep away...the stumbling blocks with the wicked' ESV mg.), a judgment that affects *all creation* (see France 1985: 226; Robertson 1990: 259-60).

[39]The phrase in Matthew 7:23b is very close to that in 13:41b. The first uses a participle of *ergazomai* ('to work'), the second a participle of *poieō* ('to do'). Whereas the judgment of Zephaniah 1:2-3 is *cosmic* in scope (see the previous note), verses 4-6 foretell judgment upon Judah and Jerusalem (i.e., upon *the church*).

[40]Jesus 'proclaims a terrible judgment upon all hypocrites and reprobates, who now seem the leading citizens in the Church, to awake them from their sleep and their dreaming boasts' (Calvin 1995a: 77). See 1 Corinthians 1:2-9, together with 2 Corinthians 13:5. Cf. Ezekiel 3:27 (akin to Matthew 13:43b), and, in that light, the commands in 3:16-21 to warn both wicked and righteous in Israel. On the issues raised in the above paragraph, see Hendriksen 1973: 572-74; Hagner 1993: 393-95; Wenham 1989: 58-59. On the distinction of the invisible church from the visible, see WCF 25; Calvin 1960: 1021-22 (4.1.7). Cf. Davis 2002: 28-31 on 'eliminating the kingdom's enemies' in Solomon's time.

image of God's Son, and radiant with his glory.[41] The Son's kingdom (13:41) and the Father's (13:43) are one and the same; those who belong to the Son belong to his Father as well.[42]

'He who has ears, let him hear,' concludes Jesus (13:43b). He spoke these very words to the crowd in 13:9; here he addresses disciples. Here, as there, he calls for action (see p. 684, n. 12): let these disciples – among whom Judas is still numbered – reflect soberly upon the warnings implicit in this exposition, lest at the end they be excluded from the heavenly kingdom. And are not the crowds being admonished as well, albeit indirectly? Are not unbelievers past and present free to read this parable (13:24-30), *together with* its explanation (13:36-43)? Does not Jesus speak here both of the *inevitability* of judgment and of its *delay*? There is therefore time for people in the crowds to become Jesus' followers, and to be numbered among 'the sons of the kingdom' at the end. And there is therefore need for people in the church to exercise caution, lest they presume to make conclusive judgments about others within and beyond the church, and arrogate to themselves an authority reserved for the Son of Man.[43]

E. The Parables of the Treasure and the Pearl (13:44-46)

These parables are paired linguistically and conceptually. The opening six Greek words of Matthew 13:44 are repeated in verse 45 (after *palin*, 'again'). Each parable speaks of a man (*anthrōpos*, 13:44, 45) who finds (*heurōn*, 13:44, 46) an object of

---

[41] Cf. Romans 8:29-30; 2 Corinthians 3:18; Philippians 3:20-21. Matthew 13:43 contains the single instance of the verb *eklampō* ('shine, blaze') in the NT.

[42] Cf. Matthew 6:9-10; 12:28; 16:28; 20:21. Messiah is King in the kingdom of God (see pp. 132-33). There are several allusions to Daniel in this passage, including the references to the Son of Man (Matt. 13:37, 41; Daniel 7:13-14), the fiery furnace (Matt. 13:42; Dan. 3:6), and the righteous (Matt. 13:43; Dan. 12:3); cf. Wenham 1989: 64. Kistemaker 1980: 39 also refers to Malachi 4:1-2.

[43] 'The parable is not merely about judgment but about the delay of judgment' (Hagner 1993: 392). 'The delay in the separation of true and false till the last judgment makes a prohibition against rigorism in church discipline, particularly against private judgments' (Gundry 1994: 262, cf. 264). Similarly Bruner 2004b: 32 (with 29-33). See Matthew 5:21-2; 7:1-5; 18:15-20; 1 Corinthians 4:5; James 5:7-9; Calvin 1960: 1030 (4.1.16); Kistemaker 1980: 41-2.

great value (*thēsauros*, 'treasure', 13:44; *margaritēs*, 'pearl', 13:46), and who therefore goes away (*hypagei*, 13:44; *apelthōn*, 13:46), sells (*pōlei*,13:44; *pepraken*, 13:46) all (*panta hosa*, 13:44, 46) that he has (*echei*, 13:44; *eichen*, 13:46), and buys (*agorazei*, 13:44; *ēgorasen*,,13:46) his discovery.[44] *Anthrōpos* and *agros* ('field') in 13:44 recall the parable explained in 13:36-43 (see v. 24), *kekrymmenō* ('hidden') in 13:44 recalls *kekrymmena* in the quotation of verse 35. Moreover, these two parables are linked to those about the mustard seed and the yeast (see p. 685). The treasure, like the yeast, is hidden; and the pearl, like the mustard seed, is small.

The Pictures

The first parable speaks of a treasure (*thēsauros*) hidden in a field (13:44a). Valuables stored in the house could more easily be found by thieves (6:19, with *thēsauros*) or by marauding armies. In this instance, the treasure – probably silver coins or jewels placed in a pottery jar – is buried before the present owner's lifetime or acquisition of the property. The man who finds the treasure is probably a day laborer (as in the parable of 20:1-16) or perhaps a tenant farmer (as in the parable of 21:33-41). He makes the discovery when plowing the field (did his ox sink into a hole?), digging a ditch or planting a tree. Instead of removing the treasure, he buries it again – both to protect it and to keep it hidden from the owner, who might claim to have hidden the treasure himself.[45] Then 'out of his joy [*apo tēs charas autou*] he goes [*hypagei*] and sells [*pōlei*] all that he has, and buys [*agorazei*] that field' (13:44b). The phrase 'out of his joy' is placed first for emphasis. The three Greek verbs here indicated express the man's resolution. The accent

---

[44]The lexical forms of these respective verbs are *heuriskō* ('find'), *hypagō* ('go away'), *aperchomai* ('go away'), *pōleō* ('sell'), *pipraskō* ('sell'), *echō* ('have') and *agorazō* ('buy').

[45]For one or more of the above points, see Jeremias 1963: 198-99; Kistemaker 1980: 54; Gundry 1994: 276, 278. 'The morality of his action is not under consideration. Nevertheless, it is worth noting that his action was formally legitimate' (Jeremias 1963: 199); cf. France 1985: 229. (Had the owner buried the treasure, he would not have sold the field, or would have removed the treasure before doing so.) In Matthew 25:18, the servant digs a hole in the ground and hides his master's money; behind 'hides' is *kryptō*, twice used in 13:44.

is not on what he relinquishes but on what he *acquires*: the value of this treasure, together with the field, exceeds all that he formerly possessed.[46]

The nature of that *thēsauros* is not indicated, but the object in the second parable is a precious, exceptionally valuable pearl (*polytimos margaritēs*). Pearls were highly prized in antiquity, and could be esteemed above gold. Secured by divers or nets from the Red Sea, the Persian Gulf and the Indian Ocean, pearls were used for adornments, especially for necklaces. Some were worth millions in today's currencies.[47] In that light, we can better understand Jesus' words in Matthew 7:6 (about throwing pearls to pigs), and Paul's in 1 Timothy 2:9 (about wearing gold, pearls and expensive clothes). Whereas the first man stumbled upon his treasure, this exceptional pearl is found by a merchant (*emporos*) in the habit of searching (the verb *zēteō*) for fine pearls (*kaloi margaritai*).[48] This man's holdings would far exceed those of the worker in the previous parable. Nevertheless, to acquire a single pearl he too sells all his possessions – which shows that the pearl is valuable to the

---

[46]He 'sold from self-interest, in order to buy something far greater' (France 1985: 229). 'The necessity of selling all to purchase the field shows the poverty of the day laborer' (Gundry 1994: 278).

[47]For these points, and examples, see F. Hauck, *TDNT* 4: 472-73; BAGD s.v. *margaritēs*, 1.; Jeremias 1963: 199-200; Keener 1999: 392. Cf. the use of *margaritēs* in Revelation 17:4; 18:16.

[48]*Emporos* (here only in Matthew) 'marks the merchant as a wholesale dealer, a big businessman who travelled to such places [as the Red Sea, Persian Gulf and Indian Ocean], not a small-time, shop-keeping retailer [*kapēlos*]' (Gundry 1994: 279); cf. Jeremias 1963: 199. Merchants and pearls are again joined in Revelation 18:11-12.

[49]There is 'deliberate hyperbole' in Matthew 13:46 (Hagner 1993: 397). The verb behind 'sold' is the perfect indicative *pepraken*, an 'aoristic' or 'dramatic' perfect, used 'in a rhetorical manner to describe an event in a highly vivid way' (*GGBB*, 578).

[50]'The kingdom of heaven is like a treasure [*thēsaurō*]' (Matt. 13:44); but 'the kingdom of heaven is like the situation of a merchant [*anthrōpō emporō*]' (13:45; translations by Hagner 1993: 395), because it is the pearl (not the man!) that corresponds to the treasure. Still, the *whole* of verse 44 describes the working of the kingdom (cf. p. 707). Cf. the comments on 7:6. Not so

point of being priceless, and that no price is too great for so precious an object.[49]

The Teachings
The *treasure* in Matthew 13:44 and the *pearl* in 13:46 both stand for the *kingdom* of God, as offered in Jesus' *gospel* of the kingdom.[50] Jesus calls listeners to *incalculable gain* and *great joy*.[51] For persons who perceive this kingdom for what it truly *is* (13:10-17), all else pales by comparison. To the onlookers, especially slaves of wealth (6:24; 13:22), the act of selling all one's possessions for the sake of a single – invisible – object, would doubtless appear wildly impractical and foolishly extravagant. For the rich man of 19:16-22 to sell all his possessions would be excruciatingly painful for him (and utter folly to his wealthy friends), because he does not – even in face of Jesus' promise of heavenly *thēsauros* – recognize the kingdom of God for what it really is. Like the treasure in the field, the kingdom is *hidden* from such people's view; it is like a pearl, too *small* for them to notice. But for persons granted insight into the realities of which that gospel speaks – and gripped by the mercies and powers of God and his Messiah – acquiring the kingdom of heaven at the cost of worldly goods is like purchasing a mansion for the price of a shanty. The object of Jesus' preaching is to convince people 'that the Kingdom is the most precious thing conceivable.... It is wealth which demonetises all other currencies.'[52] 'Like a hidden treasure or a pearl that can be held in one's hand, the kingdom is known only to its joyful possessors.'[53]

---

likely is the view that the treasure and the pearl stand for Jesus himself (cf. *ACC* 1a: 285-87; Kistemaker 1980: 56), though it is he who makes the kingdom a priceless treasure.

[51]Cf. Wenham 1989: 208. As noted, 'out of his joy' (13:44) is stated emphatically. Jeremias 1963: 200-01 judges that this phrase applies to both the laborer and the merchant.

[52]Manson 1957: 196; cf. Job 28:18; Psalm 119:162; Proverbs 3:15; 8:11. Manson adds that compared to the kingdom's wealth 'all other goods lose their value' (ibid.). But in fact it is those who prize the kingdom who can enjoy earthly wealth: see comments on Matthew 6:19-34. Cf. 10: 34-39; 13:18-23; 19:23-30; Phil. 3:7-8 (with 4:10-20). Recalling Jesus' words in 13:22

F. The Parable of the Net (13:47-50)

This is the third parable addressed to disciples exclusively; the Greek which introduces the other two (13:44, 45) appears here too (13:47, like v. 45, opens with *palin*, 'again'). This parable is also to be paired with the one about the weeds (13:24-30, 36-43; see p. 685); only here the explanation is attached directly to the parable (compare 13:49-50 to vv. 40-42), since Jesus is alone with disciples (13:36).

The Picture

A net (*sagēnē*) is cast (the verb *ballō*) into the sea (*thalassa*), whence it gathers (the verb *synagō*) fish of every kind (*ek pantos genous*; Matthew 13:47). Once it is full (the verb *plēroō*), it is dragged (the verb *anabibazō*) to the shore (*aigialos*), where the fishermen gather (the verb *syllegō*) the good fish (*ta kala*) into containers (*angē*), and throw away the bad ones (*ta sapra*; 13:48).

A *sagēnē* was a large drag-net (or seine-net) with floats on the top edge and weights on the bottom, for vertical use. It could be thrown into the water from the land or a boat, or from between two boats. (In 4:18, Peter and Andrew are casting a net into the sea: the verb *ballō* appears with the phrase *eis tēn thalassan*, as in 13:47.) Once the fish were caught, the net was dragged to shore with long ropes (as here), or towed in by a boat (as in John 21:4-11); or its contents were emptied into a boat (or boats) and brought to shore (as in Luke 5:4-11).[54] Naturally, fish 'of every kind' are gathered by that means; so once the net is brought to shore, the fishermen must separate the worthless from the good. Unclean and inedible fish would be discarded, and the rest kept for sale.[55]

---

about wealth's deceitfulness, Bruner 2004b: 49 says the parables of 13:44-46 call for 'economic simplicity.'

[53]Hagner 1993: 397. Cf. 1 Corinthians 2:6-16.

[54]Jeremias 1963: 225; Davies and Allison 1991: 440-41; Hagner 1993: 399. This is the only instance of *sagēnē* in the NT (it is the source of the Middle English word 'seine'). The word in Matthew 4:18 (here alone in the NT) is *amphiblēstron*, a circular or pear-shaped net (cf. BAGD and GT s.v.). Used in 4:20, 21 (and 10 more times in the NT) is *diktyon*, which 'seems to be the general name for nets of all kinds' (GT s.v.).

The Teaching
This parable, like the one about the weeds, speaks of the judgment to be executed 'at the close of the age' (13:39-40); the seven opening Greek words of 13:49 all occur in verse 40b and in the same order. The ones who sort out the fish are not the apostles (*hoi apostoloi*), as we might have expected (4:18-22; 10:1-42; 28:16-20), but the angels (*hoi angeloi*), as in 13:41. Here, as there, they act at the bidding (it is implied) of the Son of Man. As they were said to gather the wicked out of his kingdom (13:41), so now 'they separate [*aphoriousin*] the evil ones [*tous ponērous*] from the midst of the righteous [*ek mesou tōn dikaiōn*]' (13:49). When explaining the previous parable, Jesus described what awaits both the wicked (13:42) and the righteous (13:43). Here he focuses exclusively on the punishment of the evil (*hoi ponēroi*; 13:49) i.e., the sons of the evil one (*ho ponēros*; 13:38). Verse 50 exactly repeats the Greek of 13:42 (see those comments).

In the matching parable, the field was expressly identified as the world (*kosmos*; 13:38); so too by implication is the sea (*thalassa*; 13:47).[56] But whereas in the earlier parable it was the Son of Man who sowed good seed and the devil who sowed weeds (Matt. 13:37-39), here it is Jesus and his followers (including the fishermen of 4:18-22) who cast their nets into a global sea and gather 'fish of every kind' (13:47). Moreover, whereas in the other parable the angels gather the lawless out of the *kingdom* (*basileia*; 13:41), here they separate evil persons from the midst of the *righteous* (*dikaioi*; 13:49). The judgment described in verses 39-42 affects both church and world (cf. p. 718, points 1. and 2.); verses 49-50 focus exclusively on the visible church. As both good (*kala*) and bad (*sapra*) fish are gathered (cf. Jesus' choice of Peter and Judas), so the visible church consists of true and false disciples, whose fruit (whether *kalos* or *ponēros*) will reveal their true identity (whether *agathos* or *sapros*; 7:16-20; cf. 12:33; 13:8, 23). In this

---

[55]For unclean fish, see Leviticus 11:9-12. Inedible marine creatures included crabs (Jeremias 1963: 226, who notes that twenty-four different species of fish have been counted in the Sea of Galilee).
[56]Gundry 1994: 279.

respect, the parable anticipates 22:1-14; there, in response to a widespread invitation (22:9), both evil (*ponēroi*) and good (*agathoi*) fill the wedding hall (22:10), but some who come are banished (22:11-14).[57]

G. Two Opposing Responses (13:51-58)

The persons in 13:51-52 and 13:54-58 respectively, represent the groups that are distinguished in 13:10-17, and that are to be recognized and separated at the Last Judgment (13:40-42, 49-50). Verse 53 signals that this discourse of parables has concluded (see p. 51).

The School of Disciples (13:51-52)

Jesus' opening question – 'Have you understood all these things?' – is addressed to his disciples (cf. v. 36). This inquiry is serious indeed, for these disciples are not exempt from the judgment depicted in 13:49-50; and let us remember that Judas is still among them. Their unadorned affirmative reply – 'Yes' (*Nai*; 13:51b) – suggests assurance on their part. Yet, how well they truly understand (the verb *syniēmi*) will be ascertained not merely from their intellectual grasp of the kingdom's mysteries, but also from their active obedience to these parables' implicit commands: see especially 13:23, where understanding (*syniēmi* again) is closely joined to bearing fruit.

The designation in Matthew 13:52a – 'every scribe [*grammateus*] who has been discipled [*mathēteutheis*] for the kingdom of heaven' – applies potentially to all disciples: this passive participle comes from *mathēteuō*, a verbal counterpart (like *manthanō*) to *mathētēs*, 'disciple.' As we saw, it applies especially to Matthew. He would show his true understanding by *inscribing* Jesus' teachings. Not every disciple would become a *grammateus* in that sense; but each was to become a *teacher* – a *discipler* – of others (28:19-20; with both *mathēteuō* and *didaskō*, 'teach'). Every true disciple has discovered the treasure (*thēsauros*) of the kingdom (13:44); and each of them

---

[57]The later parable also depicts persons who are judged for refusing to enter the church (Matt. 22:2-7). See comments on 13:36-43 and 22:1-14; Hagner 1993: 399; Wenham 1989: 67.

will in time have a full treasury (*thēsauros* again) from which to impart things both new and old (13:52b), including things formerly learned but now freshly illuminated by the foregoing parables and explanations.[58]

The People of Nazareth (13:53-58)

Jesus now leaves Capernaum (13:53a) and comes to his home town (*patris*), i.e., Nazareth, where he teaches in the synagogue (13:54a). This is probably the same visit recorded in Luke 4:16-30.[59]

The people in the synagogue are astonished at Jesus' teaching (Matt. 13:54a): the verb is *ekplēssō*; here, as in 7:28 (the only prior instance in Matthew), it expresses listeners' recognition of Jesus' great authority. So they wonder (13:54b) how he acquired 'this wisdom' (*hē sophia hautē*) evidenced in his teaching and what enables him to do 'the mighty works' (*hai dynameis*) they have heard about (cf. Luke 4:23).[60] The question of 13:54b is virtually repeated in verse 56b: 'Whence therefore [*oun*] did all these things [*tauta panta*: i.e. wisdom and miraculous powers] come to this man?' The intervening questions about Jesus' family (13:55-56a) all expect positive replies: 'Is not... Are not ...?' Which is to say: 'This man

---

[58]Gundry 1994: 281. See above, pages 43-45 (comments on Matthew 13:52); 64 *et seq.* (Matthew's 'drawing out things new,' namely Jesus' teachings), 91 *et seq.* (his 'drawing out things old,' OT teachings in light of Jesus' own use of the OT). 'The new is not added to the old; there is but one revelation, and its focus is the "new" that has fulfilled and thereby renewed the old' (Carson 1984: 333). Carson, 332, takes the 'treasury' (13:52) to be the human heart; thus is *thēsauros* in 12:35 to be understood (see my comments on that verse).

[59]Jesus has been in Capernaum since 13:1 (see p. 682, n. 2). Both in Matthew's account (akin to Mark 6:1-6a) and in Luke's, Jesus teaches in the synagogue (Matt. 13:54; Luke 4:16); the people are astonished and offended by his words, and refer to his family (Matt. 13:54-57; Luke 4:22, 28); Jesus speaks of the prophet's rejection in his *patris* (Matt. 13:57; Luke 4:24); the people's unbelief is a barrier to miracle-working (Matt. 13:58; Luke 4:23, 25-27); and Nazareth is linked to Capernaum (implicitly in Matthew 13:53-54; explicitly in Luke 4:16, 23, 31). But the visit of Matthew 13 and Mark 6 may be later than that of Luke 4. See comments in Carson 1984: 335; Morris 1992: 364.

[60]A demonstrative adjective (*hautē*) is attached to *sophia*, but not to *dynameis*; so it is misleading to translate 'this wisdom and these mighty

cannot be what he seems to be, because we know who he is and where he comes from.'[61] Jesus also appears to have *deserted* the familiar and the familial (cf. 12:46-50): 'Someone or something has stolen "our" boy.... He who was one of Us has become one of Them. What right had anybody to do it? He is *ours*.'[62] This shows that amazement is mingled with skepticism in the enclosing questions of 13:54b and 13:56b (note how the opening *oun* in verse 56b founds this question on the preceding three). The result is predictable: 'and they were offended [*eskandalizonto*] by him' (13:57a). This same verb (a passive form of *skandalizō*) appears in 11:6 (where Jesus threatens to offend John) and in 15:12 (where he actually offends the Pharisees). Because of whom Jesus is and what he does, persons who are *offended* by him are in grave danger of *falling into sin*.[63] As those who are impressed by Jesus' wisdom and mighty works, but who nonetheless remain skeptical about him and are finally scandalized, these townspeople may fall prey to the Pharisaic propaganda of 12:24.

In response, Jesus says, 'A prophet is not without honor [*atimos*] except in his home town [*en tē patridi*] and in his house [*en tē oikia autou*]' (Matt. 13:57b). This instance of *patris* echoes that of 13:54; despite widespread unbelief in Galilee (cf. chs. 11–13), the people's response to Jesus elsewhere – notably in and around Capernaum – contrasts sharply with his reception in Nazareth. The people have just mentioned Jesus' family: they identify him as son of the carpenter (*tektōn*), who is probably now deceased; and they speak of his mother *Miriam*, his brothers *Iakōbos*, *Iōsēph*, *Simōn* and *Ioudas*, and his sisters, none of whom are named. Jesus' subsequent reference to his own household (*oikia*; 13:57) indicates that at least some persons in his family share in the Nazarenes' unbelief (*apistia*; 13:58). John 7:5 expressly says that Jesus' brothers [*adelphoi*, as in Matt. 13:55] did not believe [*oude...*

---

works' (so ESV). The imperfect verb *edidasken* (Matt. 13:54a) is probably progressive ('he was teaching'), though possibly ingressive ('he began to teach'); for these usages, see *GGBB*, 543-45.

[61]Cf. Hooker 1991: 152, on the parallel in Mark 6:2-3.

[62]Lewis 1960: 72. Cf. the comments on Matthew 10:34-37; 12:46-50. See also John 6:42!

[63]The passive of *skandalizō* bears both meanings: see page 606, with n. 18.

episteuon] in him.' But that would change (Acts 1:14); and, in time, two of these brothers – *Iakōbos* and *Ioudas* – would contribute to the writings of the NT.[64]

'And he did not do many mighty works [*dynameis*] there, because of their unbelief [*dia tēn apistian autōn*]' (13:58). Thus does Matthew conclude this chapter. The parallel in Mark 6:5 states that Jesus 'was not able [*ouk edynato*] to do a mighty work [*dynamin*] there, except that he laid hands on a few sick people and healed them.' It is not that Jesus' power, having recently been expended (Mark 5:30), is now utterly depleted from raising Jairus' daughter (5:41-42) and healing 'a few sick people' in Nazareth. Rather, Jesus *could* not do many miracles because he *would* not do so in face of the townspeople's unbelief. Mark 6:5 is explained in verse 6: 'and he marveled because of their unbelief [*dia tēn apistian autōn*],' the exact phrase of Matthew 13:58. Just as Jesus judged the crowds' unbelief by refusing to explain his parables to them, he judges the Nazarenes' unbelief by withholding from them his miraculous powers.[65] That he nonetheless chooses to accomplish *some* mighty works (13:58; Mark 6:5), testifies to his marvelous grace and mercy.

---

[64]For arguments that these men are the authors of the Epistles of James and Jude, respectively, see Guthrie 1990: 746 (with 723-46), 905 (with 902-5). For this James, see also, e.g., Acts 12:17; 15:13; 1 Corinthians 15:7; Galatians 1:19. The brother here named *Iōsēph* (for the Hebrew *yôsēp*) is called *Iōsēs* ('Joses') in Mark 6:3 (*yôsēy* being the Galilean pronunciation for *yôsēp*); cf. *TC*, 28 (on Matthew 13:55). The NT says nothing more of Joseph and Simon, or of the sisters (it will be argued that Matthew 27:56 ['Mary the mother of James and Joseph'] speaks of different persons). *Miriam* is Semitic (this was the name of Moses' sister); the usual spelling is *Maria*, 1:16, etc. (on the different spellings, see BDF, par. 53). Since Mary's husband *Iōsēph* is named only in 1:16-20, it is highly probable that he died before Jesus' public ministry began. A *tektōn* might be a carpenter or a builder; Joseph probably worked for a thriving construction company, as did Jesus for a time (see Mark 6:3); for details, see Albright and Mann 1971: 172-73; Keener 1999: 395, n. 2.

[65]'As before (cf. 12:38-39), Jesus will not perform miracles to counteract unbelief' (Hagner 1993: 406). 'Jesus' power is neither magical nor automatic' (France 1985: 233). The connection between the people's unbelief and Jesus' refusal is yet tighter in Matthew 13:58 than in Mark 6:5-6 (Gundry 1994: 284). Cf. Isaiah 59:1-4 (and Motyer 1999: 364).

Other books of interest in the
Mentor Imprint
from
Christian Focus Publications

Matthew

A MENTOR COMMENTARY

Volume: 2 Chapters 14-28

Knox Chamblin

Matthew
Volume 2 (chapter 14–28)

A Mentor Commentary

Knox Chamblin

This second volume completes Chamblin's commentary and includes Scripture and subject indices for Volumes 1 and 2.

This thoughtful and thorough commentary on the First Gospel comes from a scholar who has obviously spent many years at the feet of Matthew the teacher, and even more importantly, at the feet of the One to whom Matthew bears witness.

**Jonathan Pennington,
Assistant Professor of New Testament Interpretation,
The Southern Baptist Theological Seminary,
Louisville, Kentucky**

What, you might say, am I to do with 2 volumes and 1,400 pages on Matthew? Well, what should you do if given two million pounds? Spend it, of course–but not all at once. So with Chamblin's Matthew. Preach an Advent series – and use Chamblin on chapters 1–2; then preach from the Old Testament and come back to the Sermon on the Mount – and use Chamblin on chapters 5–7; then map out a series on Matthew's passion narrative – and use Chamblin on chapters 26–28. I'm not a hypocrite – I'm using him on Matthew 13 even as I write this!

**Dale Ralph Davis, Pastor,
Woodlands Presbyterian Church, Hattiesburg, Mississippi**

978-1-84550-379-6

Proverbs

A MENTOR COMMENTARY

John Kitchen

Proverbs

A Mentor Commentary

John Kitchen

To cope with modern life we must have wisdom! There is no better starting point than the Book of Proverbs. Its *purpose* is to impart wisdom to those who want it. From its pages God promises to set us on 'The path of life' (Prov. 15:24).

John Kitchen is clear and probing on the text and always practical. His Appendix on wisdom vs folly is powerful and his Thematic Index of Proverbs opens up the only real preaching possibility for expositors beyond chapter nine of the book. This is a solid and substantial piece of work, which will deservedly take its place as one of the finest contemporary treatments available.

**David L. Larsen, Professor Emeritus of Preaching,
Trinity Evangelical Divinity School, Deerfield, Illinois**

Committed to the full integrity and authority of the Bible as the written Word of God, to careful exegesis of the text, and to practical application of the truths of biblical wisdom to everyday life.

**Eugene H. Merrill, Professor of Old Testament Studies,
Dallas Theological Seminary, Dallas, Texas**

Kitchen combines careful attention to the text with a warm pastoral concern for his readers. He is familiar with the scholarly discussions on the book, but he avoids technical jargon as he interprets Proverbs for the life setting of the twenty-first century. This book will prove helpful for laypeople, students, and scholars alike.

**Daniel J. Estes, Distinguished Professor of Bible,
Cedarville University, Cedarville, Ohio**

John Kitchen is the Senior Pastor at the Stow Alliance Fellowship, Stow, Ohio. He is also the author of *Song of a Satisfied Soul* (ISBN 978-1-85792-942-3) and *Embracing Authority* (ISBN 978-1-85792-715-3)

978-1-84550-059-7

Christian Focus Publications
publishes books for all ages

Our mission statement –
STAYING FAITHFUL
In dependence upon God we seek to impact the world through literature faithful to His infallible Word, the Bible. Our aim is to ensure that the Lord Jesus Christ is presented as the only hope to obtain forgiveness of sin, live a useful life and look forward to heaven with Him.

REACHING OUT
Christ's last command requires us to reach out to our world with His gospel. We seek to help fulfill that by publishing books that point people towards Jesus and help them develop a Christ-like maturity. We aim to equip all levels of readers for life, work, ministry and mission.

Books in our adult range are published in three imprints.

Christian Focus contains popular works including biographies, commentaries, basic doctrine and Christian living. Our children's books are also published in this imprint.

Mentor focuses on books written at a level suitable for Bible College and seminary students, pastors, and other serious readers. The imprint includes commentaries, doctrinal studies, examination of current issues and church history.

Christian Heritage contains classic writings from the past.

Christian Focus Publications, Ltd
Geanies House, Fearn, Ross-shire,
IV20 1TW, Scotland, United Kingdom
info@christianfocus.com
For details of our titles visit us on our website
www.christianfocus.com